Clinical Applications of the Polyvagal Theory

The Norton Series on Interpersonal Neurobiology

Louis Cozolino, PhD, Series Editor

Allan N. Schore, PhD, Series Editor, 2007–2014

Daniel J. Siegel, MD, Founding Editor

The field of mental health is in a tremendously exciting period of growth and conceptual reorganization. Independent findings from a variety of scientific endeavors are converging in an interdisciplinary view of the mind and mental well-being. An interpersonal neurobiology of human development enables us to understand that the structure and function of the mind and brain are shaped by experiences, especially those involving emotional relationships.

The Norton Series on Interpersonal Neurobiology provides cutting-edge, multidisciplinary views that further our understanding of the complex neurobiology of the human mind. By drawing on a wide range of traditionally independent fields of research—such as neurobiology, genetics, memory, attachment, complex systems, anthropology, and evolutionary psychology—these texts offer mental health professionals a review and synthesis of scientific findings often inaccessible to clinicians. The books advance our understanding of human experience by finding the unity of knowledge, or consilience, that emerges with the translation of findings from numerous domains of study into a common language and conceptual framework. The series integrates the best of modern science with the healing art of psychotherapy.

A Norton Professional Book

Clinical Applications of the Polyvagal Theory

The Emergence of Polyvagal-Informed Therapies

STEPHEN W. PORGES
DEB DANA

W. W. Norton & Company
Independent Publishers Since 1923
New York • London

POLYVAGAL INSTITUTE PVI POLYVAGAL INFORMED

Certified by Polyvagal Institute as accurately representing the principles described in Polyvagal Theory.

Printed in the United States of America
First Edition

For information about permission to reproduce selections from this book, write to Permissions, W. W. Norton & Company, Inc., 500 Fifth Avenue, New York, NY 10110

For information about special discounts for bulk purchases, please contact W. W. Norton Special Sales at specialsales@wwnorton.com or 800-233-4830

Manufacturing by LSC Harrisonburg
Production manager: Christine Critelli

Library of Congress Cataloging-in-Publication Data

Names: Porges, Stephen W., editor. | Dana, Deb, editor.
Title: Clinical applications of the polyvagal theory : the emergence of polyvagal-informed therapies / [edited by] Stephen W. Porges, Deb Dana.
Other titles: Norton series on interpersonal neurobiology.
Description: First edition. | New York : W.W. Norton & Company, [2018] | Series: Norton series on interpersonal neurobiology | "A Norton professional book." | Includes bibliographical references and index.
Identifiers: LCCN 2018013159 | ISBN 9781324000501 (hardcover)
Subjects: | MESH: Stress Disorders, Traumatic—therapy | Autonomic Nervous System—physiology | Psychological Theory | Physician-Patient Relations | Sensory Art Therapies
Classification: LCC RC552.T7 | NLM WM 172.5 | DDC 616.85/21—dc23
LC record available at https://lccn.loc.gov/2018013159

W. W. Norton & Company, Inc., 500 Fifth Avenue, New York, N.Y. 10110
www.wwnorton.com

W. W. Norton & Company Ltd., 15 Carlisle Street, London W1D 3BS

7 8 9 0

To the passionate authors of the chapters in this book
and to the extended family of compassionate therapists
who are actively transforming the lives
of those disrupted by trauma.

Contents

Contributors

Stephen W. Porges, PhD is Distinguished University Scientist at Indiana University, where he directs the Traumatic Stress Research Consortium in the Kinsey Institute. He holds the position of Professor of Psychiatry at the University of North Carolina and Professor Emeritus at the University of Illinois at Chicago where he directed the Brain-Body Center. Dr. Porges is also Professor Emeritus at the University of Maryland where he served as Chair of the Department of Human Development and Director of the Institute for Child Study. He is a former president of the Society for Psychophysiological Research and also of the Federation of Behavioral, Psychological, and Cognitive Sciences. He is a former recipient of a National Institute of Mental Health Research Scientist Development Award. He has published more than 250 peer-reviewed scientific papers across several disciplines including anesthesiology, critical care medicine, ergonomics, exercise physiology, gerontology, neurology, obstetrics, pediatrics, psychiatry, psychology, space medicine, and substance abuse. In 1994 he proposed the Polyvagal Theory, a theory that links the evolution of the vertebrate autonomic nervous system to the emergence of social behavior. The theory provides insights into the mechanisms mediating symptoms observed in several behavioral, psychiatric, and physical disorders. The theory has stimulated research and treatments that emphasize the importance of physiological state and regulation of the autonomic nervous system in the expression of several psychiatric disorders and provides a theoretical perspective to study and to treat stress and trauma. He is the author of The Polyvagal Theory: Neurophysiological foundations of Emotions, Attachment, Communication, and Self-regulation (Norton, 2011) and The Pocket Guide to the Polyvagal Theory: The transformative power of feeling safe, (Norton, 2017).

Peter A. Levine, PhD is a forerunner in body-oriented approaches to trauma. He is the developer of Somatic Experiencing® a naturalistic, approach to healing trauma which he has developed during the past 45 years. He has received the Lifetime

Achievement award from the US Association for Body Psychotherapy, and an honorary award as the Reiss-Davis Chair for his lifetime contribution to infant and child psychiatry. Dr. Levine served as a stress consultant for NASA in the early space shuttle development and has served on the APA task force for responding to large scale disasters and ethno-political warfare. He is currently a Senior Fellow and consultant at The Meadows Addiction and Trauma Treatment Center in Wickenburg, Arizona. He is the author of several best-selling books on trauma, including *Waking the Tiger: Healing Trauma* (published in 26 languages), *In an Unspoken Voice: How that Body Releases Trauma and Restores Goodness,* as well as *Trauma and Memory: Brain and Body in a Search for the Living Past.*

Bessel van der Kolk, MD, is a Professor of Psychiatry at Boston University Medical School. He is a past president of the International Society for Traumatic Stress Studies. Though he identifies primarily as a clinician, he has published well over 150 peer reviewed scientific articles on various aspects of trauma, including yoga for treating PTSD, the use of theater for violence prevention in the Boston public schools, the mechanisms of EMDR, sensory integration, and the use of neurofeedback in PTSD. He is author of the New York Times Science bestseller *The Body Keeps the Score,* which has been translated into 19 languages.

Pat Ogden, PhD, is a pioneer in somatic psychology and the Founder and Education Director of the Sensorimotor Psychotherapy Institute, an internationally recognized school specializing in somatic–cognitive approaches for the treatment of posttraumatic stress disorder and attachment disturbances. Her Institute, based in Broomfield Colorado, has 19 certified trainers who conduct Sensorimotor Psychotherapy trainings for mental health professionals throughout the US, Canada, Europe, and Australia. The Sensorimotor Psychotherapy Institute has certified hundreds of psychotherapists throughout the world in this method. She is cofounder of the Hakomi Institute, past faculty of Naropa University (1985-2005), a clinician, consultant, and sought after international lecturer. Dr. Ogden is the first author of two groundbreaking books in somatic psychology: *Trauma and the Body: A Sensorimotor Approach to Psychotherapy* and *Sensorimotor Psychotherapy: Interventions for Trauma and Attachment* (2015) both published in the Interpersonal Neurobiology Series of W. W. Norton. She is currently working with colleagues on a third book *Sensorimotor Psychotherapy for Children, Adolescents and Families.*

Her current interests include developing training programs in Sensorimotor Psychotherapy for children, adolescents and families, Embedded Relational Mindfulness, culture and diversity, couple therapy, working with challenging clients, the relational nature of shame, presence, consciousness and the philosophical/spiritual principles that guide Sensorimotor Psychotherapy.

Bonnie Badenoch, LMFT, therapist, mentor, teacher, and author, has spent the last 14 years integrating the discoveries of relational neuroscience into the art of therapy. In 2008, she cofounded the nonprofit agency Nurturing the Heart with the Brain in Mind to offer this work to the community of therapists, health-care providers, and others interested in becoming therapeutic presences in the world. For 25 years, she has supported trauma survivors and those with significant attachment wounds to reshape their neural landscapes for a life of meaning, resilience, and warm relationships. These days, Bonnie takes joy in offering immersion trainings for therapists and others. These groups cultivate the capacity for presence through the development of deep listening and the embodiment of the principles of interpersonal neurobiology. Her conviction that wisdom about the relational brain can support healing experiences for people at every age led to the publication of *Being a Brain-Wise Therapist: A Practical Guide to Interpersonal Neurobiology* in 2008 and *The Brain-Savvy Therapist's Workbook* in 2011. Bonnie's latest writing is *The Heart of Trauma: Healing the Embodied Brain in the Context of Relationships.* These books seek to make a bridge between science and practice with clarity, compassion, and heart.

Joe Tucci, BSc, BSW, PhD is a social worker and psychologist. He is the CEO of the Austrlian Childhood Foundation. **Angela Weller, BSW** is a social worker and manager of the Child Trauma Service for the Australian Childhood Foundation. **Janise Mitchell, BSW, MSW** is a social worker and deputy CEO of the Australian Childhood Foundation. The foundation is a not-for-profit organization that delivers therapeutic intervention to children who have experienced trauma related to abuse and family violence.

Shari M. Geller, PhD is an author, clinical psychologist, and creator of the Therapeutic Rhythm and Mindfulness Program (TRM™). With over 20 years' experience weaving psychology and mindfulness, Shari coauthored the book *Therapeutic Presence: A Mindful Approach to Effective Therapy.* She has released a companion CD on cultivating presence, with guided practices using the healing power of music and the health benefits of mindfulness. Shari's second book, *A Practical Guide to Cultivating Therapeutic Presence,* offers practical guidance for cultivating and strengthening therapeutic presence as a foundational approach. Shari serves on the teaching faculty in health psychology at York University and for the Applied Mindfulness Meditation program at University of Toronto, and is an adjunct professor in the faculty of music at the University of Toronto, in association with Music and Health Research Collaboratory. Shari is the codirector of the Centre for MindBody Health, in Toronto, Canada. She offers training and workshops internationally on the art and science of cultivating therapeutic presence.

George S. Thompson, MD, FAPA, is Associate Professor of Psychiatry at the University of Missouri-Kansas City School of Medicine, where he directed the CUES to Medical Communications course for 12 years and conducted research in medical education, focusing on how medical professionalism is modeled and learned, and how the climate of professionalism at a medical school promotes or detracts from learning professionalism. His award-winning research has been published in *Academic Medicine*. Dr. Thompson is Chief Medical Officer at KidsTLC, Inc., a child behavioral health agency in Olathe Kansas. KidsTLC provides a full array of psychiatric services, in particular for children who have experienced early trauma and abandonment and for those who have been diagnosed with Autism Spectrum Disorder. His most recent clinical interest is helping foster children build bonds of attachment through Dyadic Developmental Psychotherapy. He is a past president of the Greater Kansas City chapter of the American Academy of Child and Adolescent Psychiatry. For 17 years, he has taught and practiced the exercises of the Avatar® Course, authored by Harry Palmer, which increase a person's internal locus of control with regard to their beliefs and schemas, their attention and will, and their ability to compassionately serve others.

Moira Theede, BScN, MSc, is a retired nurse who lives in Saskatchewan, Canada. Her nursing experience includes surgical wards, operating room, medical imaging, health counseling, and teaching undergraduate nursing students. She is an accomplished photographer and has created a collection of video metpahors that visually represent the experience of neuroception. Through her longtime study of Polyvagal Theory and neuroplasticity Moira developed a series of presentations titled *The Science of Connectedness*.

Alan Theede, DVM, is a retired large-animal veterinarian living in western Canada. His education in anatomy, embryology, and mammalian physiology combined with his experience working with animals provides a strong foundation to understand and appreciate Polyvagal Theory. Al enjoys presenting basic mammalian neurophysiology as part of introductory workshops. He is particularly interested in the positive health benefits of the bidirectional human–animal bond now supported by the science of Polyvagal Theory.

Deb Dana, LCSW, is a clinician and consultant specializing in working with complex trauma. She is the Coordinator of the Traumatic Stress Research Consortium in the Kinsey Institute and the developer of the Rhythm of Regulation clinical training series. Deb is the author of *The Polyvagal Theory in Therapy: Engaging the Rhythm of Regulation* (Norton, 2018) and lectures nationally and internationally on ways in which Polyvagal Theory informs work with trauma survivors.

Deb Grant, LCSW, RSMT, is a psychotherapist, registered somatic movement educator, and yoga teacher, specializing in working with complex traumatic stress. She is certified as a Body-Mind Centering® Somatic Movement Educator and holds two yoga teacher certifications. Deb is the creator of a daylong workshop for dancers and laypeople titled Dancing in Vagus.

Amber Gray, MPH, MA, LPCC, BC-DMT, NCC, is a pioneer in the use of dance movement therapy, Somatic Psychology, and Continuum with survivors of trauma, particularly torture, war, and human rights abuses. Amber's expertise is represented in many published articles and chapters, keynote addresses, professional collaborations, and presentations around the world. Since the late 1990s, Amber has provided clinical training to programs worldwide on integrating refugee mental health and torture treatment with creative arts, mindfulness, and body- and movement-based therapies for survivors of human rights abuses. She originated a resiliency-based framework and clinical approach, Restorative Movement Psychotherapy, for somatic, movement, and arts-based therapies with survivors of trauma in cross-cultural, low-resource contexts; and she codeveloped polyvagal-informed dance movement therapy with Dr. Porges.

Sandra Lindaman, MA, MSW, LSLP, LCSW, LISW, is a certified Theraplay® therapist, supervisor, and trainer, and the senior training advisor for The Theraplay® Institute in Evanston, Illinois. Sandra has been with The Theraplay® Institute since 1990, and coauthored three chapters in the 2010 third edition of *Theraplay: Helping Parents and Children Build Better Relationships Through Attachment-Based Play* as well as a number of chapters in the play therapy and psychotherapy literature. Sandra has been very involved in Theraplay curriculum development, training, and supervision of professionals in the Theraplay model internationally.

Jukka Mäkelä, MD, is a child psychiatrist and senior expert at the National Institute for Health and Welfare. Jukka has trained in psychoanalytic child psychotherapy in the Tavistock tradition and in various techniques of child–parent relationships, and acts as a trainer in Helsinki, Finland. He is a trainer-level Theraplay therapist who brought Theraplay training to Finland and the other Nordic countries. In addition to articles on Theraplay and Polyvagal Theory, he has written widely in Finnish on themes of positive parenting, promotion of child mental health, and ways of preventing child abuse. Currently he is an adviser on the strategic government program for reforming child and family services.

Stuart Daniel, MA, PGCE, PGDip, is a play therapist and researcher based in Devon, U.K. Having a passionate interest in early communication, severe learning difficulties, and medical trauma, he has authored scientific and therapy articles in these areas, along with coediting the book *Rhythms of Relating in Children's Therapies: Connecting Creatively With Vulnerable Children*. **Kieran Donovan** is a school student and the focus of the clinical case presented in Chapter 14. He is currently studying for his final school exams with the hope of studying biomedical sciences at university. **Angie Masters, BA,** is an author and the mother of Kieran.

Robert Schwarz, PsyD, DCEP, has been a licensed psychologist working with trauma for over 30 years. He is author of *Tools for Transforming Trauma*. He speaks internationally and has organized over 20 conferences on treating trauma, brief therapy, and energy psychology. For the past 9 years Dr. Schwarz has been the executive director of the Association for Comprehensive Energy Psychology (www.energypsych.org).

Ralf Vogt, PhD is a psychoanalyst working in private practice in Leipzig, Germany specializing in work with complex trauma. Since 2000, he and his wife, Irina, have been working on the development of their own treatment program for dissociative disorders, the SPIM 30. Together, they founded the Trauma Institute Leipzig in 2002 as a center for training and research. Dr. Vogt is a past board member of the International Board of the International Society for the Study of Trauma and Dissociation (ISSTD). In 2011, he was conferred the status of ISSTD Fellow for outstanding contributions to the field of dissociation, and in 2017 received the Cornelia B. Wilbur Award from ISSTD for outstanding clinical contributions to the treatment of dissociative disorders. He is the author of numerous books on the subject.

Tom Bunn, LCSW is the founder and president of SOAR Inc., which provides programs for overcoming fear of flying. His postgraduate study includes the Gestalt Center of Long Island, the New York Training Institute for Neurolinguistic Programming, and the Masterson Institute for Psychoanalytic Psychotherapy. Tom was a U.S. Air Force pilot and later flew internationally for Pan Am. He worked as a volunteer on the first fear of flying program started by Captain Truman Cummings and in 1982 founded SOAR to develop advanced methods for treating flight phobia. Tom is the author of *SOAR: The Breakthrough Treatment for Fear of Flying*.

Candyce Ossefort-Russell, LPC-S, is a psychotherapist, grief advocate, writer, trainer, and speaker in private practice in Austin, TX. She has actively lived, studied, and trained in psychological, spiritual, and scientific perspectives of suffering and transformation for over 25 years. She has extensive experience working with, writing about, and teaching about individuals and groups from an attachment-based perspective in the areas of trauma, grief, life transition, depression, and parenting. She is known for her warm and emotionally engaged style that creates a safe and connected atmosphere for growth and learning.

Gary Whited, PhD, LMFT, is a psychotherapist, philosopher, and poet. He has a private psychotherapy practice in Boston, Massachusetts, working with individuals, couples, and groups. He presents workshops in the United States, Europe, and Russia, focusing on the practice of deep listening as a vehicle for healing trauma, grief, and shame wounds. He incorporates poetry into his workshops and into his work with clients. His book of poems, titled *Having Listened*, was selected as the winner of the 2013 Homebound Publications Poetry Contest.

Marilyn Sanders, MD, FAAP, has spent the past 30 years caring for critically ill and fragile newborns, infants, and young children. Dr. Sanders is board-certified in pediatrics and perinatal-neonatal medicine. She is an attending neonatologist at Connecticut Children's Medical Center, where she provides intensive care services, transitional medical care services, and neurodevelopmental follow-up. Dr. Sanders is a frequent invited speaker for conferences featuring trauma-informed care, ethical decision making, and social and emotional development of infants and children.

Liza Morton, CPsychol, PhD, MSc, is a chartered counselling psychologist in independent practice in Stirling, Scotland. She also leads the Professional Practice Module on Strathclyde University's Clinical Health Psychology MSc and is an Honorary Senior Research Fellow at the University of Suffolk's Congenital Cardiac Research Centre. Liza is passionate about using psychological knowledge to improve both the quality of care and wider experience of living with a heart condition from birth. Her experience in this area bridges academia, lifelong personal experience and engagement with key stakeholders and policy makers. Liza campaigns voluntarily for improved care for adults born with a heart condition as the Somerville Foundation's Scottish campaign manager. Liza has complete congenital heart block and an atrial septal defect, and as the youngest recipient of an implantable cardiac device (at 11 days old) in the late 1970s, she has received pioneering medical treatment for her condition since birth.

Preface

Why Polyvagal Theory Was Welcomed by Therapists

Stephen W. Porges

POLYVAGAL THEORY WAS unveiled to the scientific community on October 8, 1994. On that date in Atlanta, a polyvagal model with its theoretical implications was introduced in my presidential address to the Society for Psychophysiological Research. A few months later the theory was disseminated as a publication in the society's journal, *Psychophysiology* (Porges, 1995). The article was titled "Orienting in a Defensive World: Mammalian Modifications of Our Evolutionary Heritage. A Polyvagal Theory." The title, crafted to cryptically encode several features of the theory, was intended to emphasize that mammals had evolved in a hostile environment in which survival was dependent on their ability to down regulate states of defense with states of safety and trust, states that supported cooperative behavior and health.

The theory, as initially presented, did not propose applications to mental health and psychiatric disorders. The theory was proposed to generate testable hypotheses and to stimulate research expanding our understanding of how the autonomic nervous system influenced mental, behavioral, and physiological processes. Polyvagal Theory was generated as an expansive brain-body model that emphasized the bidirectional communication between the brain and the body. The theory, with its strong evolutionary and developmental perspectives, was proposed as a framework to explore links among observable behaviors, psychological processes, and autonomic state.

When the theory was initially presented, I was unaware that clinicians would embrace it. I had conceptualized the theory as a structure for generating testable hypotheses within the research community. Consistent with my initial expectations, the theory has had an impact in science and has been cited in several thousand peer-reviewed publications representing several disciplines, including neonatology, obstetrics, anesthesiology, biomedical engineering, internal medicine, psychology, psychiatry, dentistry, human factors, sociology, and philosophy. However, I did not anticipate that the main impact of the theory would be to provide plausible neurophysiological explanations for experiences described by individuals who have experienced trauma. For these individuals the theory provided an understanding of how, after experiencing life-threat, their neural reactions were retuned towards a defensive bias and they lost the resilience to return to a state of safety.

Since the first presentation of Polyvagal Theory, there has been a great interest in applying the theory in clinical practice. This interest greatly expanded with the publication in 2011 by Norton of *The Polyvagal Theory: Neurophysiological Foundations of Emotions, Attachment, Communication, and Self-Regulation.* The publication of the book provided an opportunity for clinicians to obtain information on the theory that previously was available only through academic and digital libraries.

During the 20-plus years since the publication of my presidential address, thousands of scientists have cited the theory in their research. However, more surprising has been the reception by the nonacademic clinical world. An inspection of the number of web pages mentioning Polyvagal Theory is in the tens of thousands, and my talks on YouTube have cumulatively received several hundred thousand hits. Moreover, I have been interviewed on several podcasts including *Dr. Drew, Bulletproof Radio, Darma Café,* and *Shrink Rap Radio.*

The turning point for the transition of Polyvagal Theory from academic research to clinical application occurred on May 21, 1999, when Bessel van der Kolk invited me to talk at his annual Boston trauma conference. Bessel structured the program to focus on how neuroscience informed research on trauma. Being naive about trauma and the clinical histories of survivors of trauma, I was unaware that Polyvagal Theory could provide insights into understanding reactions to trauma and could inform treatment.

A critical component of Polyvagal Theory is focused on the shift in neural regulation of the heart that occurred during vertebrate evolution, especially during the transition from the now-extinct primitive reptiles to the first mammals. Through evolution, the neural regulation of the vertebrate autonomic nervous system progressed through three global stages, with the third stage being present only in mammals. By the time mammals evolved, all three stages were represented: 1) a uniquely mammalian circuit that calmed and cued others to calm; 2) a circuit that supported mobilization behaviors including the fight-or-flight system; and 3) an ancient immobilization circuit represented in virtually all vertebrates that was capable of rapidly shutting down behavioral and physiological systems requiring metabolic resources. The mammalian calming circuit involved a vagal pathway as well as neural pathways regulating striated muscles of the face and head. The mobilization system involved the sympathetic nervous system and the adrenals. The ancient shutdown circuit involved a vagal pathway originating from a brain stem area different from the calming vagal pathway.

Polyvagal Theory provided an understanding of how mammals could shift from an aggressive fight-or-flight state to a calm state that would promote intimacy and optimize health, growth, and restoration. However, the theory also identified a very ancient defense system that, unlike the fight-or-flight system, was mediated by a vagal pathway that originated in an area of the brain stem different from the vagal pathway that calmed and down regulated defense. Thus, the origins of the polyvagal theory were rooted in the neuroanatomical and neurophysiological shifts in the regulation of the vertebrate heart that occurred through evolution. These phylogenetic transitions resulted in mammals having two vagal pathways: one related to calm states and social communication and the other related to an immobilization defense reaction.

Within Polyvagal Theory, the newer mammalian vagal circuit was codified as the social engagement system (see Porges, 2001). This circuit was most accessible during states of trust and safety. Withdrawal of this system enabled the efficient expression of a fight-or-flight system, while withdrawal of the fight-or-flight system uncovered an evolutionarily ancient shutdown system. The shutdown system, when enabled in mammals, results in fainting, defecation, and, as I would learn later, dissociation. This immobilization response was the body's attempt to become inanimate in the presence of a predator. It is important to note that neural mechanisms involved in the fight-or-flight system (i.e., sympathetic nervous system) and the neural mechanisms involved in the shutdown system are also recruited during safe calm states to efficiently support homeostasis and to enable play and intimacy. However, when not in a state of safety, the autonomic nervous system efficiently supports defensive strategies of fight-or-flight and shutdown.

By understanding the phylogenetic changes in the neural regulation of the vertebrate autonomic nervous system, Polyvagal Theory proposed a hierarchy of reactions to challenges that paralleled evolution in reverse. This strategy was consistent with the construct of dissolution, or evolution in reverse, proposed by John Hughlings Jackson (1884) to explain the disinhibition of "older" brain structures when "newer" brain structures were damaged. The mechanism through which cues in the environment reflexively (without awareness) triggered massive adaptive shifts in autonomic state was subsequently added to the theory with the construct of neuroception (Porges, 2003, 2004).

After presenting the theory at Bessel's Boston trauma meeting, I was informed that Polyvagal Theory provided a missing construct in the explanation of experiences following trauma. Prior to my presentation, the scientific explanation of the effects of trauma focused on the assumption that the trauma reactions were fight-or-flight reactions, mediated by the sympathetic nervous system and the hypothalamic–pituitary–adrenal (HPA) axis. In general, these reactions have been clustered in the term *stress*. Consistent with this prevalent global stress model, survivors of trauma were categorized and diagnosed with a disorder known as post-traumatic stress disorder (PTSD).

The word *stress* within the diagnostic label fit nicely with an assumption that the trauma-related disruptions to homeostatic functions were due to alterations in sympathetic nervous system and HPA axis function. However, physiological data and personal experiences did not support this contention. Slowly, a different narrative emerged for survivors of trauma, which included a down regulation of the sympathetic nervous system and HPA axis, convergent with personal experiences of shutdown, immobilization, and dissociation. Polyvagal Theory provided a neurophysiological model that coincided with the experiences of many survivors of trauma.

Personal communications, such as the quote below, illustrate how Polyvagal Theory has provided survivors of abuse and trauma with a better understanding of bodily reactions.

> I read about the body immobilizing instead of fighting or fleeing. I am now 69 and when I was 18 I was nearly strangled and then sexually assaulted. Years later I was speaking with my daughter about this incident and she was disbelieving that I did what I did and that I froze. I felt so ashamed and judged. After reading your theory I cannot tell you how excited and vindicated I feel. I am crying right now. (Personal communication, 2013)

Unlike many of my colleagues, who treat and study trauma, trauma was not a focus of my research or part of my theoretical agenda. Without traumatologists being interested in Polyvagal Theory, there would not have been an entrée for the theory to contribute to the understanding and treatment of trauma. This entrée was due to three pioneers in traumatology: Peter Levine,

Bessel van der Kolk, and Pat Ogden. Each has graciously welcomed me on their journey to understand and rehabilitate the disruptive effects of trauma. It was through their passion to help their clients, their commitment to learn, and their curiosity to understand the processes involved in experiencing and recovering from trauma that they embraced insights from the theory in their treatment models.

My interactions with Peter started in the late 1970s, when Peter's curiosity led him to call me and discuss models of homeostatic function. At that time, I was developing time series statistical models to describe and quantify the vagal regulation of the heart from beat-to-beat heart rate variability. Peter and I became good friends, and in the late '70s and early '80s participated in think-tank workshops on the neurobiology of emotion regulation. Over the years, I have seen Peter's insights crystalize and evolve into a powerful treatment model that became the basis of Somatic Experiencing. Through Peter I was drawn into the community of somatic therapy.

As I started to be invited to give talks in the more interdisciplinary and eclectic area of somatics and psychotherapy, I was on programs with Pat and Bessel in the 1990s. Pat was developing Sensorimotor Psychotherapy as a bridge between somatic therapy and psychotherapy. She, like Peter, emphasized the potent role of appropriately accessing and managing implicit memories. I met Bessel in the world of somatic therapists as he was on his passionate journey to help his clients. Through Pat, I was a frequent speaker at the annual meetings on attachment and trauma at UCLA organized by Marion Solomon and the Lifespan Learning Institute. These meetings now form the focal point for clinicians interested in interpersonal neurobiology. At the Boston trauma meetings organized by Bessel and the UCLA meetings organized by Marion Solomon, I became good friends with Dan Siegel, Norman Doidge, Allan Schore, Diana Fosha, and Louis Cozolino. As the circle of colleagues expands, our understanding of trauma is enriched. Frequently, several of us are on the same program and have had the opportunity to conduct joint workshops.

Through these interactions, I became informed about the profound disruptive impact of trauma on a significant portion of the population. I became aware that survivors of trauma often go through life without an opportunity to understand their bodily reaction to the trauma or to recover the ability to regulate and to co-regulate their physiological and behavioral state. Many of these individuals are revictimized when discussing their experiences and are often reprimanded for not fighting or fleeing. Others are chastised for not psychologically recovering when there is no apparent physical damage.

The theory stimulated interest in clinical applications. This prompted invitations for me to talk at clinically oriented meetings and to conduct workshops on Polyvagal Theory for clinicians. During the past few years, through the publication of *The Polyvagal Theory* (Porges, 2011) and talks, there has been an expanding awareness of Polyvagal Theory across several clinical areas. This welcoming by the clinical community identified limitations in my knowledge. Although I could talk to clinicians and deconstruct their presentations of clinical cases into constructs described by the theory, I was *not* a clinician; I was limited in how I related the theory to clinical diagnosis, treatment, and outcome. Consistent with these limitations, I continually receive requests to provide more clinical examples in presentations. These experiences have served as the motivation to edit a volume in which clinicians describe how they have applied Polyvagal Theory in their own work.

The current volume evolved through interactions with clinicians who shared with me their enthusiasm and creativity in integrating aspects of Polyvagal Theory into their work. As I discussed clinical applications with many clinicians, the idea of an edited book took form. The goal was not to have authors recapitulate the theory, but to explain how the theory enabled them to expand their work. The authors of the chapters were invited to focus their chapters on how Polyvagal Theory provides insights into their clinical practice; how the theory offers an organizing principle that facilitates a better understanding of clinical conditions and enhances communication with their clients.

My coeditor, Deb Dana, is one of the gifted therapists that I have met on my journey. Deb has an intuitive grasp of Polyvagal Theory and has creatively expanded aspects of the theory into the training models that she teaches in her workshops. Her skillful translation of Polyvagal Theory into exercises and subjective experiences provides clinicians and their clients with a broader understanding how the theory relates to clinical features and treatment outcomes. Deb has played a major role in coordinating this volume by providing editorial guidance and support to our authors. As coeditor, she has created a network of insightful and compassionate clinicians who are generating the models and strategies for polyvagal-informed therapies.

Following this preface are brief chapters from Peter Levine, Bessel van der Kolk, and Pat Ogden. Peter, Bessel, and Pat have welcomed Polyvagal Theory into the world of trauma therapy. Without their interest and foresight, Polyvagal Theory may have languished in my laboratory and not readily transitioned into traumatology. I am sincerely grateful for their passion for improving the quality of life of their clients and their commitment in bringing Polyvagal Theory into their models of therapy.

Since all authors were asked not to retell Polyvagal Theory, I have written an overview chapter on the theory. Following the overview are chapters illustrating and documenting how insightful clinicians have incorporated aspects of the theory into diverse clinical settings. The chapters provide vivid examples of how Polyvagal Theory provides a language of the body that has enabled the authors to passionately express their desire to understand and to optimize the human experience. It is our hope that this edited volume fulfills the need for clinical examples of how Polyvagal Theory can improve the treatment and understanding of clinical conditions.

References

Jackson, J. H. (1884). The Croonian lectures on evolution and dissolution of the nervous system. *British Medical Journal, 1*(1215), 703–707.

Porges, S. W. (1995). Orienting in a defensive world: Mammalian modifications of our evolutionary heritage. A Polyvagal Theory. *Psychophysiology, 32*(4), 301–318.

Porges, S. W. (2001). The Polyvagal Theory: Phylogenetic substrates of a social nervous system. *International Journal of Psychophysiology, 42*(2), 123–146.

Porges, S. W. (2003). Social engagement and attachment. *Annals of the New York Academy of Sciences, 1008*(1), 31–47.

Porges, S. W. (2004). Neuroception: A subconscious system for detecting threats and safety. *Zero to Three (J), 24*(5), 19–24.

Porges, S. W. (2011). *Norton Series on Interpersonal Neurobiology. The Polyvagal Theory: Neurophysiological foundations of emotions, attachment, communication, and self-regulation.* New York, NY: Norton.

Part I

The Introduction of Polyvagal Theory Into the World of Trauma Therapists

1

Polyvagal Theory and Trauma

Peter A. Levine

Abstract: This chapter tells a personal story of the parallel and interactive journeys between two longtime friends and colleagues, as well as an application of Polyvagal Theory involving the understanding of emergent properties of complex systems, bottom-up processing, self-regulation, and the resolution of traumatic experiences. It also discusses how this application of Polyvagal Theory has an impact on the fields of internal medicine and trauma-related chronic pain.

The map may not be the territory, but it sure helps you to get around.
—Peter A. Levine

IN ADDRESSING THE vital role played by Polyvagal Theory, as it informs trauma-based therapies, I have chosen to take a somewhat personal and historical perspective. I begin by reflecting on a four-decade relationship with the senior editor of this volume, a special filial friendship that developed around our shared interests and passion for bottom-up processes, emergent properties, self-regulation, and playful laughter. Since our first meeting in 1978, Stephen Porges and I have remained kindred spirits and willing co-conspirators. His work on Polyvagal Theory developed a key holistic concept he called *neuroception*. This organismic perception was an emergent property of three distinct autonomic, visceral, and somatic states signaling safety, danger, and life-threat. During the decades that Porges was evolving his visionary theory, I was developing my life's work, called Somatic Experiencing.

For most of the previous centuries, with the notable exception of William James and Carl Lange at the turn of the 20th century, the autonomic nervous system and visceral organs were believed to be unconscious, far outside the realm of awareness. However, it was becoming evident to me that this understanding of internal perception was limited, if not fundamentally incorrect. I learned that not only are people able to become aware of their visceral states, but that cultivating this perception is essential to taming various traumatic and other difficult sensations and emotions, including fear, rage, grief, and shame. Indeed, it became increasingly evident that these problematic affects are derivative of habitual muscular and visceral states. Crucially, in order to change our emotional states, it is first necessary to alter the underlying autonomic, visceral, and kinesthetic sensations. For this transformation, it is essential to develop a reliable *interoceptive awareness*. Interoception is any sense that is normally stimulated from within the body. This involves numerous sensory receptors in the muscles and in the internal organs. These receptors are neurologically linked to nuclei in the brainstem as part of a complex feedback system. Interoception is thought to be abnormal in clinical conditions such as PTSD and alexithymia. So, while mine was a clinical body awareness approach, it was clearly mirroring Porges's Polyvagal Theory, as this short chapter will, hopefully, elucidate.

This unfolding story traces back to an unexpected and pivotal event that occurred in 1969 as I was developing a body-mind stress treatment modality. At that time, I was in the midst of a doctoral program in the Department of Medical and Biological Physics at UC Berkley. In this interdisciplinary program, I was free to study in my elected fields of neurophysiology, stress research, zoology, physics, and math, as well as continuing with my clinical practice. Ed Jackson, a psychiatrist friend, knowing of my keen interest in stress and in mind-body healing, asked me to see a patient of his I'll call Nancy. At the time, I had been experimenting with a series of body awareness exercises on a group of 15 people who had significantly elevated blood pressure indicative of chronic sympathetic arousal. I had found that teaching them how to relax certain muscles in their neck, jaw, and shoulders often brought their high blood pressure to a normal level (120/70), sometimes in a matter of 20 minutes. This shift would imply that a dynamic balance between the sympathetic and parasympathetic branches of the autonomic nervous system was restored.

Nancy had been suffering from what would now be called fibromyalgia, chronic fatigue, irritable bowl syndrome, migraines, severe premenstrual syndrome, and urinary problems. She had also been plagued with debilitating panic attacks and agoraphobia to the extent that she was unable to leave her house without being accompanied by her husband. Even with this critical support, such an excursion was terrifying and exhausting. Her life had become a living hell. My psychiatrist friend thought that perhaps some of my relaxation exercises might at least help with her severely limiting anxiety.

With the best of intentions, I began a relaxation session with Nancy. On arrival, her heart rate was pounding at about 120 beats per minute (as seen by observing her carotid artery pulse), indicating sympathetic arousal. Her head and eyes were cast downward, assiduously avoiding any eye contact with me. I cautiously taught her how to relax certain muscles in her neck and jaw and, to my self-satisfaction, her heart rate slowly dropped to a more normal 75 beats per minute, indicating a balanced and reciprocal relationship between sympathetic and parasympathetic. I wasn't only pleased with the efficacy of my techniques, but I was grateful for her comforting improvement. However, just as she seemed to be settling, her heart rate abruptly skyrocketed to about 160 beats per minute (hyperactivation of the sympathetic system), followed by a gradual descent, much to my relief. However, my reprieve was short lived, as her heart rate rapidly plummeted to a frightful 50 beats per minute (seeming to indicate the onset of an unexpectedly powerful parasympathetic dominance). At this point, her face became deathly pale and her fingers turned icy cold. Her eyes desperately locked onto mine as she pleaded, "I'm dying. Don't let me die. Help me . . . Don't let me die!" At that dark moment of peril, just as her pulse reached the slowest rate yet, I was able to guide her to envision an effective motoric action of escape. Out of the blue, a fleeting image of a tiger, readying to spring at its prey, had appeared to me. Following my intuition, without fully understanding the significance, I engaged her in mobilizing an active defensive response by commanding, "Nancy, there's a tiger chasing you! Run, run fast, climb those rocks and escape!" Later, when she described her experience in the session, Nancy reported how, at first, her legs couldn't move; that they "felt like lead." But then she noticed that her body was "filling up with energy." She noted that, with my encouragement, she was able to stay with these challenging sensations; she could feel herself starting to move and then running, full-out, culminating in a triumphant escape. Nancy reported that after climbing the rocks, she turned and looked down, and instead of seeing the tiger, she saw herself at the age of 4, held down by several doctors and nurses who were forcing an ether mask over her face for a tonsillectomy. Nancy had been completely terrified and overwhelmed at that time. Her body had, for 20 years, needed to mobilize an active escape. She finally did this, retrospectively, in response to the evocative image of the tiger, introduced at the critical moment of her collapse. Her successful escape was now embodied in the emergence of a new (reconsolidated) procedural memory engram; one of power and agency, instead of helplessness and defeat (Levine, 2015).

During the session, Nancy experienced waves of shaking and trembling, cycles of heart rate changes, and changes in temperature—from cold to hot and finally to an even, warm skin tone. Each of these cycles was followed by deep spontaneous breaths. At the end of her session, she opened her eyes and looked toward me, this time without fear and grasping, but rather with the spontaneous delight of mutual connection. As we shared this soft gaze together, she reported that she felt, in her body, as though she was "being held in waves of tingling warmth."

We continued with a few more sessions. Afterward, she reported that many of her physical symptoms had resolved or greatly improved, and she was able to resume her doctoral work (ironically, in physiology). Later at a 2-year follow-up, she had not experienced any further panic attacks and was enjoying exploring the many interesting things that Berkeley had to offer. Needless to say, I began to try to understand her extreme physiological changes and the salubrious effect at the end of the session. In order to comprehend what had happened in the session, as well as her long-term improvement, I was pulled in several directions.

First, I was finding pieces of the puzzle in the field of ethology, the study of wild animals in their natural environments, as well as my evolving understanding of the autonomic nervous system. In 1969, some months before my encounter with Nancy, I was participating in a weekly seminar on animal behavior in the zoology department. One of the professors, Dr. Peter Marler (an ethologist), had mentioned an obscure biological phenomenon. He described how, when a wild animal is physically restrained without a struggle, it enters a dramatically immobilized state called *tonic immobility*, known by the colloquial phrase "playing possum." During tonic immobility, the animal's respiration is so faint that one can barely detect life. To the naked eye it looks dead. However, it is not just playing dead; instead the animal has entered a profound physiological state, one sometimes called *thanatosis*, because of its apparent similarity to death. In this state, an animal's heart rate typically drops to an extreme low because of parasympathetic dominance. Such an animal spontaneously recovers from this paralytic state in a matter of seconds to minutes (usually after the predator has left the scene). However, if the animal is frightened before or during the restraint, it remains locked in this deathlike state for a much longer time. This, I reasoned, was what had happened to Nancy when she was held down—physically immobilized and terrified.

When visiting a physiology laboratory at the Federal Medical University of Brazil, one of the few groups studying the neural substrates of immobility, I had the rare opportunity to observe guinea pigs who were first frightened and then physically restrained. As these terrified animals struggled to escape, their heart rates, like Nancy's, were initially very high, just as you would expect in an animal activating a fight-or-flight response (i.e., sympathetic dominance). However, as their frantic struggles continued, their heart rates and respiration suddenly dropped, precipitously, to a very low level (i.e., parasympathetic dominance). Unlike relaxation, which is typically associated with parasympathetic activity, these animals' reactions (like Nancy's) were hardly relaxed ones. They appeared terrified, frozen, and/or collapsed. I was intrigued by the additional observation that the guinea pigs, who were repeatedly spooked every time they started to come out of tonic immobility, succumbed to immobility for an even more extended period of time. In one instance, this extended tonic immobility lasted well over 24 hours, rather than the seconds to minutes of the tonic immobility that I had first learned about in my zoology seminar. This induction of prolonged tonic immobility, known as *fear-potentiated immobility*, was first elucidated by Gallup and Maser in their 1977 book (Maser & Seligman, 1977). A fortuitous example of the blending of clinical and experimental occurred when a stranger appeared at the conclusion of a lecture I was giving at a psychiatric conference. With an impish grin, the man announced himself as Jack Maser, the very man I had just quoted in my speech and video demonstration. He expressed sheer delight that his academic research from decades before helped to support a clinical application for healing human trauma. Such synchronicity never ceases to delight me.

Together, Maser's research and the guinea pig experiments I had observed in Brazil gave me a clearer understanding of the healing trajectory of clients such as Nancy, what kept them stuck, and how they finally resolved their traumas. What was the similarity between immobilized mammals and traumatized individuals? In particular, what is it that kept humans in this frozen or collapsed state, seemingly indefinitely? My epiphany came when I realized that my clients, like the spooked guinea pigs, were being repeatedly frightened. However, these traumatized humans were spooked by the very bodily sensations that would have arisen as their immobilized state began to proceed toward a natural resolution. The initial sensation, as the thaw began, was a re-encounter with the high sympathetic charge that was present prior to the onset of immobility. Their fearful reactivity to their own internal sensations of release from the freeze state and into high sympathetic charge was sending them back into immobility, keeping them trapped indefinitely, like the repeatedly frightened guinea pigs who were locked in terror. This was the difference between immobilized animals in the wild who are not frightened and frightened again, and who quickly return to homeostasis when the threat is past, and traumatized humans who continue to frighten themselves repeatedly, and thus can stay stuck in trauma for a lifetime. In the words of the 1960s band Dan Hicks and His Hot Licks: "It's only me I'm afraid of; I won't scare myself."

After my epiphany of how internalized fear maintains the state of immobility, seemingly forever, my life's work was reoriented to a relentless pursuit of an effective, gentle, and precise method to guide clients into, and then out of, the sensations of immobility, so that they could befriend these restorative sensations. In this way, they could gradually move out of shutdown into hyperarousal (flight-fight) and then, with guidance, restore homeostatic equilibrium and inner balance (see Figure 1.1). My passion for refining this process redirected my pursuits from an academic career to that of a clinician and gentleman scientist. It is here that Stephen's and my roles diverged, but our interests nonetheless converged.

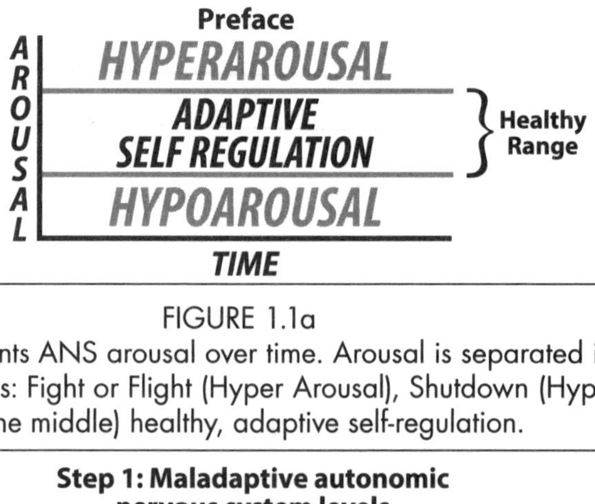

FIGURE 1.1a
This chart represents ANS arousal over time. Arousal is separated into three distinct states: Fight or Flight (Hyper Arousal), Shutdown (Hypo Arousal, and (in the middle) healthy, adaptive self-regulation.

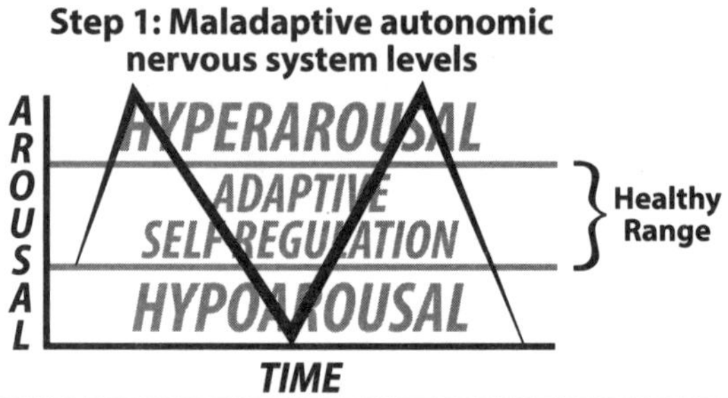

FIGURE 1.1b
A traumatized individual is unable to regulate their ANS arousal, jumping rapidly between extreme Hyper-Arousal and extreme Hypo-Arousal.

There were several lessons that I took from the chance event with Nancy and the animal observations that followed. One of my first unsettling realizations was how close I had come to retraumatizing Nancy. By exposing her to the most frightening part of a traumatic experience, I had inadvertently risked returning her right to that original state of overwhelm, freeze, and collapse (similar to the guinea pigs in Brazil who were spooked and respooked). I could have essentially abandoned her to even greater depths of helplessness and despair.

Another strong influence, at this time of my life, was the disastrous human toll taken on the returning veterans from the Vietnam War. As a healer and clinician, I was addressing the invisible injuries of this war as well as sequelae to the trauma "cure du jour" called exposure therapy, which was being liberally applied to the traumatized vets. In this sledgehammer approach to treatment, these vets were instructed to relive the worst, most horrific parts of a traumatic

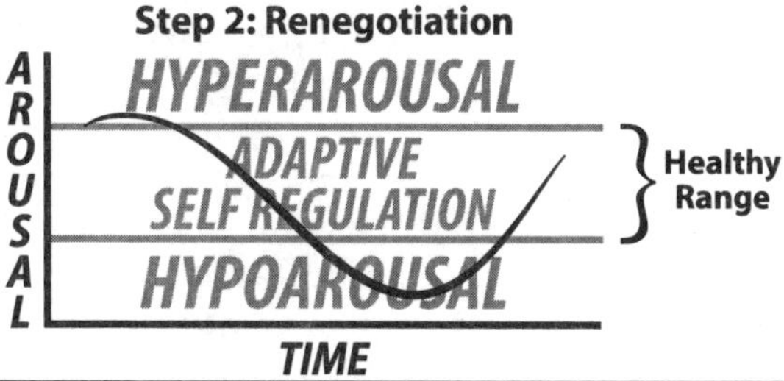

FIGURE 1.1c
We help contain these erratic fluctuations by slowing down their experience and curbing their intensity. As a person is able to experience a sense of control of their arousal, they renegotiate their relationship to the trauma.

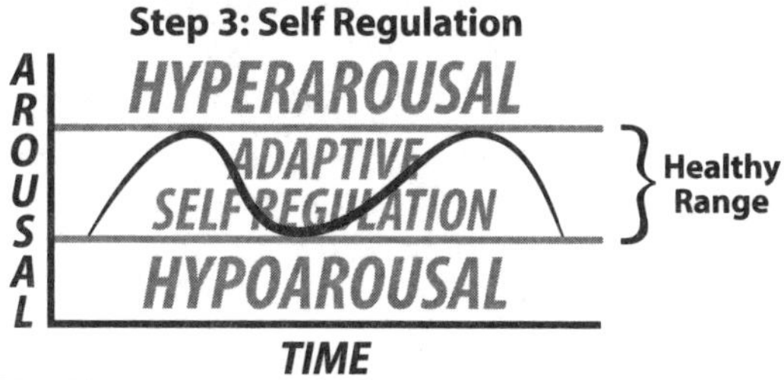

FIGURE 1.1d
As the individual is better able to modulate their arousal, they are more able to flexibly adapt to the stress of everyday situations, and return to adaptive self-regulation.

episode, over and over, until the "swamp" was somehow drained. However, based on my observations of their continuing shell shock, I felt that this kind of flooding carried an unnecessary risk of retraumatization. (The diagnosis of PTSD was still a decade away. Shell shock was an honest, graphic term left over from the disastrous effects of World War I.) Therefore, as I continued to develop Somatic Experiencing, I incorporated a fundamental principle that I called titration. This intentional slowdown of dynamic processing involves working with the types of physiological and emotional responses that I had observed with Nancy. However, with the use of titration, these responses are engaged in a much milder, softer form. Gradually, the person is guided to experience only small parts of a traumatic imprint, cushioned between orienting and settling phases. The subtle interoceptive awareness that is evoked allows the client to minimize the very real and dangerous risk of flooding, and instead offers the opportunity to successfully digest and integrate (i.e., renegotiate) these pieces, one small element at a time (Levine, 2010).

One of the biggest mysteries of my session with Nancy concerned the abruptness (and directions) of her heart rate changes. These reflected discontinuous (and paradoxical) shifts in autonomic activity. What perplexed me about her heart rate was that it went from a very high activation level (indicating sympathetic preparation for flight) to a much lower rate, seeming to portend death. At the time, it was believed that there was a reciprocal (a linear, inverse) relationship between the sympathetic and parasympathetic nervous systems. In meeting stress or threat, there was a charging of sympathetic activation, followed by a sympathetic discharge, along with parasympathetic rebound and deep relaxation (see Figure 1.2). Let us utilize the following analogy to convey this flexible reciprocity: Imagine a finely tuned car in which you gradually accelerate (foot gently on the gas), and then remove your foot from the accelerator and lightly transfer it to the brake, steadily increasing the pressure until the car is gently brought to rest.

However, in Nancy's case, a very dissimilar chain of events had her heart rate swinging wildly between a very highly sympathetic state and an even higher parasympathetic state. Parasympathetic dominance, which appeared to override the high sympathetic activation, caused her heart rate to plummet precipitously to the deathlike state. If her parasympathetic system was asserting itself properly, then she should have felt relaxed. Instead, she went into total paralyzing terror. This just didn't make sense. Clearly, her nervous system was not functioning in a balanced way, but why?

It was apparent that the parasympathetic system had overridden the effect of the sympathetic, even while Nancy's sympathetic system remained fully engaged. It was as though, in the car analogy, the (sympathetic) accelerator

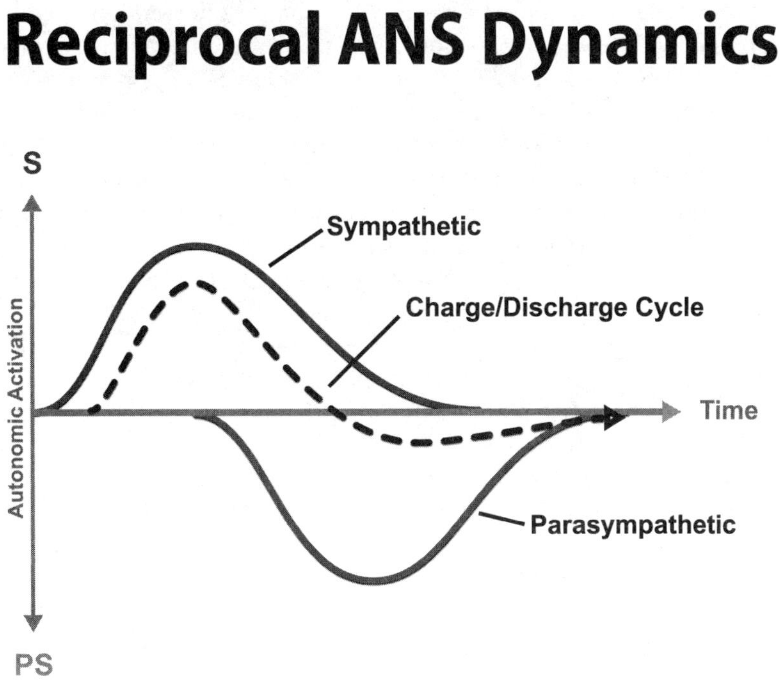

FIGURE 1.2

and the (vagal) brake were both fully on, simultaneously. The car was immobilized until the brake was released, at which point the car would abruptly lurch forward. Likewise, Nancy's response seemed to indicate a concurrent sympathetic/parasympathetic response, where a (dorsal) vagal brake had her immobilized, but with an underlying high sympathetic charge (i.e., she was frozen in terror; see Figure 1.3). The image of the tiger seemed to help the sympathetic system break through the override (the freeze), and organized that charge into a coherent active escape response, thus completing a meaningful course of action: escape. This allowed her to come back into the balanced sympathetic and parasympathetic (ventral vagal region) linear reciprocal range where she could experience profound relaxation.

Though the image of the tiger rescued Nancy (and myself) from the disastrous likelihood of retraumatization, it was at this point merely an intuition drawn, in part, from my zoological and physiological studies. The puzzle continued to plague me. I still needed a clear map of the internal autonomic states of my clients to know precisely what kind of intervention would be appropriate; when, where, and how. This understanding was particularly important as I had begun to teach my nascent method to a small group of Berkeley students in 1972.

The missing pieces finally came together in 1995. Stephen Porges addressed this autonomic paradox when he published his landmark work positing the existence of a second parasympathetic system controlled by the 10th cranial nerve from the dorsal motor nucleus of the mid–brain stem. This primitive, unmyelinated vagus system appeared to be able to operate in parallel and somewhat independently of the sympathetic one (Levine, 1977). The pieces of this confounding enigma were finally coming together. However, let me return to the chronology of our historical perspective, once again revisiting the 1970s when I was confronting the conundrum in my doctoral research.

During the middle of that decade I had noticed an interesting relationship between breath and variations in heart rate. In healthy individuals, there was a smooth relationship between inhalation and an increase in heart rate; and then, on exhalation, there was a decrease in heart rate. This seemed to be associated with the reciprocal sympathetic/parasympathetic balance. However, as an individual's stress and anxiety levels increased, there was little or no change in the heart rate in response to inhalation and exhalation. And then, with the chronically stressed and traumatized people that I was working with, there was often a paradoxical and opposite response. The heart rate actually decreased on inhalation and increased on exhalation. This observed reversal, I reasoned, was associated with individuals demonstrating concurrent sympathetic and parasympathetic activation (see reference to spillover in Figure 1.3). This relationship between breath and heart rate was called *respiratory sinus arrhythmia*, which is a robust index of parasympathetic (vagal) tone to the heart. What was most intriguing was that, as my clients resolved their traumas and inner autonomic balance was restored, their respiratory sinus arrhythmia also demonstrated parallel positive changes. However, as much as I tried, I couldn't find a precise way to quantify respiratory sinus arrhythmia so that I could track the degree of clinical improvement as manifested by the change from dysfunction to restoration of healthy autonomic balance. At that time I received a copy of an obscure article on ADHD by Stephen Porges (Porges, Walter, Korb, & Sprague, 1975). In this article, Porges described mathematical measures he called *vagal tone*. This measure reflected the amplitude of respiratory sinus arrhythmia and "weighted coherence," indicative of the "phase locking" between the spontaneous oscillations in respiration and heart rate. This

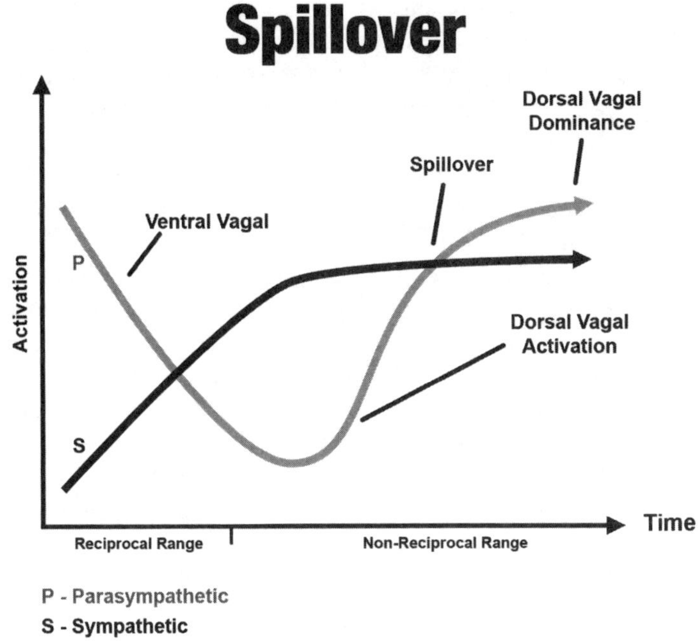

FIGURE 1.3

indication of coherence was precisely the type of measure that I had been searching for.

I immediately sought out the young Dr. Porges. Then I (the once-young Peter Levine) hurriedly described some of my clinical observations, and sent him my doctoral dissertation on accumulated stress. One week and several long-distance-landline phone calls later, Stephen and I met at UCLA, where he was beginning a sabbatical. We hit it off immediately and have remained colluding subversives over the following decades. However, allow me to indulge you with some selected details of this quixotic meet-up and connection.

For this part of our shared story, I must defer primarily to Stephen's recollection of this amusing tale. When he offered to pick me up at the Los Angeles airport, I told him that I would wear a red carnation prominently displayed in the lapel of my white sports jacket so that he could easily recognize me. With that in mind, he was surprised to see this eccentric hippie accosted by a young damsel dispensing the Hare Krishna version of the Bhagavad Gita while loudly proclaiming, "God loves you, and I love you." To this impassioned declaration, I apparently swept her up and planted a hearty kiss on her cheek, with the rejoinder, "I love you, too!" She reversed direction and fled in apparent distress. Steve watched this strange occurrence from a distance before tentatively approaching me. With a bit of uncertainty and curiosity, we made our introductions before heading off to the UCLA campus, thus beginning our 40 years of brotherly collaboration.

The day of our first meeting was spent in a nearly hypomanic excitement. When I showed Stephen some of my clinical and theoretical data regarding these strange autonomic effects, particularly those of parasympathetic spillover, where there is concurrent activation of high sympathetic and even higher parasympathetic tone, he echoed my previous thoughts that it just wasn't possible; it didn't make any sense. But this is what I had clearly observed. Perhaps, for both of us, a seed was planted. In any case, Stephen Porges first proposed his Polyvagal Theory about 20 years later (Porges, 1995). This unifying theory would forever change the landscape of clinical and theoretical work in trauma (Levine, 2010; van der Kolk, 2014). It would also contribute to a number of medical, social, and educational fields. Most importantly, for me, it provided the remaining piece of the puzzle. It is for this work that I am honored to present my perspective on his immense and unique contribution.

Polyvagal Theory offers us a clear map of the basic physiological states that drive specific perceptions, particularly those regarding safety, opportunity, danger, and life-threat. It demonstrates how neuroception is an emergent property of certain core (autonomic) neurobiological systems. Just as maps are useful in finding particular parts of a city, maps of the human organism are important in navigating the landscape of trauma and informing its healing. It is here that Porges's groundbreaking work provides an eloquent, well-reasoned, and broadly supported treasure map of the psychophysiological systems that implicitly govern traumatic states. The same systems also mediate core feelings of safety, goodness, and belonging. In this regard, Polyvagal Theory illuminates the pathways for integration, recovery, and transformation (Porges, 2001). In addition, his model clarifies why certain common approaches to trauma therapy frequently fail.

Briefly, Porges's theory states that three basic neural energy subsystems underpin the overall state of the autonomic nervous system and their emergent behaviors, emotions, and perceptions (see Figure 1.4). The most primitive of these three systems, the *dorsal-vagal system*, stems from about 600 million years ago and finds its origin in early (vertebral/segmental) fish species, including cartilaginous fish such as sharks and rays. The function of this primitive system is immobilization, metabolic conservation, and overall shutdown. Its target is the internal, visceral organs. The next stage in evolutionary development is the *sympathetic nervous system*. This global arousal system evolved from the rep-

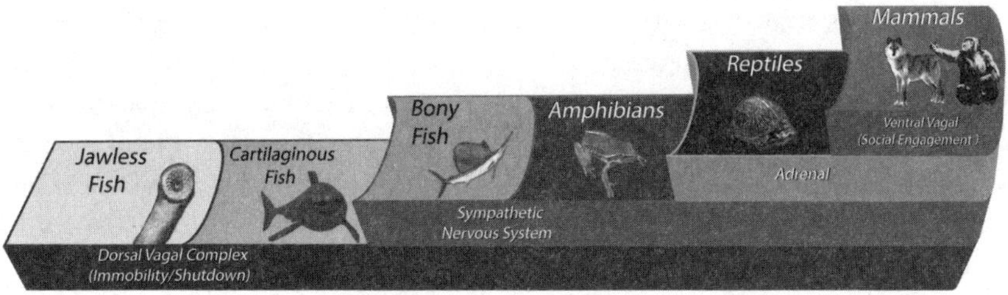

FIGURE 1.4

tilian period of about 400 million years ago. Its function is mobilization and enhanced action (as in fight or flight); its target in the body is the limbs. Finally, the third and phylogenetically most recent system (deriving from about 200 million years ago) exists only in mammals, and particularly in the later social mammals (from about 100 million; see Figure 1.4). This neural subsystem shows its greatest refinement in the primates, where it mediates complex social and attachment behaviors. It utilizes the ventral branch of the parasympathetic nervous system, the so-called mammalian or smart vagus nerve. These nerve fibers are myelinated for better speed and precision. This ventral system is linked neuroanatomically to the cranial nerves that mediate acoustic tuning, vocalization, and facial expression. Porges has aptly referred to this integrated function as the *social engagement system*. This mammalian system came online when Nancy initiated the soft mutual gaze at the end of her session.

In the Consulting Room

About a decade after my encounter with Nancy (in 1980), the definition of PTSD was entombed in the nomenclature of the *DSM* (the diagnostic manual for mental illness) as a psychiatric disorder. Here the listed symptoms were largely about hyperactivation of the sympathetic branch of the autonomic nervous system. These included hyperarousal, hypervigilance, exaggerated startle, flashbacks, sleep disorders, and intrusive thoughts. However, my clinical observations in the 1970s and 1980s made it absolutely clear that many of my clients also suffered from symptoms of shutdown, involving (as it is now known) the unmyelinated dorsal-vagal parasympathetic system. These individuals, rather, presented as being depressed, apathetic, lethargic, dissociated, and lacking vitality. They also suffered from various physical (functional) complaints similar to Nancy's, including unexplained chronic pain, gastrointestinal disorders, cardiac arrhythmias, and various urinary tract symptoms.

Around this time, a few of my Berkeley students asked me to observe how they worked with their trauma patients. One thing that stood out to me was that they were all directly facing their clients and looking, compassionately, toward them. This empathy, however, was to no avail as their clients looked away and downward, seeming to purposefully avoid any kind of benevolent eye contact, almost as if they feared that they were going to be be shamed by their therapist.

Dogma had it that trauma was created by a betrayal of trust, a rupture within the context of a relationship, and by someone who was supposed to care for and protect the client. Hence, it was assumed that empathy, and the building of a caring relationship with the therapist, were necessary and sufficient to repair the trauma. This caring and emotional holding was expressed through eye contact, reassuring vocal prosody, and the compassionate facial expressions of the therapist. However, in my observations of the dyadic body language between my students and their clients, this clearly wasn't helping. Rather, the clients seemed to become even more withdrawn and stuck when such eye contact and kindness were offered.

In a published study, Ruth Lanius, one of the most original neuroscientists studying trauma (along with her colleagues), conducted the following simple experiment (Steuwe et al., 2014). They showed the picture of a kind, friendly face to a nontraumatized control group of subjects who were positioned in a high-powered brain scanner. Not surprisingly, the prefrontal cortex increased its activity, while the activity in the amygdala decreased. This was an expected example of a compassionate face having a calming effect on an individual. In stark contrast, however, when Lanius showed the same photograph to a group of chronically traumatized individuals (with relational rupture), that area of the prefrontal cortex actually decreased its activity, while an area in the brain stem, the periaqueductal gray, significantly increased activity. This is the very area of the brain responsible for immobility, shutdown, and terror. Indeed, the kind, empathic face, with its invitation to eye contact, seemed only to make the traumatized subjects feel worse, probably much worse. Further, from my clinical experience, the friendly face activates postural and psychophysiological states of shame, including acute vasodilation, loss of muscular tonus, loss of vital energy, and averting of the eyes. These states need to be worked with by gradually deconstructing the psychophysiological and postural shame state and reconstructing those of pride and dignity.

This experiment, though conducted decades later, clarified what I had previously observed with many of my clients and then taught to my students. It explained why the clients would look down and away from my face, or, if they did look at me, it was as though they were looking through me, as though they were looking behind or past me. Because of this problematic interface, I had learned to position my chair at a 90-degree angle to the client's. I showed my students how this gave the client the choice to easily look away, to look interoceptively inside of themselves, or, if the client wished, to initiate eye contact.

It was here that my intuition was confirmed by Polyvagal Theory and the aforementioned work of Ruth Lanius. The avoidance of eye contact, I reasoned, was because when people are in a state of vagal shutdown (hypoarousal), they will perceive nearly everything in their external environment as a life-threat, and they will continue to perceive this overwhelming threat until their internal state changes. The avoidance of eye contact by prey, in the face of a lethal predator, is seen throughout the animal kingdom. Direct eye contact by prey is very likely to incite a lethal attack. Indeed, we Colorado hikers are instructed by the local fish and game wardens, if we should encounter a bear, to look away and down, and then to slowly back away.

In addition, shutdown (hypoaroused) individuals frequently experience pervasive shame. This corrosive and debilitating emotion is also locked in the shutdown autonomic nervous system and in a particular collapsed somatic posture. Indeed, until this pattern is altered (deconstructed and renegotiated), it is difficult if not impossible to exit those debilitating shame states. Hence, for these reasons, the therapist should not initially try to engage eye contact or make too many compassionate, contact-full, reflective statements. However, after clients have shifted from states of hypoarousal and shutdown into states of hyperarousal and hypervigilance, it is possible to engage them with a limited degree of eye contact and prosody. This can be useful to help guide them through these difficult energetic sensations and then to support them as they settle from sympathetic hyperarousal into relaxation and restored equilibrium. After this cycle of activation and discharge, clients will often, and spontaneously, seek out and sustain soft eye contact, and/or will orient around the room—as though they are seeing it for the first time.

In my efforts to explain how to navigate these inner states to my students, the Polyvagal Theory framework provided a clear map of the client's autonomic nervous system mode, indicating just where an individual was operating. This way the therapist could identify and time interventions appropriately and guide the client effectively. For example, hyperarousal is manifested by more active indicators of autonomic state, such as increased heart rate, rapid and high chest breathing that sometimes borders on hyperventilation, furtive glances, fidgeting, dilated pupils, wide eyes, and edginess, often described as "jumping out of one's skin," as well as other intense body sensations. On the other hand, some of the basic signs of hypoarousal (dorsal-vagal) are appearing spaced out, being dissociated, lacking vitality, having a flat or frozen face, exhibiting facial pallor, and manifesting a slowed heart rate, though this can be unstable—that is, switching abruptly between fast and slow (tachycardia and bradycardia). In addition, the client's chronic physical symptoms often give an indication of dorsal-vagal shutdown. These include chronic fatigue, gastrointestinal and urinary problems, cardiac arrhythmias, episodes of dizziness, and some types of asthma, as well as certain autoimmune disorders.

During Somatic Experiencing trauma therapy, when the client is hyperaroused, the therapist can support downregulation of this sympathetic charge using the principle of *pendulation* (Levine, 2010). Pendulation refers to the natural oscillation between opposing forces of contraction and expansion. This innate rhythm helps a client experience a sense of flow that contradicts the fixity of trauma. This dynamic principle embodies the ever-familiar, but often ignored, axiom "what goes up, will come down." What hyperaroused clients usually do, however, is brace against the contraction associated with increased arousal. This prevents an expansion that would reduce the hyperarousal. Another strategy to facilitate pendulation is to bring clients' attention to their extremities (e.g., their hands or feet). This awareness will often provide some sense of containment and internal safety, thus enhancing ventral vagal activity, which, according to Polyvagal Theory, reduces sympathetic hyperactivation. Prosody, along with some eye contact and gentle reassurance from the therapist (a joining), helps the client to open to these intense hyperarousal sensations and settle through pendulation. For such joining to be coherent and authentic, it is essential for therapists to also feel their own sensations and regulate their own sensations and emotions. This somatic resonance is a basic principle of body psychotherapies and facilitates the benefits of pendulation. In terms of Polyvagal Theory, the therapist is able to use her calm, centered social engagement capacity to track and guide the client from the hyperaroused (sympathetic) state toward internal regulation and the neuroception of safety.

To summarize, pendulation implies that every contraction (fearful sensation) will be followed by an expansion (a sense of pleasure and release). However, this can also be frightening or unsettling, but in a different way. This is because this release is, initially, so unfamiliar to the client. This restoration of the ventral vagal parasympathetic relaxation response reestablishes autonomic balance. During this settling phase, the therapist (and client) may notice easier, spontaneous breathing, an even coloring of the face and hands, and a stable heart rate of approximately 74 beats per minute with some discernible heart rate variability. The therapist will also become aware of the client's desire to seek soft eye contact and will respond appropriately to meet that need. Another clear indication of ventral vagal restoration is that the client begins looking around and taking in the now-safe environment. With these signs and behaviors, we can be confident that the social engagement system has come online.

Now that we have some basic guidelines for how to work with hyperarousal, we can examine some strategies to employ with individuals when they are in the shutdown state. The ability of these clients to become aware of internal sensations is severely limited. Trying to guide a hypoaroused client to settle via tracking internal sensations is usually counterproductive and could potentially exacerbate the shutdown. Instead, the therapist must first guide the client out of shutdown and into a small and manageable, hyperaroused state. In the car analogy, it is like taking the pressure off the brake just enough to smoothly move forward, and doing this a few times until there is a stable settling. I call this developing a contained (safe) sympathetic charge. The goal here is to produce, and draw awareness to, the physical sensations of a small, self-generated, sense of excitement and power. In working with shutdown, I use a variety of special techniques and tools to develop this safe charge, including movements and exercises that are adapted from qigong and other movement and martial arts. One of my favorite simple tools for shifting out of the (dorsal) vagal shutdown, and which can be utilized in the seated position (the more common setting in psychotherapy), is the Voooo sound/breath.

Along with multitudes of other people, I have experienced various chanting and ancient sound practices that facilitate healing and help open the doors of perception. Singing and chanting are used in religious and spiritual ceremonies in every culture for lightening the load of earthly existence. When you allow yourself to chant or sing in deep, resonant lower belly tones, you pleasurably stimulate the many serpentine branches of the vagus nerve, including the gut, heart, lungs, chest, mouth, and throat.

In his research, Porges confirmed early neuroanatomical findings that over 80% of the vagus nerve was afferent; that is to say, conveying sensory information from the various organs to the brain. It is essential to use these afferent feedback circuits to interrupt the shutdown signals of extreme distress and thus help move the client out of a self-reinforcing immobility. Certain Tibetan chants have been used successfully for thousands of years. In my practice, I use a sound similar to some of these chants. One of these sounds, in particular, helps open, expand, and vibrate the viscera and diaphragm in a way that provides new sensory signals to a shutdown or overstimulated nervous system. The practice is quite simple: take an easy, full breath and then make an extended "vooo . . . " (soft *o*, like *ou* in *you*) sound on the exhalation, focusing on the vibrations stimulated in the belly as you complete a full expiration of breath.

When I introduce the "vooo" sound to my clients, I may additionally ask them to imagine a foghorn in a foggy bay as it resounds through the murk to alert ship captains that they are nearing the land, and thence guiding them (like the boats) safely home. This image works on different levels. First of all, the image of the fog represents the fog of numbness, dissociation, and shutdown. The foghorn represents the beacon that guides the lost boat, or soul, back to safe harbor, to home—in breath and belly. This image also inspires the client to take on the heroic role of protecting sailors and passengers from imminent danger, as well as giving him or her permission to be silly and thereby play. Most important are the image's physiological effects. The sound vibrations of vooo enliven sensations from the viscera and diaphragm (as well as the throat), while the full, easy expiration of the breath produces the optimal balance of oxygen and carbon dioxide (R. Whitehouse, personal communication, October 5, 2008).

Let me guide you through this brief vooo exercise:

> Begin the exercise by finding a comfortable place to sit. Then slowly inhale, pause momentarily at the end of your full inhalation, and then, on the out-breath, gently utter "vooo . . . ," sustaining the sound throughout the entire exhalation. Vibrate the sound as though it were coming from your belly. At the end of the breath, pause briefly and allow the next breath to slowly fill your belly and then chest. When the in-breath feels complete, pause momentarily, and again make the vooo sound on the exhalation until it feels complete. It is important to let sound and breath expire fully, and then to pause and wait for the next breath to enter on its own when it is ready. Repeat this exercise first once, allowing the sensations and feelings to settle, and then if you wish, do it a few more times before resting. Next, focus your attention on your body, primarily on your extremities and your abdomen.

This sounding, with its emphasis on both waiting and allowing, has multiple functions. First of all, directing the sound into the belly evokes a particular type of sensation while also keeping the observing ego online. People often report various qualities of vibration and tingling, as well as changes in temperature—generally from cold (or hot) to cool and warm. These sensations are generally pleasant, although they may initially seem a bit unpleasant (i.e., unfamiliar); for example, mild waves of nausea and tingling are common. Most importantly, these new sensations contradict the twisted, agonizing, highly nauseating, deadening, numbing sensations associated with the fear-potentiated immobility state. Oftentimes this exercise is followed by sounds of gurgling and burps. I validate and support these involuntary responses (which might otherwise be judged uncouth), as they signal that the client's rhythm of digestion and assimilation is coming back online. This also allows access to a wide range of pleasurable sensations and gut instincts (the intuitive sense). This indicates that the client's body has successfully returned to a low-stress state, with a more balanced equilibrium between the sympathetic and parasympathetic branches of the autonomic nervous system.

Because the vagus nerve is primarily afferent, the predominant role of this enormous nerve is to relay information from the viscera to the brain. It seems likely that the change in the sensory messages (from organs to brain) along the (ascending) vagus nerve powerfully influences the messages being sent, in turn, from the brain back to the organs. As the organs report safety and pleasure, sensed through interoception, the brain sends commands to initiate normal regulatory, digestive, sensory, and social functions. Thus, homeostatic balance is restored. Porges (2009) concurs on this key regulatory system: "The afferent feedback from the viscera provides a major mediator of the accessibility of prosocial circuits associated with social engagement behaviors."

Beyond Psychosomatic Medicine: How Polyvagal Theory Informs Internal Medicine

As mentioned previously, many of the clients that I was seeing for prolonged stress and trauma also exhibited symptoms of chronic pain, chronic fatigue, digestive disorders, and a variety of other respiratory and cardiocirculatory problems. These clients were often dismissed by the medical system, as their conditions had no clearly defined organic cause. Their seemingly endless array of unpredictable, labile, and mutating symptoms confounded and frustrated their physicians, who often branded them as psychosomatic or, pejoratively, as attention-seeking malingerers. This is where mind-body dualism has deeply abandoned these, very real, sufferers.

The role of chronic stress and trauma in understanding and treating these types of physical, behavioral, and emotional symptoms is revealing. These signs and symptoms can be traced to the survival-based behavioral and physiological (somatic and autonomic) reactions associated with fight-flight and tonic immobility. In this regard, it is worth briefly mentioning the survival (evolutionary) value of these responses. First, tonic immobility creates an increased likelihood that the predator won't notice the prey if it is motionless. Further, many predators will not attack prey that does not put up a fight or appears to be dead. This is likely a protective response of the predator, because eating dead or sick animals could expose them to various pathogens. In addition, intense dorsal vagally mediated fecal expulsion (diarrhea) and vomiting also makes the prey a far less than desirable meal. Then, when the prey animal becomes mobile, there is a surge of intense sympathetic activity. This prepares the prey animal for what is called undirected flight or rage counterattack. This makes sense because the predator is unlikely to be fooled a second time. I have on several occasions witnessed a cat capture a mouse that immediately succumbed to immobility. However, the cat, seeming to want the game to go on, gently swatted the mouse with its paws, bringing it out of immobility. Then in a split second the frantic mouse scurried off, wildly (ultra-high sympathetic), in the direction it was pointed. On a few occasions, when the batted mouse came out of immobility directly facing its feline predator, it ran straight into the cat's nose, startling the cat as it scurried wildly away free to live another day.

Thanks to the contributions of Porges and Polyvagal Theory, we now have a clear model that can provide a better system of assessment, diagnosis, and treatment for these fluctuating presentations that have autonomic, somatic, and emotional components. Although it is essential to investigate their possible organic origin, it is equally important to recognize that these perplexing symptoms (sometimes called medically unexplained symptoms) may have a common root as a stress-related disorder of regulation; that is, they may constitute a single underlying syndrome, which can be effectively treated when properly identified.

I have proposed to call this seemingly confounding collection of symptoms autonomic dysregulation syndrome. The crucial identifier, *dysregulation*, suggests that the opportunity for treatment lies in interventions that reestablish organismic self-regulation through a reciprocal balance between the sympathetic and parasympathetic systems. Notwithstanding the primary importance of the autonomic nervous system in this disorder, it is crucial to note that, in addition to affecting multiple organ systems through the autonomic nervous system, this core disturbance also involves hypothalamic–pituitary–adrenal (HPA) axis dysregulation as well as an imbalanced muscular (hyper- or hypo-) tonus (Levine, 2010; Gelhorn, 1967).

The symptoms of this frequently misdiagnosed autonomic disorder, autonomic dysregulation syndrome, can be readily understood from the Polvagal Theory perspective. What is interesting, from a medical standpoint, is that these global reactions are engaged in a variety of ways, whether from encounters with an inescapable external threat, from ongoing stress, or from an internal threat such as serious illness or injury (Levine, 2010; Scaer, 2014).

During increased sympathetic arousal, our muscles tighten, and heart rate, blood pressure, and respiration increase. Features of the dorsal-vagal state include marked energy conservation and a lack of muscle tone (shutdown) associated with illness or injury. Such was noted by the pioneering stress researcher Hans Selye when he was a young medical student. Selye observed that while his professors would rattle off the many assorted symptoms of their patients' different conditions, they had one striking feature in common: all of them simply looked sick (Selye, 1955, 1956). These nonspecific signs of shutdown include flat facial expression, facial pallor, bodies that appeared collapsed, and shuffling movements that were labored and without energy.

To summarize, the survival-based instinctual reactions (either mobilization or immobilization) are designed to be temporary, and to turn off (reset) after the threat has passed or the illness or injury has been resolved. However, when these reactions do not resolve by restoring core autonomic homeostasis in a timely manner, individuals are left with ongoing stress accumulating in the autonomic nervous system (Levine, 1997, 1986). This *allostatic load* gives rise to the varied signs and symptoms of the autonomic dysregulation syndrome and may help explain such mysteries as why individuals sometimes develop chronic fatigue syndrome and fibromyalgia in the aftermath of such seemingly diverse triggers as illness, trauma, or prolonged stress (Levine, 1977; McEwen, 2002).

Recall that while the symptoms of sympathetic hyperarousal include tension, pain, (Levine & Phillips, 2012), fibromyalgia, vasoconstriction (cold hands, i.e., Raynaud's syndrome), excessive sweating, and racing heart (tachycardia), those of vagal hypoarousal include shutdown, numbness, chronic fatigue, irritable bowel syndrome, gastric reflux, low heart rate or blood pressure, syncope (postural orthostatic tachycardia syndrome, or POTS), light-headedness, migraines, and certain cardiac arrhythmias (Scaer, 2014; Chang et al., 2009).

Some syndromes appear to be manifestations of a sequential or concurrent interplay between sympathetic and parasympathetic (vagally mediated) symptoms. For example, migraines appear to have a sequential phase of vasoconstriction (increase in sympathetic tone) followed by abrupt vasodilation (withdrawal of sympathetic tone). Some cardiac arrhythmias involve both tachycardia and bradycardia. Similarly, irritable bowel syndrome may involve sympathetic contraction of the internal anal sphincter, concurrent with abnormally high levels of (vagally mediated) peristalsis of the (longitudinal) intestinal smooth muscles. These manifestations of autonomic dysregulation syndrome frequently lead to profound and debilitating distress (Razran, 1961; Scaer, 2014; Porges et al., 1975).

It has been shown that up to 70–90% of all primary care visits are driven by so-called psychological factors (Bruns, 1998). While fluctuating presentation can be confounding to clinicians, the varying symptoms are acutely problematic, wildly expensive, and often deeply demoralizing to the patient. When patients present with myriad mutating symptoms, they are frequently referred to multiple specialists who may order a wide array of expensive and invasive diagnostic tests. Alternatively, the clinician may suggest that the patient's condition has psychological or psychosomatic origins. While it is true that these conditions do have emotional and developmental components, unfortunately, this is likely to seem dismissive to the patient, rendering him or her defensive and resistant. This adversarial positioning will indeed add tension to the already frustrated patient-doctor relationship. If, however, the underlying neurobehavioral stress response syndromes can be accurately identified through Polyvagal Theory, and then treated appropriately so that the dynamic homeostatic function of reset can be accessed, far more efficacious outcomes will be achieved.

Epilogue

Our dialogue between the academic scientist and the trauma clinician concludes for now. I hope that this collaboration has been fruitful, with its playful tension, and will continue to be so until one or both of us give up the ghost. What began with hypomania in the 1970s, between the Berkeley–Big Sur free spirit and the academic rising star, has come together, again, here in this midlife tome. With the winds of change, Stephen has now contributed deeply (as recognized in this and hundreds of other publications) to all sorts of innovative therapies and alternative healing approaches, worldwide; and, ironically, my creative endeavors have included contributions to academic journals. In one more turn of the continuous spiral of life, our circle of friendship and collaboration completes itself, for now at least.

In conclusion, I would like to believe that we have inspired each other in our parallel explorations and discoveries, and that these peregrinations will somehow contribute to the alleviation of suffering. But, without question, I submit that the dialogue between Polyvagal Theory and clinical psychotherapeutic approaches to trauma, and to internal medicine, offers a rare opportunity to bridge the scientific with the clinical worlds. Most importantly, it leads to more precise and consistent clinical work. Further, this exchange represents a potential to advance both realms of inquiry, the academic and the healing-clinical ones. If this chapter contributes to that dialogue and synthesis, then my load will have been lightened and my goal will have been met.

References

Bruns, D. (1998). Why did Kaiser change? Retrieved from http://www.healthpsych.com/practice/ipc/primarycare3.html

Chang, L., Sundaresh, S., Elliott, J., Anton, P. A., Baldi, P., Licudine, A., . . . Mayer, E. A. (2009). Dysregulation of the hypothalamic-pituitary-adrenal (HPA) axis in irritable bowel syndrome. *Neurogastroenterology and Motility, 21*(2), 149–159. doi:10.1111/j.1365-2982.2008.01171.x

Gallup, G. G., Jr. & Maser, J. D. (1977). Tonic immobility: Evolutionary underpinnings of human catalepsy and catatonia. In J. D. Maser & M. E. P. Seligman (Eds.), Psychotherapathology: Experimental Models. San Francisco: Freeman. pp. 334–357.

Gellhorn, E. (1967). *Principles of autonomic-somatic integrations: Physiological basis and psychological and clinical implications.* Minneapolis: University of Minnesota Press.

Levine, P. A. (1977). *Accumulated stress, reserve capacity and dis-ease* (Doctoral thesis, UC Berkeley, University Microfilm 77-15-760, Ann Arbor, Michigan). Retrieved from http://somaticexperiencing.com/wp-content/uploads/2010/07/Peter_A_Levine-Thesis.pdf

Levine, P. A. (1986). Stress. In M. Coles, E. Donchin, & S. Porges (Eds.), *Psychophysiology: Systems, processes, and application; a handbook.* New York: Guilford.

Levine, P. A. (2010). *In an unspoken voice: How the body releases trauma and restores goodness.* Berkeley, CA: North Atlantic.

Levine, P. A. (2015). *Trauma and memory: Brain and body in a search for the living past: A practical guide for understanding and working with traumatic memory.* Berkeley, CA: North Atlantic.

Levine, P. A., & Phillips, M. (2012). *Freedom from pain: Discover your body's power to overcome physical pain.* Boulder, CO: Sounds True.

Maser, J. D., & Seligman, M. E. (1977). *Psychopathology: Experimental models.* San Francisco: W.H. Freeman.

McEwen, B. S. (2002). Introduction: Protective and damaging effects of stress mediators: The good and bad sides of the response to stress. *Metabolism, 51*(6), 2–4. doi:10.1053/meta.2002.33183

Porges, S. W. (1995). Orienting in a defensive world: Mammalian modifications of our evolutionary heritage, a polyvagal theory. *Psychophysiology, 32*(4), 301–318. doi:10.1111/j.1469-8986.1995.tb01213.x

Porges, S. W. (2001). The polyvagal theory: Phylogenetic substrates of a social nervous system. *International Journal of Psychophysiology, 42*(2), 123–146. doi:10.1016/s0167-8760(01)00162-3

Porges, S. W. (2009). The polyvagal theory: New insights into adaptive reactions of the autonomic nervous system. *Cleveland Clinic Journal of Medicine, 76*(Suppl. 2). doi:10.3949/ccjm.76.s2.17

Porges, S. W., Walter, G. F., Korb, R. J., & Sprague, R. L. (1975). The influences of methylphenidate on heart rate and behavioral measures of attention in hyperactive children. *Child Development, 46*(3), 727. doi:10.2307/1128571

Scaer, R. C. (2014). *The body bears the burden: Trauma, dissociation, and disease.* New York: Routledge.

Selye, H. (1955). Stress and disease. *Science, 122*(3171), 625–631. doi:10.1126/science.122.3171.625

Selye, H. (1956). *The stress of life*. New York: McGraw-Hill.

Steuwe, C., Daniels, J., Frewen, P., Densmore, M., Pannasch, S., Beblo, T., . . . Lanius, R. (2014). Effect of direct eye contact in PTSD related to interpersonal trauma: An fMRI study of activation of an innate alarm system. *Social Cognitive and Affective Neuroscience, 9*(1), 88–97. doi:10.1093/scan/nss105

van der Kolk, B. A. (2014). *The body keeps the score: Brain, mind, and body in the healing of trauma*. New York: Penguin.

2

Safety and Reciprocity: Polyvagal Theory as a Framework for Understanding and Treating Developmental Trauma

Bessel van der Kolk

Abstract: Polyvagal Theory provides a framework to understand and treat developmental trauma. The theory, by defining an integrated biobehavioral social engagement system, highlights the features of dysfunction manifest in individuals who have experienced developmental trauma and provides insights into normalizing these features through contextual cues of safety and social reciprocity.

In the year 2000, the U.S. Congress mandated the establishment of the National Child Traumatic Stress Network (NCTSN) with the intent of increasing awareness of the effects of trauma on child development, and to stimulate the development of effective treatment methods for traumatized children and adolescents. This new network put my colleagues and me in a good position to document what we had long suspected, namely that the hundreds of thousands of children in the United States who have been abused, neglected, and otherwise traumatized at the hands of their own caregivers develop a rather consistent set of psychological and behavioral disturbances.

The NCTSN currently consists of over 150 clinical and research institutions in almost every state, and it has collectively treated and studied well over 200,000 traumatized children and adolescents. As we started to take a closer look at the kids who were seen in the network, it soon became clear that they suffered from a vast array of psychological and behavioral problems that went well beyond any existing classification systems. In fact, the average child turned out to carry between three and seven distinct co-occurring diagnoses in the *Diagnostic and Statistical Manual of Mental Disorders* (*DSM*). Yet, from the vantage point of developmental psychopathology, almost all their problems could be accounted for by developmental injuries in the context of their caregiving system.

After collecting data on about 20,000 children within the network at numerous different sites,[1] we proposed a new diagnosis to be included in the *DSM-5*: developmental trauma disorder, consisting of pervasive problems with (1) affect regulation, such as an inability to tolerate, manage, or recover from extreme affect states, including temper tantrums and immobilization, as well as an inability to properly regulate bodily functions such as sleep and appetite; (2) attention and concentration, such as preoccupation with threat, difficulty appraising danger, attention, and pathological attempts at self-soothing, such as rocking, deliberate self-injury, and compulsive masturbation; (3) severe disturbances in negotiating harmonious relationships with themselves and the people around them, such as self-loathing, impulsive aggression, overcompliance with the wishes of others, and difficulties playing and imagining novel possibilities (van der Kolk, 2005; Cloitre et al., 2010; D'Andrea, Ford, Stolbach, Spinazzola, & van der Kolk, 2012; Ford et al., 2013).

Our submission to the American Psychiatric Association's *DSM* committee (on which I had been quite active in previous decades) included the results of four 25-year prospective studies of abused and neglected children, as well as direct interview data of 20,000 children treated within the network. A few months later, the *DSM-5* committee rejected the proposed developmental trauma diagnosis with the statement, "The notion that early childhood adverse experiences lead to substantial developmental disruptions is more clinical intu-

---

1 Participants included doctors Joseph Spinazzola, Julian Ford, Marylene Cloitre, Wendy D'Andrea, Robert Pynoos, Frank Putnam, Brad Stolbach, Cassandra Kisiel, Alexander McFarlane, Martin Teicher, Dante Cicchetti, Marla Zucker, Margaret Blaustein, Gosh Ippen, Alicia Lieberman, Tracy Fahrenbach, T. McClellan, J. Henry, W. Harris, J. Hawke, J. Griffin, J. Chapman, J. Briggs-King, J. Fairbairn, S. Ostrovsky, and others.

ition than a research based fact. This statement is commonly made but cannot be backed up with prospective studies.

The rejection of a developmental trauma diagnosis in our diagnostic manual leaves clinicians in the curious position of having a plethora of options to diagnose the traumatized children they treat, as well as adults with early childhood histories of abuse, neglect, and abandonment: PTSD, disruptive mood dysregulation disorder, reactive attachment disorder, ADHD, dissociative identity disorder, nonsuicidal self-injury, intermittent explosive disorder, disinhibited social engagement disorder, oppositional defiant disorder, conduct disorder, or borderline personality disorder, none of which ever seem to occur in isolation, and none of which have actually met solid scientific criteria to be properly considered valid diagnoses. Yet all of these so-called diagnoses capture some aspects of developmental trauma, while none of them provides a clue about what has really gone wrong, nor do they offer any suggestions about what can be done to help patients who have them.

Why has psychiatry been so blind to the impact of abandonment, neglect, and abuse on the developing human psyche? One possible answer is that there has been an excessive (and potentially lucrative) focus on finding a magic pill to change unacceptable behaviors, at the expense of keeping up with the remarkable advances in developmental psychopathology, attachment studies, and developmental neuroscience. The quest for the magic potion so far has been largely a dry well, while the effort to create a diagnostic system that actually incorporates what we have learned about the developing mind, brain, and attachment system continues unabated.

My favorite psychology course in college focused on Harry Harlow and his monkeys, particularly on Harlow's demonstration of the devastating effects of maternal deprivation on self-regulation, peer relationships, and the capacity to play—incidentally, exactly the behavioral problems that showed up again in the NCTSN's studies of abused and neglected children 50 years later. Maybe it's no accident that since our undergraduate days, Stephen Porges and I have both closely followed the subsequent work of Harlow's student Stephen Suomi, chief of the Laboratory of Comparative Ethology at the National Institutes of Health, and of attachment researchers such as Ed Tronick, Beatrice Beebe, Karlen Lyons Ruth, and Colwyn Trevarthen. Why was that work so compelling? Because these researchers were elucidating the relevance of the social engagement system and the vital role of rhythmical, synchronous face-to-face and voice-to-voice interactions in the development of mind, brain, and self, in which the Polyvagal Theory—Stephen Porges's life's work—plays such a pivotal role.

The Polyvagal Theory (Porges, 2011) provided us with a coherent framework to understand the multiplicity of disturbances, emotional states, and behaviors in the abused children we see in the NCTSN. While almost all our children have experienced horrendous traumas, only a few of them clearly have PTSD. What characterizes most of our kids is that their traumas pretty much occurred in the family (and other caregiving systems): they have witnessed terrible violence between parents, or had to look after caregivers who were too stoned, depressed, or out of it to take care of them. Many have suffered beatings and molestation at the hands of the very people who are supposed to guarantee their safety. The work of our attachment research colleagues and the primatologists made it clear that the problems and behaviors we are trying to treat seem to be the net result of an accumulated lack of safety within a frightening caregiving system.

We gradually have learned how dependent children are on consistent and predictable care (start wrapping your head around the fact that 2.3 million American children have incarcerated parents). Living in a safe and predictable environment is essential for normal mental and physiological development, and, as Porges adds, for being able to turn off defensive systems, making it possible to feel intimate, to play, to collaborate with others, and to lovingly parent your offspring. Even as adults, we continue to depend on each other for safety, security, predictability, and meaning. We are social creatures through and through: when we are threatened and endangered, we automatically turn to others for help and comfort. And, as research studies have shown over and over again, as long as one's social engagement system is fully intact, people rarely develop lasting adverse reactions to potentially traumatizing experiences.

However, as Porges frequently points out, social engagement is not identical to social support—we can be terribly nice to people, but if their receptors for the milk of human kindness are blocked, they cannot take it in and reciprocate. The hallmark of a well-functioning social engagement system is mutuality and reciprocity. Thus, a central focus of treatment and repair needs to be helping people to be able to mutually engage and reciprocate. This can be an arduous undertaking. Over the last few years, we have learned that people who have been most severely injured in the context of their early caregiving relationships may be best helped by learning resonance and synchrony from other mammals, such as horses, dogs, or even dolphins—we can easily understand how those mammals may be experienced as much less threatening and treacherous than humans.

Human beings simply cannot live in isolation. Social isolation per se is traumatic and has been shown to severely compromise people's health and well-being. Our source of pleasure and meaning is almost completely dependent on our social interactions—in fact, that is what we have brains for. Our most painful injuries are inflicted by the people we love and depend on. That is the source of the deepest human grief, as well as of most psychiatric disturbances. If, as happens in the kids we study within the NCTSN, the very sources of comfort simultaneously are the sources of danger, this creates complex disturbances. Polyvagal Theory provides a clear neurobiological model that links difficulties in spontaneous social behavior to reciprocal behaviors, as manifested in both facial expression and the regulation of visceral state.

Polyvagal Theory (Porges, 2015) posits that children and adults are able to feel safe, physiologically calm, mentally clear, and socially engaged by activating their social engagement system, which is mediated by reciprocally engaged voices and faces. When the social engagement system fails, for example, when our cries go unheard and our pleadings don't stop the abuse, this automatically releases the sympathetically based fight-flight system, or the parasympathetic, unmyelinated immobilization shut-down response. It thus makes sense that children with trauma histories suffer from both externalizing and internalizing behaviors; they display both various degrees of unmanageable behaviors (these squeaky wheels attract the most grease—and diagnoses such as ADHD and oppositional defiant disorder), and withdrawn self-isolation. Both adaptations interfere with play, formation of friendships, social awareness, emotional responsiveness, and language development.

When people are scared, they automatically activate their fight-flight response: they need to move, run, or fight. Many of the children we treat seem to be stuck in habitual flight-flight behaviors for which they frequently are treated with drugs or restraints. But when people are isolated or restrained, our ancient parasympathetic nervous system shuts us down. Forced immobilization, such as in medical procedures and forced physical restraint in psychiatric institutions, discussed in detail in our research on awareness during anesthesia (Osterman, Hopper, Heran, Keane, & van der Kolk, 2001), prevents access to the moderating support of friendly faces and soothing voices, which our nervous system ordinarily uses to self-regulate and to feel safe.

Lack of adequate caregiving often is the result of intergenerational transmission of trauma. As Charles Darwin pointed out as early as 1872, in his magisterial book *The Expression of the Emotions in Man and Animals*, escape and avoidance are helpful for survival throughout the animal kingdom, but getting stuck in escape or avoidance, that is, being traumatized, interferes with the most elemental life processes, including feeding, mating, and nurturance, on which the survival of the species depends. In this context it is not surprising that John Hackman won the 2000 Nobel Prize in Economics for showing that for every $1 invested in helping mothers take care of their babies and infants, society in the long term reaps $7 in benefits in reduced medical, legal, and prison costs, and increased tax revenues from productive citizens. At this point, mother-child intervention therapy has been shown to be the single most effective mental health intervention known. Any intervention that can improve the neural regulation of the social engagement system would theoretically enhance spontaneous social behavior, enhance state and affect regulation, reduce stereotypical behaviors, and improve vocal communication.

Most clinicians are aware that their patients' faces and the quality of their voices (their prosody, which is controlled by muscles of the face and head) accurately convey their physiological state and use this information to choose interventions. We also gradually have become aware that our own facial expressions, tone of voice, and body movements can have profound effects on the state of mind of the people we treat. When we work with traumatized kids and adults, we tend to carefully track how the content of their narratives affects their tone of voice, facial expressions, and body movements—as well as our own. For many of us, those are the primary modes of communication that we pay attention to and work with.

Given the basic issues about safety, reciprocity, and synchronicity that are spelled out by Polyvagal Theory, it seems obvious that the various therapies that social workers, psychologists, and psychiatrists currently learn in their professional trainings present just a fraction of potentially effective self- and mutually regulatory methods. My lab has already shown that yoga tends to be more effective for the treatment of PTSD than any currently used medications. But how about tango dancing? Martial arts? Drumming? One study showed the dramatic effects of choral singing on brain activation in depressed individuals (Petchkovsky, Robertson-Gillam, Kropotov, & Petchkovsky, 2013). The challenge for both clinicians and researchers is to discover the optimal way in which we can help people who suffer from developmental trauma to activate their capacity for self-regulation, reciprocity, and mutuality. The infusion of insights from Polyvagal Theory into clinical treatment is providing a critically important guide for this journey.

References

Cloitre, M., Stolbach, B. C., Herman, J. L., van der Kolk, B. A., Pynoos, R. S., Wang, J., & Petkova, E. (2010). A developmental approach to complex PTSD: Childhood and adult cumulative trauma as predictors of symptom complexity. *Journal of Traumatic Stress, 22*, 399–408.

D'Andrea, W., Ford, J., Stolbach, B., Spinazzola, J., & van der Kolk, B. A. (2012). Understanding interpersonal trauma in children: Why we need a developmentally appropriate trauma diagnosis. *American Journal of Orthopsychiatry, 82*, 187–200.

Ford, J. D., Grasso, D., Greene, C. R., Levine, J., Spinazzola J., & van der Kolk, B. A. (2013). Clinical significance of a proposed developmental trauma disorder diagnosis: Results of an international survey of clinicians. *Journal of Clinical Psychiatry, 74*(8), 841–849.

Osterman, J. E., Hopper, J., Heran, W. J., Keane, T. M., & van der Kolk, B. A. (2001). Awareness under anesthesia and the development of posttraumatic stress disorder. *General Hospital Psychiatry, 3*(4), 198–204.

Petchkovsky, L., Robertson-Gillam, K., Kropotov, J., & Petchkovsky, M. (2013). Using QEEG parameters (asymmetry, coherence, and P3a novelty response) to track improvement in depression after choir therapy. *Advances in Mental Health, 11*(3).

Porges, S. W. (2011). *The Polyvagal Theory: Neurophysiological foundations of emotions, attachment, communication, and self-regulation.* New York: Norton.

Porges, S. W. (2015). Making the world safe for our children: Down-regulating defence and upregulating social engagement to "optimise" the human experience. *Children Australia, 40*, 114–123.

van der Kolk, B. A. (2005). Developmental trauma disorder: Toward a rational diagnosis for children with complex trauma histories. *Psychiatric Annals, 35*, 401–408.

3

Polyvagal Theory and Sensorimotor Psychotherapy

Pat Ogden

Abstract: This chapter describes the different but somewhat parallel paths of two colleagues and friends in their mutual quest to understand the intelligence of the body and to help others. Polyvagal Theory has become essential in conceptualizing and teaching Sensorimotor Psychotherapy. It elucidates why the bottom-up, somatic interventions we teach and practice in Sensorimotor Psychotherapy are critical to help clients heal from trauma and attachment wounds, and reengage with the world and with others. This chapter illustrates the author's early discoveries of bottom-up interventions with patients, explaining these discoveries in terms of Polyvagal Theory, and describing the transformative power of the term *neuroception*. The chapter concludes by exploring the nature of love as it applies to Polyvagal Theory and Sensorimotor Psychotherapy.

There is more wisdom in your body than in your deepest philosophy.
—Nietzsche

MY FIRST ENCOUNTER with Steve Porges and his research took place before there was a Polyvagal Theory. In 1988, Steve coauthored two articles about what Rolfers call the pelvic tilt, a soft-tissue mobilization of the pelvic and sacral area, that showed the effects of this intervention on the autonomic nervous system, particularly that it could quiet the sympathetic nervous system. I myself am certified in the Rolfing method, a form of hands-on bodywork that aims to release fascial layers so that the body can attain its natural alignment and range of motion. For years I had witnessed the calming effects of the pelvic tilt in my own bodywork practice. Steve's article was the first scientific research that explained why, which was uniquely exciting and validating for me as a bodyworker.

I began my professional life in an alternative world, studying and practicing various forms of bodywork (Rolfing, Reichian, Swedish, Lomi, Shiatsu massage, postural integration), movement approaches (Rolf movement, Continuum Movement, dance), and yoga (primarily Hatha, Bikram, and, more recently, yin and restorative yoga). These disciplines are the solid ground upon which I stand as a body psychotherapist. My own work grew out of such alternative experiential training and what I learned from my clients, not from science or even psychology theory. In the 1990s, I had the good fortune to meet Bessel van der Kolk, who introduced me to a more conventional psychotherapy world—the more traditional fields of trauma, attachment, neuroscience, and dissociation. Steve, although he is not a psychotherapist, also travels in both worlds, and his ability to bridge these two worlds was exciting and personally validating.

In the mid-1990s, I briefly heard Steve speak in person at the founding conference of the United States Body Association of Psychotherapy. I have a vivid image of him leaning forward in his chair, speaking to an enthralled audience gathered on the floor around him. The room was full to the brim, and since no more seating was available, I only heard a few words. But I remember the tone of his voice, his gentleness and earnest engagement with this group of nonscientists, and the enraptured attention of the listeners, whose expressions were alight with enthusiasm and the ah-ha of recognition. At that time, it was rare to hear someone who could explain the science of how the body works in an engaging and accessible manner to a group of nonscientists. I immediately thought that Steve was someone I wanted to know and learn from.

Our next encounter was in the late 1990s, at Bessel's trauma conference in Boston, where we were both invited to deliver keynote speeches, and both received standing ovations. Steve brought the nuances of Polyvagal Theory to life in a friendly, personable voice that instantly captured the hearts and minds of the clinicians in the audience, myself included. I became more and more riveted the longer Steve spoke. The most moving part of his keynote, which has made an indelible impression on my memory, was the video he showed of a child with autism whose therapist was trying to engage him in blowing soap bubbles. In the first clip, this boy was clearly in his own world, and he was not responsive to the practitioner, despite her best efforts. The next clip showed the child wearing headphones. Steve explained that as the music engaged the neural regulation of the middle ear muscles, the child would also become calmer. As I became more familiar with Polyvagal Theory, I learned that these effects occurred as the brain stem area known as the ventral vagal complex integrated the neural regulation of middle ear muscles with the regulation of the heart through myelinated vagal pathways. I also became aware that this system regulated other features including facial expression and voice intonation to form an integrated social engagement system.

The theory behind the intervention focused on stimulating the tiny muscles of the middle ear to vitalize the ventral vagal complex and stimulate social engagement. Indeed, in the third clip, the child was engaged and smiling as he blew bubbles with his therapist. Having worked with special needs children in the late 1960s and early 1970s, seeing such dramatic results brought tears to my eyes. I knew firsthand how miraculous an achievement this was. I was hooked. Later, I learned more about the Listening Project Protocol that Steve pioneered in his laboratory to test his hypothesis that specific interventions that stimulate the muscles of the middle ear could improve spontaneous social behavior.

Sensorimotor Psychotherapy, which I developed, builds on traditional psychotherapeutic understanding but includes the body as central in the therapeutic field of awareness, using body-reading observational skills and interventions not usually practiced in talk therapy (Ogden, 1997, 1998; Ogden & Minton, 2000; Ogden, Minton, & Pain, 2006; Ogden & Fisher, 2015). Steve's ideas expressed in his Polyvagal Theory elucidate why the bottom-up, somatic interventions we teach and practice in Sensorimotor Psychotherapy are critical to help clients heal from trauma and reengage with the world and with others. Polyvagal Theory explains in scientific terms much of what I do in my own work as a therapist and trainer.

In this chapter, I want to write about our very different but somewhat parallel paths in our mutual quest to understand the intelligence of the body and to help others. And I hope to elucidate why, upon hearing Steve speak in those years long ago, I had the sense of therapeutic ideas and neuroscience coming together, bridges being built, and connections being made. Because of this, Polyvagal Theory has become critical in conceptualizing and teaching the interventions and approach of Sensorimotor Psychotherapy.

Mobilization and Immobilization Without Fear

In 1974, I was employed at Vanderbilt University Medical Center's psychiatric unit in Nashville, Tennessee. The hospital's approach at that time consisted primarily of medication and problem solving through talk therapy, which I thought was odd since many of the patients were incapable of rational conversation. The diagnosis of PTSD was not yet included in the American Psychiatric Association's *Diagnostic and Statistical Manual of Mental Disorders*, but we know now that many psychiatric patients have suffered trauma. Trauma-related disorders have long been characterized by a vacillation between intrusive reliving of past trauma and numb avoidance of traumatic reminders, accompanied by hyperarousal and hypoarousal, respectively. In retrospect, it is obvious that many of these hospitalized patients experienced profound dysregulation, accompanied by terror, rage, despair, and suicidality. But in the early 1970s at this short-term inpatient psychiatric hospital, no one talked about the nervous system, or dysregulation, or trauma for that matter.

These dysregulated, sometimes violent and often loud behaviors were frightening to the staff, who were desperate to find ways to control the patients. Doctors instructed us to point out inappropriate behavior, require that the patient only use appropriate behavior, and revoke privileges such as receiving visitors or going on outings if patients were unable to comply—in other words, if they were unable to regulate their arousal. Noncompliance was grounds for locking a patient in a padded isolation room and administering strong doses of tranquilizers and antipsychotic medications, often forcefully, that had severe side effects. Sometimes behavior was demanded that seemed traumatic in and of itself: for example, one patient who for periods of time became immobile and could not speak was forced to scrub the floor with a toothbrush in a futile effort to induce her to speak. Doctors and nurses were baffled and frustrated at the ineffectiveness of their interventions, and no one seemed to understand why patients got better or worse.

The director of the unit encouraged me to follow my own interests, so I experimented with leading various group activities, including art therapy (which I learned about from library journals), group therapy, and yoga and dance classes. Attendance was voluntary, and no demands were placed on the patients who attended these classes. I noticed that art therapy was more popular than the groups where we sat and talked, presumably because clay, paint, and collage gave patients a means to express implicit phenomena that they could not find the words to articulate. The talk therapy sessions were short lived; what I remember most about them were the long, awkward silences.

The groups that seemed the most successful and that intrigued me most were the ones that directly involved the body. I already had a great affinity for dance, having studied it since age 7, so I was excited to teach simple but energetic line dance routines that were so popular in the nightclubs of the 1970s. I also taught relaxing yoga classes, which I learned from Swami Satchidananda's *Integral Yoga Hatha* (Satchinanda, 1970). No one had heard of yoga at that time, so I called the yoga class a "stretch and relaxation" group. These two classes were the most popular among the patients, and these were the activities that seemed to support their well-being. The hospital staff noted that those patients who became regular participants in both yoga and dance classes seemed to make the most progress. They appeared more energetic, calmer, and more integrated. But of course, it might have been that the patients who came to the classes were going to get better anyway.

I didn't know much about the nervous system in the 1970s, let alone the detailed nuances of the autonomic nervous system embedded in Polyvagal Theory. But, in retrospect, Polyvagal Theory may explain the positive effects of the yoga and dance classes. During these activities, patients were encouraged to do what felt right to them. There was no requirement to stay—some came and went freely—or to do anything that they didn't want to do. There was no criticism because there was no right or wrong way to dance or do the yoga stretches. The atmosphere was safe, and patients were relatively regulated and engaged with themselves and with me and, to the best of their capacity, tuned into their bodies. Their social engagement systems were online, particularly in the dance classes, at least more so than during most of the day.

Through yoga, they learned simple, easy stretches that helped them relax in a calm, peaceful room away from the chaos of the hospital unit. Yoga sessions were conducted in silence, often with eyes closed, so auditory and visual stimulation was reduced. Everyone was instructed to wear loose, comfortable clothing that didn't restrain breath or movement. They all, as best as they were able, followed my slow instructions to breathe deeply, move gently, go at their own pace, never force the body, and let go into the pose.

In contrast, the dance classes were energetic and rhythmic, conducted at a faster pace to rousing dance club music. There was an atmosphere of camaraderie and fun. The patients became more talkative and interactive. Spontaneous, nonhostile, often friendly vocalizations emerged as everyone tried to follow the steps and turns. Sometimes people bumped into each other when they made the wrong move, and there would be shrieks of laughter (which frightened some folks and sent them rushing out of the room, only to return once they had calmed down). As we moved rhythmically together, keeping up with the pace of the music, arms and legs moved more freely, heart rates increased, eye contact was sometimes made, and faces became more expressive. Those in the room who were watching often tapped their feet and joined in the fun vocally.

I think that Polyvagal Theory explains why these classes seemed to help the patients. Trauma survivors, as we well know, often suffer from profound autonomic dysregulation, both hyper- and hypoarousal. Polyvagal Theory explains how these extremes of arousal in trauma survivors are related to mobilization and immobilization coupled with fear. Mobilization with fear refers to the rise of sympathetic tone when threatened, which supports the active defenses of fight and flight (and also the "cry for help" defense, an attempt to get others who are stronger to protect us). The "vehement emotions" (Janet, 1925) of rage, terror, and panic that fuel the vigorous activity needed for defense were common emotions of these patients. Hyperarousal and these strong emotions maximize our chances of survival by enabling us to carry out aggressive actions of protection. When vigorous physical responses, such as running or fighting, are successful, not only is the level of threat reduced, but the cascade of danger-related neurochemicals is metabolized through these energy-consuming actions.

One of the great gifts of Polyvagal Theory is teaching us that there are two branches of the vagus (not one as previously thought): the myelinated ventral vagal branch that regulates the heart and is integrated into the regulation of facial muscles, middle ear muscles, larynx, and pharynx, and the primitive, unmyelinated dorsal vagal branch that slows everything down. The dorsal vagal branch mediates immobility and energy conservation, in contrast to mobilizing, active defensive strategies mediated by the sympathetic nervous system. Many functions of the body begin to slow down when the dorsal vagal system is activated—the heart rate decreases, breathing slows, and, in trauma, all this is often accompanied by fear and a sense of numbness and shutting down. This immobilizing hypoarousal can ensure survival in the wild, since most predators will not eat an immobile animal, and it also stimulates endorphins that mediate pain.

Increased sympathetic tone, without the fear, enables us to engage in highly stimulating activities such as sports, dance, energizing debates, or performances and feel high-arousal emotions, such as joy, elation, or excitement. Increased dorsal vagal tone, without the fear, allows us to enjoy low-arousal activities, such as relaxation, dreamy states, meditation, and yoga and low-arousal emotions, such as peaceful, calm, tranquil, and contemplative states. Traumatized people, however, often cannot enjoy either extreme of arousal because these extremes are coupled with fear.

In the yoga and dance classes, the sympathetic and dorsal vagal branches of the autonomic nervous system were also activated, but without fear. Some patients who felt fearful or anxious simply left, often to return a few minutes later when their nervous systems had calmed down. Stimulating these extremes of arousal without fear may have been inherently healing, especially since there is quite a bit of evidence that most psychiatric patients have experienced trauma and thus dysregulated arousal. Perhaps the yoga classes enabled patients to access dorsal vagal states in a safe atmosphere and experience immobilization without fear. The mobilizing, rhythmic activity of dance and the accompanying high arousal, in a safe environment, possibly helped the nervous systems of these patients tolerate high arousal without fear.

In trauma, we need to utilize hyper- or hypoarousal to fuel adaptive mobilizing and immobilizing defensive strategies. However, these patients had developed habitual autonomic responses to triggers that they experienced daily, keeping them in prolonged dysregulated states. They had come to depend upon these defensive mechanisms to navigate daily life, which compromised their ventral vagal complex, or social engagement system, rendering it much less accessible.

Social engagement was evident in both these classes. When safety and choice are paramount, the evolutionarily newer ventral vagal branch of the parasympathetic system that regulates the heart, calms the viscera, and governs the muscles of the face is activated, enabling positive social behavior. This open system is affected by interactions with others. I think these classes enabled patients to feel safe in nonthreatening atmospheres of both high and low arousal. Their social engagement systems were stimulated, and perhaps their nervous systems recalibrated as they learned to tolerate the extremes of arousal, to the degree that many staff noticed improvement in social behavior.

Somatic Resources/Neural Exercises

In the 1970s when working at Vanderbilt, I met Ron Kurtz, a body psychotherapist whose approach validated my intuition that the body's posture, gesture, expression, and movement were valuable avenues to explore in psychotherapy. Ron was the first body psychotherapist I had met, and meeting him changed my professional trajectory as well as my personal life. I moved to Boulder, Colorado, within the year of our meeting to become his apprentice, his first assistant, and, later, cotrainer and cofounder of the Hakomi Institute. A few years after moving to Boulder, I became the referral body therapist for the University of Colorado's Wardenburg Clinic for female college students who suffered from sexual nonresponsiveness. In the 1970s, women who were not yet able to experience sexual pleasure or orgasm were identified as "preorgasmic." I found out later that virtually all of them had been sexually abused. However, my colleagues and I were not aware of trauma at that time—it wasn't until 1980 that PTSD was added to the *DSM*. Thus, our practice was not trauma informed in the least. We concentrated on making the unconscious conscious, working with regressive states, the negative belief systems learned in childhood, and the strong affect related to these limiting beliefs and attachment failures (although *attachment* was also not a term we were familiar with). With an emphasis on an attuned, empathic therapeutic relationship, I used interventions that helped clients reexperience early memories and express painful emotions. I faithfully used approaches that I'd been taught to use, and my clients had powerful, expressive, cathartic sessions. However, to my dismay, they often became more dissociated and dysregulated than they had been when they started working with me. For some, symptoms such as panic and nightmares increased; for others, despair and spacing out were on the rise. I began to question my competence as a psychotherapist and mistrust my approach to clinical practice.

Intuitively, I came up with this concept: perhaps if I just helped them stay connected with their bodies, followed the body's lead, and didn't try to reexperience painful childhood memories, their symptoms might improve. Instead of only regressive emotional work, I began to implement simple body exercises that I had learned in my bodywork and movement training simultaneously with accessing childhood memories. The grounding, centering, breathing, touch (their own and mine), lengthening the spine, and eye contact exercises, along with following the movements their bodies wanted to make (pushing pillows, walking around, kicking, and so forth) were my version of what Steve calls "neural exercises," designed to help these clients regulate their physiological states. They were always done as a little experiment to find out what changed somatically, and their purpose was to quiet the defensive responses, bring arousal into the "window of tolerance" (a term coined by Dan Siegel in *The Developing Mind* in 1999), and increase their engagement with me. My sessions moved much more slowly. Clients became less dramatic, more embodied, and less emotional as our primary focus was to stay grounded, centered, and present as old memories were addressed. Symptoms lessened, overwhelming affect and numb states decreased, and social engagement and daily life functioning improved.

It was these clients, rather than trauma theories or neuroscience, that first taught me about PTSD and the efficacy of bottom-up interventions in regulating dysregulation. Focusing on what we now call stabilization rather than regressive work was a huge change in my approach. Rather than expressing the terror and rage related to the abuse they had suffered, we explored neural exercises together, which I later called "somatic resources," to discover which ones would help a client regulate extreme emotions and dysregulated arousal. Janet coined the term "vehement emotions" to describe the rage and terror that fuel the mobilizing of defensive strategies. He taught that trying to work with vehement emotions directly or expressing them was ineffective and only led the patient around in circles. However, I noticed that when clients began to experience these emotions, they often had an impulse to hit out or move their legs. When we executed these actions, the dysregulated emotions seemed to dissipate.

But it was also a difficult time personally because neither I nor my peers understood trauma. In those days, in my world, emotional catharsis was the name of the game, and some of my peers and mentors thought I was avoiding my clients' strong emotions. The importance of neural exercises to quiet the defensive systems and help people notice features of the environment that helped them feel safe was not in our awareness in the 1970s.

The Modulation Model and Neuroception

Polyvagal Theory identified that there are two branches of the vagus nerve, and that the branch that developed most recently in evolution (the ventral vagal complex or VVC) could inhibit both the older branch (the dorsal vagal complex or DVC) and the sympathetic nervous system (SNS). I came up with a graph (Figure 3.1), variations of which are widely used, that illustrates these three zones of arousal: hyperarousal (SNS), hypoarousal (DVC), and optimal arousal (VVC).

The graph first grew out of my background in music. My mother, an amateur pianist, taught me to read music before I learned to read words. In fact, I can remember learning to read letters in school, but I don't remember learning how to read musical notation. Although I never became an accomplished musician, I often think in musical terms. In the late 1980s or early 1990s, as I was reflecting on my clients' inability to modulate arousal, I thought of the power of music to change our state. In music, modulation refers to changing keys, which affects the mood of the piece, and thus of the musician and the listener. Moving from a higher or lower key, from major to minor key, and speeding up or slowing down the pace all have the power to affect one's state. Tempo (e.g., largo versus allegro), dynamics (e.g., pianissimo versus forte) and changes such as decrescendo or crescendo can downregulate or upregulate arousal and emotions. I thought about how clients suffered chronic dysregulated arousal and could not up- or downregulate as needed or transition smoothly between arousal states. They often experienced abrupt changes into very high or very low arousal states, and rarely were their arousal and mood optimal for daily life functioning. Out of these musings, the graph, called the "Modulation Model," emerged, and versions of it have been used in Sensorimotor Psychotherapy trainings since the 1990s.

The model describes the signs of autonomic arousal within each of the

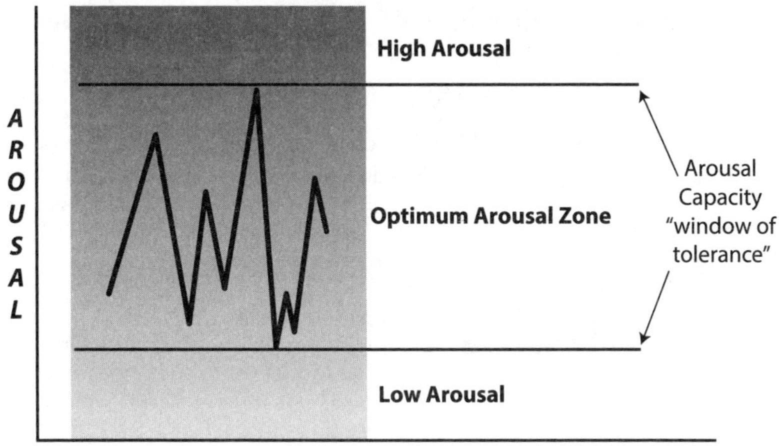

FIGURE 3.1
The Modulation Model: Optimal Arousal Zone (Ogden & Minton, 2000).

three zones: sympathetic hyperarousal, dorsal vagal hypoarousal, and the ventral vagal window of tolerance. Eventually, it evolved to illustrate the Polyvagal concept of neuroception (Porges, 2004), the innate ability of the nervous system to detect features in the environment that signal safety, danger, and life-threat (Figure 3.2).

Neuroception is an invaluable concept in working with clients and in teaching Sensorimotor Psychotherapy because it explains the innate intelligence of the body and makes sense of confusing dysregulated behaviors. Understanding neuroception decreases clients' self-judgment and shame about their dysregulated reactions. Often traumatized clients report, "I can suddenly feel unsafe," "I feel dead," "I get so overwhelmed." Or they report symptoms and impulsive actions that they don't understand: "I'm having panic attacks," "If someone touches me I hit them before I even think," or "I passed out when this girl hugged me." These symptoms usually reflect a nervous system biased to neurocept cues of danger and threat rather than safety, which is triggered by reminders of a perilous history. Clients are relieved when symptoms and behaviors are reframed as the result of faulty neuroception, a survival mechanism conditioned to assess present-moment reminders of the past as current threat, rather than as a personal shortcoming or deficit. When clients understand that neuroception is automatic and unconscious and can't be changed through cognition, their embarrassment and self-deprecation immediately lessens.

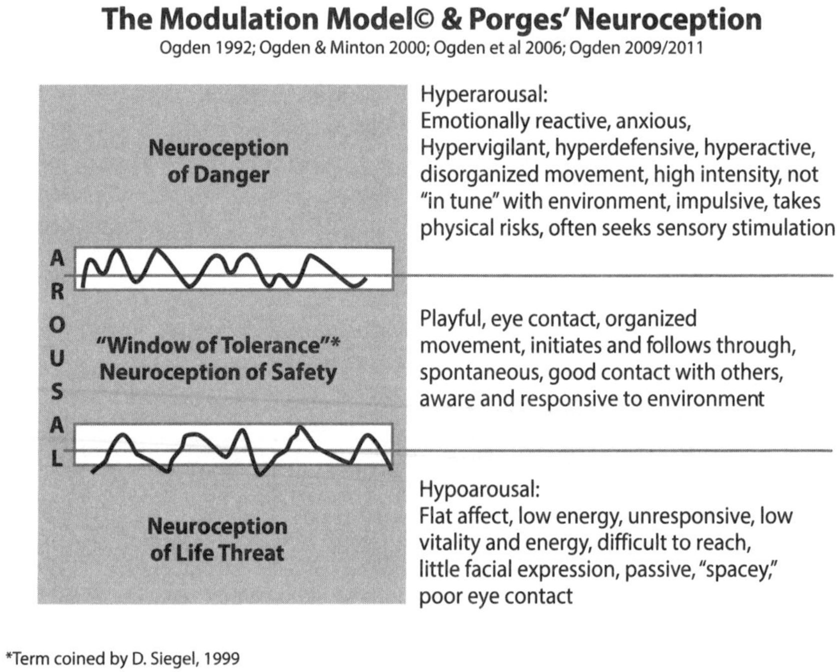

FIGURE 3.2

Figure 3.2 is a helpful psychoeducation tool to teach clients about the instinctive intelligence of their neuroception and to identify triggers and symptoms of faulty neuroception. Those who feel empty or dead inside learn that these states fall in the hypoarousal zone on the graph, and they can often identify the environmental cues that they neurocept as threatening. Those who have been paralyzed by fear are relieved to learn that their immobility results from faulty neuroception that elicits instinctive dorsal vagal responses of hiding, feigned death strategies, or disappearing.

Conversely, clients whose hyperarousal causes them to be impulsive, self-destructive, or enraged are relieved to understand these reactions as related to faulty neuroception, triggered by current reminders of past danger. When they are ashamed of their impulsivity, understanding that hyperarousal is designed to mobilize defensive action quickly without contemplation can generate appreciation of the adaptive root cause of their impulsive behavior.

Polyvagal Theory and neuroception are commonly thought of as particularly significant in understanding trauma and treating PTSD. However,

Polyvagal Theory helped me understand that they are equally relevant to attachment. The social engagement system is available to the full-term infant before attachment bonds are formed, and is further developed through interactions with an attachment figure who responds with motor and sensory contact to the infant's signals long before communication with words is possible. Thus, attachment and social engagement build upon each other. Socially engaged interactions of attunement and mutual pleasure strengthen attachment bonds and future capacity for affiliation (Porges, 2004, 2005, 2009, 2011), and a secure attachment with sufficient interactive repair when misattunements occur develops a healthy social engagement system. Neuroception of safety is reflected both in the inhibition of defense systems and in the ability to engage with others through eye contact, facial expression, and the voice.

Children can become frightened when their attachment figures criticize them for making mistakes, push them to excel, indicate they are disappointed in them, or punish them if they are idle or fail. Children neurocept danger in these situations because at a primitive level, parental disapproval implicitly threatens them since they are dependent on their caregivers for survival, safety, and a sense of belonging. These dynamics cause a degree of emotional distress, but not always so severe as to result in an insecure attachment or in the strongly dysregulated arousal of traumatized children.

All children learn early on what is expected in relationships with their attachment figures, and they will instinctively adjust their inner needs and behavioral and bodily responses to parental demands and preferences. In a conversation about this in 2013, Steve Porges pointed out that parental expectations inevitably leave a young child with two (nonconscious) choices: One, to remain safe and win approval of attachment figures by meeting their expectations; or, two, to risk danger in the form of rejection, criticism, disappointment, or worse by failing to meet expectations. When possible, living up to expectations would be the best choice because doing so reduces the presence and frequency of the behavioral features in the attachment figure that cause children to instinctively neurocept danger. Survival, security, and social engagement are preserved when meeting parental expectations allowing the child to neurocept safety.

Even clients with securely attached histories present with relational troubles rooted in mildly unsatisfactory (in comparison with insecure attachment) relational experiences, such as inadequate attention from parents who were too busy, or treatment that was slightly harsh, critical, inconsistent, insensitive, or fault finding.

The following is an example of how a therapeutic model incorporating the modulation model and neuroception can be useful in a clinical session.

> Darrell did not understand why he became so reactive in one of his classes in graduate school. He had a good relationship with his professor, and he was at the top of his class. But when his professor used a loud voice, Darrell neurocepted danger. He began to anticipate criticism and became hyperaroused at the slightest indication that he might not be doing well in this class. Darrell was happily married, had grown up with attentive, caring parents, and remained close to them as an adult. As he and his therapist tried to understand his current reactivity, Darrell recalled that his parents sometimes raised their voices in heated debate, which frightened him as a child. He identified the current cue that caused him to neurocept danger: his professor's loud voice. He learned to recognize the physical signs of faulty neuroception that occurred when his professor raised his voice: tension in his shoulders, shortness of breath, and an increase in heart rate. When he became aware of these signs, Darrell could learn to take measured, deep breaths, sit back in his chair, and relax his shoulders to help him calm himself and return his arousal to a window of tolerance. These neural exercises calmed his physiology, and as he could neurocept safety again, his social engagement system came back on line.

Clients learn to become aware of features in their current lives that cause them to neurocept threat. These are typically cues reminiscent of their attachment figure's inattentiveness, disapproval, criticism, disappointment, and the like. They learn to distinguish their own bodily signals that indicate that their arousal is approaching the edges of, or outside of, the window of tolerance. Once these triggers and signs of even slight dysregulation are identified, these clients will benefit from the neural exercises that bring arousal into the window of tolerance and thus enable prosocial behavior. No matter if triggers are trauma or attachment related, or both, understanding the automaticity of faulty neuroception challenges cognitive schemas of defectiveness, inadequacy, and unworthiness.

On Love

Now we get to the part that is most meaningful for me personally, the topic of love, and the underlying principles that inform the practice of Sensorimotor Psychotherapy beyond technique. The principles guide our way of being in relationship, including with our clients. To give you some history: I introduced Steve Porges to Ron Kurtz, my best friend and mentor, several years ago in Boulder, Colorado. They had an immediate affinity for one another, which pleased me immensely. I think the foundational root of their work (and mine) is the same: both were primarily interested in a state of being that embodies connection and love. The science and psychotherapy emerge out of that foundational interest.

I was lucky enough to meet Ron in the 1970s at the start of my career, when I was working for Vanderbilt's psychiatric hospital. I learned from him that therapy starts with the presence of the therapist, which allows clients to neurocept enough safety to embark upon the often-frightening journey of self-discovery—although at that time the term *neuroception* had not yet been invented. Ron taught me to look for something in my relationships with my clients that brought me pleasure, that inspired me in some way and evoked a loving state in me. He wrote, "My first impulse is to find something to love [in the client], something to be inspired by, something heroic, something recognizable as the gift and burden of the human condition, the pain and grace that's there to find in everyone you meet" (Kurtz, 2010). What better intention could there be to implicitly convey acceptance and security to another person? If the therapist keeps this in mind, certain nonverbal cues—a gentle facial expression, compassionate, loving eyes and prosody to match, open body posture, relaxed muscles—are neurocepted by the client. A loving atmosphere is created that is conducive to healing.

Many times, I've heard Steve talk about the neural love code, which he describes as a metaphor to understand attachment, bonding, and that in-love feeling that falling in love elicits in all of us. Our bodies seek out safe face-to-face interactions and immobilization without fear, which promote intimacy. This can only occur when we neurocept safety. Safety, whether with a friend, lover, or client, is created not through verbal but through nonverbal exchanges. Body cues are neurocepted unconsciously: resonant prosody, face-to-face expression, body-to-body affective signals. As Steve says, when we see another person's face and hear their voice, we know if they understand us, and we know if we are safe. The nonverbal expressive and auditory cues are neurocepted automatically, without conscious thought. As Steve says, the bodily feelings generated by the neuroception of safety turn off defensive strategies and critical thoughts, and promote connections and feelings of compassion.

Similarly, Ron emphasized safety, created by what he called "loving presence," cues of which are also conveyed nonverbally. Ron wrote, "Loving presence is a state of being. It is pleasant, good for your health, rewarding in and of itself. It's a state in which you feel open-hearted and well-intentioned. In its purest form, it is spiritually nourishing and sensitive to subtleties" (Kurtz, 2009, p. 1). Loving presence implicitly acknowledges the dignity of the human spirit, setting the stage with compassion so that clients can feel safe, much the way Steve also does in his work and personhood.

When loving presence is embodied by the therapist, clients pick up on cues, like a soft expression or gentle prosody, and feel understood and safe. When this happens, healing has already begun. As Polyvagal Theory explains, clients feel safety viscerally, outside of awareness, as their social engagement system comes online. I feel that embodied loving presence creates a way of being, and it is this being, not doing, that is the essence of healing. This gives clients the courage to enter the challenge of reworking their painful pasts. The therapist then must simultaneously accompany clients into the painful present-moment reexperiencing of the past to some degree, often accessing state-specific memories that elicit sympathetic and dorsal vagal responses in the present. Simultaneously, therapists must ensure that clients neurocept cues of safety in the here-and-now relationship, track and recover when safety is compromised, and interactively repair and reestablish social engagement when this occurs. This concurrent evocation of trauma-related dysregulation, relational disappointments, and failures of the past, mixed with social engagement, can result in a depth of intimacy in the relationship which exceeds that which ensues from conversation alone. The therapeutic encounter often becomes more deeply resonant emotionally, and the person-to-person connection becomes more palpable.

Polyvagal Theory offers a brilliant and heartfelt map and explanation for this process of relationship and healing that is easily accessible to Sensorimotor Psychotherapy students and clients. The felt sense comes to life in the science of Polyvagal Theory, which teaches that the wisdom we need is within our bodies and nervous systems, and is deeper than our cognitive explanations or mental assessments of danger and safety. Polyvagal Theory describes the drive for connection and intimacy as a nonconscious biological imperative situating any relationship, including the therapeutic relationship, in a new realm. Through safe connections, faith in organicity, a guiding concept of Sensorimotor Psychotherapy, becomes evident. This principle assumes that each person is free to choose their own path and has the intelligence, particularly somatic intelligence, within themselves that will yield the answers they are seeking. Polyvagal Theory has given us a language and a science that describes not only why we do what we do in Sensorimotor Psychotherapy, but why connection is the essence of healing. The state of being-in-relationship that is inherently healing is cultivated by loving presence that includes all aspects of a person. This is the foundation of Ron's work and of Sensorimotor Psychotherapy. At its core, Polyvagal Theory is about love and identifies the physiology behind it. It puts meat on the bones of Nietzsche's assertion, "All virtues are physiological conditions. Our most sacred convictions are judgments of our muscles."

References

Janet, P. (1925). *Principles of psychotherapy*. London: George Allen and Unwin.

Kurtz, R. (2009). *Loving presence*. Unpublished manuscript.

Kurtz, R. (2010). Readings in the Hakomi method of mindfulness-based assisted self-study. Retrieved from http://hakomi.com/wp-content/uploads/2009/12/Readings-January-2010.pdf

Ogden, P. (1997). Inner body sensation: Part one. *Somatics, 11*(2), 40–43.

Ogden, P. (1998). Inner body sensation: Part two. *Somatics, 11*(3), 42–49.

Ogden, P., & Fisher, J. (2015). *Sensorimotor psychotherapy: Interventions for trauma and attachment*. New York: Norton.

Ogden, P., & Minton, K. (2000). Sensorimotor psychotherapy: One method for processing traumatic memory. *Traumatology, 6*(3), 1–20.

Ogden, P., Minton, K., & Pain, C. (2006). *Trauma and the body: A sensorimotor approach to psychotherapy*. New York: Norton.

Porges, S. W. (2004). Neuroception: A subconscious system for detecting threats and safety. *Zero to Three, 24*(5), 19–24.

Porges, S. W. (2005). The role of social engagement in attachment and bonding: A phylogenetic perspective. In C. S. Carter, L. Ahnert, K. E. Grossmann, S. B. Hrdy, M. E. Lamb, S. W. Porges, & N. Sachser (Eds.), *Attachment and bonding: A new synthesis*. Cambridge, MA: MIT Press.

Porges, S. W. (2009). Reciprocal influences between body and brain in the perception and expression of affect: A polyvagal perspective. In D. Fosha, D. Siegel, & M. Solomon (Eds.), *The healing power of emotion: Neurobiological understandings and therapeutic perspectives*. New York: Norton.

Porges, S. W. (2011). *The Polyvagal Theory: Neurophysiological foundations of emotions, attachment, communication, and self-regulation*. New York: Norton.

Satchidananda, S. S. (1970). *Integral yoga hatha*. New York: Holt, Reinhart and Winston.

Siegel, D. (1999). *The developing mind*. New York: Guilford.

4

Polyvagal Theory: A Primer

Stephen W. Porges

Abstract: This chapter provides an overview of the Polyvagal Theory. The chapter is organized to facilitate an understanding of the constructs embedded in the theory that are relevant for clinical application. The chapter is organized with headings identifying important constructs within the theory, many of which are used by the authors of the chapters that follow.

Overview

Although Polyvagal Theory is the focus of this volume, the contributing authors were requested not to restate the details of the theory within their chapters. Instead, this chapter provides an overview of the theory. Although this chapter is dense and scientific, we hoped that by providing information on the theory in beginning of the book, we would allow the authors to be less encumbered by the science and to write in a more personal voice that would convey how Polyvagal Theory influenced their work. To facilitate the generalizability of Polyvagal Theory to clinical application, the chapter is organized with headings identifying important constructs within the theory.

Polyvagal Theory describes an autonomic nervous system that is influenced by the central nervous system and responds to signals from both the environment and bodily organs. The theory emphasizes that the human autonomic nervous system has a predictable pattern of reactivity, which is dependent on neuroanatomical and neurophysiological changes that occurred during evolution. Specifically, the theory focuses on the phylogenetic changes in the neural regulation of bodily organs during the evolutionary transition from ancient extinct reptiles to the earliest mammals.

Evolution of the Vertebrate Autonomic Nervous System

As mammals evolved, their behaviors differentiated them from their primitive reptilian ancestors. Unlike the solitary behaviors and lack of nurturance of their vertebrate ancestors, mammals expressed a broad range of social behaviors, including caring for offspring and cooperation. These behaviors supported the survival of mammals. However, in order for these behaviors to occur, the mammalian nervous system had to selectively down regulate defensive reactions. This convergence was dependent on the coevolution of modifications in the neural regulation of the autonomic nervous system and the sociality that defines mammalian behavior.

To understand Polyvagal Theory, it is first necessary to understand three contingent points: first, the relationship between autonomic state and defensive behaviors; second, the changes that occurred during vertebrate evolution in the neural regulation of the autonomic nervous system; and third, the physiological state, which enables bodily responses and feelings of safety, optimizes social behavior and concurrently optimizes health, growth, and restoration.

In most vertebrates, the two primary defense systems are fight-or-flight and immobilization. Fight-or-flight behaviors enable the organism to flee or defend when threatened. These behaviors require the rapid accessibility of resources to mobilize through the activation of the metabolically costly sympathetic nervous system. Immobilization is a more ancient defense system, which is shared with virtually all vertebrates. In contrast to the metabolically costly mobilization strategy, immobilization is an adaptive attempt to reduce metabolic demands (e.g., reduced options for food and oxygen) and to appear inanimate (e.g., death feigning). Juxtaposed with the rapid activation of the sympathetic nervous system required to promote fight-or-flight behaviors, immobilization defense behaviors required a massive shutting down of autonomic function via a vagal pathway within the parasympathetic nervous system.

Over time, a second vagal pathway evolved that had the capacity to down regulate both forms of defense. This second vagal pathway is observed in mammals and not reptiles. In addition, the anatomical structures regulating this component of the vagus interacted in the brain stem with structures regulating the striated muscles of the face and head to provide an integrated social engagement system. This emergent social engagement system provided the mechanism for co-regulation of physiological state, as mammals conveyed cues of safety and danger—via vocalizations, head gestures, and facial expressions—to conspecifics. The social engagement system enabled mammals to co-opt some of the features of the vertebrate defense systems to promote social interactions such as play and intimacy. These changes in the autonomic nervous system provided mammals with neural mechanisms to promote the biobehavioral states necessary for caring for offspring, reproducing, and cooperative behavior. In contrast, the adverse behavioral and psychological effects of trauma appear to target a disruption of the social engagement system, its management of defense reactions, and its contribution to co-regulation and cooperative behaviors, including intimacy and play.

Origin of Polyvagal Theory: The Vagal Paradox

Polyvagal Theory emerged from research studying heart rate patterns in human fetuses and newborns. In obstetrics and neonatology, the massive slowing of heart rate known as *bradycardia* is a clinical index of risk and assumed to be mediated by the vagus. During bradycardia, heart rate is so slow that it no longer provides sufficient oxygenated blood to the brain. This type of vagal influence on the fetal and neonatal heart could potentially be lethal. However, with the same clinical populations, a different index of vagal function was assumed to be a measure of resilience. This measure was beat-to-beat heart rate variability and was the focus of my research for several decades. Animal research demonstrated that both signals could be disrupted by severing the vagal pathways to the heart or via pharmacological blockade (i.e., atropine), interfering with the inhibitory action of the vagus on the sinoatrial node (for review see Porges, 1995). These observations posed the paradox of how cardiac vagal tone could be both a positive indicator of health when monitored with heart rate variability and a negative indicator of health when it manifests as bradycardia.

The resolution to the paradox came from understanding how the neural regulation of the autonomic nervous system changed during evolution, especially through the transition from primitive extinct reptiles to mammals. During this transition, mammals evolved a second vagal motor pathway. This uniquely mammalian pathway is myelinated and conveys a respiratory rhythm to the heart's pacemaker, resulting in a rhythmic oscillation in heart rate at the frequency of spontaneous breathing known as *respiratory sinus arrhythmia*. Myelin is a fatty substance that surrounds the fiber. Myelin provides electrical insulation for the fiber, which enables the signal to be transmitted with greater specificity and speed. This branch of the vagus originates in an area of brain stem known as the *nucleus ambiguus*, travels primarily to organs above the diaphragm, and interacts within the brain stem with structures regulating the striated muscles of the face and head. The other vagal motor pathway does not have a respiratory rhythm, is observed in virtually all vertebrates, is unmyelinated, travels primarily to organs below the diaphragm, and originates in an area of the brain stem known as the *dorsal nucleus* of the vagus.

Phylogenetic Shifts in Vertebrate Autonomic Nervous Systems

By tracking the evolutionary changes in the vertebrate autonomic nervous system, I identified a phylogenetic pattern consisting of three evolutionary stages. During the first stage, vertebrates relied on an unmyelinated vagus with motor pathways originating in an area of the brain stem resembling the dorsal vagal complex. During the second stage, an excitatory spinal sympathetic nervous system developed, which complemented the down regulation functions of the ancient vagal pathway. During the third stage, defined by the emergence of mammals, an additional vagal pathway evolved, during which cells of origin of the vagus migrated from the dorsal nucleus of the vagus to the nucleus ambiguus; many of the vagal motor fibers originating in the nucleus ambiguus became myelinated and integrated in the function of the brain stem regulation of a family of motor pathways (i.e., special visceral efferent pathways) that control the striated muscles of the face and head (see Figure 4.1).

In mammals, the unmyelinated vagal pathways originating in the dorsal nucleus of the vagus primarily regulate the organs below the diaphragm, though some of these unmyelinated vagal fibers terminate on the heart's pacemaker (sinoatrial node). Polyvagal Theory hypothesizes that these unmyelinated vagal fibers primarily remain dormant until life-threat, and they are probably potentiated during hypoxia and states in which the influence of the myelinated vagal input to the heart is depressed. This sequence is observable in human fetal heart rate, in which bradycardia is more likely to occur when the tonic influence of the myelinated vagal pathways, manifest in respiratory sinus arrhythmia, is low (Reed, Ohel, David, & Porges, 1999). This also may be the mechanism mediating trauma-elicited dissociation, defecation, and syncope (i.e., fainting).

In ancient vertebrates, an unmyelinated vagal pathway emerging from the brain stem was a critical component of the neural regulation of the entire viscera. This bidirectional system reduced metabolic output when resources were low, such as during times of reduced oxygen. The nervous systems of primitive vertebrates did not need much oxygen to survive and could lower heart rate and metabolic demands when oxygen levels dropped. Thus, this circuit provided a conservation system that in mammals was adapted as a primitive defense system manifested as death feigning and trauma-driven responses of syncope and dissociation. Since this defense system could be lethal in oxygen-demanding mammals, fortunately it functions as the last option for survival. The phylogenetically older unmyelinated vagal motor pathways are shared with most vertebrates and, in mammals, when not recruited as a defense system, function to support health, growth, and restoration via neural regulation of subdiaphragmatic organs (i.e., internal organs below the diaphragm).

The "newer" myelinated ventral vagal motor pathways regulate the supradiaphragmatic organs (e.g., heart and lungs) and are integrated in the brain stem with structures that regulate the striated muscles of the face and head via special visceral efferent pathways resulting in a functional social engagement system. This newer vagal circuit slows heart rate and supports the states of calmness required for social interactions. The ventral vagal circuit coupled with other autonomic circuits supports social play (i.e., ventral vagal coupled with sympathetic activation) and safe intimacy (i.e., ventral vagal coupled with the dorsal vagal circuit). Thus, the mammalian vagus has properties that promote states that contain the range of responding of all components of the autonomic nervous system and functionally restrains the system from moving into states of defense.

The Emergence of the Social Engagement System

The integration of the myelinated cardiac vagal pathways with the neural regulation of the face and head gave rise to the mammalian social engagement system. As illustrated in Figure 4.1, the outputs of the social engagement system consist of motor pathways regulating striated muscles of the face and head (i.e., somatomotor) and smooth and cardiac muscles of the heart and bronchi (i.e., visceromotor). The somatomotor component involves special visceral efferent pathways that regulate the striated muscles of the face and head. The visceromotor component involves the myelinated supradiaphragmatic vagal pathway that regulates the heart and bronchi. Functionally, the social engagement system emerges from a face-heart connection that coordinates the heart with the muscles of the face and head. The initial function of the system is to coordinate sucking, swallowing, breathing, and vocalizing. Atypical coordination of this system early in life is an indicator of subsequent difficulties in social behavior and emotional regulation.

When fully developed, two important biobehavioral features of this system are expressed. First, bodily state is regulated in an efficient manner to promote growth and restoration (e.g., visceral homeostasis). Functionally, this is accom-

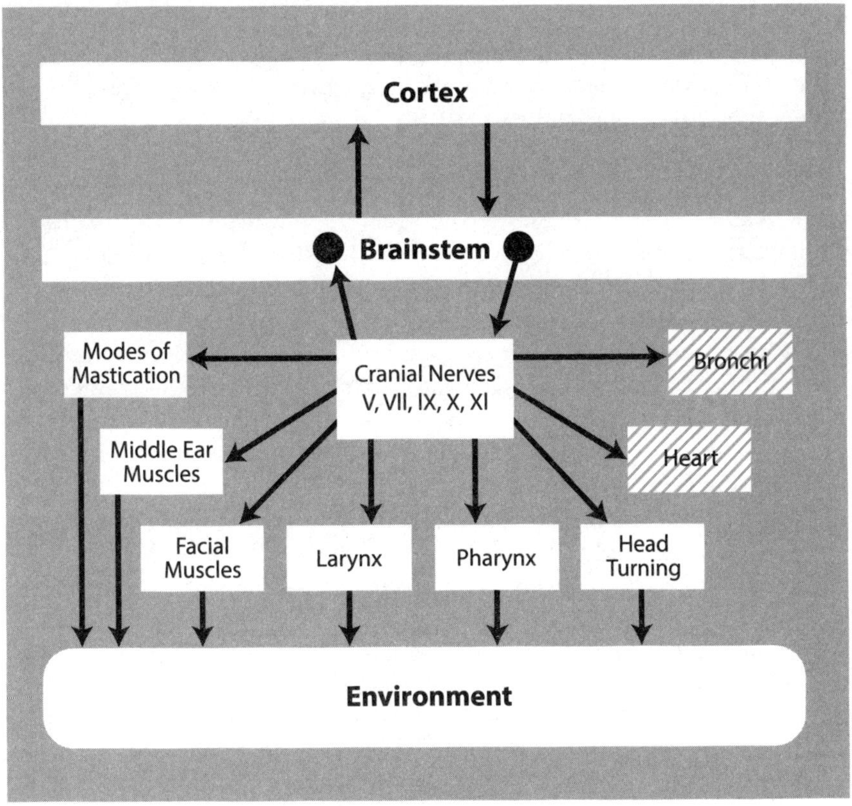

FIGURE 4.1
The social engagement system consists of a somatomotor component (solid blocks) and a visceromotor component (dashed blocks). The somatomotor component involves special visceral efferent pathways that regulate the striated muscles of the face and head, while the visceromotor component involves the myelinated vagus that regulates the heart and bronchi.

plished through an increase in the influence of myelinated vagal motor pathways on the cardiac pacemaker to slow heart rate, inhibit the fight-or-flight mechanisms of the sympathetic nervous system, dampen the stress response system of the hypothalamic–pituitary–adrenal (HPA) axis (responsible for cortisol release), and reduce inflammation by modulating immune reactions (e.g., cytokines; for review see Porges, 2007). Second, the phylogenetically mammalian face–heart connection functions to convey physiological state via facial expression and prosody (intonation of voice), as well as regulate the middle-ear muscles to optimize species-specific listening within the frequency band used for social communication (Kolacz, Lewis, & Porges, in press; Porges, 2007, 2009, 2011; Porges & Lewis, 2010).

The brain stem source nuclei of the social engagement system are influenced by higher brain structures (i.e., top-down influences) and by sensory pathways from visceral organs (i.e., bottom-up influences). Direct pathways from cortex to brain stem (i.e., corticobulbar) reflect the influence of frontal areas of the cortex (i.e., upper motor neurons) on the medullary source nuclei of this system. Bottom-up influences occur via feedback through the sensory pathways of the vagus (e.g., tractus solitarius), conveying information from visceral organs to medullary areas (e.g., nucleus of the solitary tract) and influencing both the source nuclei of this system and the forebrain areas, via the insula, that are assumed to be involved in several psychiatric disorders, including depression and anxiety (Craig, 2005; Thayer & Lane, 2007, 2009). In addition, the anatomical structures involved in the social engagement system have neurophysiological interactions with the HPA axis, the social neuropeptides (e.g., oxytocin and vasopressin), and the immune system (Carter, 1998; Porges, 2001).

Sensory pathways from the target organs of the social engagement system, including the muscles of the face and head, also provide potent input to the source nuclei regulating both the visceral and somatic components of the social engagement system. The source nucleus of the facial nerve forms the border of nucleus ambiguus, and sensory pathways from both the facial and trigeminal nerves provide a primary sensory input to nucleus ambiguus (see Porges, 1995, 2007). Thus, the ventral vagal complex, consisting of nucleus ambiguus and the nuclei of the trigeminal and facial nerves, is functionally related to the expression and experience of affective states and emotions. Activation of the somatomotor component (e.g., listening, ingestion, vocalizations, facial expressions) could trigger visceral changes that would support social engagement, while modulation of visceral state, depending on whether there is an increase or decrease in the influence of the myelinated vagal motor fibers on the sinoatrial node (i.e., increasing or decreasing the influence of the vagal brake), would either promote or impede social engagement behaviors (Porges, 1995, 2007). For example, stimulation of visceral states that promote mobilization (i.e., fight-or-flight behaviors) would impede the ability to express social engagement behaviors.

The face–heart connection enabled mammals to detect whether a conspecific was in a calm physiological state and safe to approach, or in a highly mobilized and reactive physiological state during which engagement would be dangerous. The face–heart connection concurrently enables an individual to signal "safety" through patterns of facial expression and vocal intonation, and potentially calm an agitated conspecific to form a social relationship. When the newer mammalian vagus is optimally functioning in social interactions, emotions are well regulated, vocal prosody is rich, and the autonomic state supports calm, spontaneous social engagement behaviors. The face–heart system is bidirectional, with the newer myelinated vagal circuit influencing social interactions and positive social interactions influencing vagal function to optimize health, dampen stress-related physiological states, and support growth and restoration. Social communication and the ability to co-regulate interactions, via reciprocal social engagement systems, lead to a sense of connectedness and are important defining features of the human experience.

Vagal Brake

The vagal brake reflects the tonic inhibitory influence of the myelinated vagal pathways on the heart, which slows the intrinsic rate of the heart's pacemaker. The intrinsic heart rate of young, healthy adults is about 90 beats per minute. However, baseline heart rate is noticeably slower due to the influence of the vagus, which functions as a "vagal brake." When the vagus decreases its influence on the heart (i.e., the vagal brake releases), heart rate spontaneously increases. This is not due to an increase in sympathetic excitation; rather, the release of the vagal brake allows the rate intrinsic in the pacemaker to be expressed. The vagal brake represents the actions of engaging and disengaging the vagal influences to the heart's pacemaker. In addition, the release of the vagal brake on the heart also enables tonic underlying sympathetic excitation to exert more influence on the autonomic nervous system. Polyvagal Theory specifically assumes that the vagal brake is mediated solely through the myelinated ventral vagus and can be quantified by the amplitude of respiratory sinus arrhythmia. The theory acknowledges other neural (e.g., dorsal vagal pathways) and neurochemical influences that can slow heart rate (e.g., clinical bradycardia), which are not included within the construct of the vagal brake.

Dissolution

The human nervous system, similar to that of other mammals, evolved not solely to survive in safe environments, but also to promote survival in dangerous and life-threatening contexts. To accomplish this adaptive flexibility, the mammalian autonomic nervous system, in addition to the myelinated vagal pathway that is integrated into the social engagement system, retained two more primitive neural circuits to regulate defensive strategies (i.e., fight-or-flight and death-feigning behaviors). It is important to note that social behavior, social communication, and visceral homeostasis are incompatible with the neurophysiological states that support defense. Polyvagal response strategies to challenge are phylogenetically ordered, with newest components of the autonomic nervous system responding first. This model of autonomic reactivity is consistent with John Hughlings Jackson's construct of dissolution, in which he proposed that "the higher nervous arrangements inhibit (or control) the lower, and thus, when the higher are suddenly rendered functionless, the lower rise in activity" (1882, p. 412). In this hierarchy of adaptive responses, the newest social engagement circuit is used first; if that circuit fails to provide safety, the older circuits are recruited sequentially.

Neuroception

Polyvagal Theory proposes that the neural evaluation of risk does not require conscious awareness and functions through neural circuits that are shared with our phylogenetic vertebrate ancestors. Thus, the term *neuroception* was introduced to emphasize a neural process, distinct from perception, capable of distinguishing environmental and visceral features that are safe, dangerous, or life-threatening (Porges, 2003, 2004). In safe environments, autonomic state is adaptively regulated to dampen sympathetic activation and to protect the oxygen-dependent central nervous system, especially the cortex, from the metabolically conservative reactions of the dorsal vagal complex (e.g., fainting).

Neuroception is proposed as a reflexive mechanism capable of instantaneously shifting physiological state. Feature detectors, located in areas of or near the temporal cortex, which are sensitive to the intentionality of biological movements including voices, faces, gestures, and hand movements, might be involved in the process of neuroception. Embedded in the construct of neuroception is the capacity of the nervous system to react to the "intention" of these movements. Neuroception functionally decodes and interprets the assumed goal of movements and sounds of inanimate and living objects. Thus, the neuroception of familiar individuals and individuals with appropriately prosodic voices and warm, expressive faces frequently translates into a positive social interaction, promoting a sense of safety. Although we are often unaware of the stimuli that trigger different neuroceptive responses, we are generally aware of our body's reactions.

Autonomic State as an Intervening Variable

Polyvagal Theory proposes that physiological state is a fundamental part, and not a correlate, of emotion or mood. According to the theory, autonomic state functions as an intervening variable biasing our detection and evaluation of environmental cues. Depending on physiological state, the same cues will be reflexively evaluated as neutral, positive, or threatening. Functionally, a change in state will shift access to different structures in the brain and support either social communication or the defensive behaviors of fight-or-flight or shutdown. Contemporary research on the impact of vagal nerve stimulation on cognitive function and emotion regulation supports this model (Groves & Brown, 2005). The theory emphasizes a bidirectional link between brain and viscera, which would explain how thoughts change physiology, and physiological state influences thoughts. As individuals change their facial expressions, the intonation of their voices, the pattern in which they are breathing, and their posture, they are also changing their physiology through circuits involving myelinated vagal pathways to the heart.

The Role of Sensations From Bodily Organs in the Regulation of Autonomic State

The prevalent focus of research investigating the neural regulation of the heart has focused on motor pathways emerging from brain stem nuclei (i.e., vagal pathways) and the sympathetic nervous system. Limited research has been conducted on the influence of sensory feedback from bodily organs (i.e., visceral afferents) in the neural regulation of the autonomic nervous system, and how these influences are manifested in the heart and other visceral organs. This is, in part, due to a top-down bias in medical education that limits the conceptualization of the neural regulation of the heart and other bodily organs by emphasizing the role of motor fibers and minimizing the role of sensory fibers. However, this bias is rapidly changing due to research on the applications of vagal nerve stimulation, a bottom-up model that focuses on the vagus as a sensory nerve (approximately 80% of the vagal fibers are sensory). Interestingly, the side effects of vagal nerve stimulation are frequently due to the influence of vagal nerve stimulation on motor pathways. These side effects are primarily noted on features of the social engagement system, including changes in voice and difficulties swallowing (Ben-Menachem, 2001). However, in some cases, the stimulation has been manifested in subdiaphragmatic organs, resulting in diarrhea (Sanossian & Haut, 2002). As vagal nerve stimulation becomes more commonly applied to medical disorders, there is an emerging awareness of the influence of the sensory pathways of the vagus on neurophysiological function (e.g., epilepsy), emotional state (e.g., depression), and cognition (e.g., learning and attention; Howland, 2014).

According to Polyvagal Theory, the social engagement system is regulated by complex neural circuits, involving both sensory pathways from visceral organs (i.e., bottom-up) and higher brain structures (i.e., top-down) that influence the brain stem source nuclei controlling both the myelinated vagus and the striated muscles of the face and head. As the surveillance role of sensory pathways providing feedback from bodily organs to the brain stem is incorporated into an understanding of the autonomic nervous system, clinicians and researchers will begin to recognize manifestations in the vagal control of the heart in patients with a variety of disorders of peripheral organs. With that understanding, rather than interpreting the atypical neural regulation of the heart as a cardiovascular disease, comorbidities may be explained as manifestations of "system" dysfunction consistent with the prescient views of Walter Hess (1949/2014).

Several chronic diseases manifested in specific subdiaphragmatic organs (e.g., kidney, pancreas, liver, gut, genitals, etc.) have identifiable features that have led to treatments that target organs (e.g., medication, surgery). However, other disorders that have an impact on quality of life, such as irritable bowel syndrome and fibromyalgia, are defined by nonspecific symptoms. The literature links these nonspecific chronic disorders with atypical vagal regulation of the heart, reflected in diminished heart rate variability (Mazurak, Seredyuk, Sauer, Teufel, & Enck, 2012; Staud, 2008). Consistent with these findings, heart rate variability has been proposed as a biomarker for these disorders.

Polyvagal Theory proposes an alternative interpretation of this covariation. Consistent with the integrated model of the autonomic nervous system described in the theory, atypical heart rate variability is not interpreted as a biomarker of any specific disease. Rather, depressed heart rate variability is proposed as a neurophysiological marker of a diffuse retuning of the autonomic nervous system, indicating a withdrawal of the ventral vagal circuit following an adaptive complex autonomic reaction to threat. Compatible with this interpretation, there are strong links between the prevalence of a history of abuse, especially sexual abuse in women, and the manifestations of nonspecific clinical disorders such as irritable bowel syndrome and fibromyalgia. In addition, emotional stress intensifies symptoms and hinders positive treatment outcomes, and trauma may trigger or aggravate symptoms (Clauw, 2014; Whitehead et al., 2007). The initial adaptive neural response to threat, via sensory feedback from the visceral organs to the brain stem, may result in a chronic reorganization of the autonomic regulation observed in vagal regulation of the heart (i.e., depressed heart rate variability) in conjunction with altered subdiaphragmatic organ function and pain signaling.

A New Perspective of the Autonomic Nervous System

Polyvagal Theory uses an inclusive definition of the autonomic nervous system that includes sensory pathways and emphasizes the brain stem areas regulating autonomic function. The theory links the brain stem regulation of the ventral vagus to the regulation of the striated muscles of the face and head to produce an integrated social engagement system (see Figure 4.1 on the ventral vagal complex and social engagement system).

In contrast to the traditional model that focuses on tonic motor influences on visceral organs, Polyvagal Theory emphasizes autonomic reactivity. Polyvagal Theory accepts the traditional model of interpreting *tonic* autonomic influences on several visceral organs as the sum of a paired antagonism between vagal and sympathetic pathways. However, Polyvagal Theory proposes a phylogenetically ordered hierarchy in which autonomic subsystems *react* to challenges in the reverse of their evolutionary history, consistent with the principle of dissolution.

The theory postulates that when the ventral vagus and the associated social engagement system are optimally functioning, the autonomic nervous system supports health, growth, and restoration. During this ventral vagal state, there is an optimal "autonomic balance" between the sympathetic nervous system and the dorsal vagal pathways to subdiaphragmatic organs. When the function of the ventral vagus is dampened or withdrawn, the autonomic nervous system is optimized to support defense, and not health. According to Polyvagal Theory, these defense reactions may be manifested as fight-or-flight or shutdown. As fight-or-flight defense, there is an increase in sympathetic activity to promote mobilization strategies while inhibiting digestion (and other dorsal vagal functions). In contrast, when manifested as shutdown, sympathetic activation is depressed, while there is a surge of the dorsal vagal influences that would promote fainting, defecation, and an inhibition of motor behavior often seen in mammals feigning death.

Cues of Safety Are the Treatment

Polyvagal Theory proposes that cues of safety are an efficient and profound antidote for trauma. The theory emphasizes that safety is defined by feeling safe and not simply by the removal of threat. Feeling safe is dependent on three conditions: 1) the autonomic nervous system cannot be in a state that supports defense; 2) the social engagement system needs to be activated to down regulate sympathetic activation and functionally contain the sympathetic nervous system and the dorsal vagal circuit within an optimal range (homeostasis) that would support health, growth, and restoration; and 3) cues of safety (e.g., prosodic vocalizations, positive facial expressions and gestures) need to be available and detected via neuroception. In everyday situations, the cues of safety may initiate the sequence by triggering the social engagement system via the process of neuroception, which will contain autonomic state within a homeostatic range and restrict the autonomic nervous system from reacting in defense. This constrained range of autonomic state has been referred to as the *window of tolerance* (see Ogden, Minton, & Pain, 2006; Siegel, 1999) and can be expanded through neural exercises embedded in therapy.

Neural Exercise as Intervention

Polyvagal Theory focuses on specific neural exercises that provide opportunities to optimize the regulation of physiological state. According to the theory, neural exercises consisting of transitory disruptions and repairs of physiological state through social interactions employing cues of safety would promote greater resilience. Play, such as peek-a-boo, is an example of a neural exercise that parents frequently employ with their children. Play provides an example of a therapeutic model in which autonomic state is disrupted and then stabilized through the recruitment of the social engagement system. This model can be generalized to the clinical setting, in which the client experiences disrupted changes in autonomic state, which are stabilized through the support of the therapist. Functionally, therapy becomes a platform to exercise the capacity to shift state by recruiting features of the social engagement system to keep the autonomic nervous system out of prolonged states of defense. This process is initialized through co-regulation between the client and the therapist. Subsequently, when the client experiences reliable co-regulation, the potency of transitory shifts in state as triggers of defense is reduced and self-regulation spontaneously emerges.

Through the metaphor of play, the social engagement system is coupled with the sympathetic nervous system. This coupling enables bodily cues of mobilization to be contained within a social setting and not to erupt into aggression. However, these eruptions or tantrums frequently occur in children and adults with behavioral problems and psychiatric disorders. Research documents a consistency of a down regulated social engagement system (e.g., lack of prosody, blunted facial expression, auditory hypersensitivities, poor eye gaze) in individuals with state regulation disorders (see Porges, 2011).

Polyvagal Theory emphasizes that the vulnerability to these disruptions is due to a physiological state shift characterized by sympathetic activation without the resource of efficient self-soothing or calming through the social engagement system.

The metaphor of play is also useful in deconstructing intimacy. Intimacy is a state-dependent behavior. Intimacy involves coupling the social engagement system with the dorsal vagal circuit to enable immobilization without shutdown. Intimacy requires a state in which touch and proximity do not trigger defense. For mammals, immobilization is a vulnerable state. For intimacy to occur, neuroception has to interpret proximity and contact as safe and shift the body into a state that is welcoming. This coupling of two bodies initially occurs through cues of safety, such as prosodic vocalizations and gentle contact. Intimacy is often associated with a form of play, foreplay. However, similar to the positive attributes of play, which functions as a neural exercise optimizing the ability of the social engagement system to regulate the sympathetic nervous system, foreplay and truly safe experiences of intimacy provide a neural exercise optimizing the ability of the social engagement system to regulate the dorsal vagal pathway. This form of neural exercise may have long-term beneficial effects on the regulation of bodily organs by supporting homeostasis. Moreover, safe foreplay and intimacy may also be a preparatory neural exercise for women that, by enabling immobilization without fear, would optimize the reproductive behaviors and processes, including facilitating childbirth.

Listening as a Neural Exercise

Polyvagal Theory emphasizes how listening is a portal to the social engagement system. Based on Polyvagal Theory, the Listening Project Protocol is a listening intervention designed to reduce auditory hypersensitivities, improve auditory processing, calm physiological state, and support spontaneous social engagement. The intervention is currently known as the Safe and Sound Protocol and is available to professionals only through Integrated Listening Systems (http://integratedlistening.com/ssp-safe-sound-protocol/).

The Safe and Sound Protocol is based on an "exercise" model that uses computer-altered acoustic stimulation to modulate the frequency band passed to the participant. The protocol was theoretically designed to reduce auditory hypersensitivities by recruiting the antimasking functions of the middle-ear muscles to optimize the transfer function of the middle ear for the processing of human speech. Modulation of the acoustic energy within the frequencies of human voice, similar to exaggerated vocal prosody, is hypothesized to provide cues of safety to the client. Hypothetically, these cues are processed, via neuroception, and reflexively recruit and modulate the neural regulation of the middle-ear muscles. Based on the theory, this process would functionally reduce auditory hypersensitivities, stimulate spontaneous social engagement, and calm physiological state by increasing the influence of ventral vagal pathways on the heart. The intervention stimuli are listened to on headphones. The protocol consists of 60 minutes of listening on five consecutive days in a quiet room without major distractors, while the clinician, parent, or researcher provides social support to ensure that the participant remains calm. The neurophysiological basis of the intervention is elaborated in other publications (see Porges, 2011; Porges & Lewis, 2010).

Since the late 1990s my research group has been evaluating and refining the protocol. We have tested the protocol on several hundred children with a variety of disorders including children with autism spectrum disorders, speech/language delays, auditory hypersensitivities, and behavioral regulation disorders. The outcomes have been positive with noticeable increases in spontaneous social engagement behaviors, reduced sound sensitivities, improved organization of social behaviors and emotional state, and improved and more spontaneous verbal communication highlighted by more expressive voices. We have also conducted and published two peer-reviewed publications describing our findings (see Porges et al., 2013; Porges et al., 2014). During the past few years we have organized several clinical trials, which are currently registered on ClinicalTrials.gov. These new clinical trials are evaluating the intervention with different populations including children with abuse histories, individuals with attention and concentration difficulties, and children with Prader Willi Syndrome.

Since the release of the Safe and Sound Protocol, we have received feedback from therapists that matches the positive behavioral changes in children that we observed in our research. During the 20 years that we have tested the Safe and Sound Protocol with children, we have not observed any major adverse effects. Occasionally, we have observed an initial tactile sensitivity to the headphones, which would rapidly resolve. Also, perhaps due to previous unpleasant experiences with sounds and headphones, the combination of sounds and context might provoke minor anxiety in the child, which has rapidly resolved. This success is, in part, due to the "safe" context in which the intervention is delivered. For children, the safe context is efficiently structured by creating a 'safe' clinical environment with a therapist who projects welcoming cues of warmth to the child. This sense of a 'safe container' is supported by a safe and protective parent or caregiver accompanying the child, while the child experiences the Safe and Sound Protocol.

The Safe and Sound Protocol as an intervention has two components: first, structuring a safe context in which the intervention is delivered; and second, delivering the acoustic features of the sound presented during the intervention that serve as a neural exercise. The safe component is managed by the practitioner delivering the intervention. The sound component is embedded in the acoustic stimuli. It is important to acknowledge successful implementation of the intervention requires both components. For the Safe and Sound Protocol to be effective, it is necessary to maintain the client's nervous system in a state of safety.

For the Safe and Sound Protocol to be effective with adults, similar to applications with children, it is necessary to maintain the nervous system in a state of safety. Maintaining the adult's nervous system in a state of safety may be challenging, especially adults with trauma histories. Unlike the 'safe containment' that children experience in the presence of a caring and supportive adult, adults frequently arrive at a clinic without a supportive partner. Suggesting that a trusted friend, who would be available for support and regulation, accompany the client would be helpful in maintaining the client in a state of safety. Vulnerability to state changes might be exacerbated if the adult comes alone to the clinic.

Emotional and physiological reactions to the intervention are a potent signal that the stimuli are effectively triggering neural circuits. However, for the stimuli to trigger and exercise neural circuits that promote spontaneous social communication, improved state regulation, and reduced auditory hypersensitivities, the nervous system has to be in a safe state. More accurately, the nervous system has to feel protected and sufficiently trusting not to move into states of self-protection, hypervigilance, and defense. This may require a titration of the acoustic stimuli with the client temporarily pausing the intervention stimuli when the sounds elicit a strong emotional or visceral reaction. If the client feels discomfort, the client should be empowered to pause the intervention to allow their nervous system to stabilize. Although the fixed protocol works extremely well with children, adults may have a complicated history and may have difficulties feeling safe. As we move into the treatment of adults, we will continue to learn through the detailed comments from the therapists about variations in responses. This important feedback will allow us to modify the protocol to optimize the client's outcome.

Passive and Active Pathways

The human nervous system provides two pathways to trigger neural mechanisms capable of downregulating defense and enabling states of calmness that support health, spontaneous social behavior, and connectedness. One pathway is *passive* and does not require conscious awareness (see neuroception), and the other is *active* and requires *conscious voluntary behaviors* to trigger specific neural mechanisms that change physiological state (see neural exercise).

Both the passive and active pathways regulate the social engagement system. The passive pathway recruits the social engagement system through cues of safety such as a quiet environment, positive and compassionate therapist-patient interactions, prosodic quality (e.g., melodic intonation) of the therapist's vocalizations, and music modulated across frequency bands that overlap with vocal signals of safety used by a mother to calm her infant. Successful therapists, regardless of their orientation, often intuitively manipulate the passive pathway in treatment. In contrast, the active pathway recruits the social engagement system when the patient engages in reciprocal dialogue and other practices, such as vocalizations, voluntarily controlled breathing, movements, or postures. Access to the client's active pathway is dependent on the passive pathway effectively triggering a state of safety in the client.

The passive pathway is an effective and efficient method to recruit the social engagement system to spontaneously transition the client into a ventral vagal state. The passive pathway provides the client with feelings of safety. The active pathway provides the neural exercises to empower the client to efficiently move into and out of a ventral vagal state. Through effective interventions the client may have transitory experiences in states previously associated with defense and dominated by either the sympathetic nervous system or the dorsal vagus. The exercises enable the client to functionally contain previously disruptive autonomic states by accessing the social engagement system and the ventral vagus. The passive pathway provides the client with feelings of safety, while the active pathway challenges these feelings of safety by 'exercising' the neural resources of the social engagement system. These sequential processes expand resilience and provide resources to calm, to co-regulate, and self-regulate when challenged.

Polyvagal Theory: Trauma Only Makes Sense in the Light of Evolution

At the core of the evolved features that define mammals is the role that social interaction plays in their survival. Functionally, the ability to establish feelings of safety within a social interaction underlies their survival and acts as a prepotent biological imperative. This important attribute and a refinement of the meaning of "survival of the fittest" was emphasized by the evolutionary biologist Dobzhansky (1962), when he stated that "the fittest may also be the gentlest, because survival often requires mutual help and cooperation." For the survivors of trauma, their lives reflect a loss of these mammalian qualities.

As Polyvagal Theory has deconstructed several of the mechanisms through which trauma retunes the nervous system, an understanding of evolution and dissolution provides insights into the physiological and psychological experiences and helps the client generate a plausible personal explanatory narrative. This emphasis on evolution in understanding trauma reactions is reminiscent of Dobzhansky's most famous quote, "Nothing in biology makes sense except in the light of evolution" (1973, p. 125). Consistent with Dobzhansky, a polyvagal perspective explicitly assumes that *the response to trauma only makes sense in the light of evolution.*

Synthesis

Polyvagal Theory emphasizes that humans, similar to other mammals, consist of a collection of dynamic, adaptive, interactive, and interdependent physiological systems. From this perspective, it becomes apparent that the autonomic nervous system cannot be treated as functionally distinct from the central nervous system. Consistent with Polyvagal Theory, the heart and other organs are not "floating in a visceral sea," but are metaphorically anchored to central structures by motor pathways and continuously signaling central regulatory structures via an abundance of sensory pathways. This dynamic, bidirectional communication between brain structures and bodily organs influences mental state, biases perception of the environment, prepares the individual to be either welcoming or defensive of others. These processes simultaneously support or disrupt health, growth, and restoration.

The theory provides a plausible explanation of how a response to life-threat could retune the autonomic nervous system to lose resilience and to remain in defense states. This retuning might lead to disruptions in homeostatic function with manifestations in visceral organs (e.g., heart disease, irritable bowel) or diffuse symptoms of dysregulation (e.g., fibromyalgia, dysautonomia), while simultaneously limiting access to the social engagement system that would compromise the ability to co-regulate through social interactions. These common consequences of trauma are highlighted by difficulties in feeling connected and safe with others. Polyvagal Theory explains how both aspects of disruption (i.e., lack of safety with others and disorders of bodily organs) are manifestations of a retuned autonomic nervous system, and offers insights into rehabilitation. Thus, Polyvagal Theory provides an optimistic strategy for therapy, which would be based on a "retuning" of the autonomic nervous system through portals of the social engagement system.

References

Ben-Menachem, E. (2001). Vagus nerve stimulation, side effects, and long-term safety. *Journal of Clinical Neurophysiology, 18*(5), 415–418.

Carter, C. S. (1998). Neuroendocrine perspectives on social attachment and love. *Psychoneuroendocrinology, 23*(8), 779–818.

Clauw, D. J. (2014). Fibromyalgia: A clinical review. *JAMA, 311*(15), 1547–1555.

Craig, A. D. (2005). Forebrain emotional asymmetry: A neuroanatomical basis? *Trends in Cognitive Sciences, 9*(12), 566–571.

Dobzhansky, T. G. (1962). Mankind evolving: The evolution of the human species. *The Eugenics Review, 54*(3), 168–169.

Dobzhansky, T. G. (1973). Nothing in biology makes sense except in the light of evolution. *The American Biology Teacher, 35*(3), 125–129.

Groves, D. A., & Brown, V. J. (2005). Vagal nerve stimulation: A review of its applications and potential mechanisms that mediate its clinical effects. *Neuroscience & Biobehavioral Reviews, 29*(3), 493–500.

Hess, W. (1949/2014). The central control of the activity of internal organs. Nobelprize.org. Retrieved from http://www.nobelprize.org/nobel_prizes/medicine/laureates/1949/hess-lecture.html

Howland, R. H. (2014). Vagus nerve stimulation. *Current Behavioral Neuroscience Reports, 1*(2), 64–73.

Jackson, J. H. (1882). On some implications of dissolution of the nervous system. *Med Press Circ*, 2, 411–414.

Kolacz, J. K., Lewis, G. F., & Porges, S. W. (In press). The integration of vocal communication and biobehavioral state regulation in mammals: A polyvagal hypothesis. In S. M. Brudzynski (Ed.), *Handbook of ultrasonic vocalization.* London, England: Elsevier.

Mazurak, N., Seredyuk, N., Sauer, H., Teufel, M., & Enck, P. (2012). Heart rate variability in the irritable bowel syndrome: A review of the literature. *Neurogastroenterology and Motility, 24*(3), 206–216.

Ogden, P., Minton, K., & Pain, C. (2006). *Trauma and the body: A sensorimotor approach to psychotherapy.* New York, NY: Norton.

Porges, S. W. (1995). Orienting in a defensive world: Mammalian modifications of our evolutionary heritage. A Polyvagal Theory. *Psychophysiology, 32*(4), 301–318.

Porges, S. W. (2001). The Polyvagal Theory: Phylogenetic substrates of a social nervous system. *International Journal of Psychophysiology, 42*(2), 123–146.

Porges, S. W. (2003). Social engagement and attachment. *Annals of the New York Academy of Sciences, 1008*(1), 31–47.

Porges, S. W. (2004). Neuroception: A subconscious system for detecting threats and safety. *Zero to Three (J), 24*(5), 19–24.

Porges, S. W. (2007). The polyvagal perspective. *Biological Psychology, 74*(2), 116–143.

Porges, S. W. (2009). The Polyvagal Theory: New insights into adaptive reactions of the autonomic nervous system [Supplementary material]. *Cleveland Clinic Journal of Medicine, 76*, S86.

Porges, S. W. (2011). *Norton Series on Interpersonal Neurobiology. The Polyvagal Theory: Neurophysiological foundations of emotions, attachment, communication, and self-regulation.* New York, NY: Norton.

Porges, S. W., Bazhenova, O. V., Bal, E., Carlson, N., Sorokin, Y., Heilman, K. J., Cook, E. H., & Lewis, G. F. (2014). Reducing auditory hypersensitivities in autistic spectrum disorder: Preliminary findings evaluating the listening project protocol. *Frontiers in Pediatrics*. doi:10.3389/fped.2014.00080

Porges, S. W., & Lewis, G. F. (2010). The polyvagal hypothesis: Common mechanisms mediating autonomic regulation, vocalizations and listening. *Handbook of Behavioral Neuroscience, 19*, 255–264.

Porges, S. W., Macellaio, M., Stanfill, S. D., McCue, K., Lewis, G. F., Harden, E. R., . . . Heilman, K. J. (2013). Respiratory sinus arrhythmia and auditory processing in autism: Modifiable deficits of an integrated social engagement system? *International Journal of Psychophysiology, 88*(3), 261–270.

Porges, S. W., Bazhenova, O. V., Bal, E., Carlson, N., Sorokin, Y., Heilman, K. J., Cook, E. H., & Lewis, G. F. (2014). Reducing auditory hypersensitivities in autistic spectrum disorder: preliminary findings evaluating the listening project protocol. *Frontiers in Pediatrics*. doi:10.3389/fped.2014.00080

Reed, S. F., Ohel, G., David, R., & Porges, S. W. (1999). A neural explanation of fetal heart rate patterns: A test of the Polyvagal Theory. *Developmental Psychobiology, 35*(2), 108–118.

Sanossian, N., & Haut, S. (2002). Chronic diarrhea associated with vagal nerve stimulation. *Neurology, 58*(2), 330–330.

Siegel, D. J. (1999). *The developing mind: How relationships and the brain interact to shape who we are*. New York, NY: Guilford Press.

Staud, R. (2008). Heart rate variability as a biomarker of fibromyalgia syndrome. *Future Rheumatology, 3*(5), 475–483.

Thayer, J. F., & Lane, R. D. (2000). A model of neurovisceral integration in emotion regulation and dysregulation. *Journal of Affective Disorders, 61*(3), 201–216.

Thayer, J. F., & Lane, R. D. (2007). The role of vagal function in the risk for cardiovascular disease and mortality. *Biological Psychology, 74*(2), 224–242.

Whitehead, W. E., Palsson, O. S., Levy, R. R., Feld, A. D., Turner, M., & Von Korff, M. (2007). Comorbidity in irritable bowel syndrome. *The American Journal of Gastroenterology, 102*(12), 2767–2776.

Part II

Safety as the Core of Therapy

5

"Safety *is* the Treatment"

Bonnie Badenoch

Abstract: These reflections explore the years-long developmental experience of integrating Polyvagal Theory with interpersonal neurobiology, Iain McGilchrist's work on the divided brain, social baseline theory, affective neuroscience, and coherence psychology. One valuable outcome of interweaving and embodying these theories over time is an increase in our capacity to offer a kind of nonjudgmental presence that fosters emotional safety, which is the foundation for healing, both in our therapeutic relationships and in daily life.

THE MOST USEFUL new learning we do involves a process of integration with what we already know, and this takes time as well as attention. In 2004, I first began to hear about Polyvagal Theory. For about a year, I had also been going further into the study of interpersonal neurobiology in a group with Dan Siegel, and developing a much deeper appreciation for how we are constantly shaping one another's brains, how devoted our systems are to maintaining ongoing connection with one another at every stage of life. It felt like these two theories—Polyvagal Theory and interpersonal neurobiology (IPNB)—shared some important common ground, although I was initially far from clear exactly how. This lovely intersection of Siegel (1999/2015) and Porges (2004) was augmented in 2011 by the eloquent and unique work of Iain McGilchrist (2009) on the two hemispheres of the brain. As he described the relationship between our right-centric relational experience and left-centric stabilizing but limiting knowledge, I gradually recognized that the state of our autonomic nervous system correlates with a certain kind of integration between the hemispheres. This is the story of how these three strands have gradually woven a shift of perception into my mind, heart, and body that has profoundly affected the quality of relating that unfolds in the space between me and the courageous people who come for help as well as with all others in my life.

What I want to share here is a developmental story that moves from an initial sense of being intrigued by this new view of our autonomic nervous system, to a rudimentary conceptual understanding of Polyvagal Theory, to a slowly deepening felt sense for the movement of the three branches of the autonomic nervous system, to applying this emerging embodied knowledge as I could feel and understand more of what was happening with my patients, and finally to a transformation of the patterns of relationship emerging between us. This unfolding process is more of a series of interlocking circles than a straight line, with application leading back to study, and embodiment of the principles clarifying my experience with patients. The main point is that I have learned to give these beautiful discoveries time to have their way with me; seeds planted and this garden emerging in unexpected ways when given time to germinate.

During my first acquaintance with Polyvagal Theory (Porges, 2004), I was immediately struck by how much more at home I felt with these three hierarchical pathways than I did with the picture of two complementary circuits (sympathetic and parasympathetic) that were seeking balance with each other. It was as though my body felt the truth of its functioning being reflected and was saying yes to this new way of seeing our autonomic nervous system. The next strong recognition was that Porges's vision of the polyvagal circuits seemed to be describing another way in which our systems are dedicated to supporting the ongoing possibility of connecting with one another, of shaping one another's neural firings in the direction of integration, a central principle of IPNB (Siegel, 1999/2015). I was hearing that our system has a preference for ventral vagal parasympathetic, the social engagement system, the essential circuitry for joining with one another. These pathways remain active until we need to adaptively move into sympathetic activation or even dorsal vagal parasympathetic collapse in response to a sense of danger emerging internally, externally, or both.

In addition, once we have adaptively left the calm physiological state mediated by ventral vagal pathways, we can be helped to return to the possibility of connection by being in the presence of another person who is in a ventral[1] vagal state. Because of this preference for social engagement, we are always leaning toward one another, seeking to settle into warm relationships even when there are considerable obstacles from previously encoded experience or current challenges. That this system fostering attachment and ongoing connection emerges automatically in response to conditions of safety was deeply reassuring for me as a therapist. It felt as though we had an ally in the room, our two ventral systems seeking one another in their quiet, usually unseen way. I was comforted that my ventral presence in and of itself would be healing. Even with just this rudimentary conceptual understanding of the polyvagal system, I believe the sense of support it offered was already helping me stay in social engagement more often. For my patients, this meant I could offer a more steady invitation into safety.

I found myself wanting to take in more details to build on these few broad concepts. The ways we telegraph safety or danger to one another and the embodied wisdom of neuroception particularly drew me at this stage. While it had always been so, I was now becoming a bit more aware of how we constantly reflect the state of our autonomic nervous system to others through the prosody of our voices, the quality of our gestures, the tension or relaxation in and around our eyes, and the quality of our listening. These communications are simultaneously being received by those with us, filtered through their own current state, and affecting their emerging sense of safety or danger. It was also becoming clear that these signals emerged automatically from the activations of our autonomic nervous system in response to this unique moment. A ventral state is not something that can be willed into existence. In fact, any effort to create a ventral experience likely involves sympathetic activation. Instead, our own sense of emotional and relational safety would reveal itself through these signals. This depth of entanglement between ourselves and others began to strengthen my sense of the importance of attending to our own mental health so that ventral activation becomes our baseline, and we could more consistently offer an island of safety for those near us, not only in the counseling room but in our homes and even walking down the street.

---

1 Throughout this chapter, the words *ventral* or *ventral state* and *dorsal* or *dorsal state* are used in the place of the full descriptions of the vagal processes occurring when the sympathetic nervous system is not recruited in defense. Specifically, being in a ventral state reflects the recruitment of the ventral vagal pathways, which promote a physiological state supportive of feeling safe and an ability to socially engage in response to a neuroception of safety, while being in a dorsal state reflects the recruitment of the dorsal vagal pathways, which promote a physiological state of withdrawal, collapse, and dissociation in response to a neuroception of life-threat.

Beginning to understand neuroception was deepening my respect for the innate wisdom we carry in our bodies, largely out of conscious awareness. Porges (2003) coined this term for our system's powerful embodied process for assessing safety and danger, which is distinct from perception, the conscious experience by which this awareness sometimes comes into working memory. It is as though we have an inner guardian constantly in touch with what is emerging within our implicit memory system, blending that with what is coming to us from the outside via our senses. This system then adjusts our biological universe to prepare us to meet these conditions in the most adaptive way. All this is happening rapidly and continuously in ways that our much slower conscious processing could never manage.

As I stayed with this experience of neuroception through becoming more aware of my body's subtle shifts, the primacy of this adaptive process became more of a lived reality. In addition to deepening my sensitivity to these changes in my patients, I also found that my compassion was expanding, as I could feel that these experiences of moving in and out of an ability to connect weren't chosen and didn't reflect the moral character of the person who was exhibiting this movement toward and away from being receptive. Instead, they were a reflection of automatically adapting to inner states and outer conditions of safety and danger emerging from moment to moment.

I remember speaking with a couple about this process as they shared an ongoing struggle that was separating them and bringing on a good deal of anger. The husband arrived home before his wife almost every day. They had made a commitment to greet one another warmly before beginning to talk, and that was going well. However, as he started sharing about his day, which often included considerable stress, his wife would often drift away toward the mail or dinner preparations. As she broke eye contact and turned her back, while reassuring him that she was listening, he felt a wrenching sensation in his belly and chest, accompanied by the unspoken words *What a jerk!* He would turn away in anger, while she felt bewildered and hurt by him breaking contact. Her inner monologue said, *He's just being a selfish baby! Can't he see that I'm tired but still listening?*

These painful judgments came from the assumption that the other person was making a choice to move out of connection, that the unwillingness (which is different from inability) to stay engaged was simply bad behavior. We talked some about our autonomic nervous system's sensitivity to the emergence of safety and danger, and the automatic shifts that occur when there is a neuroception of threat. There was an immediate softening toward one another with the understanding that the behaviors weren't chosen, and the pain they both felt when they disengaged was a reflection of their deep desire to stay close to one another.

We asked a question: "At what point in your journey back toward one another in the evening do you begin to feel unsafe?" With support, they were able to deepen into their bodily sensations when they thought of coming back together. He could feel his belly tightening when he knew she was on her way home in anticipation of her inability to receive him, and she felt warmth and eagerness when she first saw him. This seemed to make their initial greeting possible, as her ventral state activated his. She also realized that she then experienced a kind of whole-body shrinking away when he began to talk about work, simply because she was already overloaded with tension from the day and didn't have room for more in that moment. This reliably led to a cascade of sympathetic arousal in both of them, leading to the familiar disruption in their capacity for social engagement. What a relief to discover that these interactions had nothing to do with their love for one another or their wish to be closer. On this foundation of understanding and compassion, their deep care for their partner's experience of safety became central for them, and they found they could more often move toward one another when behaviors of separation emerged. Once the burden of moral judgment lifted, it felt natural to be present with their partner in times of distress. They also noticed that they responded to their children's upsets differently. Rather than correcting behavior, they moved toward warm curiosity about the roots of the disruption, listening in receptivity until connection was reestablished. The behaviors seemed to take care of themselves at that point.

Just like this couple, I was experiencing a significant shift toward growing trust in the adaptive nature of our embodied systems, and this was making its way into my counseling room with my patients more regularly. Almost all of my people were survivors of significant wounding, and would often come in filled with shame at their inability to control their emotions and reactions. As I shared appropriate bits and pieces of what I was learning about the protective, adaptive nature of our autonomic nervous system, not only at the time of the wounding but also later to continue to guard that unhealed injury, compassion and gratitude for even the uncomfortable aspects of our autonomic nervous system could often expand. A man who felt devastated and filled with self-hatred and shame at the rage that regularly erupted toward his friends began to understand and sense how the anger was protecting the unhealed terror he felt in the presence of his own violent father. When inner and outer circumstances threatened to reactivate these feelings, his sympathetic system would rescue him from dropping into the terrified helplessness and dorsal collapse he had experienced as a very young child by awakening his capacity to fight. On the foundation of understanding the adaptive nature of his rage, which significantly reduced his shame, we were able to work together to heal these old, deeply embedded traumas. The rage response receded when there was less and less terror to protect. As his whole system felt safer, more ventral responses became possible even in times of interpersonal challenge.

Anything we are able to offer that lifts shame has the potential to open the doorway to connection and healing. As we can probably all feel in our bodies, shame lies at the edge of dorsal withdrawal, a state including physiological shifts that feel and look like restriction and collapse, accompanied by a profound loss of connection. The physiological changes that are associated with the dissolution of shame—restored eye contact, opening of our shoulders and chest, deeper breathing, and others—are signs that the ventral pathway is activating so that a renewal of co-regulation is possible. This in itself offers the opportunity for some trauma repair. Some would say that the essence of trauma has more to do with our felt sense of aloneness in times of pain and fear than with the events themselves (Badenoch, 2017; Kohrt et al., 2010). From the viewpoint of our autonomic nervous system, being moved out of ventral in the presence of threat means that we will also feel disconnection and isolation. As we sense being understood without judgment in our experience of dysregulation and shame and take in a different viewpoint on the wisdom of our system, the increased sense of safety, acceptance, and accompaniment begins to activate our social engagement system, relieving the implicit experience of aloneness. Porges's statement that "safety *is* the treatment" comes into view at this point. I was beginning to realize that this autonomic shift was an indispensable condition for integrating traumatic experiences that had been held in isolation in subcortical and bodily circuits. Therefore, my capacity to support such a space needed to be a priority.

Perhaps because my practice was almost exclusively with people who had experienced some form of trauma, I was now also being drawn into a deeper understanding of the connection between our autonomic nervous system and the regulatory pathways between the orbitofrontal cortex and amygdala. In other words, the polyvagal perspective and IPNB were enjoying a more thorough and complex integration as I was lingering with both. I had often imagined that our autonomic nervous system would become calmer as the circuitry of regulation grew stronger—and this is true. However, now I began to see that the presence of a strong social engagement system, the ventral vagal parasympathetic branch of the autonomic nervous system, fostered in safe interpersonal connections, was also a primary builder of these neural connections. Because of our sensitivity to one another, the two-person system of therapy or friendship offers the opportunity for two nervous systems to shape one another in the direction of neural integration. I could feel this myself when, at a time when I was upset, a friend could receive me without judgment and hold a loving, attentive, reflective space for me until I settled down. I realized that these bodily sensations of relaxation and opening indicated that the potential trauma was integrating rather than being sent away into limbic and bodily isolation until another opportunity for healing might come. With each experience of such co-regulation, the neural pathways between prefrontal and limbic regions were also strengthening in permanent ways.

Between what I was studying and what I was personally experiencing, the picture and feeling of the interconnections between these circuits was developing, and now more often accompanying me into my counseling room. I believe this gradually made me more sensitive to what my patients needed as a primary condition for healing—a nonjudgmental, receptive, and reflective partner to provide support for their wise system to find its way toward the inherent health waiting within the pathways of their complex co-organizing brains. But I am getting ahead of myself a bit. It took many years of dwelling with these ideas and experiences for me to embody this overarching shift in how I was present with others. These days, I find that my natural response to sympathetic arousal or dorsal collapse in my patients is to become quietly receptive of their experience, rather than responding to the urge to shift something, even while feeling resonance with those states. It is one thing to have an idea about this, and, I say with ever-deepening humility, quite another to practice in this way. There is little within our culture or training that helps us cultivate our capacity be present without agenda. This is where Iain McGilchrist (2009) enters the scene.

He talks about our two hemispheres not in terms of *what* each does (because both hemispheres fire for everything), but of *how* each experiences—and then creates—the world based on the different way each side of our brain attends and perceives. Right and left literally offer different perspectives concerning what matters, and as a result, shape the way we interact with each other, the kinds of institutions we create, and the values we hold.

In a very brief summary drawn from McGilchrist's (2009) work, our right hemisphere orients us toward the space between, the relational space, as it is unfolding moment to moment. As such, everything it sees is held in context and finds its meaning there. The flow of novel experience comes to us here as rich streams of a continuously changing felt sense in the body. This perspective is aware of the uncertainty of the next moment and the next, and keenly attuned to both the suffering and the potential meaningfulness of life. There can be a broad acceptance of paradox, a both/and way of meeting what comes, and deep respect for the fullness of implicit experience. It is also here that we make and sustain living connections with one another, and here that the guiding vision for a humane society might arise. The individual, the unique, the unrepeatable, the irreplaceable, the unpredictable, the interpersonal all live here. I began to wonder if this described the ventral experience, and in fact, Porges did point to an article from 1994 detailing the research through which he and his colleagues had found that the ventral vagal parasympathetic state lateralizes to the right hemisphere (Porges, Doussard-Roosevelt, & Maili, 1994).

The dovetailing of these two perspectives provided such strong support for the value of cultivating a right-centric, ventral state with my patients, and really with everyone. In these moments of deep and respectful meeting, without judgment or agenda, the other people's systems might find the safety, resonance, and reflection needed to deepen into greater contact with their inner worlds. It may be important to sit with this way of relating for a moment. What would it be like for us to be with our people with fewer judgments and consciously letting go of our own agenda? It would require deep trust in the power of relationship to surface the innate healing capacities of our patients. This would most likely be built on our own experience of healing, in which being heard and held without judgment or agenda were the agents of change. Entering this familiar place of deep listening, together we might also sense the best supports for moving toward healing. Might eye movement desensitization and reprocessing (EMDR) meet this emerging need? A sand tray, perhaps? Continuing to attend closely to what is arising? All of these possibilities can be offered in a tentative way, with the most important part being listening to the inner response of our patient as our guide to how to proceed. Rather than following a premade treatment agenda, our path could emerge organically and fluidly in the moment. A safe space between the two of us is the indispensable foundation for that possibility.

When we are in this right-centric process of fluid connection, we are also in the territory of the unknown, which can be frightening, bringing on sympathetic activation, since we don't know what will emerge next. At these moments, our left hemisphere's way of attending can become a vital support, an emissary, as McGilchrist would say, potentially serving our right-centric, ventral vagal way of relating. What characteristics do our left hemispheres bring? To begin with, it is the realm of greater fixity, of creating systems that can potentially bring the right's vision into manifestation. When we learn a step-by-step process for facilitating access to traumatic memories or study aspects of neuroscience that give us a clearer vision of how our systems work, we are nourishing our left hemispheres with knowledge that can help relieve anxiety about how to help our patients, and thus help us stay in ventral more of the time. I saw this clearly with both the interns and experienced therapists at our agency in California. As our knowledge of relational neuroscience grew, our capacity to be quietly present in the midst of uncertainty expanded. It was as though a solid foundation grew beneath our feet, quietly, often without our awareness, offering its stabilizing understanding.

At this point in our cultural history, this relationship between the hemispheres is not well supported (McGilchrist, 2009). Instead, research suggests that about 75% of us are experiencing a separation between the hemispheres that puts our left-centric mode in the lead, rather than the right-centric relational perspective (Fredrickson et al., 2013). When this happens, the other characteristics of the left hemisphere viewpoint take over. To begin with, our relational circuitry is right centric, so because the isolated left has no felt sense of "we," there is a cascade of biological responses that arise from moving out of ventral co-regulation into sympathetic activation. To be concrete about this, if I open the door to greet my patient with my own idea about which techniques will best help this person, my ventral vagal parasympathetic will most likely be offline, a condition that will communicate lack of safety to my client. Probably none of this will rise to the level of conscious awareness, but it will cause a neuroception of lack of connection and therefore danger, influencing what will unfold between us. All of this can happen while I am also experiencing a lot of care for my patient and a strong wish to relieve suffering.

I began to understand that our current emphasis on evidence-based practice implemented by various interventions, protocols, treatment plans, and expected outcomes is both a creation of our culture's left-centric bias and the means by which we remain confined to that viewpoint and separated from the living reality of our patients' unfolding experience. Our left hemispheres, when robbed of connection with the right, are drawn to focus on tasks and behaviors, on autonomy and self-reliance, and on getting specific results from particular techniques with less regard for the individuality and emerging experience of our patients. In addition, the left is prone to judgments, which almost inevitably induce shame in those on the receiving end, even when these judgments are unspoken. I so often hear colleagues lament particular patients' inability to implement or respond to particular protocols, sometimes with the air of criticism that arises side by side with left-centric expectations. In those moments, we are helplessly locked out of true connection with the people we want to serve.

At least in part, what drives this shift into dominance of our left hemispheres is fear. When there have been insufficient resources of emotional and relational safety both in our childhoods and in the culture at large, a neuroception of danger arises, along with a need to control, one of the specialties of left-centric attending. In our profession, this leads to states of mind and autonomic nervous system in which we can't trust that our human systems have an innate healing capacity that is just waiting for the needed support to arrive. This inherent movement toward health is carried by our preference for ventral, our ongoing openness to warm attachments, our brain's capacity for responsiveness to offers of co-regulation, and many other neural streams as well (Badenoch, 2017). At this point, our personal and cultural fears that lead to the need to control are embedded in the basic assumptions of our training, and subtly separate us from our own ventral capacity and thus from true connection with our patients. It becomes the institutionalized norm to practice in this pattern of taking charge of the therapy and looking for specific outcomes, often setting up a painful and draining internal struggle with our own system's tendency to move into the fluid realm of responsive relating in the present moment.

It was gradually becoming clear to me that a Polyvagal perspective points the way back toward reinhabiting and expanding our capacity to regulate our behavior and emotions and to promote connectedness through the ventral vagal pathways. To enhance this ventral capacity, rather than trying to generate safety alone, we need our own support in the form of people who can deeply listen to us, without agenda or judgments. When people can be present with us in this way, what Porges called the "passive pathways" (Porges, Badenoch, & Phillips, 2016) that foster entry into a ventral state have a strong probability of being activated. We humans are built for co-regulation, and offers of deep safety made by one person's ventral state may awaken this longing for connection within us. This opens the doorway to the inner explorations that foster healing. We can then experience and begin to embody the kind of healing we want to offer our patients. It is so much easier and more natural to share at many levels what is already living in us rather than offer more disconnected ideas about healing. As we experience being held in safety, our right and left hemispheres have the potential to come back into relationship with one another, the right-centric, ventrally supported experience leading the way (or being the Master, as McGilchrist, 2009, said), with the left-centric repository of wisdom being the stabilizing emissary in service of deepening safety. All the protocols and interventions we have learned now have the potential to become a rich storehouse of supplies that we can draw on in the moment in response to our patients' emerging needs. We may begin to experience our work more as a unique dance of call-and-response rather than as a set of instructions about how to undo certain symptoms.

Between my earliest days of encountering Polyvagal Theory and the current profound change the polyvagal perspective has wrought in my way of being present in the room, several other pieces of research have augmented this developing universe of understanding what it is to be human, to be wounded and to heal. Bruce Ecker and his colleagues (Ecker, Ticic, & Hulley, 2012) gave us insight into how the felt-sense quality and behavioral patterns of implicit memories can change. This healing pathway is built on our capacity to trust that symptoms are meaningful protectors of our wounds and on our ability to be fully present to our patients so that their implicit world can come into view. In other words, such healing is facilitated by our left-centric emissary's knowledge of how implicit memories change, leading to trust, accompanied by us holding an emotional and relational safe space for our clients so their deeper mind can emerge.

To imagine holding this kind of space continually can feel so daunting that it activates sympathetic arousal all on its own. Ed Tronick's (2003) work on rupture and repair can help us ease back toward ventral. He talked about how secure attachment arises when we are able to respond to our child's need for resonance and reflection about 33% of the time on the first try, with all the rest being a matter of recognizing ruptures and moving toward repair. This pattern is optimal because it encodes an expectation that when connections are broken, someone will arrive to help us reestablish the bond. This process is equally applicable to our familial and therapeutic relationships. Perhaps we can feel ourselves taking a deep, relaxing breath as permission to be far less than perfect arrives.

Lane Beckes and James Coan (2011), developers of Social Baseline Theory, drew on research suggesting that in the presence of a trustworthy other person, our amygdalae quiet all on their own in times of stress and danger because of our inherent physiological expectation that we will be embedded in a nest of warm relationships. To find ourselves out of connection is to violate the core assumptions of our biology. These discoveries provide further support for what Porges (Porges & Phillips, 2016) said: Connectedness is a biological imperative, the gift of our evolved mammalian autonomic nervous system. As we listen to these gathering streams of support, we can perhaps begin to settle into a sense of reassurance about the centrality of cultivating an ever-expanding capacity for returning to a ventral baseline after adaptively moving into sympathetic or dorsal activation. The further encouragement is to seek it in the company of others rather than alone.

At the beginning of my journey with Polyvagal Theory, I had no idea where it would lead me. I believe I was first intrigued by my own biological response to the truth of what Porges was saying. What followed was a journey into the basics, the education of my left hemisphere into the ways of the polyvagal system. This produced a particular kind of graphic that was perhaps useful for my patients and students at the time. It looked like this.

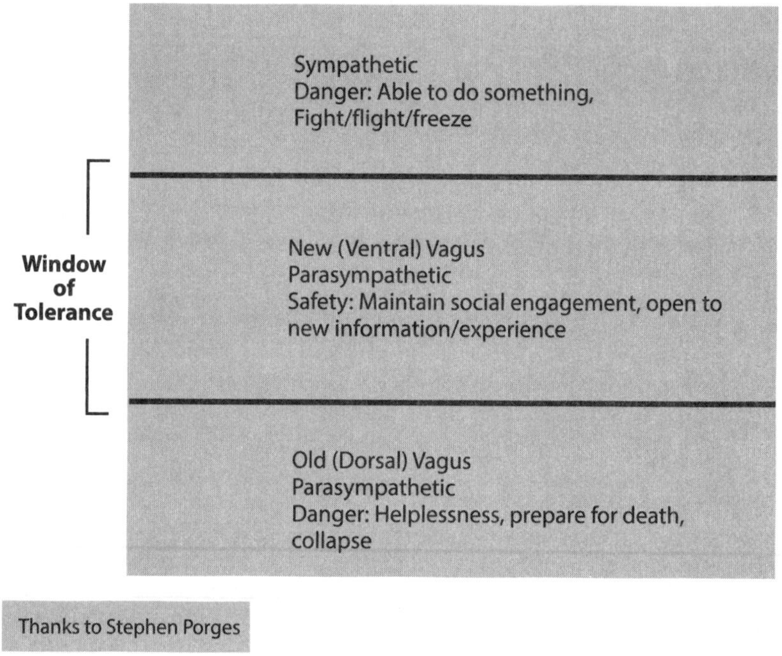

FIGURE 5.1

A second image included the autonomic state of both patient and therapist, and the experience of potential co-regulation. It was seeking to capture the space we offer our patients when our ventral window holds their dysregulation even while we also participate in their arousal, so that our brains join and become a single healing system (Hasson, Ghazanfar, Galantucci, Garrod, & Keysers, 2012).(Figure 5.2)

Now, many years into this experience of the flow and complexity offered by Polyvagal Theory, new images have arrived. (Figure 5.3)

Over time, just by staying with the experience of my own autonomic nervous system, learning from my patients as we attended to theirs, and continuing to study, the sense of constantly shifting conditions in our autonomic nervous system seemed to ask for a different, less boxy kind of image. Here, the attempt is to convey the movement from wide to narrow window of tolerance (top to bottom) as well as the continual flow from moment to moment between dorsal, under the management of ventral, and sympathetic, under the management of ventral (right to left and back). Our autonomic nervous system is never fixed, but is continually responsive to internal and external events, continually emerging. It invites us to follow its movement with quiet attention, and as we notice with kindness, it often responds to being seen by coming toward ventral.

As this ability to attend expanded over time, the nuances became more visible. Along the diagonal lines of Figure 5.3 are some words that seek to name the experience of crossing from ventral safety to sympathetic arousal or dorsal withdrawal with the arrival of fear. If we watch children (or mice) play, we can sense that moment when the back-and-forth of rough-and-tumble excitement becomes dominance by one partner. Play stops as social engagement resources are withdrawn (Panksepp & Biven, 2012). It is a very fine line, and when children are allowed free play, they explore this line over and over again, learning how to read the autonomic nervous system's signals of face and voice that say when the line has been crossed. Over time, such learning may lead to less bullying because there has been so much practice with reading faces and slowing things down to return to connection in the midst of the joy of play.

On the "dorsal" side, there is a similar line where deep rest can slip into dissociation. If our lives have led us to be adaptively drawn into dorsal collapse to protect ourselves in times of helplessness, the quiet of rest can remind us of the former danger. One of my patients with a dedicated spiritual practice talked with me about her frustration as she repeatedly fell into dissociation when she would sit for meditation. As the embedded traumas of terror gradually came to the surface within the safety of our relationship, her capacity to become still while remaining present also expanded. This dorsal experience was able to remain under the management of ventral, as there was more safety within

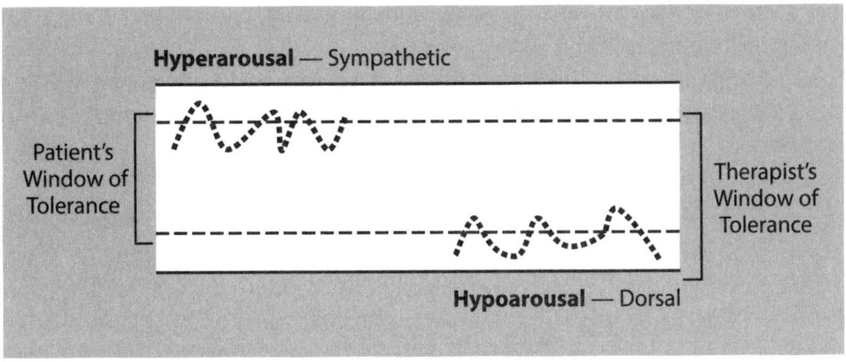

FIGURE 5.2

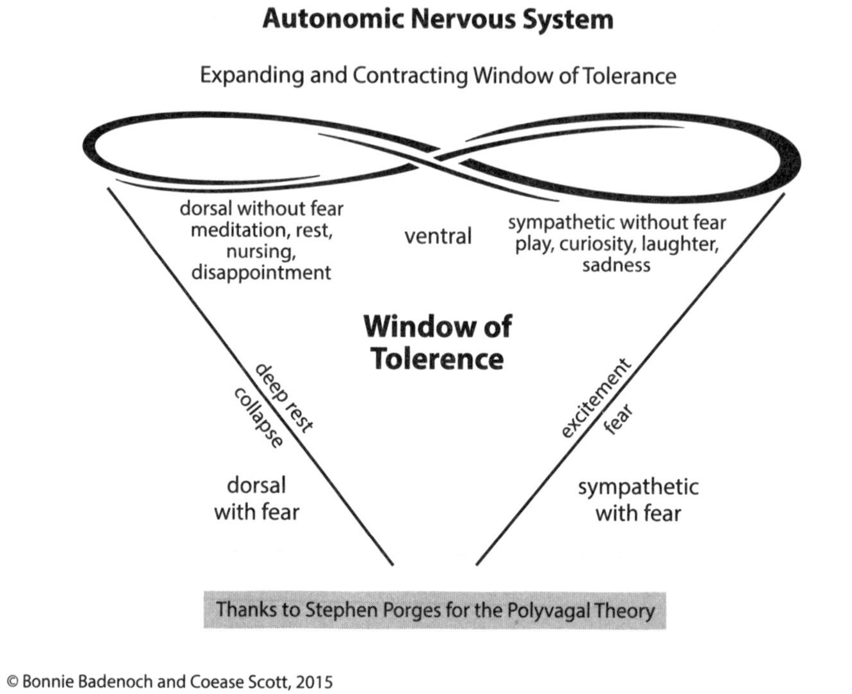

FIGURE 5.3

her system. For her, it was the most significant gift of the healing process that was unfolding in the space between us.

A companion image including patient and therapist also arrived (Figure 5.4). The second pair of diagonal lines forms the embrace of one person's autonomic nervous system by another's broader capacity for remaining in ventral in this moment, even while the two people are resonating with each other. When this occurs in therapy or friendship, a healing space opens where disconfirming experiences may naturally occur. Embodied memories that would be dysregulating were we on our own experience being joined and held in the safety of ventral. At these moments, the conditions for potentially integrating embedded traumas and changing the felt-sense experience and behavioral patterns of implicit memory are met.

I imagine that as I continue to linger with the growing aliveness of Polyvagal Theory in my mind and body, new images might emerge again, ones I can't imagine at this point. Over time, I suspect there will be a continued

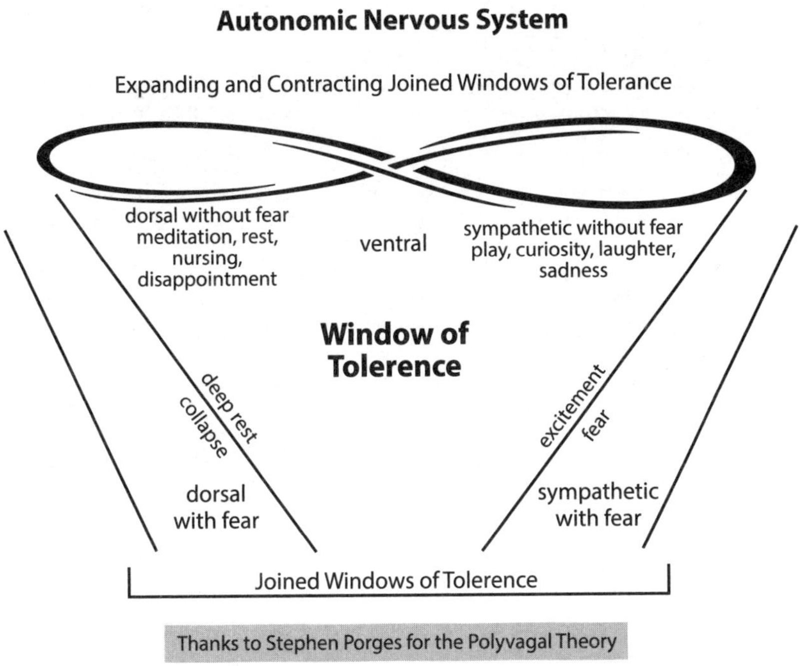

FIGURE 5.4

deepening into the inner, trusting stillness that facilitates the diminishment of judgments and release of agendas. I believe that more ways of sharing with my patients the wisdom of our autonomic nervous system will also likely come as experience and knowledge continue their beautiful integration. Most of all, I trust that as each of us finds the nonjudgmental, safe support we need to heal our own wounds, we will experience more deeply that safety *is* the treatment.

References

Badenoch, B. (2017). *The heart of trauma*. New York, NY: Norton.

Beckes, L., & Coan, J. A. (2011). Social Baseline Theory: The role of social proximity in emotion and economy of action. *Social and Personality Psychology Compass, 5*(12), 976–988. doi:10.1080/10926771.2013.81388

Ecker, B., Ticic, R., & Hulley, L. (2012). *Unlocking the emotional brain: Eliminating symptoms at their root using memory reconsolidation*. New York, NY: Routledge.

Fredrickson, B. L., Grewen, K. M., Coffey, K. A., Algoe, S. B., Firestine, A. M., Arevalo, J. M. G., . . . Cole, S. W. (2013). A functional genomic perspective on human well-being. *PNAS, 110*(33), 13684–13689. doi:10.1073/pnas.1305419110

Hasson, U., Ghazanfar, A. A., Galantucci, B., Garrod, S., & Keysers, C. (2012). Brain-to-brain coupling: A mechanism for creating and sharing a social world. *Trends in Cognitive Sciences, 16*(2), 114–121. doi:10.1016/j.tics.2011.12.00

Kohrt, B. A., Jordans, M. J. D., Tol, W. A., Perera, E., Karki, R., Koirala, S., & Upadhaya, N. (2010). Social ecology of child soldiers: Child, family, and community determinants of mental health, psychosocial well-being, and reintegration in Nepal. *Transcultural Psychiatry, 45*(5), 727–753. doi:10.1177/1363461510381290

McGilchrist, I. (2009). *The master and his emissary: The divided brain and the making of the western world*. New Haven, CT: Yale University Press.

Panksepp, J., & Biven, L. (2012). *The archaeology of mind: Neuroevolutionary origins of human emotions*. New York, NY: Norton.

Porges, S. W. (2003). Social engagement and attachment. *Annals of the New York Academy of Sciences, 1008*(1), 31–47.

Porges, S. W. (2004). Neuroception: A subconscious system for detecting threat and safety. *Zero to Three: Bulletin of the National Center for Clinical Infant Programs, 24*(5), 19–24.

Porges, S. W. (2007). The polyvagal perspective. *Biological Psychology, 74*, 116–143. doi:10.1016/j.biopsycho.2006.06.009

Porges, S. W., Badenoch, B., & Phillips, M. (2016). Feeling and expressing compassion [Webinar]. Retrieved from http://bestpracticesintherapy.com/silver-month-long-july/

Porges, S. W., Doussard-Roosevelt, J. A., & Maili, A. K. (1994). Vagal tone and the physiological regulation of emotion. *Monographs of the Society for Research in Child Development, 240/59*(2–3), 167–186.

Porges, S. W., & Phillips, M. (2016). Connectedness: A biological imperative [Webinar]. Retrieved from http://bestpracticesintherapy.com/silver-month-long-july/

Siegel, D. J. (1999/2015). *The developing mind: How relationships and the brain interact to shape who we are* (1st and 2nd ed.). New York, NY: Guilford Press.

Tronick, E. Z. (2003). Of course all relationships are unique: How co-creative processes generate unique mother-infant and patient-therapist relationships and change other relationships. In *New Developments in Attachment Theory: Application to Clinical Practice*, proceedings of conference at UCLA, Los Angeles, CA.

6

Realizing "Deep" Safety for Children Who Have Experienced Abuse: Application of Polyvagal Theory in Therapeutic Work With Traumatized Children and Young People

Joe Tucci, Angela Weller, and Janise Mitchell

Abstract: Safety is foundational to processes that support children to recover from experiences of trauma associated with abuse and family violence. Polyvagal Theory provides an insight into how safety is viscerally experienced in relationship with others. In this chapter, we examine how themes of deep safety are interwoven into therapeutic processes that resource connectedness. We articulate an emerging framework for intervention that is based on a number of practice principles that integrate our own clinical experience and the insights offered by Polyvagal Theory. We show how relationally oriented safety is resourced and facilitated through a sequenced therapeutic process that connects physiology and metaphors in a form of reflective praxis. In each phase, we provide examples of questions and activities that illustrate the application of the approach in practice.

Your voice is a place I want to take shelter in, a place that makes me feel safe and soft.
—Zaeema J. Hussain, *The Sky Is Purple* (2014)

Introduction

SAFETY IS A basic human right. It creates the conditions in which the experience of being human is given the time and potency to flourish. It is integrated into narratives of meaning that offer metaphors rich in resources about predictability, security, and stability. Safety is associated with powerful memories of home, of important people, of experiences that are full of warmth, love, and nurture. It weaves interconnection. In its absence, danger lurks. Threat is perceived and felt. Fear overwhelms the senses and cripples the capacity for protection. It unleashes hurt, trauma, and loss. After such disruption, states of safety are pursued in an inherent drive to recapture what was lost. Relational experiences calm and soften the pervasiveness of vulnerability. Safety searches for familiarity. It harnesses the strength of interdependence. It ritualizes care and empathy.

Safety Restores Life

Over the past two decades, our collective line of sight into the core meaning of safety has become even more profound. Those of us working with children and young people affected by the intense violation of safety arising from abuse and family violence owe a significant debt of gratitude to the work of Stephen Porges culminating in his proposal of Polyvagal Theory (Porges, 1995, 1998, 2001, 2003, 2009, 2011; Porges & Carter, 2016).

As a result, we now have a granular understanding of the physiology that gives rise to states of safety and states of threat and how, as humans, we transition from one to the other. According to Porges, safety is a deeply visceral experience. It is felt in our hearts. It is held in our lungs as we breathe. It is also a connected experience. It lies in the familiar tone of voices of those who love us. It is found in their gazes and their hand gestures. Safety is embedded in the dynamic tensions associated with autonomic homeostasis. It is the perpetual quest of our brain-body systems to engage, and to connect.

In this chapter, we explore the centrality of "deep" safety as a conceptual cornerstone in therapeutic work with children and young people affected by the developmental trauma that results from experiences of abuse and violence. We articulate an emerging framework for intervention that is based on a number of practice principles that integrate our own clinical experience and the insights offered by Polyvagal Theory. Its aim is to embed resonant experiences of safety within the everyday interactions with the important adults who care for, educate, and engage traumatized children and young people. We show how relationally oriented safety is resourced and facilitated through a sequenced therapeutic process that connects physiology and metaphors together in a form of reflective praxis. In each phase, we provide examples of questions and activities that illustrate the application of the approach in practice.

What Are the Principles That Underpin a Practice Framework That Centralizes Safety?

Safety Is a Relational Experience

Safety is experienced in and between people. According to Porges (2011), the evolutionary path from reptile to mammal led to the emergence of cooperative orientations in species to support the achievement of social, collective benefits and survival.

Over the course of such adaptation, a number of emergent needs required resolution. Mammals needed to be able to signal to others of their species that they were open to engagement in order to perform various survival-oriented functions, such as reproduce and care for their young. They evolved extensive neural regulation over muscles that enabled social communication and gestures. As Porges illustrated, such control enabled humans, in particular, to "make eye contact; vocalise with an appealing inflection and rhythm; display contingent facial expressions; and, modulate the middle-ear muscles to distinguish the human voice from background sounds more efficiently" (2011, p. 15).

The performance of these interdependent functions placed mammals in vulnerable positions involving physical proximity with one another, which would normally have activated phylogenetically older physiological systems for responding to danger. Consequently, they had to develop the capacity to turn off the more primitive (reptilian) responses to perceived threat. The myelinated ventral vagal pathway evolved as a link to adaptive social, affective, and communicative behaviors.

The social engagement system that connected humans to other humans became linked with the capacity to regulate the activation of the sympathetic branch of the autonomic nervous system, enabling fight-or-flight actions of protection. The myelinated vagus regulates the striated muscles of the head and face, including emotional expressiveness, eye gaze, listening, and prosody, which are part of the social engagement system. They influence and shape our physiological state through interpersonal communication.

In the face of triggers in the environment or in ourselves that alert us to danger, other people have the capacity to calm us down by connecting with us through displaying their regulated physiological state as a cue that signals interpersonal safety. The softness in their tone of voice; the way their head and face turn toward us, inviting closeness; and the comforting look in their eyes serve as powerful supports in shutting down our threat response system.

We come to find in others a multidimensional embrace that soothes our terror and alarm. We touch the safety that is held in the corporeal experience of others—the rhythm of their heart rate, the depth of their breath, the steadiness of their gaze, the melody of their voice. We source safety in the memories of shared activities of strength, love, and nurture. We hear safety through collective narratives of oppression and resistance, struggle and resolution, pain and release. We sense safety in the activated states of our organs and their manifestations. We know safety when we trust someone, when they are predictable and consistent. We experience safety when our fears are understood and validated by others through their patience, tolerance, and empathic posture.

We are safe in relationships that are safe and communicate safety.

Safety Is Embedded in Our Physiology

According to the Polyvagal Theory (Porges, 2011),

> The detection of a person as safe or dangerous triggers neurobiologically determined prosocial or defensive behaviours. Even though we may not be aware of danger on a cognitive level, on a neurophysiological level, our body has already started a sequence of neural processes that would facilitate adaptive defense behaviours such as fight, flight or freeze. (p. 11)

Because our experience of safety is so intertwined with the physiological state of others with whom we relate, it is a survival imperative that we are able to identify people who are safe or who represent a threat to us. Porges's concept of neuroception reflects how significantly embedded safety is in our physiology.

Neuroception describes "how neural circuits distinguish whether situations or people are safe, dangerous, or life-threatening" (Porges, 2011, p. 11). Porges has argued that at deep, physiological levels, the vagal system is the primary vehicle for visceral surveillance (Porges & Carter, 2016). It provides a dynamic, moment-to-moment monitoring of the major states of our organs through the nervous system, adjusting their metabolic responses to changes in demand arising from our need to stay vigilant or roar into action to protect ourselves; or shut down totally in the face of danger that is so overwhelming that any form of defense is futile; or, ultimately, slow down to rest and restore our expended body's resources.

Our physiology evaluates risks posed by others and our environment. Neuroception empowers the readiness of our body to be engaged by neural circuits that give us the best chance to survive in any given circumstance. It realizes adaptation to threat without conscious awareness.

This intrinsic, body-grounded subjectivity forms the basis for our psychological experience as humans. It seeps into our language. It permeates the stories we tell about ourselves and how we engage with the world and others. It shapes the reflections we make about why and how we have grown to become the identities we claim. It is expressed in our perceptions, the way we interpret them and give voice to the expectations that we derive from them. It delivers us the judgments we make about our past and the approach we will hold into the future. It informs our beliefs about how relationships work; what they can offer; how we should feel in them; and whether or not they will offer us the resources we need to continue to live, along with the courage we need to change the very same physiological patterns that have evolved as adaptations to danger.

Safety is more than the absence of risk. At its core, it occurs in relationships that engage the neural circuits underpinning physiological renewal and growth. It is found in our spontaneous seeking out of proximity with others, our playfulness and curiosity as we explore intimacy, and our attunement to the comfort of others. It also emerges when our bodies find themselves giving peaceful priority to sleep, rest, and nurture.

We find safety in the embodiment of our vulnerability in the heart of a loved one.

Child Abuse Is a Deep Violation of a Child's Sense of Safety

Abuse is an abrupt and forceful denial of safety for children at multiple levels. Children are frequently hurt by people who should be protecting and caring for them. These adults can be their parents, extended family, teachers, coaches, caregivers. For many abused children, these adults have acted as havens for children's mobilized systems of danger for periods of time. For others, these relationships are a constant source of alarm within which safe haven is never experienced. Children rely on these relationships for co-regulation to help soothe and comfort them. When the adults in their lives are sources of abuse, they not only cause pain and fear; they also leave children exposed to threat without the regulatory resources they require to return to states of physiological and psychological safety. Adults have been unpredictable in their actions and their language. Children have been engaged on adults' terms and at the mercy of their agendas.

When abuse involves force and violence, it compels children's mobilization system to stay activated. Terror fills their hearts. They are not sure when their father will next come home drunk on a rampage against them or their mother. They are not sure when next they will be hit with a pipe or a hose because they did not finish their dinner. They cannot predict when they will next be pushed onto the bed and raped. Their home, their room, the family kitchen hold the sensory elements that evoke cascades of overwhelming danger. Every exchange with the adult who has abused them triggers fear. They must be ready to defend themselves, their bodies in a constant state of preparedness for action. Mobilization becomes the steady state for a child. At least, until such threat is so overwhelming that there is little hope of changing it, stopping it, running far enough away from it. And then children collapse. They immobilize to survive. They disconnect. Their physiology moves to conserve whatever resources it still has. They become small, lose their voice. Their bodies and minds give up on safety.

In these states, the resources of their social engagement system that could provide relief are so distant as to be nonexistent. Offers of interpersonal regulation—a comforting word in a calm tone, a soft touch, a caring and open look—have little chance of registering. Polyvagal Theory identifies this vividly as it unraveled our evolutionary responses to danger. "Mammals have evolved to be able to move efficiently between the social engagement and fight-flight systems. But we do not move out of shutdown/feign death response as efficiently or effectively" (Porges, 2016).

Worse still, children abused through psychological manipulation have the power of the social engagement system used against them. People who perpetrate sexual abuse distort children's regulatory experiences—violating them by offering the very kindness and softness that they would expect from a loving adult. They use the potency of the body's social engagement system to overcome children's physiological and psychological sense of safety. They make the experience of danger feel like it is safe. They corrupt children's neuroceptive capacities. Safety does not feel like it should. Their own physiology lies to them. They are left without the means to accurately know danger and therefore how to prepare for it. Some children will mobilize resources when there is the smallest infraction in intimacy. Others will misread overt signs of danger in someone who has a long history of violence and control over them. These children, and the adults they can become, live with an intolerable lack of safety.

For all abused children, their visceral experience is overbalanced to danger and their physiologies' reaction to it. Threat permeates the tension in their muscles, the rhythm of their heartbeat, their breathing, their digestion—the very feeling of their body. They inhabit the two older phylogenetic responses to peril—mobilization and immobilization with fear (Porges, 2011). There is little opportunity for their physiologies to rest and regenerate. They are tired. They have little energy to adapt to new environments and new information. They struggle to learn—so much so that they come to resist change. They lock down their range of responses to the forms of action they have always taken just to survive. They shut out the world, and in particular, others who pose a threat. It is no wonder, as Porges has pointed out, that they lose the protective vagal tone to their visceral organs (Porges & Carter, 2016). Trauma diminishes the ventral vagal system's function in homeostatically regulating the body's internal organs. Children become more attuned to the sounds of threat and less able to differentiate the comfort of the human voice. Their gestures are more erratic. They suffer from stomachaches. They struggle to sleep. They disengage from eye contact. Their tone of voice is not reciprocal to those around them. The lack of safety that they experience around them in the external world is paralleled in their internal neurophysiology.

Such corporeal experiences of themselves and their interactions with others become narratives filled with fear, rejection, isolation, shame, and humiliation. The stories that others tell about these children lack awareness of the ways the autonomic nervous system activates adaptive survival responses. People find it difficult to bring empathy to understanding the devastating impacts of these children's trauma. *They are ungrateful. They push us away. They are argumentative. They do not listen. They try to control everyone around them. They are manipulative. They will never learn. They are unlovable.*

In response, these become the narratives that children believe about themselves. *I am stupid. I cannot be trusted. I am bad. I hate myself. I have to run away. I am not safe.* These themes find their way into children's interpretations of relationships. *People are untrustworthy. Relationships are not reliable. They hurt. They are not predictable. They are dangerous. There is no one who can protect me. The only one I can rely on is me. Relationships are not safe.*

Children who have suffered abuse show all of this in their behavior. They show us with rage, anger, frustration, and irritability. They express it in sadness and withdrawal. They also communicate the internalization of the pain they have endured by activating the threat systems of those of us who work to support them. Their behavior is often challenging and frightening. Those who care for and support traumatized children are often left feeling confused, overwhelmed, and unsafe. We respond in kind, treating them as dangerous, reacting from our own well-worn paths of defense and self-protection. We blame them and each other for not effecting change. Formal and informal systems of care and support around these children often become organized around disconnection, defensiveness, and control rather than collaboration, empathy, and care.

Safety is missing. It has disappeared for so many children who have experienced abuse—in their bodies, in their relationships, in their sense of what is in fact possible for them now. It is also often missing in the systems of care and support around them.

Safety Is at the Core of Healing Trauma

Safety is the experience of a profound physiological and relational harmony. It is the ventral vagal activity that is continuous and stable, enlisting the activation of the parasympathetic branch of the autonomic nervous system. It is experienced in relationships that offer an interdependent and regulatory ambience expressed in mutual and contingent activation of social engagement systems. Safety is perceived psychologically and experienced physiologically.

The experience of safety for traumatized children is compromised. Relational safety is both the goal of intervention and a major resource in the healing process. Relationships that heal are trustworthy and enduring. They offer predictability. They stabilize. They regulate. They interpret and reinterpret identity. They allow new meanings to emerge that are based in the grounded visceral experience of comfort. They recruit our phylogenetically new systems to connect and stay connected. They help to create new memories of care and trust. They support the generation of narratives that make the world feel less dangerous and help children feel more capable.

Safety is the biologically determined pathway to healing children's trauma.

What Is Therapeutic Intervention That Centralizes Safety for Traumatized Children?

In our work at the Australian Childhood Foundation, we provide therapeutic intervention to children and young people traumatized by experiences of physical abuse, sexual abuse, and family violence. Many have also often suffered chronic early neglect and emotional abuse. We engage children and the important adults in their network who provide relationships that care for, educate, and support them.

Our therapeutic approach has been influenced by the pioneers of the trauma and attachment fields, such as Schore, Siegel, van der Kolk, Tronick,

Ogden, and Hughes. Increasingly, we have turned to the work of Porges and Polyvagal Theory for the knowledge base for our interventions. Safety has become the core construct in our approach.

In this section, we describe our way of working that centralizes safety as the theme for healing the physiological and psychological consequences of abuse and violence for children and young people. It is a sequenced process that weaves safety into the physiological fabric of relationships as regulatory experiences, while creating narratives of "deep safety" in the descriptions given by adults and children to the shared experiences that emerge during the process. Its aim is to merge the relational systems of children and their caring adults to support and nurture safety as embodied resources found in their interpersonal exchanges.

Retrieving the Lived Experience of Safety for Adults

The adults in the networks of traumatized children are parents, grandparents, uncles, aunts, foster caregivers, residential care workers, teachers, coaches, mentors, child protection workers, therapists. Some of them have experienced the same violence that the children have suffered. All of them have experienced the mobilization of their bodies through the activation of the sympathetic branch of the autonomic nervous system in response to danger. Some will have become frozen with fear as their system becomes totally immobilized in the face of unassailable threat. Some will have had relationships as children and as adults that have helped them to find and experience safety. Safety may be a conscious quality in their lives. Others will not have experienced safety consciously or unconsciously. Danger may have been a predominant experience of their lived experience. Danger acted to shape their physiology, as it was dependent on the presence or absence of a kind and comforting other person.

In order to offer safety, it is our belief that adults need to orient themselves to its feel, its dimensions, its reverberations. There can be no openness to the child's experience if there is no openness to one's own experience. They need to find the experiences in themselves and their relationships of moments of shared safety that have given way to a sense of relief, comfort, and restoration. These are themes that can be examined directly and indirectly with these adults. Such exploration brings into their awareness the reactions of their bodies, their thoughts, and the descriptions they hold about the experience. All of these are important facets of knowing and experiencing safety. As they do this, they are more likely to be able to integrate safety as a resource into their interactions with the child we are all supporting.

We have developed some questions and practices that explore the theme of safety with the adults in the child's network. They are presented here as options for working with parents and caregivers. They can be adapted to suit other adults with different roles or relationships with children.

- How does someone find their way to your heart? How do you know you feel safe with someone? What do you sense in your body that tells you that?
- How do you find your way to your child's heart? What does your child know about you that has been safe for him?
- When you were younger, how and who made you feel protected? What were some of the things they did to help you feel safe? Who looked after you whom you knew you would always feel safe with? What was it about this person that helped you to know that feeling with such confidence?
- When you were not sure about things in your life, whom have you always turned to? What is it about the way that this person relates to you that lets you know that you can turn to them?
- Whose voice do you hear when you want to feel safe, calm, and protected?
- When you think about your child, what is it about her that you hold in your heart that makes you want to protect her?
- What does being comforted feel like for you? What have been some times in your life that you remember where someone comforted you in the face of being frightened? How did they do that? What was important in what they said? What was important in the way they interacted with you that gave you the message that you were special enough to them that they would try really hard to help you feel better?
- Imagine or bring something with you to a counseling session that you believe is important to your child's safety. It can be a toy, photo, or book, for example. Hold this item and imagine your child holding it or playing with it or being comforted by it. What will your child be feeling the most? What will his breathing be like as he holds it and plays with it? What will the look in his eyes tell you about how he is feeling? What will he be saying to you about it? What will his tone of voice sound like?
- What does this experience of deep safety remind you of in your life? How do you know what you know about this kind of deep safety? Who helped you to know it and to experience it when you were younger? Who helps you know and experience safety now? How does safety feel now for you?

- What feels the same about the safety that you feel now and the safety your child feels when she holds this object? What is your tone of voice like now? How do you think one would describe the look in your eyes?
- When you clasp your hand to your heart, what can you feel about your child and the closeness you feel with him? If you and your child were holding each other softly, what would it feel like in your heart? What words would you use to help your child know that he is safe?
- Trace a story from your life where safety in the face of fear was an experience you really valued. How did it start? What did it mean to you? What do you still carry with you about that experience?
- Consider a time when you were able to share the feeling of safety with your child in a way that you knew she felt it deeply. How do you know that she shared that feeling and experience with you then? What was it like for you to share this feeling of safety with your child in such an intensive way?
- When you hear your child's voice, what do you hear when he is distressed? What do you hear when he is feeling connected to you and you to him? What do you hear when he is feeling safe with you? What do you hear when he is scared or worried?
- Are there moments when you feel really close to your child? How is being safe part of that? What do you look for in your child's expression to tell you that she is feeling safe? What does she show you in a spontaneous way that would tell you that she is feeling safe and close to you?
- If feeling safe was difficult for someone you knew, how would you help him? What would you say to him? How would you say it? What would you show him in the way you interacted with him?
- If you knew that feeling safe was difficult for your child, what would you do to help her? What would you change about the way you are with her? What would you try to do more of? How important is it for you and your child that you share a sense of safety together?

These questions, and the ensuing conversations, promote reflective engagement with the lived experiences of safety. They are not psychoeducational—instead, they act to empower these vitally important adults to use their experiences of safety as corporeal, metaphorical, and as a relational resource for the children for whom safety has been so distressingly violated. It is a form of therapeutic praxis—enlisting the potency of the regulatory parallels between therapist and parent or caregiver with those embedded in the relational experiences of caregiver and child. As adults' own neuroceptive capacity strengthens, they come to know safety from the inside. They find it easier to trust their own physiology. They sense safety closer to themselves and even appreciate what it can offer them. Safety is teased from places outside of awareness into the consciousness of the adult with the view to it being able to be used more intentionally in interactions with the traumatized child.

Tempting Safety Back Into the Experiences of Traumatized Children

For children who have experienced abuse, the offer of relational safety is the most tender of invitations. It starts softly, with the adult paying careful attention to how the children perceive visceral information and feelings from their bodies. Here, therapist and select important adults in the children's network spend time noticing how the children respond to disruptions in their environment and relationships that might feel distressing, dislocating, or perturbing. The intent of this phase is for these adults to attune to the internal neuroceptive activity of the children as they subconsciously evaluate external risks and their own inner visceral states of safety and danger. We have found the following questions to be central to this orientation.

- How does the child react to any changes in her routine, environment, or relationships?
- What have you noticed that seems to trigger any behavior associated with the child feeling upset, angry or distressed? How long does it take for the child to calm down after he has become distressed or upset about something?
- What kind of behavior does the child engage in when she is upset, angry, or distressed? Are there patterns in this behavior?
- What does it take to calm down or change the way the child feels when he is upset, angry, or distressed? How does the child seek out comfort from others to change the way he is feeling? What does the child need from you at those times to assist him to calm and soothe?
- When the child is upset, angry, or distressed, how does she listen to instructions or statements from those around her?
- Has the way the child reacted to change or any triggers shifted over time? Has it become more intense, less intense, or stayed the same?
- Under what circumstances does the child spontaneously try to involve others in his play? What is the most evident behavior that the child uses to seek out closeness with another? Are there circumstances in which the child shows contingent eye contact with others?
- Under what circumstances does the child feel distant from any form of social connection? How does she express this withdrawal or distancing

experience? What behavior does she engage in that reflects her feeling separate from the experience that is being shared?
- How does the child communicate internal states related to the perception of danger? What does he show in his eyes, breathing, tone of voice, head turning? What does he say (if anything) that lets you know that danger is being experienced?
- How does the child communicate internal states related to the perception and experience of safety? What does she show in her eyes, breathing, tone of voice, head turning? What does she say (if anything) that lets you know that safety is being experienced?

This process of building the adult's relational harmony to the child's internal state is critical. Children experience their own bodies as a site of the danger. They do so because they no longer trust their bodies. They find it difficult to be able to differentiate the reactions of terror they experience that reverberate in their bodies from the actual sources of the danger external to them. To these children, they are one and the same. There is a neuroceptive mismatch between the internal cues and the experiences of danger or safety in the child's environment. The goal is for adults to support clearer internal states of safety in the child, and support them being distinguished from states of terror.

The internal states of children are softly validated by their important adults using their own social engagement systems as a common scaffold toward increasingly mutual experiences of shared regulation. Adults use their tone of voice, their gaze, their regulated slow and rhythmic breathing to tempt the child's physiology away from mobilized and immobilized states and back to safety.

As this occurs, the traumatized child comes to experience this caring adult as a source of shared intention and volition. In the relational space between adult and child, there is a togetherness through which they come to experience common anticipation of a moment of laughter or joy. They find it in synchronous moments, when the adult finishes off the words to a song that the child really enjoys; or the child finds the perfect spot on the chest of the parent or caregiver to rest her head; or they hold hands and swing their arms in unison; or they play basketball and feel the way their hearts pound in response to the demands of the game.

The relational experience at the edge of activation of the child's fight-or-flight/flop response (mobilization and immobilization with fear systems) is the meeting point where corporeal experiences of danger change to embodied experiences of safety. This shift toward attuned, regulated states in both the child and adult offers opportunities for rehearsal and practice of discovering the nuanced experiences of deep safety.

It holds the physiological boundary over which change is sensed and realized. As this occurs, the process is captured with language and expression that makes it more tangible and real. For the child and the adult, the repetition of the movement in neurophysiological activation forms the basis for reexperiencing dimensions of deep safety that can accompany predictability and stability. Children learn to tolerate the boundary of activation so that their physiologies can be coaxed back into the safe zone of proximity and relational connectedness.

Children come to feel themselves as being safe through their experience in a relationship with a caring and protective adult. They become more open and less fixed. They use their own social engagement systems to approach the adult and seek mutually satisfying interactions. They play and experience curiosity. They test the reliability of the safety being offered. They reach out and begin to hold on to safety for what it offers them. They change. They begin slowly to shed the habitual patterns of activation that have been defined by their trauma-based responses to the world. Their hearts open to the adult's affection.

Merging Safety Deep Into the Relational World of Adults and Children

In this final phase, what has been a gradual retuning of the physiological circuits that shape the child's experience of safety progresses to the explicit exploration of safety within the merged relational experiences of the child and the adult. The central tenet here is that safety reemerges as shared embedded experiences from synchronous engagement by protective adults with a child followed by joint enactments of reciprocity.

As therapists, we actively direct opportunities for playful exchanges that promote matched behavioral patterns between the child and the important adult. This is followed by supported acts of turn taking and mutual recognition of each other's responses. Each parcel of intervention ends with a cognitive reflection exercise that attempts to give collective meaning to how safety is experienced in the bodies and minds of the adult and child. This narrative resource is logged as a reminder to be used at times of relational disruption and misalignment. The bigger the bank of experiences, the greater the predictability of the shared experiences of relational safety in the child and the adult.

The following five activities are examples of how joint experiences of play that combine sensory, narrative, and metaphorical dimensions promote the shared movement underpinning relational safety.

YOU AND ME ON A TREASURE HUNT

In a room, the therapist creates imaginary landmarks that need to be navigated to find a hidden treasure. Each landmark is represented by a sensory object that resembles the features of that point in the landscape. Vines in a jungle are represented by soft ropes. Muddy flats are represented by wet sand. Windy plains are represented by a fan blowing into a corner of a room. A land of bubbles is represented by balloons. The child and adult are invited to traverse each of the landmarks and at every point take notice of how they are keeping themselves safe. They are also asked to describe to each other how they are helping each other to stay calm and keep on track. They are encouraged to talk about how their bodies feel as they approach a new challenge and how safety helps them to take each step and find the treasure.

JOINING UP THE STARS IN THE SKY

In a darkened room, the child and the adult are each given a flashlight. The child is asked to make stars appear on the ceiling by switching the light on and off. The adult is invited to join up the stars in the sky created by the child by matching the rhythm of the stars' twinkles. The child and adult take turns to create different twinkles rhythms (slow, fast, dancing, skipping) and repeat what the other has created. As the child and adult share in matching their experiences, the therapist asks them to describe how the rhythms are different and feeling words that best describe them. They explore how they can make their bodies synchronize in real life—at moments of fun, safety, calm. This is an activity that explores the embodied experiences of cooperative social engagement systems of the child and the adult.

SANDY TOGETHERNESS

The child and the adult are each given a container with sand and a bucket. They are guided to pour the sand over each other's hands, draw collaborative pictures in the sand with their fingers, make symbols in the sand that represent shared experiences of feeling safe. As they do this, they are invited to reflect on the fun that they are having now. They trace fun and safety through stories that they can tell each other.

FEEL THE MUSIC

The child and the adult listen to different examples of classical music. The music chosen for this activity spans a range of tones, rhythms, and arrangements. The child and the adult are asked to take turns choosing tracks that represent to them a feeling, such as happy, sad, excited, scared, lonely, proud, frustrated, surprised, safe. The child and adult are invited to describe the dimensions of the music that they believe characterizes the feeling. For example, fear can be represented by loud, low notes with deep vibrations. Safety can be represented by violins playing softly in harmony with other instruments. The feelings that the music evokes are traced into bodies of the child and adults with questions that explore the location and reaction to each track. The child and adult explore how safety can be found in many of the tracks if you listen deeply enough.

SQUIGGLE AND GIGGLE

The child and the adult are provided with a tray containing colored shaving cream. The child and the adult take turns making different shapes that have to be matched by the other. They compare their shapes. They reflect on how they can best work together to make their shaving cream shape be as identical to each other as possible. They choose a shape that represents a shared memory or feeling of safety they can both recognize. They finish the activity by creating a shared picture that explores children and adults feeling safe together.

In all these examples, the children and adults are given the opportunity to share internal states reflective of an open and active social engagement system. This is represented in reciprocal exchanges filled with fun. Children are led through what Porges has increasingly referred to as *neural exercises* embedded in such play (Porges & Carter, 2016). Caring adults support the activation of mobilized states at the very border of relational safety. Soft tones of voice, shared movements, mutual gaze recruit the child's physiology toward down-regulated states of calm and interdependence. This back-and-forth exposes children's fight-or-flight reactivity to the influence of the social engagement system offered by caregivers. With repeated experience, children's physiologies tip toward the resources of the ventral vagal system that affirm the potency of connection.

Safety is the theme that draws a relational line that joins their respective physiologies and cognition. Narratives of mutuality become a base on which an articulated sense of safety is autonomically known and understood. It is available to be used as a resource when perceived or real threat may reemerge.

Relational safety builds on repetition. It sets up a "neural expectancy" (Porges & Carter, 2016) in children that a reliable, attuned adult can regulate their activated states of distress and fear. The inherent physiological risk for children of being left to try and soothe their own pain is substantially lowered when the presence of a safe adult is affirmed. The predictability of responses by adults to the child's physiological and psychological needs makes clear to the child the intent of the adult to act protectively. The games and activities are the sparks transforming the future relational experiences for both child and adult.

Safety Is a Biological Imperative

Porges has often repeated, as an eloquent conclusion to his years of research, that connectedness is a biological imperative (Porges & Carter, 2016). It serves significant survival functions. It is resourced by a mammalian neurophysiology that has evolved to ensure that such interdependence is achievable.

Underscoring this simple truth is an even more obvious one. Safety, as the emergent property of an interwoven physiology between humans that regulates and facilitates growth and restoration, is equally a biological imperative. Deep relational safety is certainly the means through which children who have suffered abuse and violence come to settle and find the comfort and love they need to recover from its traumatic effects.

Realizing such deep safety is both the intervention and the end goal of therapy with traumatized and vulnerable children and the important adults who care for, educate, and support them.

References

Hussain, Z. (2014). *The sky is purple*. Self-published.

Porges, S. W. (1995). Orienting in a defensive world: Mammalian modifications of our evolutionary heritage. A Polyvagal Theory. *Psychophysiology, 32*(4), 301–318.

Porges, S. W. (1998). Love: An emergent property of the mammalian autonomic nervous system. *Psychoneuroendocrinology, 23*, 837–861.

Porges, S. W. (2001). The Polyvagal Theory: Phylogenetic substrates of a social nervous system. *International Journal of Psychophysiology, 42*, 123–146.

Porges, S. W. (2003). Social engagement and attachment: A phylogenetic perspective. *Roots of Mental Illness in Children, Annals of the New York Academy of Sciences, 1008*, 31–47.

Porges, S. W. (2009). The Polyvagal Theory: New insights into adaptive reactions of the autonomic nervous system. *Cleveland Clinic Journal of Medicine, 76*, 86–90.

Porges, S. W. (2011). *The Polyvagal Theory: Neurophysiological foundations of emotions, attachment, communication, self-regulation*. New York, NY: Norton.

Porges, S. W., & Carter, S. (2016). *The neuroscience of safety in treatment: Clinical applications of the Polyvagal Theory.* Master class presented at the Second International Childhood Trauma Conference, Australian Childhood Foundation, Melbourne, Australia.

7

Therapeutic Presence and Polyvagal Theory: Principles and Practices for Cultivating Effective Therapeutic Relationships

Shari M. Geller

Abstract: Therapeutic presence involves being in the moment, receptive, and attuned with clients on multiple levels. Research demonstrates that therapeutic presence is necessary to facilitating positive therapeutic relationships and effective therapy. This chapter explains why this happens through the lens of Polyvagal Theory. There is a neurophysiological activation of safety in present, centered relationships via the ventral vagal pathways of the parasympathetic nervous system, which elicits clients' neuroception of safety. In turn, health and optimal growth are promoted. Practices are offered to strengthen relational presence, including mindfulness, attunement, and drumming exercises based in the therapeutic rhythm and mindfulness program.

I've learned that people will forget what you said, people will forget what you did, but people will never forget how you made them feel.
—Maya Angelou (in Booth & Hachiya, 2004, p. 14)

Working effectively in psychotherapy is only possible when clients feel safe and secure in relationship with their therapist. To promote safety and optimal therapy, therapists need to focus on *how* they are with clients as more primary than what they *do* in the therapy session. This is affirmed by decades of psychotherapy research demonstrating the relationship as the most consistent predictor of change (Norcross, 2011). Yet what contributes to a positive therapy relationship has been less clear until recently.

Emerging research suggests that therapeutic presence is a necessary and preliminary step to facilitating positive therapeutic relationships and effective therapy (Geller, 2017; Geller & Greenberg, 2002, 2012; Geller, Greenberg, & Watson, 2010). And Polyvagal Theory (Porges, 2011) explains *how* therapists' presence evokes clients' safety, strengthening these therapeutic relationships.

When therapists are fully in the moment and attuned with their clients, their receptive and safe presence sends a neurophysiological message to clients that they are being heard, met, felt, and understood, which elicits a feeling of safety (Geller & Porges, 2014). According to Polyvagal Theory, when clients feel met and felt by another person, they not only feel aligned with them, but the brain likely establishes a neuroception of safety (Porges, 1998, 2011). Clients who have experienced misattunement or trauma are often wired to perceive unsafety even when safety is present (Geller & Porges, 2014). They relate to the world with a heightened state of fear and protection as their sympathetic nervous system is aroused; or if it is overaroused, the dorsal vagal wing of the parasympathetic nervous system kicks in, evoking a state of shutdown or freeze. When therapists relate with their clients as a calming presence, it activates the social engagement system and invites calm and connection in the ventral vagal wing of their clients' parasympathetic nervous system, and over time clients feel safer and regulated in the relationship. Therapeutic presence elicits a reciprocal experience of safety between both therapist and client, which allows clients to open up and engage in the necessary therapeutic work.

This chapter will focus on understanding (a) the value of therapists' presence in creating safety for clients and in deepening the therapeutic relationship; (b) how presence elicits a neurological and physiological feeling of safety, which is the foundation for healing, as viewed through the lens of Polyvagal Theory; and (c) practices that help to cultivate therapeutic presence using relational approaches such as mindfulness and rhythm-based modalities. Overall, this is all a call for more ventral vagal therapy through emphasizing the need for training and cultivation of this foundational approach of therapeutic presence.

What Is Therapeutic Presence?

Therapeutic presence is a way of *being* with client that optimizes the *doing* of therapy (Geller, 2017; Geller & Greenberg, 2012). It involves therapists bringing their whole self to the encounter and being present on multiple levels—physically, emotionally, cognitively, relationally, and spiritually (Geller & Greenberg, 2012). Therapeutic presence involves being grounded in one's self, while receptively taking in the verbal and nonverbal expression of the client's in-the-moment experience.

Therapeutic presence is a way of *preparing* for therapy (Geller, 2017). As therapists become present in their personal and daily life and prior to session, it allows presence to be experienced with greater ease in session. Through practice and care to their own well-being and relationships, therapists can more finely attune their nervous systems so their ventral vagus nerve is activated and they are ready to engage with clients in a healing and attuned manner. Ongoing self-care as well as taking a few minutes prior to session to center inside and invite a state of presence and ventral vagal activation can support therapists to be in an optimal state to facilitate their clients' healing. This is supported by research that suggests that just 5 minutes of centering prior to session improves session outcome and reduces clients' psychological distress (Dunn, Callahan, Swift, & Ivanovic, 2013).

Therapeutic presence is an *internal experience*. Therapists' experience includes feeling (a) *grounded*, centered and in contact with one's self, while being (b) *immersed* in the moment with clients' pain and suffering. There is a simultaneous experience of (c) *expansion*, in which there is a felt sense of a larger perspective and spaciousness, and of compassion, as therapists are (d) *with and for* the other, in service of their client's healing process. This internal experience of therapists' presence is an expression of their ventral vagal system being ideally tuned so that therapists can be a safe presence for their clients.

Therapeutic presence is a *process* or way of doing therapy (Geller, 2017). This process involves (1) being open and *receptive* to clients' experience, attuning to their verbal and nonverbal expressions; (2) *attuning inwardly* to therapists' resonance with clients' in-the-moment experience, which serves as a guide to (3) *extend and promote contact* through both verbal and nonverbal expression. Therapists' inner sensory systems inform them of how their client is receiving their responses and interventions and what is occurring moment to moment in the relationship (Geller, 2017). This helps therapists recognize the optimal moments for particular responses or interventions so they are offered with the greatest impact and precision, and in resonance with what is emerging in the moment. The moment-to-moment attunement that is inherent in the therapeutic presence process serves two important purposes. First, it allows clients to feel felt, heard, and calmed as their nervous system comes into alignment with their therapist's calming presence. Through the bidirectional communication between the nervous systems of the therapist and client, growth and healing are supported. Second, it allows therapists to sense and feel their clients' experience so they can respond with what is most needed in the moment to support clients' growth.

Therapeutic presence is also highly *relational*. When clients perceive their therapist as present with them, they become more present within and in the relationship. The bidirectional communication that is central to Polyvagal Theory reflects this process where the nervous systems of people affect each other, and as the therapist's presence activates clients' presence and back again, they engage in a feedback loop where a larger state of shared presence begins to emerge, and therapists' and clients' bodies and brains become in sync. This supports an intersubjective consciousness or sharing of the same emotional landscape (Stern, 2004), which deepens safety and leads to therapeutic change.

Therapeutic presence is *growth promoting* for therapists, clients, and the therapeutic relationship. It includes self-care and balance for therapists. Clients feel heard, understood, and safe, which is experienced on a neurophysiological level, and even outside of conscious awareness (Geller & Porges, 2014; Porges & Carter, 2014). Clients' defenses then soften, and natural growth and healing unfolds.

Background Research on Therapeutic Presence

An empirically validated model of therapeutic presence was developed (Geller & Greenberg, 2002) that includes the preparation, process, and experience described above. From this model came the development and validation of a psychotherapy measure, the therapeutic presence inventory (therapist and client versions; Geller et al., 2010). Research with the therapeutic presence inventory suggests that therapeutic presence is a positive predictor for the therapeutic alliance (Geller et al., 2010; Pos, Geller, & Oghene, 2011). It was found that clients' experience of their therapists' presence matters most—those who experienced their therapist as present had a positive alliance and a successful session outcome across three modalities of therapy (cognitive behavioral, emotion-focused, and person-centered therapies; Geller et al., 2010). It is valuable, then, to be skillful in nonverbally communicating presence so that clients receive their therapists' presence. Polyvagal Theory helps us to understand how to do this through prosody of voice, open body posture, and a face-to-heart connection that evokes connection and safety.

Research affirms that therapeutic presence is related to yet distinct from empathy (Pos et al., 2010; Geller et al., 2010); and presence precedes empathy

(Hayes & Vinca, 2011). Therefore, the ventral vagal activation in therapists that ensues from therapeutic presence is proposed as a necessary precondition to being empathic and sustaining a positive therapeutic relationship.

How Does Therapeutic Presence Promote Effective Therapy?

We can best answer this question through the lens of Polyvagal Theory as well as therapeutic presence research. Presence and attunement to one's self and others activates safety, which improves the therapeutic relationship and overall outcome. Also, therapists who are grounded and present serve as an emotional regulator for clients, given that the bidirectional communication and interaction between therapists' and clients' nervous system and viscera (the brain and the body) is mediated by the relational environment (Geller & Porges, 2014; Porges, 2011). The following brief explanation shows how this occurs in the psychotherapy process (see Figure 7.1).

First, the therapists become present, prior to session, through grounding, centering, breathing, and attuning within their self in the moment. This then allows therapists to openly receive and attune with their clients. Clients begin to feel safe from a neurological, physiological, and emotional perspective (Allison & Rossouw, 2013; Cozolino, 2006; Geller & Porges, 2014; Porges, 2011; Schore, 2012). This process has three important effects (Geller & Porges, 2014).

1. Clients' defenses drop away, and an optimal portal opens up to engage effectively in the work of therapy.
2. Clients' nervous systems begin to calm in resonance with their therapists' calm, grounded presence, and they feel more present and accepting within and more connected with their therapists.
3. Therapists' responses and interventions are offered in attunement with what is poignant in the moment for their clients, including their readiness to receive.

Through repeated experiences of safety, clients can potentially generate a greater sense of safety in other relationships, which is central for well-being, growth, and health (Geller & Porges, 2014).

Co-Regulation: Creating Safety Through Presence in Relationship

The regulators of emotions and physiology are embedded in relationship (Cozolino, 2006; Geller & Porges, 2014; Porges, 2011; Schore, 2012). Experiencing the attuned presence of another person can change the brain (i.e.,

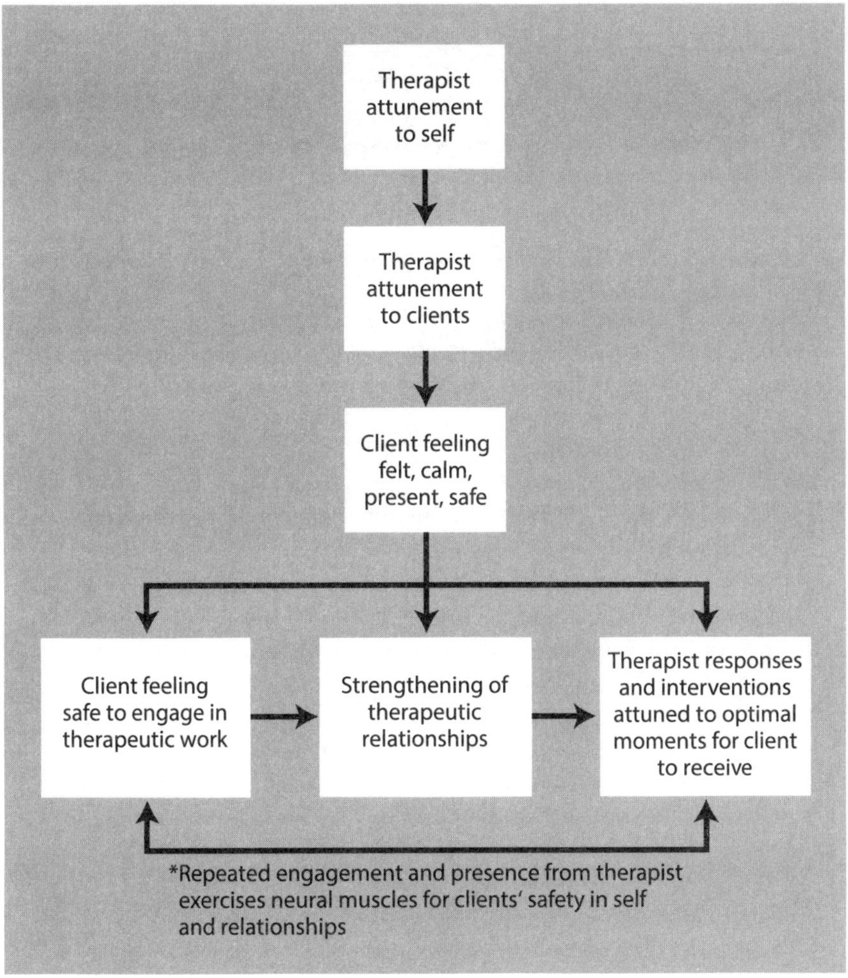

FIGURE 7.1
How Does Therapeutic Presence Promote Safety and Therapy Effectiveness?

the client) and the experience of the person they are in relationship with (i.e., their therapist). This can in part occur through co-regulation, which has been defined as the bidirectional linkage of oscillating emotions between different partners, contributing to the emotional stability of both (Butlar & Randall, 2013). So in clinical terms, if therapists are calm, then their clients will become calm in resonance with their grounded presence, as emotions, bodies, and brains are bidirectionally linked (Geller, 2017; Geller & Porges, 2014). Alternatively, if therapists are not grounded and present, then they can be thrown off or dysregulated when their clients are emotionally overwhelmed. Polyvagal Theory helps to understand how this happens, and its insights have direct application to the clinical setting.

Indicators of Safety: Bidirectional Communication Within and Between People

Polyvagal Theory describes the evolution of the mammalian nervous system to include a third wing beyond the fundamental fight-or-flight and immobilization responses, called the *social engagement system* (Porges, 1995, 1998, 2003, 2011). The fight-or-flight portion of the autonomic nervous system depends on sympathetic activation. Immobilization and social engagement are parasympathetic responses, but their divergent outcomes depend in part on the portions of vagus nerve they activate (Porges, 2011). The ventral (or "smart vagus") supports face-to-face communication, and helps to inhibit sympathetic excitation (which triggers fight-or-flight behavior) so that emotions are well regulated. Having the ventral vagus activated supports having positive social interactions.

Polyvagal Theory further explains that potent cues of safety or danger outside of conscious awareness are detected by cortical areas, and can shift physiological states (Geller & Porges, 2014; Porges, 2011). Shifting physiological states are communicated from visceral organs to the brain via the vagus. These cues are also communicated from the regions to which the vagus nerve has projections—such as the striated muscles of the face and head (Porges, 2011). Because of these connections to the face and running all the way down to the subdiaphragmatic region, the way that people use their faces, voices, breathing, and bodies can say a lot about how calm or activated they are feeling in a given moment. When vocal prosody (pitch, rhythm, and timbre of voice) is rich, the body is open, and the face is at ease, a general state of calmness is being experienced, and this supports spontaneous social engagement behaviors (Geller & Porges, 2014).

Not only is there a bidirectional communication between brain (i.e., central nervous system) and body—there is also a bidirectional communication between the nervous systems of people who are in relationship with each other (Cozolino, 2006; Porges, 2011; Schore, 2012; Siegel, 2010). This communication is not necessarily in conscious awareness; it is more of a "gut" (visceral) sense that informs us of how we are feeling in an interaction. In this way, safety and unsafety are experienced and mediated by physiological states (for example, bodily felt agitation when unsafe, internal sense of ease when feeling safe). This process of automatic evaluation of safety or risk in relationship is called *neuroception* in Polyvagal Theory (Porges, 2003).

Emotional dysregulation and physiological reactivity to others can develop in response to trauma or misattuned relationships. Yet current safe relationships can heal and exercise the neural muscles of safety, such as with a person who is present, caring, and in sync. The bidirectional nature of the social engagement system means that positive interactions between therapists and their clients can influence their vagal function to dampen stress-related physiological states, and support growth and restoration (Geller & Porges, 2014).

Promoting Regulation and Growth in the Therapeutic Relationship

A helpful way of looking at how to promote regulation in relationship is through attuned right-brain-to-right-brain communication (Schore, 2009, 2012; Quillman, 2012). In relationship, while there is often a verbal narrative that is being communicated (which is primarily left-brain activity), there is an additional nonverbal way that emotions and experiences are expressed. *Right brain to right brain* refers to these nonverbal ways that promote regulation, as highlighted in Polyvagal Theory, such as body posture, vocal expressions, facial expressions, and gestures.

In interactions with therapeutic presence, therapists listen with their bodies and senses (right brain) to what is expressed via the bodies of their clients (their right brain's communication). Informed by Polyvagal Theory, it is important that therapists are actively using nonverbal communication to show that they are listening, connected, and want to understand their clients and help them to feel safe.

Polyvagal Theory proposes that cues of safety or danger are communicated interpersonally from the upper part of the face, eye contact, prosody of voice, and body posture. The therapeutic encounter is filled with nonverbal messages that are outside the realm of our awareness, yet clients are interpreting their therapists' way of relating with them in a physiological or gut-sense way. The neuroception of safety is detectable by physiological markers.

Through therapists' warmth and prosody of voice, soft eye contact, open body posture, and receptive and accepting stance, clients can receive their calm and safe therapists and feel safer to open and engage. The work of therapy is significantly enhanced. Attuning to the moment-to-moment encounter allows therapists to recognize (e.g., in the facial expressions of their clients) when their client is (a) feeling open and ready for an intervention, and it is appropriate to proceed with such; or (b) not feeling safe, and therefore it is necessary to pause and not proceed with an intervention and instead focus on enhancing safe contact in the relationship. Therapeutic presence also helps therapists regulate their own reactivity so they can maintain their ventral vagal activation within themselves, and authentic connection with clients.

Research suggests that a safe therapeutic environment facilitates the development of new neural pathways for the client, which in turn contributes to the repair of attachment injuries and provides the positive social interactions that are essential for health and growth for the client (Allison & Rossouw, 2013). So when clients feel that their therapist is present, open, and centered, and willing to hear, feel, and hold their pain with a caring and grounded presence, it can actually deactivate the trauma response and over time give their brains an experience of safety that eventually extends to other relationships. This helps to strengthen clients' ventral vagal systems, and creates flexibility in their vagal brakes (Porges et al., 1996) so they can open and close with greater fluidity and control. Therapists' presence can both reduce distress and provide a soothing comfort that changes the structure of the brain to feel safe, grow, and restore healthy functioning. So how can therapists activate presence and encounter their clients in session in a way that maximizes safety and healing?

The Process of Presence in Session

The process of presence reflects what therapists do when they are present with clients to activate that state of safety and connection as well as facilitate therapeutic growth. This is not about actual techniques but about how therapists are with their clients. Cultivating presence in therapeutic relationships begins with the therapists, so that they enter into the therapy encounter feeling grounded, open, and receptive.

Starting With Cultivating Presence in the Therapist

An array of practices to cultivate therapists' presence in daily life can be found in the book *A Practical Guide to Cultivating Therapeutic Presence* (Geller, 2017) and from suggestions below. Diaphragmatic breathing with long exhalations, relaxation practices, yoga, chanting, music, mindfulness, grounding or centering exercises, and deep listening all help to activate presence. Polyvagal Theory affirms these ancient practices, as they soften sympathetic activation and strengthen the newer vagal circuit through play, positive activity, and vocal stimulation. Cultivating presence within therapists helps them to confront painful or difficult events (such as clients' suffering or personal hardship) with less reactivity, and helps build the autonomic and neural structure to be present with their clients.

Preparing Prior to Session

Prior to session, therapists need to cultivate presence so they are ready to meet their clients as a safe other, ready to receive them without judgment. This allows their nervous systems to meet their clients in a state of calm. This starts before therapists even arrive at the office. It includes allowing time to open up the space, gather thoughts, get nourished, and center inside, rather then checking messages, texts, and e-mails.

Setting an intention for presence at the start of a day or session can be powerful and simple. Standing in stillness, feeling the soles of the feet as they touch the floor, and taking a few deep and slow breaths can facilitate this process. Words can also support the intention for presence, such as "Letting go of stress" with your exhale, and "Arriving into now" on your inhale. Therapists can engage in a tree pose or a centering practice to activate a sense of presence in the body. It also helps to take a brief time between clients, such as taking three full breaths to let go of the last contact and open to the next meeting in this new moment.

The Process of Presence Within a Session

Throughout the session, therapists are going through a reciprocal process to optimize their presence in relationship with their clients: They are (1) receiving from the client (2) attuning within to what is being received, and (3) allowing this blend of experiences to inform their understanding and response. This includes tracking moment to moment their clients' experience and the relationship, as well as assessing when clients feel safe or unsafe and adjusting when needed to promote contact and safety.

RECEIVING, READING, AND ATTUNING WITH CLIENTS

Once the session begins, present therapists are receiving their clients, actively listening to all of their ways of expressing, and attuning with them to activate an experience of feeling heard, felt, and seen. This includes attending to verbal and nonverbal expressions as therapists offer gateways to understanding their clients' experience.

Attuning to facial expressions and eye gaze is helpful from a Polyvagal perspective to reading the state of the other. For example, eyes that are widened may suggest fear and unsafety. A soft eye gaze may indicate that the client feels safe and at ease. Leaning on Polyvagal principles, a shared gaze between a warm and present therapist and the client can evoke a sense of safety and regulation.

Polyvagal Theory sheds light on why nonverbal communication like vocal prosody, body posture, and facial expressions are consistently such powerful conveyers of an individual's physiological and psychological state. We are all equipped with the integrated system that Polyvagal Theory describes, connecting cues in our environment to our internal sense of safety or unsafety. These manifest in how we use our faces, voices, breathing, and body. But the physiological changes that give us an internal sense of security or dis-ease are mediated by features in social interactions that are, in general, outside the realm of our awareness. An interaction with another (i.e., with client or therapist) can trigger a broad range of observable bodily changes; while we may be unaware of them in ourselves, we can and do interpret them in each other.

Why is this important for therapeutic presence? Think of a situation, for example, when you (or imagine a therapist) had a momentary lapse in attention when listening to a client. A tightness in the edges of the client's eyes or a distant gaze would inform the therapist that their client has noticed and is having a reaction—they might feel unsafe or disconnected. The momentary lapse in attention can be experienced as rejecting, which triggered physiological changes of unsafety, as revealed through the client's face.

The neuroception of unsafety can be expressed in other ways in the therapeutic relationship. For example, a therapist who looks down in reflection could be perceived as rejecting what the client is saying; a therapist who raises her arm to reach for a glass of water could be perceived as preparing to strike. It is helpful for therapists to develop the ability to attune with their clients so they can read the cues to help guide their responses.

PRACTICE FOR ATTUNING WITH CLIENTS: MIRRORING GESTURES

Attuning to others can be developed with practice, such as with this two-person exercise (Geller, 2017). Person A is asked to connect to a particular feeling. Then person A is guided to create different movements, facial expressions, and gestures reflecting that feeling. Person B is invited to mirror or imitate these gestures, speech patterns, or movements. Person B can express what he feels as he mirrors person A's experience to see if it is similar. Partners can then switch roles and repeat the steps above. Debriefing helps to make sense of what is being experienced in mirroring another and reflect on the accuracy.

Attuning Inwardly

As therapists receive their clients' moment-to-moment experience, they are also attuning with their selves to understand what is being received. This inner attunement with acceptance and awareness is a part of keeping the ventral vagus online in therapists and remaining a grounding presence for clients. In this state of sensing without reactivity, the therapist's body acts as an antenna or a tuning fork. Therapists use their bodies to detect states of autonomic resonance with their clients in order to sense and listen to clients' experience, and then listening internally to determine how to respond. Therapists can also tune in to how they may not be present (i.e., distraction), and invite their attention back to the moment. Scanning one's inner experience can occur in a split second, once the ability to be present strengthens through practice.

There are multiple things that therapists can turn their attention to internally as they read and resonate with their clients. Emotions, body sensations, breathing patterns, images, and insights are all venues for therapists to attend to within themselves. For example, a quiver in the therapist's chest or moisture in their eyes may inform them that his client is feeling sad. An accelerated heart rate or a tight, anxious feeling may be an autonomic resonance with their client's anxiety. Attending to breathing patterns also provides cues of what is occurring in the session. A therapist's restricted breath may reflect their own absence or disconnection, or it is a resonance with their client indicating that the client is unsafe or emotionally disconnected. When therapists are present, the body acts as an empathic indicator of clients' experience, which may in part be a function of the bidirectional communication inherent in Polyvagal Theory.

Therapeutic presence requires that therapists have an embodied sense of self-awareness and capacity for interoceptive (sensing inwardly) awareness. Embodied self-awareness is the ability to pay attention to ourselves, including our experience, bodily sensations, movements, and inner sensory world in the present moment (Fogel, 2009). This capacity is a key source of information when therapists are in bidirectional attunement with their clients.

PRACTICE FOR ATTUNING TO YOUR OWN RHYTHM: MINDFUL DRUMMING

Mindful drumming can heighten interoceptive capacities, helping attune to your internal bodily terrain, first by noticing your bodily rhythm, and then by externalizing those rhythms through movement and sound (Geller, 2017). Drumming also helps to release stress and tension by activating the vagal brake, quieting the mind as the ventral vagal is optimized, and strengthening the rhythmic alignment and communication between brain and body.

Slowing down external rhythm can encourage bodily rhythms to slow down in sync with your playing, which creates a calmer and more stable feeling inside. Mindful drumming is a wonderful integration practice too. Coordinating both right and left hands with the heart, breath, and bodily rhythms helps to syncopate right-brain and left-brain hemispheric activity. This supports balance and mental acuity, enhancing your focus and attention. The following practice can be done on a hand drum (e.g., djembe or ashiko) or on the top of a desk or on your lap. An empty large jug of water turned upside down can serve as a useful rhythm tool as well.

1. Place your nondominant hand on your heart, neck, or wrist to sense your heartbeat or pulse, trying to listen to the rhythm of heart or pulse as it is right now. Notice if it is fast or slow, deep or shallow.
2. With your dominant hand, play the rhythm of your heart or pulse with a soft tap on your instrument.
3. When that feels comfortable and natural, tune in to the rhythm of your breath.
4. Play the rhythm of your breath with your nondominant hand by tapping at the beginning of each inhale and each exhale. Notice the difference in the rhythm of breath from heart or pulse, and how these rhythms relate with each other.
5. Continue playing the rhythm of your heart and breath for 10–15 minutes, at times inviting yourself to slow down and continue the same rhythms but at a slower pace. Notice your experience as your external rhythms slow.
6. As you close this practice, rest with your hands on your instrument and rest in silence, sensing what is true in your experience and bodily rhythms.

Responding and Promoting Contact

We have been exploring the first two parts of the cyclical process of therapeutic presence. The third reflects extending and maintaining contact with clients, such as with an empathic understanding or silent gesture. When therapists are attuning to the nonverbal elements of clients' experience, they are supporting an autonomic attunement with clients that allows them to respond with ways to calm and promote safety as needed, and strengthen the connection and the therapeutic process. For example, if therapists feel tension and sense it is an autonomic resonance with their clients, they can genuinely reflect that and ask clients what is going on for them emotionally (assuming they do so in a way that expresses their ventral vagal connection through vocal prosody and soft facial features).

In the therapeutic presence process, therapists use the cues they receive from reading clients and within themselves to guide their responses. These cues can inform whether they need to slow down and reestablish safety and connection, or if it is okay to proceed to an intervention. The insights of Polyvagal Theory allow therapists to assess their clients' sense of safety through nonverbal communication. In the clinical encounter, therapists can notice clients' state of safety or unsafety by recognizing their physiological expressions—for example, are their eyes downcast? Is their face relaxed? And importantly, therapists can then use physiological modes of expressing and connecting to induce feelings of safety and ease in the clients.

So how, exactly, can therapists use this information as a basis for responding and communicating therapeutic presence? If therapists register that their clients are feeling safe, then it is an optimal time to proceed with facilitation of the therapeutic process by engaging in an intervention. If they perceive that clients are unsafe, then they may want to pause and inquire what is going on for them, causing the unease. The possibilities are that the client is feeling scared, resistant, or disconnected, or perhaps that the therapist is not present. Therapists can enhance safety through offering practices grounded in Polyvagal Theory, such as entraining their breathing with that of their clients, inviting long exhalations, a kind and caring look, or leaning forward (Geller, 2017). Clients can also benefit in and out of session from neural exercises that promote experiences of inner safety, such as deep breathing or bodily relaxation practices like qigong or yoga.

ENTRAINMENT IN BODY, BRAIN, AND RELATIONSHIPS

Entrainment is based on a physics phenomenon of resonance. Independent rhythms (or oscillating bodies) join in synchronized movement as one speeds up while the other slows down. For example, the second hands of clocks will eventually move in unison when positioned next to each other, independent of any intervention. Entrainment helps us understand the psychological, physiological, and neuronal synchrony in therapeutic presence that promote regulation and growth in therapeutic relationships.

Purposely entraining our body movements with someone else's can increase our sense of unity (Geller, 2017). Like the hands of the clock, bodies tend to naturally fall into these rhythms in relationship as well (Marsh, Richardson, & Schmidt, 2009). In the therapy context, intending for presence can invite this synchrony between brain and body rhythms, along with a positive sense of interpersonal connection (Geller, 2017).

When therapists use their presence to autonomically attune and resonate with clients' physiology and experience, synchrony emerges as their bodies come into rhythm with each other. Their heads move in temporal coordination, and vocal rhythms are reflective of each other (Ramseyer & Tschacher, 2014; Imel et al., 2014). Coming into sync on a physiological level builds a sense of trust and safety. Movement synchrony at the start of psychotherapy has predicted client ratings of the alliance at the end of each session, as well as symptom reduction (Ramseyer & Tschacher, 2011).

Synchrony between the bodies of the therapist and client can emerge naturally in therapeutic presence and in moments of deep relating. For example, research suggests that people in dialogue who feel connected may begin to breathe in sync, and those engaged in joint tasks requiring interpersonal trust show heart rate synchrony (Warner, 1996; McFarland, 2001; Mitkidis, McGraw, Roepstorff, & Wallot, 2015; Koole & Tschacher, 2016). The more partners expected the other person to show reciprocity in the joint task, the more synchronous their heart rate rhythms became. This research suggests that trust builds synchrony and synchrony builds trust. Synchronization of physiological rhythms could be considered a "proxy for trust-building process" (Mitkidis et al., 2015, p. 105), a process that lies at the core of the therapeutic alliance. Therapists can use their ventral vagal, attuned presence to intentionally express to their clients that they are present and safe.

Practices and Tools for Promoting Contact

The following suggestions fine-tune how therapists can promote contact and express presence nonverbally.

USING NONVERBAL CUES TO PROMOTE CONTACT AND SAFETY WITH AND FOR CLIENTS

Therapists can use nonverbal expressions to promote contact with clients that inspires a neurophysiological experience of safety (Geller, 2017), including:

- prosody (rhythm) in voice;
- soft facial expression;
- soft and direct eye gaze;
- open and forward-leaning body posture;
- visual focus and attention attuned to clients.

Research supports these nonverbal elements of safety in the clinical encounter. For example, direct and attentive eye gaze results in clients feeling present and empathically attuned to (Marci & Orr, 2006; Marci, Ham, Moran, & Orr, 2007). Clients' and therapists' physiological arousal was measured as in sync when therapists' eye gaze was attentive and in contact with their clients (Marci et al., 2007). Alternatively, clinicians who shifted their eyes and attention away from the clients left clients feeling distanced, less empathically attuned to, and in discord or out of sync with their clinicians. Clients can sense when their therapists maintain or lose their presence and attention.

It is helpful if therapists bring their attention in interactions with their clients to these elements. If they notice a tension in the body, they can adjust and soften to a more present-centered focus, to help ensure nonverbally that clients feel safe with them.

ENTRAINMENT BREATHING

Therapists can intentionally mirror their breath with their clients as a way to read their experience and to promote connection and contact. Entrainment breathing communicates to clients that they are not alone in their experience, promoting a neuroception of safety and activating the social engagement system (Geller & Porges, 2014).

Entrainment breathing is when therapists mirror the clients' breathing rhythm. It creates a neurophysiological synchronization of rhythm in the brain and body between people (Cozolino, 2006; Siegel, 2010; Porges, 2011, 2014). This both supports empathic attunement with clients' emotional experience and invites clients to feel safe as their ventral vagal system comes online and in rhythm with their therapists' calm and grounded presence.

LONG EXHALATIONS TO ACTIVATE A CALM PRESENCE

Long exhalations are efficient ways of turning off therapists' (and clients') sympathetic nervous systems and vagal pathways of defense, inviting a sense of calm, openness, and trust (Geller & Porges, 2014; Porges, 2011). In contrast, longer inhalations with shorter exhalations can increase tension, yet can also increase state of alertness in the body if greater wakefulness and energy is needed. Through long exhalations, therapists can invite their own bodies into presence and invite clients to attune to their therapists' calming presence. It is also a helpful practice for clients to do directly to activate greater calm and safety.

Therapeutic Relational Presence

I described in this chapter a process where the therapists are present with their clients that activates an experience of presence and safety in clients and strengthens the therapeutic relationship. This process of relating can deepen into profound moments of relating, termed *therapeutic relational presence* (or *relational presence*; Geller, 2017; Geller & Greenberg, 2012). As both people become present with each other, a portal opens up to an "I–Thou" encounter that is larger than each individual (Buber, 1958).

This transformative state engages a triad of relationships between therapists, clients, and a larger sense of spirituality. Therapists experience a sensitivity and access to the inner world of their clients, as if they are sharing the same space. There is an interpersonal synchrony in these moments, which unfolds to a form of intersubjective consciousness (Stern, 2004). The consciousness of one overlaps with and partially includes the consciousness of the other, so that when one person has an experience, it activates almost the same experience in the other person too (Geller, 2017).

How Does Relational Presence Create Change?

Neuroscience research, such as the discovery of mirror neurons at the end of last century, may illuminate what happens in relational presence (Ferrari & Rizzolatti, 2014; Gazzola, Aziz-Zadeh, & Keysers, 2006; Glenberg, 2010; Siegel, 2010). In shared moments of presence, therapists' mirror neurons and adaptive oscillators activate in relation to clients' expressed experience, which manifests in an experience of knowing the other through direct engagement. Like two people dancing together, there is a reading and a sharing of experience. This shared neural experience is a form of interbrain synchrony (Behrends, Müller, & Dziobek, 2012; Llobera et al., 2016), which can deepen into relational presence.

Feeling attuned to and deeply connected with their therapists can activate clients' social engagement systems (ventral vagal activation), reducing defenses and evoking a neuroception of safety. The hormone oxytocin (Carter, 2014; Porges, 1998) may also be released and contribute to a loving therapeutic relationship infused with healing.

Cultivating Relational Presence: Therapeutic Rhythm and Mindfulness

Therapeutic Rhythm and Mindfulness (TRM™)[2] combines evidence-based practices of group drumming, mindfulness, visualization, and emotion-focused awareness (Geller, 2009, 2010, 2017) into a unified program that offers multiple benefits. It is designed to release positive emotions such as joy, vitality, and social connectedness, while reducing stress, tension, anxiety, and depression. It provides an opportunity to build relationships and to feel a sense of belonging in community with other therapists.

The mechanisms in TRM likely exercise therapists' social engagement systems through the playfulness of drumming, rhythmic movement, breath awareness, and group entrainment. The neural pathways can be strengthened that support social connection, growth, and healing (S. W. Porges, personal communication, 2014). TRM is an efficient and positive practice to cultivate relational presence, as it enhances intrapersonal and interpersonal connection as well as

2 http://rhythmandmindfulness.com/

a connection with something larger. Group drumming helps therapists become more synchronized with their own rhythms as well as the rhythms of others, as it involves an improvisational emergent way of communicating with rhythm. Research suggests that improvisational music played in relationship involves a brain-phase-locking process within a person and between people, increasing brain coherence in self and brain synchronization in relationship (Lindenberger, Li, Gruber, & Müller, 2009; Sänger, Müller, & Lindenberger, 2012). Group drumming has been shown to increase brain hemispheric synchronization and social connectedness (Winkelman, 2003), manifesting in increasing connectedness with the self and others, while promoting a larger state of group connection.

Practice: Relational Mindfulness With Rhythm (Geller, 2017)

Drumming practices are particularly powerful in relationship (dyad or group), as the experience of entrainment quickly occurs. Entrainment promotes a subjective sense of synchrony, supporting therapists to attune to clients' experience without getting caught up in words. Drumming also promotes synchronicity of left-brain and right-brain hemispheres, eliciting a clearer sense of focus, concentration, and inner harmony (Winkelman, 2003).

This practice can be done with another person or in a larger group. It helps to use a small percussion instrument, such as a hand or tongue drum or shakers.

1. Sit across from your partner.
2. Each of you can close your eyes and attune to your breath.
3. Then open your eyes, staying connected to your own rhythm of breathing.
4. Extend awareness to the rhythm of your partner's breathing, perhaps noticing the rise and fall of your partner's belly or chest.
5. After a few moments of breath entrainment, pick up your instrument.
6. Begin to play a gentle rhythm in relation, allowing a rhythm of conversation to emerge between the two of you—allow space for listening and expressing/playing.
7. Notice what you feel inside—play your present moment experience of being in relationship with your partner.
8. After 5–10 minutes of playing, close your eyes and begin to soften the volume of your rhythm back in attunement with your breath, until it is barely perceptible.
9. Return awareness to your breath.
10. When this feels complete, open your eyes and thank your partner for this practice.

Final Remarks: The Fertile Ground of the Present Moment

We are interconnected beings, resonating moment to moment on the level of dialogue and in our bodies, emotions, and brains. This sense of connection exercises the social engagement system defined by Polyvagal Theory (Porges, 2011), releasing the barriers to relationship, eliciting safety, and promoting growth. In psychotherapy, therapists' attunement to the fertile ground of the present moment, and to both the visible and invisible expressions of a client's experience, allows clients to feel deeply felt, seen, and understood, activating a sense of safety in relationship.

Polyvagal Theory helps to explain the neural mechanisms of how presence evokes safety and growth. The bidirectional communication of brains and bodies allows therapists with intention for presence to serve as regulators in relationship with their clients. An understanding of how therapists affect their clients' neurophysiology helps them to be intentional in using nonverbal means to attune with their clients in a way that facilitates a positive and effective therapeutic relationship.

As a foundation to optimal therapeutic effectiveness, I propose that therapeutic presence grounded in Polyvagal principles be provided as an essential part of psychotherapy training. Understanding the components and functioning of the mammalian nervous system gives the therapist a whole new set of tools to use in establishing and communicating presence with and for their clients. The larger sense of interconnection that ensues from this foundational state invites a healthy state for both therapists and clients.

References

Allison, K. L., & Rossouw, P. J. (2013). The therapeutic alliance: Exploring the concept of "safety" from a neuropsychotherapeutic perspective. *International Journal of Neuropsychotherapy, 1*(1), 21–29. doi: 10.12744/ijnpt.2013.0021-0029

Behrends, A., Müller, S., & Dziobek, I. (2012). Moving in and out of synchrony: A concept for a new intervention fostering empathy through interactional movement and dance. *The Arts in Psychotherapy, 39*(2), 107–116. doi:10.1016/j.aip.2012.02.003

Booth, D., & Hachiya, M. (2004). *The arts go to school.* Markham, Canada: Pembroke.

Buber, M. (1958). *I and Thou* (2nd ed.). New York, NY: Scribner.

Carter, C. S. (2014). Oxytocin pathways and the evolution of human behavior. *Annual Review of Psychology, 65,* 17–39. doi:10.1146/annurev-psych-010213-115110

Cozolino, L. J. (2006). *The neuroscience of relationships: Attachment and the developing social brain.* New York, NY: Norton.

Dunn, R., Callahan, J. L., Swift, J. K., & Ivanovic, M. (2013). Effects of pre-session centering for therapists on session presence and effectiveness. *Psychotherapy Research, 23,* 78–85.

Ferrari, P. F., & Rizzolatti, G. (2014). Mirror neuron research: The past and the future. *Philosophical Transactions of the Royal Society B, 369*(20130169), 1–4. doi:10.1098/rstb.2013.0169

Fogel, A. (2009). *The Psychophysiology of self-awareness: Rediscovering the lost art of body sense.* New York, NY: Norton.

Gazzola, V., Aziz-Zadeh, L., & Keysers, C. (2006). Empathy and the somatotopic auditory mirror system in humans. *Current Biology, 16*, 1824–1829.

Geller, S. M. (2009). Cultivation of therapeutic presence: Therapeutic drumming and mindfulness practices. *Tijdschrift Cliëntgerichte Psychotherapie, 47*(4), 273–287.

Geller, S. M. (2010). *Clearing the path of therapeutic presence to emerge: Therapeutic rhythm and mindfulness practices.* Unpublished manuscript.

Geller, S. M. (2017). *A guide to cultivating therapeutic presence.* Washington, DC: American Psychological Association.

Geller, S. M., & Greenberg, L. S. (2002). Therapeutic presence: Therapists' experience of presence in the psychotherapeutic encounter. *Person-Centered & Experiential Psychotherapies, 1*, 71–86.

Geller, S. M., & Greenberg, L. S. (2012). *Therapeutic presence: A mindful approach to effective therapy.* Washington, DC: American Psychological Association.

Geller, S. M., Greenberg, L. S., & Watson, J. C. (2010). Therapist and client perceptions of therapeutic presence: The development of a measure. *Journal of Psychotherapy Research, 20*(5), 599–610.

Geller, S. M., & Porges, S. W. (2014). Therapeutic presence: Neurophysiological mechanisms mediating feeling safe in therapeutic relationships. *Journal of Psychotherapy Integration, 24*(3), 178–192.

Glenberg, A. M. (2010). Embodiment as a unifying perspective for psychology. *WIREs Cognitive Science, 1*, 586–596. doi:10.1002/wcs.55

Hayes, J., & Vinca, J. (2011). *Therapist presence and its relationship to empathy, session, depth, and symptom reduction.* Paper presented at the meeting of the Society for Psychotherapy Research, Bern, Switzerland.

Imel, Z. E., Barco, J. S., Brown, H. J., Baucom, B. R., Kircher, J. C., Baer, J. S., & Atkins, D. C. (2014). The association of therapist empathy and synchrony in vocally encoded arousal. *Journal of Counseling Psychology, 61*(1), 146–153. doi:10.1037/a0034943

Koole, S. L., & Tschacher, W. (2016). Synchrony in psychotherapy: A review and an integrative framework for the therapeutic alliance. *Frontiers in Psychology 7*(862), 1–17. doi:10.3389/fpsyg.2016.00862

Lindenberger, U., Li, S., Gruber, W., & Müller, V. (2009). Brains swinging in concert: Cortical phase synchronization while playing guitar. *BMV Neuroscience, 10*(22), 1–12. doi:10.1186/1471-2202-10-22

Llobera, J., Charbonnier, C., Chagué, S., Preissmann, D., Antonietti, J., Ansermet, F., & Magistretti, P. J. (2016). The subjective sensation of synchrony: An experimental study. *PLoS ONE, 11*(2), 1–18. doi:10.1371/journal.pone.0147008

Marci, C. D., Ham, J., Moran, E., & Orr, S. P. (2007). Physiologic correlates of perceived therapist empathy and social-emotional process during psychotherapy. *The Journal of Nervous and Mental Disease, 195*, 103–111.

Marci, C. D., & Orr, S. P. (2006). The effect of emotional distance on psychophysiologic concordance and perceived empathy between patient and interviewer. *Applied Psychophysiology and Biofeedback, 31*, 115–128.

Marsh, K. L., Richardson, M. J., & Schmidt, R. C. (2009). Social connection through joint action and interpersonal coordination. *Topics in Cognitive Science, 1*, 320–339. doi:10.1111/j.1756-8765.2009.01022.x

McFarland, D. H. (2001). Respiratory markers of conversational interaction. *Journal of Speech, Language, and Hearing Research, 44*(1), 128–143. doi:10.1044/1092-4388(2001/012)

Mitkidis, P., McGraw, J. J., Roepstorff, A., & Wallot, S. (2015). Building trust: Heart rate synchrony and arousal during joint action increased by public goods game. *Physiology & Behavior, 149*, 101–106.

Norcross, J. C. (2011). *Psychotherapy relationships that work: Evidence-based responsiveness* (2nd ed.). New York, NY: Oxford University Press.

Porges, S. W. (1995). Orienting in a defensive world: Mammalian modifications of our evolutionary heritage: A Polyvagal Theory. *Psychophysiology, 32*(4), 301–318.

Porges, S. W. (1998). Love: An emergent property of the mammalian autonomic nervous system. *Psychoneuroendocrinology, 23*, 837–861.

Porges, S. W. (2003). Social engagement and attachment: A phylogenetic perspective. *Annals of the New York Academy of Sciences, 1008*, 31–47.

Porges, S. W. (2011). *The Polyvagal Theory: Neurophysiological foundations of emotions, attachment, communication, self-regulation*. New York, NY: Norton.

Porges, S., & Carter, S. (2014, June). *The Polyvagal Theory: The physiology of love and social behavior and clinical applications*. Lecture conducted from Leading Edge Seminars, Toronto, Canada.

Pos, A., Geller, S., & Oghene, J. (2011). *Therapist presence, empathy, and the working alliance in experiential treatment for depression*. Paper presented at the meeting of the Society for Psychotherapy Research, Bern, Switzerland.

Quillman, T. (2012). Neuroscience and therapist self-disclosure: Deepening right brain to right brain communication between therapist and patient. *Clinical Social Work Journal, 40*, 1–9.

Ramseyer F., & Tschacher, W. (2011). Nonverbal synchrony in psychotherapy: Coordinated body movement reflects relationship quality and outcome. *Journal of Consulting and Clinical Psychology, 79*(3), 284–295. doi:10.1037/a0023419a

Sänger, J., Müller, V., & Lindenberger, U. (2012). Intra- and interbrain synchronization and network properties when playing guitar in duets. *Frontiers in Human Neuroscience, 6*(312), 1–19. doi:10.3389/fnhum.2012.00312

Schore, A. N. (2009). Right-brain affect regulation: An essential mechanism of development, trauma, dissociation, and psychotherapy. In D. Fosha, D. Siegel, & M. Solomon (Eds.), *The healing power of emotion: Affective neuroscience, development & clinical practice* (pp. 112–144). New York, NY: Norton.

Schore, A. N. (2012). *The science and art of psychotherapy*. New York, NY: Norton.

Siegel, D. J. (2010). *The mindful therapist: A clinician's guide to mindsight and neural integration*. New York, NY: Norton.

Stern, D. (2004). *The present moment in psychotherapy and every day life*. New York, NY: Norton.

Warner, R. M. (1996). Coordinated cycles in behavior and physiology during face-to-face social interactions. In J. H. Watt & C. A. VanLear (Eds.), *Cycles and dynamic patterns in communication processes* (pp. 327–352). Newbury Park, CA: Sage.

Winkelman, M. (2003). Complementary therapy for addiction: "Drumming out drugs." *American Journal of Public Health, 93*(4), 647–665.

8

Brain-Empowered Collaborators: Polyvagal Perspectives on the Doctor–Patient Relationship

George Thompson

Abstract: Brain-Empowered Collaborators describes applications of Polyvagal Theory to understand physician–patient relationships. Awareness of the neurophysiology underlying reactions to illness and medical treatment informs physicians of when to build trust and when to gather medical information. By attuning to their polyvagal state and sending verbal and nonverbal signals of safety, physicians can activate the patient's social engagement system, the optimum neurophysiology for decision making, comfort, and collaboration. A grounding in Polyvagal Theory enriches the tender and heroic partnership between patients and their physicians, offers insight into physician well-being, and suggests pathways to peace for the planet as well. Relationship becomes medicine.

Mark Roberts, a pediatric oncologist, knew that the boy could die before the day was over. Fourteen-year-old Tannor had been diagnosed with leukemia a year earlier. Now he was lying in a hospital bed with a fever and a tender belly, his mother a wary guardian at his side. The two doctors going off duty told

Dr. Roberts that they were worried about appendicitis, potentially fatal when leukemia and chemotherapy have conspired to destroy the immune system. When those doctors had tried to examine him, Tannor had thrown them out of the room.

It was Dr. Roberts's turn. Tannor's mom was stationed in a chair to the right of his head, where she could see Dr. Roberts through a window well before he arrived. Tannor was motionless, his sheet pulled up to his shoulders, his legs extended stiffly down the bed. "When I entered," Dr. Roberts told me later, "Tannor's mother glared at me, but he kept staring straight forward, not even acknowledging my presence. Had he made the smallest gesture, she would have told me, 'It's time for you to go.'"

Tannor's brain had made a critical and potentially lethal error. It gauged the doctors to be dangerous, and summoned defensive systems to protect him from potential harm. These defensive systems were preventing him from allowing the examination and treatment that could save his life. He was in the midst of a neurophysiological crisis, on top of his surgical emergency. For Tannor to survive, his brain needed to immediately reevaluate what was safe and what was dangerous. But this neurophysiology arises below the cortex, outside the thinking and speaking brain. In short, Tannor couldn't control his reaction because he was not aware that it was taking place.

Polyvagal Theory, originated and developed over the past 40 years by neuroscientist Stephen Porges (2011), describes brain processes essential to understanding and resolving Tannor's impasse. As we have seen in other chapters, Dr. Porges proposed that an instantaneous, automatic, and unconscious neurological assessment determines whether a given situation is safe or dangerous. The process, which Dr. Porges called *neuroception*, then immediately initiates changes in the autonomic nervous system to match the perceived needs of the moment. If the system detects safety, the ventral vagal social engagement system comes online, allowing us to relax, calm down, and prepare to engage with others. Perceived threat, on the other hand, triggers fight-or-flight activation of the sympathetic nervous system and prepares our bodies to run or attack.

Porges proposed that inescapable life-threat triggers dorsal vagal collapse, fainting or "death feigning," a survival mechanism, which appeared in early in vertebrate evolution (e.g., fish, amphibians, and reptiles), presumably to make the animal a less appealing target to predators (2011). *Partial* dorsal vagal shutdown responses, as in Tannor's case, can appear as immobility, emotional numbing, difficulty thinking, inability to put thoughts into words, and losing touch with one's surroundings, (i.e., dissociation; McKinnon et al., 2016). These three systems together are known as the *autonomic nervous system* (ANS).

Dr. Roberts could have told the boy, "Your brain has made an error. Those people aren't out to get you. You need them to survive." But Tannor saw Dr. Roberts as a threat. If Dr. Roberts tried to reason with him, Tannor would simply have kicked Dr. Roberts out of the room too. In order to save Tannor's life, Dr. Roberts needed to first reengage Tannor's ventral vagal system, the calm, connected, openhearted and open-minded state in which more thoughtful reflection could take place. It was not a matter of simply telling him it was safe. Dr. Roberts needed to send enough signals of safety to the boy's ANS that his brain concluded that things truly were safe now. Only then would Tannor be able to rationally consider whether to let the doctors examine him.

The Physiology of the Doctor–Patient Relationship

Much attention has been paid to the robust benefits of the physician–patient relationship and how to make it even stronger (Fortin, Dwamena, Frankel, & Smith, 2012). But, because we have only just started to look at the physician–patient relationship through the lens of Polyvagal Theory, neither Dr. Roberts nor the physicians that Tannor dismissed had been trained to consider the neurophysiology underlying the boy's refusal of help. They had not been trained to consider that a patient's neuroception automatically scans for cues of safety and danger. They had not been trained to consider that a patient's abilities can vastly differ in states of ventral vagal social engagement, sympathetic fight-or-flight, and dorsal vagal shutdown. Finally, the doctors had not been trained to consider the neurobiological rationale for reversing the patient's shutdown and reviving awareness, connection, and initiative.

In short, these physicians had polyvagal blindness.

I met Dr. Roberts just as I began writing this chapter. Our conversation about his work with children who had cancer revealed his natural ability to address patients' sense of safety and move them into a ventral vagal state. But he knew little of Polyvagal Theory and its application to a physician's interpersonal work with patients and their families. He agreed to allow me to interview him and explain Polyvagal Theory as we went along.

Even though when he saw Tannor, Dr. Roberts could not yet use Polyvagal Theory as a tool of understanding, predicting, and problem solving, he did know how to proceed effectively. In his years of pediatric oncology practice, he had met with thousands of children and their parents. All were shocked to receive a cancer diagnosis and terrified that the malignancy would kill the child. Dr. Roberts listened to these families to understand their experiences and be of genuine help. Over time, he developed a philosophy and approach that he and his patients found valuable. He described it to me this way:

> Treat patients with respect, dignity and honesty. Give them facts; let them know what's happening to them. Create an open relationship where they can talk about cancer and death. Keep balancing realism and optimism. Give them a chance to be cured and have a happy life. Establish a profoundly human partnership to ease the burden of knowing that this is a kid that could die. (personal communication, 2015)

Dr. Roberts was describing the calm and engaged ventral vagal state without knowing it. The ventral vagal state establishes the neurophysiological foundation for a vital human relationship: the tender and heroic partnership between patients and their physicians as they navigate the rough waters of illness, injury, and death. When these storms of life are interpreted as threats, they rally the sympathetic nervous system to fight or flee or even cause dorsal vagal shutdown. Shutdown is where Dr. Roberts found Tannor.

Several years ago, I got real-life experience in how Polyvagal Theory plays out from the patient's perspective. I was diagnosed with a very aggressive lymphoma that threatened to end my life much too soon. Now and then, my nervous system abruptly swung into high gear, and an "emotional hijacking" (Goleman, 2005) swept me along in the turmoil. Test results were potential death sentences. I was afraid I would not enjoy this lifetime, with my wife, AnnMarie, and our children, that we had imagined. Sometimes, when the worries got the best of me, the fear was physical—chest tightening, heart pounding, and sweating. Because I had already begun studying Polyvagal Theory, I kept one interested eye on what was happening in my brain, even while my other eye was fixed on survival.

Patients and Physicians: A Duet of Fear

Patients experience any number of threats when seeking medical care. Colleen Sweeney, who has surveyed patients extensively about their fears, reported that they worry about the severity of their condition, the pain that a procedure might cause, inability to pay their medical bills, or humiliation for failing to follow their treatment plan (Sweeney, in press). They fear that they will not be able to adequately communicate their needs, that there will be a mix-up in their procedures, or that the people caring for them are not competent. So when patients arrive at the clinic or in the emergency room, they are often in a state of vulnerability (Elmqvist, Fridlund, & Ekebergh, 2012), their nervous systems activated to defend against the threats they fear.

Ultimately, a person is either open or defensive (Baylin & Hughes, 2016). In ventral vagal engagement, people open up to each other. In sympathetic arousal and dorsal vagal shutdown, people are defensive. Defensive people make others uneasy.

Physicians, striving to remain open, must recognize and negotiate their own internal danger signals. In preparation for writing this chapter, I asked physicians about the threats *they* face in their work with patients. One physician, whom I'll call Dr. M, said that not knowing the diagnosis or how to answer a question threatens her, as does attempting a difficult intubation without backup. In these situations, she feels agitated, annoyed, even a little angry. She can feel it in her heart and hands. Her thought processes don't move like she wants them to—she feels thick headed. Even though she might not know what to do or how to do it, she has multiple backup plans.

Another physician I'll call Dr. C also told me that he feels threatened when there is a rapidly changing and confusing clinical picture that he is not able to diagnose. He also feels vulnerable when he is not able to reach his patient and form an alliance, as he feels he should. About these situations, he said, "It's like you are walking through mud. I don't want to walk into that room. It's almost twice as hard—dealing with the situation and the mud."

Several physicians talked about the effect of nurses' neurophysiology on the team. Dr. C said, "The other night we had a patient who was tanking. We had to intubate, use pressors, all the things you learn to do. If we have nurses who are calm, who know how to handle the problems, that makes all the difference. An anxious nurse makes you put attention on them rather than the patient." Marilyn Sanders, neonatologist and author of Chapter 20 in this book, said, "During what I call my worst day, with a baby dying and the room in chaos, a senior nurse looked me in the eyes, and very steadily said, 'What do you need me to do?' She gave me her steely determination." Dr. Sanders's husband Peter added, "That's when you became confident that you could be confident."

When I asked Dr. Roberts his reaction to Tannor's situation, he described a different reaction: "There's a calm that comes over you—you think, 'I'll panic later. It's time to go in there and be effective. Failure could mean death of a child.'" Dr. Sanders, who understands Polyvagal Theory, said, "For me, I have to allow the vagal brake to come off, to allow the energy to come to handle the crisis." She needs to relax her ventral vagal activation just a bit to unleash enough sympathetic activity to meet the challenges she faces.

Doctors told me that threats come from outside the doctor–patient relationship as well. Insurance companies deny payment for needed medical services. Government inspectors enforce burdensome regulations. Administrative glitches impede positive action. And there are always legal hazards lurking—medical malpractice, HIPAA violations, and so on. One physician told me,

> Lawsuits don't bother me much. But things that are so unrelated to my clinical duties, like an administrator telling me to discharge a patient from the hospital in the next 48 hours when they need another week or two—that gets me sympathetically activated. I have to work really hard to stay regulated, and the nurses protect me some. But I may have to go from that situation, talk with a family whose loved one is dying, then run a code. You may get a few minutes to grieve a loss. And sometimes not. Things cluster and the beeper goes off. (personal communication, 2015)

Given the multiple threats facing both physicians and patients, and the built-in tendency of neuroception to mobilize protective measures when it detects danger, it is a minor miracle that a patient ever shows up to a clinic to ask for help at all—and that a physician is there to offer it.

Facing a Dilemma

When I interviewed Dr. Roberts, I had been teaching doctor–patient communication to medical students and psychiatric residents for more than 20 years. My goal in teaching was to support students to be fully present with their patients, attending to their needs. I wanted to empower students to express the compassion that had inspired most of them to go into the medical profession in the first place, which medical education and practice could grind down and even destroy (Dyrbye & Shanafelt, 2016). I also wanted to introduce my students to the powerful working partnership that I knew physicians and patients could develop, and the joy that such partnerships could bring, even, or especially, in the face of sickness.

Some of my students dove into the learning. They had gone into medicine intending to offer compassionate care to patients. Many had been to doctor visits with their loved ones—a grandmother with Alzheimer's, a brother with heart disease, a parent who had died. In most cases, the physicians of these students' family members had been humane, caring, and sensitive, as well as skilled in diagnosis and medical intervention. The students had also seen what happened when insensitive doctors had ignored the human aspects of their family's situation. They winced at the demoralizing effects such ignorance had had on their loved ones' spirits. In my view, these kinds of students were humanists.

Another group of students had gone into medicine with a completely different—and no less valuable—set of interests and aspirations. These were the scientists. They loved reading about the discoveries made in labs and clinics of years past. They relished the great intellectual mysteries and the elegant ways that medical insights were coaxed from the depths of the unknown. But, because they were focused on the physical world of the body and biology, the course often made little sense to them. They asked, "Why do I need a course in talking? I have been talking since I was two!" They had not yet discovered the inner, experiential world of hopes and fears, beliefs, feelings, stories, and faith. How could I awaken them to the magic of the human?

Building Bonds of Attachment

The answer to my question came from an unexpected direction. Several years ago at KidsTLC, Inc., the Kansas City–area behavioral health agency where I work as a child psychiatrist, my colleagues and I came to the realization that many of the children we worked with had suffered early abuse, trauma, neglect, and abandonment, adverse experiences known to cause what Bessel van der Kolk and his colleagues call *developmental trauma disorder* (2005). Dr. van der Kolk says that psychologically harmful experiences disrupt the child's normal process of acquiring fundamental capacities: for example, the capacity to form stable, trusting relationships; to allow caregivers to help regulate their intense emotional states; and to make sense of experiences in coherent, understandable ways. Although we succeeded in helping a number of these children, there were others whom we could not find a way to reach.

We learned that psychologist Dan Hughes had created an approach, called Dyadic Developmental Psychotherapy (DDP), that effectively addresses these children's underlying issues (2006). Because abused children have understandably concluded that adults are not trustworthy, the goal of DDP is to help these children learn to trust the good foster and adoptive parents who are raising them now. KidsTLC invited Dr. Hughes to train us in this approach.

Dr. Hughes introduced us to Polyvagal Theory. Although aware of fight-or-flight and shutdown, we had never learned about ventral vagal responses and the signals of safety that elicit them. Like Tannor's doctors, we were missing the polyvagal perspective that was critical to helping our patients heal. We too had polyvagal blindness.

Dr. Hughes taught us to be playful, accepting, curious, and empathic, a deportment known by the acronym PACE (2006). The PACE attitude actively signals to the child's nervous system that the adult is safe, moving the child into a ventral vagal, socially engaged relationship. When adult and child are both in ventral vagal social engagement, we clinicians can help the child build trusting relationships, learn new social skills, and process trauma. Likewise, we can teach direct-care staff and parents to become what we at KidsTLC call a *competent companion*, a person who stays ventral vagal while accompanying someone through life's trials and tribulations with compassion and expertise (Thompson & Mock, 2016).

Teaching the Interpersonal Neurobiology of the Doctor–Patient Relationship

Many days I drove from KidsTLC to teach medical students in the CUES (communication, understanding, education, and self-assessment) to Medical Communications course at the University of Missouri–Kansas City (UMKC) School of Medicine. My emerging learnings traveled with me. I saw that Polyvagal Theory could be applied not only to the parent–child relationship but to the doctor–patient relationship as well. In fact, Dr. Sue Carter, the behavioral neurobiologist who first identified the physiological mechanisms responsible for social monogamy, says that the mother–child interaction is the prototype for all nurturing relationships (2014).

It occurred to me that I could reach those science-oriented students by presenting polyvagal neurophysiology as an understandable rationale for exploring medical communication skills. Experience had shown me that if I could get students to try these communications strategies with their patients in clinic, their patients' positive feedback would provide more and more reasons for them to keep developing these skills. The good results they produced would stoke a self-rewarding cycle: Success with patients would motivate more communication skills practice, leading to further success with patients.

My heart stirred with a growing recognition that this work was part of my life purpose: to awaken people to the power and grace and interconnectedness that arises from wholeheartedly embracing our humanity.

I envisioned training science-focused students to be competent companions, able to attend compassionately and faithfully to patients and their families, while understanding their biology as well. Their patients would feel well cared for, both medically and emotionally. And students would awaken to the uplifting feelings of satisfaction that come from caring for the whole person, as a whole person.

Soothing Tannor's Brain

Dr. Roberts continued telling me what happened with Tannor.

> I sat in the chair at the foot of Tannor's bed for 15 minutes before anyone said anything. I was in a heightened state of awareness, watching for cues about what was happening. He was sick; he was in pain. I had decided that I

> was not the one to talk first. Eventually Tannor demanded, "So, why are you here?" I simply told him, "I am the on-call doctor," and then returned to a friendly and calm silence. Another 15 minutes went by before Tannor asked a bit more quietly, "Well, what are you going to do?" I said, "I am not going to do anything without your permission." (personal communication, 2015)

Dr. Roberts explained that more minutes passed, but not as many as before, then:

> Tannor asked, with some measure of curiosity, "So, what is it that you want to do?" Still in my chair, I said, "I am concerned that you have an infection in your appendix that is making you feel so bad. I want to find out exactly what's going on." Tannor asked me, "What will that take?" I explained that I needed to listen to his belly with a stethoscope. I needed to press on his belly too, and he could tell me to stop if it hurt. I promised to tell him everything I was learning, every step of the way. He agreed to let me examine him. Then his mother dropped her guard as well. (personal communication, 2015)

When Dr. Roberts finished the story, I described Polyvagal Theory to him, clarifying that Tannor's shutdown was a dorsal vagal response and his mother was experiencing sympathetic mobilization to defend her son. Dr. Roberts's behavior sent signals of safety to Tannor's brain. As the boy's neuroception slowly accepted these signals, indicating that danger was receding and that the environment was becoming safe, he was able to generate new responses that were appropriate to a safe context. The brain could tell other organs: *Calm down. No need for alarm. Danger has passed. Let Dr. Roberts approach. He represents no threat. Listen to what he is saying.*

We talked about Tannor's mother. She was keenly attuned to Tannor's frozen panic. Only when her polyvagal neuroception determined that Tannor was not defending himself from danger did it conclude that the situation was becoming safe. That's when she relaxed too.

When Tannor's and his mother's nervous systems moved from sympathetic fight-or-flight into ventral vagal, the shift activated a number of physiological responses that Porges (2011) describes: Heart rate, blood pressure, and breathing were normalizing. Pupils were constricting, not needing so much light. The eardrums were tuning to the human voice rather than to lower-pitched frequencies associated with predators and dangers (think a growl or low roar of an earthquake or landslide). Facial muscles were looser and more animated. Musicality was returning to their speech. The mother's and boy's neurophysiologies were now preparing them to work as productive, trusting partners with Dr. Roberts.

Thinking With Polyvagal Theory

I have taught in the CUES to Medical Communications course since 2002. We always start the course by teaching nonverbal communication skills, which are the very skills that Dr. Roberts instinctively employed with Tannor. They include putting the patient at ease by placing oneself in nonthreatening positions and stances, and using tone of voice and facial expressions that telegraph safety.

When we teach students Polyvagal Theory, they realize that their own calming nonverbal communication conveys a neurobiologically effective sense of safety and connection to the patient. We teach them to "think with the theory" (Schon, 1983) by observing whether their interventions help their patients let go and open up as they'd predicted. With polyvagal awareness, the students begin to better understand how to "translate" various patient behaviors. The "fight" response often looks like an angry or resistant patient. The "flight" response often looks like submissive acquiescence without follow-through.

The act of understanding brain function can generate a fuller comprehension of human experience as well. One student, noticing nonverbal signs of fearfulness, discovered that his patient heard gunshots in her apartment complex day and night. She had been enduring a life-threatening situation and the physiological panic responses that went with it. Given what my student had learned about Polyvagal Theory and fear, he could put himself squarely into her physiological and emotional shoes.

Equally, as human experience is illuminated, our understanding of brain function deepens too (Hughes, 2012). For example, that same student, empathizing with the experience of his patient's chronic stress, developed a vivid grasp of what happens in the brain of a person who is relentlessly confined to a dangerous situation.

Patients experience states of alarm in non-life-threatening situations as well. While undergoing chemotherapy, I recognized a fear of needles that I had simply endured. Each time my blood was to be drawn, I got anxious and my chest tightened, even though I told myself that the needles wouldn't injure me or hurt very much. One study found that 22% of patients had a fear of needles, and over half of those had sympathetic symptoms (dry mouth, sweating, and shortness of breath) or dorsal vagal symptoms (feeling nauseated, faint, and dizzy) (Wright, Yelland, Heathcote, Ng, & Wright, 2009). The study authors point out that, because each year globally people get around 12 billion injections, the cumulative impact of this fear is enormous.

Letting the Patient Lead

As it turned out, the textbook we chose for the CUES to Medical Communications course presented an approach to the doctor–patient relationship that implicitly addressed polyvagal concerns, though we had not heard of Polyvagal Theory at that point. The approach and the text, both called Patient-Centered Interviewing, began by asking the patient what concerns brought her to clinic—both medical symptoms and how they affect her life (Fortin et al., 2012). They encouraged the physician to look for the emotions that the situation has stirred up and to use empathy skills to help manage these emotions. Although the text did not explicitly conceptualize the empathy skills as addressing the patient's polyvagal state, in my experience, using this approach sends calming signals of safety. The stage is now set for physician and patient to work together to clarify threats to health, diagnose the medical and psychosocial issues, and make a plan to address the situation.

The patient-centered portion of the interview demonstrates to patients that the physician is interested in them as a whole person, both in their symptoms and in the personal and emotional impact that the symptoms have had. This approach is patient centered because *the physician follows where the patient leads*. Dr. Roberts, in allowing Tannor to be in charge, was patient centered. In physician-centered interviewing, *the physician leads and the patient follows*—into questions about past medical history, family medical history, social factors, and a general review of symptoms. After patient-centered interviewing, the patient is ready to turn control over to the physician because the physician has demonstrated that she is prioritizing the patient's needs and experiences, and is therefore worthy of the patient's trust. In practice, control of the interaction may switch back and forth between patient and physician many times during a visit, in a process that Dr. Hughes calls "follow-lead-follow" (Baylin & Hughes, 2016, p.168).

After the interview comes the physical exam. Abraham Verghese, a noted proponent of a collaborative doctor–patient relationship, pointed out that the exam can be experienced as dangerous, because it may involve disrobing as well as touch (Verghese, Brady, Costanzo Kapur, & Horwitz, 2011). But, he said, the exam is not only a potential threat; it is an opportunity to increase safety. Dr. Verghese believes that "when a sick patient is examined with skill, it goes a long way in earning trust and authority. It may affirm the personal commitment between doctor and patient at a deeper level—the unspoken, 'I will always be with you. I will not let you suffer'"(p. 552). The depth of this commitment sends a powerful signal that the physician is dedicated to supporting the patient's well-being.

Even after patient-centered interviewing induces a patient to feel calmly connected to his doctor, a sense of danger can reawaken, for example, if his physician touches a painful body part, or asks a question that inadvertently touches a sensitive subject. Consequently, we teach students to observe the patient's facial expression and tone of voice for nonverbal cues of upset, because they are readable and reliable indicators of a person's autonomic state (Porges, 2015a). Addressing how the patient is feeling in that moment and sending signals of safety prepares the patient for a return to clinical questioning. Again, this is the "follow-lead-follow" strategy that Dr. Hughes encouraged.

Caroline Dawson, my partner in the CUES course, teaches students a lovely way to empathically inquire about these shifts in patient's experiential reality by asking, in effect, "What happened that *that* happened?" For example, "I noticed that when I asked about your family history of heart disease, the expression of your face changed, and you started looking at the floor. What was going on for you when I asked that?" This refocusing on patient experience again sends signals of safety to the patient's autonomic nervous system, especially when accompanied by calming facial expressions and vocal intonations on the part of the physician.

When I asked Dr. Roberts to reflect some more on what happened with Tannor, he said, "I knew that two doctors had been thrown out of the room. So obviously my first goal was, 'Don't get thrown out.' In my mind I could see Tannor and his mother in a World War I foxhole. They had tense posturing." That made him think, "If I am overly active, I will be shot at." He went on, "I made a quick calculation. I sat below the physical level of the patient." Then Dr. Roberts realized a key factor. "Sitting down broke the dynamic. Tannor felt that others were trying to control him. By sitting down, I showed him that I wasn't going to dominate. With me, Tannor had control over the situation."

Relationship as Medicine

Dr. Roberts's ventral vagal social engagement system saved Tannor's life. This dramatic statement is true for two reasons. First, Dr. Roberts's ventral vagal state supported Tannor to relax and reflect. It was as if a scene from an old war movie played out, as the sentry of Tannor's neuroception demanded: "Hark, who goes there! Friend or foe?" Dr. Roberts, in the role of the approaching soldier, had to give the designated nonverbal countersign to demonstrate that he was a friend. As Tannor's neuroception received these nonverbal signals, the boy's autonomic nervous system grasped that there was safety in the midst of danger. It lowered its defenses and prepared for collaboration.

Second, because Dr. Roberts's mind was open and clear, he could see that Tannor was a desperate boy, clinging to his very life. The physician could free-associate; he could see solutions. Dr. Porges said, "Safe states are a prerequisite not only for optimal social behaviour, but also for accessing the higher brain structures that enable humans to be creative and generative" (2015a, p.115). The safe state of Dr. Roberts's own autonomic nervous system gave him the interior freedom to find an approach that would help Tannor.

Surgeon Glenn Talboy tells CUES students that emergency situations demand a particularly advanced level of communication skill. In surgical emergencies, he must connect quickly with the patient and family, help to calm them as much as possible, and provide the necessary information clearly, succinctly, and compassionately. Complicating the situation, the more threatening the medical situation, the more fearful and shut down the patient typically is.

In the emergency situation, neither Dr. Talboy nor Dr. Roberts has the luxury of long months to get to establish trust with his patient, as does a primary care physician treating a patient with a chronic condition. Yet in Tannor's emergency, Dr. Roberts took the time to help the boy move into a ventral vagal state. In its way, it was as important a step as taking the time to induce anesthesia before operating. The good cognitive functioning Dr. Roberts fostered is crucial when a life is in jeopardy.

Physicians don't always have even the little time that Dr. Roberts took to connect with Tannor. When the medical needs of the situation demand immediate action—for example, when an unconscious patient has life-threatening bleeding—ethics, regulations, and laws allow intervention without the patient's consent. These necessary violations of the patient's right to decide can cause ruptures in her sense of safety and trust. After the crisis, the physician can seek to repair any break in the relationship by asking the patient about her experience of having decisions made on her behalf, listening compassionately, and making apologies when appropriate.

Today, we teach medical students not only to observe their patients' nonverbal cues, but also to be aware of their own autonomic state. Dr. Hughes said that whenever two people relate to each other from different polyvagal states, whoever stays in his own state the longest will bring the other into that state (2012). If the physician stays calm and engaged long enough, the patient will usually move from fight-or-flight (or shutdown) into the social engagement system as well. This is neurophysiological leadership—and relationship as medicine. Dr. Jon Baylin, Dr. Hughes's coauthor of *The Neurobiology of Attachment-Focused Therapy* (2016), highlighted the importance of being able to shift to more adaptive states by cleverly observing, "It is all about Interstate travel!" (J. Baylin, personal communication, November 2, 2016).

Bringing patients into ventral vagal has another benefit. As Porges put it, the nondefensive ventral vagal state "provides neural opportunities for us to learn and to form strong social bonds while simultaneously supporting health, growth and restoration" (2015a, p. 115). Not only does ventral vagal allow one to think and collaborate, it also benefits the body at a physiological level as well.

Aequanimitas Means "Composure"

A physician who is in fight-or-flight activation is concerned primarily with his own survival and protection. He may be inconsiderate and abrasive, or even desperate and reckless. He cannot regulate his autonomic nervous system, and his emotions will be dysregulated as well. He may yell at a patient, throw a clipboard at a nurse, or leave the room in a huff.

Dr. Louise Arnold, my mentor at UMKC, has used her long and distinguished career to study the nature of medical professionalism and how to advance it. Along with NYU professor of internal medicine David Stern, she described professionalism as including four necessary *aspirational* principles: excellence, humanism, accountability, and altruism. Drs. Arnold and Stern also described three *foundational* elements of professionalism: clinical competence, ethical understanding, and communication. The foundational elements comprise the attitudes, knowledge, and skills required to enact the aspirational principles. Drs. Arnold and Stern depicted this definition of medical professionalism as the steps and columns of a Greek temple. The three foundational elements are the steps of the temple, and the four aspirational principles are columns rising from steps (2006).

From a polyvagal perspective, medical professionalism requires the ability to maintain and regain a ventral vagal state no matter how threatening the circumstances. As Dr. Arnold and I have observed before (Arnold & Thompson, 2010):

> The value of professionalism is most visible when the stakes are high, information is incomplete, and no predictable solution to the situation exists . . . (Patterson, Grenny, McMillan, Switzler, & Covey, 2002). These circumstances can be associated with harmful reactions and emotions and unhelpful thought patterns that diminish one's ability to act professionally.

Ventral vagal social engagement enables the physician to maintain critical cognitive faculties (excellence), facilitate the emotional and neurologic well-being of the patient (humanism), and remain open and engaged when instinct prompts running, fighting, or hiding responses (altruism). Adequate ability to override more evolutionarily primitive reflexes in favor of an open and engaged outlook demands self-initiative and self-development (accountability).

Because the autonomic and emotional regulation found in ventral vagal social engagement appears necessary to deploying these aspirational virtues, we propose adding the ability to maintain and regain the ventral vagal as an additional foundational element, a fourth step of Drs. Arnold and Stern's Greek temple of professionalism.

In his valedictory address to the University of Pennsylvania School of Medicine graduates in May 1889, William Osler (n.d.) exhorted new physicians to develop a warmly genuine and autonomically regulated composure:

> Cultivate, then, gentlemen, such a judicious measure of obtuseness as will enable you to meet the exigencies of practice with firmness and courage, without, at the same time, hardening "the human heart by which we live" [cf. Wordsworth, 1807; reference not in the original]. . . . Hence the need of an infinite patience and of an ever-tender charity toward these fellow-creatures.

Though in 1889, Dr. Osler could not have been familiar with the term *ventral vagal*, he was nonetheless describing just that—the nonreactive, openhearted, caring and concerned, body-mind state of a competent social engagement system.

Physician, Heal Thyself

How do we physicians develop such composure ourselves? Dr. Arnold and I have spent numerous hours talking about how to help students develop professional virtues. Only partly in jest, we dreamed aloud of a medical training that was part lab, part clinic, and part monastery, where character is developed along with mental alacrity and physical dexterity.

Dr. Porges maintains that one can enter the ventral vagal through the doorways of meditation and religious practice (2014). For example, Dr. Ronald Epstein, a physician who studies how to improve communication between clinicians, patients, and their families, proposed that practicing mindfulness increases a physician's ability to maintain reflectiveness even in emotionally stressful situations (1999). He says that the goal of mindfulness practice for physicians is the ability to join in "compassionate informed action in the world, to use a wide array of data, make correct decisions, understand the patient, and relieve suffering" (1999, p. 838).

Over the past 15 years, my own self-development practice has been to start the day with exercises from Harry Palmer's Avatar® Course (Palmer, 2011; Palmer, 2012). Avatar teaches people to live deliberately by acting with purposeful determination, controlling attention skillfully, replacing self-denigrating beliefs with self-empowering perspectives, and relating to others with compassion, tolerance, and understanding. My personal objective in practicing the exercises has been to increase my sense of calmness, connection, and self-efficacy. This practice has likely had a neurophysiological effect of increasing my ability to be in a ventral vagal state.

Another result of practicing Avatar exercises is the development of what Palmer calls the witness viewpoint, "a quiet viewpoint that can watch consciousness" (2007). Jon Kabat-Zinn, who has studied and taught mindfulness meditation to patients and physicians alike, instructs us that "assuming the stance of an impartial witness" (2009, pp. 33–34) enables us to step back from our judgments and fearful reactions, while providing relief from stress as well.

I believe the witness viewpoint to be firmly centered in the social engagement system, providing a place of awareness from which to experience biology happening. It can observe while safely allowing adrenaline to pump, the heart to race, and muscles to tremble. For example, in a moment when large clumps of my hair were falling out due to chemotherapy, and with AnnMarie as support, I used an Avatar exercise to let wave after wave of visceral revulsion flow through me and be released. As Mr. Palmer said, the witness viewpoint is "sufficiently disengaged from your own consciousness that you can even watch emotion without becoming agitated" (2007).

A half hour later, I went to the Downtown Barbershop, where a man I'd never met before cut off what hair of mine remained. Learning of my situation, Jay told me I owed him nothing. He said, "You can pay me when your hair grows back!" I felt such loving companionship in those words. Jay touched my heart and moved me to tears. I was experiencing the emotion of elevation, a warm and open feeling in the chest that makes you want to be around people and become a better person (Haidt, 2003). Elevation theory postulates that vagal pathways play a role in this emotion. And the compassion Jay was most likely experiencing, in response to my suffering, may have its own connections to the vagus as well (Stellar, Cohen, Oveis, & Keltner, 2015). As I discovered so poignantly that day, the ventral vagal state may be filled with tenderness and blessings that transcend our ability to describe (D. Dana, personal communication, August 21, 2016).

I have not spoken much professionally of my self-development practice and the states of grace I have experienced. I feel a flush of embarrassment as I write about it even now, as I sense taboos against talking about intimate experiences in the presence of colleagues. But how will we physicians recognize the benefits of self-development if we don't speak of it with each other? Knowing what we now know about the positive impact of calm ventral vagal connectedness on the doctor–patient relationship, we cannot afford to remain silent about our own experiences any longer.

Accordingly, I teach medical students the Avatar Compassion Exercise (Palmer, 2008; also cf. www.theavatarcourse.com/compassion), which involves placing one's attention on another individual and then contemplating five statements, such as, "Just like me, this person is seeking some happiness for his/her life." "Just like me" is the most vital part of this practice, for it acknowledges that both you and another person seek these goals, and helps you to feel an authentic connection with him or her. The students who do the exercise say they feel calmer, more present, and more empathic toward the person they were considering. Some say that the exercise is their favorite part of the course. They carry a small card with the compassion instructions in their white coat pockets, pulling it out when they need a calmer and broader perspective.

The Physician as Patient

Experiencing illness personally can expand a physician's perspective as well. My first symptoms of lymphoma appeared in December 2012. My belly had swollen, and I was sweating day and night. My primary care physician, Loree Cordova, made time to see me during her lunch break. She examined me thoroughly and encouraged me to get a CT scan. In a state of dorsal vagal shutdown, I refused. Her help felt threatening, as I confused her efforts to diagnose my condition with the danger that the diagnosis itself represented. She did blood tests to get further information and to keep me engaged. Later that day she called with the lab results, which were inconclusive, but she continued to talk to me until she found a way to get through. She wondered how I was going to go on a family trip that weekend, not knowing the cause of my swollen belly? Her calm insistence in offering help, staying connected, and encouraging the scan, despite my efforts to push her away, enabled me to take action.

Three hours later I lay on a gurney, AnnMarie by my side, in the radiology department of the community hospital where I do occasional psychiatric consultations. Dr. Cordova came in to give my wife and me the news. The scan showed that I had more than 20 masses throughout my abdomen, including a 2 × 4 in. mass in my small intestine, right where it joins the colon.

Dr. Cordova didn't know what the masses were, but she had spent the previous half hour arranging a colonoscopy for the next morning to biopsy the largest one. Scheduling the colonoscopy was part of her philosophy of always giving patients a "next step" to evaluate or treat their symptoms or illness. The next step, after the colonoscopy, was an appointment with an oncologist. And so the next steps continued, all the way through chemotherapy and recovery. Dr. Cordova's consistent concern, thoughtfulness, and deliberate action plan conveyed the same message that Dr. Verghese attributed to skillful physical exam: "I will always be with you. I will not let you suffer." Her promise of presence was a compelling and potent hallmark of safety that moved me out of the dorsal vagal and into action.

After my fourth round of chemotherapy, I awoke in the middle of the night with nausea, vomiting, and a fever of 102.9 degrees. My oncologist had given me a card instructing my local doctors, if I got a fever, to look for infection and start antibiotics immediately afterward. For me, like Tannor, infection in that situation could be fatal. So I woke AnnMarie, looked for the card, and started to panic when I couldn't find it. "We need to get to the hospital," my wife said urgently. "Let's go!" Angrily, I refused to get in the car. She insisted. I refused again. I could hear her telling our neighbor what the oncologist had told her: "Do whatever you need to get him in the car. Pick him up and carry him. Call an ambulance if necessary." After what seemed like eons, I found the card and got in the car. AnnMarie made the two-minute drive to the hospital.

A few weeks later, AnnMarie and I were still blaming each other for almost killing me. We took some quiet minutes to connect and talk about what had happened from each of our perspectives. Listening to each other with care, my wife and I moved back into ventral vagal compassion and companionship. We realized that both of us had been trying to keep me alive, but our brains had shut down. This situation gave the physician and medical educator in me much more empathy for patients. Who knows what states of alarm and shutdown people have suffered in the process of getting themselves to the doctor!

Trusting Collaboration in the Ventral Vagal

Tannor, AnnMarie, and I had all experienced a state of alarm that prioritized defense and prevented us from communicating. Dr. Porges has proposed that the key factor in calming our alarm and preparing us to engage and collaborate is the ventral vagal state (2015a). Calmness allows us to approach each other in peace. This is the neurobiology of safe working relationships.

Safe partnership has benefits beyond what working together achieves. Drs. Lane Beckes and James Coan, cognitive and affective neuroscientists, posit that human brains operate more efficiently and effectively in collaboration with each other (2011). When people work together, their brains use less energy than when they work alone. Aligned with Polyvagal Theory, Drs. Beckes and Coan observe that signals of safety allow transition to this collaborative mode. They cite a remarkable experiment (Schnall, Harber, Stefanucci,

& Proffitt, 2008) in which standing next to a friend makes a hill look less steep than when one views the hill alone. And *the longer the friendship, the less steep the hill appears*. What an extraordinary metaphor for how companionship influences our outlook on the challenges of life.

Dr. Peter Fonagy is a psychoanalyst who is advancing our understanding of what creates secure and trusting relationships. Along with fellow psychoanalyst Dr. Liz Allison (2014), he wrote that humans' ability to form trusting relationships develops during childhood, when parents repeatedly recognize and understand that their children have their own experiences and intentions. Drs. Fonagy and Allison proposed that, even when adults did not experience such understanding in childhood, they may still learn to trust later in life—for example, when they feel that an empathetic therapist repeatedly grasps their subjective experience. In describing these phenomena, Drs. Fonagy and Allison highlighted the nature and characteristics of epistemic trust, which is "an individual's willingness to consider new knowledge from another person as trustworthy, generalizable, and relevant to the self" (2014, p. 373).

We see here other benefits of patient-centered interviewing: understanding the patient's perspective and experiences promotes epistemic trust, a sense of safe interaction and the brain efficiencies of collaboration.

The Neurobiology of Peace

Stepping back from what Polyvagal Theory has taught us in this chapter, we may glimpse even larger lessons about the world and our place in it. Years ago, I saw a 10-year-old boy who had been abused by his family, then moved from one foster home to another. I am not sure today what brought him to my clinic, but one fragment of his visit stands out clearly. After we had talked for a bit, he took a deep breath and asked sincerely why he had been treated so badly, why no family would have him, and why he had to suffer so. I deliberated before speaking, feeling what was in my heart, knowing the magnitude of the moment. After what seemed like an eternity, I took my own deep breath and told him with equal sincerity that I did not know why he had to endure so much when he was yet a boy. Truly I had no answers.

He looked more deeply into my eyes—I can still see him today—held that gaze for another long moment, then let go and relaxed. Why? Maybe I had passed a test. Maybe my inability to make sense of his situation led him, in Dr. Dan Siegel's words, to "feel felt" (2010). Or maybe he moved into that impartial witness consciousness that could, with equanimity, allow the reasons for his life's tragedies to remain a mystery.

Whatever it was that happened, I experienced a palpable feeling of connection that goes beyond description. Something vital awakened in both patient and physician, something mighty, rejuvenating, and life-affirming. It was sublime.

Spiritual practices are, according to Dr. Porges, "doorways to the ventral vagal" (2014). Perhaps the ventral vagal is a doorway to our experience of the divine as well. In *The Doubter's Guide to God* (2016), my friend Roger Martin beautifully described the joining of souls he has experienced in his own spiritual journey, along with echoes of the sanctuary to be found in ventral vagal. He observed:

> The soul knows that life within the house of the body could be less tumultuous. It longs for us to find ease. It would have us bring forward our best, evince humility and gentleness, forthrightness and integrity, calm and patience. It mourns the deformation of love, as love twists into cruel words and deeds that betray our original tenderness and vulnerability. The soul is the angel in us waiting to meet the angel in another, so that these angels, like drops of mercury, can rejoin. (p. 214)

We live in a world that can be tumultuous and cruel. A relentless parade of danger signals pervades daily life, Porges warns, signals that notify us, in effect, that threat looms ever present (2015a). He says that institutions, not understanding our "biobehavioral need for safety," often do little to promote the kind of warm, face-to-face connection that could mitigate this generalized neuroception of danger. In the face of disconnected menace, humanity as a whole is pressured to fight or flee, rather than to cooperate in the mutual understanding of epistemic trust.

Many people today are bucking this cultural current of danger, which hurries us toward fear and disengagement, by creating and participating in activities designed to foster a more harmoniously connected world. As we have seen in this chapter, these efforts include research, education, and training in how to create safe, collaborative, and life-affirming relationships.

When Dr. Arnold and I were preparing a chapter on medical professionalism, we realized that the doctor–patient relationship "provides a world-wide model for reducing intolerance, cruelty, and violence and expressing a humanism that encompasses all of us" (Arnold & Thompson, 2010, p. 18). Now we see that physicians, practicing medical professionalism, enter the ventral vagal state to help their patients become open and engaged. Face-to-face physician–patient meetings, which likely number in the millions each day around the world, have the potential to create ever-widening circles of ventral vagal signals of safety. If enough people stay in the social engagement system for a long enough time, that accord is likely to spread to larger and larger groups.

From the perspective of Polyvagal Theory, physicians can play a crucial role in creating a widespread neurologic shift that will—we hope—usher in peace on the planet.

References

Arnold, L., & Stern, D. T. (2006). What is medical professionalism? In D. T. Stern (Ed.), *Measuring medical professionalism* (pp. 15–37). Oxford, England: Oxford University Press.

Arnold, L., & Thompson, G. S. (2010). Defining and nurturing professionalism. In J. Spandorfer, C. A. Pohl, S. L. Rattner, & T. J. Nasca (Eds.). *Professionalism in medicine: The case-based guide for medical students* (pp. 7–21). New York, NY: Cambridge University Press.

Baylin, J., & Hughes, D. A. (2016). *Norton Series on Interpersonal Neurobiology. The neurobiology of attachment-focused therapy: Enhancing connection & trust in the treatment of children & adolescents.* New York, NY: Norton.

Beckes, L., & Coan, J. A. (2011). Social baseline theory: The role of social proximity in emotion and economy of action. *Social and Personality Psychology Compass, 5*(12), 976–988. doi:10.1111/j.1751-9004.2011.00400.x

Carter, S. (2014, November). The endocrinology of compassion and love: An oxytocin hypothesis. In S. Brown (Moderator), panel discussion at the CCARE Science of Compassion 2014: The Psychophysiology of Compassion conference, San Francisco, CA. Retrieved from https://www.youtube.com/watch?v=VAL-MMYptQc

Dyrbye, L., & Shanafelt, T. (2016). A narrative review on burnout experienced by medical students and residents. *Medical Education, 50*(1), 132–149. doi:10.1111/medu.12927

Elmqvist, C., Fridlund, B., & Ekebergh, M. (2012). On a hidden game board: The patient's first encounter with emergency care at the emergency department. *Journal of Clinical Nursing, 21*, 2609–2616. doi:10.1111/j.1365-2702.2011.03929.x

Epstein, R. M. (1999). Mindful practice. *Journal of the American Medical Association, 282*(9), 833–839. Retrieved from http://jamanetwork.com/pdfaccess.ashx?url=/data/journals/jama/4685

Fonagy, P., & Allison, E. (2014). The role of mentalizing and epistemic trust in the therapeutic relationship. *Psychotherapy, 51*(3), 372–380. doi:10.1037/a0036505

Fortin, A. H., Dwamena, F. C., Frankel, R. M., & Smith, R. C. (2012). *Smith's patient-centered interviewing: An evidence-based method.* New York, NY: McGraw-Hill.

Goleman, D. (2005). *Emotional Intelligence: Why it can matter more than IQ.* New York, NY: Bantam Books.

Haidt, J. (2003). Elevation and the positive psychology of morality. In C. L. M. Keyes & J. Haidt (Eds.), *Flourishing: Positive psychology and the life well-lived* (pp. 275–289). Washington, DC: American Psychological Association.

Hughes, D. A. (2006). *Building the bonds of attachment: Awakening love in deeply troubled children* (2nd ed.). Lanham: Jason Aronson.

Hughes, D. A. (2012, July). Dyadic developmental practice, psychotherapy, and parenting: Level 2. Training, Colby College, ME.

Hughes, D. A. & Baylin, J. (2012). *Norton Series on Interpersonal Neurobiology. Brain-based parenting: The neuroscience of caregiving for healthy attachment.* New York, NY: Norton.

Kabat-Zinn, J. (2009). *Full catastrophe living: Using the wisdom of your body and mind to face stress, pain and illness.* New York, NY: Bantam Dell.

Martin, R. P.. (2016). *A doubter's guide to God.* Topeka, KS: Woodley Press.

McKinnon, M. C., Boyd, J. E., Frewen, P. A., Lanius, U. F., Jetly, R., Richardson, J. D., & Lanius, R. A. (2016). A review of the relation between dissociation, memory, executive functioning and social cognition in military members and civilians with neuropsychiatric conditions. *Neuropsychologia, 90*, 210–234. doi:10.1016/j.neuropsychologia.2016.07.017

Osler, W. (n.d.). *Aequanimitas* (3rd ed.). New York, NY: McGraw-Hill.

Palmer, H. (2007). *Source beingness* [Video talk]. Star's Edge International, Altamonte Springs, FL. Retrieved from http://avatarepcmedia.com/Video/sourcebeingness.html

Palmer, H. (2008). *ReSurfacing®: Techniques for exploring consciousness*. Altamonte Springs, FL: Star's Edge International.

Palmer, H. (2011). The Avatar® path: The way we came. Altamonte Springs, FL: Star's Edge International.Palmer, H. (2012). *Living deliberately: The discovery and development of Avatar®*. Altamonte Springs, FL: Star's Edge International.

Porges, S. W. (2011). *The Polyvagal Theory: Neurophysiological foundations of emotions, attachment, communication and self-regulation*. New York, NY: Norton.

Porges, S. W. (2014, November). Vagal pathways: Portals to compassion. In S. Brown (Moderator), panel discussion at the CCARE Science of Compassion 2014: The Psychophysiology of Compassion conference, San Francisco, CA. Retrieved from https://www.youtube.com/watch?v=VAL-MMYptQc

Porges, S. W. (2015a). Making the world safe for our children: Down-regulating defence and up-regulating social engagement to 'optimise' the human experience. *Children Australia, 40*(2), 114–123. doi:10.1017/cha.2015.12

Porges, S. W. (2015b). Play as neural exercise: Insights from the Polyvagal Theory. *The Power of Play for Mind Brain Health*, 3–7.

Schnall, S., Harber, K., Stefanucci, J., & Proffitt, D. R. (2008). Social support and the perception of geographical slant. *Journal of Experimental Social Psychology, 44*(5), 1246–1255. doi:10.1016/j.jesp.2008.04.011

Schon, D. A. (1983). *The reflective practitioner: How professionals think in action*. New York, NY: Basic Books.

Siegel, D. (2010). *Mindsight: Transform your brain with the new science of kindness*. New York, NY: Bantam Books.

Stellar, J. E., Cohen, A., Oveis, C., & Keltner, D. (2015). Affective and physiological responses to the suffering of others: Compassion and vagal activity. *Journal of Personality and Social Psychology, 108*(4), 572–585. doi:10.1037/pspi0000010

Sweeney, C. (2017). The patient empathy project: A study of patient fears. In D. L. Zimmerman & D. G. Osburn-Harrison (Eds.), *Person-focused healthcare management: A foundational guide for healthcare managers* (pp. 193–201). New York, NY: Springer.

Thompson, G., & Mock, B. (2016, November). *The competent companion: Dyadic developmental practice in psychiatric residential treatment and doctor-patient communication*. Presentation at DDP Study Days, sponsored by DDP Institute, Stony Point, NY.

van der Kolk, B. A. (2005). Developmental trauma disorder: Toward a rational diagnosis for children with complex trauma histories. *Psychiatric Annals, 35*(5), 401–408.

Verghese, A., Brady, E., Costanzo Kapur, C., & Horwitz, R. I. (2011). The bedside evaluation: Ritual and reason. *Annals of Internal Medicine, 155*(8), 550–553. Retrieved from http://annals.org/

Wordsworth, W. (1807). Ode: Intimations of immortality from recollections of early childhood. In Wordsworth, W. *Poems, in two volumes*. Retrieved from http://www.bartleby.com/101/536.html

Wright, S., Yelland, M., Heathcote, K., Ng, S., & Wright, G. (2009). Fear of needles: Nature and prevalence in general practice. *Australian Family Physician, 38*(3), 172–176.

9

Polyvagal Theory Affirms the Importance of Nursing

Moira Theede

Abstract: Polyvagal Theory provides a framework to understand the spectrum of behavioral responses of patients whose neuroception is one of danger or life-threat. Polyvagal Theory provides nurses with new science underlying the neurophysiology of what happens during stress states, illness, and trauma. It expands health professionals' "response abilities" to recognize shifts in the autonomic nervous system of self and others. Polyvagal Theory and the social engagement system provide a new platform for understanding person-to-person relational skills, cues of safety and caring that contribute to a patient's recovery.

> *Nursing is more than the sum of its parts. Any health system needs nurses who are intellectually able and emotionally aware and who combine technical skills with a deep understanding and ability to care, as one human to another: This is a constant of nursing. It is the value base on which public trust rests and the profession is grounded.*
> —Christine Beasley (2006, p. 4)

I WAS FIRST introduced to Polyvagal Theory in 2007 when beginning studies in Self Regulation Therapy® and later when studying Peter Levine's Somatic Experiencing®. My work experience included orthopedic, general surgery, operating room, and nursing in a medical imaging department. I worked as a nurse educator both in New Zealand and in Canada, where I live. The bio-psychosocial, spiritual approach was the foundation for my master's studies in health promotion. As a grandmother now, my self-reflective process from the polyvagal perspective has allowed me to spiral back to my basic personal and nursing philosophies, affirming both the old and the new.

Polyvagal Theory affirms nursing theories and all levels of nursing expertise. "In the context of caregiving, the quality of the person-to-person interactions between a caretaker [*caregiver*] and those being cared for is critical for survival. Often this involves contingent and 'appropriate' gesture, facial expression, prosody, proximity, and touch" (Porges, 2011, p. 295). Polyvagal Theory provides nurses with the underlying neurophysiology of what happens during stress states, illness, and trauma. "At the heart of mammalian survival is the concept of safety and the ability to distinguish whether the environment is safe, and whether other individuals are friend or foe" (Carter, Harris, & Porges, 2009, p. 173). I believe Polyvagal Theory provides a functional framework for nurses as they understand their nursing presence and how they respond to patients while providing care. Polyvagal concepts explain how safety from the patients' perspectives influences their autonomic nervous system.

My psychiatric nursing classes and communication theories were based on Carl Rogers's person-centered approach. Humanistic psychologist Sidney M. Jourard, in *The Transparent Self*, emphasized the importance of authenticity in dialogue and empathy within the nurse–patient relationship rather than presenting a professional mask. Jourard wrote, "Empathy—the ability to guess what a patient is experiencing in a given situation—is an outgrowth of insight, or self-awareness" (1971, p. 186). Polyvagal Theory deepens our capacity for empathy and how we interpret behavioral responses when safety is understood from an autonomic nervous system perspective. Polyvagal Theory and its elaboration of the social engagement system provides the neurobiology underlying what Jourard proposed—that "patient behaviors, inner experience and physical status" can be influenced by nurse–patient relationships.

Florence Nightingale is considered the founder of the nursing profession (1860), and Hildegard Peplau is considered the first nurse theorist, publishing her *Interpersonal Relations in Nursing* in 1952. Nursing theories have evolved and expanded over the six decades since Peplau's work of studying nursing as an interpersonal process, and Polyvagal Theory reinforces her view that nurse–patient relations are a vital part of the treatment for recovery. Peplau's theory "is profoundly important because it was the first to propose that instead of *doing things to* a patient, a nurse must *provide care in partnership with* the patient" (Sitzman & Eichelberger, 2017, p. 140). Polyvagal Theory provides the lens to view the "quality of exchanges" between caregiver and those for whom care is provided. Cues of safety from the nurse (especially from the upper half of the nurse's face) "enable the sick or compromised person not to be in a defensive state" (Porges, 2011), but rather to feel calm and connected.

Polyvagal Theory describes for the nurse how the patient's autonomic nervous system is orienting for safety, danger, or life-threat. Feeling safe is necessary for strong social relationships to be established—the foundation for social support. "It is important to remember that neuroception of danger or a threat to life can occur with respect to the external environment (e.g. a dangerous person or situation) or the internal environment (e.g. fever, pain, or physical illness)" (Porges, 2011, p. 15). The neuroception of danger or life-threat is relevant to patients' internal environment when they experience medically related challenges including infections, surgery, medication side effects, diagnostic procedures, and chemotherapy. Some obvious external environmental factors that may disrupt the patient's internal environment and compromise the body's ability to heal may include: HVAC (heating, ventilation, air-conditioning) sounds, visitor traffic, the noises of technology (beeps and alarms), rushed health care staff, the constantly changing faces of ward personnel with rotating shift workers, and overhearing incivility between health care providers.

I fully recognize the current challenges and tensions between "fostering the coexistence of caring philosophy and economics in today's health care system," as discussed by Cara, Nyberg, and Brousseau in a 2011 *Journal of Nursing Administration* article. A multidisciplinary and interdisciplinary understanding of Polyvagal Theory has the potential to change attitudes across the wide scope of health care by bridging nursing specialties and educational levels and giving a common polyvagal language and platform for interprofessional dialogue.

Safety Optimizes the Human Experience

Polyvagal Theory deepens our understanding and appreciation of safety, describing how our mammalian autonomic nervous system monitors both internal and external environments, while operating at a nonconscious brain stem level. "Safety optimizes the human experience" (Porges, 2013).

> My mother worked as a registered nurse in a 40-bed rural hospital that provided emergency, labor and delivery, pediatric, medical, surgical,

cardiac, and palliative care, serving a community of 2,000 people and the surrounding area. She worked night shifts. She kept all her work in complete confidentiality for all those years, but we could always tell when a baby was born on her shift, as she would come home in the morning beaming with delight. New beginnings seemed to balance the community losses. After my mother died, in talking with people and in the letters and cards that we received, there was one theme: *safety.* People shared memory after memory of how important it was for them to know that "D" was on duty while they were in the hospital. Women were thankful she had been with them during labor and delivery for their children's births, expressing how safe they felt in her presence. She believed in care, compassion, and comforting touch, but also knew how to be kind and firm when she needed to be. When I was 11, my great-grandmother, age 88, had a stroke (hemiplegic—no speech) and we cared for her at home for a year. I watched my mother provide tender, loving care. It was only in hindsight that I realized how much I had learned from her about compassion, connection, and the use of touch (massage) to enhance physical comfort.

From a polyvagal perspective, my mother engaged with people with a smile that provided a strong face–heart connection. She had a reassuring manner, and patients came first. Being present at a baby's birth was a sacred moment for her, and I saw the eye-to-eye connection she made with all her grandchildren, especially when they were newborns. She always wore Clinic brand shoes because they were comfortable and quiet and she could silently walk into a patient's room on her rounds with her tiny flashlight in hand. I can imagine her soft eye gaze and prosodic voice with patients when she answered a call bell, conveying to them that their needs were important. The connection would have created a sense of safety, contributing to comfort, rest, and sleep.

Virginia Henderson's definition of nursing provided the main framework used by my professors in the 1970s. Henderson responded to a request from the International Council of Nurses to define a basic nursing platform independent of technology or medicine, and the *Basic Principles of Nursing Care* was published in 1960 and translated into over 20 languages. It stated that a person has physical, mental, emotional, and spiritual needs, and a person needs to be in relationship with others to meet those needs. In Henderson's definition of nursing, "empathy coupled with knowledge and interest on the part of the nurse will enhance the healing process" (Sitzman & Eichelberger, 2017, p. 38). The expansion of neurophysiology and knowledge about emotional and autonomic states (Polyvagal Theory) explains how the social engagement skills and reciprocity between nurse and patient affect recovery. In polyvagal language, co-regulation between nurse and patient is how safety is defined.

Key elements in establishing nursing rapport with patients and families occur when "individuals share a feeling of mutual trust, affinity, understanding and connectedness" (Gregory, Raymond-Seniuk, Patrick, & Stephen, 2015, p. 600), in other words, ventral vagal social engagement. Acceptance and safety allow the patient to trust the nurse's integrity and reliability.

> I clearly remember a chance meeting with a former professor who told me, "I hear you are wasting your time in the operating room," and my response, with no hesitation, was, "Quite the opposite. I know how to establish rapport with patients before surgery, and that makes a difference." I had set a goal for myself to maximize even the short moments of connection to provide for the mental and emotional needs of patients before their surgeries. One of my duties as an operating room (OR) circulating nurse was to greet the next patient waiting (face-to-face, with no mask on), introduce myself, check identity, chart, and so on, with usually a few minutes of conversation, and then accompany the patient into the operating room. I would position myself beside the patient, making eye contact (soft eyes), touching the patient's arm, talking, and being able to assist the anesthetist at the same time. In retrospect, those moments were providing cues of safety (as in Polyvagal Theory) and a regulating presence for patients.

Relationships Influence Physiological States and Healing

Jean Watson's nursing Theory of Human Caring from 1979 (care of body, mind, and spirit) certainly took into account the influence of interactions between human beings, but it would be 15 years later that Polyvagal Theory explained the neurophysiology of connectedness and the social engagement system. Dr. Watson wrote, "When the nurse and the patient come together, they experience a caring moment. It is through the caring moment of connection between the two that transformation and healing can occur. These moments are shaped by the nurse's attitude and competence" (Gregory et al., 2015, p. 199). Sitzman and Eichelberger (2011) described Watson's theory as one of mindful, in-the-moment, committed caring where the nurse–client exchange is mutual and reciprocal. Relationships influence physiology. Understanding the science of connectedness through Polyvagal Theory provides the language and neurophysiology to describe what the nursing tradition, old and new, views as caring.

When an individual feels safe, body physiology is regulated in an efficient manner to promote growth, restoration, and health. Cranial nerves V, VII, IX, X, and XI, forming the social engagement system, are linked in the brain stem and control facial expressions, the ability to discern the frequency of human voice, prosody and intonation of speech, and head turning for face-to-face gaze and eye contact. These neural circuits also simultaneously influence heart rate, respiration, and visceral regulation. This face–heart connection provides humans with an ability to calm physiological states in the self and others (Porges, 2011). A nurse using the social engagement system to provide prosocial communication with face-to-face eye gaze, engaging facial expressions, attuned listening, and calming prosody in vocalizations, gestures, proximity, and touch conveys cues of safety to the patient's autonomic nervous system, enhancing the recovery process.

A patient's feeling of safety while in the hospital takes on a new emphasis in the context of Polyvagal Theory. Is face-to-face dialogue being minimized with the increasing number of machines that need attending? Or in this age of rapidly increasing technology, are we minimizing face-to-face connection and dialogue without recognizing the consequences to each other's human nervous systems? How does technology divide our attention?

The following poem (Barss, 1999, p. 15), written by a nursing educator, gives voice to the patient's need to be seen, heard, and understood as the patient copes with a hospitalization that may have potentially life-changing consequences. It demonstrates the need for understanding the social engagement system.

Accompany Me

Efficient, skillful, learned one,
On whom I must depend,
Please see the person sitting here,
Not just a wound to mend.

Please focus less on tests and tasks
And more on how I feel;
It really gives a lift to know
That your concern is real.

And though it may be that it is,
I sometimes wonder when

You come and go and do your work,
But no warmth and caring lend.

And don't forget it cuts me deep
And undermines my grace
When you advise and condescend
And don't respect my space.

I'd really like to see a glimpse
Of you—the real you—
The one who can relate to pain
And share some insight, too.

I really wish you'd notice all
The things I leave unsaid;
I'd love to talk about them
If I were safely led.

You need to know that helping me
Takes more than concrete skill;
You need to show some competence
In listening to my will.

For I'm the one who's living
With challenges and risk;
I need some understanding,
Not interventions brisk.

I am so very vulnerable;
I need to find my stride
If you will walk along with me,
We both can walk with pride!

(Used with permission, Karen Scott Barss, RPN BHSc MA.)

Touch as Nonverbal Communication

The work of Tiffany Field of the Touch Research Institute in Miami over the last 35 years documents the importance of touch. One of her research studies correlates weight gain and increased cardiac vagal tone with medium-pressure massage given to premature infants (Field, 2006, p. 48). It would never occur to us to stop touching our dog because it outgrew puppyhood. Healthy attunement and attachment for infants, children, and adults includes touch (contact), essential for establishing social bonds. "We readily think of stressors as consisting of various unpleasant things that can be done to an organism. Sometimes a stressor can be the failure to provide something to an organism, and the absence of touch is seemingly one of the most marked of developmental stressors we can suffer" (Sapolsky, 2004, p. 8). Our sense of touch is the first to develop in utero and "functions even after seeing and hearing begin to fade" (Field, 2003, p. 8). How might our awareness shift if we were to remember that the skin and nervous system, brain included, develop from the same embryologic tissue—the ectoderm? "Our bodies have eighteen square feet of skin, which makes skin our largest sense organ . . . it is in a constant state of readiness to receive messages—it is always on . . . and touch continues to be the primary means of experiencing the world through infancy and well into childhood, even into aging" (Field, 2003, p. 10). In polyvagal terms, the skin is always ready for connectedness.

Touch can calm and ground patients. Touch influences the ventral vagal regulation of the heart and lungs. Appropriate, respectful, and compassionate touch is nonverbal communication that conveys to infants, to children, to the sick, to the injured, to the grieving, or to the dying that they are not alone and someone cares. "Soothing touch, whether it be applied to a ruffled cat, a crying infant, or a frightened child, has a universally recognized power to ameliorate the signs of distress. How can it be that we overlook its usefulness on a jangled adult as well? What is it that leads us to assume that the stressed child merely needs 'comforting,' while the stressed adult needs 'medicine'?" (Juhan, 1998, p. 56).

Field, well-known for her touch research with premature infants, also did extensive research on the value of massage for age groups across the life span for numerous conditions (2006). How might the information gained from her studies be integrated into nursing health care for all ages? As technology has developed, we aspire to be "touchless" (we can just talk to Siri), and we literally "touch less" and become "out of touch" with ourselves. "Touch" has become associated with a device (touch screens) rather than humans. Perhaps we need to reinvent the importance of touch using heart rate variability technology to provide evidence that compassionate touch, providing comfort measures, increases the ventral vagal tone of the patient.

Social Engagement

I felt affirmed recently when I learned that a handshake is worth 3 hours of face-to-face time and builds rapport (Heller, 2016). I come from a family of handshakers. My grandfather was one of my role models, and his delight of connection through handshakes with others is an understatement. It was his way of saying Welcome, come on in. *I also grew up knowing that although my father loved me dearly, he had given me a name others found difficult to pronounce: Moira—challenging phonetics for many to hear and pronounce unless you understand Gaelic. It seems I kick-started the social engagement system by extending a handshake and an introduction. "Good morning. My name is Moira—Moy-ra. I will be looking after you today." Every shift would begin with a quick round to connect patient names with faces and reconnect with those patients cared for on the previous shift.*

Handshakes and purposeful face-to-face introductions using the muscles of the upper face, especially the muscles around the eyes, provide a connection and offer a regulating influence to the patient's autonomic nervous system. This increases ventral vagal tone, engages the social engagement system, and establishes nursing presence at the beginning of a shift. This personal face-to-face connection helps the patient's neuroception of safety, and, as Porges (2015) said, "without caring face-to-face interactions that include cues such as warmly modulated voices, the patient or student shifts rapidly into a bodily state that supports defense and limits the ability to understand the information words convey."

Nurses who provide continuity of care for hospitalized patients are caring for individuals who are vulnerable in many ways. However, we place expectations on the patient to adjust to the hospital environment. Consider the altered sense of identity, loss of independence, and confinement that are associated with a gown, wristband, room number, bed number, and side rails. The latest iteration of technology, scanning wristbands, could result in patients feeling objectified and reduced to a bar code if no social engagement and cues of safety are initiated by the nurse. For example, how easy it would be for the nurse to look at the patient's face as she walks into the room, smile and say in a prosodic tone of voice, "Hello, Sam, I have your medications and, as per hospital protocol, I will again need to ask your name and birth date," while holding the patient's wrist at the same time. Imagine how this simple style of engagement might change the experience for the patient. It could enhance the social engagement behaviors of the patient, establishing the base for effective interpersonal communication.

The hospital environment includes both low-frequency sounds (such as mechanical HVAC noises), which are phylogenetically associated with predators, and high-frequency alarms and buzzers that can trigger the sympathetic nervous system. When patients experience a neuroception of danger or life-threat, their eyes may roll up and have a glazed, disconnected look; their eyelids may droop; their voice may lose inflection; any positive facial expressions dwindle; and the ability to discern the sound and intent of human voice becomes less acute (Porges, 2011). The challenge of adapting continually to new faces, lights, and the din of noises are constant stressors to the patient's autonomic nervous system. What happens when polyvagal-informed care providers understand that neuroregulators of the face are the neuroregulators of the heart and communication, which provide a calming effect for the patient's autonomic nervous system (Porges, 2014)? How might seeing the faces of familiar staff throughout the day support the patient's neuroception of safety, recognizing the nurse as friend rather than foe? If a handshake is equivalent to 3 hours of face-to-face social engagement, then I wonder the time value of supporting a patient's hand or wrist with one hand while using the fingers of the opposite hand to take (skin to skin) the patient's radial pulse; assessing rate, strength, and rhythm for 15–30 seconds or even a full minute. There is much to be learned from taking a manual pulse—a nuanced type of experience not possible from looking at screens. What kind of attunement, resonance, and energy exchange could happen? Can it be that the person-to-person touch with pulse taking, once considered a routine nursing assessment, was providing the essential energetic connection between nurse and patient, creating the autonomic foundation for trust and sense of safety?

Neuroception: A Core Concept for Compassionate Nursing

As Porges (2013) wrote, "Feeling safe is a necessary prerequisite before strong relationships can be established and before social support can be effective in 'healing' physical and mental illnesses." The neuroception of safety, danger, or life-threat is at the interface between patients, health care professionals, technology, diagnostic equipment, and the hospital facility, and shapes the patient experience as either a caring one or a traumatic one. Understanding neuroception will help prevent assumptions and negative labeling of patient states and behavior. Polyvagal Theory supports our understanding that the experience of trauma is not a cognitive state of mind or limited to motor vehicle accident injuries, burns, fractures, wounds, and so on. Trauma is a physiological state that the body experiences at a nonconscious level. According to Peter Levine (2013), "trauma is held in the nervous system." When we feel vulnerable and stressed and our neuroception is one of danger, the sympathetic nervous system is triggered and reactivity increases. In hospitals, fight-or-flight is not usually an option, although individuals experiencing panic may become aggressive or defensive in their attempt to regain a sense of safety. If helplessness and overwhelm are detected in the patient's autonomic nervous system, it increases the possibility of a shift into dorsal vagal dominance. Polyvagal Theory describes the state of dorsal vagal shutdown as the response to a neuroception of life-threat that results in bradycardia, compromised respiratory function, and compromised subdiaphragmatic visceral function. If severe enough, this response can be lethal. By understanding the possibility of dorsal vagal shutdown and knowing how to bring cues of safety through their calm, prosodic voice tones, nurses may positively counteract this. None of us want to be considered a health risk factor in another person's life. The need for connectedness is important to humans and all the more essential when experiencing a health challenge at any age. Connectedness within a caring relationship provides a bidirectional influence, supporting the autonomic nervous system of both the nurse and patient. The work of nurse researcher Sigridur Halldorsdottir shows that patient perceptions of caring or uncaring are on a spectrum between life-giving and life destroying. "Being uncared for in a dependent situation develops feelings of impotence, a sense of loss, and a sense of having been betrayed by those counted on for caring" (in Smith, Turkel, & Wolf, 2013, p. 203). In the context of Polyvagal Theory, being uncared for creates helplessness and negatively affects the patient's autonomic nervous system. In a paper titled "Why Does Social Exclusion Hurt? The Relationship Between Social and Physical Pain" (MacDonald & Leary, 2005), the authors state, "Most people have experiences in which socially mediated pain is so great that they are not only in agony but are overwhelmed or incapacitated." (p. 202). This feeling of being overwhelmed is magnified when social exclusion happens in a hospital, a place the patient anticipates will be hospitable.

When we are in a ventral vagal state, we have the capacity to use our mammalian evolutionary inheritance for positive social engagement—face-to-face in the same physical space, feeling calm and connected. Our neuroceptive experience is one of safety in our internal and external environments. We play, care, and share together. We enhance our social engagement system with our eye gaze, facial expressions, prosody and voice intonations, attuned listening and hearing each other, proximity, gentle touch, mirroring, and presence (Porges, 2011). "The soothing system is therefore able to signal to the threat system: It's okay here. We're cared for and safe" (Gilbert, 2009, p. 173).

In an optimal ventral vagal state, in which we are mindful and grounded, we convey cues of safety through tone of voice, what we are saying with our faces, and the mood and affect that we bring to an interaction. Prosocial skills, supported by our ventral vagal state, allow us to recognize feelings, be mutually respectful, encourage others, extend apologies when necessary, encourage a growth mindset of curiosity, provide a listening ear, and convey a sense of hope. Empathy and compassion support physical comfort and emotional connection.

John Coates (2012), author of *The Hour Between Dog and Wolf*, drew from Polyvagal Theory when he wrote,

> Speaking in a calm and reassuring voice, making eye contact, displaying facial expressions that broadcast cooperation rather than confrontation, all these help avoid a metabolically expensive and potentially damaging fight; and crucially they calm our visceral arousal. The vagus nerve, it could be said, forms the diplomatic core of the body. (p. 231)

The vagus knows before cognition, and this means that neuroception precedes cognition.

Nurses at the front lines experience what nurse scholars refer to as "the incongruities between the staff nurse's caring ethics and the health care industry's focus on competition, profits and productivity" (Cara et al., 2011). I recently was saddened to read the words of an author suggesting that empathy be used as the latest marketing tool to cure the U.S. health care crises and to help organizations have a competitive advantage. Empathy and competition seem at the opposite ends of the motivational spectrum, and the vagus will know! Genuinely engaged nurses, who listen to patients while they create safety for the patients' autonomic nervous system, need to be acknowledged. Providing dialogue with empathy, care, and compassion, a skill that many nurses would consider part of the art of nursing, requires time and may appear at odds with systems focused on task efficiency or manualized care. Reliability and trust provide a sense of safety when equal value is given to the technical skills and the social engagement skills of the nurse. Both contribute to patient outcomes.

> As a surgical nurse caring for postoperative patients, before laparoscopic surgeries were commonplace, it was very important to do routine deep breathing exercises, especially for patients with abdominal incisions. I would walk into the patient's room with a calm smile, make eye contact, and ask, "How are you doing?" and pause for a response. I would assess the patient's facial expressions and possible tension around the jaw, tone of voice, body posture, and signs that would indicate pain and discomfort (attunement to their autonomic state). I would make contact by taking their pulse, and then in a modulated voice ask, "Okay if I have a look at your dressings? Looking good. While I am here, let's do some deep breathing exercises." Patients naturally tend to "hold" the diaphragm when in pain, or afraid of pain, when asked to inhale. I took an opposite approach and would have patients focus on their exhalation first.

"Let's try something a little different. I'd like you to groan like this"—I'd demonstrate for the patient—"on the out breath. Let's do it together." I would coach them to deliberately groan and extend the exhalation while I supported the sides of their rib cage or abdomen with my hands as we groaned together. The in breath would then take care of itself. After each focused out breath and groan, I would watch and feel each corresponding inhalation and the progressively increased chest expansions. After several breaths, patients would usually sigh deeply, indicating increased comfort. Extended exhalation improves ventral vagal regulation (Porges, 2014). My supportive touch and comforting dialogue while ensuring that their call bell was easily within reach, implying my availability, supported the patient's sense of safety, influencing their ventral vagal tone.

Mobility of the patient is a nursing fundamental. From a polyvagal context, early mobilization after anesthesia and surgery may be doing more for patients than decreasing venous stasis in order to prevent deep vein thrombosis or paralytic ileus alone. As patients regain the ability to move, first with the assistance of the nurse and then gradually on their own, they not only gain independence but also influence the ventral branch of the vagus nerve. I have a friend in New Zealand who gives all the credit for her recovery after hip replacement surgery to a student nurse who "came to take me for walks whenever she could"—the social engagement of the student nurse was important to her. My friend regained confidence in her own legs as strong and supportive. She was able to "mobilize without fear" (increasing ventral vagal tone). The student nurse conveyed cues of safety and ongoing help with each additional "walk down the hall." My friend felt that she was in safe hands, cared for by a student who consciously engaged and recognized that frequent walks would contribute to a faster recovery for her patient. This student knew that mobility is extremely important for patients' healing after orthopedic surgery. Independent mobility (moving) is important for mammalian autonomic nervous system regulation.

Immobilization With Fear Versus Immobilization Without Fear

"Immobilization with fear" versus "immobilization without fear" (Porges, 2014) are powerful phrases. Hospitalization implies limitation and immobilization on many levels. How might we change the way we carry out medical interventions and nursing care to minimize the neuroception of danger or life-threat in the patient's autonomic nervous system? Noise levels are just one example.

Hospitals are becoming progressively noisier. As Norman Doidge wrote, "A direct link exists between the auditory cortex and the threat systems in the brain, which is why unexpected, startling noise can trigger immense, immediate anxiety" (2015, p. 327). Alarm buzzers on patient-controlled analgesia or intravenous pumps, frequently not attended to, are an example that triggers the sympathetic nervous system fight-or-flight reaction in the patient's nervous system. Hospital staff may not be aware of how they tune out the alarms and fail to recognize that patient and family anxiety increases when staff appear to be ignoring the alarms. Research from the University of Oxford (Darbyshire & Young, 2013) showed that the decibel levels in five intensive care units exceeded 85 decibels 16 times per hour during the night and more frequently during the day, and had a detrimental effect on patients' quality of sleep and cognition. Research from Johns Hopkins University (Kamdar et al., 2013) also showed that simple common-sense measures to reduce noise and lighting levels reduced patient delirium in the intensive care unit. In her book *The Sleep Revolution*, Arianna Huffington wrote, "Welcome to the hospital, where we've created a healing environment that's a cross between an active construction site and a horror movie" (2016, p. 253). Harsh words or reality? Understanding Polyvagal Theory provides valuable insights into intensive care syndrome.

How might the high-decibel noise levels in hospitals be influencing the autonomic nervous systems of the nurses, doctors, and other staff? How might understanding the nervous system from the polyvagal approach provide insight into alarm and alert fatigue? Imagine the changes that could be made to foster the health for patients and their health care providers if everyone, from architects and engineers to hospital administrations, were polyvagal informed.

When viewed from the polyvagal perspective, trauma is not cognitive. Trauma happens at a nonconscious level. In medical imaging, machines may come toward the patient from the ceiling, patients may be moved into confined spaces with possible restraints, and endoscopes may be used for diagnosis and interventions. "Trauma is defined by its effect on a particular individual's nervous system, not on the intensity of the circumstance itself" (Levine & Kline, 2007, p. 37). Polyvagal Theory provides nurses with a user-friendly framework to understand the wide spectrum of behavioral responses of hospitalized patients whose neuroception is one of danger or life-threat. It also expands health professionals' "response abilities" with their new ability to recognize shifts in the autonomic nervous system of self and others (Dana, 2016).

Human-factor engineering (e.g., engineering, ergonomics, and psychology) can assist with newer designs when considering the neurophysiology of Polyvagal Theory. A good example is the MRI, a confined space with possible restraints. Lying in a supine position, patients are slowly moved backward into the MRI machine. This can be activating for the nervous system, as it is a vulnerable orientation. Communication between the technician and client is done through a speaker system. Headphones with music are available, but they do little to eliminate the background sounds. MRIs are loud machines. What instructions can be given to patients before they enter the MRI, to give them advance information for their neural expectancy, rather than contributing to overwhelming startle and a sympathetic nervous system fear response or panic? We interpret new environments in the context of our past experience, and neuroception is individually unique. A rural grain farmer might really believe the MRI was falling apart, and react to all the clanging and banging noises that, if they were coming from a threshing machine, would definitely be signaling a breakdown. Some sounds are similar to that of a garden tiller, and other sounds could be described as a couple of one-string guitars not in tune, creating only high-pitched twangs, while other sounds are loud and booming. Patients may be asked to hold their breath during the scans. The presence of someone who understands Polyvagal Theory and knows how to coach patients to breathe in a regulating way between scans, reassure with touch, and converse using a prosodic tone of voice can influence the patient's ventral vagal state.

Face–Heart Connection Versus Biological Rudeness

"We wear our hearts on our face" (Porges, 2013). Do you know what your face feels like and looks like when you are conveying care and compassion? Patients anticipate that nurses will be their safe havens and advocates. Many nurses have been personally told that patients remembered their kind, caring eyes. Looking with soft, kind eyes communicates intentions of caring and helping within the nurse–patient relationship and conveys attention, comfort, safety, and hope—an example of the face–heart connection.

Hospitals have increasingly more and more technological equipment that requires attention from nurses and others. British scholars Foster and Hawkins from the Faculty of Health, Wellbeing, and Science at Suffolk College published an article in 2005 in the *British Journal of Nursing* titled "The Therapeutic Relationship: Dead or Merely Impeded by Technology?" One of the authors shared a personal experience after orthopedic surgery: "Throughout the day a number of nurses enter the room and fail to acknowledge or engage with the patient, rather focusing their attention to the drip (IV)." How does the patient's nervous system respond to not being seen, and what thoughts may go through the patient's mind when this exclusion happens? When social engagement and reciprocity are not evident, patients could conclude, *The machine seems more important than I am.* And question—*Who are these strangers?*

The term *biological rudeness* is a construct created by Dr. Stephen Porges to describe social disconnection. When we are engaged in a conversation with another person and they just walk away without terminating the social interaction we feel it in our bodies. It is a situation we do not tolerate well - a violation of our expectation of the social interaction. You may have experienced this. Have you been engaged in a conversation with a friend and their cell phone rings and they turn away from you to chat with the caller? Or you watch a friend check an e-mail or text and their face takes on what is called flat affect (no facial expression), and they are gone somewhere else, so to speak? These moments of "biological rudeness" are a violation of neural expectancy and create the potential for defensive behaviors (Porges, 2014).

Sherry Turkle's (2015) research at MIT indicates that divided attention occurs in the presence of personal devices even if they are turned off. Our habit of always responding to cell phones, texts, social media, and e-mail diverts us from engaging. Lulls in conversation have become triggers to check cell phones even if they aren't ringing. The development of empathy requires face-to-face conversation. When the nurse enters the patient's room, where does the attention first focus if technology is present? On the patient's face or on the machines? Would you consider the scenario described by Foster and Hawkins two paragraphs up an example of "biological rudeness"? What happens to the patient's neuroception of safety and visceral response when biological rudeness and divided attention meet?

Offering a Regulating Influence

Before infants can speak, they connect with their mother or father through eye gaze and facial expressions—attunement. Eye gaze is a part of the mammalian social engagement system. "According to the Polyvagal Theory, the face and voice are powerful conduits through which safety is communicated to another" (Geller & Porges, 2014). "Looking at the face of the other and listening to voice are central to human relating, dialogue, and presence" (Geller & Greenberg, 2012). Failure to provide face-to-face eye gaze becomes a stressor for the patient, but *when my nurse looks at me and socially engages, I know he is looking after me.* Each one of us orients to our environment, looking for safety through the process of neuroception. Paul Ekman said, "It requires a well-developed capacity for compassion to respect, feel sympathetic toward, and patiently reassure someone who is afraid of something which we are not afraid of. Good nurses understanding their patient's fear, are able to see the patient's perspectives, they are able to reassure them" (2003, p. 153). Peter Levine added, "The human nervous system is designed and attuned to receive and to offer a regulating influence to another person" (2010, p. 75). These quotations will be affirming for nurses who know from experience that their calm groundedness, their centeredness, and their resonance provides a trustworthy base, a non-threatening regulating resource, for the patient. To do this requires that nurses understand their own nervous systems and become skilled in recognizing their own autonomic state changes, as this gives insight into the effect each of us has on another's affect. In polyvagal language, nurses who initiate prosocial engagement (eye gaze, prosodic speech, facial expression, reciprocity, gestures, touch) and are conscious of conveying cues of safety as they interact with patients support ventral vagal tone in both patients and themselves. Nurses who intuitively know how to be with, and walk with, a fellow human will understand the energetic presence of the face–heart connection.

Polyvagal Theory provides the neurophysiological evidence that supports the importance of care, empathy, and attunement at the core of the nursing profession. Attention and attending creates presence and safety. "The interaction that never happened is labeled as a non-caring interaction" by the patient (Reiman in Smith et al., 2013, p. 296). Polyvagal Theory is a key factor in deeply understanding how influential our social engagement skills, or lack thereof, affect patient outcomes. Nurses can positively influence the regulation of the heart, lungs, and viscera by the way they socially engage, communicate with prosody, and touch patients during hospitalizations or, to use Peter Levine's words, "provide a regulating influence" when they understand Polyvagal Theory.

What happens for nurses as the old understanding of the autonomic nervous system has changed? Now there is new physiology! And how does this influence the platform used for nursing assessments? Nurses can feel empowered further in their care paradigms with new understandings of the ways parasympathetic networks of the autonomic nervous system affect nursing theory and practice. Polyvagal Theory is embraced by psychologists, therapists, trauma experts, play therapists, Self Regulation Therapy® and Somatic Experiencing® practitioners. Verbal and nonverbal communication skills and social engagement skills that convey cues of safety are at the heart of nursing. Nurses need to know the science that affirms the therapeutic interpersonal relationship and affirms the value of their courageous nursing presence.

The real voyage of discovery consists not in seeking new lands but seeing with new eyes.
—Marcel Proust

It is a very interesting time when knowledge from across disciplines expands visions for a better future. Old wisdom? New awareness? New possibilities? Neuroscience? Neuroplasticity? Revised anatomy and physiology texts? Changing mindsets? Active hope?

We each have our own unique, kaleidoscopic moment-to-moment combination of life events and experiences that influence how we see the world and how we come to adopt ways of trying to find and maintain safety. Polyvagal Theory, for me, provides a key to intrapersonal wisdom and understanding our interdependent need for connection, love, compassion, and cooperation.

Enjoy the comings and goings each day,
Crossing thresholds,
Seeking prosocial engagement,
Enhancing "growth, restoration and health"
For yourself and those you meet along the way
Creating a polyvagal-friendly world.

—*Moira*

References

Barss, K. S. (1999). *Healing images: Reflections on a healing journey.* Muenster, Canada: St. Peter's Press.

Beasley, C. (2006). Modernizing nursing careers: Setting the direction. London, England: Department of Health.

Cara, C. M., Nyberg, J. J., & Brousseau, S. (2011). Fostering the coexistence of caring philosophy and economics in today's health care system. *Nursing Administration Quarterly, 35*(1), 6–14.

Carter, C. S., Harris, J., & Porges, S. W. (2009). In J. Decety & W. Ickes (Eds.), *The neuroscience of empathy.* Cambridge, MA: MIT Press.

Coates, J. (2012). *The hour between dog and wolf: How risk-taking transforms us, body and mind.* Toronto, Canada: Vintage.

Dana, D. (2016, June). The rhythm of regulation: Building safety from a polyvagal perspective. Presented in Saskatoon, SK, Canada.

Darbyshire, J. L., & Young, J. D. (2013). An investigation of sound levels on intensive care units with reference to the WHO guidelines. *Critical Care, 17*(5), R187.

Doidge, N. (2015). *The brain's way of healing: Remarkable discoveries and recoveries from the frontiers of neuroplasticity.* New York, NY: Viking.

Eckman, P. (2003). *Emotions revealed.* New York, NY: Henry Holt.

Field, T. (2003). *Touch.* Cambridge, MA: MIT Press.

Field, T. (2006). *Massage therapy research.* Philadelphia, PA: Churchill Livingstone Elsevier.

Foster, T., & Hawkins, J. (2005). The therapeutic relationship: Dead or merely impeded by technology? *British Journal of Nursing, 14*(13), 698–702.

Geller, S. M., & Greenberg, L. S. (2012) *Therapeutic presence: A mindful approach to effective therapy.* Washington, DC: American Psychological Association.

Geller, S. M., & Porges, S. W. (2014). Therapeutic presence: Neurophysiological mechanisms mediating feeling safe in therapeutic relationships. *Journal of Psychotherapy Integration, 24*(3), 178–192.

Gilbert, P. (2009). *The compassionate mind: A new approach to life's challenges.* Oakland, CA: New Harbinger.

Gregory, D., Raymond-Seniuk, C., Patrick, L., & Stephen, T. (Eds.). (2015). *Fundamentals: Perspective on the art and science of Canadian nursing.* Philadelphia, PA: Wolters Kluwer Health.

Heller, D. (2016, April). DARE to connect training, Boulder, CO.

Huffington, A. (2016). *The sleep revolution: Transforming your life one night at a time.* New York, NY: Harmony Books.

Jourard, S. M. (1971). *The transparent self.* New York, NY: Van Nostrand Reinhold.

Juhan, D. (1998). *Job's body: A handbook for bodywork.* Barrytown, NY: Barrytown.

Kamdar, B. B., King, L. M., Collop, N. A., Sakamuri, S., Colantuoni, E., Newfeld, K. J., . . . Needham, D. M. (2013). The effect of a quality improvement intervention on perceived sleep quality and cognition in a medical ICU. *Critical Care Medicine, 41*(3), 800–809.

Levine, P. A. (2010). *In an unspoken voice: How the body releases trauma and restores goodness.* Berkley, CA: North Atlantic Books.

Levine, P. A. (2013). Trauma and spirituality: A marriage of body and spirit. Presented at Breath of Life Conference, London, England.

Levine, P. A., & Kline, M. (2007). *Trauma through a child's eyes: Awakening the ordinary miracle of healing.* Berkeley, CA: North Atlantic Books.

MacDonald, G., & Leary, M. R. (2005). Why does social exclusion hurt? The relationship between social and physical pain. *Psychological Bulletin, 131*(2), 202–223.

Porges, S. W. (2011). *The Polyvagal Theory: Neurophysiological foundations of emotions, attachment, communication, self-regulation.* New York, NY: Norton.

Porges, S. W. (2013). A neural love code. Presented at Breath of Life Conference, London, England.

Porges, S. W. (2014). The transformative power of feeling safe. Presented at Cape Cod Institute, Eastham, MA.

Porges, S. W. (2015). Making the world safe for our children: Down-regulating defence and up-regulating social engagement to 'optimise' the human experience. *Children Australia, 40*, 114–123. doi:10.1017/cha.2015.12

Sapolsky, R. M. (2004). *Why zebras don't get ulcers.* New York, NY: Henry Holt.

Sitzman, K., & Eichelberger, L. W. (2017). *Understanding the work of nurse theorists: A creative beginning.* Burlington, MA: Jones & Bartlett.

Smith, M. C., Turkel, M. C., & Wolf, Z. R. (2013). *Caring in nursing classics: An essential resource.* New York, NY: Springer.

Turkle, S. (2015). *Reclaiming conversation: The power of talk in a digital age.* New York, NY: Penguin.

Watson, J. (1997). The theory of human caring: retrospective and prospective. *Nursing Science Quarterly, 10 (1), 49-52.*

10

Presence, Prosody, and Touch: Engaging the Mammalian Autonomic Nervous System

Alan Theede

Abstract: Veterinarians pay close attention to the autonomic nervous system states of the animals they examine and treat. Careful observation of behavioral patterns and examination of physical signs is essential in making diagnoses and determining individualized treatments. The author uses Polyvagal Theory as a platform to understand the mammalian social engagement system, to minimize the neuroception of danger, and to provide ethical care for animals.

POLYVAGAL THEORY DESCRIBES the evolutionarily developed mammalian autonomic nervous system. Humans are mammals, and the human autonomic nervous system shares a similar structure with all other mammals. We coexist and share the earth with the animals that are our companions and pets, the creatures that provide food and clothing for mankind, creatures that provide transportation and recreation, and the "wild" animals in our environment. Human–animal interactions and the depth of relationships vary. It is the neuroception of safety, in both the animal and the human, that allows for the building of relationship and the co-regulation of their nervous systems. Although domesticated animals (pets) have their own epigenetic inheritance and experience of living in close contact and being cared for by humans, these animals "live in the moment" (in the now), and their autonomic nervous systems respond in the moment to the owner's nervous system. When strong, healthy relationships are present, pets will initiate contact and engagement (lick, paw, wag their tail) or initiate play with their owners. The friendly excitement of a pet happy to see its owner at the end of a long day offers a ventral vagal boost. Social engagement connections exist between the mammalian autonomic nervous systems of pets and their owners. Pets have a positive impact on human health (Serpell, 1991). The physiology of one influences the physiology of the other. Polyvagal Theory outlines the social engagement system and the neuroception of safety as the basis for co-regulation.

The purpose of veterinary medicine is to ensure the health, wellness, and welfare of all animals except humans. The majority of animals (more than 95%) treated by veterinarians are mammals. Birds, reptiles, and fish are occasionally examined and treated by veterinarians, but they generally make up a small percentage of the caseload for most practitioners. Polyvagal Theory speaks to the phylogenetic development of the mammalian autonomic nervous system. Therefore, the discussion and examples presented in this chapter are about mammals. Mammals are vertebrate animals; they have a neocortex, hair, detached middle-ear bones, and mammary glands. I have used the wording *mammal* and *animal* interchangeably throughout the chapter. The animals used as examples in this chapter—dogs, cats, horses, and cattle—are all mammals and share the polyvagal nature of the parasympathetic nervous system (myelinated ventral vagal branch and primitive dorsal vagal branch of the vagus nerve) described by Polyvagal Theory.

I have been a veterinarian throughout my working career. After studying Polyvagal Theory, I realize that much of the work done by veterinarians is to provide cues of safety to the animals they are treating. These cues of safety allow veterinarians and animal owners and caretakers to safely and compassionately engage with their animals and to perform the care, feeding, examinations, procedures, and treatments that are necessary to maintain health and well-being. Animals are healthier and recover more quickly and completely when attention is paid to understanding and regulating their autonomic nervous systems. It is especially important to minimize activation of the animal's sympathetic nervous system and the metabolically expensive fight-or-flight state. When people assume the responsibility to keep, care for, and manage animals, which we do with our pets, farm animals, and zoo and research animals, we also assume the moral and ethical obligation to provide a comfortable, calm, reasonably natural, and safe existence for these animals.

Humans share similar physiology, nervous system anatomy, visceral organs, metabolism, and body systems with other mammals. Therefore, the medical care of mammals in general, and the care of their nervous systems in particular, provides striking parallels between veterinary and human medicine. The 2012 book *Zoobiquity: What Animals Can Teach Us About Being Human* (Natterson-Horowitz & Bowers, 2012) describes the importance of sharing experiences, research, and the techniques used in health care professions across all of the species. Each chapter describes diseases and conditions where animal health research and experience can provide insights into human healing and methods to maintain wellness. The book calls on all health care providers, including physicians and veterinarians, to look beyond their own experiences and expertise to consider the common health circumstances of all animals. Polyvagal Theory and the evolutionary mammalian nervous system we have in common with animals is an example of the value of sharing interspecies knowledge.

Animals cannot tell us their thoughts, their feelings, or where it hurts. They can't discuss or explain their health status. Veterinarians work in an exclusively nonverbal world (no spoken language). Veterinarians respond to the animal's symptoms and nervous system state moment to moment within the current time frame. Nothing is predetermined or assumed, because the relationship with the animal occurs in the present moment. Careful observation and examination of the animal is necessary to provide answers and insight about injury, disease, or health status. Veterinarians are trained to observe subtle changes in physiology and behavior that are clues to the animal's condition. They see these subtle changes every day in their animal patients. When there are no words exchanged, an understanding of the neuroception within the animal becomes essential. Polyvagal Theory describes how understanding and observing the regulation of an animal's nervous system provides valuable insights into the metabolic and behavioral states of the animal. With experience, it is possible to observe subtleties in the muscle tension around the animal's eyes, mouth, and in the limbs; to see bristling of body hair; and to hear vocalizations; all assisting in making a judgment about the state of the animal's autonomic nervous system. When the animal is calm, relaxed, and quiet, it is picking up cues of safety from the veterinarian, and the environment and is under ventral vagal influence. Through a polyvagal perspective, we understand the importance of providing safety.

My veterinary career has been spent working for the improved health and wellness of food-production mammals. My own experience is with group, community, or herd medicine. I placed an emphasis on disease prevention, disease treatment, optimal nutrition, housing or shelter, and welfare for the animals under my care. For this chapter, I have consulted my colleagues who are companion-animal, equine, and animal-behavior specialists.

Approaching and Relating to Animals

Veterinarians are taught to approach animals slowly and calmly with an intention to do no harm; to make contact allowing the animal to feel safe; to not startle an individual or a group of animals triggering their survival instinct to escape. Polyvagal Theory explains that when a mammal is frightened, it becomes "dependent on the neural circuits that evolved to provide adaptive defensive behaviors," and "when, on the other hand, there is a neuroception of the environment being safe . . . mechanisms of defense are disabled" (Porges, 2011, p. 19). With a neuroception of safety, an animal remains calm and approachable. From a polyvagal perspective, slow movements and gestures, prosodic voice, and soft eye gaze support the animal's social engagement system and help regulate its nervous system, allowing the animal to settle and adjust to human presence. The hearing range for most herd and pet mammals (not rodents that hear higher frequencies) largely overlaps the hearing range of humans. These mammals are sensitive to human voice intonation or prosody and can hear and decode the intention and emotion being conveyed when people speak to them. Since animals cannot verbally tell us how they feel or where they hurt, careful observation is needed to assess their physical and behavioral state during an approach. It is fairly easy to see sympathetic activation and determine if more time is needed for the animal to orient to its surroundings, including the approaching veterinarian, to minimize arousal and defensive actions. When entering a pen of cattle, sheep, or pigs, or when approaching a single animal such as a horse, dog, or cat, veterinarians learn to establish presence slowly and attentively. Speaking softly, with a calm tone of voice, and maintaining visual contact while moving slowly toward the mammal engages the animal's social engagement system and contributes to the sense of safety.

Grazing animals have a wide angle of vision because their eyes are located on the sides of their heads. Their visual field is over 300°, compared to approximately 120° for humans. Horses or cattle in an open field or pasture will see people from a great distance. The eye location for dogs and cats can vary greatly depending on the breed, although most have a forward orientation for their vision. Understanding that vision is an important sense, ensuring that an animal can see a person approaching, is an important strategy to avoid creating the cues of danger and surprise that can trigger a defensive sympathetic nervous system response.

In my experience with large animals, I found that once my presence was established, the animals would often move toward me, as their natural curiosity was aroused—an example of their active social engagement system. I would then move toward the animals while avoiding making sudden movements and startling gestures. Moving slowly through a group, or around an individual animal, I could do a visual examination. An animal such as a horse that is accustomed to being touched and held can be gently restrained to allow a closer examination such as palpation, listening with a stethoscope, and taking body temperature. Often it is sufficient for the owner to hold the horse with a halter around the head. The presence of the owner in close contact with the horse is a strong cue of safety for the animal helping to regulate its autonomic nervous system and remain calm throughout the examination.

Touch is an important part of establishing relationship with an animal. Gentle touch is an important cue of safety. My practice was to touch an animal, stroking the neck, head, and back, when I made initial contact. Proximity, safe presence, and touch help settle the mammal into a calm, ventral vagal–dominant state. I cannot imagine being close to an animal or carrying out a procedure without placing my hand on the animal, usually along the neck or back, providing reassuring touch. Owners pet their dogs or cats; horses and cattle enjoy being stroked and groomed with combs and brushes. Youth groups such as 4-H clubs teach young club members the intrinsic value of touch in establishing relationship and engagement with their animals.

Over time, owners and their pets form social bonds; what Dr. Porges (2013) described as the "Neural Love Code." Close proximity, social engagement, touch, play, and loving care between the owner and pet create a condition of safety and connection, and a strong social bond is established. Owners are naturally concerned when their pets are injured or sick and require veterinary care and treatment. There is often sympathetic arousal, and sometimes dorsal vagal arousal, in both the animal and the owner. The veterinarian comes into contact with both the pet and the owner, and a triad is formed: pet, owner, and veterinarian. Developing trust within this triad is vital, although the dyad between the veterinarian and animal comes first. A close friend, a companion-animal veterinarian, described "moments of meeting" with sick or injured pets, establishing a primary relationship with the animal through eye gaze, prosodic speech, and soothing touch, while listening with a third ear to comments from the owner. The veterinarian observes the nervous system and the behavioral state of the pet and changes the pacing of the examination as needed to mitigate the animal's autonomic dysregulation. When the owners experience their pets being examined and handled with care, and they observe a positive shift in the pet's autonomic state, trust and engagement are built between the owners and the veterinarian. The owner's physiological state shifts as well. Information and clear explanations about the diagnosis, prognosis, and treatment plan, provided in a calm and engaging manner, build on this foundation of trust and strengthens the owner–veterinarian relationship. Owners in a calm, regulated, ventral vagal state are able to co-regulate their pets' physiology, enhancing recovery and healing. This is an important factor, since the owners are the primary caregivers for the pets when they return home. The owner's ventral vagal state also enables the optimal tension in the muscles of the middle-ear bones, thus facilitating improved hearing and comprehension (Porges, 2011) of the ongoing care instructions given by the veterinarian. Although the veterinarian's primary role is the diagnosis and treatment of the pet's disorder, taking into consideration the veterinarian–owner–pet triad, supporting owners in their autonomic regulation ultimately supports the recovery of the animals.

Approaching and handling animals in a calm, slow, and focused manner, a regulated ventral vagal manner, is a safety factor for the veterinarian and owner. A fast or aggressive approach can trigger an animal's startle and arousal response, putting the people who are present at risk. The animal's autonomic nervous system can easily become dysregulated, triggering an adaptive survival response of fight (bite, scratch, kick) or flight (trying to run). A large farm animal in a sympathetic nervous system flight state can be dangerous and unpredictable. Not only may its health be further compromised, there is an additional occupational health and safety aspect for their caretakers and for the veterinarian. Animals in a fear response are much more likely to injure both themselves and their handlers than are animals that are calm, with minimal sympathetic arousal. As an example, a veterinarian working with a 1,500-lb (700 kg) dairy cow or an over-2,000-lb (1,000 kg) draft horse must be aware of signs of sympathetic activation (ears back, nostrils flared, reluctance to stand still) and adjust their work accordingly. Imagine the risk to the veterinarian when lifting a front or back leg of a horse or cow to examine for lameness.

Companion animals have strong attachments to their owners. When a pet and owner are together and there is a neuroception of safety, a ventral vagal state is shared by owner and pet as their two mammalian autonomic nervous systems co-regulate. Both pet and owner seek this enjoyable, homeostatic, restorative state. There are numerous stories exemplifying the loving and dedicated connections formed between people and their pets. Miraculous stories abound of long-distance travel, the passage of time, or the complexity of the separation, in which dogs have returned home and found their owners despite extreme circumstances.

PAWS YOUR STRESS! is a unique title on a poster I saw at our local university Health Sciences Library. The university encourages students during final exams to "take time to de-stress with some of St. John Ambulance's wonderful therapy dog volunteers." Therapy dogs are brought to various university libraries, where students can take a break from studying to pet, hold, and cuddle them. This co-regulation is an example of human–mammal interconnections reinforcing the neurophysiology described by Polyvagal Theory.

The co-regulation and ventral vagal influence between three pet owners and their dogs can be seen in a YouTube video produced by Dr. Craig Duncan and Mia Cobb (2016) in Australia. The dogs and their owners were separated. Heart rate monitoring sensors were placed on each owner and their dog. When the dog and owner were physically reunited with hand stroking, cuddling, and with what could be called prosodic verbal communication (speaking petese—as mothers speak to their babies with motherese); the heart rates of both the person and the dog slowed quickly and showed a remarkable amount of coherence in heart rhythm tracings. The myelinated ventral branch of the vagus nerve was energized by the reunification. The resulting synchronization of heart rates demonstrated the strong and rapid connection that exists between the social engagement system and the heart in both pet and owner. A similar result is reported on the HeartMath Institute's website by Dr. Rollin McCraty based on the interactions of his son Josh and their dog Mabel.

Dogs or horses are frequently used as therapy animals, and the human–mammal interaction has an impact on the social, emotional, cognitive, and physical functioning of the person undergoing pet therapy or equine-assisted therapies. I have watched equine therapy sessions where the horse continually adjusted its gait and movement to compensate for the motor challenges and poor balance of the brain-injured rider. The horse, responding to the rider's weight shifts, and the therapeutic riding instructor walking alongside were working together to regulate and support the rider. The horse's ventral vagal state provided stability and reassurance (cues of safety) to the rider. After the rider dismounted, the engagement between the two was demonstrated when the horse moved over, nudging the rider's shoulder, looking for touch. The previous examples demonstrate how effective human–mammal interactions are in helping to co-regulate the autonomic nervous systems of both persons and animals.

The term *zooeyia* was coined by Hodgson & Darling (2011) to encompass the positive mental, physical, and social benefits to human health from interactions with animals, with a focus on companion animals. "Zooeyia extends beyond the benefits to the individual pet owner; companion animals also strengthen communities. Pets facilitate social interactions; they promote a sense of safety. Companion animals encourage reciprocity—the give and take among neighbors that builds a sense of community" (Hodgson & Darling, 2011, p. 190). The conditions necessary to establish co-regulation, calming, and trust are based on both human and animal neuroception of safety. Safety, social communication, engagement, and co-regulation coexist simultaneously in each. Mammals can be a tremendous asset to support the nervous systems of humans who are experiencing stressful and challenging circumstances.

Mooo . . . d Music

Did you know dairy cows produce more milk when listening to slow-tempo and classical music? Farmers have played music in dairy barns and milking parlors for decades. A research report from Adrian North and Liam MacKenzie at the University of Leicester in the United Kingdom confirmed the advantages of music in a 2001 research paper. In their study of a large dairy herd, the cows were exposed to fast-tempo music (over 120 beats per minute), slow-tempo music (under 100 beats per minute), or no music for 12 hours each day. The animals hearing the slow-tempo music produced 3% more milk as compared to the other two groups. This equates to 0.73 extra liters (25 fl oz) of milk per cow per day. For this entire herd of 1,000 cows, this works out to 730 liters (190 U.S. gal) extra milk production and an added value of approximately $300 to $400 worth of milk each day. These results were statistically significant, confirming that milk yields can be increased by playing certain types of music for the cows. The cows are content, seemingly relaxed, and calmed by the music. Their metabolic and homeostatic processes are enhanced, resulting in increased production of milk.

The researchers found that cows responded to a pleasant auditory environment. Believe it or not, the study went so far as to suggest a playlist for the dairy cows, including Simon and Garfunkel's "Bridge Over Troubled Water," Henry Mancini's "Moon River," and Beethoven's "Pastoral Symphony"! The Dairy Producers in British Columbia, Canada (2012), hosted a contest for composers to write music for dairy cows. The cows' choice, as measured by improved daily milk production, was a new composition having a similar slow beat to that indicated in the U.K. research.

A calm and relaxing environment, in part established by the tempo of the music, supports mammals (dairy cows) in regulating their autonomic nervous system, improving ventral vagal tone, achieving a more homeostatic metabolic state, and producing more milk. The enhanced milk production is a practical example of restoration and health (Polyvagal Theory language) or improved metabolic energy use for body maintenance and milk production (veterinary and animal science language).

Polyvagal-Informed Veterinary Clinic: An Animal-Friendly Clinic

A trip to a veterinary hospital is stressful for a pet. A polyvagal-friendly veterinary clinic is a place where the cues of danger, risk, and challenge that could be detected by a visiting animal's neuroception system are removed or mitigated. As an example, a local companion-animal veterinary hospital describes their "cat-friendly" facility. They sponsor a radio advertisement featuring a dramatic scene in which a cat is frightened by the "big scary dog" across the waiting room. The cat escapes from the owner and is very difficult to catch. There is a significant sympathetic activation with mobilization and flight. The clinic advertises a separate entrance for cats and their owners, as well as separate "cat-only" examination and treatment facilities. There are also separate doors, examination rooms, and treatment rooms for dogs and other species of animals. This is a polyvagal-friendly facility, where many of the cues of danger have been reduced or eliminated. Polyvagal-friendly facilities include awareness of challenges to autonomic regulation and a commitment to reducing cues of danger while increasing cues of safety. A program supported by the American Association of Feline Practitioners provides education and sets standards for cat-friendly clinics. Often these clinics are feline only or, as described above, have completely separate facilities from those handling dogs and other animals. Aspects of these clinics include nonslip examination tables; tables or counters where owners can place the cat carrier basket at tabletop height, rather than placing the cat carrier on the floor, where the cat feels more vulnerable; and cat-friendly hospitalization cages that have soft and comfortable bedding, a shelter within the hospital cage where the cat can retreat into its own space, and a perch shelf where the animal can sit. In years past, veterinary examination rooms would almost always have had stainless steel tables that, although easy to clean and sanitize, were very slippery, disorienting, and fear inducing. This is a potentially overwhelming cue of danger for animals. Now clinics have nonslip tabletops, yoga mats, or other animal-friendly surfaces. These ideas and innovations are examples where there are dividends both to the animals and to the people around the animals when comfort, safety, and reduction of risk and fear are addressed. These advances in creating polyvagal-friendly environments foster an atmosphere that supports the ventral vagal regulation of the animal's autonomic nervous system. Pet owners are more at ease, as they recognize that their pets are less anxious and aroused when visiting the veterinary clinic. A better place for the animal, a better place for the people who visit and work in the building, and better for the clinic business.

A veterinarian is often called upon to perform euthanasia services to alleviate severe pain and suffering for animals. Doing this work is a spiritual experience, and I believe most veterinarians approach the moment from a state of ventral vagal regulation that allows them to be with animals and owners with reverence and presence. Progressive companion-animal hospitals are now providing a comfortable and private "quiet room" within the clinic where the pet and the family can spend their last time together. This room offers a separate, safe space during this very stressful time. The pet is kept comfortable, often wrapped in its own blanket or on its own bed brought from home by the family. This environment creates, as much as possible, a neuroception of safety for both the animal and the family members. The drug products are administered carefully and gently, avoiding any sense of danger or sympathetic activation for the pet. The owner and family can be present if they wish, and the process is explained step-by-step so there are no surprises for family members. The quiet, comfortable environment; slow, gentle, and paced (mindful) actions; prosodic voice; gentle touch; and minimum restraint of the pet all support engagement between the pet and the family members. By paying close attention to the autonomic nervous systems of the pet and the family, the veterinarian can facilitate peaceful and meaningful final moments. This respectful way of dealing with end of life and the mitigation of pain and suffering is important for all involved: the pet, the owner, the family, the animal hospital staff, and the veterinarians. An awareness of Polyvagal Theory assists in understanding the importance of creating this safe and supportive space.

Recently I listened to a talk radio announcer describe how his 12-year-old dog had to be put to sleep during the past weekend because of failing health and advanced cancer. It was a live, on-air emotional moment as he thanked the veterinarian who provided the service. He had his second dog, a longtime companion to himself and the other dog, on the floor beside him in the radio studio. He said both he and the surviving dog needed the close connection to each other. He also thanked the radio station management for allowing him to bring his dog to work that day. In fact, he and the dog were supporting and regulating each other's autonomic nervous systems through proximity and connectedness. No doubt the announcer was frequently touching and petting his dog under the table beside him.

Relationships Between Human–Animal Interactions and Animal Health

The veterinary and animal science literature has many examples where researchers and animal-behavior specialists have examined the details of relationships between animals and their human caregivers. There is a correlation between the care animals receive and the attitudes and behaviors of their caretakers. People provide food, water, temperature and ventilation control, safe movement of animals from place to place, and the identification of sick or injured animals leading to appropriate veterinary attention and the administration of prescribed treatments and procedures. Beyond providing these basic services, caretakers of animals need to care about animals and be comfortable around them. They must bring their own ventral vagal regulation to their interactions with the animals. The caretakers' calm and regulated nervous systems allow them to co-regulate and provide cues of safety to the animals under their care. The cues of safety allow the pet or large animal to maintain a ventral vagal–influenced nervous system that supports their homeostatic physiology. The result is better outcomes for all—the triad of the animal, caretaker, and veterinarian.

Paul Hemsworth, from Melbourne, Australia, has studied for many years the interactions between dairy cattle, pigs, and pets with their caretakers or stockpersons. His paper in the *Journal of Animal Science* states: "The significant correlations between stockpersons' attitudes and behavior and the cow behavior and productivity indicate the possibility of targeting these human characteristics to reduce fear responses in dairy cows to humans and improve the cows' productivity" (Hemsworth, Coleman, Barnett, & Borg, 2000, p. 2821). This quote describes the importance of co-regulation between the human's autonomic nervous system and the mammal's autonomic nervous system.

People who recognize the necessity and importance of reducing fear in the animals under their care are much more successful as owners and caretakers of the animals. Caretakers have the capacity and the responsibility to create these safe spaces. All animals do better when their neuroception of danger and threat is reduced. Other animal-behavior studies, with both pigs and cattle, have shown that animals can remember and will change their behaviors following "fear inducing—bad" experiences with individual caretakers (Hemsworth, Barnett, & Hansen, 1987, p. 245). The ability to retain these memories is a fascinating example of the capacity of the mammal's autonomic nervous system to adapt based on the animal's past experiences and the present environment.

These examples highlight the importance of providing a comfortable, calm, and safe environment. In polyvagal language, the mammal's neuroception system is detecting a safe environment, allowing ventral vagal tone to increase in order to achieve a relaxed, calm, and homeostatic physiological state. By improving ventral vagal tone and the neuroception of safety for our pets, domestic animals, and ourselves, we are facilitating health, growth, and restoration for all.

Animal Care and Welfare

The Five Freedoms is a core concept in animal welfare that originated in a United Kingdom government report in 1965 and was further refined by the U.K. Farm Animal Welfare Council in 1999. These Five Freedoms have become the bedrock guidelines and reference points for the care of farm animals, animals used in research settings, and other confined animals such as those in zoos, as well as those we keep at home as companion pets. Research groups complete "Animal Care" protocols as a required part of the application process with funding and granting agencies. Approval by the institutions and the payment of grants are not obtained unless the care and welfare of the research animals is ensured. These protocols and guidelines are based on the Five Freedoms concept.

An animal's primary welfare needs can be met by safeguarding the following freedoms:

1. Freedom from hunger and thirst—by ready access to fresh water and a diet to maintain full health and vigor.
2. Freedom from discomfort—by providing an appropriate environment, including shelter and a comfortable resting area.
3. Freedom from pain, injury, or disease—by prevention and/or rapid diagnosis and treatment.
4. Freedom to express (most) normal behavior—by providing sufficient space, proper facilities, and company of the animal's own kind.
5. Freedom from fear and distress—by ensuring conditions and treatments that avoid mental suffering (see Watson, 2010).

These fundamental concepts, describing what is necessary to define the appropriate care and welfare of animals, were developed and published without the benefit of an understanding of Polyvagal Theory. Polyvagal Theory and the science of the mammalian autonomic nervous system that supports Polyvagal Theory validate the Five Freedoms. Each of the freedoms is, at its core, about the neuroception of safety. Safety, comfort, security: words to describe an animal able to regulate its autonomic nervous system and move into a ventral vagal–supported state with its physiology and metabolism in homeostasis. This, I believe, would describe the state of maximal welfare for the animal.

One Health

The goal of health for all species is encompassed by the global One Health concept. There is a growing recognition that the health of humans is directly connected to the health of animals and the health of the environment. "The One Health concept is a worldwide strategy for expanding interdisciplinary collaborations and communications in all aspects of health care for humans, animals, and the environment." (One Health Initiative, 2006). Although the primary focus of One Health is infectious zoonotic disease (infections emerging in animals and transferred to people or visa versa), there is a recognition in the One Health Initiative mission statement of the importance of the human–animal bond.

> Recognizing that human health (including mental health via the human-animal bond phenomenon), animal health, and ecosystem health are inextricably linked, One Health seeks to promote, improve, and defend the health and well-being of all species by enhancing cooperation and collaboration between physicians, veterinarians, other scientific health and environmental professionals and by promoting strengths in leadership and management to achieve these goals. (One Health Initiative, 2006)

"Pets benefit human health (zooeyia) in four ways: as builders of social capital, as agents of harm reduction, as motivators for healthy behavior change, and as potential participants in treatment plans" (Hodgson et al., 2015, p. 526). Therapy dogs are increasingly being used in different settings to build therapeutic bonds between animals and people. Examples include within prison populations, at methadone treatment clinics, and as accompanying animals for military veterans (Dell & Chalmers, 2017). Zooeyia is an essential component of One Health.

I believe the examples described in this chapter exhibit the co-regulation that occurs between humans and animals (mammals). Pets in particular provide owners with a direct experience of the human–animal bond. Pets demonstrate the nonverbal features of the social engagement system as they communicate and co-regulate with their owners within a safe environment. The demeanor of each pet is unique, and pets frequently initiate nonverbal engagement features, including eye gaze and presence, proximity, gestures and touch (e.g., pets will approach and nudge their owners), and vocalizing (e.g., purring). The owners' reciprocity is evident when they respond to their dog, cat, horse, and so on, in kind with prosodic voice tones (petese); reach out to stoke their pets; or cue their pets for play activities (e.g., play fetch with their dogs). The reciprocal dynamics between the pet and the owner increases ventral vagal tone and regulation as described in Polyvagal Theory, influencing the owner's physiology and mental health. The One Health concept links human, animal, and environmental health. We are all together on this planet. Incorporating the key concepts of Polyvagal Theory into our everyday lives will help build our personal safety and develop healthy, strong, and resilient nervous systems for the people and animals around the globe.

Conclusion

The care, handling, medical attention, and treatment of mammals as well as other animals requires an extensive and varied skill set. The skill set for the maintenance of health and wellness in animals as well as the diagnosis and treatment of disease and injury is primary to the profession of veterinary medicine. The Veterinarian's Oath approved by the Canadian Veterinary Medical Association in 2004 states, in part, "I will strive to promote animal health and welfare, relieve animal suffering, protect the health of the public and environment, and advance comparative medical knowledge." The people responsible for animals have an ethical and moral responsibility to provide for the animals' needs and to keep them safe. This shared mammalian autonomic nervous system is the basis for understanding the bond between people and animals. Polyvagal Theory and its reconceptualization of the autonomic nervous system applies across the broad spectrum of animal health, veterinary medicine, reproduction, housing and shelter, nutrition, handling, care, animal welfare, and wellness. I believe Polyvagal Theory is, and will be, a critical component of animal, human, and environmental health, One Health, into the future.

References

Dell, C., & Chalmers, D. (2017) Bringing One Health to life: 2017 discussion series. University of Saskatchewan, Saskatoon, Canada.

Duncan, C., & Cobb, M. (2016, April 26). Pedigree—hearts aligned [Video file]. Retrieved from https://www.youtube.com/watch?v=8Y3ct0SYwro

Hemsworth, P. H., Barnett, J. L., & Hansen, C. (1987). The influence of inconsistent handling by humans on the behaviour, growth and corticosteroids of young pigs. *Applied Animal Behaviour Science, 17*, 245–252.

Hemsworth, P., Coleman, G. J., Barnett, J. L., & Borg, S. (2000). Relationships between human-animal interactions and productivity of commercial dairy cows. *Journal of Animal Science, 78*, 2821–2831.

Hodgson, K., Barton, L., Darling, M., Antao, V., Kim, F. A., & Monavvari, A. (2015). Pets' impact on your patients' health: Leveraging benefits and mitigating risk. *Journal of the American Board of Family Medicine, 28*, 526–534.

Hodgson, K., & Darling, M. (2011). Zooeyia: An essential component of "One Health." *Canadian Veterinary Journal, 52*, 189–191.

Natterson-Horowitz, B., & Bowers, K. (2012). *Zoobiquity: What animals can teach us about being human*. Toronto, Canada: Doubleday.

North, A., & MacKenzie, L. (2001, June). 'Moosic study' reveals way of increasing milk yields. *University of Leicester press release, 67.*

One Health Initiative. (2006). One Health initiative - one world one medicine one health. Retrieved from http://www.onehealthinitiative.com

Porges, S. W. (2011). *The Polyvagal Theory: Neurophysiological foundations of emotions, attachment, communication, self-regulation.* New York, NY: Norton.

Porges, S. W. (2013). A Neural Love Code, presented at Breath of Life Conference, London, England.

Serpell, J. (1991). Beneficial effects of pet ownership on some aspects of human health and behaviour. *Journal of the Royal Society of Medicine, 84*, 717–720.

Watson, J. (2010). Animal welfare. Retrieved from http://ocw.jhsph.edu/courses/humanescience/PDFs/CAATLecture8.pdf

Part III

Therapeutic Approaches and Clinical Applications

11

The Polyvagal PlayLab: Helping Therapists Bring Polyvagal Theory to Their Clients

Deb Dana and Deb Grant

Abstract: The Polyvagal PlayLab brings together neuroscience, expressive arts, and somatics to teach therapists Polyvagal Theory and its application to clinical work. Designed to help participants learn the theory by engaging experientially with their autonomic nervous systems, therapists experiment with ways to "map" their autonomic patterns, attune to their neuroception of safety, and tone their social vagus. This chapter describes elements of the Polyvagal PlayLab, inviting readers to experiment with the material and create a more deeply polyvagal-informed approach to their work with clients.

AS THERAPISTS, WE know that unconscious experiences of safety, danger, and life-threat become woven into personal narratives. Polyvagal Theory is essential for understanding how physiological state influences and shapes this process. How might psychotherapists apply this new understanding, which bridges psychological experiences with physiological states, in their clinical work?

In the Polyvagal PlayLab, we set out to "play" with Polyvagal Theory with a group of therapists. The PlayLab brings together neuroscience, expressive arts, and somatics to teach Polyvagal Theory and its application to clinical work. This chapter describes several elements of the Polyvagal PlayLab so readers can experiment with the material and integrate aspects of the PlayLab with their current treatment approaches, bringing a more deeply polyvagal-informed approach to their work with clients.

According to Polyvagal Theory, maintaining a ventral vagal state is a basic physiological requirement for growth and learning (Porges, 2003b). Creating an environment where the passive pathways of neuroception signal safety and activate the social engagement system is necessary to establish a foundation for participants to absorb the workshop material. The experiential nature of the workshop promotes processing from the bottom up as felt experience in the body. Integrating embodied experience with a cognitive understanding of Polyvagal Theory is the goal for the PlayLab.

Polyvagal Theory suggests that beneath our conscious awareness, the nervous system scans for risk features in both our internal and external environments. Based on detection of risk, the autonomic nervous system is recruited to respond and promote states of safety or defense. This process linking the identification of risk to specific autonomic reactions is known as *neuroception* (Porges, 2003a, 2004). Neuroception detects cues of safety, danger, or life-threat. Although we are profoundly aware of these massive physiological state shifts mediated by neuroception, we are often clueless as to the specific cues that triggered the response. Therapists, similar to clients, are vulnerable to neuroception and the consequential physiological reactions.

Within any group of therapists, as well as in the general population, a percentage of participants are likely to have had traumatic experiences as part of their history, affecting their neuroception of safety within a training context. Vicarious trauma is an expected and manageable experience for therapists who treat trauma (Harrison & Westwood, 2009). The PlayLab is a structured experience for therapists to gain insight into the ways autonomic awareness can function as a protective factor against this common challenge.

Understanding that moments of defense (e.g., mobilization and immobilization) would likely be triggered during the workshop, we incorporate principles and activities to support participants' smooth return to a state of safety via ventral vagal mechanisms. Fight-or-flight and immobilization defensive responses to neuroception occur reflexively in micromoments. State shifts can be subtle; and even astute, skilled therapists who are adept at tracking behavior changes in their clients might be unaccustomed to tracking nuances of their own state shifts and how these state shifts may impact the client. Throughout the PlayLab, we support participants in learning to track awareness by attending to their autonomic state.

Polyvagal Theory, as an integrated theory involving both top-down and bottom-up processes, has greater relevance, application, and impact when psychotherapists have mindfully explored their own polyvagal patterns, mapped their autonomic nervous systems, and somatically experienced and influenced state shifts in their personal explorations of body-based interventions. The following guidelines support learning, practicing, and playing with Polyvagal Theory in a safe "laboratory" with other therapists.

Create a structure and format that allows workshop leaders to attune to participants' varying needs in a learning environment. Educational settings can evoke a neuroception of a loss of safety for adults based on past experiences in school and learning environments. Experiences in childhood and adulthood often lead to fear of being incompetent, difficulty with processing new material, or an obsessive need to be perfect. Therapists' autonomic states may become dysregulated when they are required not only to learn something new or unfamiliar but to learn experientially. Experiences of autonomic dysregulation are manifested in familiar stories such as "But it's just a workshop, I shouldn't be triggered." or "Everyone else can do this—I'm a failure." Identifying mobilization and immobilization triggers as adaptive autonomic responses and normalizing them as a commonly shared human experience invites participants to recognize their state shifts and respond with compassion.

Provide opportunities for safe group connection, sense of belonging, and comfort. New groups can bring cues of danger and challenges around fitting in, safety, belonging, and worthiness. In both personal work and work with others, the neural platform for cognitions is as worthy of attention as the cognitions themselves. Each moment of the workshop presents an opportunity to support ventral vagal regulation to ensure feelings of safety and connection. This means attention to the placement of, and flow between, segments of the workshop that use intentionally activated state shifts as a learning tool to give the nervous system time to "take a breath," rest in a ventral vagal state, and experience the feeling of safety; thoughtfulness about physical comfort and cues of safety and danger in the workshop environment knowing that the passive pathways of neuroception are continuously taking in information; and repeated invitations to participants to notice their autonomic state and follow that information in meeting their individual needs for comfort.

Actively track participants' autonomic responses. Since the autonomic nervous system is a relational system toned in experience with others, participants each bring their own unique neural profiles to the learning environment. For some participants, the PlayLab and its experiential content will be a day of comfortable engagement through neural exercises that bring the right degree of challenge. For other participants, the experiential components will evoke intense experiences that bring too much of a neural challenge. When cues of danger override cues of safety, participants experience the predictable cascade of physiological state shifts that take them out of connection into states of protection. If an exercise pulls a participant into an adaptive survival response, co-regulation through engaging the pathways of the social engagement system is the first response offered. As group leaders, we extend our own active engagement and also support other group members in reaching out to offer ventral vagal connection.

Prioritize ventral vagal regulation as a part of the group process and awareness. Therapists' skills for maintaining a state of ventral vagal regulation are necessary to lead a workshop, facilitate a group, or engage clients in individual therapy. The PlayLab provides a setting to model conscious use of Polyvagal Theory to regulate and demonstrate skills in the group. Skills include describing states of activation as they happen, engaging in self-regulation and co-regulation, and demonstrating a range of regulating actions.

This chapter presents a sampling of exercises from the PlayLab. We invite the reader to explore these experiential approaches as a way to become familiar with Polyvagal Theory from the inside out.

Introducing Polyvagal Theory

Polyvagal Theory can be thought of as the science of feeling safe enough to fall in love with life and take the risks of living. Through the concept of "neural surveillance," we understand that the autonomic nervous system and the higher brain structures regulating and monitoring the autonomic nervous system are always running in the background, listening and moving us along a continuum of adaptive survival responses. Looking at the autonomic evolutionary timeline, we can track the polyvagal hierarchy of ancient (dorsal) vagus collapse through sympathetic mobilization and into social (ventral) vagus connection. Adding anatomical images to convey the architecture of the nervous system and video clips to see it in action helps participants "see the science."

Exploring the triune nervous system in an "autonomic psychodrama," using group participants to role-play the three states of autonomic experience, brings the psychoeducation alive. Participants in the role-play act out the behavioral impulses and narrate the story of each state. Seeing the autonomic hierarchy in action and identifying the qualities of each autonomic state brings awareness to the responses that are invited or restricted in each state. What do the dorsal vagal "path of last resort," the sympathetic "on the move" energy, and the ventral vagal "safe and social" experiences bring?

Broadening the exploration of the neurobiology of experience brings the focus to the intertwining regulation within the brain stem of the myelinated ventral vagal pathway with the specific pathways (i.e., special visceral efferent) embedded within five cranial nerves. These comprise the "safety circuit" and manifest as the social engagement system. The social engagement system is linked to the moments of attunement and misattunement that are spread throughout our daily experience. Understanding the neural platform for these commonly experienced moments reduces shame and blame and increases the possibility for compassion and curiosity.

Homeostasis and the nonreactive roles of the dorsal vagal and sympathetic nervous systems are possible only with the ventral vagal system overseeing regulation. This optimal state for mental and physical health buffers the sympathetic nervous system and the dorsal vagal circuit from shifting into states of defense. The ventral vagal system has a regulating role; recognizing that unopposed dorsal vagal or sympathetic states take us out of connection into adaptive survival responses is an important part of understanding Polyvagal Theory. An integrated nervous system is necessary to support compassionate regard for others, curiosity about the world we live in, and safe emotional and physical connection with others.

Three basic elements of Polyvagal Theory are presented in the PlayLab: autonomic hierarchy, neuroception, and reciprocity/co-regulation. These are explored through the exercises described in the next sections.

Autonomic Awareness Through Mapmaking

We make maps to chart a specific territory—in this case, the autonomic nervous system as seen through the lens of Polyvagal Theory. Maps give us a way to enter into autonomic awareness by providing a structure through which we bring language to the wordless experience of neuroception. With these mapping experiences, participants explore ventral vagal, sympathetic, and dorsal vagal patterns and begin to identify their individual profiles of engagement and activation. Maps are memorable, and autonomic maps are powerful tools that help create a habit of knowing where we are. They are an anchor to return to with the orienting question, "Where am I on my map?"

The Ladder Map

From the moment you came into this world, a ladder was placed in front of you that you might transcend it.
—Rumi

This mapping exercise is based on Deb Dana's *Beginner's Guide to Polyvagal Theory* (2018). The Ladder Map brings both left-brain and right-brain capacities together by first inviting an embodied sense of the autonomic state (right hemisphere bias) and then adding language to the experience (left hemisphere bias). Tracking state shifts through the image of moving up and down the ladder has proven to be easy for people to comprehend and utilize. The question "Where am I on the ladder?" is straightforward to answer and brings with it a wealth of usable information. These autonomic ladder maps are easy to share with others, creating a mutual understanding of autonomic states and state shifts.

The ladder image invites a sense of safe transitions. Moving up and down a ladder does not require a leap across a gap but instead involves a steady progression from rung to rung. A ladder is always in contact with the ground, offering a way to safely reach higher places. In this case, the ground for our ladder are our evolutionary roots of dorsal vagal energy, and our transition upward takes us through the energized sympathetic state and into the ventral vagal state of social connection.

This mapping exercise follows the process of dissolution (Porges, 2011) to give a felt sense of the autonomic response hierarchy. The structure of the mapping sequence is designed to maintain a "critical mass" of ventral vagal control, so participants can safely activate sympathetic and dorsal vagal states, be with each state but not be hijacked by them, and intentionally shift between states. When guiding the mapmaking experience, it is important to offer cues of safety that the social engagement system watches for—warm tone of voice, eye gaze, proximity to signal connection.

Mapmaking activates the autonomic nervous system, energizing each state as it is mapped. It is essential to end the mapping exercise with the ventral vagal "safe and social" section, as this is the autonomic state we want to actively access and experience at the close of the exercise.

Begin the mapping process by moving first into sympathetic "danger," and then further down the autonomic hierarchy to dorsal vagal "life-threat," before mobilizing back up the hierarchy to end in ventral vagal safety and connection. When bringing sympathetic and dorsal vagal states to embodied aliveness, titrate the experience to allow just enough of a flavor, or taste, of these memories for them to be accessible for mapping. For the ventral vagal state, the instruction is to "fill from the core to the skin" with the memory, creating a fully embodied and alive experience.

The movement up and down the autonomic hierarchy is familiar and easily invoked. The transition from dorsal vagal back into ventral vagal requires a progression through sympathetic mobilization. A simple four-step "stretch, touch, breathe, laugh" sequence guides the return from dorsal vagal collapse through sympathetic to ventral vagal safety and connection: an arm stretch to activate extensor tone, touching fingertips with another person to bring the co-regulation of friendly touch, a long slow exhale to increase ventral vagal tone, and a shared laugh for breath control and co-regulation.

At the completion of the mapmaking exercise, participants form dyads to share their maps. The pairs travel their maps together, discussing the body, behavior, and belief landmarks they've identified. In this process, they notice together the difficulty or flexibility of transitioning between states. This is a time of ventral vagal connection, each participant bringing curiosity and compassion and actively engaging in co-regulation.

Directions for Completing the Ladder Map

Start with a blank "ladder map" and colored markers. Color is one of the first strategies we use to distinguish between things (Church, 2004), and studies show that colors evoke a physiological arousal and psychological effects (Yoto, Katsuura, Iwanaga, & Shimomura, 2007). Offering colored markers brings attention to the ways this is not only a top-down cognitive exercise and invites a shift into a different way of experiencing. "What color are you drawn to as you prepare to map sympathetic danger, dorsal vagal life-threat, ventral vagal safety?" This is an opportunity to practice making an autonomically informed choice, tuning into the information communicated by the autonomic state rather than listening to a cognitive story about color.

For each section, choose colored markers that represent that autonomic state. Interestingly, gray or black is often a dorsal vagal choice, red a sympathetic nervous system choice, and blue a ventral vagal choice. Working with each section, allow yourself time to sense your embodied experience (autonomic neuroception), and then bring that experience to awareness (cortical perception).

Remember a time when you felt the sense of activation in that state. For sympathetic and dorsal vagal, let a bit of that into your mind and body—just enough to get a flavor of it. For ventral vagal, bring the fullness of that experience into your mind and body.

For each section, fill in the space, writing what it feels like, looks like, sounds like.

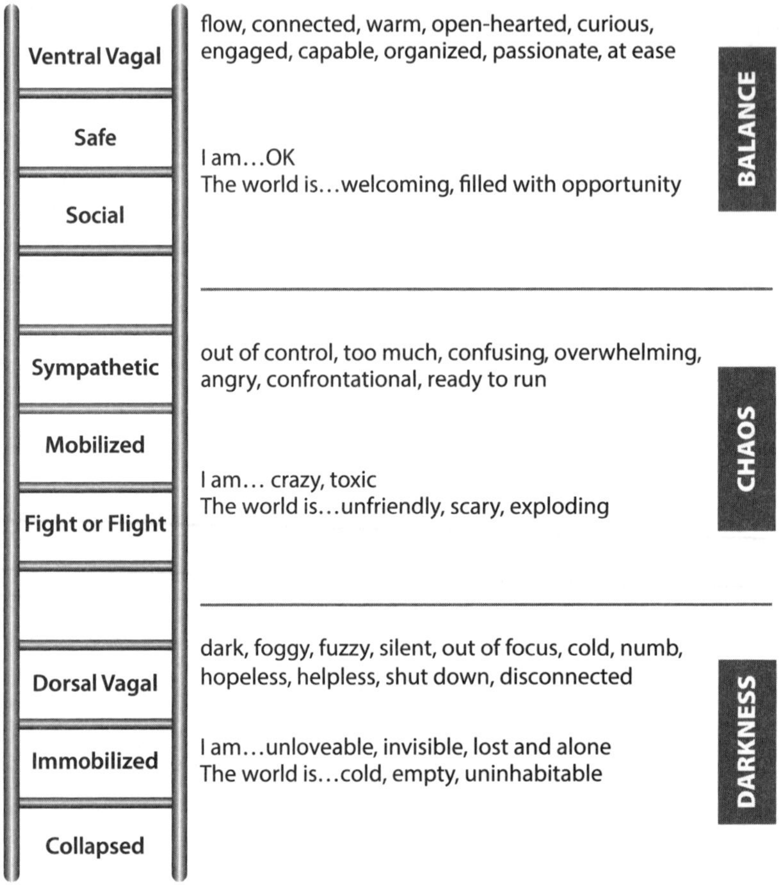

FIGURE 11.1
This sample map is a composite of common responses from clinicians and clients.

What happens in your body? What do you do? What do you feel? What do you think and say? How is your sleep, activity, food, use of substances affected?

As you finish each section, from that autonomic state, fill in the two sentences below. which identify core beliefs at work in each state:

"I am . . ."

"The world is . . ."

Creating an "Art Map"

> *I found I could say things with color and shapes that I couldn't say any other way—things I had no words for.*
> —Georgia O'Keeffe

Art is a symbolic communication system that, similar to language, conveys thoughts, ideas, and emotions (Zaidel, 2014). Making art has been shown to increase functional connectivity in the brain and bring an increase in qualities of resilience (Bolwerk et al., 2014). Creating an autonomic art map brings the right hemisphere and its love of imagery into action. And since the right hemisphere is less influenced by prediction, what emerges in an art map often brings new awareness.

Art activities bring a wide range of autonomic responses, and acknowledging that common experience helps to normalize it. You don't have to be an artist to make an autonomic art map. You only need materials and a willingness to experiment; in this case, paper and markers and enough cues of safety in the room to bring a ventral vagal state of curiosity. Using heavier-weight, large-sized art paper avoids the implicit memories from childhood that newsprint can trigger, conveys a valuing of the process, and invites people to move beyond the confines of the world so often defined by 8.5 × 11 in. paper.

To begin, participants are offered markers and paper. After dividing the paper in thirds, representing the three stages of the autonomic hierarchy, participants have 15 minutes of uninterrupted time to create their art maps. The directions are to "let your autonomic nervous system guide you." When the maps are completed, participants check to see if sharing their art map feels like a regulated, ventral vagal experience. If so, they place their maps faceup, and if not, facedown. This decision requires all participants to listen to their own autonomic needs and honor the autonomic requests. Maps faceup and facedown around the room are visual reminders that individual autonomic responses are present within a shared experience.

Embodied Autonomy: Experiencing Polyvagal Physiology From the Inside Out

Cellular Intelligence

Below personality, emotion, and physiology, we are composed of approximately 30 trillion cells (Eveleth, 2013). Each cell is both dependent and interdependent, regulating metabolic processes by determining, moment to moment, what to bring in or to send out across the cell membrane. Gazing at an image of an undifferentiated cell (easily found with an online image search) cultivates the felt sense of being a living, breathing community of cells. Imagining the feeling of an undifferentiated cell while attuning to body sensation initiates a sense of calmness and aliveness that comes from the knowledge that our cells know just what to do. The sense of natural cellular intelligence being "in charge of our systems" supports safe experiencing of the body, leading to increased ventral vagal flow.

Shared Breath

Breath is a direct, accessible way to increase ventral vagal tone. Moving from typical breathing, around 15 breaths per minute, to slow breathing, 5–7 breaths per minute, increases parasympathetic activation (Jerath, Crawford, Barnes, & Harden, 2015). As breaths per minute decrease, ventral vagal tone increases. Following the rhythmic expanding and contracting movement of a Hoberman sphere (a geometric toy that folds open and closed) offers a dramatic visual experience and creates a focus for collective breath. As the sphere is slowly opened and closed, participants match their own breath to the sphere's "breath," inhaling as the sphere expands and exhaling as it contracts. With several guided breath cycles, awareness shifts from individual breath to an experience of shared group breath. Shared rhythmic breathing seems to bring individuals into safe connection, and following the shared breath exercise, participants often identify a sense of group belonging.

Cellular Breathing

Every living cell in the body brings in oxygen and expels carbon dioxide in a process referred to as *internal respiration*. The Body-Mind Centering® embodiment practice of cellular breathing involves visualizing, sensing, feeling, and embodying this vital process of gas exchange across the cell membrane happening in every living cell of the body (Brook, 2014; Aposhyan, 2004). Typically this metabolic activity occurs beneath conscious awareness, but with the practice of "feeling into" the subtle expansion and contraction of the body's cells, it is possible to experience embodied awareness of the cells themselves. Visualizing being one cell breathing within a fluid environment helps guide our kinesthetic experience, resulting in attunement to a global sense of presence, aliveness, and vitality within the ocean of the body (Cohen, 2008).

The "vagal brake" is naturally engaged. Accessing a felt sense of cellular breathing requires calm, focused attention and curiosity about this natural metabolic regulation. Increased feelings of ease, balance, and global relaxation throughout the body reduce sympathetic activity and increases parasympathetic tone.

Feeling for and Following the Vagus

Using anatomical drawings of the vagus nerve as a guide, gently walk your fingers along the base of the skull near the ear, along the neck, and to the heart region, pausing to attune to the sense of its presence in the body. Follow "the wandering nerve" (i.e., the literal translation of *vagus*), while recalling the nerve's function and sensing its impact on eye gaze, sucking, swallowing, hearing sound, vocal tone, breath, and heart rate. Exploring the vagus nerve while feeling for it from the inside out increases interoception of the nerve itself, as well as of the surrounding tissue. Bringing attention to the physical presence of the vagus nerve increases curiosity, self-awareness, and ventral vagal tone.

Exercising the Vagal Brake

This guided movement exercise is designed to explore experiences of regulation and co-regulation. The exercise begins with the group moving in the space responding to directions to slow down (engaging the vagal brake), speed up (evoking sympathetic tone), and engage with others and the environment in distinct ways while tracking their autonomic state shifts. At points, eye contact is invited, and at other times eye contact is disallowed, helping participants experience how eye gaze influences neuroception in social interaction. Prosodic vocal sounds are encouraged—saying one another's names in singsong tones and gently tilting the head with the offer of kind eyes—cues of safety that stimulate ventral vagal tone. Then vocalization is expressed in a monotone, accompanied by rigid body posture, triggering a neuroception of danger or life-threat.

The guided explorations in this exercise bring increased awareness to the ways subtle movement and the intentional alternating of orientation between internal and external experience affects neuroception. As participants track the subtle state shifts that occur within the process of ventral vagal regulation, they learn how autonomic state affects their sense of safety and ability to connect with others. Participants are encouraged to notice and compare their experiences of co-regulation and self-regulation. Since co-regulation builds resilience and the capacity for self-regulation (Porges, 2016), experiences of collective group safety have the potential to increase the sense of individual safety.

Embodying the Muscles of the Social Engagement System

When a muscle of the social engagement system is activated mindfully, the system itself is brought further 'online,' leading to greater ventral vagal tone. Since many people don't have a sense of the muscles that make up the social engagement system, a visual anatomical map is a good starting point for exploration. The web has many easily found images that can be used to support these explorations. Begin by looking at the image, and then find and feel into your body's anatomical equivalent. Seeing the muscles of the social engagement system depicted in anatomical drawings while activating and experiencing the movement of the muscles is a powerful way of understanding material directly in the body.

Exploring the Muscles of the Pharynx and Larynx

Beginning with the muscles of the pharynx, explore the psychophysical experience of the muscle action of the levator veli palatini (CN X, XI) by swallowing mindfully, attuning to the kinesthetic experience of swallowing while sensing how this muscle action prevents food from entering up into the nasal passage. Continue by looking at images of the inner muscles of the pharynx, which control the actions of swallowing and breathing, sensing how these muscles help prevent food from entering the airway when breathing, and help safely propel food down the pharynx when swallowing.

Moving to the larynx, find the cricothyroid muscle (CN X), responsible for tensing the vocal cords and adjusting human voice pitch by gently palpating the throat. Feel for the trachea just above the sternum and then walk your fingers up until you reach the cricoid cartilage. Once this is found, soft humming can be felt in the fingers as vibration. Palpating the muscle while humming tones the vagus. Notice what state shifts can occur as you hum different melodies or tones.

Exploring the Soft Palate

Stimulate the muscles of the soft palate (CN V) by drawing the tongue down from the posterior soft surface of the roof of the mouth in a gentle sucking action, releasing it from the palate. As the tongue draws down it creates a soft clicking sound. A soft inner smile, one that can be felt inside but isn't strongly expressed on the outside, can be activated by smiling gently from the inside of the mouth, focusing at the back right and left corners of the soft palate

(Aposhyan, 2004). This also serves to tone the soft palate. Directly manipulating these muscles activates the social engagement system.

Exploring the Muscles of the Head and Neck

The large trapezius (CN XI) moves, rotates, and stabilizes the scapula. Relaxing the trapezius provides nonverbal cues of safety. Intentionally engaging and releasing the trapezius activates subtle shifts in neuroception. When engaged, upon raising the scapula the trapezius activates sympathetic mobilization and a neuroception of danger that comes with the muscular activation of readiness to defend; when relaxed, the neuroception is one of safety, as openness to connection is felt; and if collapsed, a sense of shutdown is evoked. Similar shifts in neuroception are felt when observing these movements in others. The sternocleidomastoid (CN XI) helps with movement of the head on the neck and assists with breathing by raising the sternum. When the sternocleidomastoid is engaged on one side of the body to create a gentle head tilt, the autonomic message felt internally and conveyed to others is one of curiosity, kindness, and authentic engagement, while rigidity of these muscles bilaterally produces a neuroception of danger, producing a freeze response.

Micromovements of the Head on the Neck

Exploring intentional rotations and micromovements of the head on the neck in soft and fluid movements stimulates vagal tone (Aposhyan, 2004). Imagine you are a bobblehead toy just after the head begins to slow from its frantic movements. These micromovements gently engage and release the small suboccipital muscles that attach to the base of the skull, C1 and C2. Let the actions become more subtle, eventually settling into a soft-moving near stillness, evoking a feeling of calm. Feel the social vagus working to inhibit sympathetic arousal.

Neuroception

There is a voice that doesn't use words. Listen.
—Rumi

The autonomic nervous system, through bidirectional communication pathways with the brain, is our autobiographer. Our life story is written first in the experience of the autonomic state and then translated into beliefs that structure our daily living. The mind narrates what the nervous system knows. Story follows state.

Neuroception is defined as the "evaluation of risk without awareness" (Porges, 2003a; Porges, 2004), making the important distinction between perception that involves cortical pathways and the subcortical process of neuroception that is the autonomic nervous system's way of knowing. Note that the autonomic nervous system, in polyvagal terms, provides a bidirectional communication between visceral organs within the body and the brain areas regulating and monitoring the organs within the autonomic nervous system. The sensory pathways from the organs to the brain provide the implicit gut feelings and heart-informed feelings that move us along the continuum of safety and adaptive survival response.

Many PlayLab participants are therapists who work in the field of trauma. A principle of effective work is that perception is more important than reality, and that the personal perception, not the actual facts of an experience, creates traumatic sequelae. Using a polyvagal perspective, before the brain understands and makes meaning of an incident, the autonomic nervous system, via the process of neuroception, has reacted and initiated an adaptive survival response. Polyvagal Theory challenges therapists to change their customary way of thinking about trauma and adopt a core concept from Polyvagal Theory: neuroception precedes perception, story follows state.

The following exercise creates opportunities to track both broad and nuanced experiences of neuroception and to identify the specific ways the autonomic nervous system acts in service of safety and survival. Adaptive survival responses begin with a shift of autonomic state and lead to constructing personal narratives that justify emotional states, beliefs, and behaviors. The central components of our brain regulating the autonomic nervous system listen intently to the experiences in the body and in the environment, scanning for cues of safety and danger. Information from the viscera (heart, lungs, intestines), cues from the place we are in, and the people and things around us are all important components of neuroception.

Mapping movement along the continuum of neuroception response brings attention to individual neural profiles and recognition that one person's cues of safety and danger may be similar to or very different from those of the people around them. Although we share the same continuum of safety to danger to life-threat, movement along it is an individual experience. Taking into account that the autonomic nervous system is a relational system shaped by experience, it makes sense that people will each have their own response patterns.

State shifts between the three major categories of safety, danger, and life-threat are accompanied by intense changes in somatic sensation. Since story follows state, the accompanying narrative will reflect the intensity of the state change. Once these large, between-state shifts have been identified, attention shifts to the nuances of neuroception and cultivating an awareness of the subtleties of response.

The Sunglasses Experiment

Interpreting emotions from facial expressions is a part of social reciprocity (Domes, Steiner, Porges, & Heinrichs, 2012), and people pay the most attention to eyes when processing facial features (Sullivan, Ruffman, & Hutton, 2007). This experience uses sunglasses to mask the cues the orbicularis oculi sends, and searches for, in the quest for safe connection. The exercise combines eye gaze with other elements of the social engagement system—facial expression, head turn and tilt, and vocalization—along with proximity to experiment with cues of safety and danger.

Participants are each given a pair of sunglasses with dark lenses that mask their eyes and then begin to move around the room, periodically stopping in front of another person to simply look at each other with an expressionless face, an unmoving head, and without vocalization. This is repeated several times while participants are guided into noticing their autonomic responses. The exercise is then changed so that half of the group is wearing sunglasses and half is not, and changed a third time to reverse the wearing and not wearing of sunglasses. For each of these shifts, the beginning instructions are to remain expressionless, with a fixed head, and silent. Following several minutes, the instructions are changed to first allow expression and then expression along with head turn and tilt. Finally, the entire group is asked to take off the sunglasses and connect with each other through eye gaze, smiling, and a natural tilt of the head that expresses vulnerability and a willingness to connect. Lastly, vocal bursts, the small, nonlanguage ways we connect with each other such as with *ahhh, mmmm, ohhhhh,* are added. At this point in the exercise there is a palpable sense of relief in the room, and participants often naturally laugh, move into closer proximity, and offer friendly touch, restoring the sense of ventral vagal safety.

While seemingly a simple exercise, the Sunglasses Experiment elicits powerful autonomic responses. Comments shared after this exercise highlight the power of neuroception to create stories of fear, anxiety, and mistrust: "Even though I had done dyadic exercises with this person today, I felt fearful when their eyes were hidden." "I know this person well, and yet, when I couldn't see her eyes and her face was flat, I felt like being close to her was dangerous in some way." "I could feel myself trying very hard to elicit a response, and when

I couldn't, I wanted to move away quickly." "I felt like the group had gone from feeling like a group of people I shared interests and connection with to a group of strangers who were not safe to be around." "The whole energy and tone of the room changed, and even though my brain could say it was just an exercise and just sunglasses, my body said clearly, this is not a safe place." Other comments prove the power of the social engagement system to restore safety and connection. "As soon as I could see his eyes, I felt myself relax." "When I heard her voice, even though it was just a sound and not a word, I knew I was safe." "Something about him moving his head made me feel like he was here with me." "When everyone finally took their sunglasses off and smiled, I felt like I could breathe again."

Breathing Out and Into Safety

Working with breath can be a helpful way to repattern and regulate autonomic states (Cohen, 2008). The anatomy of the thoracic diaphragm is of central importance to understanding breathing and to regulating and toning the vagus. Attuning to, influencing, and repatterning movement of the breath requires time, gentleness, and steady attention.

Observing and Guiding Diaphragmatic Breathing in Partners

The "receiver" (referring to the partner who is receiving the floor, attending to the breath, and exploring repatterning the breath) lies on the floor in a prone posture. The upper arms rest along the floor above the head parallel to one another, elbows along the ground and bent at 90°. Each hand rests on top of the opposite forearm near the elbow. This positioning brings gentle pressure to the region of the thoracic diaphragm, supporting easeful diaphragmatic breathing and therefore ventral vagal tone. Even for people who might typically have restricted or upper chest breathing and a tendency for more sympathetic arousal, this position often brings a shift in breath that increases ventral vagal tone.

The supporter helps the receiver listen autonomically for comfort and ease throughout the exercise and make adjustments to bring more safety. Attending to the receiver in this way offers not only a cognitive message but also an autonomically received message that their sense of ease and safety is important.

Upon each inhalation, the receiver is invited to direct breath into the area of the front body that makes most contact with the ground, feeling this area press downward into the support of the floor underneath. Both the receiver and the supporter note movement they observe related to initiation of breath at the diaphragm. Attention is given to the changing movement sensations at the level of the diaphragm as well as the softening of the belly and other areas of the body that might habitually hold tension. These actions serve to tone the vagus nerve and reduce sympathetic recruitment of energy.

Once the receiver has explored and experienced diaphragmatic breathing in a prone position, she gradually moves to standing, pausing at various levels (in yoga terms, this could be child's pose, to table pose or downward-facing dog pose, to standing) to again investigate initiation of the breath from the diaphragm. Changing postures slowly gives the autonomic nervous system time to adapt to the needs for increased output of energy necessary for movement and supports the shift from inner sensing to sensing surroundings.

In addition to the somatic experience of working with diaphragmatic breathing to tone the ventral vagus, the partnering experience offers an opportunity to explore attunement and reciprocity. In order to guide this exercise safely, the supporter must track her own movement along the neuroceptive continuum and engage the vagal brake to ensure an ongoing state of regulation, skills that are necessary for working effectively in the therapist–client dyad.

Changing breathing patterns takes time. For many people, breath exploration is an uncomfortable experience and can be especially difficult if not done with postural support. Therapists are encouraged to know and understand their own limitations as supporters of breath work. Therapists' exploration of and comfort with breath for themselves is essential. From an autonomic perspective, the therapist must be familiar with, and able to regulate, her own breath patterns.

Moving Through the Model: Somatic Movement and the Ventral Vagal Complex

When an infant is fortunate to have general physical health, a safe environment, and a "good enough" caregiver, she develops healthy vagal tone and increased capacity for modulation of inner and outer experience (Tronick & Reck, 2009). The infant experiences the world with a sense of safety and connection, where the needs of her inner environment are met by her external environment. Co-regulation leads to self-regulation and, over the course of thousands of interactions in the safety of the infant–adult dyad, the infant develops the physiological capacity to dampen sympathetic tone through the vagal brake. In the absence of safety within the infant–adult dyad, sympathetic and dorsal vagal activation threaten attunement and reciprocity and lead to patterns of distressed attachment. By using somatically based exercises designed to support embodiment of the social engagement system, protective responses created in early infant–adult patterns of misattunement can be repatterned in favor of adaptive responses in a safe environment.

Establishing and Attuning to Somatic Comfort

One participant acts as "receiver," who will receive a soft greeting and soothing sounds from their partner, who will act as "caregiver." The receiver is guided to lie on her stomach, using cushions or blankets as needed in order to assure comfort. As the receiver yields her weight to the ground and feels into the softness of her front body, she is instructed to notice and follow the sensations of movement that are present with her breath, digestion, circulation, and from the natural movement that occurs while lying still in a prone position. Provided that participants' neuroception at the start of the exercise is one of safety, this awareness exploration offers an experience of homeostasis. The quiet activity of lying prone engages the braking function of the vagus, leading to decreased sympathetic arousal. Additionally, the position of lying along the front body supports increased awareness of sensation of organs, offering an opportunity to settle and to track pleasant sensation.

Exploring Lifting of the Head from a Comfortable and Engaged Base of Support

Lying prone, the receiver is invited to explore gradually pressing the sternum into the floor until she begins to feel an initiation of the lifting of the head. When performed with whole-body engagement rather than just lifting the head from the neck, this action introduces extensor tone throughout the body. Physiological extension, essential for normal infant development, is seen when the extensor muscles along the back increase their tone, leading to a fully arched posture through the spine. In infants, expression and modulation of healthy flexor and extensor tone develops in relationship with the caregiver through attunement and co-regulation (Brook, 2014). Extensor tone is both an indication of and supportive of babies' physiological readiness for increased interaction with others and the environment. The "social vagus" in turn is toned as the social engagement system develops.

Auditory Receiving and Responding

Continuing the exercise, the caregiver begins to gently interact with the receiver, softly calling their name. This part of the exploration is adapted from an exercise described by Body-Mind Centering® teacher Annie Brook in her book *Birth's Hidden Legacy, Volume 2*. The receiver is guided to "reach" with her ears for the caregiver's voice, engaging the muscles of the middle ear associated with the social engagement system. She is then invited to track the sound. By turning the head to follow what the ears are tracking with their reach, a second element of the social engagement system is activated.

Lifting the head from the engaged sternum and the whole-body base of support allows for mobility of the head and neck, enabling the receiver to track and respond to what she hears. By turning the head in the direction of the sound, the receiver may then make contact with the caregiver visually, who is ready and smiling receptively with kind eyes. The tracking of the voice, the turning of the head, the integration with and engagement of the eyes, and the reciprocity of facial expression all activate the muscles associated with the ventral vagal complex and tone the social engagement system.

Exploring Variations of "Call and Response"

This exercise often evokes implicit memory. Autonomic responses to these exercises range from adaptive protection to social connection. Participants register implicit memory upon hearing their name called which, depending on past experiences, produces experiences of ventral vagal flow, sympathetic mobilization, or dorsal vagal immobilization. At times a participant's name might have been spoken by family members in loving ways, and at other times in criticizing or shaming ways. The activation of these implicit memories drives a neuroception of safety, danger, or life-threat. To support safe experiencing of implicit memory, the receiver has been invited to listen autonomically to her changing experience of neuroception, track restimulation of memory, and slow down as needed in order to keep up with changing internal states.

To support working with uncomfortable material, it can be helpful to intentionally explore increasing ventral vagal tone by changing positioning, sequencing movement differently, or asking the partner for a change in her behavior. With support of the caregiver, the receiver can titrate her level of activity by attuning to her internal environment, leading to increased sensation, awareness, and calm (activating the vagal brake); or she can attune to her external environment, leading to increased energy and outer-directed expression, exploration, and playfulness. She is encouraged to communicate requests to the caregiver for more or less volume with her voice, for increased or decreased overall energy level in the interaction, including facial expression, and for proximity or distance, including touch if felt to be ventral vagal toning from a sense of attunement and connection. The caregiver attunes to the receiver, through prosody, movement, proximity, and nonjudgmental responsiveness to what the receiver communicates about her experience or needs. The intent is for the dyad to increase attunement by cultivating conscious use of reciprocity.

The movements of the receiver and the interaction between caregiver and receiver are fairly simple in this exercise, yet it can be surprising how powerful it is to weave together the elements of the ventral vagal complex and the social engagement system experientially through the exploration of developmental movement. For the receiver, hearing his or her name spoken in a way that feels safe and connecting may be a first-time experience.

Ending in Play

Play only occurs when one is safe, secure and feeling good, which makes play an exceptionally sensitive measure for all things bad.
—Panksepp and Biven (2012, p. 355)

Play is possible when the social engagement of the ventral vagal complex and the mobilization of the sympathetic nervous system work together (Porges, 2009). Imagine these two systems metaphorically "holding hands," and if that connection is lost, the liveliness of play turns from feeling safe to feeling frightening. Play is meant to be a neural exercise strengthening the ability to flexibly transition between activity and calm (Porges, 2015). However, for many people, rather than a ventral vagal–supported anticipation, opportunities for play bring the dysregulating energies of a survival response. We can move from judgment to self-compassion through understanding that autonomic responses to play are shaped by personal histories. Play evokes responses along the continuum of protection to connection, sometimes enlivening the social engagement system and sometimes triggering an adaptive survival response.

Peacock Feather Dancing

The PlayLab play experience is a peacock feather dance. This is adapted from the work of Robert Macy, president of the International Trauma Center, who uses peacock feathers in his work with children who have survived natural disasters to help them return to a feeling of safety in their bodies and on the earth. Each participant is given a peacock feather to balance on the tip of a finger and shown how movement keeps the feather from falling. We add music and invite participants to begin to move around the room with their "dancing" feathers. As participants become more adept with the new experience, individual dances expand into group choreography and playfulness naturally emerges. As attunement to the group, the music, and the activity of balancing the feather builds, the task of balancing the feather becomes more fluid and easeful, a natural result of increased ventral vagal tone.

Conclusion

The Polyvagal PlayLab is designed to help therapists engage experientially with their autonomic nervous system, the platform upon which human behavior, including behaviors and symptoms targeted in psychotherapy, rests. Through the exercises presented in the PlayLab, therapists become better able to map their autonomic patterns, attune to their neuroception of safety, and tone their social vagus, thus learning how they might become more regulated during sessions with clients. With increased ventral vagal tone, therapists are better able to attune to their clients' experiences and to project cues of safety, leading to clients' increased sense of connection and trust in the therapeutic relationship. Through this process of co-regulation and reciprocity, clients experience micromoments of ventral vagal regulation and, over time, their autonomic map begins to change.

When therapists offer clients education and regulation tools based on Polyvagal Theory, their clients benefit from having a nonblaming, nonshaming model for understanding their behavior and are better able to track and influence their autonomic state. The Polyvagal PlayLab informs the therapist's clinical practice from a physiological perspective, giving opportunity for deeper experiences of safety, connection, and healing, the results of which can then be brought into their work with others.

References

Aposhyan, S. (2004). *Body-mind psychotherapy: Principles, techniques, and practical applications.* New York, NY: Norton.

Brook, A. (2014). *Birth's hidden legacy: Treat earliest origins of shock and attachment trauma in adults, children and infants* (Vol. 2). Boulder, CO: Smart Body Books.

Church, E. (2004, September). What a colorful world. *Scholastic Parent and Child*, pp. 52–54.

Cohen, B. B. (2008). *Sensing, feeling, and action: The experiential anatomy of body-mind centering.* Northampton, MA: Contact Editions.

Dana, D. (2018) *The polyvagal theory in therapy: Engaging the rhythm of regulation.* New York, NY: Norton.

Domes, G., Steiner, A., Porges, S., & Heinrichs, M. (2013). Oxytocin differentially modulates eye gaze to naturalistic social signals of happiness and anger. *Psychoneuroendocrinology, 38*, 1198–1202.

Eveleth, R. (2013, October 24). There are 37.2 trillion cells in your body. Retrieved from http://www.smithsonianmag.com/smart-news/there-are-372-trillion-cells-in-your-body-4941473/

Harrison, R. L., & Westwood, M. J. (2009). Preventing vicarious traumatization of mental health therapists: Identifying protective practices. *Psychotherapy: Theory, Research, Practice, Training, 46*(2), 203–219.

Jerath, R., Crawford, M., Barnes, V., & Harden, K. (2015). Self-regulation of breathing as a primary treatment for anxiety. *Applied Psychophysiology and Biofeedback, 40*, 107–115.

Panksepp, J., & Biven, L. (2012). *The archaeology of mind: Neuroevolutionary origins of human emotions*. New York, NY: Norton.

Porges, S. W. (2003a). Social engagement and attachment. *Annals of the New York Academy of Sciences, 1008*(1), 31–47.

Porges, S. W. (2003b). The Polyvagal Theory: Phylogenetic contributions to social behavior. *Physiology & Behavior, 79*, 503–513.

Porges, S. W. (2004, May). Neuroception: A subconscious system for detecting threats and safety. *Zero to Three* (J), 24(5), 19–24.

Porges, S. W. (2009). *Reciprocal influences between body and brain in the perception and expression of affect: A polyvagal perspective*. In D. Fosha, D. Siegel, & M. Solomon (Eds.), *The healing power of emotion: Affective neuroscience, development, clinical practice*. New York, NY: Norton.

Porges, S. W. (2015). Play as a neural exercise: Insights from the Polyvagal Theory. In D. Pearce-McCall (Ed.), *The power of play for mind brain health* (pp. 3–7). Retrieved from http://mindgains.org/

Porges, S. W. (2016). A conversation with Stephen Porges [Webinar]. Retrieved from http://proactivemindfulness.com/zug/transcripts/Porges-2016-09.pdf

Sullivan, S., Ruffman, T., & Hutton, S. B. (2007). Age differences in emotion recognition skills and the visual scanning of emotion faces. *Journal of Gerontology Series B: Psychological Sciences and Social Sciences, 62*(1), P53–60.

Tronick, E., & Reck, C. (2009). Infants of depressed mothers. *Harvard Review of Psychiatry, 17*(2), 247–156.

Yoto, A., Katsuura, T., Iwanaga, K., & Shimomura, Y. (2007). Effects of object color stimuli on human brain activities in perception and attention referred to EEG alpha band response. *Journal of Physiological Anthropology, 26*, 373–379.

Zaidel, D. (2014). Creativity, brain, and art: Biological and neurological considerations. *Frontiers in Human Neuroscience, 8*, 389.

12

Roots, Rhythm, Reciprocity: Polyvagal-Informed Dance Movement Therapy for Survivors of Trauma

Amber Gray

Abstract: Polyvagal-informed Dance Movement Therapy (DMT) offers survivors of extreme human rights violations opportunities to restore meaning and a sense of belonging through the integration of Polyvagal Theory with DMT. Movement, rhythm, and dance promote connection, social engagement, and reciprocity. The case presented in this chapter describes the restorative process of "Rita," a survivor of torture who initially presented in a state of complete terror and shutdown. Rita's road home to her body integrated the following core components of polyvagal-informed DMT: restoring relative safety, yield, core rhythmicity, the markers of engagement, and her ability to state shift more fluidly.

Introduction

The sound of the balls bouncing against the cold tile floor at first is dull.

Thud.

Thud.

Thud.

Like a heart beating only because it has to. I have been invited to Leawood Elementary

School in Littleton, Colorado, just a few days after the Columbine shootings, to work with the elementary school children who remain terrified from the things they heard, saw, and experienced on that day. When I walked into the science lab, where three 8-year-olds whom teachers had identified as "particularly traumatized" met me, I asked what they wanted to do. Looking at my menagerie of supplies—puppets, balls, stretch bands, art supplies—they said, "Can we bounce those balls?"

That's where we began.

We bounced. We bounced the balls, and at first the bouncing varied between highly energetic, almost aggressive throwing to limp, apathetic, dropping the ball on the floor. Thud. *As we began to process the bouncing, the children decided they wanted to make as many bounces as necessary to help those slain in the shootings to get to heaven. In other words, we were bouncing a "stairway to heaven." We bounced over 100 bounces before the children, who were now bouncing more evenly and cohesively, in a more unified rhythmic process, decided to "build" the stairway.*

The sound of the bouncing had shifted from a dull thud to a lighter, crisper staccato. When we were done, there was an awkward silence, and one of the children said, "Maybe we should also bounce for the boys who did this."

Another silence.

Another child said, "I don't think they can go to heaven."

We paused in silence.

The first child: "Maybe if we bounce for both for them, God will forgive them and they can go to heaven and help the ones they hurt."

We bounced over 500 times.

Rhythm is a fundamental component of all life. The oscillations of birth and death, fast and slow, awake and asleep, in and out may all be conceptualized as basic rhythmic patterns and processes that define our movements as an individual, a family, a community, a species, and a very small thread in the web of life. For years, ancient cultures and indigenous peoples have engaged in social and communal rites of passage and rituals with rhythm as a fundamental connecting, organizing, and healing force.

Polyvagal Theory illuminates the evolution of the mammalian nervous system as an influence on human behavior. It describes social engagement as an emergent, adaptive behavior arising from the development of the multibranched vagus nerve. The need for increased oxygen as we "complexified" through our species evolution guided (and perhaps still guides) this evolution. Evolution itself may be seen as a rhythmic dance of engagement with the environment and its inhabitants that calls us to adapt to the ever-changing nature of life.

Building on the intelligence of this hierarchical, adaptive outcome of evolution, neurological and physiological survival circuitry offers many creative adaptations to the usual ideas about therapy and healing that evidenced-based practice for survivors of trauma promote. One way to conceptualize Polyvagal Theory is as a physiological response and regulation system set in place by advances in our biology and a template for how we can adapt our behavioral health interventions to support and enhance the very creative survival and "thrival" strategies afforded us by evolution.

Trauma treatment as a professional field is fairly young. As our understanding of the impact of trauma on human experience grows through neuroscience with conceptualizations such as Polyvagal Theory (2011) and research on the brain and memory (Levine, 2015; Herman, 1997, Perry, 2017; Siegel, 1999; 2012 & van der Kolk, 2001, 2014), the essential role that somatic and movement-based therapies play in the restorative process is now widely accepted (Johnson, Lahan, & Gray, 2009; Gray, 2015b; & Gray 2016). To remain connected to our embodied experience, we must relearn to work through trauma with movement, the primary language of the body. Rhythm, a component of movement, is the organizing principle for all life. We begin and end with the most fundamental rhythm of all: our breath.

Knowledge that the brain responds, grows, and changes in response to experience, and knowledge of the nervous system's regulatory role in our response to dangerous and life-threatening situations, has promoted recognition of the crucial role dance and movement-based therapies play in work with survivors of trauma. Polyvagal-informed DMT (2015, 2016) integrates the intelligence of the nervous system's response to socially safe, dangerous, and life-threatening environments into movement practices and processes that promote a restoration of social engagement through "state shifting."

If human experience is defined as a continuum originating with basic sensorimotor impulses culminating in our transpersonal perspectives and experiences, some of the layers that connect the most basic foundational to the more expansive mental and spiritual aspects of human experience are movement, emotion, and cognition. Movement, as described by Perry (2017), may be the most direct pathway to promote brain plasticity and therefore promote learning capacities, healing, and a sense of well-being. Working with movement, we access the neurological underpinnings of all human thoughts, feelings, behaviors, and actions and restore our ability to be a conductor in the symphony or "play" of our ongoing interaction with the larger world. For people with unresolved trauma, neuroception—the name coined by Stephen Porges for the subcortical process that detects safety or danger or life-threat in our environment—can misappraise the environment as unsafe, even when it is safe. A traumatized system, locked down in fear or terror, sends signals of fear even when there is no viable threat. This faulty neuroception contributes to thoughts, feelings, behaviors, and actions that are rooted in past experiences of fear rather than what's current, present, and accurate. Movement gives us direct access to the nervous system, and from the tiniest micromovement to large, expressive gross motor movements can initiate shifts in physiological state via the nervous system. Movement helps us regain mastery over our body's day-to-day function and engagement with the world.

Dance Movement Therapy

DMT's history begins with rhythm. Marian Chace, a modern dancer who is considered the North American pioneer of this field, worked closely with psychiatrists in St. Elizabeth's Hospital from 1942–1966. One of her many creative "interventions" for working with severely psychotic patients, then locked in the back wards of insane asylums, was to mirror their movements and actions, which promoted a sense of what is now known as *social engagement.* Coining the term *kinesthetic empathy* to describe the connection that occurred between herself and the clients, she observed that meeting them in their movement world—no matter how fragmented and strange their movements were—sparked a connection. As this connection deepened, she would slow down, speed up, and "cohese" the movements so that they were more coherent and organized. This alteration in rhythm, tempo, pace, frequency, and all other elements of movement seemed to promote increased organization of the clients' movement vocabularies and, eventually, verbal communication.

Later, she invited these clients to participate in group dance movement therapy, which is where the classic Chacian group was born (Levy, 1992). In these groups, she used simple 4/4 rhythms to invite the clients to clap, step, stomp, and move together. Over time, the vitalization, cohesion, and synchrony (Schmais, 1985) that occurs in all DMT groups as a direct result of rhythmic activity encouraged these forgotten patients to express themselves in relationship to one another.

Marian Chace went on to work with veterans returning from the Second World War who were too psychologically damaged to benefit from mainstream psychiatric interventions, and this work contributed to the solidification of DMT as a therapeutic approach. The increased movement, verbal, and behavioral coherence observed in these early years of trauma treatment is what I now refer to as "body prosody" (2016) from the perspective of polyvagal-informed DMT. Body prosody refers to a healthy, diverse range of movement "tones" that allow us to express the full range of our internal world, including our feelings, emotions, and thoughts. Congruence in movement, affect, and cognition are a sign of well-being and social engagement in safe contexts. The interactions that took place in those back wards where Marian Chace pioneered DMT likely engaged or reengaged what Dr. Porges described in his "rules of engagement" as nonverbal cues or markers of engagement that become observable deficits in human behavior when there is a disorder: facial expressivity; prosody, eye contact, or gaze; mood and affect, state regulation, and posture in social engagement (Porges, 2013).

From the perspective of Polyvagal Theory and polyvagal-informed DMT, social engagement is possible to "read" through the aforementioned markers of engagement. I would expand this to include movement prosody—the fluidity and dimensionality of movement itself—and body prosody. Body prosody is the more global expression of the body: posture, shaping, action (embodied behaviors), and the congruency between movement and emotional and verbal expression that can literally be silenced by the horrors survivors of trauma have endured. Recruiting body prosody in a dyadic interaction can function as a neural exercise that may promote social engagement and therefore increase the ability to remain in a state of embodied presence. Embodied presence would be based on maintaining a ventral vagal state that heightens the ability to pay attention to what is occurring in this very moment, suspend judgment and interpretation and simply bear witness, and be willing to be courageous and curious enough to ask questions that may not have answers. Presence is a ventral vagal state that reflects our mindful ability to be compassionate toward ourselves and our clients (Geller & Porges, 2011) and to communicate safety. In work with the survivors of human rights abuses described in this chapter, presence can communicate our humanity.

Core Rhythmicity

The core rhythms that promote well-being are heart rate (60–80 beats per minute), respiration (12–20 breaths per minute, resting), and vascular feedback loops, which occur every 15–30 seconds. Oscillations of rhythms, especially when they are reinforced by externally changing tempos (i.e., with different types of music), can provide a feedback loop to core rhythms of the human body. These rhythms change in states of social engagement, mobilization (which can feel and appear like fast, sharp, or energetic movements), and immobilization (which can feel and appear slow or heavy, like molasses). Movement as felt experience, and as it may appear to an observer, requires shifts in autonomic state that are manifested in changes in heart rate, heart rate variability, respiration, and vascular feedback to slow down or speed up and maintain fluidity.

Berrol summarizes several studies that demonstrate how rhythm affects physiological responses: "Emotional perception of music has a significant effect on autonomic responses—e.g., changes in pulse rate, galvanic skin response, and blood pressure. Bodily rhythms and activities appear to regulate to external rhythmic stimuli, matching tempi" (Berrol, 1992, p. 25), which can help regulate emotions. Because the primary influence on our core rhythmicity is our biology, the observations of therapists working in many cultures inform us that culture is a secondary but profound influence. As we develop, cultural experiences influence how we express emotions and move in and out of space, what music we listen to, how we dance and posture, and appropriate demonstration of eye contact and facial expressivity. The markers of social engagement are the primary ways we communicate safety. Facial expression, prosody, and gaze are literally reflections of our heart (Porges, 2017). It is not language; it is our biology that communicates safety. Fear is the final layer that can undermine the positive biological and cultural influences on our core rhythmicity.

The following case describes polyvagal-informed DMT with an adult survivor of severe trauma (torture) for whom all observable markers of social engagement were compromised. Polyvagal-informed DMT is my unique adaptation of DMT to work with survivors of extreme trauma. Based on core theories and principles of DMT, the work is adjusted, titrated, and expanded to include the important foundations of Polyvagal Theory:

1. The role of safety in establishing trust, and trust as the basis of meaningful human relationship and reciprocity.
2. Multidirectional state shifting: Physiological state shifts create emotional and psychological state shifts. The states are related to the pathways of social engagement, mobilization and immobilization.
3. Restoring core rhythmicity through the exploration of external rhythm (song, movement, dance, drumming) so that clients have a restored sense of mastery over their responses to the environment (i.e., trauma triggers).
4. Restoring the markers of engagement (facial expressivity, gaze, vocal and movement prosody, posture during social engagement and mood, affect and state regulation) in culturally relevant ways.

Rita's Dance to Freedom

Rita is a 52-year-old East African woman who, prior to her captivity and torture, was a community leader, potato farmer, mother and homemaker, and deeply committed to her church. She described her life in Africa as one of "many friendships, and much love for my family and God." She loved growing potatoes and was proud of having taught many people to grow their own food.

In the then-growing violence that continues to engulf her country and community, she was accused of conspiring against the government. Many members of her community were similarly accused despite having no history of, or involvement in, antigovernment activities. Rebels frequented her community and often stole or asked for food, but Rita did not support their cause. Rita was captured and imprisoned for seven years. During this time, she was held in a prison cell that "was built for only 10 people but often held as many as 60."

When she was initially assessed at our program, she was unable to share her history, and said nothing of her pretorture life. This is not uncommon for survivors of torture. Often the benign past is consumed by the horror of their more recent history. People, places, positive events are all buried under the overwhelming terror that seems to fill every moment.

Rita's seven years of abuse at the hands of her government included daily beatings, cutting and scarring, rape, sensory and food deprivation, forced labor, and extreme environmental conditions. She did not elaborate on any of these atrocities. She did not need to. *She embodied them.*

Her initial clinical presentation was one of complete shutdown. She was immobilized in terror. Since her release from prison, she isolated herself, as she could no longer bear human interaction. She refused calls from family back home, would not leave her house, and often spent days alone in her room. She refused to attend the local church. She described an inability to trust, and a loss of faith through statements like "I do not know where God went" and "I am all alone now." As with many survivors of trauma whose dorsal vagal circuit activates immobilization, Rita experienced emotional disconnect from her family and lost interest in social activities.

Her clinical presentation of dissociation, flat affect, severe pain and numbness, and reduced range of motion in her arms, legs, and hips created a clinical complexity that was overwhelming to the therapist who completed her intake. The therapist chose not to work with Rita because being in her presence had overwhelmed her emotionally. This extreme dysregulation, or "loss of core rhythmicity," can make it impossible for survivors to self-regulate, increasing the intensity of the clinicians' need to co-regulate. Even the most mindfully present clinician can be overwhelmed by the depth and intensity of fear, or terror, that is expressed through the client, whose inability to maintain or access a state of social engagement, or any safe state (i.e., immobilization without fear/rest and settle, or mobilization without fear/play) is overwhelming. Even the most experienced therapists can become overwhelmed by the complete absence of the usual markers of engagement, which connect us to our humanity.

Rita's face was frozen in terror and withdrawal, watching her move was painful, and there were long periods of silence as she struggled to stay present in sessions. The isolation that living in fear creates is exacerbated by the response of the world. People often withdraw from those with silent, nonexpressive faces who appear metaphorically like the walking dead. Rita's symptoms were overwhelming. She made no eye contact and simply "went away" during any conversation. She also had several large, disfiguring scars on her right shoulder blade, upper right thigh, and the back of her left calf. The one on her shoulder blade still oozed pus.

It was difficult to know where to begin, so I invited Rita to complete two movement baselines: kinesphere (Tortora, 2006), and pushing and reaching, from the developmental progression (Bainbridge Cohen, 2012). Kinesphere can be described as the space in which we can move by reaching and extending our limbs, while standing in place on one foot or two feet if balance is severely affected, as it often is with trauma. Pushing and reaching are based on Bonnie Bainbridge Cohen's (2012) work, as expressed in my Poto Mitan ("centerpost") Framework for the Restorative Process (Gray, 2015a,b). Pushing is a developmental action that helps establish a "boundaried" sense of self and relates to playful (including competitive) mobilization states. Reach is an action that supports the physiological state of social engagement through safe connection with others and the environment.

When I began treatment, I had no idea where to start. Rita was frozen. Her eyes locked in terror; she was withdrawn and mumbled toward the floor. Her social and relational capacities were shattered. She had virtually no kinesphere. She walked with visible suffering. The markers of engagement were absent—no prosody of voice or movement, no facial expressivity, flat affect, depressed mood, and a misshapen, collapsed posture. Attempts to "resource" by finding what helped her survive, or even remember and describe what she loved, were futile. She "did not know." And she did not appear to care.

I asked her where she wished to begin. When she didn't know, I asked what bothered her the most. Her response was *pain*. To begin with, such intense pain is challenging, and it's not unusual for clients to disappear from treatment when they perceive it as the place they "have to feel the pain all over again."

She offered me no other options, so we began by exploring her pain. I asked her if she could tell me where the worst pain was; it was behind her right shoulder. She said the pain at the scar in her right thigh also hurt, but a little less. I suggested we begin where the pain was a little less, and perhaps more tolerable. Because she was collapsed, depressed, and immobilized, beginning in her lower extremity—the subdiaphragmatic innervation of the dorsal vagus—I thought we might initiate an increased ability to "rest and settle." Resting and settling is a calm, relaxed parasympathetic, dorsal or "old" vagus mediated state, which allows us to be quiet and introspective. Increasing energy in her legs—that is, a slight mobilization through the play of her interaction with a therapy ball—seemed like a relatively safe way to increase engagement in the direction of mobilization without fear, and then return to a rest state. This state shifting between relatively safe immobilized and mobilized states promotes self-regulation in clients who present initially as shut down and disconnected. Immobilization, by definition, means no movement, so even seemingly micromovement explorations and processes begin to shift state toward social engagement. While the dissolution that occurs in service of survival is hierarchical, the pathway to healing rarely follows a straight line. It is not usually possible, or even recommended, to state shift terrified, shut down clients immediately into social engagement. While it may seem logical to work "backward and upward" to a mobilization state and then to social engagement, the imprint of terror that caused the shutdown can be experienced like memory shards layered throughout a body and mind that have become a minefield. Attempting to find refuge in this internal minefield can be terrifying. While both the ventral vagus and the dorsal vagus provide a brake on the sympathetic adrenal system, immobilization in defense is the result of an immediate loss of social engagement and ventral regulation on the entire nervous system, resulting in the dorsal vagal shutdown. There is no sympathetic charge wedged in between, so feelings of mobilization can be challenging to tolerate, whether they are tinged with fear or playful pleasure. Mobilization without fear is play, and play states exist on a continuum that includes "edgy" or competitive play (sports), gentle play (e.g., with a new puppy), and intimate play—like foreplay. Shifting into safe dorsal vagal immobilization was the safest pathway for Rita to begin to experience nonfear states, so that we could begin the journey toward social engagement. Tolerating enough moments of "rest and settle" allow a client like Rita to begin to yield into self-safety, as a step toward experiencing safety in relationship.

Rita was unable to stand for any period of time and preferred to remain seated. Chairs are not the best structures to invite a supportive relationship between belly and back muscles. This can be even more true for survivors of rape, whose abdomens are often distended due to hypertonicity in their low back and sacrum and hypotonicity in their bellies. This distention creates a simultaneous compression and inward contraction in the pelvic floor. Sitting on a chair can increase the discomfort and reduce relational capacities because they do not support postures of social engagement. A compressed or rigid sacrum is not a neutral sacrum, and therefore can interrupt cardiac vagal tone (via ventral vagal complex) and the naturally fluid, dimensional movement of the sacrum.

Research (Cottingham, Porges, & Lyons, 1988) in the 1980s demonstrated a restoration of cardiac vagal tone with the Rolfing pelvic lift. Deep abdominal pressure and tactile stimulation to the back and sacral nerve roots produce "PNS [parasympathetic nervous system] cardiovascular reflexes and alterations in respiratory patterns" (p. 355). Shifts in posture, spinal and sacral movement, and orientation affect cardiac vagal tone. From the perspective of dance movement therapy, a sacrum capable of full range of motion (not just flexion and extension but wheel-like rotations and dimensional movements, such as those core to Haitian, Afro-Caribbean or Latin dancing) supports restoration of vagal tone and may promote emotions associated with social engagement such as happiness. This sacral "movement enticement" may even contribute to the discovery of meaningful relationships, which support a sense of belonging.

Wishing to invite this state of yield/relaxation/rest and settle, which is synonymous with a state of effortlessness or even grace, I asked Rita if there was any body position she had discovered that relieved some of the pain she felt in her thigh.

She described how she sometimes lay in her bed, with her head leaning against the headboard and her right leg propped up on pillows. This relieved the pain somewhat. An important note: She never referred to her leg, or thigh, as hers. It was always the leg, or the thigh. She did not experience the right leg as being connected to the rest of her body.

I introduced her to a therapy ball. The larger balls (55–75 cm) are very effective for promoting yield, absent in the tonic imbalance that sitting in chairs creates. Yield is a Body-Mind Centering (2012) term that describes the physiological action of relating to gravity in a way that allows us to relax into it, be supported, and mobilize to use our gravitational push, if necessary. I invited her to sit in her chair, the place where she was most comfortable, and rest her right leg on the ball. She discovered that this reduced the pain in her leg, and was relatively comfortable. We spent the next four sessions working with the idea of a state of comfort, and after two weeks, I gave her a ball to take home and practice.

Initially, I sat beside her, several feet away. In each of the eight sessions we had over four weeks, I slowly moved closer to her, and positioned myself more directly in front of her, so she could see me and relate to me. I smiled with encouragement, looked into her eyes enough to let her know I saw her, but did not stare or maintain contact for extended periods of time. I often used what I call the soft gaze of compassion, allowing my eyeballs to literally "rest" into the "hammock" of my eye sockets. This soft gaze opens panoramic vision, which creates spaciousness in witnessing. I believe this practice is a meaningful way to invite our clients to grow into more dimensional presence without pressure to "do the right thing" or fear of being judged. My facial expressivity was intentionally warm with just enough of a smile to encourage connection. Changing my body's placement (spacing and placing) was a nonintrusive way to begin to reestablish boundaried relationship, toward a goal of a relatively safe reciprocal relationship.

Boundaries are always ruptured in trauma. Interpersonal traumas, especially human rights violations, create extreme boundary ruptures that contribute to an ongoing sense of the world as unsafe. Boundaries that are either too rigid (i.e., unapproachable) or too loose (i.e., enmeshed) can be evidence of past boundary violations. Discernment regarding how long these maladaptive patterns must remain intact to support the establishment of healthier boundaries is essential to promote social engagement. Healthy boundaries in a human are like a cell's semipermeable membrane: We have some volition regarding what enters and exits. When we lose this permeability due to violation, persecution, displacement, and perpetration, we lose our ability to move volitionally in and out of relationships.

As the pain in her leg dissipated, she began to describe a "reacquaintance" with her leg. I invited her to tell me stories of times she had relied on both of her legs for strength, mobility, and ground. By the end of the four weeks, she finally used "my" in describing her leg. We agreed we would continue to work with her leg, and also begin to work with other areas of her body. My treatment plan was the reintroduction and reintegration of her "lost" body parts into her whole body: somatic reintegration toward social engagement. Her treatment plan was to reduce pain.

We agreed to begin working with the pain in her right shoulder blade, which severely reduced range of motion in her right arm. She felt that this pain had reduced somewhat, although it was still the most troubling pain in her body.

She continued to support her right leg with the ball while we addressed the pain and lost range of motion in her right arm. We processed the meaning of the pain in the arm, and she described this as the place that held "the struggle" and therefore still held fear. Naming fear was important for her, and later on this became a portal into her trauma history and processing. To externalize the struggle, we tied a stretch band to the door, and she used varying amounts of effort to stretch and release the band resting between exertions. We integrated breath into this practice, inhaling while contracting and pulling, and exhaling while releasing and letting the band go. Eventually, she took a band home, and after eight weeks, she referred to both her thigh and shoulder as her body parts.

This oscillation of relatively safe immobilization and mobilization states increased her willingness to talk about the changes in her pain levels and range of motion without her usual dissociated immobilization. Her posture had changed. She sat up more erectly, and occasionally, peeked up at me and held my gaze for several seconds. During the time that we focused on her arm and shoulder, we also worked with making facial expressions to match the feeling of pulling (resisting) and releasing (letting go of) the stretch band. By the end of the initial eight weeks of therapy, her face, which previously showed no expressivity, began to move when she spoke. She had not yet begun to speak of either her benign or her traumatic history, and mention of her torture still elicited a dissociative state and deficits in the markers of engagement. Shutdown was her go-to behavioral strategy.

It was at the eight-week mark that she came in, walking with a slightly but visibly more animated pace, and announced that she was "coming home to my body." I asked her what she meant, and she simply said, "I have less pain, and I can move my arm and my leg." Observing the state shift that had occurred, I witnessed a woman whose posture had changed to one of increased engagement. She was standing straighter. While her movement was still stiff in her core, she was moving her entire body when she walked, stood, and spoke. The integration of her body parts had begun. She was able to look at me, holding gaze for almost the whole time we spoke. Her face showed more expressivity; she smiled, there was light in her eyes, and her forehead had more movement when she spoke or smiled. Her voice had only a little more prosody, but she was more "present" when she spoke. I could hear her in her voice. Her breath supported her voice and she spoke with more definitiveness and strength. Her state was no longer completely immobilized. Her breath, voice, and movement were coordinated when she spoke. She was inching toward safe social engagement. She approached me more closely than she ever had before.

Recognizing the restoration of her markers of engagement, and feeling energized myself, I decided to begin the process I call *weaving the narrative*, the meaning-making phase of the restorative process: reconnecting her body to her history and to the present, and preparing her for the future. I have found that working across cultures, it is most effective to do this through a combination of somatic and movement-based therapies with narrative or storytelling processes.

I began with a question that was fashioned in the tradition of the Brief Solution-Focused "Miracle Question": How can we arrive all the way home to your body? Her first response was to heal herself of the "ugly scars" that she had on her body. I realized she had defined herself as this ugliness. She felt deep shame about these disfigurements, and this was a major contributing factor to her desire to disappear and remain alone. I asked her to draw pictures of herself without scars, at home in her body. She drew smooth, coffee-colored skin; this was Home. I then asked her to draw herself now, and she drew an ugly scar: a coffee-colored circle mangled by black and red streaks and dots. This was Now.

I asked her to put the ugly scar drawing (Now) in a place in the room that felt like Now, and she did. She then placed the Home drawing on the other side of the therapy room, although before doing so, she also placed it behind the Now drawing and stood on it, as if remembering.

I sent her home with "home play": to define the steps between Now and Home. When she returned, she carried with her a drawing she made at home with paper and crayons I loaned her. We converted it into four separate drawings. They were:

Patience
Struggle
Time
Strive

For the next eight months, working together weekly, we traveled these steps on her "road to home" through a process that integrated rhythmic sequences related to the feeling, or physiological state, of each step. We explored stories of her benign past, and identified resources from those stories that sustained her now. We began with Patience, her identified first step. We followed this process for each step:

1. Baseline: Place the Now and Home drawings where they belong, in relation to one another, today.
2. Baseline: Rita chose her beginning place. She either stood on Home or Now first. She stood on Home and Now in the order that felt correct to her, at the beginning and end of each session. Then she placed herself where she belonged, today, in relation to the drawings, and it was here we would begin.
3. Engagement: Rita would share her experience of standing on Home and Now. We chose the word "share" intentionally. I initially invited her to "report out," but she preferred to share, a first indication of social engagement.
4. Engagement: Her sharing included a description of her general feeling

states, bodily sensations (which took some time to learn to describe), and any thoughts, images, and memories that arose for her. Her ability to utilize interoception (somatic awareness), which is "non-evaluative with respect for feedback from the viscera to the brain" (Porges, 2013), and share her internal process (conceptual awareness; Hindi, 2012) improved over time, indicating increased embodied awareness and self-engagement. As her affective expression increased, she began to name her emotions, which promotes brain integration (Siegel, 2013).

5. Engagement: After our opening, and before our closing practice of standing on the newly placed Home and Now, we would work with her steps to arrive home. While standing on each step, we would:
   a. "Check in" with her body, including neuroception of safety, and notice sensations, feelings, images, memories, thoughts that arose. She shared what she noticed verbally, or with rhythm, movement, or gesture.
   b. Movement, voice, and body dialogue. Depending on what Rita noticed, we would either work nonverbally or talk about it, and then create a movement, movement sequence, rhythmic sequence, or song.

Following are examples of how we worked with Patience and Struggle.

Patience

We did not spend much time on Patience, because Rita believed in, and exemplified, this attribute. The four weekly sessions (one month) we worked on Patience consisted of her describing the importance of patience as a Christian value, and how she required patience to survive prison. She shared that patience helped her survive endlessly long days in a dark cell so crowded that the women would take turns squatting (sitting was not possible because of human and other filth on the floor). She did not want to remember what it felt like to be in the eternal squat she often held for hours at a time.

She described it as a relief when they had to leave the cell to work. The prison was so dark that the only light they saw, unless outside, was a tiny sliver of sunbeam that shone on the wall through a crack in the prison wall. She related her patience to waiting to see this light every day, which reminded her that the sun was outside, and "another day was born." Later, she would recall that this sliver of light was her hope. Her posture in Patience was either to sit quietly, in a dorsal vagal "rest and settle" state, or sometimes she stood with this sense of quiet and calm. Sometimes she would visibly slump into sadness as she recalled her time in prison. She would then grow very quiet, and her initial state of immobilization would creep in for a few moments. She seemed to "disappear," often after a brief moment of tensing up and then losing muscle tone. She would sometimes return on her own or come back when I coached her to find her feet, or seat, or to breathe.

Struggle

Standing in Struggle, she remembered her pain. The pain began in the tightly crowded, filthy, rank prison cell that stank of blood, excrement, and death. Holding her body's posture to stay as far off the floor as possible hypercontracted her muscles, and the things she and the women experienced contributed to her psychic pain. She witnessed many women die of exhaustion and injuries they sustained; she was beaten daily, creating layers of physical and psychic pain. Living like filthy animals, she described each moment as a struggle. She knew that some element of struggle would be necessary for her to return "all the way home" to her body. When we began the Struggle work, her muscle tonus would often rigidify, and she would appear tense and stressed. She shifted quickly into a strained, mobilized state, and it appeared as if fear was physically streaming through her body.

Standing on Struggle, Rita began to talk more about her torture experiences. To avoid dissociation, I invited her to punctuate her verbal narratives with movements that expressed the fragments of her story. In Struggle, her movements were quite jagged and strong, and she used a lot of dysrhythmic movements to express her movement narrative and internal feeling states. One movement she used was a fist clenched with a hypertonic contraction of her arm muscles, trying to "lift up, up and out of this place." We repeated this movement, alternating between me mirroring her directly and responding to her with my own movement (an attunement dialogue that helps form a movement narrative). I also invited her to adjust tension or effort level (softer, lighter), strength (strong, light), shape (big, small, just her arms, just her hands, her whole body). These oscillations relate to effort shapes in Laban Movement Analysis (Tortora, 2006) and are an effective way to assist survivors in state shifting. It is not possible to shift emotional and psychological states without shifting physiological states. These variations in the way she moved, pushed, and stomped her story allowed her to move with more coherent rhythmicity, and eventually increase her movement repertoire. This enhanced her emotional expression and connection to her own movement narrative, and eventually, her own body and life story. Because Struggle contained movement sequences that were expressed as stomping, pushing, and trying to lift or rise in a highly contracted muscle tonus, she shifted from immobilization to mobilization states, initially abruptly, but following the explorations of effort and shape and speed, the sequences became more fluid over time.

Our work with Struggle continued for three months. We periodically went back to the movement sequences and a song associated with Patience, when needed. Patience became a resource for Rita to delve into her past and her current struggle as a survivor of political torture. Her initial Patience movement was simply standing or sitting still. Over time, she was able to do this without tensing and without dissociating. This stillness also became punctuation for her Struggle movements. After three months of speaking her trauma narrative in bits and pieces, moving her narrative, and weaving them together to integrate past, present, and her future goal of coming home to her body, Rita was ready to move on to Time. She realized time was a force beyond her control, and described it as "God's domain." She also wanted to prepare herself for Strive, which she saw as the final step, because she would strive her whole life to be whole again. Rita considered Strive as an ongoing act of faith in God—that is, striving to be a better person, striving to be a good Christian, striving to be a good family and community member.

We worked in this way for another several months. We sometimes returned to a previous step because the play we engaged in on a later step brought up something from her past that she believed required a "revisit" to one of her steps. As we progressed through each step, she demonstrated more interest in reading her Bible. Rita began to relate her movement sequences to aspects of her own story, and then relate her own story to Biblical stories and parables. I eventually invited her to bring her Bible to our sessions and suggested we begin each session with a reading, chosen by her, which she found in the week between our sessions. This request invited her to engage with "homeplay," an essential step in making therapy real by taking it into meaningful action and integrating it into clients' lives. Homeplay helps restore social engagement and "bio-engagement" (my term for engagement with our entire planet and ancestry, through family *and* through evolution) in the broad context of the world. Rita also continued to practice the movement exercises we did in our sessions at home.

We began to create body narratives (a series of gestures, or movement sequences that can become a "small dance" that tells a story) representing both the resources and the trauma narratives of her life. We created a full narrative for each step. Each narrative had its own rhythmicity varying on a continuum from stillness to highly mobilized, energetic rhythms (within her abilities). Sometimes music, or songs she taught me, would accompany these rhythms, and sometimes they would inspire brief choreographies. We would then weave the body narratives into her overall body and life story. One activity that supported this process was the creation of a "river of life." A lifeline was constructed of colored yarn and small objects borrowed from my sand tray collection to mark both the benevolent, life-affirming, and hope-filled times in her life, as well as the challenging, painful, or traumatic times in her life. As we wove narratives into a story, her movements and transitions from narrative to narrative became more fluid. The restoration of fluid movement that both promotes and accompanies state shifting is essential to the restorative process in polyvagal-informed DMT.

At the end of every process, we discussed her body story—the history she carried from her past, her life now, and her dreams for the future. As Rita remembered and told stories, themes emerged that related to her leadership in her church community and her strong sense of faith. When we were working with Strive, I asked her to relate a story or teaching from the Bible to her life and at first, she could not think of any. I asked her a series of questions about her scars, and about her identification with these scars, and a flash of recognition lit up her face. "Job's body" she said. "My story is the same as Job's body."

This realization was a pivotal moment in our work. In the next four sessions, we read, discussed, and moved Job's body. We went back through each step of her road home to her body, weaving the rhythms, movements, sounds, and songs that she related to each step, together into a series of movements that was, in her words, "my body's story of how I am alive, even when I felt dead." Rita then asked for a break from therapy. She wanted time "to think about who I am now." I supported her request, since it arose at a time when she was moving with greater fluidity, able to sustain my gaze, demonstrated increased vocal and movement prosody, and her posture was markedly more erect and strong. It seemed like a bold embodiment of empowerment.

When Rita returned, she was a changed woman. She entered the space with these words: "I am here now. I have come home to my body." She requested that I videotape her doing the same movements we did for our assessment eight months prior, and then we sang some of the songs that most inspired her journey home to her body. She led the songs, her vocal prosody restored so that her voice was melodic and clear. She faced me and sustained a posture of engagement and in one instance pointed at me, as if telling me what to do, in a gesture of leadership. Then she grabbed my hands and held them. This was the first time she had ever made this type of contact with me. She was in charge, she was present, engaged, and in relationship with me.

She came back the next time and asked me to watch her "dance to freedom"; she had prepared this "in my mind" because "I know you love to dance." This was her gift to me. Rita then squatted, a posture she had endured for a long time in prison. This was the first time a survivor has ever resumed the posture of their suffering in our work together. She squatted, breathing heavily, and then began a long, strained, oscillating between bound and unbounded (Hackney, 2002)(tight and loose, in her description) spinal roll upward, sometimes clenching her fists and contracting her arms as she did in Struggle and Strive, as we had done when we first worked with her shoulder scar. When she was midway, she went completely limp for a moment and then she resumed her body uprising, the flow or "prosody" of her movement oscillating from tense, rigid, and stiff to completely limp and lifeless, with brief moments of fluidity in between. When she was standing erect, she raised her arms upward, fists clenched in a stance that reminded me of power and pleading to God. We had explored this in Struggle, when she asked God: "Why? Why? Why? Why?"

Her arms then transformed. In an instant they were shaped like a chalice raising upward to the sky, and she was looking up at the ceiling, tears in her eyes. As she raised her arms, she extended them in a reach that extended farther than I had ever seen her reach, she smiled and brought her eyes to mine. She held my gaze. And she said again, "I am free." She was standing in a posture of complete engagement; her body prosody as steady and communicative as her vocal prosody when she had sung for me.

She then said, "This is the only time I will do this dance." I asked her if we should film it, and she said no, and repeated: "This is the only time I will do this dance." She then asked me to reflect it back to her, and when I finished, she said, "We are done." She would allow me to share this with others I teach, but said she never wished to move, or see, her dance again. Pointing to her heart, she said, "It's here. I will never forget this journey. It lives in my body, like Job's story did."

We met for another several months, and eventually Rita completed therapy. As always, my clients are invited back for check-ins, and she came a few more times to see me. The last time I saw her, she was happily working in a nursing home, tending to elders, and she loved this work. It allowed her to "give love to people who are left alone at the time when they most need it." She attended church regularly, had brought several of her children over to join her, and was actively involved in their lives. She was emerging into local leadership in her newly re-embodied life.

Summary and Discussion

Rita's Dance to Freedom describes how the markers of engagement, based on the Porges "rules of engagement" (2013), restoring relative safety through re-embodiment, and core rhythmicity through state shifting in multidirectional ways, began to restore Rita's place in the world. As with many survivors of torture, she had lost a sense of belonging and questioned the meaning of her experiences, and therefore of her life. She suffered from multiple clinical diagnoses as well as a disconnect in her relational and social capacities, creating a loss of social engagement. The journey home to her body, and to freedom, was initially based on a restoration of yield, an immobilization without fear-supported action. Rita's ability to relax and to connect to others was undermined by the extraordinary lack of safety in her body, which undermined the trust necessary to either settle into herself or relate to another. Therefore, work in the realm of immobilization without fear was not possible initially. She would either shut down completely or get too agitated and ask to finish the session. We began state shifting into gentle mobilization activities and states to avoid the scariness of deeper relaxation states requiring trust. We used rhythm, ranging from lyrical and light to staccato and strong, to promote these state shifts. She shared biblical stories, a source of meaning and belonging, in spoken word and in movement, shifting her movement and body prosody from nondimensional, fragmented and diminished, to something closer to what I imagined her baseline may have been. The pain in her scarred areas and deep damage to muscle tissue would not allow full recovery of prior range of motion. However, Rita reestablished her ability to express herself both verbally and as a body narrative to tell important aspects of her life story as a coherent narrative with movement, image, and word. She reconnected to things that gave her life meaning. She found her way home to a place of increased belonging in the world.

Each narrative had a verbal and a nonverbal component. Within Polyvagal-informed DMT, the nonverbal component was the bridge from a body that shut down in terror and disbelief to a body capable of prosodic expression in rhythm, dance, and breath. In her own words: "My Dance to Freedom taught me how to move in my body, my human body, once again."

References

Bainbridge Cohen, B. (2012). *Sensing, feeling and action: The experiential anatomy of body-mind centering*. Toronto, Canada: Contact Editions.

Berrol, C.F. (1992). The neurophysiologic basis of the mind-body connection in dance/movement therapy. *American Journal of Dance Therapy, 14*(1), 19-29. doi: https://doi.org/10.1007/BF00844132.

Cottingham J., Porges, S., & Richmond, K. (1988). Shifts in pelvic inclination angle and parasympathetic tone produced by Rolfing soft tissue manipulation. *The Journal of American Physical Therapy Association, 68*(9), 1364–1370.

Geller, S. M., & Porges, S. W. (2014). Therapeutic presence: Neurophysiological mechanisms mediating feeling safe in therapeutic relationships. *Journal of Psychotherapy Integration, 24*(3), 178–192.

Gray, A. E. (2002, May 30–June 1). Dance movement therapy: The use of rhythm as an intervention for traumatic stress. Presented at Dr. Bessel van der Kolk's 13th Annual International Trauma Conference, Boston, MA.

Gray, A. E. (2015a). Dance movement therapy with refugee and survivor children: A healing pathway is a creative process. In C. Malchiodi (Ed.), *Creative interventions for traumatized children*. New York, NY: Guilford Press.

Gray, A. E. (2015b). The broken body: Somatic perspectives on surviving torture. In S. L. Brooke & C. E. Myers (Eds.), *Therapists creating a cultural tapestry: Using the creative therapies across cultures*. Springfield, IL: C. C. Thomas.

Gray, A. E., & Porges, S. W. (2017). Polyvagal-informed dance/movement therapy with children who shut down: Restoring core rhythmicity. In C. Malchiodi & D. Crenshaw (Eds.), *What to do when children clam up in therapy: Interventions to facilitate communication* (pp. 102–136). New York, NY: Guilford Press.

Hackney, P. (2002). *Making connections: Total body integration through Bartenieff fundamentals*. New York, NY: Routledge.

Herman, J. (1997). *Trauma and Recovery*. New York, NY: Basic Books.

Hindi, F. S. (2012). How attention to interoception can inform dance/movement therapy. *American Journal of Dance Therapy 34*(2), 129–140. doi:10.1007/s10465-012-9136-8

Johnson, D.R., Lahad, M., & Gray, A. (2009). Creative Therapies for Adults. In Foa, E., Keane, T., Friedman, M. & J. Cohen (Eds.), *Effective Treatments for PTSD, Second Edition*. 2009: The Guilford Press.

Levine, P. (2015). *Trauma and memory: Brain and body in a search for the living past: A practical guide for understanding and working with traumatic memory*. Berkeley, CA: North Atlantic Books.

Levy, F. (1992). Dance movement therapy: A healing art. American Alliance for Health, Physical Education, and Recreation.

Perry, B. (2017). In H. K. Kemble (Director), *The moving child: Supporting early development through movement* [Motion picture]. Retrieved from https://vimeo.com/ondemand/themovingchildfilm

Porges, S. W. (2011). *The Polyvagal Theory: Neurophysiological foundations of emotions, attachment, communication, self-regulation*. New York, NY: Norton.

Porges, S. W. (2012). Body, Brain, Behavior: How Polyvagal Theory Expands Our Healing Paradigm. [Webinar] The National Institute for the Clinical Application of Behavioral Medicine. Retrieved from www.nicabm.com

Porges, S.W. (2017). *The pocket guide to the polyvagal theory: The transformative power of feeling safe*. New York, NY: Norton.

Rothschild, B. (2000). *The body remembers: The psychophysiology of trauma and trauma treatment*. New York, NY: Norton.

Schmais, C. (1985). *American Journal of Dance Therapy, 8*, 17. doi:10.1007/BF02251439

Siegel, D. (1999). *The developing mind*. New York, NY: Guilford Press.

Siegel, D. (2012, March 28). Bringing out the best in kids: Strategies for working with the developing mind [Webinar]. The National Institute for the Clinical Application of Behavioral Medicine. Retrieved from www.nicabm.com

Siegel, D. (2013, January 16). The mind lives in two places: Inside your body, embedded in the world [Webinar]. The National Institute for the Clinical Application of Behavioral Medicine. Retrieved from www.nicabm.com

Tortora, S. (2006). *The dancing dialogue: Using the communicative power of movement with young children*. Baltimore, MD: Paul H. Brooks.

van der Kolk, B. (1994). The body keeps the score: Memory & the evolving psychobiology of post traumatic stress. *Harvard Review of Psychiatry, 1*(5), 253–265.

van der Kolk, B. (2014). *The body keeps the score: Brain, mind, and body in the healing of trauma*. New York, NY: Penguin Books.

van der Kolk, B., Hopper, J. W., & Osterman, J. E. (2001). Exploring the nature of traumatic memory: Combining clinical knowledge with laboratory science. In J. J. Freyd & A. P. DePrince (Eds.), *Trauma and cognitive science: A meeting of minds, science and human experience* (pp. 9–31). Philadelphia, PA: Haworth Press.

13

The Polyvagal Foundation of Theraplay Treatment: Combining Social Engagement, Play, and Nurture to Create Safety, Regulation, and Resilience

Sandra Lindaman and Jukka Mäkelä

Abstract: Polyvagal Theory tells us that when individuals feel safe, they display social engagement, play, and loving behavior. It also suggests that we can help children with social behavior and attachment problems by altering the cues of safety in the caregiving environment and giving the child new neural experiences of safety. Coherence of Theraplay® structured use of child–parent social engagement, play, and nurture with Polyvagal Theory and polyvagal processes embedded in its protocol are examined. Therapeutic stages and decisions in light of Polyvagal Theory are illustrated for a child with selective mutism following medical trauma. Theraplay treatment resulted in significant improvements in state regulation, social behavior, communication skills, and quality of life.

THIS CHAPTER WILL introduce the reader to Theraplay® and discuss polyvagal processes embedded in Theraplay treatment. We will illustrate therapeutic stages and decisions in light of Polyvagal Theory in a case example of a child with selective mutism following severe medical trauma. Porges has proposed a therapeutic model with a passive stage in which therapists communicate cues of safety to the client through their own social engagement system. Once the client's neuroception triggers feelings of safety, the therapist engages the active stage. In the active stage, therapists present further opportunities for exercising the client's social engagement system. Successful implementation of these two sequential stages promotes outcomes manifested in improved state regulation, social behavior, communication skills, and quality of life (Porges, 2016). We will examine the coherence between Theraplay's structured use of social engagement, play, and nurture and Polyvagal Theory. We hope to elaborate on how methods employed in Theraplay provide efficient exercises of the social engagement system. By doing so, we wish to contribute to making the world feel safer, and thus become safer for children and families.

Theraplay is a relationship intervention modeled on healthy parent–child interaction involving moment-to-moment, sensitively responsive and regulating interactions leading to healthy development. Psychologists Ann Jernberg and Phyllis Booth created Theraplay in the 1960s for children in Head Start. Jernberg said, "The best way to understand the principles underlying Theraplay is to rediscover the basics of the mother-infant relationship" (Jernberg, 1979, p. 4). At that time, John Bowlby was developing attachment theory and suggesting that "the pattern of interaction adopted by the mother of a secure infant provides an excellent model for the pattern of therapeutic intervention" (Bowlby, 1988, p. 126).

Theraplay started by teaching secure adults to be present with aggressive or withdrawn high-risk preschoolers in an engaging, caring, and playful way to relieve the children's distress so that they would have a more positive experience of themselves and others. The key elements of this kind of interaction were described as: Structure (warm adult guidance and organization); Engagement (personal connection through eye contact, vocalizations, proximity, and physical contact); Nurture (soothing activities such as feeding and tending to hurts); and Challenge (simple cooperative games focused on the child's success). Many of the young clients improved dramatically. Based on that initial success, Theraplay focused on helping parents and children build better relationships through these kinds of interactions (Booth & Jernberg, 2010). Currently Theraplay is practiced in many social and mental health settings in 60 countries to treat dysregulated behavior arising from attachment insecurity (Weir et al., 2013; Booth, Lindaman & Winstead, 2014; Salo, Lampi, & Lindaman, 2010). Dyadic family and group Theraplay have effectively improved caregiver responsiveness and reduced problems of emotional regulation, aggressive behavior, and social interaction (Substance Abuse and Mental Health Service Administration, 2017; California Evidence Base Clearinghouse, 2009; Siu, 2009, 2014; Wettig, Coleman, & Geider, 2011; Cort & Rowley, 2015; Tucker & Schieffer, 2017).

The Coherence Between Polyvagal Theory and Theraplay

Polyvagal Theory. adds an important piece to the understanding of the autonomic regulatory processes underpinning child development and attachment formation as well as the therapeutic experiences of Theraplay's social engagement, play, and nurture. Polyvagal Theory identifies evolutionary changes from which three primary neural circuits emerged that form an ordered response hierarchy to regulate behavior and physiological adaptations to environments. These neural circuits are recruited by the nervous system via neuroception (i.e., the nervous system's capacity to evaluate risk without awareness), which detects contexts as safe (i.e., recruits the ventral vagal complex), dangerous (i.e., recruits the sympathetic nervous system) or life-threatening (i.e., recruit the dorsal vagal complex). Polyvagal Theory also describes how the development of an integrated social engagement system is related to maintaining a state of safety and how the social engagement system contributed to other social processes including play and intimacy (i.e., immobilization without fear; Porges, 2011). Throughout life, we calm our physiological defense systems by seeking cues in the faces and voices of others and forming trusting relationships with those who emit cues of safety. The capacity and flexibility of the social engagement system requires exercise and begins with early interactions with caregivers when there is reciprocal interaction between the newborn's limited behavioral repertoire and the parent's responsive facial expressions, vocalizations, listening, and head gestures.

When the parent's voice is prosodic and face warmly expressive, it activates the child's social engagement system, which downregulates defensive states and enables feelings of safety. This has been described "as neural exercises that enable social cues of safety, emanating from the mother, to regulate the infant's physiology and behavioural state. As the infant calms, cues from the infant calm the mother. These bidirectional and reciprocal interactions strengthen the social bonds between mother and infant and foster a capacity to co-regulate" (Porges, 2015, p. 116).

Play

Play is not merely pleasurable activity. Polyvagal Theory defines play as requiring "reciprocal interactions and a constant awareness of the action of others" (Porges, 2011, p. 276). Play involves reciprocal movement, proximity, and touch, which are potential cues of danger that mobilize the sympathetic nervous system. If unchecked, this could activate a survival response of fight-or-flight. Play also requires synchronous face-to-face interactions; the social engagement systems of the players regulate the mobilization of their sympathetic nervous systems. And so, during play an individual is exposed to alternating cues of danger and safety. Play provides repeated practice opportunities for the social engagement system to efficiently downregulate sympathetic activation. Play begins in the parent–infant relationship with "baby games" that move the child from calm engagement to mobilization and back to calm again (e.g., "this little piggy"). The more times this game is played, the less overwhelmed the baby will become at the tummy tickle at the end and the faster she will return to a calm state. Participating in this type of play with another person gives us practice using social cues to regulate our physiological state so that rather than reacting defensively, we can form trusting relationships.

Immobilization Without Fear

In normal development, a parent and infant often are in close body contact, inhibiting movements. When awake, this closeness also involves gentle face-to-face and vocal exchanges, rocking and singing and often feeding. These activities promote calmness through the oxytocinergic system and both the ventral and dorsal vagal complexes, leading to immobilization without fear. Polyvagal Theory describes how the social engagement system enables physical contact to occur while immobilized without fear, and how this state "maintains a physiological state that supports health, growth and restoration, optimizes the ability to rest, relax, sleep and perform bodily processes, and enables feelings of trust, safety and love" (Porges, 2015a, p. 2). This reciprocal process of giving and receiving of caregiving has the capacity to protect, heal, and restore (Porges, 2011).

When There Is Inadequate Parent–Child Neural Exercise

We are born with the potential for social behavior to regulate our physiological state, to calm us and shift defensive behaviors to trusting relationships. However, these pathways need to be exercised to be strengthened. This occurs when the mother or caregiver is "available to reliably provide the infant with opportunities of high-quality reciprocal interactions" (Porges, 2015b, p. 116). The ability to co-regulate is optimized with adequate exercise of these neural pathways and at risk if the exercise is inadequate, disrupted, or unreliable. Even when the cues of danger no longer exist, "the social engagement system may remain dormant unless it is appropriately stimulated with safety cues" (Porges, 2015b, p. 120). Children who have experienced trauma may have faulty neuroception; their nervous system may incorrectly appraise safe situations as dangerous. When this occurs, they react defensively and cannot engage socially. For trusting relationships to develop, the child must experience cues of safety via appropriate social engagement, enabling proximity and contact.

Many children present with problems of dysregulation of physiological state manifested in mobilized hyperarousal or immobilized hypoarousal. When expressed as mobilized hyperarousal aggression, irritability or trouble concentrating is observed. When expressed as immobilized hypoarousal, there is a constricted range of emotional expression and a stilling of behavior. Many of these dysregulated children live in psychologically toxic environments with caregivers who do not feel safe and regulated themselves. Parents, teachers, and even therapists do not have sufficient information about what contextual cues our nervous system needs to feel safe. They do not typically see dysregulated behaviors as dependent on physiological state or as result of the physiological experience of not feeling safe. Rather, they interpret these behaviors as volitional and attempt remediation through interventions based on cognitive explanations and "learning" exercises. A greater knowledge of Polyvagal Theory could help by providing a template for understanding and intervening at the most basic level of the autonomic nervous system to take actions that support the neuroception of safety.

Polyvagal Processes in Theraplay

Polyvagal Theory informs therapists to develop new intervention paradigms focused on providing contextual cues that would shift the child's physiological state to help children regulate behavior:

> We can alter the caregiving environment so that it will appear and be safer for children and less likely to evoke mobilization or immobilization responses. We also can intervene directly with children, exercising the neural regulation of brainstem structures, stimulating the neural regulation of the SES [social engagement system] and encouraging positive social behavior. (Porges, 2011, p. 19)

Theraplay directly intervenes with both the caregiver and the child. It exercises the neural pathways that allow social behavior to regulate physiological state through providing high-quality reciprocal structured sequences of social engagement, playful challenge and nurture. The therapist's primary responsibility is to create a safe and rewarding experience of being with another person for the child, for the parent, and for the child and parent together. The therapist's primary tool is his social engagement with the participants. Theraplay strengthens synchronization processes in the autonomic and limbic systems through the creation of moments of meeting between the therapist and child and the parent and child (Mäkelä & Hart, 2011). These experiences need to send clear cues of safety and be interpreted via neuroception as safe and different from earlier experiences in which social interaction felt dangerous or life-threatening.

At the Seventh International Theraplay Conference (July 2016, Evanston, IL), Stephen Porges described the polyvagal processes in Theraplay as seen in Figure 13.1. We describe below how participation in Theraplay creates a neuroception of safety and enhances autonomic flexibility and emotional regulation.

Recruiting the Passive Pathway: Creating a Neuroception of Safety in Assessment

After meeting with a therapist to gather history, the parents and child participate in a video-recorded assessment of parent–child interaction, the Marschak Interaction Method (MIM) (Marschak, 1960; Booth, Christensen, & Lindaman, 2011). The MIM assesses parent–child strengths and challenges in the areas of Structure, Engagement, Nurture, and Challenge through a structured observation of nonverbal and verbal interaction. The MIM assesses the very elements outlined in communicating through the social engagement system: the dyad's facial expressions, vocalizations, movements, proximity, contact, guidance, co-regulation, synchrony, contingent responsiveness, attunement, misattunement, and repair. It assesses whether the participants appear calm and relaxed, hyperaroused, or shut down, and what kinds of interactions led to these states. After the MIM, these observations are discussed with the parents while viewing portions of the video to hear the parents' view of the interaction and their thoughts about their child's behavior and experience. In addition to describing the Theraplay process to the parents, we practice Theraplay activities with them so they can experience for themselves the nature of the social engagement, play, and nurture that we will employ. The therapist assesses the

Polyvagal Processes in Theraplay	
Stage	**Polyvagal Process**
1. Recruit passive pathway • Deliver therapy in a safe context • Witness and respect initial biobehavioral (physiological) state of child • Use social engagement to trigger a state of safety through neuroception	• Neuroception of safety • Remove predator cues • Express acoustic cues similar to a loving mother (prosodic voice) • Express positive facial expressions and gestures
2. Recruit active pathway • Synchronous reciprocal interaction (e.g., play) as a neural exercise (active pathway) • Develop resilience by expanding the window of tolerance	• Exercise 'vagal brake' to enhance autonomic fexibility and emotional regulation. • Resilience emerges while moving between states of immobilization, mobilization, and safety.

FIGURE 13.1

parents' reactions to this interaction, and the parents can ask questions and tell the therapist how they feel and how their child might feel and react.

Social Engagement in Treatment

In Theraplay, we give both the child and the parent new ways of coming into, and staying within, the safe state. As therapists, we use our own ventral vagal mediated prosodic voice and positive facial expressions and gestures to activate the child's and parents' neuroception of safety. We position ourselves with our faces toward the child and come close enough for the child to see the calming emotional expression around our eyes. With the child, we verbalize what is happening in a relaxed, melodic voice described as "parentese." This is to eliminate the cues of danger, such as a frightening voice or angry or flat face, they may have encountered in the past. We look for the right degree of neural challenge that will engage the client's social engagement system and not activate an adaptive survival state.

The following describes a typical sequence.

After greetings and entering the treatment room in a playful activity guided by the therapist, the therapist creates an opportunity to further assess the child's and parents' states and to use social engagement to trigger a state of safety by engaging the clients in a "checkup."

After the child and parent settle next to each other on floor cushions, the therapist sits facing them and "checks up" on all of the wonderful things the child brought with her that day, saying: "There you are!" *(Acoustic cue of warm, prosodic voice.)* "Looks like you and Mom had haircuts since the last time I saw you." *(Visual cue of positive facial expression.)*

The child touches her hair and nods her head.

The therapist says, "Yep, *(contingent gestural cue of head nod)* I'll bet it feels a little different." *(Acknowledgment of child's physical sensation.)* "Which finger had a scratch last week?" *(Demonstrates that therapist has kept child in mind.)*

The child shows finger with a smile. *(Child reacts with facial expression of social engagement.)*

"Oh, look how much better it is!" *(Contingent facial expressions of concern and then relief.)* "Today you have different hair and a finger that's better. Mom, let's check if her eyes are still that same dark brown. Yay! They are!" *(Therapist continues to use own social engagement system of eye contact, positive facial expression, and prosodic voice to create a neuroception of safety; and acknowledges not just new events but enduring characteristics of the child.)*

The therapist assesses the child's autonomic state and comfort with this interaction by observing the child's face, voice, breathing, and body posture. If the child seems uncomfortable or nonreceptive, the therapist downregulates defensiveness by shifting the focus to a "checkup" that uses less face-to-face interaction while maintaining warm, appreciative acoustic cues, for example: "We checked your hair, your eyes, and your finger, but how about your toes?" *(Keeps child in social engagement system by allowing a break from eye contact while maintaining prosodic acoustic cues.)* "I wonder if we can see you wiggle them even inside your shoes—yes, we can, they are strong toes!"

The parent is our client too. Parents often begin to imitate the therapist's manner of social engagement. Parents learn simple routines and activities to exercise the social engagement system with their child; they come to experience and understand the power of the engagement tools they have at their disposal. Some parents have not experienced safe co-regulation in their own childhoods, nor do they have these kinds of positive social engagement activities in their current lives. They may have difficulty with, or devalue, speaking to and looking at their child in this engaged way. With these parents, the therapist makes time for additional support, discussion, and practice.

Recruiting the Active Pathway

Play: Synchronous Reciprocal Interaction as a Neural Exercise of the Vagal Brake

Play is another way to enter into, and stay in, the safe state. Within a Theraplay session, play consists of therapist-guided reciprocal activities paired with an active presentation of cues of safety from the therapist's social engagement system. By recruiting the child's social engagement system, the child experiences both sympathetic activation to support the physical activity and the influence of the vagal brake, via the social engagement system, to restrain aversive mobilization. The resulting interaction is experienced as safe, pleasant, somewhat exciting, with a sense of accomplishment. A Theraplay session will contain a number of these play sequences, resulting in exercising the vagal brake in ways that will, over time, enhance autonomic flexibility and emotional regulation.

The following describes a typical play sequence.

After the "checkup" described above, the Theraplay therapist engages the child in synchronous reciprocal play as a neural exercise. The therapist sits face-to-face across from a child on the floor and, with a smile and widened eyes, places a soft stuffed toy on her own head. *(Continues therapist's social engagement system cues of positive facial expressions; the activity itself encourages eye contact.)* She extends her hands, palms up, toward the child and nods *(social engagement system cue of positive head gesture)*, inviting the child to do the same, and places her hands below the child's hands. *(The therapist judges that there is sufficient social engagement system activation of child to allow greater proximity and brief physical contact associated with the game.)* In a melodic voice, the therapist says, "One, two, three . . ." and then tilts her head forward so that the toy drops into their hands with a soft plop *(encouraging reciprocity while maintaining synchrony)*. The therapist exclaims, "Wow, we caught it!" The child laughs and eagerly says, "My turn!" *(The child's positive response indicates she remains in social engagement even after experiencing mobilization.)* After several rounds, the therapist says, "Mom, now it's your turn, sit right here." *(The parent has her own opportunity to use the social engagement system in play, guide the child, and maintain safety.)*

Theraplay provides repeated practice opportunities for the social engagement system to efficiently downregulate sympathetic activation. If it weren't for the powerful constraining role of the social engagement system, the activity could end in fight-or-flight or freeze. This happens with many of our clients who have difficulty playing with their families or peers. Some are bossy and controlling, blow up, melt down, or become aggressive—signs of an autonomic shift toward the fight-or-flight state of sympathetic activation. Some children withdraw, isolate themselves, and play alone. These may be preliminary signs of dorsal vagal activation shutting down the capacity to stay in contact. These shifts reflect the child's adaptive survival responses and affect the child's ability to feel safe and stay in social engagement.

For many children with regulatory problems, live play with an attuned adult and the experience of co-regulation is novel. In Theraplay we set up activities that have the qualities of preverbal parent–child play: face-to-face, back and forth, rhythm and rhyme, proximity with gentle and playful touch (i.e., activities that are synchronous, reciprocal, and containing safety cues). The play activities can be mildly mobilizing, as with "catch the beanbag" described above, or more physically active such as jumping off pillows into a parent's arms. The therapist leads the interaction first with the child, then involves the parent as a coplayer, and eventually the parent takes over leadership and the therapist assists.

Our goal for parents is to help them understand the value of interpersonal play in supporting the child's capacity for social engagement, and to be able to use this kind of play to strengthen their relationship with their child and co-regulate the child's state and behavior. Sometimes this type of play is unfamiliar or difficult for parents. They may devalue play, question its usefulness to regulate behavior, or be focused on more chronologically appropriate issues such as more complicated games, competition, humor, sportsmanship, and fairness. The therapist provides support to the parent through discussion and practice in these situations. This is an opportunity to teach parents about the basics of Polyvagal Theory. This can help parents come to terms with their own issues concerning regulation of their autonomic state, which in turn affects their capacity for co-regulating the child's state.

Social engagement creates space to play, learn, and interact socially. An active social engagement system provides the co-regulation needed to play. Through Theraplay treatment, difficulties with playing often improve dramatically. Both parent and child experience enhanced autonomic flexibility and emotional regulation; parents gain new knowledge, skills, and reflective capacity about their child as an active, participating, and creative person. The child's ability to play with peers often improves without ever bringing another child into the treatment room to practice peer skills directly.

Experiencing Immobilization Without Fear

Giving and receiving nurture is another way to enter into and stay in the safe state. Theraplay helps the child and parent experience the positive state of immobilization without fear. Prosocial use of the voice and face plus proximity and gentle contact is the essence of Nurture, which allows for intense downregulation of arousal toward a "rest and digest" state (dorsal vagal), while staying in connection (ventral vagal). Many children with physical or attachment trauma cannot immobilize without fear. Since their history frequently includes danger that has occurred in contact with others, proximity or touch often leads to either sympathetic nervous system or dorsal vagal activation. In Theraplay, we constantly work to offer the right degree of proximity and contact for the child to feel safe, using our social engagement system to signal that our intentions are good. This strengthens the child's neuroception of safety and the ability to relax in the proximity of another. In addition to using play as a neural exercise, the Theraplay therapist also creates several opportunities for immobilization without fear in each session. Over the course of a session the therapist leads the child and parent between states of mobilization, immobilization without fear, and safety.

Continuing our example from the play section.

After several rounds of Mom and child dropping the toy into each other's hands, the therapist looks carefully at the child's hands. *(Therapist begins to move from mobilizing play toward immobilization without fear by initiating greater proximity along with positive facial and acoustic cues that activate the social engagement system.)* She says, "My goodness, what great hands you have—they're warm." *(Given the child's acceptance of proximity, the therapist initiates contact and feels the child's hands briefly.)* The child smiles at the therapist and nods. The therapist tells the child, "You have one-two-three-four-five fingers." *(Given the child's calm breathing and positive social engagement system cues, the therapist makes gentle contact by touching each finger lightly.)* "And look, *(leans forward, points)* there is a special freckle on your thumb!" *(Therapist finds a specific feature of the child to attend to and care for.)* "Mom, I'll give you a cotton ball. You can give a soft touch to that freckle and see if you can find two more on your girl's hand." *(Therapist provides a model for making gentle contact with the child while giving safety cues, and directs the parent to do the same and then extend that contact.)* Child and parent resilience emerges while moving between states of mobilization, immobilization without fear, and safety.

Nurture conveys care and attention. We make an active statement of this intention by the rule of "no hurts" in Theraplay. It is the responsibility of the therapist to be sure that the play activities he sets up are safe. When the child is ready, touch is an important element, as warm touch raises the levels of the hormone oxytocin, a calming and antiaggressive hormone supporting the ventral vagal complex. When touch and pleasant stimulation are coordinated with warm facial expressions and vocalizations, the child's level of oxytocin produces a warm, light, loving feeling, which helps create the calm needed to engage in social interactions and attachment formation (Mäkelä & Hart, 2011). We may rub our hands together to warm them and place them over the child's cold hands in winter. We take care of small bruises that a child may have by caring for them with a cotton ball or lotion. We sing songs about the child and give them blanket swings. Rocking promotes calmness by influencing the myelinated vagus.

We always have a beverage and food snack at the end of sessions and work toward the parent feeding the child the snack. Feeding promotes calmness by activating the muscles of mastication via the trigeminal nerve that connects to the ventral vagal complex. When a child is not comfortable accepting nurture directly, positive attention and care are conveyed in more playful ways. The therapist and child can put lotion on their hands and try to hold slippery hands, or feeding is done with a taste test or contest. No child or parent is ever required to eat or to allow touch they are not comfortable with. It is imperative to understand the subtle expressions of discomfort as seen in state shifts from social engagement system to sympathetic nervous system to dorsal vagal, not just directly expressed verbal cues. Here, knowledge of Polyvagal Theory helps the therapist in responding to the child or parents in a more comprehensive way. One result of a successful therapy is for the child to feel "safe to cuddle and immobilize in the arms of another, no longer vigilant about activity from behind" (Porges, 2016).

Again, parents may not have had positive experiences with the state of immobilization without fear themselves. They may tell us that caregiving is babying or spoiling, creates dependency or rewards bad behavior, is unimportant or contrary to their desire to "toughen" their child. They may tell us they are uncomfortable with nurture. These parent responses invite additional investigation, support, and practice.

Moving Between States of Immobilization Without Fear: Mobilization and Safety to Enhance Resilience

The Theraplay therapist structures the sequencing of social engagement, play, and nurturing care. In early child–parent relationships, the adult has more responsibility and more abilities than the child. Adults make safety, play, and nurture happen, and, if they don't, the child misses opportunities to learn to self-regulate. The Theraplay therapist takes the stance of initiating social engagement with the child (ventral vagal), while guiding the child into higher activation (sympathetic nervous system) and lower activation (dorsal vagal and vagal brake). In the session the therapist briefly explains one activity at a time while leading the child through the activity. If a child is reluctant to interact, the therapist demonstrates with the parent. The therapist decides when and how much to ask the parent to lead activities. When activities become familiar, explanations are not necessary, and the therapist introduces small variations to maintain interest. Increasingly, the parent helps guide and co-regulate, and eventually the child learns to self-regulate. As parents and children experience Theraplay's new ways of coming into, and staying in, the safe state, their autonomic flexibility and emotional regulation are enhanced, as described by one parent:

> My 6-year-old daughter struggles with attention deficit disorder and difficulty processing and using language. As I practiced Theraplay with her, I realized that these activities were affecting me as well. I felt intrinsically rewarded, almost elated to have actual directions of what to do in order to achieve a meaningful connection with my own daughter. Although I needed to redirect her back to me several times, she pretty quickly allowed me to guide her for continued interactions—something that is usually very challenging for me and for others who care for her. It felt good to know that simple activities can empower me to feel more confident in knowing how to interact with her in the ways that she needs.
>
> I found that utilizing these activities also helped me to remain focused and in the moment, which is difficult for me to maintain with my own attention deficit disorder. I believe I may be feeling some similar, if not the same, effects of a much-needed playful connection that stimulates parts of my brain that were rarely triggered as a child. After the activities, I come away feeling calmer, more connected, with a sense of deeper love and understanding of my child—a satiating experience of true contentment (personal communication, February 2015).

In the following sections, we present a Theraplay treatment analyzed in terms of the Polyvagal processes. The child's parents agreed to and contributed to this publication, and her name was changed for confidentiality. Assessment and treatment sessions were videotaped, allowing verbatim reports and analysis of the specifics of our reciprocal interactions in light of Polyvagal concepts. The therapist and author (Sandra Lindaman) refers to herself as "me" or "I."

Background and Assessment

Five-year-old Nora did not speak in school. She often cried and was unresponsive when spoken to; she did not interact with other children. Nora was active and talkative at home with her immediate family, but severely restricted her communication with them elsewhere. Her parents showed me two photos: one taken at home shows Nora with sparkling eyes and a wide open smile; in her school photo her facial expression is blank and her lips are pursed.

Nora had experienced extensive medical trauma in infancy. She had an emergency major surgery at three weeks of age with multiple complications, resulting in ten months of hospitalization. She was dependent on a ventilator and feeding tube into her second year with delayed ability to eat and speak. Her parents reported that Nora often appeared fearful during necessary procedures by various medical providers during her early years. Nora also was sensitive to loud noises, voices, and laughter.

The Marschak Interaction Method

When I met Nora for our parent–child interaction assessment, I made the setting as similar to Nora's home environment as possible. I hoped that she could experience the Theraplay office as a place safe enough to engage with her parents and eventually with me. Typically I would be more involved in greeting and getting to know the child while explaining the assessment to the parents; with Nora I minimized her initial exposure to me, as I felt she would see me as another possibly frightening provider.

Nora entered the room and approached the materials cautiously, with a wary expression and tightly closed mouth. She initially communicated through gestures and pointing. Although Nora eventually spoke in short sentences, her vocalizations had a panting quality and her body movements were jerky. Sometimes Nora did not respond immediately, and her parents had to repeat statements. Nora appeared to start the assessment with dorsal vagal–induced immobilization and later moved between it and sympathetic nervous system–mediated hyperarousal and mobilization. She interacted and cooperated with all tasks but did not appear calm and relaxed at any time.

A Brief Theraplay Trial

After the family finished the assessment, I joined them on the floor to play a few activities. My hope was that in the safe context of being with her parents and involved in play, Nora could begin to tolerate social interaction with me. I used my social engagement system, speaking in a calm but melodic tone, smiling warmly, looking at the parents more than at Nora. I blew bubbles, and the family worked as a team to pop them. We held a blanket at chest height and rolled a ball between the four of us. I showed them how to raise the blanket up high and briefly look at each other before lowering it. Nora looked at me and smiled a bit and silently cooperated in these activities that combined the sympathetic nervous system and social engagement system. When I tested for her ability to experience a downregulating nurture task with her parents in my presence, she refused and looked down. Because I sensed that she was returning to the immobilized state, I removed myself from the family circle and suggested an activity that would put Nora in a more comfortable state of sympathetic mobilization with the social engagement system. I instructed that they stack floor cushions, so that Nora could jump off of them into her dad's arms. She did this joyfully; on that positive note, they went home.

Nora's behavior indicated that she frequently experienced both freezing and high arousal levels. This was understandable, as she had perceived so much danger and life-threat that her social engagement system was unavailable to her except at home. She demonstrated a number of deficits of the social engagement system: lack of vocal prosody, poor eye contact, difficulties in social communication, blunted facial expressivity, sound sensitivities, difficulties in listening, and oral-motor defensiveness (Porges, 2016). My initial goal was to support her neuroception of safety so that she could experience emotionally engaging moments of vitality, pleasure, and soothing with me present. I hoped that after a sufficient experience with this neural exercise, she would be able to engage more comfortably with others and ultimately speak outside of her home.

In the assessment, I could see that Nora's relationship with her parents was comfortable and joyful. Nora's parents were well informed about attachment theory and child development and had devoted themselves to establishing a secure relationship with Nora despite the medical and separation challenges. Their good relationship could be used in the Theraplay sessions to support Nora and bring her into social engagement in this novel surrounding, and explains much of her relatively fast progress. Consistent with Nora's case, a report in the play therapy literature (Glibota, Lindaman, & Coleman, 2018) describes the positive outcome of a child with selective mutism and parent–child relationship issues treated with a Theraplay treatment strategy informed by Polyvagal Theory and attachment theory.

The First Session

To increase the safe context of therapy, I planned to reduce the intensity of my relationship with Nora by demonstrating activities with her parent rather than directly with her. We played games as a threesome instead of my pairing directly with Nora. I arranged the play materials on the floor, so they were all visible. I chose objects that were familiar from the earlier assessment. I added a sheer scarf and cotton balls for new activities. As an invitation to a more familiar and mobilizing and less proximal form of play, I added a balloon and small plastic rackets.

When Nora and her dad came in for the first Theraplay session, I greeted them with a smile and a warm hello and then stood to the side. Nora did not look at me; her lips were pursed and her body movements stiff, indicating her defensive immobilization. At the door to the treatment room I had arranged the pillows in a path on the floor, inviting a move from an immobilized dorsal vagal state to interactive play involving the synergistic involvement of the sympathetic nervous system and the social engagement system. In a calm but inviting voice, I asked Nora's dad to hold her hand while she jumped on the pillow path to the spot where I had arranged the play materials. She chuckled while jumping. When we sat down, her facial expression indicated more curiosity, a sign of increased activity in her social engagement system. We sat on the floor in a triangle formation, close enough to play together. Again, I used my ventral vagal–mediated eye contact and prosodic voice to trigger Nora's neuroception of safety. I titrated the neural challenge of how directly I engaged Nora. To tone down the neural challenge of direct engagement, I often addressed my comments just to Dad. I gestured to the materials and named them, wondering aloud what Nora might like to do. After some encouragement from her dad, she pointed to the rackets. After a few hits by Dad and me, Nora began to bat at the balloon. We hit it around for several minutes. I made sure that my voice was not too loud when commenting on the skill and speed of the play. I wanted to continue to offer cues of safety to Nora's nervous system.

Dad chose cotton balls for the next activity. We held the blanket between us and bounced the cotton balls up and down like making popcorn—a game with greater proximity and eye contact. Next I chose the bubbles; after the familiar blowing and popping, I asked Dad to pop a bubble with the body part that I named. After several turns I asked Nora how Dad should pop it. She pointed to her cheek, so I held it up to Dad's face. This was her first communication directly to me, indicating a greater safety in engaging. Next she chose the small stuffed animals, and we sat in a circle. This time I presented a neural challenge by demonstrating an unfamiliar game involving face-to-face interaction and synchrony: We put the animals on our heads and dumped them to the floor between us on the count of three. Synchrony stimulates social engagement and helped her cope with the challenge. Then I chose the sheer scarf and had Nora sit on her dad's lap. I held the scarf up in front of them and pretended that I could no longer see them. She seemed pleased with this, so I gently put it over their heads and wondered where they were. Dad made some tongue clucks to answer my question and Nora clapped her hands—and so I found them. Her initiative to find a way to signal "I'm under here too" was a further sign of her social engagement system activating. Next I suggested we use the cloth like a rope in a gentle tug-of-war. When I drew close, stressing her sense of safety in proximity, she drew back quickly. I immediately backed away from Nora and switched to rolling the ball back and forth on the cloth between us while I made sounds resonating with the ball's movements. We were still facing each other, which challenged her social engagement system, but she reacted to my vocalizations with smiles, so the reduced proximity while maintaining face-to-face contact seemed to offer the right degree of neural challenge.

After this successful activity, I offered Nora a food snack, a typical ending in a Theraplay session. Unsurprisingly, she declined the snack. Ingesting food in the proximity of another requires a strong neuroception of safety. I thought that offering this possibility might help her to accept such "rest and digest" situations later—hopefully at school, too. I told her she would never have to do things she didn't want to do and asked Nora and her father to take the snack home for later. To end on a positive note, I had Dad stuff her pockets with more cotton balls so that she could show her mom the popcorn game at home.

Treatment Progression

In the next two sessions, I increased the time of face-to-face contact, exercising Nora's capacity to relax in proximity to me. After these three sessions, the teacher at school wrote, "This past week . . . I have noticed how responsive she has been to her peers . . . She was working on a snow man at the table with three other children. She was silently laughing to the things they were saying. She was more interactive than she has been in the past." Theraplay is a way to exercise the vagal brake by working the boundaries of feeling safe, using both the joy of play and the pleasure of nurture to set these new boundaries for staying within the social engagement system.

Over the next four sessions, Nora's smiles and vocalizations of pleasure increased. I used the same activities for predictability, but I always had one new material present. When I introduced a new game, Nora at first looked quite uncomfortable, demonstrating a difficulty shifting from a defensive dorsal vagal or sympathetic nervous system state to ventral vagal; over time she joined in new activities more quickly and took more chances. Since relaxation in the proximity of others (requiring both dorsal vagal and ventral vagal) was her major issue, I had powder and lotion visible to offer the possibility of soothing care, but never insisted on using them on Nora. She did participate in putting these materials on her parents. I could see her ventral vagal functions slowly but surely strengthen; she could look in my face, use her voice in nonverbal and later verbal utterances, and stay in proximity with others initially while playing and then during relaxed immobilized states. Over time, I focused more on my direct social engagement with Nora, while her parents sat with us and observed. I did this to help her feel safe enough to reach out to others in situations in which her parents would not be present.

Play as a neural exercise of the vagal brake to enhance autonomic flexibility and emotional regulation. Nora became very physically active in the sessions. She initiated and showed pleasure in moving, rolling, tumbling, and all forms of rough-and-tumble play, clearly sympathetic states of arousal. Her insistence on playing this way also warded off slow, resting things that could activate a dorsal vagal state of collapse. Sluggish vagal brake reactivity to a physical exercise challenge was found in children with selective mutism, indicating "a more universal difficulty in dynamic autonomic adjustments required to move between states requiring mobilization and those requiring social engagement behaviors" (Heilman et al., 2012, p. 248). I accommodated her need; I also made sympathetic nervous system activities into opportunities to include our social engagement systems. I arranged for Nora to jump off pillows and tunnel under them to her parent. When she rolled and somersaulted on the mats and jumped up and down, I started copying her movements—and then she copied mine. She liked watching herself in a large mirror while moving about; I held up a big scarf between her and the mirror—and then whisked it away with an "abracadabra," to have her magically reappear again, to her delight. Over the sessions, Nora's movements became more fluid and coordinated—a mark of better regulation of high arousal through the continued use of social engagement system co-regulation.

Developing resilience: Moving between states of immobilization, mobilization, and safety. Initially Nora rejected downregulating activities and soothing in my presence. They probably felt like they were bringing her to the brink of primitive immobilization, reminiscent of the shutdown states she activated to handle the terror related to painful medical procedures and the physical restraint she experienced at those times. My aim was to strengthen her capacity for immobilization without fear. After a high mobilization activity, like jumping off pillows into her parent's arms, I did small soothing actions like fanning Nora's "jumping feet" and the parent's "catching arms" with a paper fan. Nora began to accept these without shutdown.

Even though she declined the snack provided in the first three sessions, in the fourth session she fed herself one small chocolate chip cookie. Her mother's reaction was: "This is huge." Nora had always been very self-conscious about eating in front of others. Sharing a treat quickly became a comfortable part of the session. One time she started the session with, "When are we eating? I'm starving."

After seven sessions, Nora spoke to her mother in the waiting room in front of me. In session nine, when her mother and I said the color of the balloons as we batted them around, Nora joined in with "Green . . . red . . . pink." From then on, Nora increasingly spoke in the sessions; she sang, joked, and acted out various events. Then, in session 11, she invented silly stories about her family. As she left the room she stopped and pointed to herself and said, "I talk—I'm a talker." I responded, "Yes, you sure are a talker." Speech gives such strength in personal relations that this description of herself was a clear sign of resourcefulness and resilience, demonstrating a pride in her being. In just 11 sessions she had become able "to regulate her own physiology so that she could access her higher level functions" (Stephen W. Porges, Personal communication, February 2015).

Increasing social flexibility and emotional regulation in and out of session. Nora began to demonstrate improvements in state regulation, social behavior, communication skills, and quality of life. For example, she became more secure at school. After 12 sessions, Nora's teacher reported, "When [I] asked the class who wanted to come to the board during an activity, Nora raised her hand and went up to the board to identify a rainbow color. This is the first time she has participated like this." After 20 sessions, Nora had her first-ever playdate. Her mother reported, "They had so much fun. Within minutes, Nora was talking to Sara and was completely her 'true' self."

After 28 sessions, Nora demonstrated emotional reflectivity and willingness to share concerns. During a balloon game, Nora said, "I like to play this; I happy." A little later in the session she said, "I like school, but on my first day I scared." Nora began to talk about the feelings she experienced inside and outside of the therapy room.

At the end-of-the-year picnic, Nora spoke to her father in front of her classmates and teachers for the first time. At the end of summer, Nora's mother reported the following: "She appears more confident in social settings and talks in the presence of anyone, meaning she doesn't care who might be hearing her talk. She asked to order her food at a restaurant. She is even more spontaneous in engaging/talking with familiar and unfamiliar children."

Nora continued her gains in speaking in public and began to speak freely in kindergarten the following spring after continued Theraplay sessions, a period of EMDR, and medication (Lindaman, 2014). Polyvagal Theory tells us that the face reflects the individual's physiological state (Porges, 2016). In the photo taken at the beginning of first grade, Nora looks directly at the camera with laughing eyes and a wide, confident smile.

Summary

Polyvagal Theory informs us that when individuals feel safe, they display social engagement, play, and loving behaviors; their physiological state is controlled by the ventral vagal pathways, and the ventral vagus moderates the sympathetic and dorsal vagal pathway fibers. The vagal brake on the heart works efficiently, and a calm, well regulated, related state is possible. Polyvagal Theory also suggests that we can help children with social behavior and attachment problems by altering the cues of safety in the caregiving environment and giving the child new neural experiences of safety.

Theraplay offers direct neural exercises to strengthen social engagement pathways. Through these, children can regulate their physiological state though experiencing social engagement, play, and nurture. Theraplay's structured combination of these three positive physiological states supports the neuroception of safety, and thus keeps humans in optimal arousal and allows engagement, connectedness, and reciprocal synchrony.

References

Booth, P., Christensen, G., & Lindaman, S. (2011). *Marschak Interaction Method (MIM) manual and cards* (Rev. ed.). Evanston, IL: Theraplay Institute.

Booth, P. B., & Jernberg, A. M. (2010). *Theraplay: Helping parents and children build better relationships through attachment-based play*. San Francisco, CA: Jossey-Bass.

Booth, P., Lindaman, S., & Winstead, M. (2014). Theraplay in reunification following relational trauma: Isaiah's journey home. In C. Malchiodi & D. Crenshaw (Eds.), *Creative arts and play therapy with attachment problems*. New York, NY: Guilford Press.

Bowlby, J. (1988). *A secure base: Parent-child attachment and healthy human development*. New York, NY: Basic Books.

California Evidence Base Clearinghouse. (2009, December). Theraplay. Retrieved from cebc4cw.org/program/theraplay

Cort, L., & Rowley, E. (2015). A case study evaluation of a Group Theraplay intervention to support mothers and their preschool children following domestic abuse (Research in Brief). British Psychological Society, Debate 156.

Glibota, L., Lindaman, S., & Coleman A. R. (2018). Theraplay as a treatment for selective mutism: Integrating the Polyvagal Theory, attachment theory, and social communication. In C. Schaefer & A. Drewes (Eds.), *Play-based interventions for childhood anxieties, fears, and phobias*. New York, NY: Guilford Press.

Heilman, K. J., Connolly, S. D., Padilla, W. O., Wrzosek, M. I., Graczyke, P. A., & Porges, S. W. (2012). Sluggish vagal brake reactivity to physical exercise challenge in children with selective mutism. *Development and Psychopathology, 24*, 241–250.

Jernberg, A. M. (1979). *Theraplay: A new treatment using structured play for problem children and their families*. San Francisco, CA: Jossey-Bass.

Lindaman, S. (2014). Theraplay for selective mutism. *Newsletter of The Theraplay Institute*. Retrieved from www.theraplay.org

Mäkelä, J., & Hart, S. (2011). Theraplay: An intensive, engaging, interactive play that promotes psychological development. In Hart, S. (Ed.), *Neuroaffectiv psykoterapi med born* [Neuroaffective psychotherapy for children], (pp. 1–28). Denmark: Hans Reitzels.

Marschak, M. (1960). A method for evaluating child-parent interactions under controlled condition. *Journal of Genetic Psychology, 97*, 3–22.

Porges, S. W. (2011). *The Polyvagal Theory: Neurophysiological foundations of emotions, attachment, communication, and self-regulation*. New York, NY: Norton.

Porges, S. W. (2015a). Clinical applications of the Polyvagal Theory: The transformative power of feeling safe. Presented at Cape Cod Institute, Eastham, MA.

Porges, S. W. (2015b). Making the world safe for our children: Down-regulating defence and up-regulating social engagement to 'optimise' the human experience. *Children Australia, 40*, 114–123.

Porges, S. W. (2015c). Play as neural exercise: Insights from the Polyvagal Theory. In D. Pearce-McCall (Ed.), *The power of play for mind brain health* (pp. 3–7). Retrieved from http://mindgains.org/

Porges, S. W. (2016, July). Presentation at the 7th International Theraplay Conference, Evanston, IL.

Salo, S., Lampi, L., & Lindaman, S. (2010). Use of the emotional availability scales to evaluate attachment-based intervention—Theraplay—in substance abusing mother-infant dyads in Finland. *Infant Mental Health Journal, 32*, 77.

Siu, A. F. Y. (2009). Theraplay in the Chinese world: An intervention program for Hong Kong children with internalizing problems. *International Journal of Play Therapy, 18*(1), 112.

Siu, A. F. Y. (2014). Effectiveness of group Theraplay® on enhancing social skills among children with developmental disabilities. *International Journal of Play Therapy, 23*(4), 187–203.

Substance Abuse and Mental Health Service Administration (2017). National registry of evidence-based programs and practices: Theraplay. Retrieved from http://nrepp.samhsa.gov/ProgramProfile.aspx?id=156

Tucker, C., & Schieffer, K. (2017). Enhancing social-emotional skills in at-risk preschool students through Theraplay-based groups: The Sunshine Circle Model. *International Journal of Play Therapy*. 26, (4), 185-195

Weir, K. N., Lee, S., Canosa, P., Rodrigues, N., McWilliams, M., & Parker, L. (2013). Whole family Theraplay: Integrating family systems theory and Theraplay to treat adoptive families. *Adoption Quarterly, 16*(3–4), 175–200.

Wettig, H. G., Coleman, A. R., & Geider, F. J. (2011). Evaluating the effectiveness of Theraplay in treating shy, socially withdrawn children. *International Journal of Play Therapy, 20*(1), 2637.

14

When Pediatric Medical Trauma Presents as Asperger's Syndrome: Polyvagal Explanations and Polyvagal Therapeutic Play

Stuart Daniel, Angie Masters, and Kieran Donovan

Abstract: Kieran's childhood, a clinical case, is presented, in which a late diagnosis of Asperger's syndrome is questioned and the possibility of infant pediatric medical trauma as the primary disorder is considered. Polyvagal Theory explains the neurophysiological and developmental mechanisms underpinning this possibility. Kieran's subsequent progress in play therapy, especially in prosocial behavior, coupled with a reinterpretation of initial diagnostic parameters, has led the authors to accept the primary medical trauma hypothesis. The polyvagal concept of play as a mutual exercise of the vagal brake is discussed in the context of Kieran's therapy.

I think one of the most important things that I would change (if I could) would be an acknowledgment from the medical profession that what we are doing to these tiny babies will affect them for the rest of their lives.
—Angie Masters

Introduction

I WORK IN a room filled with toys. There's lots of space to move, relate with each other, and also hit things as and when needed! Often, I work with traumatized children, helping them to move on from that trauma through play therapy. Polyvagal Theory has a great deal to say about trauma—its nature, onset, developmental implications, and diagnostic place within the spectrum of developmental disorders. Together with Kieran and Angie, I will be exploring all these aspects in detail, as we tell Kieran's story. Kieran is a teenager who from birth endured a great deal of trauma. Angie is his mom.

Here, to begin with, I want to give an introductory overview on how Polyvagal Theory can inform our understanding of therapeutic play. The principles discussed here will become the language of Kieran's story.

The Face–Heart Connection

Polyvagal Theory (Porges, 1995, 2001, 2007, 2009, 2011a, 2018) emphasizes the lifelong human drive to calm neural defense systems by detecting features of safety in others. This drive is present from birth, when an infant communicates the need to be soothed and regulated in partnership with her caregiver. This drive is the impulse within social behavior, the drive for relationship.

Porges (2003) coined the term *neuroception* to describe the reflexive process by which we automatically and continually scan our environment for features of danger or safety. Humans have evolved a three-tiered hierarchy of survival-oriented adaptive systems, each system a well-tuned, organism-wide response to the immediate environment. Our two defense systems are the mobilization system (fight-or-flight behavior) and the immobilization system (metabolically conservative, death-feigning behavior)—more on these later. When there is a neuroception of safety, our defense systems are dampened down and our social engagement system comes online (Porges, 2007, 2011a). When this happens, two important dynamic responses are expressed. First, bodily state is regulated in an efficient manner to promote health, growth, and restoration (visceral homeostasis). This occurs when the influence of mammalian myelinated vagal motor pathways on the cardiac pacemaker increases. Increasing the influence of these vagal pathways slows heart rate, inhibits the fight-or-flight mechanisms of the sympathetic nervous system, dampens the stress response system of the hypothalamic–pituitary–adrenal (HPA) axis, and reduces inflammatory reaction. Second, system-wide influences promote effective prosocial behavior, co-regulation, and relationship. How? Through evolutionary bootstrapping processes, the brain stem nuclei that regulate the myelinated vagus were integrated with the nuclei that regulate the striated muscles of the face and head—specifically, the muscles controlling facial expression, listening, and prosodic vocalizations. This link enables a bidirectional coupling between spontaneous social engagement behaviors and bodily states—the face–heart connection (2007). Simply put, a human who feels safe is an effective social being, while a human who feels threatened is severely compromised socially.

Therapeutic Play and Polyvagal Theory

The face–heart connection provides us with an ability to convey physiological state via facial expression and prosody (intonation of voice). This gives us the potential to use social interactions to calm physiological state in others, through the facial expressions and vocalizations that form the core of social interactions. For example, a mother's voice has the capacity to soothe her infant.

> The sounds of the mother's vocalisations signal safety, which is detected by higher brain structures. The higher brain structures dampen defense systems and facilitate the calming effect on the heart by ventral vagal influences. In parallel to this calming effect, the regulation of the muscles of the face and head are enhanced to enable reciprocal interactions between mother and infant. The reciprocal interactions function as a neural exercise between their Social Engagement Systems. The result is an infant–mother dyad that efficiently uses social communication to co-regulate, with both participants feeling calm and bonded. This neural exercise builds capacity for the infant to develop relations with others and to deal with state regulation challenges and disruptions through the lifespan. (Porges & Daniel, 2017, p. 116-117)

From the polyvagal perspective, this creative, co-regulatory neural exercise—in which two or more humans sensitively explore the functional limits of safety, risk, and calm—*is* play (Porges, 2015; Porges & Daniel, 2017). During healthy play, children will often seek the vulnerable edges of their safety and comfort. With a play-partner, a child will experience this vulnerability and learn to self-regulate through the discomfort and back down to a calm, enlivened state. Through the neural exercise of play a child is engaging over and over in the exercise of her *vagal brake* (Porges, Doussard-Roosevelt, Portales, & Greenspan, 1996; Porges 2015). In this way, the child's autonomic system is slowly entrained towards a dampening of defensive responses and an awakening of the Social Engagement System (Porges, Doussard-Roosevelt, Portales, & Greenspan, 1996; Porges 2015). In healthy human development, the journey from safety to risk and back again is hugely important. Social life will always involve difficult times—moments (sometimes extended) of disconnection. These experiences will be uncomfortable, disruptive, disturbing, or even shocking. How a child learns to transition these moments safely, through repeated playful neural exercise, is crucial for developing a sense of trust and an integrated sense of self (Hughes, 2004; Schore, 1994). "The core of the (*healthy*) self lies in patterns of affect-regulation that integrate a sense of self across state transitions, thereby allowing for a continuity of inner experience" (Schore, 1994, p. 33). In healthy play, moments of vulnerable disconnection are sought out by both partners. Deeply, we know that we need to practice this edge. Both mother and infant naturally initiate games that play in and around vulnerability. In peek-a-boo and hide-and-seek, for instance, moments of vulnerability are sought, created, extended, survived, and repaired, all in synchronous play.

Within playful therapy, this neural exercise is engaged in consciously (Porges & Daniel, 2017; Daniel, 2018). Dan Hughes (2004) talks of natural moments of *disruption* in any therapeutic relationship.

> The attachment sequence of attunement, disruption, and repair occurs frequently in an attachment-based model of therapy, just as it does in the parent-child relationship. The therapist does not avoid these . . . disruption(s), but rather provides a safe setting in which they can occur and then the therapist repairs the relationship before proceeding (p. 269).

The *safe setting* is provided through a consistent environment, through the therapist's ability to respond sensitively to the child's communication (to engage in the neural exercise of play), and above all through the therapist's dedication to accepting and understanding the child's ongoing biobehavioral state (Hughes, 2000; Landreth, 2012; Porges & Daniel, 2017). The *repair work* is done by the therapist consciously leveraging the power of her social engagement system to communicate calm, playful states to the child. In turn, the child's defense systems are dampened via the vagal brake, the social engagement system comes online, and the relationship is reinforced through resultant positive social behavior. Put together well, these elements aggregate as a "containing" experience for the child (Winnicott, 1971). Contained co-regulation, through the playful exercise of the vagal brake over time, will expand a child's window of tolerance (the range of autonomic state in which they can remain stable) and promote emotional and social flexibility (Porges, 2015, 2018; Porges & Daniel, 2017).

Polyvagal Theory gives us deep insights into the nature of healthy play and therapeutic play. It can also help us explore the biobehavioral and developmental roots of trauma, look specifically at how a traumatized child might present in therapy, and make suggestions as to how to tweak the above therapy process of attachment-disruption-repair (Hughes, 2011) when working with a child who has been traumatized from birth. We explore these factors as we move to Kieran's story.

Meeting Kieran

Kieran was 11 years old when we were introduced. Our first meeting was held in a small, beige clinic room in the Royal Hospital for Sick Children in Edinburgh, Scotland. Kieran and his mother, Angie, were present, along with a pediatric psychiatrist and me, a play therapist.

> *Kieran (age 14 at the time of writing):* When we decided to meet Stuart, it was because I wasn't feeling like I fitted in. I wanted to feel better about myself and feel more able to cope with my past and all the reminders of it that I just wanted to let go of.

Kieran had been referred for therapeutic input with the following profile: overwhelming distress and anger, self-harm, a fear of busy social spaces, psychological and physiological distress in response to medical appointments, sleep disturbance, and significant impairments in reciprocal social interaction.

> *Angie:* Kieran had been struggling with anger issues for quite some time. He was prone to verbal outbursts and agitation (particularly when faced with noisy, chaotic, unpredictable situations). Kieran was having an extremely difficult time, and one day a friend came to me and told me that Kieran had hurt himself and that his arm was bleeding. After some time speaking with Kieran, he disclosed to me that hurting himself helped to block out the noise, that when he did it, the pain blocked out the noise.

Kieran displayed disturbances in organized prosocial impulse, including flat affect, awkward prosody, problems turn taking and initiating conversational turns, some asynchronous eye contact and gaze tracking, and an aversion to physical comfort and contact.

> *Kieran:* I only had about three friends and found it extremely hard to make new friends because I didn't know how to start conversation, maintain conversation, or even approach a person.
>
> *Angie:* Kieran did not make friends during his early childhood. He would play by himself and exclude other children. As his behavior became more known, the other children would actively avoid interacting with Kieran.

At age 9, Kieran's difficulties with reciprocal social behavior became evident in a manner that brought up the possibility of a specific disorder. Following the standard Autism Diagnostic Observation Schedule (A-DOS; score: 8, moderate) and a social responsiveness scale—both assessing criteria based on *DSM-IV-TR* and ICD-10 diagnostic algorithms—Kieran was diagnosed as having Asperger's syndrome. It is important to note here that a "moderate" A-DOS score can often represent a significantly debilitating condition, as outlined above.

After our initial introductions and a brief case history, I decided to try a role-reversal assessment game that I often find useful. I asked Kieran:

"Do you reckon your Mum can pretend to be you?"

Kieran gave a small smile. "Yeah."

Throughout our meeting I used my calm but melodic "story-tellers" voice when relating to Kieran. He was, of course, a little nervous, a little on edge, and I was aware that the impact of possible trauma could leave him either dissociated (dorsal vagal state) or hypervigilant (sympathetic nervous system activation)—we will explore these possibilities in more detail later on. Polyvagal Theory explains how my melodic voice can calm and engage Kieran—his neuroception of my signals of safety downregulating his heightened defenses and enabling his social engagement system to come online (Porges, 2011a, 2015). And a note for other male therapists like me—it is good to be careful that your calm voice does not tend too much toward a low, deep tone. Polyvagal Theory explains how low, resonant tones can easily be perceived as the tone of a predator (Porges, 2011b).

I continued: "And if I ask her when she's being you, 'What is the thing that worries you most?' Do you reckon she might get it right?"

"Yeah, I think she knows," said Kieran.

"But," I said, "I won't know if she's got it right. Will you be 'Official Kieran' and, if I ask you, will you tell me if she's got it right?"

"Yeah, no problem," replied Kieran.

I then proceeded to ask Angie (as Kieran) a series of personal questions. In order to check in with Official Kieran, I used only minimal eye movements and facial gestures as nonverbal prompts. Each time, Kieran responded without hesitation. Here Kieran showed a relaxed understanding of rapid nonverbal prompts, of a three-way role reversal of immense theory-of-mind complexity, and of microemotions as they relate to himself and others—each of these levels of understanding apparently contraindicating a diagnosis of autism spectrum disorder (ASD) including Asperger's syndrome (Baron-Cohen, 1989, 2008; Papagiannopoulou, Chitty, Hermens, Hickie, & Lagopoulos, 2014). Kieran then asked if he could show me something he was proud of. He had brought with him a piece of creative writing he had completed in class. It was a wonderful description of a roller-coaster ride and was characterized by an impressively delicate employment of emotive adjectives; again, a skill that is markedly absent even in higher-functioning autism (Brown & Klein, 2011; Baron-Cohen, 2008). It is fair to say that I was questioning Kieran's diagnosis from day one.

It seemed that Kieran had little difficulty with the *receptive* side of social interaction; he understood others with sensitivity and subtlety. This was contrary to a diagnosis of ASD. He did, however, present with Asperger's-like difficulties with the *production* of fluid prosocial behavior. When he was relaxed, these difficulties were more subtle in Kieran. They were highly debilitating when he found himself in stressful social situations. What could explain Kieran's particular profile? Could there be an alternative developmental model to explain his matrix of difficulties? How can Polyvagal Theory help us here? To find out, we need to begin at the start of Kieran's story.

By the way, the two answers—that came via Angie-pretends-to-be-Kieran—to the question "What worries you most?" were "being frightened in the busy stairwell at school," and "not being able to control my anger." Kieran desperately wanted to be in control, to not be frightened, to change.

Kieran's Early Life and Iatrogenic Trauma

When Angie was younger, she suffered retinoblastoma (RB)—cancer of the eyes. When Kieran was born, there was a high chance that he would develop the same disease; he did. After a normal delivery, Kieran was immediately diagnosed as having bilateral retinoblastoma (cancer in both eyes).[1]

Almost all medical procedures are experienced as aversive by children and, sadly, many procedures are still undertaken in ways that can have traumatic effects (Azeem et al., 2015). The dynamics of childhood medical trauma may be described by the co-occurrence of two qualities: overwhelming fear and inescapability (either physical or perceived; Kazak et al., 2006; Levine, 2010; Porges & Daniel, 2017). Understanding the significance of the co-occurrence of these two particular factors leads to a recognition of the phenomenon of pediatric medical traumatic stress (Kazak et al., 2006), a type of iatrogenic trauma. Several categories of medical experience have the potential to meet these co-occurring criteria of fear and inescapability: primarily, any frighten-

1 Here, it is important to note that after Kieran's initial treatment, his eyesight was not affected. As we move on to discuss the quality and patterns of Kieran's social interactions, please bear this in mind.

ing procedure that involves being physically restrained or intense and immobilizing toxic or physical shock, but also potentially MRI scans with limited anesthetic restraint (not including a general anesthetic). Despite many intelligent child-friendly hospital protocols, physical restraint continues to be used on a daily basis in most pediatric oncology wards. Studies by Diseth (2005) illustrate that children forced to undergo medical procedures, particularly in the context of their families holding them down, present with significantly more dissociation than children treated less invasively. As many as 30% of medically ill children go on to develop symptoms of post-traumatic stress (Forgey & Bursch, 2013).

Between 6 weeks and 20 months of age, Kieran experienced multiple potentially traumatic experiences, all of which met the criteria of co-occurring fear and inescapability. These included being physically restrained for the administration of painful cyclopentolate and phenylephrine dilating eye drops, being physically restrained for inhalant anesthesia prior to examination under anesthetic, extensive radiotherapy blocks (including a block of one month involving a daily general anesthetic), and being physically restrained for injections.

> *Angie:* The two main traumatizing experiences for Kieran throughout his treatment for RB have always been the examination eye drops and the anesthesia mask. From his very first examination under anesthetic until the last time inhalant anesthesia was given (at around 3 years old), Kieran was physically (and aggressively) restrained. There were very tight time restraints placed on the staff who worked the examination under anesthetic clinic. They had a lot of children to "process" and very little time to do it. This necessitated a "conveyor belt" approach. From his first examination under anesthetic at age 5 weeks, Kieran was wrapped like a burrito, his head laid in the nurse's lap with me holding his body, his eyes pried open and the eye drops administered. "Numbing" eye drops, used with older children to reduce pain and discomfort, were never used. I am unsure why this was the case: Time? Money? A 5-week-old baby won't remember the pain, so why bother? All of the above? There was no time available for staff to spend supporting the child (or, indeed, their parents); no time to potentially minimize the trauma caused.

Our current understanding of pediatric trauma (Kazak et al., 2006; Levine & Kline, 2006; van der Kolk, 2005), including the implications of the polyvagal perspective (Porges, 2011a, 2011b; Porges & Daniel, 2017), tells us that trauma minimization *is* possible. Engaging, relaxing, informative, and empowering play *can* be used to prepare a child for potentially traumatic procedures.

Leveraging the power of childhood attachment helps here (Azeem et al., 2015; Levin & Kline, 2006)—a parent or caregiver is best placed to engage the child's social engagement system. Helping to minimize fear, and so downregulate the sympathetic nervous system's preparation for fight-or-flight behaviors, reduces the buildup of mobilization energy. It is this trauma energy, if not minimized, that becomes "locked in" through physical or emotional restraint and can lead to chronic trauma. In an ideal world, this preemptive play would work well enough to remove the need for physical restraint completely. Unfortunately, this is rarely the case—sometimes "just because," but more often due to time and personnel constraints, or lack of staff training and understanding. In Angie and Kieran's case, a dangerous mixture of these limiting factors seems to have been present. Given the lack of alternative preventative measures in place, Angie naturally assumed that forceful restraint was the only option available. She made a courageous decision, sacrificing her own feelings to support Kieran in the best way she knew how.

> *Angie:* I was always the one who took Kieran in for the eye drops and helped restrain him while he was having the anesthesia. I had felt that it would be best for him to have one consistent person who always did the "bad" things, that way he would have a safe person (usually my mom, Kieran's grandma) whom he could trust not to hurt him when we were in that situation. There was a degree of me feeling responsible for Kieran going through this, so I needed to be the one who "managed" everything . . . I worried that he would hate me for doing these things to him.

In addition to Kieran's ongoing experiences of traumatic restraint, Angie remembers vividly a particular incidence of septic shock that illustrates the extremes of trauma Kieran went through at such a young age:

> *Angie:* When Kieran was about 9 months old, we went into clinic to have his 10th round of chemo. The nurse had some trouble getting draw back on his line, so she gave some Heparin and tried again. After some jiggling, she finally got some blood, and we were able to get ready for the chemo starting. Within half an hour of his line being accessed, Kieran started to shake and he lost all color, almost going gray. He began violently shaking, his temperature had spiked to over 40 °C, his heart rate was more than double normal, and his oxygen saturation was dropping. The on-call doctor was paged, and I was asked to lay Kieran on the bed so the nursing staff could work on him. This was a little boy who would scream hysterically whenever he saw a medical professional enter the

room, but at that moment he just lay there, curled on his side, and did not fight or resist at all. He was hooked up to all kinds of monitors, with an oxygen mask in place; there were three or four doctors and nurses around the bed. He was awake throughout, so I am sure he must have been terrified and confused. He was given a strong antibiotic, which worked to stabilize him after about three hours.

Polyvagal Theory and Immobilization

The human nervous system, similar to that of other mammals, evolved not solely for life in a safe environment, but also to survive in dangerous and life-threatening contexts. When there is a neuroception of risk, or when the social engagement system is compromised, two more primitive neural circuits regulating physiological state may be recruited to support defensive strategies (Porges, 1995, 2011a): the mobilization system (which orchestrates fight-or-flight behaviors) and the evolutionary ancient immobilization system. The recruitment of the immobilization system, and the corresponding shutdown of the social engagement system, can explain the phenomenon of pediatric medical traumatic stress. We can explore this with a particular example from Kieran's life.

Angie described how Kieran, at around 8 months old, began to display what she calls a "shutdown" response. In the very early stages, Kieran would fight and scream in response to restraint and pain—healthy normal protest behaviors. But from around 8 months old, Kieran shifted into a matrix of completely different neurophysiological patterning. This pattern was defined by Kieran's withdrawal from interaction: no eye contact, utterances, or crying; no gross or subtle prosocial movements whatsoever. This pattern soon became habitually associated with the hospital environment and became Kieran's norm.

Angie: Initially, Kieran appeared unaware of hospital visits, other than the effect my own stress would undoubtedly have had on him. He first started to show recognition around 5–6 months old; he was very scared of strangers and would openly react to a blue nurse's uniform, becoming very distressed and anxious. Kieran was 8 months old when I first witnessed his complete "shutting down." At the time he was a happy, chatty, lively little boy who was cruising around the furniture and didn't stay still for more than a few moments. We arrived at the clinic at 10:00 a.m., and the instant we walked through the doors, Kieran stopped moving, he kept his head dropped, making no eye contact or sounds at all. He stayed this way for about five hours until he went in for his examination

> under anesthetic, literally not moving or reacting to me or his grandma in any way. It was completely heartbreaking to see my son so broken.

The behavioral "shutdown" described by Angie, and the psychological and social dissociation described by Diseth (2005), can be explained by the triggering of the dorsal vagal immobilization system. The immobilization system is our body's phylogenetically ancient response to the detection of an inevitable and significant threat to physical integrity or imminent death. It is triggered by the co-occurrence of fear and inescapability—both registered subconsciously, via neuroception. The immobilization system recruits the unmyelinated vagal motor pathways to the heart to produce an immediate and massive slowing of heart rate (i.e., bradycardia) and often the cessation of breathing (i.e., apnea), and is often associated with vasovagal syncope (i.e., fainting). This massive shift in metabolic resources results in the organism appearing to be inanimate. This pattern is a primary defense strategy for many reptiles—a way to avoid detection from a predator. This reaction is metabolically conservative, rapidly withdrawing resources from the highly oxygen-dependent central nervous system. Once activated, the immobilization system may involve feigning death, behavioral shutdown, and dissociation.

In the polyvagal hierarchy of adaptive responses, the newest circuit (the circuit that supports the social engagement system) is recruited first; if that circuit fails to provide safety, the older circuits are recruited sequentially to orchestrate defense responses (mobilization, then immobilization). It is important to note that when these defense systems are recruited, the autonomic nervous system supports these survival-related behaviors at the expense of health, growth, and restoration. Once either of the defense systems is reflexively employed, the social engagement system is temporarily disabled, which shuts down all coordinated regulation of prosocial behavior. As Kieran was being bombarded with cues of danger, he could no longer perceive the environment as safe and did not have the ability to produce or accurately detect features of social communication.

Childhood PTSD, Development and Polyvagal Theory

It is useful here to bring in the diagnostic concept of childhood post-traumatic stress disorder. Post-traumatic stress disorder (PTSD) is an increasingly recognized childhood response to the experience of cancer and cancer treatment (Taïeb, Moro, Baubet, Revah-Lévy, & Flament, 2003; Phipps, Long, Hudson, & Rai, 2005). Recent research by Graf, Bergstraesser, & Landolt (2013) on the prevalence of childhood PTSD (onset in preschool) in cancer survivors showed that 18.8% of subjects met the age-appropriate criteria for full PTSD proposed by Scheeringa and Zeanah (2005) and 41.7% met the criteria for partial PTSD.

Drell, Siegel, and Gaensbauer (1993) give us a clinical outline of the developmental progression of the behavioral signatures of early-onset PTSD (see Table 14.1).

From Angie's extremely detailed account of Kieran's development in those first 20 months (including her firsthand, original notes written at the time), it is evident that Kieran's early developmental pattern fits Drell et al.'s outline precisely.

PTSD is a chronic condition. Severe traumatic shock is capable of skewing neurophysiological self-regulatory trends in the direction of chronic defensive patterning (Porges, 2011b; Levine, 2010). Using a polyvagal explanatory model in Kieran's case, the suggestion is that early trauma resulted in Kieran's immobilization system becoming a strong default for his self-regulation and social interactions. The suggestion is that Kieran had developed childhood PTSD. Kieran's organized impulses to engage with other people were skewed

	0–6— months	6–12— months	12–18— months	18–24— months	24–36— months
• Hypervigilance, exaggerated startle response, irritability, physiologic deregulation and/or withdrawal	*	*	*	*	*
• Increased anxiety in strange situations, angry reactions, sleep disorders, active avoidance of specific situations		*	*	*	*
• Clinginess to caretaker, over/under use of words related to the trauma			*	*	*
• Nightmares, verbal preoccupations with symbols of trauma				*	*
• PTSD symptoms seen in older children, as defined in the DSM-IVr					*

TABLE 14.1

Symptoms of PTSD in children 0–36 months—a developmental progression. Summarized from Drell et al. (1993).

in the direction of impairment from before he could talk. Here we have a trauma-based interpretation of the initial developmental features of social impairment in an autism-like presentation.

The unfolding over time of this initial matrix of social impairments can be seen as an ever-widening web of mutually compounded experiences. In this complex narrative, the following all play an interdependent part: the impact of Kieran's initial social impairment, the effect of such on the attachment relationship, the early disturbance to the attachment relationship due to Angie's necessary "restrainer" role and her related and understandable guilt, the ongoing experience of retraumatization shared by Kieran and Angie in Kieran's twice-annual eye examinations (from 2.5 years to 11 years old), and the negative feedback cycle of Kieran's play. The latter we can expand on with Porges's (2015) notion of play as a neural exercise. Above we saw how, in healthy development, play acts as a neural exercise in which both participants reinforce each other's calm, creative, prosocial responses in the face of potentially stressful experience. Over time, this becomes a cycle of positive feedback. Sadly, the opposite is also possible. When initial social impairment (through immobilization) skews play in a negative direction, this can quickly result in a negative feedback loop. Both partners become less responsive, less sensitive, and less creative, not only in their play but also in their wider social lives. This negative, looping neural exercise seems to have had an impact on Kieran in severely disabling ways.

At 3 years old. Kieran went to nursery school for the first time. It was here that it became clear that Kieran's shutdown pattern had transcended the immediate trauma context and was affecting his life in a chronic way. At school, Kieran had difficulty socializing, often lashing out physically at other children or withdrawing to a corner.

> *Kieran:* The first day of nursery school was difficult because I hadn't been exposed to people properly, I didn't know how to act in a social situation; and whenever someone came close, I always felt like they were coming to cause me some harm.
>
> *Angie:* When Kieran started school he initially seemed to be fine, not suffering from separation anxiety or upset in any way. But I soon started to feel that something wasn't quite right. He was a chatty, bright boy but would walk into school every day with his head down. I soon started to get negative feedback from the staff that Kieran was hitting and biting the other children. This was completely at odds with the extremely placid and gentle boy I saw at home. I absolutely could not understand

> what was happening, and I had no idea what to do about it. This continued through his first year of school—it was a sad and horrible time for Kieran. His second year brought a new teacher who was able to see things from a different viewpoint. She explained that Kieran was not coping with the chaos, noise, and unpredictability of the school setting. She explained that he was very regimental in his use of the nursery school space (beginning every day in the same place and then following a pattern: start at the art table, then books, then water play), and that he did not cope with the other children's more random play. He struggled particularly during group times.

Later, in therapy, Kieran described his earliest memory of nursery school in terms of "becoming lonely to protect myself"; he was impelled to remove himself from the social environment (which was overwhelming and too loud), but in doing so he felt lonely. This contradiction, loneliness through protection, remained the significant theme of Kieran's life until he was 12 years old.

Asperger's Syndrome, PTSD, or Comorbidity: Assessing the Core Deficit

There is an extremely high level of comorbidity between PTSD and other disorders. In adult and child populations, PTSD occurs with at least one other disorder 80–90% of the time (van der Kolk, 2005). However, Scheeringa (2011) explains, "despite the overlap of some PTSD symptoms with other disorders, there are pathognomonic symptoms of PTSD that make it distinct . . . if one conducts a careful interview, it should not be difficult to diagnose PTSD even in the presence of other disorders" (p. 185). The challenge for diagnosis is to assess the *core* traumatic response (Scheeringa, 2011) and, if PTSD is core, minimize the risk of clinicians focusing on comorbid elements and potentially "applying treatment approaches that are not helpful" (van der Kolk, 2005, p. 406).

Prior to therapeutic input at age 11, semistructured PTSD interviews and observational records (Scheeringa & Zeanah, 2005) were undertaken with Kieran and Angie to ascertain a detailed developmental history for Kieran; his current behavioral, educational, and emotional functioning; and the occurrence and description of any potential traumatic events (essential to a diagnosis of PTSD). Angie gave access to her firsthand notes written at the time of Kieran's original traumatic episodes. Eight nondirective play assessment sessions were undertaken, documented, and analyzed to support this information. The above ascertained that Kieran's developmental and presenting profiles fulfilled current diagnostic criteria for *full* PTSD within the PTSD preschool subtype (onset in infancy) as defined now[2] by the *DSM-V* (see Table 14.2).

PTSD had explanatory power for *all* of Kieran's symptoms (including those that overlapped with a diagnosis of Asperger's syndrome based on *DSM-IV-TR* and ICD-10 diagnostic algorithms). Kieran had experienced multiple PTSD-specific traumatic events (direct experiences of a life-threatening condition), and Asperger's syndrome exclusively *could not* explain many of Kieran's symptoms (including Criteria B: 1, 2, 3, 4, 5; Criteria C: 1, 2; and Criteria D: 1, 5—see Table 14.2). As such, a therapeutic formulation was made on the tentative basis that PTSD was the etiological core of Kieran's presenting symptoms.

Kieran in Therapy: Insights from Polyvagal Theory

Kieran and I worked together in therapy for 1.5 years. Our work was based on nondirective play therapy (Landreth, 2012) and on Dyadic Developmental Psychotherapy (Hughes, 2004, 2011). We spent time developing our relationship—chatting, having fun. Kieran enjoyed his sessions and felt at ease; he trusted me and felt safe. The basic principles of nondirective play therapy and Dyadic Developmental Psychotherapy—interacting playfully, sensitive attunement to the child's biobehavioral state and communication, clear appropriate empathy, and acceptance—enabled me to give Kieran cues of safety and connection. These cues from my social engagement system, experienced through neuroception, dampened Kieran's potential to dissociate and awakened his social engagement system to support his fluid prosocial behavior. From here, the place of safety and trust, we could move on to playful neural exercise of the vagal brake (Porges, 2015) in which we confidently approached challenging moments of attachment-disruption-repair (Hughes, 2011). We could also work sensitively with the themes of fear and inescapability within Kieran's play and conversation. We could work toward rewriting Kieran's trauma narratives in a new light—a light cast by the safety of acceptance in play.

> *Kieran:* The therapy experience as a whole seemed like sitting down and talking to a family member or friend to try and give them an understanding of what things were like for me. It was the one time that I would feel excited about an appointment, and I always seemed to enjoy

---

2 The *DSM-V* PTSD preschool subtype was developed directly from Schreenga and Zeanah (2005), which was the recognized authority at the time of Kieran's diagnosis.

• **Criterion A: 1.** Directly experiencing the traumatic events(s).
• **Criterion B: 1.** Recurrent, involuntary, and intrusive distressing memories of the traumatic event(s). **2.** Recurrent distressing dreams in which the content and/or affect of the dream are related to the traumatic event(s). **3.** Dissociative reactions...in which the child feels or acts as if the traumatic event(s) were recurring. Such...re-enactment may occur in play. **4.** Intense or prolonged distress at exposure to internal or external cues that symbolize or resemble an aspect of the traumatic event(s). **5.** Marked physiological reactions to reminders of the traumatic event(s).
• **Criterion C: 1.** Avoidance of or efforts to avoid activities, places, or physical reminders, that arouse recollections of the traumatic events(s). **2.** Avoidance of or efforts to avoid people, conversations, or interpersonal situations that arouse recollections of the traumatic event(s). **3.** Substantially increased frequency of negative emotional states (e.g. fear, guilt, sadness, shame, confusion). **4.** Markedly diminished interest or participation in significant activies, including constriction of play. **5.** Socially withdrawn behavior. **6.** Persistent reduction in expression of positive emotions.
• **Criterion D: 1.** Irritable behavior and outburst (with little or no provocation) typically expressed as verbal or physical aggression toward people or objects (including extreme temper tantrums). **2.** Hypervigilance. **3.** Exaggerated startle response. **4.** Sleep disturbance.
• **Criterion E:** The duration of the disturbance is more than 1 month.
• **Criterion F:** The disturbance causes clinically significant distress or impairment in relationships with parents, siblings, peers, or other caregivers or with school behavior.
• **Criterion G:** The disturbance is not attributable to the physiological effects of a substance (e.g. medication or alcohol) or another medical condition.

TABLE 14.2

A list of all the *DSM-V* PTSD preschool subtype diagnostic algorithms that accurately corresponded to Kieran's developmental and presenting symptoms prior to therapeutic input at age 11. Please note that Table 14.2 is not simply a list of all of the diagnostic childhood PTSD criteria—it is *only* those that corresponded with Kieran's profile. The list represents *nearly all* of the diagnostic criteria—indeed, there are *far more* positive correlations than are technically required for a diagnosis of full childhood PTSD.

them and come out feeling glad to have gotten another little thing off of my chest.

Angie: I think from the very first meeting I realized that this would be a different experience. There was an instant understanding about Kieran's background and the significance of that. The focus was on the "why" rather than the "what," so instead of it being just about Kieran's self-harming, or other issues, there was a focus on his history and how much he had been through. This immediately put me at ease, as I always felt that the reason for Kieran struggling with certain aspects of life was directly linked to his early childhood. I just never knew how to help, and there were absolutely no structures in place to support Kieran with this. Stuart's report after the initial assessment period was a great thing to read. It felt as though someone had finally listened and paid attention to what Kieran was trying to say. I was relieved and hopeful.

In conversation, through sand-tray configurations, through reenactment drama, through games supporting energetic emotional release and grounding, through creating timelines, memory books, and using memory aids from Kieran's past, Kieran and I visited and revisited his early difficult experiences many times. All of this work was "held" by our safe relationship within the neural exercise of play and flourished throughout sensitive experiences of attachment-disruption-repair. Kieran was courageous, emotionally intelligent, and enthusiastic in his explorations. Very quickly he began to progress.

After 10 months, I asked Kieran if he would like to have some sessions where Kieran, Angie, and I would all work together. Kieran was aware of, and communicative about, certain feelings of pain and ambiguity toward his mother—particularly in relation to her role in some of his early difficult experiences. I explained to Kieran that we could explore some of these feelings together and that he would have a chance to understand his mother's motives in more depth. Kieran was keen to go ahead and decided on a schedule where we would alternate nondirective play therapy sessions (Kieran and me) with Dyadic Developmental Psychotherapy sessions involving the three of us. Angie was understandably a little nervous to move into these sessions, but also very courageous. She was willing to do anything that would help her son progress. I made sure that before and after each session, Angie and I would have time to talk over her feelings and concerns. The work that Kieran and Angie did together was moving and powerful.

The aim of the Dyadic Developmental Psychotherapy model (Hughes, 2004, 2011) is to encourage a safe, playful environment and to support healthy, synchronous interaction in the caregiver–child relationship. Above we described how, from the polyvagal perspective, playful interaction is seen as a reciprocal exercise of the vagal brake—an exercise to downregulate defense systems, promote a robust autonomic nervous system, and support health and sociability. Here, some of the polyvagal principles we discussed above are leveraged in Dyadic Developmental Psychotherapy, as the therapist supports the caregiver to relate well with her child. To do this, the therapist will model cues of safety within her own social behavior. She will also create a "containing" environment in which new levels of emotional vulnerability and reciprocity can be explored. The safety inherent in the therapist's behavior is a powerful example of a proactive attempt to invigorate the social engagement system of both the caregiver and the child. This dual activation promotes an environment in which the caregiver connects to her motherly instincts (naturally offering cues of safety and connection) and the child becomes more open to attachment behavior. Then, into this safe, connected dynamic, challenging memories can be brought up and held. New pathways and relationship dynamics can be fostered through direct experiences of a retelling, a reexperiencing of the past. A new emotional narrative can be written and shared with positivity and safety by child and mother. This new narrative can define a new level of attachment.

> *Angie:* Before we had the sessions together I was apprehensive, worried about the effect it would have emotionally on both Kieran and me. Stuart had explained the theory and the hopes for the sessions, and I was unsure that Kieran would be able to achieve this. The sessions themselves were in some parts difficult. I was surprised at how well Kieran was able to express his emotions and how he was able to go back to that period in his life emotionally. I was obviously very saddened by some of the things he was saying but really felt that this was a positive opportunity to begin to heal—both of us—from that time in our lives. The hardest thing for me during the sessions (and afterward too) was to not fall into my usual pattern of distancing myself from the difficult emotions and putting up a barrier—this was very much a conscious effort on my part. I think they did help, especially for Kieran, giving him a safe space to express things he would never have been able to in any other situation.
>
> *Kieran:* I'd say these sessions were important for me because I got an understanding of how tough things were for my mom; I always pictured her being strong and smiling through, but the truth, if anything, was the exact opposite. I think that now I find it easier to talk to my mom.

After 1.5 years in therapy, with associated support at home, Kieran is now calm and happy most of the time. Kieran does not respond anxiously to social environments, can easily self-regulate in situations that previously would have triggered overwhelming anger and violence, does not self-harm, and is sleeping better. From a polyvagal perspective, Kieran has experienced enough safety, and engaged in enough iterations of playful exercise of his vagal brake, to change his life. His experiences have swayed his autonomic system toward a habitual favoring of the social engagement system—instead of the trauma habit that previously favored his immobilization system. As described above, this social engagement patterning is organism-wide and has moved Kieran into widespread patterns of health and well-being. It seems that he has overcome his childhood medical trauma.

> *Kieran:* The therapy has been a positive experience because it has made me more comfortable with talking about myself and my past, and explaining what effect everything that happened has had on me. I have also found it easier to make friends and find people who are understanding and extremely supportive. Above all, though, it has made me more comfortable in areas of loud noise and areas that are extremely crowded, even though I still find it slightly difficult sometimes, it is nowhere near as bad as it used to be for me. I am very glad that it has helped me out with those things, because for a very long time, they were major issues that I was starting to think I would simply just need to live with.
>
> *Angie:* At the end of the 18-month therapy sessions with Stuart, Kieran was a completely different child. A large number of the things that were previously preventing him from having a good quality of life were no longer affecting him, he was emotionally dramatically more stable, and his self-confidence was improved hugely. He was able to better handle day-to-day situations, such as crowds and noise, which were previously extremely distressing. He was calmer and more independent. We still have anxieties surrounding medical appointments, specifically eye drops, which can cause us to take a few steps back as the time approaches and I see the "old" behaviors reappear (verbal outbursts, mostly, and anger at having to go to the appointments). Kieran is also faced with a growing knowledge that being a carrier of the mutated RB1 gene and having received radiation dramatically increases his chances of developing another cancer. He has a close friend (his age) who is currently battling neuroblastoma as a result of RB and radiation, so he is seeing this firsthand. He is coping well with this, and I think his time

with Stuart has given him a solid foundation to manage the emotions around this.

Perhaps most marked of all are the changes in Kieran's social life. Kieran now presents with fluid prosocial behaviors; his prosody, affect, and turn taking in conversation, and his eye contact and gaze tracking are all relaxed and rhythmically in sync with others. As Polyvagal Theory predicts, as Kieran's autonomic responses have shifted away from trauma and toward health, so his relational abilities have changed from Asperger's-like to fluid sociability. Both Kieran and his mother describe a new ability in Kieran to make friends and to relate with an emotional depth that wasn't available before. Kieran still has a relatively restricted range of interests and hobbies—the only borderline A-DOS criterion still significant to his presentation—but he now shares these interests with social ease and a sense of humor. A series of standard discharge clinical psychology assessment interviews, undertaken by a case-fresh pediatric psychiatrist and clinical psychologist with Kieran and Angie, both together and separately, indicated that no further input or assessment was required. At age 13, Kieran was discharged on the basis that his presentation clearly no longer fit the diagnostic criteria for any condition—PTSD or Asperger's.

In Conclusion

This is, of course, a single case report, and we make no assertion as to the generalizable efficacy of the particular combination of therapies used here in the treatment of childhood PTSD. The only comparative study of a wide range of treatment practices for childhood PTSD (including nondirective play therapy) concludes that there is little clinical consensus regarding the effectiveness of the many modalities used (Cohen, Mannarino, & Rogal, 2001).

Kieran's subsequent and significant improvement in therapy, specifically in the key area of reciprocal social interaction, gave added weight to the diagnostic relevance of PTSD as the core deficit. It is rare that a child with a diagnosis of autism spectrum disorder can improve significantly in their fundamental ability and impulse to relate (Baron-Cohen, 2008). People with Asperger's can adapt—many can adapt brilliantly—but the idea of fundamental change in the face of higher-functioning autism is seen as a neurophysiological impossibility (Baron-Cohen, 2008). As I first began to question Kieran's early ASD diagnosis, it was this "incurability factor" that bothered me most. Remember that Kieran was desperate to change. But if Kieran had believed he was incurable, if he believed it was impossible for him to change, then he probably would not have been able to. In the absence of a DSM diagnostic criterion for a developmental trauma disorder or equivalent, I looked elsewhere for working models. The concept of pediatric medical traumatic stress (Kazak et al., 2006) was useful. But it was the accompanying polyvagal explanatory model, outlining the developmental implications of immobilization and the possibility of therapy through playful exercise of the vagal brake, that gave me the confidence to go ahead with therapy for Kieran.

References

Azeem, M. W., Reddy, B., Wudarsky, M., Carabetta, L., Gregory, F., & Sarofin, M. (2015). Restraint reduction at a pediatric psychiatric hospital: A ten-year journey. *Journal of Child and Adolescent Psychiatric Nursing, 28*(4), 180–184.

Baron-Cohen, S. (1989). The autistic child's theory of mind: a case of specific developmental delay. *Journal of Child Psychology and Psychiatry, 30*(2), 285–297.

Baron-Cohen, S. (2008). *Autism and Asperger syndrome (the facts)*. Oxford, England: Oxford University Press.

Brown, H. M., & Klein, P. D. (2011). Writing, Asperger syndrome and theory of mind. *Journal of Autism and Developmental Disorders, 41*(11), 1464–1474.

Cohen, J. A., Mannarino, A. P., & Rogal, S. (2001). Treatment practices for childhood posttraumatic stress disorder. *Child Abuse and Neglect, 25*(1), 123–135.

Daniel, S. (2018). Play Therapy and Polyvagal Theory: Towards Self-Regulation for Children with Paediatric Medical Trauma. In: P. Ayling, H. Armstrong, & L. Gordon Clark (Eds.). *Becoming and Being a Play Therapist*. Routledge, UK.

Diseth, T. H. (2005). Dissociation in children and adolescents as reaction to trauma: An overview of conceptual issues and neurobiological factors. *Nordic Journal of Psychiatry, 59*, 79–91.

Drell, M. J., Siegel, C., & Gaensbauer, T. J. (1993). Posttraumatic stress disorder. In C. H. Zeanah (Ed.), *Handbook of infant mental health* (pp. 291–304). New York, NY: Guilford Press.

Graf, A., Bergstraesser, E., & Landolt, M. A. (2013). Posttraumatic stress in infants and preschoolers with cancer. *Psycho-Oncology, 22*(7), 1543–1548.

Hughes, D. (2000). *Facilitating developmental attachment: The road to emotional recovery and behavioural change in foster and adopted children*. New York, NY: Jason Aronson.

Hughes, D. (2004). An attachment-based treatment of maltreated children and young people. *Attachment and Human Development, 3*(6), 263–278.

Hughes, D. (2011). *Attachment-focused family therapy workbook*. New York, NY: Norton.

Kazak, A. E., Kassam-Adams, N., Schneider, S., Zelikovsky, N., Alderfer, M. A., & Rourke, M. (2006). An integrative model of pediatric medical traumatic stress. *Journal of Pediatric Psychology, 31*(4), 343–355.

Landreth, G. L. (2012). *Play therapy: The art of the relationship*. New York, NY: Routledge.

Levine, P. (2010). *In an unspoken voice: How the body releases trauma and restores goodness*. Berkeley, CA: North Atlantic Books.

Levine, P., & Kline, M. (2006). *Trauma through a child's eyes: Awakening the ordinary miracle of healing*. Berkeley, CA: North Atlantic Books.

Papagiannopoulou, E. A., Chitty, K. M., Hermens, D. F., Hickie, I. B., & Lagopoulos, J. (2014). A systematic review and meta-analysis of eye-tracking studies in children with autism disorders. *Social Neuroscience, 9*(6), 610–632. doi:10.1080/17470919.2014.934966

Phipps, S., Long, A., Hudson, M., & Rai, S. N. (2005). Symptoms of post-traumatic stress in children with cancer and their parents: Effects of informant and time from diagnosis. *Pediatric Blood and Cancer, 45*, 952–959.

Porges, S. W. (1995). Orienting in a defensive world: Mammalian modifications of our evolutionary heritage. A Polyvagal Theory. *Psychophysiology, 32*, 301–318.

Porges, S. W. (2001). The Polyvagal Theory: Phylogenetic substrates of a social nervous system. *International Journal of Psychophysiology, 42*, 123–146.

Porges, S. W. (2003). Social engagement and attachment. *Annals of the New York Academy of Sciences, 1008*(1), 31–47.

Porges, S. W. (2007). The polyvagal perspective. *Biological Psychology, 74*, 116–143.

Porges, S. W. (2009). The Polyvagal Theory: New insights into adaptive reactions of the autonomic nervous system. *Cleveland Clinic Journal of Medicine, 76*, 86–90.

Porges, S. W. (2011a). *The Polyvagal Theory: Neurophysiological foundations of emotions, attachment, communication, and self-regulation*. New York, NY: Norton.

Porges, S. W. (2011b). The Polyvagal Theory for treating trauma [Teleseminar transcript]. NICABM, Mansfield Center, CT.

Porges, S. W. (2015). Play as a neural exercise: Insights from the Polyvagal Theory. In D. Pearce-McCall (Ed.), *The power of play for mind brain health*. Retrieved from http://mindgains.org/

Porges, S. W. (2018). Why Polyvagal Theory was welcomed by therapists. In S. W. Porges and D. Dana (Eds.), *Clinical applications of the polyvagal theory: The emergence of polyvagal-informed therapies*. (pp. xvii–xxiii). New York, NY: Norton.

Porges, S. W., & Daniel, S. (2017). Play and the dynamics of treating pediatric medical trauma: Insights from Polyvagal Theory. In S. Daniel & C. Trevarthen (Eds.), *Rhythms of relating in children's therapies: Connecting creatively with vulnerable children*. London, England: Jessica Kingsley.

Porges, S. W., Doussard-Roosevelt, J. A., Portales, A. L., & Greenspan, S. I. (1996). Infant regulation of the vagal "brake" predicts child behavior problems: A psychobiological model of social behavior. *Developmental Psychobiology, 29*(8), 697–712.

Scheeringa, M. S. (2011). PTSD in children younger than the age of 13: Toward developmentally sensitive assessment and management. *Journal of Child and Adolescent Trauma, 4*(3), 181–197.

Scheeringa, M. S., & Zeanah, C. H. (2005). PTSD semi-structured interview and observational record for infants and young children. Department of Psychiatry and Neurology, Tulane University Health Sciences Center, New Orleans, LA.

Schore, A. N. (1994). *Affect regulation and the origin of the self*. Hillsdale, NJ: Lawrence Erlbaum.

Taïeb, O., Moro, M. R., Baubet, T., Revah-Lévy, A., & Flament, M. F. (2003). Posttraumatic stress symptoms after childhood cancer. *European Child & Adolescent Psychiatry, 12*, 255–264.

Van der Kolk, B. (2005). Developmental trauma disorder. *Psychiatric Annals, 35*, 401–408.

Winnicott, D. W. (1971). *Playing and reality*. London, England: Tavistock.

15

Energy Psychology, Polyvagal Theory, and the Treatment of Trauma

Robert Schwarz

Abstract: Energy Psychology (EP) is a family of brief, focused approaches to releasing stuck energy and unprocessed information in the mind-body system that is the result of unresolved trauma. This chapter suggests that the clinically rapid results, supported by many outcome studies, may be due to the restoration of ventral vagal regulation of the flow of information and energy in the mind-body system. Polyvagal Theory helps explain phenomenological experience of clients during EP treatment. Polyvagal Theory also explains the data that EP improves heart rate variability. Finally, EP treatment excels at creating interpersonally mediated vagal conditions that facilitate healing.

I'VE BEEN USING and teaching energy psychology approaches (aka "acupoint tapping," a way of stimulating acupuncture points without the use of needles) as a trauma treatment for years (Schwarz, 2002). For many of us involved in treating trauma, the focus of our interventions had already been shifting away from conscious thoughts and cognitions when Polyvagal Theory appeared (Porges, 2001, 2011). It provided a final piece to a puzzle, laying out a theory and biological basis for what was clinically obvious: The sense of danger that overwhelms people with PTSD wells up from below the neocortex. It is not verbal. Cognitions do not create the perception of danger. The body-based perception of danger create cognitions.

Polyvagal Theory also provided a solid theoretical and biological framework for the rapid and unusual results of acupoint tapping. It helps to explain the rapid downregulation of overwhelming affect both from the intrapersonal perspective and from the interpersonal perspective. When we integrate Polyvagal Theory with interpersonal neurobiology (Siegel, 2015), a theoretical foundation for energy psychology (EP) emerges. Instead of being framed as a strange alternative treatment, EP can now be seen as an exposure-based, body-oriented psychotherapy that restores ventral vagal regulation of the flow of information and energy in the mind-body system. In the remainder of this chapter, I will delineate this process.

EP is a family of brief, focused approaches to releasing stuck energy and unprocessed information in the mind-body system that usually is the result of unresolved small *t* or big *T* trauma. (Big *T* trauma refers to traumatic events that everyone considers a trauma—for instance, being raped or war. Small *t* trauma refers to events that overwhelm the coping strategies of a person even though the event is not necessarily huge, such as being shamed by a parent.)

The website of my organization, the Association for Comprehensive Energy Psychology, describes EP this way.

> Within an EP framework, emotional and physical issues are seen, and treated, as bio-energetic patterns within a mind-body-energy system. The mind and body are thought to be interwoven and interactive within this mind-body-energy system, which involves complex communication involving neurobiological processes, innate electrophysiology, psychoneuroimmunology (PNI), consciousness, and cognitive-behavioral-emotional patterns.

The two most well-known EP approaches are emotional freedom techniques (EFT) and thought field therapy (TFT). A basic procedure, shared by both approaches, involves tapping on a prescribed set of acupuncture points. I will be focusing on EFT and TFT in this chapter, bringing a polyvagal perspective to the well-documented (Clond, 2016; Feinstein, 2012; Nelms, 2017) ways they bring about strong clinical outcomes.

Relative to most other forms of treatment, these "tapping" approaches are quite similar. At the most basic level, they involve having the client focus on a "target" thought, memory, sensation, or feeling that is associated with distress. At the same time, the client taps on selected acupoints. Clients report changes in their unfolding experience, including their sense of distress. The process is repeated until the distress levels are eliminated or vastly reduced. It is very important to note that in TFT and in many forms of EFT, there is little to no attempt to actively and consciously change the cognitions and meaning-making activity of the clients with regard to what happened in the memory. There is no attempt to help the clients to see that they are now safe or to provide an alternative explanation or interpretation for what happened. However, the meaning making of the clients often spontaneously changes.

There is an exception to this comment. In EFT the client is asked at the beginning of each round of treatment to tap on a meridian point and use the "set up" phrase that includes the statement, "Even though __________ [the client inserts the aversive aspect of the memory being targeted], I deeply and completely accept myself." This type of statement can be regarded as facilitating self-compassion. It is important to note that there is no attempt to change any other attribution. So, for instance, if a soldier froze during battle, there is no attempt to explain the freeze response or how normal it can be.

To the casual observer, not much else appears to be happening except focusing on a traumatic event and tapping. The entire procedure is decidedly strange, and one could easily think that these approaches should not be effective. A more sophisticated observer might notice that these tapping approaches follow a very similar pattern to EMDR (Shapiro, 2001), but instead of using bilateral stimulation, the client taps on acupressure points (Schwarz, 2012).

The fact of the matter is that the research shows these approaches are remarkably fast and effective, and actually meet the criteria of evidence-based approaches, especially for PTSD and trauma (Feinstein, 2010, 2012; Nelms, 2017). While that is not the focus of this chapter, let me summarize the published research findings of 43 randomized controlled trials and 39 outcome studies:

1. Of these 82 studies, 98% have found statistically significant positive outcomes.
2. Three meta-analyses demonstrated large effect sizes (Clond, 2016; Nelms & Castel, 2016; Nelms, 2016. One meta-analysis showed moderate effect size (Gilomen & Lee, 2015).
3. Two randomized control trials showed positive effects on genetic or biologic markers (Church, Yount, & Brooks, 2012; Church, Yount, Rachlin, Fox, & Nelms, 2016). Details can be found at http://energypsych.org/research

Acupoint tapping to treat psychological issues, a procedure shared by the majority of energy psychology approaches, was introduced in the mid-1980s.

The challenge has been explaining the mechanisms that underlie the effectiveness of this approach. Clients would come for treatment with horrible traumatic events, and in as little as 30–50 minutes, the traumatic event would cease to be a problem for the person. Clinicians and researchers wanted to know how this could possibly happen.

The early interpretation was to frame things in an energetic perspective. Combining ideas from physics and Chinese medicine, thoughts were to be considered a coherent field of energy and information, termed a *thought field* by the originator of TFT, Roger Callahan (1985). So if I said, "Think about the event where you got stabbed," the patient would tune into that thought field. The concept was that psychological symptoms, such as the intense negative affect that disrupts functioning, are caused by a disruption or "perturbation" of the thought field. Tapping on acupoints was believed to somehow resolve this disruption. The explanation given for the rapid effectiveness of the technique was that the treatment was engaging the energy system of the body. This is why the term *energy psychology* was coined.

In actuality, there was much more to this energetic point of view. For instance, one explanation for the speed of symptom reduction was that the energy system of the body (i.e., the system of acupuncture points known as *meridians*) was a faster system than the electrochemical system in neuronal transmission. There is some evidence for this. One study using functional magnetic resource imaging data found that the meridian system was as much as 10 times faster than the nervous system (Cho et al., 1998). More recently, there is evidence for the actual structures of the meridian system called the primo vascular system, and that this system transports bio-photons (Stefanov et al., 2013). While energy psychology approaches were highly effective treatments, there was a need for explanatory mechanisms for how they could so rapidly and completely excise the trauma response from memories of horrible events.

Over the last 15 years, a number of neurological mechanisms for the effectiveness of EP have been proposed. Feinstein (2012) has pointed to evidence that acupoint stimulation downregulates the amygdala (e.g., Dhond, Kettner, & Napadow, 2007; Fang et al., 2009; Hui et al., 2000), thereby reducing the alarm reaction to memories of traumatic events. Several studies have shown that tapping has normalized brain wave patterns as measured by EEG (Diepold & Goldstein, 2009; Lambrou, Pratt, & Chevalier, 2003). Tapping protocols also appear to resolve traumatic memories by activating therapeutic memory reconsolidation (Feinstein, 2015; Schwarz, 2014).

Each of these explanations may in part account for EP's effectiveness. Missing, however, has been that energy psychology protocols may be mediated by the vagal system and superbly effective at creating conditions that allow for natural healing to occur.

Initial Evidence That EP May Be Mediated by the Vagal System

The major job of the vagal system in mammals and humans is to ask the following question: "Am I safe?" If the vagal system says, "I'm not safe," the sympathetic fight-or-flight or freeze system is engaged. If asked to describe fight-or-flight using a car metaphor, most people they think of "putting your foot on the gas." But that's not actually what happens. The correct car metaphor equivalent is, rather, "foot off the brake."

The ventral vagal system keeps a brake on the heart, called the *vagal braking system* because the heart left to its own devices would race. So the ventral vagal system brings the message, "You're safe. You don't need to go superfast." If you're healthy and you're feeling safe, the brake is on, and the heart beats somewhere around 72 beats per minute, in a normal, arrhythmic manner. If the vagal system perceives danger, the foot comes off the brake, the heart starts to race, you go into fight-or-flight or freeze, until you believe you're not in danger anymore. Then the foot comes back on the brake, and a calming process ensues.

One of the most important applications of Polyvagal Theory to trauma treatment is the emphasis on treating the body-based, nonverbal, noncognitive, bottom-up signals of danger in response to, or in conjunction with, the activation of a memory of a past traumatic event. Most treatment modalities will ask the client to give a subjective units of distress (SUD) rating from 0–10, measuring how distressed they are about the memory. Ideally, the goal is to get to 0. But what does 0 really mean.

The complete resolution of a traumatic event can best be defined in the following manner: In the presence of a memory of a previously traumatic event, the body reacts as if the client is safe and secure and the mind remains calm.

The obvious question is, Does the mind drive the body, or does the body drive the mind? The answer is both. However, Polyvagal Theory suggests that the body-to-mind side of the road (i.e., sensory pathways from the body to the brain) has four lanes of traffic, compared to only one lane on the mind-to-body side (i.e., motor pathways from the brain to the body). It is a lot easier to have a quiet and calm mind when the body says, "You are safe and secure." This is exactly what EP appears to do—help restore the body to a sense of safety.

In treating a traumatic event, if before treatment your distress was at 8 when thinking about the event, and then after a few rounds of a procedure you are at 0, what is the internal experience that would allow you to say, "I am at 0"? It would be the cessation of the body-based information welling up that communicates to you that you are in danger—in danger of being hurt, or in danger of loss (of something to which you are emotionally attached). Instead, the body would be communicating the neuroception of safety and connectedness, at least in part through ventral vagal activation. Yes, there would also be thoughts and verbal labels for feelings. But, if you pay close attention, these are epiphenomena, all driven by body-based, nonverbal data. Through a polyvagal perspective, the story arises from the autonomic state first, and then the top-down cognitions and narrative helps to solidify the experiential state.

Vagal Mediation of EP Fits the Phenomenology of Clients Receiving EP

After a few rounds of tapping, the client is asked to think of the original target memory that was so upsetting. The client frequently develops a quizzical facial expression and will say something like, "This is strange. I can think of the event, but it doesn't bother me anymore. It's just kind of gone." Further interviewing usually reveals that the client actually remembers the event, but no longer experiences body-based feelings of danger. In other words, there is a cessation of subcortical messages of danger, and instead there is an autonomic message of safety. Sympathetic or dorsal vagal reactivity has been replaced by ventral vagal regulation. What is interesting is that clients are deeply surprised by this turn of events. They have come to expect these "nonrational" responses of their bodies. Through a polyvagal lens, these are seen as adaptive survival responses driven by autonomic neuroception of danger or life-threat. Conscious effort and conscious attempts to change their thinking could not be successful until the autonomic state changed to support the new experience.

Clients also frequently report self-generated cognitive shifts about the meaning of the traumatic events. One could suggest that it is the change in meaning that is creating the new sense of safety. While conceivable, it is more likely the other way around. Because the mind is no longer hijacked by intense affect dysregulation, the information can be processed in a new way. Unlike cognitive behavioral therapy (CBT), EP approaches do not attempt to actively change cognitions of clients. The narrative shifts as the autonomic state shifts and as the neuroception becomes one of safety. Once clients report these changes, it is good clinical practice to stabilize these new beliefs and to connect them with other aspects of a client's social system and self-narrative (i.e., identity). In other words, we want to place energy psychology treatment within the triphasic model of trauma treatment (Schwarz, 2002). Tapping approaches themselves can be used as part of Phase 1 or stabilization. However, they are generally used as a nonabreactive approach to treating memories of trauma (Phase 2). Phase 3 focuses on helping clients reconnect with social systems. For years, I have suggested that it also includes helping clients reconnect to a more resourceful identity.

Our consciousness seems to us to be a unitary, seamless event. However it is actually a system made up of many component parts, continually shifting and changing. This includes mental, physical, and relational aspects. To paraphrase Dan Siegel (2012), the mind regulates the flow of all of these component parts. The problem with traumatic events is that they create memories that disrupt and distort the healthy flow of information and energy within our bodies and minds and between us and our social networks. At the heart of this disruption is the loss of ventral vagal control (aka *affect dysregulation*, aka a sense of being in danger). Porges (2011) described how dorsal vagal activation impairs social bonding at the precise time that social bonding would have the possibility of helping the individual shift to a calmer state.

By the time people seek psychotherapy, they have established patterns of social interaction and self-narrative that are based on the existence of and expectation of the neuroception of danger. It is simply their sense of "the way things are." To make matters worse, other people come to expect the same about them, which rigidifies the problem. For instance, a rape victim, Glenda, is anxious around men. So she avoids men and treats them as sources of danger. Men may then respond to her anxiety and associated behaviors by being less vulnerable or intimate around her. Her expectations are confirmed.

Once we have helped the client completely resolve a traumatic event during a session, we want to spread the neuroception of safety back throughout the client's consciousness. This can be done in many ways. In the case of Glenda, it might be to visualize meeting a man at a social event and discovering that she experiences no sense of danger. She could imagine how that feels in her body and mind. We could then have a conversation with her about how that makes her feel about herself. This example is decidedly simple to make the point. In fact, many approaches can be used to "spread the perceived safety" into the client's social system and self-image.

Theoretical and Experimental Evidence That Supports Vagal Mediation of EP Results

An important application of Polyvagal Theory to trauma treatment is the finding that trauma disrupts the vagal braking system (Porges, 2011). Second, insufficient vagal braking capacities are highly correlated with affect dysregulation. Third, a good way to measure the health of the vagal system is heart rate variability (HRV). HRV is greatly influenced by spontaneous breathing, which reflects the dynamic modulation of ventral vagal influences on the heart by attenuating the vagal brake during inhalation and expressing the vagal brake during exhalation. A heart that beats at exactly the same rate is unhealthy. In general, the more variability, the better this vagal braking system is working.

Fourth, several studies of thought field therapy in the treatment of traumatic events used HRV as one of the main measures (Callahan, 2001a, 2001b.) Baseline HRV measures were recorded. HRV measures were taken again after study subjects had focused on a traumatic memory and tapped on acupoints until their SUD scores were down to 0 or near 0. HRV improved substantially. While these studies faced criticism for methodological weaknesses (Herbert & Gaudiano, 2001; Kline, 2001), Callahan (2001a) argued that HRV was generally highly stable, not easy to influence, and that its improvement was a valid measure of the power of TFT. At the time, Callahan did not appear to understand HRV as a measure of the health of vagal influence over the heart or that a flexible vagal brake was a proxy for the ability to regulate affect. Still, by using HRV as an objective measure to demonstrate the effectiveness of TFT, Callahan paved the way for the hypothesis that TFT's ability to treat trauma involves vagal mediation. This hypothesis corresponds with the phenomenology of patients' experiences. Clearly, much better research is needed to confirm it.

An unanswered question, should this hypothesis hold, involves how tapping on acupuncture points actually leads to restoring ventral vagal control. It is of interest to note that six of eight points used in the EFT protocol are on the face and head at locations that lie on or very near cranial nerves that connect to the vagal nerve. One theory is that tapping on these points creates a piezoelectric effect that can be transmitted to the facial nerves and then the vagal nerve. Again, more research is needed.

EP Creates Vagal Conditions That Allow for Natural Healing to Occur

One of the important aspects of Polyvagal Theory is the interpersonal regulation of comfort and safety. In the context of trauma and trauma treatment, the in-the-moment relationship with significant others or therapists may lead to an escalation or a de-escalation of aversive emotions for both the traumatized person and the other person. The internal sense of danger is partially mediated by the interpersonal context as two nervous systems attune. In trauma treatment, the hope is that the stability and calmness of the nervous system of the therapist will calm the nervous system of the client; that the ventral vagal state of the therapist will transmit cues of safety to the client, who will

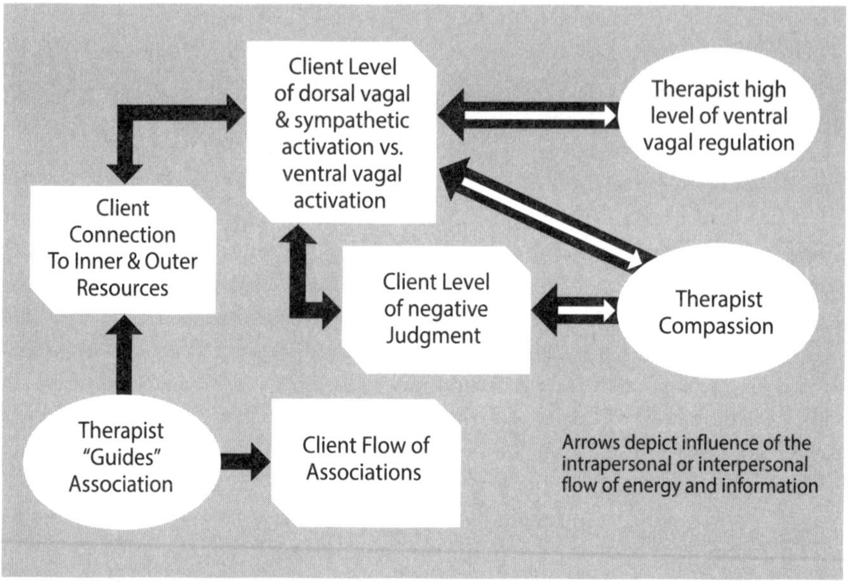

FIGURE 15.1
Therapist as "Regulator" of flow of information and energy

begin to regulate into a ventral vagal state of his own. One of the concerns of trauma treatment is that therapists listen to, and come into emotional contact with, painful to horrific events that may challenge their own capacities for regulation. If therapists become too activated, they communicate or reinforce the sense of danger to the clients. This process is depicted in Figure 15.1. The arrows depict the influence of one person upon the other.

In the Tell the Story technique of EFT, the client is asked to tell the story of a specific and time-limited traumatic event. One important difference of this approach, compared to almost all other trauma treatment approaches, is that as soon as the client begins to feel any emotional intensity, the therapist guides the client through the tapping procedure to reduce the affect to near zero before the client continues the story. From a polyvagal perspective, when the degree of neural challenge becomes too great, the client is guided to bring more ventral vagal energy to his system and come back into a state of safety before returning to work with the traumatic material.

At each stopping point, the client may tap on several different components of this segment of the traumatic event. For instance, if at a stopping point the client's father is yelling shame-infused invectives at him and the SUD level is at 8, the client might be asked to focus on the yelling and the words and do the tapping. The SUD might come down to 5. This is not below 2, so the therapist would not move to the next segment of the traumatic event. There is not enough ventral vagal capacity yet to safely continue. The therapist might ask what was making it a 5 at that point, and the client says, "The look in his eyes was full of disgust." That would be tapped on. The client would not move forward to the next part of the scene until he was at or near 0. Typically, even a short traumatic event of a couple of minutes has three to five emotional crescendos that are coupled with a reduction of ventral vagal management and increased sympathetic or dorsal vagal activation. Helping move a client's distress to 0 or near 0 at each stopping point along the way of describing a traumatic event helps a client create the necessary ventral vagal state inside the client that mediates healing and restoration.

But the traumatized client is not the only player in the equation. Generally, the EFT practitioner is also tapping on his or her own acupoints, ostensibly to lead the client in the procedure. However, there is a huge bonus. The practitioner is connecting with his or her own system, actively engaging ventral vagal energy, creating the capacity to stay calm. The client *and the therapist* share a deep sense of body-based calm and safety as they go through the entire event in a step-by-step fashion.

Over the years of training therapists in EP or other nonabreactive treatment approaches, I have become aware that a significant number of therapists are fearful of asking people to work on a specific traumatic event. They are afraid that the client will become dysregulated. And unless they know EP or another nonabreactive approach, they may have good reason to be fearful. But this very fear may be part of the problem. The therapist may communicate danger to the client through subtle facial gestures, postural shifts, or changes in tone of voice. In other words, the autonomic nervous system of the therapist communicates to the autonomic nervous system of the client that the client may be in danger. Meanwhile, the autonomic nervous system of the client is communicating to the therapist that danger is at hand. These communications are nonverbal and, for the most part, out of awareness and conscious control. This is neuroception at work, and a downward spiral can ensue.

The client's vagal brake continues to release, and the client feels increasingly more activated rather than increasingly calm. The therapist picks up on this unconsciously through his or her own neuroception or consciously through tracking external signs, and now the therapist feels more activated. One of two things happens. Possibility one is that the client begins to abreact, her sympathetic or dorsal vagal systems taking over. Possibility two is that in order to prevent this possible abreaction, the therapist begins to avoid areas of the client's experience that may be "hot." The client is often happy to accommodate this avoidance. If, however, the traumatic event is only partially treated and then avoided when dysregulation arises, pockets of negative experience are left unprocessed.

Practitioners of EP tend not to have this problem for three reasons. First, they are usually tapping themselves, so their bodies are literally less activated (this has not been experimentally verified), thereby downregulating the client as well. Second, vagal regulation allows the therapist to feel less anxious, supports presence as well as resonance with the client, and brings autonomic attunement. In particular, the Tell The Story technique in EFT allows the therapist and the client to untangle the different aspects of a specific traumatic event that would otherwise trigger a move out of ventral vagal regulation and into the "I am not safe" response. Third, once therapists have had a direct experience of being able to regulate their own autonomic responses and coregulate with their clients, they grow confident in their abilities to process traumatic events. Instead of communicating cues of danger, practitioners of EP who maintain a ventral vagal state during trauma work communicate cues of safety. The client feels the connection to the therapist's state and is better able to safely work with the traumatic memory.

The process I have depicted so far is active *during* the session. It helps to account for the rapid resolution of the negative affect associated with a traumatic event in the moment. But it does not account for the fact that once this happens, the memory of that event tends to be permanently changed. When the client thinks of the event a day, a week, or a month later, he or she is still not bothered by it. How is this possible? For this we turn to the process of therapeutic memory reconsolidation (Ecker, Ticic, & Hulley, 2012). Memory reconsolidation theory states that memories are brought in and out of long-term storage. As they are brought back into awareness, they are connected to the emotional and physiological states associated with them. If your traumatic memory is that you were attacked by a pit bull, when you remember the event, it comes back with the all of the associated body-based trauma states. When it goes back into long-term storage, it goes back with all of the body-based traumatic reactions still attached to it. However, if during the therapy, three specific conditions are met, the memory goes back into long-term storage without the body-based trauma states. Once that happens, it is permanently changed. In other words, the trauma memory is resolved permanently. The three conditions are:

1. You need to access the memory itself (have an enlivened experience of it).
2. You need to create a counterexperience so that the memory is experienced in such a way that it fundamentally contradicts the meaning of the original experience.
3. It must be repeated a number of times.

EP tapping protocols meet these criteria (Feinstein, 2015). While it is beyond the scope of this chapter to go into the details of therapeutic memory reconsolidation, I want to underscore a few points as it applies to energy psychology and Polyvagal Theory. The second criterion emphasizes the importance of creating a contradictory meaning of the original event. At first glance, this might seem like a high-level neocortical cognitive process. As discussed earlier, meaning changes occur in energy psychology treatment, often spontaneously. However, as clients focus on the memory and tap, they discover that their bodies are rapidly becoming calmer and calmer. By the time their level of distress is significantly reduced, say down to a SUD of 3 or lower, the vagal system is no longer sending the message of a clear and present danger, and a SUD of 0 corresponds with the ventral vagal system sending the message that there is no danger at all. This is not cognitive. It is in the body, powerful, palpable, and built into the fabric of the experience. And as the internal autonomic state changes, the meaning of the memory spontaneously changes.

This accounts for the typical client reaction of being surprised. In the Tell The Story technique, this process is broken down into many sets of nested loops, one set for each piece of the story that creates emotional reactions. Not only are there multiple presentations of an altered memory (Step 3), but the actual associative pathways of danger in the story become depotentiated. Each time the therapist stops the client and treats the sense of danger and upset in the path of the story, it disrupts the cascade of autonomic dysregulations and brings about ventral vagal activation. It disrupts the very flow of energy and autonomic conditions that make the memory a traumatic memory.

The third condition for memory reconsolidation, where Step 2 must be repeated multiple times, is accomplished by EP protocols in several ways. Each time a round of tapping is repeated, the client reconnects with the experience with more autonomic regulation and less agitation. Once the client is down to 0 or near 0, the capstone of successful treatment is when the therapist asks the client to test the results. The client is asked to reconnect with the memory that had previously been deeply dysregulating. Not only does this involve giving the memory an in-the-moment SUD rating, the therapist asks the client to examine every nook and cranny of the memory, scanning for places of unease.

One of two things happens. Possibility 1: The client notices a slight dysregulation calling for further attention. Possibility 2: Rather than attempting to avoid the memory, the client is now ventral vagal regulated and can safely look into every element of the memory with no subjective distress or physiological activation. By creating experiences that contradict previous instances in which the memory had led to the limbic system becoming dysregulated, the most difficult condition for bringing about therapeutic memory reconsolidation has been met. The client viscerally experiences safety in the presence of the memory, and with that sense of safety, avoidance behavior is not experienced as necessary or maintained. The ventral vagal state also supports the possibility of safely working with other traumatic memories. Either possibility is a win. If the therapist and client identify an area of unresolved affect, it's a win because they can be more thorough in the successful outcome by continuing to work on the remaining activation. If the client stays totally calm, it's a win because the resolution of this memory has been completed.

Summary

Over the last 15 years, the leading edge of trauma work has been focusing on the importance of the body and "bottom-up" factors that contribute to the creation of post-traumatic stress on the one hand and post-traumatic healing on the other (van der Kolk, 2014). During this same period, there has been a boom in the research that demonstrates the speed and effectiveness of energy psychology protocols for treating trauma. In the most popular protocols of EFT and TFT, clients focus their attention on traumatic memories while stimulating acupoints, usually via tapping. Clients who use EP describe that the memory of the event that once created tremendous dysregulation of affect simply ceases to create negative feelings. New insights and meanings tend to follow spontaneously. In this chapter, I have described how EP approaches may be helping clients switch from sypathetic or dorsal vagal activation to ventral vagal activation when consciously and unconsciously tuning into memories of traumatic events. I have suggested that Polyvagal Theory appears to account for some of the research data (e.g., changes in HRV) as well as the felt experience of clients. I have also described how the mediation of vagal activity during EP tapping protocols is both a function of intrapersonal factors as well as interpersonal factors between the client and the therapist (e.g., the therapist's self-tapping in the presence of traumatic material helps to maintain ventral vagal activation in the therapist that helps to downregulate the patient).

References

Association for Comprehensive Energy Psychology. (n.d.) *What is energy psychology?* Retrieved from http://www.energypsych.org/general/custom.asp?page=AboutEPv2

Callahan, R. J. (1985). *Five minute phobia cure: Dr. Callahan's treatment for fears, phobias and self- sabotage*. Wilmington, DE: Enterprise.

Callahan, R. (2001a) The impact of thought field therapy on heart rate variability. *Journal of Clinical Psychology, 57*(10), 1153–1170.

Callahan, R. (2001b) Raising and lowering of heart rate variability: Some clinical findings of thought field therapy. *Journal of Clinical Psychology, 57*(10), 1175–1186.

Cho, Z. H., Chung S. C., Jones, J. P., Park, J. B., Park, H. J., Lee, H. J., . . . Min, B. I. (1998). New findings of the correlation between acupoints and corresponding brain cortices using functional MRI. *Proceedings of National Academy of Sciences, 95*, 2670–2673.

Church, D., Yount, G., & Brooks, A. J. (2012). The effect of emotional freedom techniques on stress biochemistry: A randomized controlled trial. *Journal of Nervous and Mental Disease, 200*, 891–896.

Church, D., Yount, G., Rachlin, K., Fox, L., & Nelms, J. (2016). Epigenetic effects of PTSD remediation in veterans using Clinical EFT (Emotional Freedom Techniques): A randomized controlled pilot study. *American Journal of Health Promotion*.

Clond, M. (2016). Emotional Freedom Techniques for anxiety: A systematic review with meta-analysis. *Journal of Nervous and Mental Disease*. Advance online publication.

Dhond, R. P., Kettner, N., & Napadow, V. (2007). Neuroimaging acupuncture effects in the human brain. *Journal of Alternative and Complementary Medicine, 13*, 603–616. doi:10.1006/ccog.1999.0393

Diepold, J. H., & Goldstein, D. (2009). Thought field therapy and QEEG changes in the treatment of trauma: A case study. *Traumatology, 15*, 85–93. doi: 10.1177/1534765608325304

Ecker, B., Ticic, R., & Hulley, L. (2012). *Unlocking the emotional brain: Eliminating symptoms at their roots using memory reconsolidation*. New York, NY: Routledge.

Fang, J., Jin, Z., Wang, Y., Li, K., Kong, J., Nixon, E. E., . . . Hui, K. K.-S. (2009). The salient characteristics of the central effects of acupuncture needling: Limbic-paralimbic-neocortical network modulation. *Human Brain Mapping, 30*, 1196–1206. doi:10.1002/hbm.20583

Feinstein, D. (2012). Acupoint stimulation in treating psychological disorders: Evidence of efficacy. *Review of General Psychology, 16*, 364–380. doi:10.1037/a0028602

Feinstein, D. (2015) How energy psychology changes deep emotional learnings. *The Neuropsychotherapist, 10*, 39-49.

Gilomen, S. A., & Lee, C. W. (2015). The efficacy of acupoint stimulation in the treatment of psychological distress: A meta-analysis. *Journal of Behavior Therapy and Experimental Psychiatry, 48*, 140–148.

Herbert, J., & Gaudiano, B. (2001). The search for the holy grail heart rate variability and thought field therapy. *Journal of Clinical Psychology, 57*(10), 1207–1214.

Hui, K. K.-S., Liu, J., Makris, N., Gollub, R. W., Chen, A. J. W., Moore, C. I., . . . Kwong, K. K. (2000). Acupuncture modulates the limbic system and subcortical gray structures of the human brain: Evidence from fMRI studies in normal subjects. *Human Brain Mapping, 9*(1), 13–25.

Hui, K. K.-S., Liu, J., Marina, O., Napadow, V., Haselgrove, C., Kwong, K. K., . . . Makris, N. (2005). The integrated response of the human cerebrocerebellar and limbic systems to acupuncture stimulation at ST 36 as evidenced by fMRI. *NeuroImage, 27*, 479–496. doi:10.1016/j.neuroimage.2005.04.037

Kline, J. (2001). Heart rate variability does not tap putative effects of thought field therapy. *Journal of Clinical Psychology, 57*(10), 1187–1192.

Nelms, J., & Castel, D. (2016). A systematic review and meta-analysis of randomized and non-randomized trials of Emotional Freedom Techniques (EFT) for the treatment of depression. *Explore: The Journal of Science and Healing, 12*(6), 416–426.

Porges, S. W. (2001). The Polyvagal Theory: Phylogenetic substrates of a social nervous system. *International Journal of Psychophysiology, 42*, 123–146.

Porges, S. W. (2011) *The Polyvagal Theory: Neurophysiological foundations of emotions, attachment, communication, and self-regulation.* New York, NY: Norton

Schwarz, R. (2002) *Tools for transforming trauma.* New York, NY: Routledge.

Schwarz, R. (2012). Enhancing traditional therapy with energy psychology interventions. *The National Psychologist*, Jan/Feb.

Schwarz, R. (2014). *Neuroscience and the effectiveness of energy psychology (part 3 of 3)* [Video file]. Retrieved from https://youtu.be/LUQDINVN8hM

Sebastian, B., & Nelms, J. (2016). The effectiveness of emotional freedom techniques in the treatment of posttraumatic stress disorder: A meta-analysis. *Explore: The Journal of Science and Healing, 13*(1), 16–25.

Shapiro, F. (2001) *Eye movement desensitization and reprocessing (EMDR): Basic principles, protocols, and procedures* (2nd ed.). New York, NY: Guilford Press.

Stefanov, M., Potroz, M., Kim, J., Jake Lim, J., Cha, R., & Min-Ho Nam, M. (2013) The primo vascular system as a new anatomical system. *Journal of Acupuncture and Meridian Studies, 6*(6), 331–338.

Van der Kolk, B. (2014). *The body keeps the score: Brain, mind, and body in the healing of trauma.* New York, NY: Penguin

16

Trauma Severity: Parallels Between SPIM 30 and Polyvagal Theory

Ralf Vogt

Abstract: This chapter points out the psychophysiological parallels between Polyvagal Theory and the SPIM 30 (Somatic-Psychological-Interactive Model for diagnosis and treatment). Both models describe qualitative and quantitative changes in human perception, information processing, and behavior regulation under different degrees of stress. In SPIM 30, the processes eliciting these changes represent the client's different patterns of interactive relationships. SPIM-30 provides a body-oriented approach emphasizing a flexible therapeutic setting that facilitates feelings of safety and deep bodily relaxation. The SPIM-30 therapeutic strategy fosters clients to feel secure and supported as they are challenged during therapy. These bodily feelings of safety and trust are experiences that they lacked during their early development.

Introduction

FOR ME AS a trauma therapist, Polyvagal Theory provides a long-desired neurophysiological confirmation of the qualitative differences we have observed among trauma clients. In the past, neurophysiological theories of personality and emotion (cf. Hüther, 1997; Panksepp, 1998) only confirmed that there are two fundamentally different ways people process information depending on whether they experienced "normal" psychological pressure or were affected by trauma. However, there was still no corresponding neurophysiological theory that could help explain, in a holistic way, the different quantitative and qualitative stages of the traumatic and dissociative disruptions in the regulation of behavior.

The SPIM 30 model distinguishes seven stages of trauma severity, ranging from healthy to extremely disturbed experience and behavior regulation states. Prior to Polyvagal Theory there were no neurophysiological models that could be used to explain these stages (cf. Porges, 2009). Polyvagal Theory provides the first neurobiologically based model that corresponds with our many years of clinical observations. Consistent with Polyvagal Theory, we observe biobehavioral state changes in stages that we have defined. These stages depend on a person's individual stress level. In polyvagal terms, the stages would have a specific neurophysiological signature. This means that different qualities of psychological experience (subjective experiences such as joy, fear, or death threats) parallel specific neurophysiological states. From our perspective, this is a major breakthrough for our interdisciplinary research and provides an inspiration for other clinicians and scientists to engage in an expanded exploration of mechanisms and processes involved in understanding and treating trauma. In this chapter, we provide and explore some of the bridges between Polyvagal Theory and the SPIM 30 model based on our clinical work from a psychotherapeutic-phenomenological point of view.

SPIM 20

My wife, Irina, and I have been working in the field of psychotherapy for 30 years, with the last 20 years being dedicated to psychotraumatology. After comprehensively studying different psychoanalytical, depth psychology (psychodynamic), and behavioral therapy concepts, we began developing our own trauma model called SPIM 20. SPIM 20 was an abbreviation for Somatic-Psychological-Interactive Treatment Model for Dissociative Disorders in the Standard Version No. 20 (cf. Vogt, 2006, 2008). Traditional approaches to psychotherapy, such as psychoanalysis (S. Freud, 1892–1939), guided imagery (Leuner, Hennig, & Fikentscher, 1993), hypnotherapy (Erickson & Rossi, 2007), family therapy (Weiss, 1988; de Shazer, 1989; R. Schwartz, 2008) and more recent approaches in traumatology (cf. Kluft 1984, 2014; Putnam, 2003, Watkins & Watkins, 2003; Nijenhuis, Van der Hart, & Steele, 2008; Reddemann, 2012; H. L. Schwartz, 2013, and others) have been integrated into this model. As the model evolved further, key components from traditional approaches were modified and complemented by our own contributions.

To explore and expand the application of SPIM 20, we founded the Leipzig Trauma Institute in 2002 where we could explore new approaches to trauma therapy and refine new methods of treatment. When we realized that in the more advanced stages of psychotherapy, many child and adult patients could not be treated comprehensively within the therapeutic models of human-induced trauma that were available at the time, we started to develop some innovative therapeutic methods. Consistent with our institute's mission statement to constantly review conceptual elements in practice and to incorporate theoretical findings into practical methods as soon as possible, we revised the SPIM model and recently published the SPIM 30 model (i.e., the standard version of our SPIM model No. 30 in 2015; cf. Vogt, 2015).

SPIM 30

SPIM 30 is an innovative body action and attachment-orientated diagnostic and treatment approach that is complementary to the approaches mentioned above. We saw an urgent need to improve trauma treatment, because severe traumatic experiences occur in specific types of relationships that threaten the survivor's mental and physical integrity. Thus, we emphasize close links between "feelings" and body reactions (for more information on SPIM 30 and how SPIM 30 incorporates attachment theory, see Vogt, 2014, 2015, 2016). In SPIM 30, traumatic experiences are not categorized by frequency of occurrence (i.e., single vs. multiple events). Instead, we define three categories of traumatic experience based on the relationship between victim and perpetrator. In our descriptions, we label the survivor of trauma as 'victim' to emphasize the power differential with the individual (i.e., predator) in the relationship that is responsible for inflicting the trauma. In this categorization, Type I is a trauma caused by an event (such as an earthquake), where no specific victim–perpetrator relationship comes into play. Type II is caused by the perpetrator acting in a grossly negligent way, which the perpetrator later regrets (e.g., domestic violence in the course of an impulsive argument). In contrast to this, Type III is characterized by the perpetrator's intentional and deliberately malicious actions. The following table outlines this novel trauma typology (Table 16.1).

It should be emphasized that this typology puts the relationship between victim and perpetrator at the center of assessment and treatment. From a clinical perspective, this allows for a more accurate characterization of the clients' self-regulatory capacity to manage their dissociative trauma disorder. The severity of the trauma incident experienced is associated with the cumulative experience of interpersonal threats and shocks over a period of many months

Attachment-Based Trauma Classification in the SPIM-30 Model	
Type I	***Event Trauma*** Typically, a single traumatic event (e.g., earthquake, traffic accident) in which the relationship between perpetrator and victim does not play a major role.
Type II	***Negligent Trauma*** Typically, a repetitive, serial trauma in which the relationship between perpetrator and victim plays an important role. The perpetrator's behavior may vary from impulsive-careless or negligent to grossly egocentric, narrow-minded, relentless conduct.
Type III	***Intentional Trauma*** Typically, a repetitive, serial trauma in which the relationship between perpetrator and victim plays the central role. Perpetrators act consciously, intentionally, and purposefully. They are aware of their violence harming the other person, to the point that they sadistically and intentionally physically harm or psychologically threaten or torture the victim and self-righteously justify their behavior.

TABLE 16.1

or years, which elicit dissociative states that crystallize and thus become conditioned, unconscious switching patterns in the human psyche.

In the SPIM 30 model, we have associated the trauma typology with psychodynamic, interactive patterns of attachment styles (Vogt, 2016), differentiated into victim, perpetrator, and oscillating victim–perpetrator attachment style. These categories represent a trauma-psychological complement to the known attachment styles as described by Bowlby (1969), Ainsworth (1977), and Main and Solomon (1986).

This chapter will present a theoretical and practical description of the seven-stage cumulative trauma severity model. We will focus on the parallels between the neurobiological perspective of Polyvagal Theory (Porges, 2009, 2011) and our psychodynamic perspective, clinical observations, and experiences.

First, features of our active-experience therapy method will be described to provide a general perspective of SPIM 30. The SPIM 30 model includes a wider range of body and interaction-oriented psychophysiological stabilization methods than several other models. Moreover, the SPIM 30 toolbox provides structured diagnostic settings that facilitate exploratory behavior and provide opportunities for the client to become aware of relationship elicited fear or aggression, desires for support and comfort or playful interactions, and child-oriented ways of getting to know each other.

Polyvagal Theory provides further support for the neurophysiological foundations (i.e., context-dependent physiological state) of our body-oriented interventions (cf. Porges, 2009; Porges & Furman, 2011; Carter, 1998; Porges & Carter, 2016). Polyvagal Theory informs therapists of explicit features that they need to be mindful of while navigating within a sensitive interaction with trauma patients. From the many cases that my wife, Irina, and I have seen in our office on a daily basis, we know that trauma patients, particularly those suffering from dissociative trauma disorders caused by *human* violence, bring into the therapeutic setting unconscious or conscious relationship distrust and fear of commitment caused by long-term, cumulative exposure to disturbing experiences.

As psychotherapists, we should be able to respond to that with appropriate practices that would help support feelings of safety and trust. Even with adult clients, we find that the tremendous disruptions and delays in early-childhood development often lead to rather infantile relationship concepts in their adult lives, which are mostly still unconscious. Often, our trauma patients will communicate in childlike analogic (Watzlawick, Beavin, & Jackson, 1967) terms or perceive us in analogic patterns because due to the trauma, they have not learned to symbolize and abstract. Therefore, when establishing a therapeutic relationship, initially client responses are taken rather literally. As an example, in the first stage of SPIM 30 therapy with dissociative clients, we always organize interactive settings, working with movements in order to allow clients to express their needs for contact or being held, for trust and comfort. Active experiences in such settings serve as examples to make clients aware of their mostly unconscious action regulation (e.g. contact rods, holding rope, back mat, nest bag, and other contextual settings developed in our clinic and described in Vogt, 2006, 2008).

According to Polyvagal Theory, a positive, safe atmosphere in a relationship is a gate opener for prosocial contact (controlled by the ventral vagus). But severely traumatized individuals are prone to rapidly developing high levels of stress and tend to unconsciously adopt more aggressive or avoidant strategies. This process of risk assessment is consistent with the Polyvagal Theory concept of neuroception that shifts physiological state in response to unconscious cues of danger or life-threat. As these settings also serve to determine the zone of further development (Wygotsky, 1986), there is a good chance that child and adult patients will specify which forms of interaction with the therapist are acceptable for them at the time, and inform the therapist of the interactive settings in which they are currently not comfortable but might try later. The results are often therapeutically groundbreaking and highly interesting for both client and therapist. Following treatment guidelines based on the SPIM 30 model, we encourage our clients—children or adults on a partly infantile level of development alike—to sense and decide which method of interactive rapprochement seems feasible for them at any given point in time, and what they are willing to further explore. In polyvagal terms, this opportunity allows clients to sense and to explore the degree of physiological state regulation they can tolerate. It is of course our task as therapists to provide clients with the creative therapeutic activities that enable them to functionally exercise the neural capacity to regulate behavioral, emotional, and physiological state (just like good parents would for their children).

In the initial settings of the SPIM 30 contact phase, the psychological and often physiological tension pent up in trauma patients frequently prevent them from engaging in cooperative fine-tuning of biobehavioral states within the body-oriented interaction. Rather, clients will seek to control the situation out of fear, which prevents them from switching to a safe physiological state regulated by the ventral vagal pathways described in Polyvagal Theory. Functionally, their body may be detecting risk when there is no apparent risk. This process is consistent with neuroception, as described in Polyvagal Theory. However, over time the neuroception of risk may change by involving the client in the sensitive exercises in different SPIM 30 settings. These exercises may facilitate a positive, sometimes amusing, relationship experience. Severely traumatized patients of all age groups will only be able to genuinely feel such an experience and accept it with fewer feelings of shame if they can try it out with a therapist who is psychologically and physically available. This applies to young and old clients alike. Words alone are not sufficient to ameliorate the feelings of shame—but joint action will. When this occurs, the contextual cues of the therapeutic environment no longer elicit fear and danger, and the client's neuroception is now detecting safety in the clinical environment.

SPIM 30 involves the use of a variety of objects to elicit feelings of safety, trust, and security. We often use a back mat as a trust-building exercise. Clients ordinarily experience the back mat as a generally delightful experience, although it is significantly more challenging for trauma patients, because they can no longer use their vision to orient and control their movements especially while leaning backwards (cf. Vogt, 2008). When successful, the client returns to a calm state with feelings of safety, consistent with moving into a ventral vagal state; this state, following the challenge, can be part of a detraumatizing new experience.

With no visual information about the partner (leaning against the other side of the back mat) available, a more global physical perception ideally will work to create "blind" trust. If all goes well, allowing oneself to lean on another person's (metaphorically, the parent's) back can be very soothing. These and other settings in the first stage of therapy demonstrate how we seek to accomplish feelings of safety and trust and an enhanced ventral vagal regulation within the framework of the SPIM 30 model. When we start off with a client in a state of fear and chronic tension, we want to gradually develop a trustful relationship. Basically, we want to shift the client's neuroception from triggering a state of danger or life-threat to a state of safety.

Toward the end of the first stage of trauma therapy, clients are offered another a comprehensive psychoeducation to minimize the intrusive psychodynamic effects of perpetrator transferences and perpetrator introjects (cf. Vogt, 2012). Based on our experience, the educational component helps filter out "relationship resistance"—that is, consistent with traditional psychoanalysis, frequently manifested as anxious avoidance behavior. This is due to the fact that trauma patients with chronic disorders, suffering from human-induced trauma, are often stuck in their personal development because they lack sufficient knowledge of the psychodynamics involved. Through our body-oriented exercises, patients gain hands-on experience and proof of benefits of a two-way therapeutic relationship with mutual responsibilities that actively contributes to a shared experience. Polyvagal Theory describes this experience as a product of reciprocity. Reciprocity promotes an autonomic attunement between therapist and patient that evolves into a shared neuroception of safety with the client and therapist sharing a sense of relational safety and trust. Thus, trauma clients begin to feel that they have better control over the therapy and can actively monitor the involvement and commitment of the therapist by responding, both intuitively and consciously, to the therapist's facial expression and body movements, while in a calm (ventral vagal) state and from a safe distance.

An essential part of the therapeutic experience for our clients is to explain to them, in an age-appropriate way, the specifics of the trauma curve that evolved from the development of the SPIM models. The explanation includes a description of the curve for the person who is subordinate (i.e.,survivor/victim) in the interaction, the assumed neurophysiology mediating the stages, and how the intensity of traumatic experience determines the severity of mental disruptiveness. The explanation is provided in the seven-stage SPIM model of interactive cumulative regulation categories (Vogt, 2012, 2015), which is illustrated in Figure 16.1. We explain to our patients how Polyvagal Theory provides an understanding of the neurophysiological states that underlie the stages.

We use the trauma curve to explain (even to the youngest of our clients—with colorful images more suitable for children) that when our survival is challenged, all human beings will struggle at a certain point and eventually

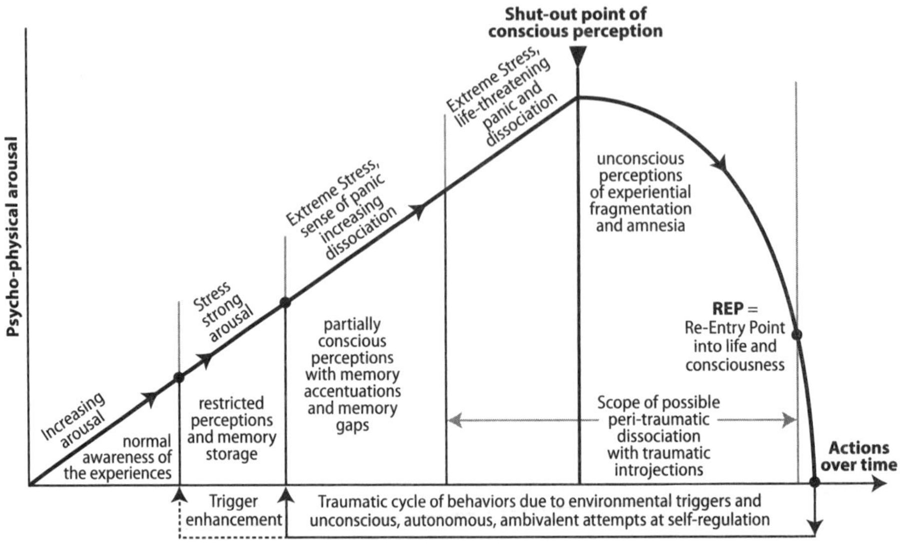

FIGURE 16.1
Sections of the trauma curve: stress levels and conscious perception of the trauma victim.

become unable to defend their psychological and physical boundaries. When overwhelmed and traumatized by a reckless or malicious person, an individual's perception will change and become increasingly constricted and focused on the perpetrator. The unbearable threat and sensory overload will eventually force the subordinated individual to dissociate. In a state of tremendous, increasing pain and panic, the subordinated person is finally left unable to remain conscious and will mentally shut down, going through a near-death situation, overwhelmed within their subjective experience of fear and physical pain. Post-traumatic repetitive compulsive thoughts and actions are often caused by fragmented representations of the trauma scenes in the mind and by the amnesic information deficit occurring while dissociated. Psychodynamically, different brain areas work together continuously and in complex ways to make sense in forming a Gestalt representation of the fragmented memories and sensations (Janet, 1901). This constant search for meaning and for ways to control the environment becomes disorganized and ineffective in response to trauma (Vogt, 2012). The repetition compulsion cannot be resolved psychologically or psychophysiologically, and thus the victim's fears become chronic and take the form of an unconscious tendency to reenact the trauma.

In the SPIM 30 approach, we have organized the trauma curve into a cumulative "slice" model to present vivid descriptors of the different degrees of mental disorders. We noticed that traumatized as well as nontraumatized individuals are able to switch into very different states of experience and behavior regulation that seem to be hard-wired into their nervous systems. These different self-regulation categories are consistent with the neurobiological principles outlined in Polyvagal Theory (Porges, 2009). It matched our experience from case studies that healthy behavior, neuroses, and psychoses share some common details and that the specific action regulation components coexist as parallel parts in the nervous system.

Trauma can happen to any human being. Currently, there is no holistic model of the underlying mechanisms through which trauma disrupts mental and physical health. In the years we have worked in psychiatry, we have had colleagues who genuinely believed that trauma patients and neurotic or psychotic patients were completely different kinds of clients and should therefore be treated by different therapeutic professionals. Informed from our many years of clinical experience, we now assume that patients sometimes share and sometimes differ in their disturbed patterns of experience and behavior as well as in memory storage and communication skills depending on the gravity of their history and their individual coping skills.

The classic psychoanalytical theories of Sigmund Freud (1892–1939) and Anna Freud (1936) or Abraham and Torok (1976) assume that people who have undergone such severe experiences cannot "digest" (i.e., process) these experiences and, as a consequence, carry in them semidigested or undigested thoughts (i.e., introjects or incorporations) that are the products of disrupted processing. We integrated these traditional approaches into the framework of the theory of boundary transgressions. According to our clinical studies and observations, the concept of attributing different degrees of severity of mental disorders to interactive experiences and the cumulative recurrence of borderline experiences is even more conclusive, and more plausible from a holistic point of view. The SPIM model focuses on the disrupted process of psychophysiological processing (i.e., the succession of the different degrees of severity in the subordinate individual due to the interactive boundary transgressions they experienced and their changing orientation toward the perpetrator, their opening up to the perpetrator as well as changes in the victim's neurophysiological processing capacities).

The trauma curve blends in with the hierarchical levels of autonomic regulation described in Polyvagal Theory by Porges (2009). Consistent with Polyvagal Theory, we can hypothetically identify plausible physiological states that will be associated with the seven stages of trauma severity described in the SPIM 30 model.

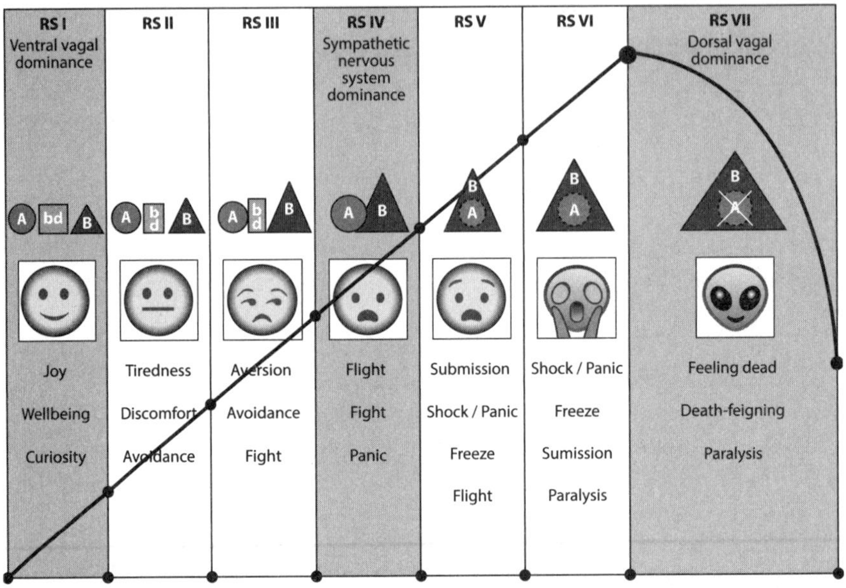

FIGURE 16.2
Neurophysiological stages of Polyvagal Theory and stages of the survivor's experience and reactions underlying the SPIM 30 trauma severity curve.

Figure 16.2 illustrates the processes through which a dependent person (such as a child) or a subordinate individual (identified as A inserted in a circle) will be imprinted by the interactions of the potentially dominant individual (identified as B inserted in a triangle). The relative size of A and B within each stage reflect the relative balance of power and control within the interaction. In regulation state category I (RS I, situationally flexible state), B fully respects A's boundaries, which is reflected in a warmhearted interaction between two engaging individuals on an equal playing field. This is similar to the role of parents playing joyful games with their children. This positive scenario develops because the dominant individual (B) does not abuse his potential power. The beautiful, lively images of such life experiences in A's mind represent a positive regulatory resource in RS I. Future interactions can be modeled on this experience if the experience is genuinely harmonic, nonviolent, and trustworthy. In Polyvagal Theory constructs, RS I is described as a state of safety supported by neurophysiological pathways involving the ventral vagus and regulating the structures defining the social engagement system (i.e., striated muscles of the face and head as well as the myelinated ventral vagal pathways regulating the heart and bronchi).

What clients experience in regulation state category II (RS II, habitual state) is that the world is generally still "in order" but not as pleasurable, peaceful, or harmonious as in RS I. What causes this slight deterioration is that B is less respectful of A's boundaries, wants to dominate the interaction to his advantage or lacks the empathy A would need. In real life, this might be a slightly narrow-minded grandfather playing with his grandchild, or helping with homework for school. Things are generally running smoothly and are friendly, but may be boring for partner A. In this stage, both interaction partners will still feel mostly satisfied. In Polyvagal Theory, RS II is described as still regulated by the ventral vagus with a possible retraction of the vagal brake and a move out of the safe and social connection felt in RS I.

In the next regulation state category, RS III (transference state), the relationship constellation changes markedly to A's disadvantage, because B is clearly dominant in an egocentric way. B in general still respects A's boundaries and tends to refrain from using violence to exert control over A. Thus, formally, A's boundaries are respected most of the time. Although interaction partner A will often experience a feeling of unilaterally having to meet B's demands, while A's own needs are being neglected. Against the backdrop of such stressful, frequently recurring life experiences, various negative psychodynamic transferences may develop, which in turn will influence A's interpersonal expectations, behavioral responses, and evaluations of interactions. In classic psychoanalysis, this is defined as *neurotic transference* (S. Freud, 1892–1939). In the SPIM 30, we describe a quantitative and qualitative dissociation concept (for more detail, see Vogt, 2012, pp. 25–74, and Vogt, 2015, pp. 1–22). An important feature of RS III is that the now-weakened individual A can develop dissociative symptoms of a remarkable scope, although we would not categorize this as a qualitative dissociative disorder. In Polyvagal Theory, RS III is characterized by a loss of ventral vagal regulation and the concomitant neuroception bias toward detecting threat.

In RS IV, due to poor interactive regulation, the cumulative negative experiences imprint with a critical impact on subordinate individual A. Often, A's psychological and physical boundaries will be overrun at this point and distort perception. Psychological and physical violence are frequently employed by B as a means to dominate A. A is often humiliated in their interpersonal relationship, destabilizing A's sense of security. From this stage of cumulative negative formative experiences, we describe psychodynamic (often already dissociative) introject images in the victim's experience and memory. This means that, due to frequent boundary violations, individual A no longer has adequate control over the psychodynamic internalization of intrinsically foreign, ego-dystonic experiences and action information and cannot accurately articulate A's personal contribution in the interaction. Functionally, A cannot answer questions such as: What was really my part in this? What is part of my own experience and value system? What is not?

In the interaction, fight-or-flight behavior occurs without a genuine sense of security or of a reliable relationship. To make clients aware of the psychodynamics of the confusing interactive experiences the subordinate individual (e.g., a child) will undergo in regulation patterns III and IV, we often use *beseelt* (animated) therapy settings with stuffed animals or other symbolization objects customized for the SPIM 30 therapy approach (Vogt, 2006, 2008).

These SPIM 30 settings with *beseelbar* (animate) objects help to illustrate the trauma clients' infantile or unconscious transference experiences and to depict them more clearly. In human-induced traumatic imprints, we often have to deal with a powerful person B determining all the features of the interaction. Attempts to prevent B's abuse of power from becoming obvious will heighten A's childlike state of powerlessness. During a retrospective exploration of the traumatic relationship experiences, we found that *beseelbar* objects that convey body-oriented information (which clients can intuitively relate to and grasp) support clients in facilitating their communicative development by learning to "read" feelings through the language of *beseelbar* objects. In Polyvagal Theory, RS IV can be viewed as having a low threshold to recruit the sympathetic nervous system to support fight-or-flight behaviors and a loss of access to the social engagement system with its calming ventral vagal pathways.

At the next stage, RS V, individual A's chronic experience of frustration and powerlessness is expressed even more dramatically. A's boundaries are forcefully overrun on a regular basis. B is the sole determiner, ruling with verbal, physical, and often sexual violence. Yelling and cynical, sadistic humiliation are considered acts of verbal violence. We also assigned the more passive forms of violence, such as emotional blackmailing, to severity degree RS V in SPIM 30. This would include children who, due to their natural need for attachment, find themselves forced to empathize with their caregivers' unstable mental structures—as would be the case with an addicted father or depressed mother. These children will inevitably learn to give up their need for healthy boundaries. From a psychoanalytical point of view, they internalize harmful emotions and instructions as (ego-dystonic and often dissociative) introjects or (strongly ego-dystonic, completely dissociative) implants. The majority of implant regulation imprints seen in clinical populations stem from experiences of active violence (see above). In the trauma literature, these dissociative regulation implants are frequently called *ego states* or *alters* (Kluft, 1984, 2014; Putnam, 2003). Nijenhuis, Van der Hart, and Steele (2008) speak of emotional parts of personality (EP). In the SPIM 30 when explaining relational human-induced trauma, we further differentiate dissociative implants into trauma victim states and perpetrator introject states because these require different therapeutic settings (Vogt, 2008, 2012, 2015). In Polyvagal Theory, RS V is characterized by sympathetic "flooding," leading to panic and behavioral freezing while maintaining muscle tone.

Scientific discussions with our European colleagues have led to Nijenhuis, van der Hart, and Steele to also speak of perpetrator-imitating parts when referring to what Nijenhuis defines as *EP-control* (cf. Nijenhuis, 2012, pp. 124–131). Kluft (1984) and Putnam (2003) often refer to victim states as *trauma child alters*, and to perpetrator states as *perpetrator alters* (or ego states). Thus, across different theoretical frameworks, there seems to be sufficient agreement on this aspect of our RS V. In continuation of our active-experience approach according to the SPIM 30 therapy model, we have researched and empirically developed interactive body and action-oriented therapy settings. These settings are meant to reduce the main dissociative symptoms of victim memory states and perpetrator implant states, given that these patients display tremendous interactive relationship fear but also considerable aggressiveness directed against themselves or others.

RS VI represents the shift from the category of a predominantly mental struggle for existence to experiencing a threat to psychophysical survival. In an increasingly life-threatening or near-death situation, human beings will eventually all reach their switch-off point for conscious experience. In these moments (seconds or minutes) of intense stress, the subordinate subject's psyche will almost exclusively align itself to the dominant individual's influence—their violence, affect, action, message, and so on. Peritraumatically, the victim will undergo extremely dissociative states. When the victim finally caves into submission, the perpetrator can easily convey behavior instructions. Due to the victim's total breakdown of mental barriers, these will not be filtered in any way. In cases of repeated, severe violence, we call the process of influencing the victim *conditioning*. When violence is increased to torture, we speak of *programming* the victim.

Survivors of trauma of this scale struggle or are unable to build trustful relationships with other people later on. They are in a permanent state of tension and suffer from feelings oscillating between panic and submission—although they try to conceal this from the outside world. This latent, constant tension is manifested in the nervous system's regulation of autonomic state (Porges, 2009).

RS VII represents inner, or mental, life after the switch-off point. While in

RS VI, there will still be fragmented records of the violent scenes in memory, or sensory memories that can later be connected with each other in a safe therapeutic environment, there are no splinters of consciousness left in the mental representation level of RS VII until, in the case of survival, consciousness is regained. There is dissociative amnesia for the trauma. For trauma processing according to SPIM 30, this means that, with RS VI, we have a focused structured action enactment for psychotrauma exposure (FSAP) and other methods to choose from. But in the case of RS VII, we need to resort to the most regressive of associative techniques, such as the SPIM 30 floor mat, to be able to help our trauma clients via implicit body-association fragments. Here, patients will find in their psyche's subconscious branched information stores a mixture of diffuse, general near-death information of physical decay, traces of perpetrator-oriented impressions of violence or dissociative mental switch-off fantasies that are hard to classify scientifically because they are just analogical and atmospheric data. After the mental death experience, these data constellations continue to run on the psyche's hard drive, so to speak, but cannot be accessed by the survivor. Therefore, we classified blueprints of RS VII as dual state in order to highlight the difference from RS VI. This dual regulation state specifically will often continue to operate unconsciously and in parallel even while RS V or VI are active. We therefore propose that, in accordance with Polyvagal Theory by Porges (2009), in RS V and VI, the dorsal vagus is probably activated in parallel to the sympathetic system, while in RS VII the dorsal vagus may become more dominant and be manifested in a decrease in motor tone and a tendency toward immobilization as the client's nervous system attempts to foster an inanimate appearance.

In this chapter, we outline a small sample of our repertoire. Apart from the contact, trust building, and holding settings mentioned earlier, a number of late-nurture settings seem to be of particular benefit for fearful trauma child or victim states. The objects for late emotional nurturing provided in the SPIM 30 inventory allow for our chronically anxious patients to experience a way of peaceful, soothing deep relaxation as would be considered appropriate and beneficial for a toddler. Consistent with Polyvagal Theory (Porges & Carter, 2016), these behavioral features are supported by a neurophysiological substrate that is manifested in peaceful immobilization that would facilitate deep, restorative relaxation. To get a better idea of the states elicited by our interventions, we use the *beseelbar* (animated) therapy objects. These include the mummy's tummy roll, the huggy horse, the big paradise egg, and the nest bag described in Vogt (2008, 2012, 2015).

These large therapy objects have been hand-tailored for us and have one feature in common: They function as surrogates for the maternal body. This makes it possible for our patients to float into positive and restorative relaxation, like toddlers, babies, or even embryos. Throughout this process, therapeutic support is always underpinned by eye contact or touch of hand.

Obviously, at the outset, therapists need to carefully explore whether any of the therapy objects are associated with traumatic experiences in any way. Such objects should only be used at a later stage of therapy. In the preliminary stages of therapy, a patient's biographical history and intuitive protective or anxious behavior already show what is or is not feasible at this point and with this therapist, to accomplish peaceful, deep relaxation for this specific patient. Often trauma patients see their trauma-stressed body as their biological enemy and have ceased to believe in the capacity for self-regulation. If one or more of these psychophysiologically relieving, late-nurturing settings are effective, this will usually have a long-lasting positive effect on the entire course of trauma therapy. On the one hand, clients experience their body as still being capable of a positive deep relaxation, which will, in turn, raise their hope for better self-regulation. On the other hand, active-experience settings for late nurturing foster the process of relationship building between patients and their psychotherapist. This is something words alone could not accomplish because the clients' understanding of their disorder is still working on a presymbolic (neuroceptive) level, and important relationship information is perceived on a rather implicit, interactive testing level. Consistent with Polyvagal Theory, we could hypothesize that the objective of applying SPIM 30 late-nurturing therapeutic settings is to shift from oscillating between sympathetic and dorsal vagal–dominated regulation to more ventral vagal control. The SPIM-30 and FSAP settings work with the client's current, more conscious inner regulation stage, providing action-oriented opportunities to objectify and slow down psychophysiological tension spirals, and to work out solutions for development (Vogt, 2008, 2015).

In dissociative post-traumatic disorders, different regulation states may coexist (Vogt, 2012, 2015), and with some practice, patients can gradually gain an increased awareness of them. The SPIM 30 therapeutic settings allow for clients to deliberately enter different regulatory states, such as trauma victim, perpetrator introject or everyday manager states, in a more controlled and less impulsive or chaotic way. In SPIM 30 therapeutic settings, clients can observe their physical stress situation and the thoughts and feelings that emerge in one regulation state as compared to those in other states. In this controlled approach, they can better sense their dissociative states and become more aware of them. We would hypothesize that on a neurophysiological level, these procedures would at various times activate each of the three primary physiological states defined in Polyvagal Theory (i.e., ventral vagal/social engagement, sympathetic/mobilization, dorsal vagal/immobilization).

Consistent with Polyvagal Theory, depending on the individual's degree of anxiety and stress in a given trigger situation, the dorsal vagal system would be alternatively activated together with the sympathetic nervous system, and the therapeutic relationship, as a calming resource, would enable the ventral vagal system to quickly and partially ease the negative conditioned dominance hierarchies.

The SPIM 30 FSAP setting is aimed at activating traumatic memories in a titrated way and in parallel with the conscious control entities (everyday manager part) that have attributes of the ventral vagal system that are capable of dampening hyperarousal and panic states (trauma victim and perpetrator introject parts) and developing new action initiatives. The therapeutic aim is to reduce phenomena such as body immobilization and motoric paralysis caused by mortal fear. A hypothesis linking these phenomena to Polyvagal Theory might be that the dorsal vagal regulation knocks on the neurophysiological door but, with the help of the therapeutically led SPIM 30 settings, can be modulated by the hierarchical nature of the autonomic nervous system that enables both the sympathetic nervous system and the ventral vagal system to downregulate the tendencies for the dorsal vagal system to respond defensively.

Trauma patients, who have experienced sadistic torture and developed regulation states VI or VII, are especially prone to moving into a dorsal vagus regulation disaster with near-death dorsal vagal dominance before or after experiencing the psychophysical switch-off point for all conscious emotional experience. The complicated regulation states before and after the switch-off point are outside the scope of this chapter. Hopefully, in the future neurobiological research will contribute additional explanations.

For clients with an extreme tendency to collapse, the therapeutic objective is to work through their traumatic experiences in a state of attenuated mental arousal. Dampening arousal will enable the reliving of the trauma sufficiently to be recognized without functionally reexperiencing the trauma with the physiological reaction that initially accompanied the trauma. The aim is for the client to link these experiences, or memories of them, in time, space, and place and to be able to endure them in a much calmer psychophysiological state and with a greater certainty of survival as compared to earlier shutdown experiences. To achieve this objective requires therapeutic skills and sensitivities to guide the client through the difficult trauma-processing work. In the SPIM 30 integration phase, over and over again, we need playful settings that provide periods of relief, which help refuel positive interpersonal as well as mental and psychophysical energy. A dialogue game with stuffed animals in individual therapy, or a group raft with several play objects, can provide a welcome relief for children as well as adult trauma patients (Vogt, 2015, 2016).

In terms of Polyvagal Theory, one could say that what we seek in the SPIM 30 approach is relief for our clients through therapy scenes that allow for a recruitment of ventral vagal control with attributes of the social engagement system, which is an efficient mechanism to generate and recharge positive interpersonal energy. At the same time, such shared experiences create an authentic bond with often developmentally delayed child parts of our trauma patients in a way that we could not accomplish with all the rational reassurances in the world.

To conclude, I hope these insights into the SPIM 30 treatment have demonstrated how our therapeutic approach to *human-induced* trauma bridges to the well-established neurophysiological features of Polyvagal Theory. The SPIM model has been developed gradually during the past 20 years. These changes occurred through iterative creative processes of search, trial and error, and through our attempts to put ourselves into our clients' contexts as we became familiar with their childlike analogic way of thinking and feeling. We continue to consistently work on updating the theory and clinical settings for our treatment model and continue to be informed by our colleagues who study trauma and behavioral neuroscience.

References

Abraham, N., & Torok, M. (1976). *Kryptonymie. Das Verbarium des Wolfsmannes.* Berlin, Germany: Ullstein.

Ainsworth, M. D. S. (1977). Feinfühligkeit versus Unempfindlichkeit gegenüber Signalen des Babys. In Grossmann, K. E. (Ed.), *Entwicklung der Lernfähigkeit in der sozialen Umwelt* (pp. 98–107). Munich, Germany: Kindler.

Bowlby, J. (1969). *Attachment and loss.* New York, NY: Basic Books.

Carter, C. S. (1998). Neuroendocrine perspectives on social attachment and love. *Psychoneuroendocrinology,* 23, 779–818.

De Shazer, S. (1989). Wege der erfolgreichen Kurztherapie. Stuttgart, Germany: Klett-Cotta.

Erickson, M. H., & Rossi, E. L. (2007). *Hypnotherapie.* Aufbau, Beispiele, Forschungen. (Leben Lernen 49). Stuttgart, Germany: Klett-Cotta.

Freud, A. (1936). *Das ICH und seine Abwehrmechanismen.* Vienna, Austria: Internationaler Psychoanalytischer Verlag.

Freud, S. (1892–1939). *Gesammelte Werke. Bd.* (Vols. I–XVIII). Frankfurt, Germany: Fischer TB.

Hüther, G. (1997). *Biologie der Angst.* Göttingen: Vandenhoek & Ruprecht.

Janet, P. (1901). *The mental state of hysterical.* New York, NY: Putnam & Sons.

Kluft, R. (1984). An introduction to multiple personality disorder. *Psychiatric Annals, 14,* 19–24.

Kluft, R. P. (2014). *Pacing in der Traumatherapie.* Lichtenau, Germany: Probst, G.P.

Leuner, H., Hennig, H., & Fikentscher, E. (1993). *Katathymes Bilderleben in der therapeutischen Praxis.* Stuttgart, Germany: Schattauer.

Main, M., & Solomon, J. (1986). Discovery of an insecure-disorganized/disoriented attachment pattern. In T. B. Brazelton & M. W. Yogman (Eds.), *Affective development in infancy* (pp. 95–124). Norwood, New Jersey: Ablex.

Nijenhuis, E. (2012). Strukturelle Dissoziation—Beispiele aus der Praxis. In Kongressband, *Gesichter der Gewalt* (pp. 124–131). Stuttgart, Germany: Eigenverlag.

Nijenhuis, E., Van der Hart, O., & Steele, K. (2008). *Das verfolgte Selbst.* Paderborn: Junferman.

Panksepp, J. (1998). *Affective Neuroscience. The foundations of human and animal emotions.* New York: Oxford University Press.

Porges, S. W. (2009). The Polyvagal Theory: New insights into adaptive reactions of the autonomic nervous system. *Cleveland Clinic Journal of Medicine, 76,* 86–90.

Porges, S. W., & Carter, C. S. (2016). Soziale Verbundenheit als biologischer Imperativ—Das Verständnis von Trauma aus dem Blickwinkel der The Polyvagal-Theorie. In R. Vogt (Ed.), *Täterbindung. Gruppenpsychotherapie und soziale Neurobiologie* (pp. 124–145). Kröning, Germany: Asanger S..

Porges, S. W., & Furman, S. A. (2011). The early development of the autonomic nervous system provides a neural platform for social behavior: A polyvagal perspective. *Infant and child Development, 20,* 106–118.

Putnam, F. W. (2003). *Diagnose und Behandlung der Dissoziativen Identitätsstörung.* Paderborn, Germany: Junfermann.

Reddemann, L. (2012). Was ist gute Therapie für komplex traumatisierte Patientinnen und Patienten. In C. Firus, C. Schleier, W. Geigges, & L. Reddemann (Eds.), *Traumatherapie in der Gruppe. Grundlagen, Gruppenarbeitsbuch und Therapie bei Komplextrauma* (pp. 161–186). Stuttgart, Germany: J.G. Cotta.

Schwartz, H. L. (2013). *The alchemy of wolves and sheep: A relational approach to internalized perpetration in complex trauma survivors.* New York, NY: Routledge.

Schwartz, R. (2008). *IFS Das System der Inneren Familie.* Norderstedt, Germany: Books on Demand GmbH.

Vogt, R. (2006). *"Beseelbare" Therapy Objects. Psychoanalytic interactional approach in a body- and trauma-oriented psychotherapy.* Giessen, Germany: Psychosozial-Verlag.

Vogt, R. (2008). *Psychotrauma, state, setting: Psychoanalytical-action-related model for a treatment of complexly traumatized patients.* Giessen, Germany: Psychosozial-Verlag.

Vogt, R. (Ed.). (2012). *Perpetrator introjects: Psychotherapeutic diagnostics and treatment models.* Kröning, Germany: Asanger.

Vogt, R. (Ed.). (2014). *Verleumdung und Verrat. Dissoziative Störungen bei schwer Traumatisierten als Folge von Vertrauensbrüchen.* Kröning, Germany: Asanger.

Vogt, R. (Ed.). (2015). *SPIM 30: Treatment model for dissociative trauma disorders.* Kröning, Germany: Asanger.

Vogt, R. (Ed.). (2016). *Täterbindung. Gruppenpsychotherapie und soziale Neurobiologie.* Kröning, Germany: Asanger.

Watkins, G. J., & Watkins, H. H. (2003). *Ego-States. Theorie und Therapie.* Heidelberg, Germany: Carl-Auer-Systeme Verlag.

Watzlawick, P., Beavin, J. H., & Jackson, D. D. (1967). Some tentative axioms of communication. In *Pragmatics of human communication: A study of interactional patterns, pathologies, and paradoxes* (pp. 48–71). New York, NY: Norton.

Weiss, T. (1988). *Familientherapie ohne Familie, Kurztherapie mit Einzelpatienten.* Munich, Germany: Kösel.

Wygotsky, L. S. (1986). *Denken und Sprechen* (6th ed.). Frankfurt/Main: Fischer

17

Treatment of Flight Phobia: A Polyvagal Perspective

Tom Bunn

Abstract: Stress hormones cause an urge to run and activate executive functions. Executive functions begin assessing the situation and inhibit the urge to run. Accurate assessment depends, in part, on the ability of reflective functions to discriminate imagination from perception. If stress hormones rise too high, reflective function collapses and imagination displaces perception. A fearful flier's concern that the plane may fall out of the sky becomes the belief it is happening. Polyvagal Theory informs the treatment of flight phobia and supports the proposition that, by establishing links between feelings of arousal and a memory of neuroceptive safety, arousal triggers the ventral vagal circuit, which overrides the effects of stress hormones, protects reflective function, and limits imagination-based distress.

I'm an engineer. I have a rational, logical thinking mind 99.99% of the time. A few days before the flight, I can see and feel what's going to happen. I'm going to be on a flight that'll crash.

AIRLINE FLYING IS remarkably safe. According to a *New York Times* article, Arnold Barnett, a professor of statistics at MIT, calculated that 45 million planes operate safely for every one that crashes. This high level of safety gives confidence to people whose executive function assesses risks versus rewards based on probability. To a fearful flier, the millions of flights that flew safely are meaningless. What matters is the other part of the statistic: the flight that crashed. Fearful fliers are dependent on the mobilization system; having no other system to regulate arousal, they are comfortable relinquishing mobilization only if they believe safety is absolute.

Passengers are invited to "sit back, relax, and enjoy your flight." That isn't possible for a mobilization system–dependent person; a person who, through a polyvagal lens (Porges, 2007, Porges, 2011), is experiencing an activated sympathetic nervous system survival response. When the plane leaves the ground, this person's ability to regulate arousal is all but lost. Expectation of returning to the ground holds him together emotionally. That expectation, however, is in conflict with another expectation: Since he sees nothing holding the plane up, he expects the plane to fall out of the sky.

As the plane climbs higher, the return fantasy becomes weaker. Physically, cruise is the safest part of the flight. Emotionally, it is the most difficult. Flight at night, or in clouds, causes a crisis. When the earth can't be seen, it is as if it no longer exists. The return fantasy falls apart. Panic results.

If there is no turbulence, distraction may keep this seemingly perilous situation out of mind. But, if turbulence begins, distraction ends. Why so? Imagine being on a stepladder, concentrating on painting the ceiling. If you were to lose your balance and fall, your amygdala would react. Stress hormones would cause alarm. In a state of alarm, intense concentration—in this case, on painting—would vanish. All you would be aware of is heading toward the floor. As long as a state of alarm exists, you must focus on what the amygdala is reacting to. Similarly, when the amygdala senses the plane drop, stress hormones are released that cause alarm.

The fearful flier's ordeal continues until the plane begins its descent. Though most accidents occur during landing, anticipation of return to the ground revitalizes the person's mobilization fantasy and brings relief.

Alarm

When your phone rings, its alarm intrudes into your awareness. When you answer the phone, it stops ringing. Consider how difficult it would be to have a conversation if the ringing did not stop.

Similarly, when stress hormone release causes alarm, the amygdala grabs your attention. Alarm must be attenuated before executive function can assess the situation and determine what, if any, action needs to be taken.

Attenuation of alarm takes place far too quickly to be the result of stress hormones wearing off. What, then, could cause attenuation of alarm? Polyvagal Theory (Porges, 2011) tells us that stimulation of the vagus nerve can quickly override the effects of stress hormones by slowing the heart and activating the parasympathetic nervous system. I propose that alarm attenuation is caused by stimulation of the vagus due to experiences early in a child's life when alarm was quickly and reliably followed by a caregiver's signals of neuroceptive safety.

When in a ventral vagal state of calm, looking inward at our mental processing allows us to critique our thinking and to intuitively sense whether we are engaged in perception or imagination. This looking inward has several names—reflective function, meta-awareness, metacognition, and so on. But when stress hormones rise high enough, reflective function disappears. As the autonomic nervous system moves out of the safety of ventral vagal regulation into the adaptive survival responses of the sympathetic or dorsal vagal systems, the distinction between imagination and perception is lost. This loss causes what psychoanalyst Peter Fonagy calls *psychic equivalence*. In a state of psychic equivalence, whatever is in the mind—imagination included—is experienced as perception. In this state, says Fonagy, imagination takes on "the full force of reality" (Fonagy & Bateman, 2006, p. 9).

In the air, stress hormones are released each time the plane drops. If not well regulated, stress hormones build up. If they cause reflective function to collapse, thoughts that the plane is falling out of the sky are experienced as though it were happening.

On the ground, stress hormones are released by anxiety-producing thoughts. Stress hormones can cause psychic equivalence in a person whose vagal braking system does not protect reflective function. Before treatment, one client would panic if he glanced at his digital clock and it read 7:37 or 7:47. Some phobic fliers avoid looking upward for fear they will see a plane and panic.

For years, nothing could be done to help fliers whose alarm was not adequately attenuated. Pilots believed that knowing how safe flying is should end fear. But, for a mobilization-dependent person, only absolute safety is adequate when mobilization is blocked. Therapists insisted that rational thinking should stop fear. But rational assessment of flying is not possible when stress induces psychic equivalence. Some advocated relaxation, saying a person cannot be fearful and relaxed at the same time. But relaxation falls apart when turbulence makes it seem like the plane is falling out of the sky. Desensitization to actual flight could not be graduated. Computer-generated imagery could be graduated, but it offered no exposure—and thus no desensitization—to risk, loss of control, and inability to escape.

With its hierarchy of arousal-regulating systems, Polyvagal Theory illuminated the problem. Regulation is first attempted by the most advanced system. If that fails to regulate arousal, regulation reverts to the next most advanced system, and so on. Since the autonomic nervous system is toned in relationship with others, and early relationships have an important impact on our autonomic response patterns, how well advanced systems work varies greatly from individual to individual.

Arousal Regulation Systems

Level 1: the immobilization system; the dorsal vagal complex. Strategy: Freeze. The most primitive system defends by involuntarily feigning death when attacked. Effective for creatures that can remain immobile indefinitely. Immobilization is problematic for mammals; immobilization sharply reduces blood flow to the brain.

Level 2: the mobilization system; the sympathetic nervous system. Strategy: Fight-or-flight. In this somewhat more sophisticated system, the amygdala reacts to changes in the environment by releasing stress hormones, which urge escape.

Level 3: executive function; cognitive. Strategy: Assess and manage risk. When activated by stress hormones, executive function surveys the situation. In optimal operation, vagal braking protects reflective function mentalization. If no threat is found, executive function terminates the alert. If a threat is identified, it considers options. Upon commitment to a strategy, it ends stress hormone release. Suboptimally, in the absence of vagal braking, stress hormones cause reflective function failure, leading executive function to equate threats based on and imagination with threats based on perception.

Level 4: the social engagement system; ventral vagal system. Strategy: Externally referenced neuroception of social safety overrides the effects of stress hormones by vagal braking, activating the parasympathetic nervous system, attenuating alarm, and inhibiting the urge to mobilize. Neuroception of safety facilitates executive function by safeguarding reflective function. Maximum vagal stimulation is produced by neuroception of physical and emotional safety.

Based on work with thousands of fearful fliers, I propose that there is a Level 5, which attenuates alarm via reference to internal replicas of neuroceptively safe past experience. This view is based on the observation that thousands of persons who suffered from panic no longer do so, in the air or on the ground, after links have been established between arousal and a memory in which their guard was caused to be let down by the presence of a neuroceptively safe person.

Attenuation of arousal via memory of neuroceptive safety in my SOAR model is presented as a foundation for self-regulation (as contrasted with other regulation produced by the physical presence of a neuroceptively safe person).

> Level 5: the internal replica system. Strategy: Internally referenced memory of neuroceptive safety overrides the effects of stress hormones. Through vagal braking, it attenuates alarm, and activates the parasympathetic nervous system.

In early experience, if alarm is consistently responded to in a way that produces a neuroception of safety, the alarm-safety sequence becomes an active working model in the mind. Thereafter, alarm triggers attenuation of arousal.

The internal replica system may successfully regulate arousal. Or it may produce alarm attenuation, which facilitates executive function. When the internal replica system is resource poor, no regulation or alarm attenuation takes place at Level 5, but may be available at Level 4 through social engagement with a neuroceptively safe person.

If social engagement is unsuccessful, regulation reverts to Level 3, executive function. If alarm attenuation has taken place, executive function surveys the environment, and, if a threat is identified, assesses options. Upon commitment, whether to a plan of action or to an assessment that no action is called for, executive function signals the amygdala to end stress hormone release. The person returns to homeostasis. This is the natural flow of autonomic response moving between ventral vagal regulation, sympathetic distress, and back into ventral vagal balance.

Without the benefit of some attenuation from Level 5 or Level 4, executive function is impaired. Without attenuation, reflective function collapses and psychic equivalence takes place. Executive function is unable to differentiate imagination from perception. Imagined threats are experienced as genuine. As executive function considers options to deal with threats, the outcome seems certain. An optimist imagines success, whereas a pessimist imagines failure. Psychic equivalence causes the optimist to regard whatever plan is in mind as certain to succeed, while the pessimist sees every plan as certain to fail. This leads an optimist to a premature commitment, but renders the pessimist unable to commit at all. Without commitment, executive function cannot end stress hormone release. Unable to regulate arousal, the person slides into Level 2, mobilization's fight-or-flight.

Suffering From Imagination

Fearful fliers do not suffer from what is happening on a flight. They suffer from imagination, which, due to psychic equivalence, is experienced as happening. A neuroception of danger or life-threat activates an autonomic state of dysregulation, and the state becomes the story. There are two sources of such suffering: (a) what people believe is happening to the plane, which they cannot escape, and (b) what people believe is happening to them during panic, which they cannot escape.

Mobilization and Panic

When stress hormones cause alarm, if alarm is attenuated, the result is a slight increase in heart and breathing rates, which prepares the body to mobilize. Perspiration evaporates and cools the body, also in preparation for mobilization. Psychologically, regulated arousal produces alertness. Executive function, operating optimally, assesses the situation and regulates the autonomic response.

But when alarm is not attenuated by a neuroception of safety at Level 5 by a replica of relationship or at Level 4 by an actual relationship, the person slips into Level 3 executive function. There, the person experiences pounding heart, hyperventilation, and sweatiness. If reflective function is overwhelmed, executive function, impaired by the merging of imagination with perception, cannot regulate arousal. Following the predictable hierarchy of Polyvagal Theory, arousal regulation reverts to the Level 2 mobilization system. Relief takes place when a clear escape route is seen, hence the expression "light at the end of the tunnel."

When the Level 2 mobilization system is active, executive function is not available. The ability to think one's way through ordinary obstacles such as stairs, doors, or elevators has collapsed. Without an obvious clear escape route, panic results.

I'm reminded of an incident when I was stationed in Germany. Our squadron was flying the Air Force's first supersonic jet fighter. It was not a safe plane. One out of three F-100s built crashed. At lunch one day, a few of us were discussing what was frightening about flying the F-100. One pilot said, "You are all a bunch of candy-asses. I'm not afraid of anything." The following year, when we switched from F-100s to F-105s, he was assigned to fly one of our new planes from Mobile, Alabama, to our base in Germany. To make the trip, three external fuel tanks were fitted to the plane, one on each wing and one under the belly.

The belly tank had only a few inches of clearance with the runway. On takeoff, he raised the landing gear prematurely, causing the belly tank to scrape the runway. Fuel leaking from the tank streamed back toward the engine's exhaust, where it ignited. Since the flame was behind the plane, the pilot was in no danger. The control tower saw the plume of fire, but did not realize the fire was trailing behind the plane, and so radioed the pilot that his plane was on fire.

Fighter pilots are trained for emergencies. The first step in an emergency is to hit the panic button to jettison the external tanks. Shedding the weight of fuel in the external tanks makes the plane easy to maneuver. In spite of this training, he failed to jettison the external tanks. He turned back toward the runway so abruptly that, with the heavy load of fuel, the plane stalled and plunged into Mobile Bay. He was killed.

Why did he not think to do what every fighter pilot is trained to do automatically? Why did he not hit the panic button? When his plane stalled, why did he not eject? In the accident investigation that followed, it was discovered that he had a phobia of water. Though Air Force pilots must know how to swim, whenever there was a swimming test, he went to the base medical center, claiming to be sick. Afraid of water, an emergency situation over water caused this pilot's executive function to shut down. Emotional regulation descended to his primitive mobilization system. His mobilization system only knew how to run. It did not know how to hit the panic button. It did not know how to fly the plane. The mobilization system, demanding immediate escape, turned him abruptly—too abruptly for the plane to handle—back toward the runway he had just taken off from.

What Does Panic Consist Of?

Panic is described as pounding heart, hyperventilation, sweating, massive tension, and psychological changes such as depersonalization, derealization, dissociation, and loss of sense of identity, place, and time.

Actually, panic is none of these. Each can be experienced without panic. Instead, panic results when a mobilization system–dependent person experiences a situation as life-threatening and inescapable. For example, a person feels his heart pounding and experiences a neuroception of danger. This may trigger the thought that this might be a heart attack. The thought triggers the release of stress hormones. If the mobilization system is active, the increased arousal cannot be attenuated. Loss of reflective function leads to psychic equivalence, which causes the thought to be experienced as reality. Since the heart attack threat is within the body, the Level 2 mobilization system is unable to regulate arousal. Thus, panic—and possibly descent into Level 1 immobilization—follows. A person who experiences physiological changes may, via psychic equivalence, regard this as going crazy.

Fonagy suggested that people with good self-esteem may have as many negative thoughts about themselves as people with poor self-esteem. The difference in self-esteem may be due to how easily psychic equivalence takes place. When a negative self-image thought comes to mind, it triggers stress hormones. If reflective function is weak, psychic equivalence causes acceptance of the negative thought as if it were a fact. On the other hand, a person not prone to psychic equivalence would regard the thought as merely conjecture.

Thus the question is this: When arousal takes place and a person feels physical or psychological changes, does his reflective function remain viable? If it does, the person knows he is involved in conjecture and does not panic. On the other hand, if reflective function shuts down, either due to weak reflective function, to lack of alarm attenuation, or to a combination of the two, conjecture is experienced as reality. The physical or psychological change is experienced as a life-threatening emergency.

Through a polyvagal perspective, the difference might be conceptualized in this way. When arousal begins, the vagal brake starts to release to meet the challenge. If the vagal braking response adequately regulates the neuroception of danger, there is a return to the ventral vagal state of safety. If the vagal braking response in not able to meet the neuroceptive challenge, instead of a return to regulation, there is a shift into a survival response.

If links between each element of panic and a memory of neuroceptive safety are able to safeguard reflective function, panic can be prevented. For example, when executive function is not impaired, it recognizes that when someone is at the gym, his target heart rate to gain aerobic benefit is 140 beats per minute. However, when psychic equivalence impairs executive function, 115 beats per minute means heart attack. Similarly, hyperventilation can mean nothing or it can mean suffocation. Physiological changes may be experienced as interesting or as going insane.

Finding a Memory of Neuroceptive Safety

Full neuroceptive safety can be elusive. In social settings, people may be competitive, judgmental, or critical. Maximum override of the effects of stress hormones is produced by both a physical and an emotional neuroception of safety.

To demonstrate vagal braking, recall a time with a friend who, at that moment, had no judgment of you in mind whatsoever. As you recall the person's presence, how their facial expressions change, how their voice modulates, how their body is relaxed, do you feel your guard being let down? If so, you are experiencing the effects of vagal braking and the impact of the social engagement system. Memory of neuroceptive safety can cause one's guard to be let down and bring a return of ventral vagal regulation.

Linking Alarm to Neuroceptive Safety

Links between alarm and neuroceptive safety establish circuitry that causes alarm to trigger vagal braking and parasympathetic nervous system activation.

Typically, panic begins with one of its elements, and spreads to a second element, which triggers a third, and so on, until there is full-blown panic. Panic can be prevented by safeguarding reflective function with links between each element of panic and memory of neuroceptive safety. Links should be established between neuroceptive safety and hyperventilation, pounding heart, sweating, body tension, psychological changes, and digestive issues. When each element of panic is neutralized by a link to neuroceptive safety, clients report that panic does not develop on the plane or on the ground.

Linking a Challenging Activity to Neuroceptive Safety

Links between an activity, or to a situation, and neuroceptive safety can prevent amygdala reaction. To link vagal braking to an activity or a situation, break it down into its parts. Link each part to a memory of being with a safe person. Imagine the person is holding a black-and-white snapshot showing a part of the activity near their face. A visual link is established quickly when the person's face, voice, and body language are held in mind simultaneously with a flight situation. An auditory link can be established by imagining that you and your friend turn to the photograph and have a conversation about it. A kinesthetic link can be added by imagining, as the two of you discuss the photograph, that the other person touches your hand. Here we are using elements the autonomic nervous system responds to—facial expression, vocal prosody, movement, and touch—to activate cues of safety.

The exercise needs to be anxiety free. A small black-and-white photograph signals to the mind that this is not an actual situation and does not need to be reacted to. If more psychological distance is needed, a cartoon depicting the situation can be used instead of a photograph.

Detailed information on treatment of flight phobia based on Polyvagal Theory is found in *SOAR: The Breakthrough Treatment for Fear of Flying* (Bunn, 2013).

Reducing Mobilization System Dependency

Some people who express concern about safety when flying say they would fly without hesitation if an anesthesiologist could knock them out before takeoff and wake them up upon arrival. Though unconsciousness does not guarantee a safe arrival, it does rule out problems with regulation of arousal.

Even when physical safety is assured, mobilization dependency can make elevators, tunnels, subways, and MRIs difficult. A mobilization-dependent person may require an end seat in a theater to ensure arousal regulation. Travel on expressways and interstate highways can trigger panic when an exit is not in view.

Viewed through the lens of Polyvagal Theory, arousal-regulation systems are seen as phylogenetically hierarchical. Each newly appearing arousal-regulating system was more sophisticated than its predecessor. Regulation is first attempted by the most advanced system. If it is unsuccessful, regulation reverts to the next most advanced system. However, the more sophisticated the system, the more individual development is required for it to function effectively.

When advanced system development is not facilitated, a person must depend on the system that requires no development, the mobilization system. This dependency may be alleviated by furthering the development of the social engagement system and the internal replica system. Development can be achieved by establishing links of neuroceptive safety to alarm, high levels of arousal, and to situations that trigger arousal.

Links between alarm and neuroceptive safety attenuate alarm. Links between situation triggers and neuroceptive safety prevent alarm. Both safeguard reflective function, prevent psychic equivalence, and—by enabling executive function to regulate arousal—frees the client from dependency on the mobilization system.

I sent an e-mail asking about panic before and after a course designed for the most difficult flight phobia cases, and 21 clients responded. All 21 reported in-flight panic prior to the course. After the course, 15 were panic free, and 6 experienced much less panic. Though the course was aimed at in-flight panic, benefit generalized to panic on the ground. Prior to the course, 15 reported panic on the ground; after the course, 13 reported they were panic free on the ground. The remaining 2 said panic was much less frequent on the ground.

The Calming Effect of Neuroceptive Safety

After Polyvagal Theory had been used in fear of flying treatment, several counseling sessions with volunteer clients were taped to produce a video-based fear of flying course. One client in particular illustrated the dynamics of Polyvagal Theory with regard to arousal regulation.

The client was born during the Hungarian Revolution to parents active in underground operations against the regime. During her first months of life, the client's mother was terrified that she and her husband would be identified and imprisoned or executed. When they were told that the government suspected them, they quickly escaped. This client has had lifelong difficulties with anxiety. Her younger sister, born in the U.S., has had none.

The sister's lack of anxiety suggests that in the U.S. the mother was able to provide predictable experiences of internalizable neuroceptive safety. But prior to escaping Hungary, extreme anxiety, her own ongoing neuroception of danger, made it impossible for her to provide the first daughter with internalizable neuroceptive safety.

The following text is transcribed from a counseling session with the client in which an experience with her father was linked to arousal and to challenging moments of flight.

TOM: Something I've been doing a lot of thinking about recently is how, as soon as we get lifted off the ground, we're like a fish out of water. On the ground is where we have control, and if we have anxiety, what we want to do is get more control to get rid of it. The other way we get rid of anxiety is through an empathic connection between us and another person. *(That is, using reciprocity and co-regulation.)* When there's an empathic connection, there's a feeling of being safe. When there's an empathic connection, the other person is not a threat to us. See, if they do something that hurts us, it only hurts them. So when kids do get that empathic connection and get calmed by it—and get that built into them—they don't get anxiety problems. *(These are experiences that exercise the capacities of the vagal brake.)* They feel secure. But if you don't get that, you turn to control, to add to whatever is built inside. And on the ground, we have some of both. Some connection and some control. But in the air, we lose both. So if you think of Linus's security blanket, it's something he uses to maintain a feeling of being connected to his mother. His own internalization of what she's done to calm him is not sufficient for him. If the ground is our security blanket—what we use to feel connected to people who calm us—what can we do when it's taken away from us? What we do in the SOAR Program is the "strengthening exercise" to provide a direct connection—skip the transitional object—go straight to the feeling that gives security. *(Neuroception of safety.)* And once you get to that feeling, you want to momentarily flick on a picture of the airplane situation and go right back to that feeling. And that feeling gets wrapped around the thought. If we do it with every thought, if we wrap every thought about flying, even the terrible ones, in that feeling of connectedness which helps us take care of the anxiety, then we've got something that will help. Well, that reminds me of what worked one time with you and your father.

CLIENT: Yes. The snowman. It's as clear to me now as it was then. And the feeling that I have—had—in conveying that episode to you, I still feel the calm from that. Still feel—I don't know if calm is the right word—peacefulness, the connectedness, safety, the peacefulness internally and externally all around me. I do envision that as kind of my force field, my bubble, that I go into. It was a night in winter. And, it had snowed. It was a Sunday night, I think, and my sister and my dad and I put on our gear. We went outside and we built a snowman, and had fun, and laughs. But I felt this really strong connectedness with my dad, and it was something that I always had with him, and this may be the source of the safety that I look for. He was a source of protection to us. And for me, it's always been important, the perceived safety that I feel. And he was that for me. He was a very calming, connected, fatherly, loving, protective dad. And that night personified that. And it was just us enveloped in this darkness around us, full moon.

TOM: Like a protective sphere around you. *(Identifying the cues of safety.)*

CLIENT: Absolutely.

TOM: If you go to that feeling, let me ask you to pretend something. As you're playing in the snow, you happen to glance down, and there's a photograph lying in the snow of a plane parked at some terminal. You're not involved, because it's a photograph. And then it gets covered up by the snow and you look back at your father. And you feel that force field of protection. And then as you look at the snowman, you happen to glance down, and maybe it's a clipping in a newspaper of an airplane just about to land. And as you continue working on the snowman, you look at your dad's eyes. He looks at you. And there's this really remarkable connection. *(Cue of safety.)* And you look down and there is a magazine that's been discarded, and there's a picture of an airplane cruising, and you go back to your father again. *(Cue of safety.)* And we can do that with each of the things that happen on a normal flight. And then, during a normal flight, instead of the flight taking energy from you, it brings you to that connectedness—everything that happens on the plane gives you a sense of being with your father. *(Active use of the imagined co-regulation to maintain a neuroception of safety.)*

CLIENT: Almost like an umbilical cord. That's what I feel almost, when I'm imagining this.

Reflecting on this counseling session, we see this client had vivid recall of an experience of neuroceptive safety with her father. This experience did not, however, generalize spontaneously to other areas of her life. All that was needed to give her more sophisticated arousal regulation was to link the experience of neuroceptive safety with her father to the challenging situations in which she had, until then, depended upon the mobilization system.

I find it, indeed, remarkable that it can take only one experience of neuroceptive safety to transform a client's ability to regulate arousal. A jar of peanut butter that can be spread on as many crackers as you want to. One experience of neuroceptive safety can be linked to each aspect of alarm, and to situations that trigger alarm.

Links to Neuroceptive Safety After Exposure to Exceptional Threat

Traumatized by a turbulent flight to Mexico, a man canceled plans for a honeymoon in Greece and instead drove to South Carolina. After treatment that established links between flight and neuroceptive safety, he was able to fly successfully. A major setback occurred on 9/11. He was on the 25th floor of North Tower of the World Trade Center when it was struck. A series of counseling sessions were done in which challenging flight situations and his 9/11 experiences were linked to his wife and his son. His return to flying—as confident as before after an intensely traumatic experience—is a dramatic illustration of the calming power of neuroceptive safety.

Summary

Stress hormones trigger a sympathetic nervous system response known as the fight-or-flight response. This survival response is habitual for people who are mobilization system dependent. Fight-or-flight is the response expressed when the Level 2 mobilization system is activated. Immediate default to fight-or-flight may result when alarm is unattenuated, when arousal has been too often followed by trauma, or when there is a lack of experience-dependent learning that allows arousal to simply be experienced as arousal, and a neuroceptively safe experience.

After alarm has been linked to a memory of neuroceptive safety, ventral vagal activity attenuates alarm. Attenuation facilitates optimal executive function and assessment of the situation in order to determine the cause of the alarm, and to determine what, if any, action is called for. Experience with thousands of fearful fliers has shown that when alarm has been linked to a relational memory of neuroceptive safety, automatic ventral vagal regulation takes place and frees the person from dependency on the mobilization system.

References

Bunn, T. (2013). *SOAR: The breakthrough treatment for fear of flying.* Guilford, CT: Lyons Press.

Fonagy, P., & Bateman, A. (2006). *Mentalization-based treatment for borderline personality disorder: A practical guide.* Oxford, England: Oxford University Press.

Fonagy, P., Gergely, G., Jurist, E. L., & Target, M. (2004). *Affect regulation, mentalization, and the development of the self.* New York, NY: Other Press.

Mouawad, J., & Drew, C. (2013, February 11). Airline industry at its safest since the dawn of the jet age. *The New York Times.* Retrieved from www.nytimes.com

Porges, S.W. (2007). The polyvagal perspective. *Biological Psychology, 74,*116-143.

Porges, S. W. (2011). *The polyvagal theory: Neurophysiological foundations of emotions, attachment, communication, self-regulation.* New York, NY: Norton.

18

Grief Through the Lens of Polyvagal Theory: Humanizing Our Clinical Response to Loss

Candyce Ossefort-Russell

Abstract: Losing a loved one is excruciating. Grief's emotions are intense and difficult to control. Western culture downplays suffering and creates a desolate environment for grieving. This chapter discusses how Polyvagal Theory provides a counterpoint to ineffective cultural grief responses. The lens of Polyvagal Theory makes sense of loss responses, and describes restorative environments. It normalizes immense physical and emotional grief responses, and explains the necessity of social safety for healing, contrasting with cultural exacerbation of defensive reactions. Clinicians learn to provide a neural platform of safety that helps grievers heal and restore. A case example illustrates this approach to grief.

Person-to-person interactions that trigger neural circuits promoting calm physiological states can contribute to health, healing, and growth processes. Alternatively, threatening interactions trigger defensive strategies.
—Stephen Porges (2011a, p. 295)

NOTHING CAN PREPARE us for the reverberating silence that loss leaves in its wake. The harsh contrast between our everyday drive to connect with the people we're closest to and the harrowing reality that no connection is available is "one of the most painful experiences any human being can suffer" (Bowlby, 1980, p. 7). Losing an attachment figure disrupts our most basic physiological functions (Lewis, Amini, & Lannon, 2000), shatters foundational assumptions about ourselves and our world (Janoff-Bulman, 1992), overturns roles and routines, and unravels our identities (Horowitz, 2014), leaving even the most courageous among us afraid and overwhelmed. Having lived through grief on both sides of the therapy room, I understand this devastation well.

Twenty-five years ago, when my son was an infant, my husband suddenly died. Week after unbearable week, I collapsed into my therapist's overstuffed chair in a trembling heap, sobbing into countless tissues and screaming rage at the universe. But because I walked through the darkness of loss with a helper who never turned away, I was able to painstakingly rebuild my shattered world in a spacious, resilient, creative way.

Transformed by loss, I became a therapist privileged to offer my clients the wisdom, acceptance, and compassion I learned. Now I provide the metaphorical lap for grieving clients to fall into. I collect the wadded-up tissues and bear the screaming rage. And I help with grief that manifests as mute numbness, choked-back tears, or the need to quickly paste a self back together.

From both sides of the therapy room, I know that the key to rebuilding life after loss is having the support of at least one person who can bear to *be with* the grief process, no matter how long it takes, no matter how messy it is. "Our capacity to heal ourselves is physically linked to our relationships with other people. . . . [At times of vulnerability], the quality of the person-to-person interactions between a caretaker and those being cared for is critical for survival" (Porges, 2011a, p. 295).

Yet Western culture creates a desolate environment for grieving. Our society underplays the importance of emotions (Lewis et al., 2000), emphasizes happiness while downplaying suffering (Janoff-Bulman, 1992), and assumes that "rational men and women can keep their mourning under control by strength of will or character" (Gilbert, 2006, p. 249). A client, Tina, cried as she said, "I finally made it back to church, and people smiled saying, 'I bet it's getting better now, isn't it?' Better? Are they kidding? My son died three months ago! When I complained to the minister, he said people are upbeat because they worry I might cry. I thought crying was normal! What's wrong with me?"

Polyvagal Theory provides a much-needed counterpoint to these ineffective cultural responses to loss. What the theory reveals—about how the nervous system responds adaptively to threat, what helps us return to safety, how past experience might make recovery difficult, and how safe environments support healing and growth—shifts us away from abandoning attitudes, and toward the safety of compassion. "Within the polyvagal theory there is no such thing as good or bad responses—these are miraculous, adaptive responses. . . . This takes a lot of what I call the 'moral veneer' away from these responses" (Porges, 2013a, p. 15).

This chapter uses the lens of Polyvagal Theory to normalize and make sense of universal and individual responses to loss, and to describe restorative environments. First, I'll explore the social safety needed for rebuilding after loss and how our culture exacerbates feelings of danger instead of returning clients to safety. Then, in order to help therapists feel safe with the intensity they see in their grieving clients, I'll use Polyvagal Theory to make sense of the enormity of physical and emotional grief responses. Next, I'll show clinicians—now fortified with demystifying information—how they can understand their own reactions in order to become part of a neural platform of safety that helps grievers heal and restore. Finally, I'll give an in-depth case example that illustrates this polyvagal-informed response to loss.

Evaluation Exacerbates; Compassion Heals

Compassion is neurophysiologically incompatible with judgmental, evaluative, and defensive behaviors and feelings.
—Stephen Porges (2012)

According to Polyvagal Theory, the nervous system processes sensory information from internal and external environments, continually evaluating risk. Below conscious awareness, through a process Stephen Porges calls *neuroception*, neural circuits distinguish whether situations or people are safe, dangerous, or life-threatening (2011a). When we detect safety, our neurobiology triggers the ventral vagal circuit that generates socially engaged behavior and supports health and healing. When we detect unsafety, our neurobiology triggers either the sympathetic nervous system that activates fight-or-flight defensive strategies (mobilization with fear); or the dorsal vagal circuit that activates defensive strategies of shutdown (immobilization with fear).

As described below, loss creates "high-risk" conditions that generate overwhelming emotions and elicit innate danger and life-threat responses. Socially, we have a profound need to be understood when we experience this level of extreme emotional threat (Siegel, 2012, p. 275). So it's important that we provide understanding environments that help clients return to safety, especially since our death-averse Western culture gets caught in defensive responses that basically abandon grievers.

One way we desert them is by acting from a defensive dorsal vagal immobilization response of avoiding grief altogether. We don't mention the loss. We offer simplistic platitudes. We praise those who show little emotion as "strong." George Bonanno, a prominent grief researcher who promotes the avoidance perspective, says that resilient grievers are "those who had no signs of depression at any point before or after the spouse's death and almost no grief at any point during bereavement" (2009, p. 70). He believes that sadness that's "too strong" or "prolonged" is "pernicious and dysfunctional" (p. 96). His view is that "the pain of severe grief is real . . . but often is fueled by an illogical chain of reasoning. . . . The therapist's job is to help separate fact from fiction" (p. 111).

Another way we betray grievers is by using a sympathetic nervous system defensive mobilization response to "attempt to organize a process that is inherently chaotic" (Ericsson, 1993, p. 21). We cling to oversimplified grief stages like denial, bargaining, and so on. We believe it takes a fixed amount of time to complete the grief process, and express surprise when our friends still hurt after more than a year. We worry about family members who aren't doing their "grief work." Specialists who use this grief-task perspective, like William Worden, contend that there are certain manualized "principles and procedures that make grief counseling effective" (2009, p. 89); specific guidelines a therapist must follow to help the client accomplish the "four grief tasks" that lead to a timely, "good adaption" (p. 89).

Either way, "Western society has added another, distinctively clinical anxiety [to the anxiety of grievers]: Am I *recovering* from the *illness* of grief at a proper rate?" (Gilbert, 2006, p. 257). In fact, much grief literature compels therapists to distinguish "normal" grief from grief that's exaggerated, abnormal, complicated, excessive in duration, too strong, or prolonged (Bonanno, 2009; Neimeyer, 2001; Worden, 2009). Instead of encouraging us to offer acceptance and understanding, this evaluative process tugs us out of engaged social warmth and pushes us instead to assess the value and style of our clients' emotional states (Bowlby, 1980; Fraley & Shaver, 1999; Gilbert, 2006; Ossefort, 2000; Ossefort-Russell, 2013; Porges, 2012). Conversely, if clients come to therapy with "normal" grief, clinicians often tell them they don't need therapy and refer them instead to short-term support groups, even though their intensely disrupted nervous systems can be crying out for the dedicated attention of individual therapy.

These evaluative attitudes are neurophysiologically incompatible with compassionate, ventral vagal–engaged warmth (Porges, 2012). Traditional, diagnostic grief perspectives actually recruit therapists' defensive circuits, causing us to transmit judgmental social communication below conscious awareness. Clients viscerally and instantaneously read intentionality from therapists' facial expressions, gestures, and intonation, unconsciously discerning whether they're being received with authentic acceptance or evaluative defensiveness (Porges, 2011b).

When grieving people come to therapy—with neural circuits triggered into sympathetic fight-or-flight and dorsal vagal shutdown—our own fear or lack of acceptance will unconsciously pull us out of social engagement and into sympathetic or dorsal vagal defenses from which we will emit social cues that *increase* clients' neuroception of danger, amplifying their existing neural states of distress and defensiveness (Porges, 2011b, 2013b). And if we fail to show understanding during a time of intensity like this, we can also evoke profound feelings of shame, leading to a downward spiral of isolation and withdrawal (Siegel, 2015). Unintentionally, evaluative grief models perpetuate defensive therapist behaviors that limit grieving clients' range of emotional expression; quality of communication; and ability to regulate bodily and behavioral states, including expression of stress-related emotions (Porges, 2011a). To counter these negative effects, we need to cultivate environments of compassionate safety that are sincerely warm and loving, not defensively evaluative (Porges, 2011b).

To be fair to clinicians who help people with grief, the culture doesn't create a climate of safety for us either. Our profession's evaluative, defense-inducing stance toward grief is perpetuated in graduate programs and postgraduate training. Medical models of therapy leave us with few ways to conceive of grief *except* with evaluation. The polyvagal concept of neuroception and its role in shaping physical, emotional, and behavioral responses is a powerful new perspective for clarifying how therapists and their grieving clients respond to loss. When we have a coherent way to make sense of the intensity that's happening in front of and inside us, we can return to a safe, compassionate physiological state from which we can offer care that can return our clients to safety (Geller & Porges, 2014; Ossefort-Russell, 2013; Porges, 2013a).

A Polyvagal Lens Demystifies Grief Responses

Demystifying people's behavior helps to regulate it.
—Stephen Porges (2011b)

The enormity, unexpectedness, and duration of distressing grief responses cause them to be experienced by grievers and helpers as an undifferentiated, tangled knot of pain. Instead of evaluating this messy clump of grief responses, Polyvagal Theory helps us tease apart its separate threads, explaining how each strand makes adaptive sense and how to weave these strands together for healing.

We can explore griever and therapist responses via the concept of neuroception and how it shapes responses to the environment. Bodily, emotional, and behavioral responses (such as responses to loss) emerge from a complex interaction between the environment and an individual's neuroception (Porges, 2011a). From this perspective, it's impossible to make sense of grief responses without understanding grievers' and therapists' unique environments and neuroceptive processes.

Making Sense of Clients' Grief Responses

To understand client grief responses, we'll explore the ways that loss is universally threatening, and the ways grief responses are affected by grievers' unique external and internal environments, neuroception, and social support systems.

LOSS: AN INTRINSICALLY THREATENING ENVIRONMENT

Loss of a loved one thrusts us into a painful, chaotic environment. Whether death is expected or not, we cannot be prepared for the inexorable silence of instantaneous, irrevocable absence. Permanent absence of someone we love is the epitome of acute disconnectedness, a massive violation of expectancy in face-to-face interaction that profoundly disrupts our ability to regulate our bodies and our emotions (Porges, 2011a; 2011b; 2015). The agonizing contrast between the drive to connect and the reality that no connection is available (Siegel, 2015) is an "attachment emergency" (Bowlby, 1980) that "jeopardizes our sense of security . . . and leads to 'primal panic'" (Johnson, 2008, p. 30). Such devastating loss of connection can cause distress so powerful that it breaks through well-practiced protective strategies, unresponsive to efforts to control it, leaving us feeling powerless to get away from it (Fosha, 2000).

The experience of grief, then, is "brutally physiological. It literally takes your breath away. Its physicality is also what makes grief so hard to communicate to anyone who hasn't experienced it" (O'Rourke, 2011, Location 1670–1671). Losing an attachment figure causes "somatic disarray" (Lewis et al., 2000, p. 83), disrupting cardiovascular function, hormone levels, sleep rhythms, and immune processes (p. 80). "Insomnia is near universal; headaches, anxiety, tension and fatigue are extremely common" (Bowlby, 1980, p. 100). Many people describe "a tightness in the throat, choking with shortness of breath, need for sighing, and an empty feeling in the abdomen, lack of muscular power, and an intensive subjective distress described as tension or mental pain" (Lindemann, 1944, as cited in O'Rourke, Location 1665). Grievers commonly report dizziness; emotional numbness; loss of appetite; feelings of fear, dread, and intense sorrow; muscle spasms; concentration and memory difficulties; social withdrawal; and profound loneliness. The physicality, feared-to-be-unbearable emotional pain, and duration of typical grief responses is often shocking and overwhelming, even for people who have good social support. Encountering such intense, long-lasting responses, possibly for the first time in remembered personal history, can itself be frightening.

To make sense of unfamiliar, chaotic reactions, we develop narratives to explain what's happening (Porges, 2013a). When the reactions are distressing *and* they occur in a society that evaluates grief, the stories we create are often self-evaluative: "Something's wrong with me. I need to take a pill to make this stop." "If I were strong, I wouldn't be so overwhelmed." Therapists, friends, and family—also frightened by the intensity of the distress they're witnessing—can align with these invalidating narratives. But inaccurate, evaluative narratives exacerbate the pain and isolation of grief (Greenberg & Paivio, 1997; Porges 2013a).

Polyvagal Theory offers a healthier narrative, describing why these reactions are not only "appropriate," but intelligent under the circumstances. Multiple features of loss—huge violation of expectancy, permanent absence that generates primal attachment distress, feared-to-be-unbearable emotions we can't control, extreme physical symptoms, self-evaluative narratives—bombard the environment with signals of peril. No matter who we are or how much support we have, our neuroception is pelted with external and internal cues that shout "*danger,*" and displace social engagement behaviors with defensive reactions (Porges, 2011a, 2013a, 2015). Grief responses, as described above, are thus variations of defensive sympathetic fight-or-flight and dorsal vagal shutdown responses. (See Figure 18.1.)

These defensive reactions are the body taking care of itself in a situation fraught with danger (Porges, 2013b). Describing physiological wisdom within chaos, Polyvagal Theory offers "comfort in the paradox in which we are suspended, a gentle stroke of encouragement that will assure us we are really in the right place, even if it all looks like such a mess" (Ericsson, 1993, p. 21).

UNIQUENESS OF GRIEVERS' ENVIRONMENTS AND NEUROCEPTION SURROUNDING LOSS

Polyvagal Theory also challenges the fear- and shame-inducing assumption that that there is a singular, normative grief response. People are affected *differentially* by events. It's not about the event itself, but about the response of their viscera to the event. The responses should not be judged (Porges, 2011b). Behavioral, emotional, and physical responses to one's environment depend on a complex interaction between the cues that emanate from specific internal and external environments, and the distinctive way a body's neuroception interprets the cues. We make sense of the fact that each person's grief response is unique by exploring the specific features of external and internal environments, the factors that affect each individual's neuroception, and the nature of social support systems. (See Figure 18.1 for an overview of these concepts, elaborated in the following sections.)

External environmental features that influence neuroception after loss. Loss upends the griever's external environment in countless ways. Here, we'll explore two major external environmental features that can profoundly affect neuroception after loss: uncertainty and absence. (A third feature of the external environment that has a crucial impact on neuroception following loss is the type of social support that's available. This feature is so important that it's discussed in a separate section, below.)

Unsought external uncertainty. Our nervous systems like uncertainty only if there's safety in the background. Without an undergirding of safety, unpredictability is treacherous (Porges, 2013c). No amount of planning can adequately prepare us for the way death slams uncertainty into life, destabilizing relationships and physical places that were havens of safety. Loss overturns countless roles, routines, and identities we took for granted (Bowlby, 1980; Fraley & Shaver, 1999; Ossefort-Russell, 2011). External structural circumstances—such as financial status, living arrangements, child custody, and employment—can be thrown into disarray. And we are forced to contend with existential issues—like mortality itself and the limited control we have over illness, accidents, natural disasters, and so on—so that life itself feels fragile and unstable while we're confronting disintegration of daily routines. The more embedded our loved one was in everyday life, the more uncertain is each moment without him.

Moment to moment, this degree of uncertainty can feel foreboding, regularly cueing the nervous system for danger (sympathetic activation) or life-threat (dorsal vagal activation). These cues themselves—their number, frequency, specific manifestations—have everything to do with the idiosyncratic ways each griever's life was entwined with the specific loved one who was lost and the circumstances in which she is rebuilding life.

Physical absence of the loved one. One of the most painful aspects of loss is the acute disconnectedness it causes (Porges, 2011b, 2015). The void left by a dead loved one regularly replays the visceral experience of social expectancy violation. We constantly collide with their absence. We instinctively turn toward them in customary ways—in bed, at the dinner table, on the phone, on social media—and are repeatedly met by the slap of empty silence that harshly vio-

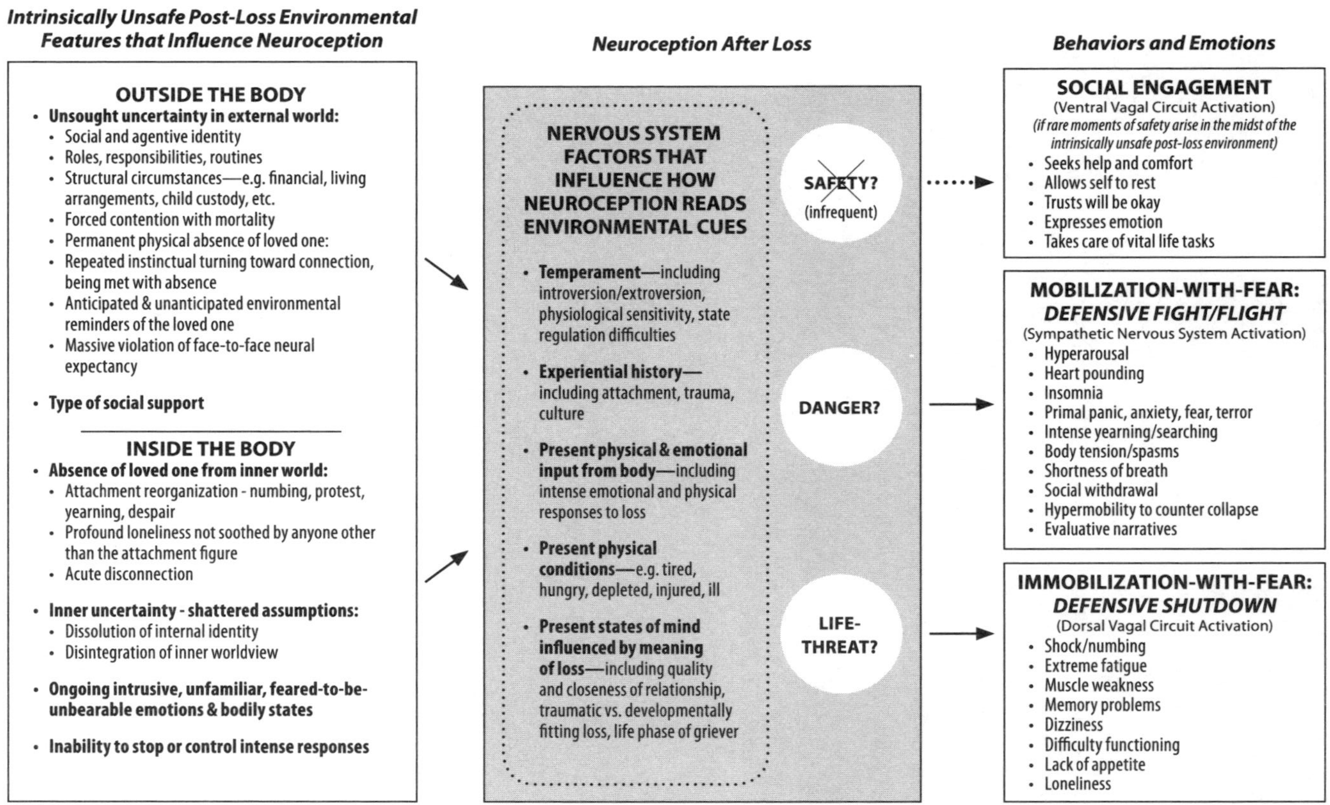

FIGURE 18.1
Environmental and neuroceptive features that affect differential grief responses.

lates expectation. Recurring exposure to absence of the loved one and sudden or consistent physical reminders can cue comfort (safety), anger or pain (danger), or shock (life-threat), depending on circumstances, timing, context, and characteristics of the grieving individual.

Internal environmental features that influence neuroception after loss. Within the internal environment, absence, uncertainty, and intensity are also hugely unsettling, cueing neuroception differently for each person. Temporary disorganization and reorganization in the inner world is a natural part of growth and change (Schore, as cited in Siegel, 2012; Spencer et al., 2006), but the vastness of self-destabilization created by loss can be agonizingly disorienting.

Absence of the loved one from the inner world. One of the most painful aspects of internal disintegration is attachment reorganization (Bowlby, 1980; Fraley & Shaver, 1999; Mikulincer & Shaver, 2007). The way attachment reorganization occurs for any individual will depend, of course, on the unique attachment relationship that was lost. But autonomically activated strategies of intense numbing, bursts of distress and angry protest, desperate yearning, despair, and profound loneliness are common. This type of loneliness stems specifically from loss of an attachment figure (Bowlby, 1980; Fraley & Shaver, 1999; Weiss, 1973/1985). "Although many bereaved individuals derive some comfort from the presence of close, supportive friends or family members, these support networks do not fill the emotional gap left by the missing attachment figure" (Fraley & Shaver, 1999, p. 737).

Internal uncertainty: shattered assumptions. We generally hold largely unconscious foundational assumptions about ourselves and about the external world, such as: "The world is benevolent; the world is meaningful, the self is worthy" (Janoff-Bulman, 1992, p. 6). We use assumptions about ourselves to know who we are and how we should behave. When we lose a close person, this internal sense of identity comes unraveled to varying degrees, causing sensations of fragmentation or disequilibrium (Gabora & Merrifield, 2013; Horowitz, 2014; Spencer et al., 2006). We use assumptions about the world to perceive events, construct plans, and forecast the future (Janoff-Bulman, 1992). These assumptions are positive illusions of certainty that protect us from perceiving the fragility and risks of life, thus helping us to remain in ventral vagal–engaged safety and giving us confidence to forge ahead into new experiences and daily life.

Secure or not, if we experience untimely or traumatic loss, or if we are new to the experience of death, losing a loved one can shatter these assumptions that have undergirded our security, creating enormous, unsafe uncertainty that plunges us into sympathetic mobilization or dorsal vagal shutdown.

> When any one of the fundamental assumptions about life is seriously challenged, an intense psychological crisis is induced. . . . The new data do not resemble . . . "normal change." . . . The [loss does not] produce the psychological equivalent of superficial scratches that heal readily, but deep bodily wounds that require far more in the way of restorative efforts. (Janoff-Bulman, 1992, pp. 51–52)

Suddenly we can become dramatically aware that bad things can happen to us, that we are not ultimately protected and safe, that the universe might contain elements of randomness and chance. We are forced to "confront [our] own fragility at a deep experiential level" (Janoff-Bulman, p. 62).

Ongoing unfamiliar, feared-to-be-unbearable emotions. The danger and life-threat cued by loss's intrinsic enormity and by the environmental impacts described above often lead to extreme fight-or-flight and life-threat responses. The very unfamiliarity and intensity of these responses, and the inability to quell them, loop back into the internal system that cues even more danger and life-threat (Fosha, 2000; Ossefort-Russell, 2011; Porges, 2011a; Siegel, 2012).

Factors that affect individual neuroception. Each person's neuroception reads the environment in distinctive ways (Porges, 2011a, 2011b; Siegel, 2012). These differential visceral responses are informed by a multitude of factors that affect the nervous system, including at least:

- *temperament*—including qualities like introversion/extroversion, physiological sensitivity, and preexisting or new state regulation difficulties;
- *experiential history*—including attachment history, trauma history, and cultural history;
- *present physical and emotional input from the body*—including intense emotional and physical activation;
- *present physical conditions*—such as feeling tired, hungry, injured, or ill; and
- *present states of mind influenced by the meaning of the loss*—including the quality and closeness of the relationship with the lost loved one, whether the loss was traumatic or developmentally fitting, and the life phase of the griever. (Losing a loved one during a time of transition can intensify destabilization, because the self is already in a state of reorganization.)

Figure 18.1 highlights these factors that color the way each individual's neuroception reads safety or danger in the post-loss environment (Bowlby, 1980;

Gilbert, 2006; Janoff-Bulman, 1992; Neimeyer, 2001; Ossefort-Russell, 2011, 2013; Porges, 2011a; Siegel, 2012).

Impact of social support. One of the most important factors, if not the most important factor, in grieving people's healing is the helpfulness or unhelpfulness of their social support (Bowlby, 1980; Calhoun & Tedeschi, 1999; Fosha, 2000; Lewis et al., 2000; Neimeyer, 2001; Ossefort-Russell, 2013; Porges, 2011a). Bowlby found that grievers who had a "good outcome" almost always reported receiving help and comfort from immediate others, and having few unhelpful interactions as they expressed their feelings about the loss (Bowlby, p. 193). The principal criteria for predicting an "unfavorable outcome" were "unhelpful interventions by relatives and others, and needs that had gone unmet" (Bowlby, p. 195).

Some grieving people have poor support systems. Others who have strong social infrastructure feel abandoned in grief if key supporters turn away because of their own fears. Others who have understanding supporters also yearn for comfort from someone who can listen without worrying about them. And even the best support systems can fall victim to rampant misperceptions about how grief is "supposed" to unfold.

The good news is that "families, friends, and others" who can remain autonomically regulated so that they are present and can provide comfort can "play a leading part in assisting the mourning process" (Bowlby, 1980, p. 191), even when the culture cannot. That's where we can use Polyvagal Theory's conceptualization of grief responses to help clients return to safety—by sifting through the strands of responses, making sense of them one thread at a time, healing old wounds in the process. However, we can only provide this safety if we can bring ourselves into a ventral vagal–based state of calm presence. Polyvagal Theory can also help us understand caregivers' responses to clients' distress so that we can more easily provide this presence.

Making Sense of Therapists' Responses to Clients' Grief

Polyvagal Theory can help us see how three features of interactions with grieving clients can trigger our own neuroception of danger or life-threat:

- *Empathic resonance*—True empathy is *feeling with* (Lewis et al., 2000; Siegel, 2012); and this inner congruence between our feeling state and that of our clients is what helps them bear what was previously unbearable (Fosha, 2000; Siegel, 2012). With grieving clients, we are called to align our internal states with overwhelming sadness, loneliness, despair, rage, and other powerful emotions (Ossefort, 2000).

- *Bidirectional social communication*—Grieving clients show up in defensive states of sympathetic fight-or-flight or dorsal vagal shutdown, often extreme, which might cause them to be unresponsive to offers of care (Geller & Porges, 2014; Porges, 2011a). Social unresponsiveness commonly elicits defensive responses.
- *The caregiving reflex*—We as mammals are wired to respond to the distress cry of people for whom we provide care (Bowlby, 1980). When clients (for whom we are caregivers) are wracked with wrenching pain from loss, loud sirens go off in our nervous system, vehemently urging us to alleviate their distress (Ossefort, 2000). The only true balm for this pain is the return of the lost loved one (Bowlby, 1980; Ossefort, 2000), so our caregiver instinct is thwarted.

Each of these features of interaction with grieving clients—alignment with enormously painful states, client unresponsiveness to our offers of care, and helplessness in response to a thwarted caregiving instinct—can yield a neuroception of unsafety within us. It makes sense that in the face of neuroceptive alarms of unsafety, the certainty of manualized grief-work protocols or the authority of evaluation might seem like the only way to return ourselves to safety.

Becoming aware of these features of grief responses can help us examine our own neuroceptive experience, and alert us to neural exercises we might need to undertake (in the safety of our own social relationships) to expand our nervous system's capacity to maintain a ventral vagal state so that we can actively bring safety, presence, and closeness to these situations. Broadened nervous system capacity can also help us bear the pain that cuts to the quick of our tender, mammalian hearts when we cannot alleviate our clients' grief, allowing us to be with their suffering instead of defensively trying to stanch it (Ossefort, 2000; Ossefort-Russell, 2013). Doing our own work to enlarge our nervous system's capacity for remaining in social engagement in these arenas will make us better therapists overall, as inner safety yields potential for creative knowledge, new ideas, and bold solutions (Porges, 2013c).

Strengthened by Polyvagal Theory's demystification of clients' grief responses and our own, we can facilitate a positive feedback loop where safety cascades bidirectionally between therapist and client, and internally between higher brain structures and bodily states (Fosha, 2000; Ossefort-Russell, 2011; Porges, 2011b, 2013a). In this state of compassionate safety, we can reassure grieving clients that their intense bodily reactions make sense and are adaptive; and we can help them learn to harness the wise neural circuits of sympathetic mobilization and dorsal vagal immobilization for healing, growth, and restoration—even while they are in severe pain (Porges, 2013a).

Recruiting Nervous System Responses for Growth and Restoration

The neural circuit of social interaction and social engagement is the same neural circuit that supports health, growth, and restoration.
—Stephen Porges (2013b, p. 11)

Inside and out, loss breaks us in two ways: (1) *Absence wounds us:* The hole left behind by our loved one is an injury in the soul that hurts, throbs, aches. And (2) *Uncertainty wrecks us:* The day-to-day life and identity we counted on before death is shattered, leaving us confused about which pieces of the wreckage are still usable and which must be discarded or rebuilt. These two types of breakage leave us with simultaneous, dichotomous needs for repair: rest to heal our wounds; action to repair the wreckage.

Isn't it interesting that automatic dorsal vagal and sympathetic nervous system responses in the face of danger (immobilization and mobilization) are in harmony with these two opposite behaviors (rest and action) that are the exact behaviors needed for repairing the wounding and wreckage of loss? In the intrinsically dangerous environment that loss thrusts us into, our bodies begin responding in automatic ways that can lead us toward repair. But these responses can do their jobs if, and only if, we're in safe environments (Porges, 2013b).

Safety, Mobilization, and Immobilization Without Fear

In the wake of loss, healing and rebuilding processes take time; and if we remain in defensive fight-or-flight or shutdown states for extended periods, there can be enormous costs to mental and physical health (Porges, 2011a, 2013b). As explored above, evaluative responses to grief can create environments that prolong and exacerbate these defensive states. Fortunately, it's possible to stabilize defensive bodily states and emotional dysregulation through attuned social interactions (Geller & Porges, 2014).

When we engage with someone who helps us feel safe, our physiological state shifts out of fight-or-flight or shutdown into a state of social engagement (Porges, 2013c). So if we therapists engage our own ventral vagal capacity to actively offer compassionate presence while helping clients understand what their bodily responses and intense emotions signify, we support them to experience their sympathetic and dorsal vagal states while at the same time activating their ventral vagal system so that they are safely socially engaged. When we couple dorsal vagal immobilization and sympathetic mobilization with safe ventral vagal social engagement, we can functionally capture and use some of our defense systems, not for defense, but instead for promoting health, growth, and restoration (Porges, 2011a, 2013b).

Immobilization without fear (nondefensive recruitment of the dorsal vagal complex) is the state we need for healing from the injury caused by the absence of our loved one.

> When we couple immobilization with social engagement, we call it falling into the arms of someone we're safe with . . . so that immobilization is no longer a defense strategy but a strategy in which we reduce metabolic demands. In our minds we say, "If you're ill . . . it's better that you don't move around too much." . . . [That you] trust, feel safe, and let [your] body do the healing. (Porges, 2013b, p. 15)

Immobilization without fear slows us down to convalesce and restore. It supports the melancholy, recuperative aspects of grieving such as resting; contemplating what has been lost; pulling inward; feeling tender and sad (Ossefort, 2000). Safe immobilization also creates space for reorganization of the attachment system via remembering, yearning, excavating meaning, and establishing internalized bonds with the lost loved one (Mikulincer & Shaver, 2007).

Mobilization without fear (nondefensive recruitment of the sympathetic nervous system) is the state we need for reconstructing our lives in a new, uncertain world. When internal and external identities have been so radically disorganized, rebuilding is an active process that requires embodied exploration of novel solutions (Spencer et al., 2006). Mobilization without fear allows us to be in "uncertainty with social engagement" (Porges, 2013c), a state necessary for active aspects of grieving such as experimenting with untried identities and behaviors. Mobilization without fear can generate courage for returning to activities without the loved one, for trying new roles, and for seeking social connections with compassionate people (Ossefort, 2000; Mikulincer & Shaver, 2007).

Supported Empowered Oscillation as a Neural Exercise

These two processes required for returning to life after loss—slowing to heal via immobilization and taking action to rebuild via mobilization—require diametrically opposed forms of energy. Both processes exert strong forces, and the sensation of being simultaneously pulled in two extreme directions can feel unbearable and confusing. People describe this sensation as "being torn in two" or "coming apart." Helping people understand their concurrent activation of two opposing circuits of the nervous system (the sympathetic and dorsal vagal) can begin to alleviate the intensity of the feeling.

Over time, upon return to ventral vagal–mediated safety, we naturally oscillate between these states. Oscillation occurs during any particular day, as well as across the passage of time (Stroebe, Schut, & Stroebe, 2005, as cited in Mikulincer & Shaver, 2007). As caregivers, we facilitate this oscillation by attending to bodily and emotional signals that indicate mobilization and immobilization needs as they arise.

When grievers are in distress and need to pull inward, we can offer soothing and emotional comfort and containment. When grievers feel angry, afraid, or uncertain as they face new challenges, we can offer encouragement and emotional scaffolding (Collins, Guichard, Ford, & Feeney, 2006). As messy and long-lasting as the process can be, with compassionate help, people can learn to recognize, allow, and bear these sizable oscillations between profound states of mobilization and immobilization without fear. These oscillations can be approached as powerful neural exercises that not only repair brokenness following loss, but also strengthen physiology and health over time (Porges, 2013c, 2015).

Grief as an Opportunity to Discover State Regulation Problems

Everyone who experiences loss brings to it characteristic nervous system responses that are a result of both inborn wiring and experiential learning (Porges, 2011a; Siegel, 2012). Some characteristic responses have caused lifelong struggles with regulating bodily and emotional states, not just during grief. Some people are so traumatized by loss that they develop state-regulation difficulties. Either way, state-regulation problems can amplify or exacerbate states of fight-or-flight or shutdown, causing recovery from loss to be especially challenging.

As we help clients traverse grief, existing or newly developed state-regulation difficulties will emerge. What if, instead of diagnosing grief itself as pathological, we seized this emergence of state-regulation problems as an opportunity to help clients both with grief and with strategies for global state regulation? We could offer them the empowering, polyvagal-informed perspective that their body's response to this acute loss situation has revealed areas where they have vulnerabilities around regulating their body and emotions. And we could help them understand that the neural exercises we practice can help them both survive loss and heal old wounds, broadening their overall mental and physical health.

To get a sense of this process, let's look at how this perspective helped Kay, a client whose body moved into defensive shutdown when her husband died.

Polyvagal Theory Informs a Humane Response to Loss

Both the giving and receiving of caregiving or love has the capacity to protect, heal, and restore.
—Stephen Porges (2011a, p. 295)

Kay—a well-behaved Southern woman in her 60s—came to me for therapy after the loss of her husband of 40 years. Kay grew up as an only child in a household ruled by a kind yet proper father who sent her to her room until she could "act right" whenever she expressed distressing emotions; and an insecure mother who virulently disapproved of behavior that didn't follow strict family rules. Embedded in Kay's neuroceptive appraisal system was experiential learning that distressing emotions should be suppressed, and independent thinking and behavior are unacceptable.

Kay's husband, Robert, provided a pleasant antidote to her rigid upbringing. He delighted in Kay's quiet, funny manner. Alone with him, she expressed emotions freely, and was herself without fearing disapproval. Socially, Robert was a liaison between Kay and others. He advocated for her desires and voiced the couple's opinions in public, bearing the brunt of disapproval that might come their way. They found a dyadic rhythm that allowed her to be authentic in private, and to remain comfortably in the background in public. Robert provided Kay with a social environment that was safe and protected, allowing her to be in ventral vagal–engaged safety, experiencing healthy immobilization and mobilization without fear.

When Robert died, Kay's dyadic safety net disintegrated, and she was thrust into acting for herself in public. She responded by retreating into a state of flattened melancholy and withdrawn inaction, except for basic functioning. She came to me isolated and paralyzed. She felt "down," she slept too much, and she rarely left her house. When she expressed grief with me, she allowed herself to cry for only moments before she suddenly hardened her face and quieted herself. Intense distress overwhelmed her system, enormous emotions kept breaking through experientially learned defenses, and making choices alone seemed impossible. These factors yielded a primary neuroception of life-threat. Unsurprisingly, her primary state reflected dorsal vagal defensive shutdown, or immobilization with fear; when emotions mobilized toward expression, she fearfully halted them.

Over a period of years, I offered Kay warmth and security, and repeatedly reflected my enjoyment of her gentle liveliness. We spent long, steady months coaxing her nervous system toward calm so she could emerge from protective emotional hiding with me. For both of us, the process was slow yet moving and rewarding. Week after week, I actively offered her safety that radiated from my ventral vagal social engagement system. Shifting her learned neuroception of danger around emotional expression and agentic action emerged from the safety that came from my patience, gentleness, and kind persistence. Relief from grief's overwhelmingness was not immediate—it grew from repeated, incremental lived experiences of soothing and encouragement that brought her ventral vagal system online.

Over time, she felt safe to express sadness and anger with me. She cried freely, and came to feel profoundly understood when I resonated with her emotions. She flowered in response to the confidence I expressed in her life choices. With this undergirding of safety, she ventured into the social world. With repeated experiences of ventral vagal–engaging safety, she became able to receive the soothing and confidence I offered. She oscillated between healthy recruitment of her dorsal vagal system for immobilization without fear by grieving, resting, and making internal connections with Robert; and healthy recruitment of her sympathetic nervous system for mobilization without fear by exploring anger about her mother's disapproval, and by taking steps toward independence. In ventral vagal–engaged safety, she began to bear expanding oscillations of restorative grieving and self-reorganization; and we repaired some deep, historic regulatory difficulties in the process.

Two years into our work, Kay joined a book group where she met a youngish man, Brian, who became a surrogate nephew. Brian added strong planks to Kay's social-safety platform, and with his help she took massive independent action: She sold her isolated rural property and moved to an in-town cottage near social activities. With healthy, ongoing social support, she grew enough to mobilize toward positive action.

Surrounded by boxes in her new home, Kay became immobilized. She came to session looking like a rag doll. She slumped into the sofa with face hanging slack, eyes drooping, and voice flat. The move created profound uncertainty and resurrected big emotions, evoking neuroception of life-threat. Her dorsal vagal complex was activated, and shutdown defenses took over.

We explored her bodily sensations of tightness in the chest, shallow breathing, and extreme fatigue; and her behavioral urge to "go in the house, lock the doors, and pull the covers over my head." She described it as "an urge to hide from what needs to be done. To become paralyzed and deny that it exists. To just block it out." I gently helped her focus on her chest and what it was trying to tell her, and her face changed. She looked sad, but animated. She frowned. Her eyes filled with tears. In safety with me, emotional expression spontaneously emerged: "I want Robert." I quietly acknowledged that, at this time of uncertainty and upheaval, she longed for him. Actively using my ventral vagal social engagement, I invited kind attention to her experience, which primed safety for her to reengage her ventral vagal system in order to feel.

"I want to be taken care of. I want him to come back and take care of me. So I don't have to do this by myself." Fully expressive, she cried out, "Come back and take care of me!" And quietly, "Tuesday was the anniversary of his death." Her neuroception perceived stark environmental cues of danger: enormous upheaval from the move, the calendar reminder of Robert's absence; emotions in response to these cues more intense than they'd been in recent months.

I shared her sadness and protest. Then positive memories began to flow. "I'm thinking of one of the wedding pictures, where I'm standing halfway behind him, like, 'You go take care of it; I'll be here when you get back.'" In ventral vagal safety with me, she retrieved an internal bond with Robert that invited her own internal support.

Making a stubborn face, she said, "I guess that's part of my inability to get going. . . . You can't make me!" This is beautiful, organic oscillation between nondefensive, dorsal vagal–based immobilization-without-fear expression of sadness and memory; and nondefensive, sympathetically based mobilized expression of angry protest.

We shared smiles about her willful protest. Then, "As so often happens with you . . . I really feel better now. . . . I feel more like getting on with it." She grinned. Her chest filled with a deep breath. Sharing safe engagement, we attended to inward-pulling sadness, then oscillated to mobilized protest. From there she accessed positive mobilization energy.

"We're acknowledging what you've been carrying around. How it affects you so deeply. How you don't know it until it gets named and felt."

"That's it. It's like magic. . . . It's one of the things he used to do for me. He could zero in on the core of something, the real meaning behind the words. And facilitate being able to name it." She is experiencing more oscillation, expanded retrieval of ventral vagal inner resources.

"What's it like remembering that now?" I'm encouraging her to fill up with this experience, to enhance her neuroception of safety and deepen into ventral vagal engagement in the present.

Soft and open, she placed her hand on her chest. "It's melancholy. Nostalgic. . . . But it feels different. It feels sad, but it's lost its paralyzing quality." With a smile, "I still have no idea what's gonna happen with the house, but it's not as scary as it was. It's not as . . . impossible. . . . It's a feeling that things will be okay, rather than I just can't do it. That's the difference." In safety her ventral vagal system remains engaged, so change is a challenge, but she's not paralyzed by it.

When we finished, Kay stood up with resolve and contacted Brian. He met her that evening to help her unpack her kitchen. The upheaval of Kay's home along with a potent loss anniversary cued her neuroception for life-threatening danger, and her body responded with defensive dorsal vagal states of shutdown. However, within our ventral vagal relational safety—an environment where we had shared deep practice of powerful neural exercises of oscillation between immobilization- and mobilization-without-fear states—a small nudge of encouragement quickly shifted her neuroception away from historic defensive regulation difficulties toward ventral vagal regulation and safety. Her state returned to fluid movement between animated emotional expression and healthy, mobilized action.

Conclusion

We make the world a better place by making people safer.
—Stephen Porges (2013c)

Our mammalian need for close attachment bonds leaves us vulnerable to intense emotions and feelings of unsafety when connections are severed by loss. Humans carry the additional vulnerability of knowing that we're mortal. What if we could openly acknowledge this vulnerability as a culture and a species, and so share compassion for each other? What if helpers had support to work through their own fears of death and the intensity of grief, so that they could harness their ventral vagal capacities to create safe spaces for anyone desiring help with facing the intrinsically dangerous environment created by loss? What if it could be viewed as normal to seek social support to bear the excruciating oscillations between sympathetic mobilization and dorsal vagal immobilization that are inherent in recovering from loss?

> We can create environmental or social structures that mimic a mammalian idealized model [of compassion and support] versus mimicking a reptilian model. A reptilian model is going to create isolation; it's not going to foster boldness. A mammalian environment will be empowering of others, more of a shared environment, and have more empathy and care for others. (Porges, 2013a, p. 14)

Creating a mammalian environment that fosters clear-eyed presence with grief is not easy. Loss is painful and grief overwhelming for even the most courageous. But even as nature has forced us to shoulder the burden of awareness of death, she has also given us the ability to discover the top-down understanding that extreme states of mobilization and immobilization make sense when we endure loss, and that responding to one another with compassionate social support when we suffer this intensely will strengthen the health of all. When we helpers can fully inhabit our ventral vagal social engagement and actively offer it to our clients in the face of this distress, we can help people not only recover but also heal old wounds and grow into creativity and confidence. Together, we can look death in the face, bear its consequences, and learn to navigate the richness of painful, challenging uncertainty. We can be part of a network of support that allows death to humble us into awe, rather than shaming us into submission.

> It seems that we are humbled before the great events of life. Events over which we have no power, no influence. . . . To be humbled like this is not meant to be a punishment, but rather Death grooming us to awaken. In this awakening of utter powerlessness over everything outside of ourselves, something miraculous occurs. We become teachable again. Humble. Graced. In touch with powers greater than us. . . . It is humanizing. (Ericsson, 1993, p. 70)

References

Bonanno, G. (2009). *The other side of sadness: What the new science of bereavement tells us about life after loss.* New York, NY: Basic Books.

Bowlby, J. (1980). *Attachment and loss: Vol. III. Loss, sadness and depression.* New York, NY: Basic Books.

Calhoun, L., & Tedeschi, R. (1999). *Facilitating posttraumatic growth: A clinician's guide.* Mahwah, NJ: Lawrence Erlbaum.

Collins, N. L., Guichard, A. C., Ford, M. B., & Feeney, B. C. (2006). Responding to need in intimate relationships: Normative processes and individual differences. In M. Mikulincer & G. S. Goodman (Eds.), *Dynamics of romantic love: Attachment, caregiving, and sex* (pp. 149–189). New York, NY: Guilford Press.

Ericsson, S. (1993). *Companion through the darkness.* New York, NY: HarperCollins.

Fosha, D. (2000). *The transforming power of affect: A model for accelerated change.* New York, NY: Basic Books.

Fraley, R. C., & Shaver, P. R. (1999). Loss and bereavement: Attachment theory and recent controversies concerning "grief work" and the nature of detachment. In J. Cassidy & P. Shaver (Eds.), *Handbook of attachment: Theory, research, and clinical applications* (pp. 735–759). New York, NY: Guilford Press.

Gabora, L., & Merrifield, M. (2013). Dynamical disequilibrium, transformation, and the evolution and development of sustainable world views. In F. Orsucci & N. Sala (Eds.), *Complexity science, living systems, and reflexing interfaces: New models and perspectives* (pp. 69–77). Hershey, PA: IGI Global.

Geller, S., & Porges, S. W. (2014). Therapeutic presence: Neurophysiological mechanisms mediating feeling safe in therapeutic relationships. *Journal of Psychotherapy Integration, 24*(3), 178–192.

Gilbert, S. (2006). *Death's door: Modern dying and the ways we grieve.* New York, NY: Norton.

Greenberg, L. S., & Paivio, S. C. (1997). *Working with emotions in psychotherapy.* New York, NY: Guilford Press.

Horowitz, M. (2014). Grieving: The role of self-organization. *Psychodynamic Psychiatry, 42*(1), 89–98.

Janoff-Bulman, R. (1992). *Shattered assumptions: Toward a new psychology of trauma.* New York, NY: Free Press.

Johnson, S. (2008). *Hold me tight: Seven conversations for a lifetime of love.* New York, NY: Little, Brown.

Lewis, T., Amini, F., & Lannon, R. (2000). *A general theory of love.* New York, NY: Vintage Books.

Mikulincer, M., & Shaver, P. R. (2007). *Attachment in adulthood: Structure, dynamics, and change.* New York, NY: Guilford Press.

Neimeyer, R. (2001). The language of loss: Grief therapy as a process of meaning reconstruction. In R. Neimeyer (Ed.), *Meaning reconstruction and the experience of loss* (pp. 261–292). Washington, DC: American Psychological Association.

O'Rourke, M. (2011). *The long goodbye.* London: Penguin Books.

Ossefort, C. (2000). *Shimmering in the darkness: Bearing witness to inconsolable suffering.* Unpublished master's thesis. Pacifica Graduate Institute, Carpinteria, California.

Ossefort-Russell, C. (2011). Individuals grieve: AEDP as an effective approach for grief as a personal process. *Transformance: The AEDP Journal, 2*(1).

Ossefort-Russell, C. (2013). Grief calls for presence, not treatment: Using attachment and IPNB to shift grief's context from pathology to acceptance. *Journal of Interpersonal Neurobiology Studies, 2.*

Porges, S. W. (2011a). *The Polyvagal Theory: Neurophysiological foundations of emotions, attachment, communication, self-regulation.* New York, NY: Norton.

Porges, S. W. (2011b). *Clinical applications of the Polyvagal Theory.* Lecture presented at a conference for Austin IN Connection, Austin, TX.

Porges, S. W. (2012, August 27). *The science of compassion: Origins, measures, and interventions* [Video file]. Retrieved from https://www.youtube.com/watch?v=MYXa_BX2cE8

Porges, S. W. (2013a). *Beyond the brain: How the vagal system holds the secret to treating trauma.* Retrieved from http://stephenporges.com/images/nicabm2.pdf

Porges, S. W. (2013b). *Body, brain, behavior: How Polyvagal Theory expands our healing paradigm.* Retrieved from http://stephenporges.com/images/nicabm_2013.pdf

Porges, S. W. (2013c, May 15). *The Polyvagal Theory* [Video file]. Retrieved from https://www.youtube.com/watch?v=8tz146HQotY

Porges, S. W. (2015). *Social connectedness as a biological imperative: Understanding trauma through the lens of the Polyvagal Theory.* Retrieved from https://attach.org/wp-content/uploads/2015/09/Attach-Porges-handout.pdf

Siegel, D. J. (2012). *The developing mind: How relationships and the brain interact to shape who we are* (2nd ed.). New York, NY: Guilford Press.

Siegel, D. J. (2015, June 27). Unpublished interview from Mindsight Immersion Weekend, Santa Monica, CA.

Spencer, J. P., Corbetta, D., Buchanan, P., Clearfield, M., Ulrich, B., & Schoner, G. (2006). Moving toward a grand theory of development: In memory of Esther Thelen. *Child Development, 77*(6), 1521–1538.

Weiss, R. (1973/1985). *Loneliness: The experience of emotional and social isolation.* Cambridge, MA: MIT Press.

Worden, W. (2009). *Grief counseling and grief therapy: A handbook for the mental health practitioner.* New York, NY: Springer.

19

Polyvagal Theory, Poetry, and PTSD: Portrait of the Poet as Trauma Therapist

Gary Whited

Abstract: This essay explores the relevance of poetry to psychotherapy. It uses the framework of Polyvagal Theory to illustrate how engaging our innate poetic sensibility can help transform trauma. Through its concept of neuroception, Polyvagal Theory illuminates how we are able to listen to our neurological and physiological experience in a way that promotes healing and the restoration of balance and well-being. The language of poetry, both in its formal literary sense and in its most essential sense shared by all humans, opens our listening to ourselves and to each other in ways that can deepen this shared healing capacity.

I RECENTLY WALKED into the gallery that holds a very old Chinese wooden statue of Kwan Yin at the Museum of Fine Arts in Boston. Kwan Yin sits on a pedestal, right knee bent and right arm resting on the knee, the body leaning in what's identified as the "royal ease" posture. The entire statue, especially the face, stuns yet quiets me with its sense of presence. I stood bathed in a sensuous feeling of calm coming from this wooden structure. Simply gazing at it, I felt kindness fill the room. How did they do this, I thought? This statued presence evoked a sense of holding and safety so compelling I didn't want to leave. What eventually occurred to me was that I was feeling listened to, generously received without judgment. Then I read the plaque nearby. In the Buddhist tradition, Kwan Yin embodies the energy of the Bodhisattva of Compassion known as "the one who pays heed to the sounds—or cries—of the world."

Isn't this what we aim to do every day in our work with our clients—to "pay heed" as we listen from an open heart, to evoke a sense of safety and regard in the presence of which another person might feel a kind and ready ear that could hear whatever wounds they come with, whatever burdens they carry.

Yet so much impinges on our listening. From too much noise around us to too much noise inside. From too many assumptions, beliefs, and biases to thinking we have none. From having a closed mind or heart to having an overwhelmed mind or heart. What are the conditions for the possibility of listening in a way that makes room for what we don't know and for what another has never told to anyone? What helps our listening open; what closes it down? And for those of us who work with trauma survivors whose stories have often not been listened to, what encourages listening, ours and our clients, to open in ways that evoke and support healing?

Though poetry in its formal sense occupies a very small portion of the daily news, as poet William Carlos Williams (1994) once put it, "It is difficult / to get the news from poems / yet men die miserably every day / for lack / of what is found there"(p. 41).

Why is it that poets are often called on for special occasions in our lives when we gather together to celebrate or commemorate a moment of joy or loss, of accomplishment or recognition, events in which we seek connection with others? Poetry and song, which were regarded as the same in early human history, are said to be the language of the heart. What do we really mean when we say that, and what might the life of poetry offer to the process of healing?

Polyvagal Theory as developed by the researcher Stephen Porges (2011) explores and maps out the phylogenetic evolution of the autonomic nervous system. It describes different aspects of this system as they activate in the face of danger or life-threat, and by contrast, what happens when we socially engage with one another and experience ventral vagal attunement. For example, when a poem touches us, or when a song shared with others connects us, we move into a ventral vagal state of awareness and feel safe enough to *open our hearts* to one another. Imagine, or remember, a concert scene when a large number of humans, most of whom don't know each other, start singing together, feeling connected with everyone in the concert hall. Poems and songs are often the vehicles through which we bear witness to our aspirations, our fears, hopes, joys, and our deepest grief; the language with which we inaugurate our presidents, sing our babies to sleep, soothe our suffering hearts at funerals. I'm reminded here of President Obama breaking into singing "Amazing Grace" when eulogizing the parishioners shot at a Southern church. The entire congregation joined in singing with him, and I suspect many of us who watched on TV were moved to sing or to tears or both. Poetry in some form is the language that naturally flows through us when we want to comfort. We do not appeal to the language of explanation for this purpose, nor to the usually more linear language of protocol and model. Poetry is the language of belonging, which for we mammals has the capacity to bring us safely together.

As is evident, I am considering poetry in its broadest sense, which includes prayer, song, and storytelling along with the traditional canon of poetry from the ancients to our time. I invite you to join me in a consideration of the ways in which poetry in all its forms has a place in this ever-changing context of our work with those who have suffered trauma, big *T* or little *t*, and who now might experience some form of post traumatic stress disorder. I also invite you to consider with me how poetry might accompany Polyvagal Theory in its relevance to our work with all our clients, especially trauma survivors.

I have been practicing psychotherapy for nearly 35 years, and have been writing poems even longer. As therapist and poet, listening has been a central theme, if not an obsession, of my professional and personal life. In this essay I want to speak for how Polyvagal Theory sheds light on these two passions in their intertwining and informing my experience of listening.

Three years ago, a book of my poems was published, the title of which is *Having Listened*. This title comes from one of its poems that speaks of the place where I grew up—the plains of eastern Montana. Many of the poems in this book speak from that place and from me in conversation with my memories of growing up on the ranch where I first began to listen. Writing those poems was in turn a listening, over and over, to the images, sounds, line breaks, and rhythms of the poems as they were being written. I noticed along the way that each poem had a sound to which I was listening. Each had a body in its lines, stanza breaks, and arrangement on the page with a discernible feel to it. Though no one was speaking, I heard the poems coming. As the voice and body of each poem developed, it resonated with the memories coming to me and to the experiences of the place and the occasions I was remembering. The inner world of my memory, which had been shaped by my experience of the prairie around me, was now manifesting in the outer world of the poems, the two worlds mingling and informing each other.

My study of Polyvagal Theory suggests to me that during my youth in Montana, which I reexperienced as I wrote the poems, my autonomic system was in resonance with what was around me on the prairie. I was seeking safe and soothing connection with the natural environment in order to move into a ventral vagal–toned state. Without knowing it, I was seeking peace through listening, a listening that I engaged with again as I wrote the poems that embodied that experience.

The renowned American poet Yusef Komunyakaa (2016), born and raised in Louisiana, has said,

> I've realized that as a young boy I was so enthused with the landscape around me because I was discovering something new every day. And maybe that's why this whole journey with poetry still exists, this discovering of something new every day. Sometimes what we discover out there has to do with reflection that is internal, getting into that interior. (p. 34.)

My effort in each of my poems was to find the words, lines, and rhythms that embodied and evoked for the reader specific details of that place of prairie and my internal experience of it. I wanted the poems to convey in sound and feel and image what that place had sounded and felt like to me. Here is one of those poems from the book:

Night Hawk's Path

It happened the first time
on the dirt cow path
when I walked

behind the milk cow,
evening chore-time light
gliding across Shadwell creek

now shadowed for the night.
When I stood still,
that hum

no one ever talked about, coming
from the earth, moved
up my legs

into my hips, turning
this body into sound.
Light flared yellow,

gathered around haystacks,
fenceposts,
the cow and me.
(Whited, 2013, p. 7)

As a child I felt an anchoring connection with the earth and everything around me, and I wanted this poem to evoke and embody the earth's sound along with the sensations of light that accompanied it, all of it holding me in a moment of peace and quiet that felt safe, as child and as adult writer. Seeing it now through a polyvagal lens, I can see that I wanted, through the poem, to share this ventral vagal state of safe connection and to invite my reader into a reciprocal exchange through the shared listening.

Along the way of making these poems, it became clear to me that the more a poem does what it says, the more accessible its message is to a reader. When a poem accomplishes this, it sets in motion, through its sound and its structure, a signal that conveys to a reader or listener the actual place, situation, or sensation to which the poem gives voice. People have often said to me after hearing me read these poems of the prairie that they felt they were there. From a Polyvagal Theory perspective, we might say a poem being read or spoken aloud evokes in a reader's autonomic system a sense of resonance with the poem, with its image or story, with the author, or with anyone who might be reading that poem aloud years after the poet has written it. How else might we make sense of being moved by Homer's *Odyssey*, Shakespeare's *King Lear*, or by a line of Rumi's, like this one: "The wound is the place where the light enters you."

After some years of working as a psychotherapist, I noticed that while sitting with clients I was experiencing something very similar to what was happening while writing or reading poems. As clients told their stories I began to hear line breaks, changes to everyday syntax and grammar, and expressive rhythms, all of which I associated with poetry. Additionally, these poetic features seemed to express themselves through the client's body signals, shifts in posture, changes in facial expression and, perhaps most importantly, changes in tone of voice. The more open my listening, the more fully these details delivered themselves into the immediacy of my autonomic awareness, enabling me to enter the world of the client as she or he experienced it. The physical and vocal presentations of the client became part of the story, along with the verbal content. All of it had to be attended to in order to get the fuller story.

What Polyvagal Theory helped me to realize is that as I attune to the client autonomically, our shared social engagement system activates, and we set out on a journey of listening together. When the client and I feel safe enough in the dialogue, we move into a felt sense of connection and reciprocity, what Stephen Porges describes as ventral vagal attunement. Ursula K. LeGuin's words on dialogue in her essay titled "Telling is Listening" speak to this: "In human conversation, in live, actual communication between or among human beings, everything 'transmitted' –everything said—is shaped as it is spoken by actual or anticipated response" (2004, p. 188). Later in the same piece, she writes:

> Mutual communication between speakers and listeners is a powerful act. The power of each speaker is amplified, augmented, by the entrainment of the listeners. The strength of a community is amplified, augmented by its mutual entrainment in speech.
>
> This is why utterance is magic. Words do have power. Names have power. Words are events, they do things, change things. They transform both speaker and hearer; they feed energy back and forth and amplify it. They feed understanding or emotion back and forth and amplify it. (p. 199)

Once this attunement between the client and myself is established, we connect back and forth through words, voice intonations, gestures, posture adjustments, all of which communicate so much that would be lost if we only harvested what our linear thinking system takes to be meaningful. Oftentimes the signal is one word that catches in my ear, as words in poems do, and seems to say, listen here to this. In this call-and-response exchange, my client and I move into co-regulation. What was transmitted, to use LeGuin's word, has been received, and our shared dialogue moves toward another door that is ready to open in the inquiry.

Particular words can seem charged, like *lost, empty, barren, loser,* and the voice tone with which they are spoken indicates an autonomic activation, perhaps a signal of danger in the client's experience. Phrases that repeat, like *I had to* or *I should have,* signal beliefs and patterns in a client's self-image or in their sense of their role in a family system. Sometimes it's a moment in which a client falls silent that sends up a signal. In my own therapy dialogue, there have been many silent places that took me back to difficult moments in my childhood on the farm. One of my charged words was *worry,* which revealed an autonomic state that took me back to many moments of fear watching my emotionally unstable mother stand at the kitchen window wringing her hands. The sound of the word *worry* carries within itself suggestions of such gestures in a way that is autonomically evocative, even in its everydayness.

Sometimes a word is accompanied by a gesture like the wave of an arm appearing to be an attempt to wave something away or pull something closer, and this might reveal an autonomic reaction that echoes an earlier trauma moment being reenacted in the client's current experience. We want to listen to these gestures no less than we do to the story as told in the verbal content. We see and feel the body's signals from the face and eyes, the postures and gestures that amplify or mute aspects of the story. As the dialogue develops over time with each client, the shape and feel of the world the client inhabits become more and more apparent. The features of this world become audible, visible, nearly touchable, like those of a poem. As client and therapist listen together, they co-regulate and move into a field of safe and reciprocal connection. Some kind of poetry is happening in this dialogue.

The story that unfolds over the course of a therapy dialogue reveals the world of the client, showing what is apparent and pointing toward what is hidden. The dialogue becomes an enactment that approximates the order and unity of that world and begins to make it more conscious for clients as well as how, and who, they take themselves to be in it. They can hear and perceive their own protective reactions to traumatic experiences in the past, notice repeated autonomic perceptions of danger or life-threat giving rise to fixed beliefs and defense structures that are carried into later life. Stories about ourselves and our self-images are both rooted in and expressed in these beliefs and patterns. Clients can actively listen to their life's story, or poem, and have the opportunity to hear it as it lives in them autonomically in company with a fellow listener.

If a client, for example, believes they are going to be, or perhaps deserves to be, abandoned because that's the message from early training, their autonomic system will be easily triggered into arousal and their body can manifest that belief in various postures and habitual movements. I have had several clients who tend to duck their head and shoulders as they walk into and out of my office, averting their gaze so as not to make eye contact with me. These gestures signal to me that they are not yet feeling safe and their social engagement system is not allowing them to connect directly with me. Once we are safely enough connected in the therapy process, I can point out these patterns. My mirroring these details and our listening to them together co-regulates the clients and enables them to calm enough to notice the repeating pattern. Once regulated, clients calm down and notice their negative regard for themselves in relation to others; they begin to hear the story they tell themselves as a story, or poetic narrative, rather than the truth about who they are, and this empowers them to actively and creatively witness rather than mechanically reenact and relive what happened to them. They are creatively separating their autonomic state from their once-fixed story.

This parallels my experience with poetry. When writing poems, I'm listening for story, for message, for belief, for anything that I'm carrying in my psyche, past or present, that feels ready to be spoken for. Through the writing, I'm finding a way to hear the story as a story and to move toward witnessing it. It's the same when I'm reading or hearing someone else's poem. In either case, I'm listening through the words, the images they create, the rhythms and line breaks, the shape of the poem on the page—all of it speaks directly into my listening with an immediacy and a granularity in the details. When I'm listening from a ventral vagal state of attunement, feeling safe enough and open, my imagination is able to actively engage and harvest the story a poem is telling. I can witness the story as such without being at the effect of it. And if it's a positive experience, like in the poem above in which I speak of the milk cow walking and the earth humming and me held by it all in a safe and nourishing way, I can witness that and metabolize what it has to offer. As a poet, my aim and my hope is that someone reading the poem can receive this nourishment as well.

Though we tend to regard being a poet as belonging to an exclusive club that includes only a small number of "writers," I want to declare that in the most essential sense there are poets and storytellers inside every one of us. I've heard that the ancient Mayans said, "We are storytelling creatures because we are grieving creatures." Every trauma survivor has experienced loss, and each part of the psyche that carries wounds and negative beliefs spawned from traumatic events is a poet or a storyteller waiting to be heard. When listened to in their own terms, without judgment or diagnostic attribution, these poets and storytellers bear witness to what actually happened and reveal familiar protective stories and beliefs.

The safe connection with another who listens with an open and sincerely curious heart enables us to shift out of autonomic arousal or shutdown in reaction to the triggering details of our story. To listen to one another when in a ventral vagal state of attunement encourages and enables our human capacity to listen self-reflexively—that is, to *listen to our listening*. It is in this that our capacity to resolve conflicts and to heal old wounds abides.

My work with clients has for some time been informed by the Internal Family Systems model as developed by Dr. Richard Schwartz (1994). This model assumes that our personality system has parts and that listening to each in its own terms with compassion and curiosity enables the client's capacity to connect and to co-regulate. Once this connection is established, tracking autonomic states with clients opens and deepens their capacity to listen to their parts and to move toward more balance and witnessing of their experience.

Cindy walked into my session room looking particularly upset one day. She reported that her new boyfriend had told her last night that he wasn't sure about going further with their relationship, and she was devastated. Her voice quavered as she spoke in hurried sentences, falling silent for long periods between each utterance. When she fell silent, her shoulders sagged and her gaze went toward the far corner of the office. Another outburst of words gushed out, and then silence again. She appeared to me to be moving from autonomic arousal to shutdown, back and forth. Cindy and I had worked together for several months and had a solid connection. At some point I could sense through my own autonomic experience that she was feeling safely enough connected to me that I said, "It sounds like some parts of your system are really triggered and understandably upset." Her gaze lifted from the corner toward me as she replied in a voice that softened ever so slightly, "Yeah, maybe. You're probably right. I hate it when they do this. I should never get close to anyone." I leaned in a little toward her and asked, "Would those parts of you that feel that way like some help?" She was silent for a few moments, then replied in a skeptical voice, "Sure."

I asked if she was aware of how fast she was speaking, and she replied that she hadn't noticed that. I then asked what she had been looking at in the corner, and she hadn't noticed that she was staring in that direction. I wondered out loud if these were signals from some part of her that wasn't feeling safe and if she was in a triggered autonomic state. As I waited for her to check in with herself, she quieted and began to look around the room and then at me. It was the first moment since she arrived that she appeared to be even a little aware of her internal process, and very soon she leaned back in her chair and tears formed in the corners of her eyes. I asked simply, "What's happening now?" She replied, "I'm sad." Then I asked, "Who are you hearing from in there?" At that point tears began to flow down her cheeks. We sat in silence for a little while as her body settled into the chair, and I sensed in my own body that she was relaxing just a little bit more. I leaned forward and asked if she'd like to speak for whoever was sad. She nodded and I waited.

I could feel myself adjusting to her pace as I sensed her internal system begin to slow down and stop cycling from states of arousal to shutdown and back to arousal. When more words came, her voice sounded less pressured and softer. As I spoke in a quiet and slow voice, I sensed she was able to relax more deeply into the field of listening we were cocreating, and that it felt safe enough for her to move into a calmer state. In short sentences, she told me how sad she'd felt last night after her boyfriend said what he'd said. I invited her to bring her attention to the place inside where she'd felt the sadness. She put her right hand on her chest and held it there. After another long pause she began to describe a memory of being 10 years old when her father was telling her and her mother that he was leaving the family. More tears came. I asked if she'd be okay speaking for that 10-year-old. For the first time in our therapy process I heard her describe this scene, how awful it was for her, how alone and unsupported she'd felt. Her mother had been terribly upset and had left the house when her father went to his room and started packing a suitcase, while she sat in the living room by herself. At this point she burst into deep sobs, and I felt a wave of empathy sweep through me as I felt the depth and energy of her sadness. I was quite moved by her telling me this story, and in a slow soft voice I said, "I'm so sorry that happened to you..

Without my thinking about it, my autonomic system was tuning to hers, and I felt compassion toward her as she began to make more eye contact with me. I sensed that she felt safe enough to allow the deep and troubling feelings she'd experienced back then to come more fully into her conscious awareness, and I felt welcoming of those feelings. She continued to cry as her body rocked back and forth. Slowly the sobs quieted and she leaned back in her chair and looked straight toward me. As our gazes met someplace in the middle of the room, there was a sense of reciprocity and steadiness in our connecting. I asked how she felt toward this 10-year-old girl, and she said she felt close to her. When I asked if the 10-year-old wanted to say anything to her, she replied, "No, it's enough just to be with her for now," her hand still touching her chest. We sat together for another few minutes, allowing her to connect with that little girl.

The ventral vagal attunement developing between us was also flowing between her and that 10-year-old girl. As I was listening to her in a connected and reciprocal way, so she was listening to her 10-year-old, and the agitated autonomic arousal states she was in when we began were not pulling her into shutdown. In Polyvagal Theory terms, her ventral vagal system had caught up with her sympathetic arousal system, braking it enough so that she could actually sense me there with her and feel safely connected with me, as well as with her little girl. She was able to calm down without being overwhelmed by the sadness, or by her defenses against it, making it possible for her to feel safely connected with the little girl and for that young part to feel safely connected with her now. Being in a ventral vagal state as she felt the grief around this old trauma allowed her to comfort the little girl. In subsequent sessions, we continued to work with this trauma and to heal the wounds she carried from that experience.

Polyvagal Theory and poetry are rooted in the reality that we mammals are communal and are able to co-regulate in the way I've just described happening for Cindy and me. We humans have evolved in such a way that when we arrive in the world, we are, as Stephen Porges, Deb Dana, Brené Brown, Peter Levine, and numerous others have said so brilliantly, *wired for connection*. As Porges explained, we depend on this capacity for connectedness and the reciprocity it affords to communicate for our survival, for our "health, growth and restoration" (Porges, 2016). When reciprocity is ruptured between people and not successfully repaired, we experience imbalance and distress. When this becomes chronic, we lose our sense of safe connection to others, which leads to autonomic dysregulation and threatens our well-being. Listening to victims of trauma in a way that evokes an experience of safe enough connection supports the individual's natural ability to balance and to heal.

Prosodic intonation is an essential aspect of our capacity to experience safe connection. Being able to raise and lower our voice along with our ability to hear these intonations and distinguish the safe from the threatening sounds guides us toward safely connecting with another. Looking at the etymology of the word *prosody* takes us back to the Greek *prosoidia*, which combines the words *pros*, meaning "toward," and *oidia*, meaning "song." The intonations of singing carry over into the reading of poetry, fairy tale, children's stories, even into everyday conversation when we speak in playful tones with others. In an interview with Jay Biles on the radio program *The Writer's Almanac Bookshelf*, the poet Dana Gioia said, "Poetry is speech heightened into music. The physical sound of a poem is part of its meaning" (2016). We often go into a deeply inflected voice when speaking to children, as well as with adults to whom we want to convey something of importance to us. When we want to let someone know that we are interested in what they are saying, we say something like, "Tell me more," and we intone it giving it accent to convey the sincerity of our desire to hear more.

The poetry of every tradition is rooted in this prosodic capacity of the human voice. *No prosody, no poetry*. As Stephen Porges said, our capacity to produce and to hear prosodic intonation is essential in our process of co-regulating, which in turn is essential in our work with trauma clients as they heal from the wounds that have engendered a sense of unsafety with others (Porges, 2012). Perhaps we could also say, *No prosody, no healing therapy dialogue*.

In my experience, the work of poetry and the insights of Polyvagal Theory cross-fertilize. When I'm writing a poem or participating in a writing workshop with other writers who read their new poems and a word or a phrase is off, or a line break isn't in the right place, I hear it and feel it more than know it in a conceptual way. In my clinical practice, I listen to what clients say in their words and in their body signals. When I sense a signal from a trauma memory, I feel it in my body, hear it and sense it energetically before I know anything about it with my thinking mind. Polyvagal Theory calls this neuroception. A subtle change in tone, a movement of the foot or the hand, a flicker of the gaze, a posture change—any of these can signal that something is happening that might be a new revelation for my client. If I catch the moment and encourage a pause for the person to listen to themself, our listening together is likely to drop to a deeper level, one where the part of their system that is signaling danger can be heard in its own terms. When enough ventral vagal energy is present in our dialogue and the client feels safe enough, habitual protecting patterns that cover things can relax so that we might hear from parts of the person's system where the wounds of trauma are stored. A memory of something painful that has been hidden can poke through and make itself known unexpectedly in a signal from the body or the voice. If my listening, or the client's listening, isn't picking up the felt signal, it goes unnoticed, unheard, and unharvested.

Guidance comes from tracking autonomic signals in the shared listening field with a client. There's a granularity to it that is always specific to each person as they tell the story they have lived through and tell it at this particular time. There's also an immediacy to autonomic information, which communicates directly into our listening without having to be processed through our thinking system in its familiar and linear way of making sense of things. The guidance of neuroception takes the listening process into uncharted territory, which is where we need to go to discover the still-hidden truth of someone's experience. Listening autonomically before going to the familiar story we have of our experience and ourselves guides us to the yet-unspoken-for places inside where trauma wounds are buried. Clients feel heard when we trust their autonomic systems to guide us into the harder places, places they have avoided. Arthur Clarke, who wrote *2001: A Space Odyssey*, said one of the laws of the universe is that " . . . the only way of discovering the limits of the possible is to venture a little way past them into the impossible" (Clarke, 1962, p. 31). To metabolize through the burdens of trauma wounds, clients have to travel into the impossible places their adaptive survival strategies have dictated they should never go.

Listening on this level of autonomic awareness deepens and optimizes the therapy process with trauma survivors. When they tell what happened to them, I encourage them to go slowly, to track autonomic responses and subtle shifts in their state as they speak. If I notice something in particular that looks like a shift in their energy, their state, their face, voice, or posture, I ask them what just happened and invite them to bring their attention to it, to stay with the experience and to listen to it until they harvest what it reveals. We join each other in this shared venture of listening neuroceptively, and together we establish a reciprocal connection that creates enough safety to explore and metabolize difficult memories.

Poetry offers a similar kind of granularity and immediacy to that of neuroception. When I hear a poem, the specifics of its images, its rhythms, line breaks, syntax, and sounds guide my listening. The poem evokes a felt sense in my body that shifts and changes each time I return to it. I'm guided into places that were uncharted and unknown to me. When I return to the poem, I feel it speaking to me like a friend, like someone I've known for a long time. At some point, the poem brings my listening back to me, as I realize that I've been listening to the author *and* to myself the whole time. Some form of ventral vagal toning activates between the poem and me, or between the author of the poem and me as I read it or hear it spoken. And when I listen to a poem that's been around a long time, it sometimes dawns on me that I'm hearing something that's been listened to many times over the centuries, and I have a sense of connection with all the humans who have been touched by this very poem. I experienced this the first time I heard this Rumi (1995) poem from the 13th century. Listen to it with me.

> The breeze at dawn has secrets to tell you.
>   Don't go back to sleep.
> You must ask for what you really want.
>   Don't go back to sleep.
> People are going back and forth across the doorsill
>   where the two worlds touch.
> The door is round and open.
>   Don't go back to sleep. (p. 36)

When Rumi speaks through these lines, translated here by Coleman Barks, we are invited to travel someplace that might feel both strange and familiar. For me it's a place where I feel the presence of someone, perhaps Rumi, who invites me to connect with myself enough to be able to notice what I really want, and I feel nourished by that, over and over. Reading this poem evokes in me a feeling of coming home to myself and a sense that I'm held in community with many others who have heard and been touched by this poem since the 13th century, when Rumi first uttered it. As I rest in the embrace of these words and in the legacy of Rumi and all who have been touched by his poems, I have a neuroceptive experience of attunement with a large community of humans whom I will never meet in the flesh though feel connected to each time this poem lands in my listening.

In its account of neuroception, Polyvagal Theory sheds light on its relevance to our work with trauma clients, and I wonder if poetry, in turn, doesn't shed light on this phenomenon of neuroception. What is happening when it occurs? Polyvagal Theory gives us the neurological account of what's happening and provides a phylogenetic account of the evolution for how that became part of our experience long ago among our ancestors. Is it possible that in the earliest stages of development in human dialogue, as members of any group were signaling danger or safety to each other, this neurological phenomenon was evolving simultaneously with the earliest forms of what we have come to identify as poetry? Rhythms, prosodic intonations, rhymes, all the basic elements of poetic dialogue were part of that early call-and-response between human beings. Could it be that poetry and the neurological development in humans that gave rise to neuroception were developing at the same time and that they are integrally tied together?

When neuroception guides our listening experience, we begin to notice things we didn't expect in our familiar way of listening that is organized according to the stories we have habitually told ourselves, the ones that have perhaps become part of our protective way of making sense of our world. When listening neuroceptively to our autonomic signals and states, we bring our listening to the immediacy of our experience rather than filtering it through our familiar stories of who we are.

Heraclitus, the ancient Greek thinker from around 500 BCE, says in one of his now-famous fragments, "If you don't expect the unexpected, you won't find it" (Heraclitus, 1957, p. 195). His words encourage us to bring curiosity to our listening. When ventral vagal toning occurs and we feel safe, curiosity along with compassion naturally arise. Therapists are always well advised to "expect the unexpected," and when the client joins the therapist in doing so on their own behalf, the cocreated listening brings details of their experience to light that optimize the potential for healing.

The ancient Greeks used an evocative word for truth: *aletheia*. It's exciting to note that this name for "truth" comes from the root verb "to cover," with the alpha privative prefix, which gives us the meaning "to uncover." Truth for the ancients was an uncovering. Listening in the fashion I'm describing, whether to a poem or a client in therapy, uncovers more of what's there. The more we notice the speaker's physical and neurological experience as they tell a story, the more of their actual experience is uncovered and witnessed, and when this happens at the optimal pace for the client, the wounds they carry in their body have a chance to be metabolized in the shared listening. Metabolization offers a useful metaphor for what happens in an active field of witnessing when two people listen to what's being told and, at the same time, listen to their listening. When ventral vagal energy activates, the field that opens has a kind of enzymatic capacity to break down, digest, and process trauma experiences and the residue they leave behind.

When exploring the conditions for the possibility of listening, another question arises for each of us: Where did our listening come from, and where did it begin to take the shape and orientation that it has? For each person this is unique. As I've already said, I'm from the prairie of eastern Montana. Visiting there this past summer called me back to the sounds of the place that first shaped and informed my listening. I visited some of the fence posts where, as a boy, I'd stand for long stretches of time fascinated and soothed by their steadiness. I remembered feeling relief from the fear I experienced when my mother would frequently appear to be losing her fight against depression and anxiety. I was her "go-to guy" in the family and was often afraid that I would fail to calm her down enough so she would be able to cook our supper. On hot afternoons when she was reading her books and magazines as her way of escaping, I would walk to the creek and lean against a fence post. I'd put my cheek next to the sun-warmed side of the post and feel soothed.

Polyvagal Theory would say I was experiencing a neuroception of safety in the fence posts. Though soothed for a while, I would often move into a dissociated state of dorsal vagal shutdown and collapse. I'd stand there for long stretches of time wishing I could trade places with the post and escape my fear. Failing to experience attunement with my mother, I'd regulate my autonomic nervous system with the cues of safety I harvested from the fence posts and the surrounding environment. I loved the stability and the trustworthiness of the posts. They never left me, turned on me, or let me down. Many of my poems have been written in honor of and in gratitude for the fence posts. Here is one of them:

To Fencepost

It knew my breath
and knew my cheek.
It was yesterday,

a long time ago,
when I stood alone
next to any old fencepost

and waited before I knew
I was beginning
a practice of listening to what stands still

a long time.
Today, standing anyplace,
that yearning might come

for a way in
to where fenceposts stay without ceasing,
each one a priest of stillness.

Any day this is so—
on a hillside where wind trembles the grass
stands a quiet gray weathered post,

crust of golden lichen
glowing
on the shadowed side.
(Whited, 2013, p. 5)

What were the cues of safety or danger in our early listening environments? What scared us? What overwhelmed us and what soothed us? How did those cues and our way of responding to them shape our listening? These questions guide us into an exploration of our listening through the lens of Polyvagal Theory. We can hear the ways in which our earlier autonomic experiences have shaped the tendencies that now manifest in our listening, which is what we take into the session room with our clients. If it's informed by our own unmetabolized wounds and grief, by protective beliefs and assumptions, these will inevitably constrain what and how we hear. The good news is that when we *listen to our listening* in this way, it naturally evolves and opens, and our personal biases become apparent as such. This is what we have to offer and to model for our clients.

One of the challenges to the domain of our work as therapists in our time is the extent to which the cognitive and conceptual have been privileged since the Enlightenment thinkers, like Descartes, whose prioritizing the mind over the body has profoundly affected Western thought and discourse. Polyvagal Theory and, in my view, poetry both offer alternatives to this bias. Polyvagal Theory shines a light on the Cartesian bias we've all inherited from generations of Western science dominating our thinking and our listening. It does this by bearing witness to this bias as a bias, and by opening a way for us to see beyond it, to actually listen to the ways it has informed and constrained our listening. Revealing the interactions between brain and body, to which Descartes did not have access, Polyvagal Theory explains how our meaning-making minds are informed by, and answer to, the neurological and physiological signals our bodies provide. It invites us to listen to the body through the awakening and development of neuroception, and it lays out what could be called an ecology of listening, which guides us into the depth of what listening, when it's open, has to offer between one human and another.

Because it's offered as a theory and not as a model, Polyvagal Theory is relevant to any and every model a therapist might employ in working with trauma survivors. It shows what is happening in the neurology and physiology of human mammals, revealing the conditions for the very possibility of connecting.

Poetry, in my view, does something similar. By introducing poetry as a resource to our work as therapists, I in no way mean to suggest that therapists should become poets, or even develop an interest in reading poetry in the formal or traditional sense. What I have tried to suggest is that poetry informs us all by virtue of the fact that each of us has inherited a particular cultural legacy that was initially articulated in poems, songs, and prayers. This mode of dialogue that stands at the beginning of every tradition, and carries down to our time the meanings made by our forebears, is poetry. It's imbedded in our psyches, embodied in our autonomic nervous systems, encoded in our verbal exchanges, maybe even in our DNA, if you will, and on all these levels we are profoundly shaped by that legacy. I would argue that we all have poetic sensibilities, and in the most essential sense, we are all poets.

What I think poetry offers us is a way of listening to our clients and to their stories in their own terms. I have been proposing throughout this essay that there is poetry in everyone's story, in the way it is told and in the way it is held inside. If my listening can access that poetry and reflect it back to them, it helps them to open their listening. Bringing the Polyvagal Theory lens to my experience as poet and therapist has deepened my understanding and my practice of the listening I have to offer my clients. Poetry has guided me to take seriously as sources of relevant information the prosodic intonations, the body signals, the rhythms, all the granular and immediate details of someone's experience, and by doing so to open and to deepen my listening when clients tells their stories. Polyvagal Theory has helped me understand why and how all of that is relevant, and what may have been happening among our earliest ancestors when they were singing our traditions into being. That ancient singing is the very fountain out of which our listening emerges, and it echoes through us as we listen to our clients and bear witness to their experience as they come to us for support in the shared endeavor to heal the wounds they carry.

References

Clarke, Arthur C. (1962). *Profiles of the Future, An Inquiry into the Limits of the Possible.* New York, NY: Harper and Row.

Gioia, D. (1969, April 22). Interview by Joy Biles. In G. Keillor (Host), *The writer's almanac bookshelf.* Saint Paul, MN: Minnesota Public Radio.

Heraclitus (1957), *The presocratic philosophers: A critical history with a selection of texts.* Cambridge, England: Cambridge University Press.

Komunyakaa, Y. (2016). Interview by Ishion Hutchinson. *American Poets: The Journal of the Academy of American Poets, 51*, 31–36.

LeGuin, U. K. (2004). *The wave in the mind: Talks and essays on the writer, the reader, and the imagination.* Boston, MA: Shambhala.

Porges, S.W. (2011). *The polyvagal theory: Neurophysiological foundations of emotions, attachment, communication, and self-regulation.* New York: WW Norton.

Porges, S.W. (2012, July). *The origins of compassion: A phylogenetic perspective.* Presented at The Science of Compassion: Origins, Measures and Interventions Conference, sponsored by the Center for Compassion and Altruism Research and Education at Stanford University, Colorado. https://www.youtube.com/watch?v=MYXa_BX2cE8&t=25s

Porges, S. W. (2016, April 11). The science of safety [Interview]. *Relationship Alive* [Audio podcast].

Porges, S. W. (2016, May 28). *Polyvagal theory: how your body makes the decision.* Interview by Gunther Schmidt. Milton Erickson Institut. https://www.youtube.com/watch?v=ivLEAlhBHPM

Rumi, J. (1995). Don't Go Back to Sleep, in C. Barks with J. Moyne (Trans.), *The Essential Rumi.* San Francisco, CA: HarperCollins.

Schwartz, Richard C. (1995). *Internal Family Systems Therapy,* New York: Guilford Press.

Whited, G. (2013). *Having listened,* Stonington, CT: Homebound.

Williams, W. C. (1994). *Asphodel, That Greeny Flower & Other Love Poems,* New York, NY: New Directions.

Part IV

Applications in Medicine

20

Strengthening the Safety Circuit: Applying Polyvagal Theory in the Newborn Intensive Care Unit

Marilyn Sanders

Abstract: Despite the technological success of modern newborn intensive care, chronic disruptions of social connectedness due to separation can be traumatic for both babies and families. Understanding and applying principles of Polyvagal Theory can benefit babies, families, and staff by fostering ventral vagal social engagement. In addition, polyvagal-trained staff can use their own ventral vagal energies to co-regulate each other and stressed families who are sympathetically activated or in dorsal vagal collapse.

The hospital is the most emo place I know . . . and the NICU is the most emo place in the hospital.
—Research nurse and parent of a former premature newborn

Introduction to Neonatology

In the United States, there are approximately 4 million births annually. Of these, about 500,000 newborns (12%; U.S. Department of Health and Human Services, 2013) require care beyond that provided in a well-baby nursery and may spend time in a newborn intensive care unit. The "lucky" babies have their medical needs met in the same hospital as their mothers. Many babies, however, need transport by a specialized team to a newborn intensive care unit across town, in a neighboring town, across the state, or even across state lines.

Neonatology is a new pediatric specialty and a modern technological success. In 1963, President Kennedy's baby son, Patrick Bouvier Kennedy, born at 34 weeks, weighing 4 pounds, 10.5 ounces, died at 39 hours of age (Altman, 2013). Today, virtually all (98–99%) babies of similar size and age survive (Matthews & MacDorman, 2013).

The babies' medical problems and severity of illness vary. Some may require only a few hours of observation. Others may need a day or two and be moved to the mother's room before being discharged home. Still more will stay in the hospital after the mother is discharged from the hospital. More than 250,000 newborns will be hospitalized for more than a week (U.S. Department of Health and Human Services, 2013).

Many newborns needing lengthy hospitalizations are premature or have lung problems. Others have congenital or genetic problems. Still others need surgeries. A very small number of newborns experience catastrophic events during labor and delivery, prolonging their hospital stay.

Despite the successes of modern newborn intensive care, a price is paid by these babies and their families—the loss of their biologically driven connectedness, for a few hours, days, weeks, or months. Families draw upon adaptive capacities they could not have previously imagined as they struggle to identify and meet their babies' needs amid the beeps, alarms, and disruptions of modern newborn intensive care.

The Expectancies of the Newborn and Young Infant

The expectancy of social engagement in mammalian species is biologically embedded. For the human newborn, this engagement typically begins when she is placed upon her mother's chest and finds the way to mother's breast. There she latches, sucks, and transfers breast milk as the mother's central nervous system releases oxytocin, bringing the mother into loving synchronicity with her baby. Together they reciprocally upregulate ventral vagal tone in each other's presence. Oxytocin's role in ensuring survival is clear, as it clamps down the uterus, preventing the mother from hemorrhaging, lets down milk to nurture the newborn, and enhances maternal prosocial and loving behaviors (Lee, Macbeth, Pagani, & Young, 2009).

Over the next hours, days, and weeks, mother and her newborn engage in an increasingly well-choreographed dance as they make meaning of their relationship and world. (Tronick, 2010). As their relationship becomes consistent, predictable, and safe, they become securely attached to each other and critical co-regulators of the integrity of each other's autonomic nervous system.

Polyvagal Theory describes the hierarchical response of the sympathetic and parasympathetic components of the autonomic nervous system through an unconscious sense of "awareness" or neuroception, active when the newborn senses "safety," "danger," or "life-threat" (Porges, 2011). When the baby senses safety, the most highly evolved ventral vagus is active. Both mother and her baby are in synchrony and engaged with facial expressions, vocalizations, and touch that blunt the hypothalamic pituitary axis and inhibit sympathetic activity. The result is a mother–baby dyad that works well, bringing pleasure, security, and nurturance to both members.

However satisfying this pleasurable state, there are frequent interruptions in the synchronicity of the well-functioning mother–baby pair, leading to disruptions even in the best of relationships. Video microanalysis reveals that typical mother–baby pairs are in sync for affective states only one-third of the time (Tronick & Cohn, 1989). It is the *repair* of the disruption—its timing, its sensitivity, its fit, its lack of intrusiveness—that will determine how well the dyad functions over time (Koulomzin et al., 2002).

A disruption that occurs with physical separation or maternal emotional withdrawal, intense anger, or anxiety signals to the newborn that he is at risk of losing the mother's availability, the preexisting condition of his unconscious sense of safety. The baby becomes autonomically dysregulated as he senses danger—a predator is in the midst. Now, seeking the return of a "safe" base, the newborn's sympathetic nervous system mobilizes, cortisol surges, heart rate and blood pressure increase, and the baby cries in protest of his felt sense of aloneness. If the mother, sensing the baby's distress and violation of expectancies, returns, cuddles, talks softly, and soothes the baby, the baby's distress often quickly resolves, and the mother–newborn pair return to safety, synchrony, and calm as ventral vagal tone is restored.

If, however, a timely repair does not occur, or the newborn becomes accustomed to chronic lack of the mother's availability due to long-term separation, severe mental illness, or chronic failures to respond, the newborn may, instead, sink into an immobilized, life-threat state modulated by the vestigial dorsal vagus. This newborn loses tone, appears passive and apathetic, and is shut down, using minimal energy to meet his metabolic demands.

Newborns and toddlers who have been raised in institutional settings where they have physically been cared for but lack safe relationships and secure attachments often display these responses. They have exhausted their cortisol reserves, manifesting low heart rates and blood pressures. They have learned all too early that expending energy for safety brings a poor return on investment. Ironically, their energy conservation mode of shutdown, in the short run, is autonomically adaptive, promoting their survival, however tenuous (Koss, Hostinar, Donzella, & Gunnar, 2014).

Polyvagal Theory and the Healthy Newborn

As ventral vagal regulation and newborn behavior mature, self-regulatory capacities come online. Porges related increasing vagal myelination and development of cortical influence upon the brain stem vagal regulating areas to postpartum adaptation of the newborn (Suess et al., 2000). Distinct from earlier, reptilian species, mammalian newborns are dependent upon caregivers for nurturance and survival. This dependency is expressed through the "ingestive-vagal reflexes" of feeding, requiring an intact brain stem and the muscles of face for mastication to ingest food. Simultaneously, the latched newborn is socially engaged through the co-regulatory capacities of maternal eye gaze, head turning, vocalization, and prosody mediated through the special visceral efferents of the vagal nerve through the face-to-heart connection. The consistent availability and predictability of the mother to co-regulate the newborn reinforces the unconscious awareness (neuroception) of safety.

Ultimately, the survival of the mammalian newborn depends upon the ventral vagal mediation of the face-to-heart connection. With evolution from reptilian to mammalian species, key components such as the detachment of the middle-ear bones from the mandible allowed both for an enlarged cranium (Rowe, 1996) and for low-amplitude/high-frequency airborne sounds such as mammalian vocalizations to be processed. At the same time, the changing spatial relationships of the vagal nuclei and the nuclei of the face, neck, and head fostered development of the social engagement system that protects, nurtures, and sustains the mammalian newborn.

Polyvagal Theory and the Premature Newborn

The premature newborn, as opposed to the healthy newborn, is challenged by the developmental trajectory of vagal myelination beginning in the third trimester of pregnancy, specifically around 32–37 weeks (Doussard-Roosevelt, Porges, Scanlon, Alemi, & Scanlon, 1997). In the 21st-century NICU, premature newborns born as early as 22–24 weeks are hospitalized many weeks before significant vagal myelination and brain stem maturity permit them to breastfeed. For these newborns, self-regulatory capacities are more limited, and their ability to participate as fully as term newborns in meaningful co-regulation is also affected. There are, however, key strategies that enhance maternal physical and emotional proximity, such as kangaroo or skin-to-skin care, discussed later, that improve co-regulatory capacity for the vulnerable newborn (Feldman, Rosenthal, & Eidelman, 2014).

Porges developed Polyvagal Theory after a question from a neonatologist (a pediatrician who specializes in the care of critically ill newborns). The neonatologist referenced the challenge of apparent "death spells" in premature newborns where the newborn abruptly drops her heart rate significantly and without intervention and resuscitation could die. Could there, he asked, be too much of an apparently good thing, or too much vagal tone?

As described and measured by Porges, vagal tone is reflected in the measure of respiratory sinus arrhythmia (RSA), a naturally occurring variability in the heart rate that is correlated with respiratory activity. Simply put, when we inhale, our heart rate increases, and when we exhale, heart rate decreases.

Of primary importance to the fetus and newborn is the role of RSA in determining fetal well-being, manifested by intact neuroregulation. In obstetrics, obstetricians assess and report fetal heart rate variability, the first cousin to RSA, for labor and delivery decision making. Heart rate variability, unlike RSA, is not indexed by respiratory activity. It is, however, a proxy easily measured with standard equipment. Alterations in fetal heart rate variability often prompt plans to deliver a newborn recognizing that diminished vagal tone may be an ominous sign of impending fetal deterioration.

The maturity of vagal tone influence measured by RSA increases throughout gestation and into infancy. Decreases in RSA are correlated with extreme prematurity, serious illness, and disease states (Doussard-Roosevelt et al., 1997; Suess et al., 2000). The premature newborn can experience a stressor that affects his immature vagal tone, reflected in his RSA, and can have a potentially lethal bradycardia.

Rather than the classic interpretation of an antagonistic relationship between sympathetic and parasympathetic systems, Polyvagal Theory presents an integrated and synergistic system with both parts working together in the service of survival. Chief among the adaptive mechanisms is the vagal brake, applied more or less strenuously to the intrinsic cardiac pacemaker as a self-regulatory mechanism to either decrease or increase energy expenditure. This led Porges to the solve the "vagal paradox."He explained that in the absence of ventral vagal tone, reflected in diminished RSA, the neural regulation of the heart could be vulnerable to a massive dorsal vagal surge producing clinically relevant and potentially lethal bradycardia. This dorsal vagal surge could be observed as a "death spell" in a premature newborn, shutdown in an older child, or dissociation in a trauma victim.

The preterm newborn, like the more mature newborn, communicates to us through her behaviors. Als's synactive theory of development recognized that newborns, including premature ones, have emerging developmental agendas, noting that their autonomic nervous systems, visceral responses and surrounding motor and state organizational systems are constantly interactive within and between each other. The entire system, embedded within the environment—in this case, the NICU—is a violation of the species expectation of transition from womb to mother's breast, or in polyvagal language, a disruption of the biologically embedded need for social engagement. Als focused upon the competencies of the preterm to communicate her needs through a hierarchy of behaviors and the primary caregiving role of the parents (Als, Butler, Kosta, & McAnulty, 2005).

When ventral vagal tone dominates, the newborn will be in a quiet, alert state, with regular respirations; be pink and well perfused; will have mild accelerations in her heart rate with handling; will show smooth movements of the arms and legs; and will engage in some self-soothing behaviors such as bringing hand to mouth, display an open face, and make sucking or mouthing movements. The sympathetically aroused newborn will be hyperalert or fussy, with fast respirations, significant increases in heart rate with handling, skin mottling, spitting up, hiccupping, and extension behaviors of the extremities and hands. Finally, the premature infant whose autonomic nervous system has strong dorsal vagal influence may have significant pauses in respiration, bradycardia or a fixed heart rate, flaccid extremities, and diminished alertness.

The synactive theory highlights the opportunities to improve ventral vagal tone by facilitating dyadic connection and safety, even while the modern NICU is providing the technologic support also necessary for survival. As premature newborns mature, so should their observed behaviors be moving from dorsal vagal through sympathetic and ultimately to ventral vagal states, even if only briefly. Since full myelination of the vagus is not achieved until close to one year of age, healthy-growing premature and term newborns will develop increasing frequency and length of ventral vagal states.

The Experience of Newborn Intensive Care for the Baby, the Family, and the Staff

Polyvagal Theory is a portal for families and caregivers to understand, both at a level of body awareness and cognition, the impact of the experience of the newborn intensive care unit on early newborn relationships and interventions to optimize the newborn–family relationship during a stressful hospitalization.

The Baby's Experience of the Newborn Intensive Care Unit

The premature or otherwise ill baby is thrust into an environment that challenges his mammalian biological imperative for connectedness. The biologically intended dyadic dance that brings mother and her newborn to connectedness is rudely interrupted for the NICU baby. The developing integrity of his autonomic nervous system is challenged by unintended violations of his evolutionary expectancies of proximity to his caregivers as well as the felt senses of safety, predictability, and reciprocity that lead to enduring connectedness.

Rather than proximity to his parents and a small number of consistent caregivers, the NICU baby receives care from a larger number of medical, nursing, respiratory, and rehabilitation providers. The baby may be cared for in an incubator that provides some buffer to harsh light and loud, unexpected sounds, but alarms go off; staff, visitors and families speak; computers on wheels are pushed around to meet the needs of the electronic health record. There is no predictability—the baby can be sleeping quietly when a code happens at the next bed or safety alarms go off and bright lights both shine and pulsate.

The timing and nature of touch is unpredictable. A baby can be resting; however, if a care time is due, and blood work needs to be done, he may be awakened by a staff member sticking his heel to draw blood. The health care provider's intention is to appropriately monitor the baby to ensure his well-being and to avoid complications of illness or even therapies. The NICU baby never knows whether the next touch will be his mother's or father's loving cuddling and stroking or the blood draw due at 2:00 p.m. In the first days of his hospitalization, he will have an average of 12 procedures daily (Carbajal et al., 2008).

The Family's Experience of the Newborn Intensive Care Unit

From an evolutionary vantage, neonatal intensive care, despite its successes, violates deeply embedded biologic expectancies of parents and their baby. The challenges for parents often begin well before the crisis of newborn intensive care hospitalization. Many struggled to conceive. Others had complicated pregnancies filled with uncertainty about outcome. For some, pregnancy was uneventful until they were rushed to an emergency cesarean section.

Rather than going from perineum to mother's chest, the typical baby who requires neonatal intensive care is whisked away into an adjoining room where medical and nursing staff evaluate, resuscitate, and stabilize the baby. Depending upon the baby's stability and the hospital environment, babies may (or may not) see their parents before going to the NICU for further care. Only infrequently does the family hold the baby prior to transfer.

Families often experience lack of privacy in ward or bay-type units. Parents are physically and sometimes emotionally distant from their newborns. They describe fear, anxiety, anger, helplessness, and powerlessness. As one mother (Leff & Walizer, 1992) said,

> I want to be with her in the NICU, but it kills me to see her so sick. . . . I'm angry, sad, frightened, exhausted all at once. . . . With whom can I be angry? Myself? My innocent baby? The doctors who practiced sound medicine? (p. 122)

Parents quickly learn that their baby's well-being depends upon the meticulous and attentive care provided by hospital caregivers. They are surrounded by neonatologists, physicians in training, advanced practitioners, nurses, and other members of the health care team. Every day, the team rounds at the bedside, armed with electronic medical records, easy access to online resources, and vast stores of knowledge to discuss the plan for the day.

In the initial days, parents are often shocked and stunned by the unexpected birth, struggling with their own medical issues, pain, and anxiety, worries about other children, and fear of the next possible impending crisis. The medical team gives a lengthy recitation of all the baby's problems, system by system. They use long words, foreign to parents. They list lots of numbers; what do they mean? They look different, set apart by their blue scrubs and white jackets. The team wraps up, summarizes briefly for the parents, and asks if they have any questions. "Is he going to be okay?" asks the mother. "It's early," says the neonatologist, who smiles gently. "We'll need to wait and see, but we're all doing everything we can to help him." The team then moves to the next bedside, often leaving a puzzled, frightened parent.

Parents of NICU babies may experience post-traumatic stress both in the NICU and potentially post-discharge. In a study of NICU parents, one third of mothers (35%) and one-quarter of fathers (24%) met criteria for acute stress disorder, and 15% of mothers and 8% of fathers met criteria for post-traumatic stress disorder (PTSD; Lefkowitz, Baxt, & Evans, 2010). Concurrent stressors and a family history of anxiety or depression were correlated with likelihood of PTSD. Of interest, there was no correlation of PTSD with the medical severity of the baby's illness.

The Experience of the Health Care Providers in the Newborn Intensive Care Unit

Who chooses to work in a high-acuity setting with unpredictability, where the work can transition from calm to frenetic in a moment? All can be stable, nurses and doctors examining babies, rounding, speaking to parents, and in a flash, they must mobilize for an emergency. In polyvagal terms, they must lift the vagal brake recruiting sympathetic tone to provide energy but maintaining a calm alert state to work collaboratively to resolve the crisis. They leverage their sense of connectedness to each other, operationalized through the common goal of saving a baby.

Ideally, health care providers spend the majority of their time in a ventral vagal state, allowing them both to care for babies, minimizing stress, and to be available to parents as a low-resistance sink for their sympathetic arousal.

However, the steady drum of high levels of stress and high sympathetic tone, for many health care providers, can result in post-traumatic stress and burnout. In a recent workplace survey of doctors and nurses in either a newborn or pediatric intensive care unit (NICU or PICU), one in six (17%) met criteria for post-traumatic stress disorder and two-thirds (66%) had lower but concerning post-traumatic stress scores. Workers reporting higher levels of emotional exhaustion and PTSD symptoms were less likely to evidence levels of resilience. (Dalia, Abbas, Colville, & Brierley, 2013).

Is the Experience of Newborn Intensive Care Traumatic, and If So, For Whom?

Trauma services abound in U.S. hospitals. Helicopters lift off, ambulances are launched, and patients from infancy throughout the lifespan who sustain serious physical injury are airlifted and ground transported to the nearest Level 1 trauma center. The meaning is explicit. Everyone who has ever watched an episode of *ER* knows. All staff members are at attention to efficiently provide high-quality intensive care services to the incoming patient.

Who broadcasts "incoming trauma" when a baby is brought from the labor-and-delivery suite, the newborn nursery, or the mother's room to the newborn intensive care unit? Is neonatal intensive care hospitalization, per se, traumatic? In a typical rupture of maternal–newborn co-regulation (e.g., the phone rings, or the mother is otherwise distracted) the disruption is brief and readily repaired, as mother and newborn soon return to their connectedness. What if, however, the disruptions are persistent and frequent? What if there is no time for repair prior to the next disruption? What if these disruptions become chronic?

Should safety and a secure base not be attainable, should these disruptions of early relationships become chronic, the newborn nervous system has two options—a state of constant mobilization, sympathetic drive, energy expenditure (danger) or immobilization (dorsal vagal tone) with death feigning, shutdown, extreme energy conservation. Neither option is growth promoting or biologically sustainable. The human newborn requires the presence of the adult caregiver to provide both her safety-promoting physical needs (warmth, nutrition, protection from the environment) and emotional needs (social engagement, connectedness, co-regulation).

For the newborn whose life depends upon connectedness, trauma is a "chronic disruption of connectedness" (Porges, 2014). Newborn intensive care, though medically life saving, is often a chronic disruption that begins at or shortly after birth. Newborn intensive care disrupts the early reciprocal caregiving relationship of the newborn, her mother, and other primary caregivers—it disrupts physical proximity of mother and newborn, and often emotional proximity of newborn and primary caregivers.

When a newborn is admitted to a neonatal intensive care unit, the family system connectedness is stressed. When the disruption of connectedness becomes chronic, newborn intensive care is traumatic. How much stress and disruption is traumatic for any newborn and family is variable and highly dependent upon individual autonomic nervous system tone resulting from prior experiences, family supports, and opportunities for repair.

Extensive research literature now documents the impact of early life stresses upon brain development and function, particularly the risk for later social emotional challenges in childhood and adulthood. Particular targets of early stress include the prefrontal cortex, the amygdala, and the hippocampus (Shonkoff et al., 2012). The prefrontal cortex and associated areas are the site of executive planning, organization, and attentional focus. The amygdala is the seat of emotional regulation, and the hippocampus is involved in learning and memory. A model for appreciating the impact of severe early developmental trauma on the fetal, newborn, and infant brain derives from long-term studies of babies raised in institutional rather than home environments. Based upon noninvasive neuroimaging studies and genetic testing, a window of 15–17 months emerges as a critical time period for establishing safe and secure relationships to diminish reactivity of the limbic system and decrease long-term psychiatric diagnoses (Tottenham & Sheridan, 2009; Zeanah et al., 2009).

The Newborn Intensive Parenting Unit (NIPU): A Ventral Vagal Informed Newborn Care Environment

How can we best create a safe and secure environment for babies who need intensive care services that promotes connectedness with their parents and family? How can we assist the families of our tiny patients feel safe and secure enough to regulate and tone their own autonomic states so they can be available to co-regulate their babies?

How can we establish therapeutic alliances that make the NICU a secure base for babies, parents, families, and staff?

The goal of the ventral vagal informed NICU is minimizing stressors and disruptions of connectedness for babies and families while affirming and celebrating the primary caregiving relationship of the baby nested safely and securely within the family. The National Perinatal Association suggests formally recognizing this paradigm shift by renaming our care environments Newborn Intensive Parenting Units or NIPUs (Hynan & Hall, 2016). Transcending the gap between the present and the future NIPU requires significant changes, including psychoeducation for families and staff, maintaining physical and emotional proximity for parents, and supporting parents in co-regulating their babies. At full implementation, a new philosophy of care, prioritizing baby and family connectedness, is the foundation for all aspects of caregiving.

Providing Psycho-Education for Families and Staff

Recognizing our own affective states is fundamental to self-regulation and participation in co-regulation. Dana's *Beginner's Guide to Polyvagal Theory* is a brief document written for a lay audience introducing the concept of neuroception and its relationship to the autonomic nervous system. It introduces the evolutionary hierarchy of dorsal vagal (reptilian, parasympathetic immobilization), sympathetic (mobilization), and ventral vagal (mammalian, parasympathetic, safe and social engagement) tone (Dana, 2015a). The simple illustrations use ladders and articulated figures, spaced either at the top (ventral vagal), in the middle (sympathetic), or at the bottom (dorsal vagal) of the ladder. Using emotional language reflecting the affective states of the position on the ladder, readers can begin identifying where on the ladder they rest in the moment or more chronically. In this simple exercise, families and staff can begin developing a common language to reflect upon their own experiences and to appreciate the triggers that may move them from ventral vagal to sympathetic and dorsal vagal states.

In addition to developing a polyvagal language culture, we need new terminology to describe the NICU experience from the baby's perspective. Most frequently, the biopsychosocial model developed by Shonkoff and colleagues (2012) elaborating the biology of stress; the continuum of positive, tolerable, and toxic stress, and the implications of "toxic stress" for the developing brain and health outcomes is referenced. This terminology is not common parlance for the lay public, and gradations of positive to tolerable and toxic stress are vague.

Trauma, however, is often chosen by parents and health care providers to describe their experience of today's newborn intensive care unit. Recent recommendations from six multidisciplinary workshops of the National Perinatal Association (Hynan & Hall, 2015) highlight the appropriateness of a trauma model in the opening paragraph of their manuscripts:

> A neonatal intensive care unit (NICU) is akin to a trauma center for all participants. Fragile babies struggle to survive and grow. Parents and families worry constantly while trying to maintain optimism and hope. Staff attempt to avoid burnout while both encouraging distraught parents and acknowledging the times of poor prognosis. Distress is the companion of everyone (p. S1).

How do we create a "holding space" within the tumult and chaos of a modern NICU, where we tune and tone the regulation of the vagal nerve and embed a sense of safety and connectedness for babies, families, and staff? Prerequisites include optimizing the NICU environment to support physical and emotional proximity for the baby and family as we affirm our own connectedness and foster self- and co-regulation.

The Newborn Intensive Parenting Unit Environment

The environment of the modern NICU violates many expectancies of the fetus, now newborn, for his newborn experience. Both the sick and healthy newborn need environmental stimuli that positively entrain their sensory organ systems, including sight, hearing, taste, touch, and smell. Common stressors in today's environment include parental separation, exposure to developmentally unexpected levels of light and sound, and frequent touch, both loving and potentially noxious. No single magic bullet will rescue sick babies and their families from their "companion distress." However, creating an environment and philosophy of care that celebrates the relationship of the baby and his family opens the door for developing the sensitive and enduring relationships that are the cornerstone for subsequent physical, and social, and emotional health.

The Newborn Intensive Parenting Unit design includes attention to the geographical layout; light and sound levels; diurnal cycles of babies, families and staff; and communication and workflow. There are comfortable spaces for parents to be with and care for their baby, to forge relationships with other families and staff, and to care for their own needs. Newly developing units include single-family room design, family lounges, kitchens, and laundry facilities. While meeting the needs of families, the layout also needs to account for space for staff and high-technology equipment, including computer workstations, given the requirements of the electronic health record.

Explicitly addressed in recent recommendations are minimum space, clearance, and privacy requirements for newborns and families, whether they are cared for in open-bay style or single-family rooms; availability of family-transition rooms; ambient lighting in newborn care areas, and availability of natural daylight. The acoustic environment should prioritize speech intelligibility and privacy (White, Smith, Shepley, Committee to Establish Recommended Standards for Newborn ICU Design, 2013).

The recognition of the needs for physical and emotional proximity as well as minimizing environmental stressors led to design of single family room NICUs. A survey by the American Institute of Architects in 2015 reported that prior to 1994, single-family-room NICUs did not exist. Since then, increasing numbers of newly built or renovated NICUs have included single-family rooms in their design. By 2011, single-family rooms were present in nearly half of new hospital construction (Sung & Shepley, 2014).

The goal of single-family rooms is strengthening the developing central nervous system by promoting parental social engagement, deepening connectedness, and a sense of mutual safety and security for parents and baby. For parents and staff to be fully present, the unit philosophy of care must be welcoming, culturally sensitive, and "safe." In polyvagal terms, the NICU must facilitate ventral vagal states for parents and staff as they reciprocally engage, connect, and attune with each other and the babies.

Evolving evidence suggests that caring for a baby and family in a single-family room promoting high maternal involvement in care optimizes at least short- and intermediate-term developmental and social emotional outcomes for babies and decreases stress for mothers. Lester and colleagues (2014, 2016) reported outcomes at hospital discharge and 18 months corrected of age of two cohorts of babies born at under 30 weeks who were cared for either in open-bay or single-family rooms. In the short run, care in single-family rooms decreased stress for mothers, babies, and staff. Mothers also reported improved satisfaction with care and spent more time with their babies. Babies whose mothers had high maternal involvement in care were also discharged sooner. If they were also cared for in a single-family room, at 18 months corrected age, they had substantive improvements in language scores.

On a sobering note, a study conducted in an urban NICU cautions us that the sensory deprivation that *may* occur without high maternal involvement may further disadvantage some newborns already at risk for poor developmental outcomes (Pineda et al., 2014). Parents must be both in physical proximity with access to their baby for co-regulation and maintain sufficient ventral vagal tone to promote co-regulation that allows them to rest in emotional proximity to their baby. Making mothers and fathers available to their babies emotionally requires addressing their own fears, worries, and prior and present traumas. Addressing these factors begins with identifying their own emotional states, whether they are "high-jacked" when sympathetically driven or "hibernate" in dorsal vagal states. These archetypes play out continuously in the NICU setting with the "hard to reach" or "infrequently present" parent who becomes "overwhelmed" or, at an extreme, even "verbally aggressive or combative" when in the NICU. For these parents, it may feel adaptive to avoid coming to the NICU when feeling states are simply too painful or devastating.

Support and Affirm Connectedness as Parents and Babies Foster Co-Regulation

The primary strategy of co-regulation for the healthy newborn is skin to skin on his mother's chest. The benefits of skin to skin to maintain autonomic nervous system stability and enhance the success of breastfeeding are well documented.

Intermittent skin-to-skin or kangaroo care was first used in NICUs in developing countries, where crowding and high infection rates threatened infant well-being, as a way of decreasing mortality and complications for premature babies (Conde-Agudelo, Belizán, & Díaz-Rossello, 2016). In developed countries' NICUs, kangaroo care is associated with improved duration of breastfeeding, decreased parental stress and feelings of helplessness (Renfrew et al., 2010), and improved autonomic regulation and maternal interactions at term (Ohgi et al., 2002). A subset of newborns followed up to 10 years old had attenuated stress responses and improved autonomic functioning (Feldman et al., 2014). These newborns were more ventral vagal and were less likely to be hijacked by stress into excessive sympathetic tone.

Kangaroo care provided during painful procedures both decreases pain scores and the amount of time for the heart rate to return to baseline after a painful procedure by 60 seconds (Johnston et al., 2008; Johnston et al., 2014). Given the number of painful procedures NICU babies experience during a day, especially during the acute phases of management, kangaroo care co-regulation holds promise as a nonpharmacologic pain therapy, along with sucrose and swaddling.

Supporting parents as primary caregivers also asks health care providers to rethink what tasks in the NICU are accomplished by families, rather than nursing staff. In a recent pilot project, a Family Integrated Care (FIC) model was tested for stable recovering babies whose parents could spend at least 8 hours a day in the hospital. Families received daily education sessions, attended rounds, and provided care to their newborns including feeding, bathing, dressing, and skin-to-skin care (kangaroo care). Nurses continued to provide technical tasks including suction, placement of feeding tubes, and so on. Parents also did basic charting and maintained a record of their own learning. Newborns who received FIC showed improved weight gain, increased breastfeeding rates at discharge, and a trend toward decreased infection. Mothers who participated had decreased maternal stress scores. The study is now being replicated in 20 sites in Canada (O'Brien et al., 2013).

Polyvagal Theory Can Help Caregivers Connect Among Themselves and With Babies

Polyvagal Theory is the neurobiological foundation of our autonomic nervous system responses to our neuroception of safety, danger, and life-threat. As a tool, Polyvagal Theory can assist families and staff to understand their own emotional responses and the responses of the others (staff, extended family, etc.), and as a barometer to measure the changing ecosystem around them. Polyvagal Theory also assists families and staff to understand babies who are trying to communicate their needs in the only language available to them: their behavior.

A deep understanding of Polyvagal Theory asks caregivers to focus their own efforts to connect with families as they "befriend," "attend," "tune," and "tone" their own and the families' autonomic nervous systems. In "befriending," staff and families learn to notice and name their own emotional states and their Polyvagal Theory correlates. Recognizing and accepting their own places on the ladder is a conduit for connection early in NICU relationships that will deepen and strengthen throughout the hospitalization. Imagine as a parent, you arrive in the NICU for the first time and are greeted by a nurse with a gentle smile who congratulates you on the birth of your baby and emphasizes the importance of your relationship before getting into an explanation of all the tubes and wires.

As we "attend," giving close and thoughtful attention, we bring perception to neuroception, considering the triggers for entering or maintaining self-states and resources that can assist transitioning from a dorsal vagal or sympathetically driven states to a ventral vagal place of ease. You now hear the nurse inquire about your feelings and concerns. The nurse reads the shock on your face as you try to return her congratulatory smile. You feel comforted as you say to yourself, "She gets it. I am terrified."

The nurse then brings over the doctor to speak with you about your new baby. The doctor sits down next to you and speaks slowly. She refers to your baby by her given name, Emma, and conveys quiet confidence as she provides basic information and answers your questions. Somehow, her calm "tunes" your own rattled, chaotic autonomic nervous system. You feel yourself, however slightly, moving up the ladder.

The doctor explains that she will be caring for your baby and you during the week and says she hopes you will join daily work rounds, where the team discusses each baby and makes a plan for the day. She tells you how important your role is in Emma's care and that your input is vital to the team. For just a moment, the chaos recedes and the discussion feels like a neural exercise in "toning" your vagal nerve (Dana, 2015b).

The 21st-Century Neonatal Intensive Care Unit

The 20th century saw the development of the field of neonatology, dedicated to supporting and caring for the sickest babies from birth to discharge (or death). Early in the history of neonatology, parents surrendered their babies to the wonders of a new technology that offered hope of survival for babies who would previously have died. With survival improving dramatically, the next frontier for neonatology is optimizing the newborn experience for both babies and their families, setting the stage for their ongoing relationships in the community.

Understanding the experience of the sick baby, his family, and the NICU staff through a polyvagal lens creates a common language for building connections to support the baby and family. Attending to our own neuroception, our unconscious awareness of our safety (or not) recognizes the elephant in the room, the implicitly perceived parent and baby experience, seen but not acknowledged by all parties. Only when we acknowledge our own safety circuits, understand our own triggers for moving down the ladder, and address our own resources for moving up the ladder will we, as staff caregivers, be able to provide the supports and kindness our patients and their families crave. "Physician heal thyself" has never been more fundamentally true than in the intensive care setting. Whether the patient is a tiny baby, a child, a previously healthy adult, or an elderly parent, the evolutionary seeds for his needs were sown when first the middle-ear bones detached from the mandible, eye-to-eye contact was established, and maternal vocalizations and prosody became the portal to social engagement and connectedness, permitting the survival of the species.

Only when we connect to our own place on the ladder and recognize the ladder rung on which our staff sit and to which our parents cling tenuously will we be able to provide the right stuff. We are wizards of technology; let us become wizards of the human spirit.

References

Als, H., Butler, S., Kosta, S., & McAnulty, G. (2005). The assessment of preterm newborns' behavior (APIB): Furthering the understanding and measurement of neurodevelopmental competence in preterm and full-term newborns. *Mental Retardation and Developmental Disabilities Research Review, 11*(1), 94–102.

Altman, L. K. (2013, July 29). A Kennedy baby's life and death. *The New York Times.*

Carbajal, R., Rousset, A., Danan, C., Coquery, S., Nolent, P., Ducrocq, S., . . . Bréart, G. (2008). Epidemiology and treatment of painful procedures in neonates in intensive care units. *Journal of the American Medical Association* 300(1), 60–70.

Conde-Agudelo, A., Belizán, J. M., & Díaz-Rossello, J. (2016). Kangaroo mother care to reduce morbidity and mortality in low birthweight newborns. *Cochrane Database of Systematic Reviews, 3*, CD002771.

Dalia, C., Abbas, K., Colville, G., Brierley, J. (2013) Resilience, post-traumatic stress, burnout and coping in medical staff on the paediatric and neonatal intensive care unit (P/NICU)—A survey. *Archives of Disease in Childhood, 98*, A26–A27.

Dana, D. (2015a) A Beginner's Guide to Polyvagal Theory. Retrieved from debdanalcsw.com

Dana, D. (2015b, November) The Rhythm of Regulation: Building Safety from a Polyvagal Perspective (Workshop), Saco, Maine.

Doussard-Roosevelt, J. A., Porges, S. W., Scanlon, J. W., Alemi, B., & Scanlon, K. B. (1997). Vagal regulation of heart rate in the prediction of developmental outcome for very low birth weight preterm newborns. *Child Development, 68*(2), 173–186.

Feldman, R., Rosenthal, Z., & Eidelman, A. I. (2014). Maternal-preterm skin-to-skin contact enhances child physiologic organization and cognitive control across the first 10 years of life. *Biological Psychiatry, 75*(1), 56–64.

Hynan, M. T., & Hall, S. L. (2015). Psychosocial program standards for NICU parents [Supplemental material]. *Journal of Perinatology, 35*, S1–4.

Hynan, M. T, & Hall, S. L. (2016, September 9). Essential care for every family: Evolving from NICU to Newborn Intensive Parenting Units. Presented at the Vermont Oxford Network Quality Congress, Chicago, Illinois.

Johnston, C., Campbell-Yeo, M., Fernandes, A., Inglis, D., Streiner, D., & Zee, R. (2014). Skin-to-skin care for procedural pain in neonates. *Cochrane Database of Systematic Reviews, 1*, CD008435.

Johnston, C. C., Filion, F., Campbell-Yeo, M., Goulet, C., Bell, L., McNaughton, K., . . . Walker, C.-D. (2008). Kangaroo mother care diminishes pain from heel lance in very preterm neonates: A crossover trial. *BMC Pediatrics, 8*, 13.

Koss, K. J., Hostinar, C. E., Donzella, B., & Gunnar, M. R. (2014). Social deprivation and the HPA axis in early development. *Psychoneuroendocrinology, 50*, 1–13.

Koulomzin, M., Beebe, B., Anderson, S., Jaffe, J., Feldstein, S., & Crown, C. (2002). Newborn gaze, head, face and self-touch at 4 months differentiate secure vs. avoidant attachment at 1 year: A microanalytic approach. *Attachment & Human Development, 4*(1), 3–24.

Lee, H. J., Macbeth, A. H., Pagani, J. H., & Young, W. S, III. (2009). Oxytocin: The great facilitator of life. *Progress in Neurobiology, 88*(2), 127–151.

Leff, P. T., & Walizer, E. H. (1992). *Building the healing partnership: Parents, professionals, and children with chronic illnesses and disabilities.* Cambridge, MA: Brookline Books.

Lefkowitz, D. S., Baxt, C., & Evans, J. R. (2010). Prevalence and correlates of posttraumatic stress and postpartum depression in parents of newborns in the Neonatal Intensive Care Unit (NICU). *Journal of Clinical Psychology in Medical Settings, 17*(3), 230–237.

Lester, B. M., Hawes, K., Abar, B., Sullivan, M., Miller, R., Bigsby, R., . . . Padbury, J. F. (2014). Single-family room care and neurobehavioral and medical outcomes in preterm newborns. *Pediatrics, 134*(4), 754–760.

Lester, B. M., Salisbury, A. L., Hawes, K., Dansereau, L. M., Bigsby, R., Laptook, A., . . . Padbury, J. F. (2016). 18-month follow-up of infants cared for in a single-family room neonatal intensive care unit. *Journal of Pediatrics, 177*, 84–89. doi:10.1016/j.jpeds.2016.06.069

Matthews, T. J., & MacDorman, M. F. (2013). Newborn mortality statistics from the 2010 period linked birth/newborn death data set. *National Vital Statistics Reports, 62*(8). 1–26.

O'Brien, K., Bracht, M., Macdonell, K., McBride, T., Robson, K., O'Leary, L., . . . Lee, S. K. (2013). A pilot cohort analytic study of Family Integrated Care in a Canadian neonatal intensive care unit [Supplemental material]. *BMC Pregnancy and Childbirth, 13*, S12.

Ohgi, S., Fukuda, M., Moriuchi, H., Kusumoto, T., Akiyama, T., Nugent, J. K., . . . Saitoh, H. (2002). Comparison of kangaroo care and standard care: behavioral organization, development, and temperament in healthy, low-birth-weight newborns through 1 year. *Journal of Perinatology, 22*(5), 374–379.

Pineda, R. G., Neil, J., Dierker, D., Smyser, C. D., Wallendorf, M., Kidokoro, H., . . . Inder, T. (2014). Alterations in brain structure and neurodevelopmental outcome in preterm newborns hospitalized in different neonatal intensive care unit environments. *Journal of Pediatrics, 164*(1), 52–60 e52.

Porges, S. W. (1992). Vagal tone: A physiologic marker of stress vulnerability. *Pediatrics, 90*(3 Pt 2): 498–504.

Porges, S. W. (2011) *The Polyvagal Theory: Neurophysiological foundations of emotions, attachment, communication, and self-regulation.* New York, NY: Norton.

Porges, S. W. (2014, December 6). *Connectedness as a biological imperative: Understanding trauma through the lens of the Polyvagal Theory.* Presented at the New England Society for Trauma and Dissociation.

Renfrew, M. J., Dyson, L., McCormick, F., Misso, K., Stenhouse, E., King, S. E., Williams, A. F. (2010). Breastfeeding promotion for newborns in neonatal units: A systematic review. *Child: Care, Health, and Development, 36*(2), 165–178.

Rowe, T. (1996). Coevolution of the mammalian middle ear and neocortex. *Science, 273*, 651–654.

Shonkoff, J. P., Garner, A. S., The Committee on Psychosocial Aspects of Child and Family Health, Committee on Early Childhood, Adoption, and Dependent Care, Section on Developmental and Behavioral Pediatrics, Siegel, B. S., . . . Wood, D. L. (2012). The lifelong effects of early childhood adversity and toxic stress. *Pediatrics, 129*(1), e232–246.

Suess, P. E., Alpan, G., Dulkerian, S. J., Doussard-Roosevelt, J., Porges, S. W., &

Gewolb, I. H. (2000). Respiratory sinus arrhythmia during feeding: A measure of vagal regulation of metabolism, ingestion, and digestion in preterm newborns. *Developmental Medicine & Child Neurology, 42*(3), 169–173.

Sung, Y., & Shepley, M. M. (2014). Neonatal intensive care unit (NICU) room type design trends. *AIA Academy of Architecture for Health Academy Journal, 17*. Retrieved from www.aia.org.

Tottenham, N., & Sheridan, M. A. (2009). A review of adversity, the amygdala and the hippocampus: A consideration of developmental timing. *Frontiers in Human Neuroscience, 3*, 68.

Tronick, E. Z. (2010). Newborns and mothers: Self- and mutual regulation and meaning making. In B. M. Lester & J. D. Sparrow (Eds.), *Nurturing children and families* (pp. 83–94). Hoboken, NJ: Wiley.

Tronick, E. Z., & Cohn, J. F. (1989). Newborn-mother face-to-face interaction: Age and gender differences in coordination and the occurrence of miscoordination. *Child Development, 60*(1), 85–92.

U.S. Department of Health and Human Services (2013). *Child health USA 2013*. Retrieved from http://mchb.hrsa.gov/chusa13/perinatal-health-status-indicators/p/infant-morbidity.html

White, R. D., Smith, J. A., Shepley, M. M., Committee to Establish Recommended Standards for Newborn ICU Design. (2013). Recommended standards for newborn ICU design, eighth edition [Supplemental material]. *Journal of Perinatology, 33*, S2–16.

Zeanah, C. H., Egger, H. L., Smyke, A. T., Nelson, C. A., Fox, N. A., Marshall, P. J., & Guthrie, D. (2009). Institutional rearing and psychiatric disorders in Romanian preschool children. *American Journal of Psychiatry, 166*(7), 777–785.

21

A Story of Stroke Recovery Told Through a Polyvagal Perspective

Deb Dana

Abstract: Interacting with medical systems is an everyday experience for millions of people. Medical offices, emergency care services, hospitals, and rehabilitation hospitals, however, are not polyvagal-informed systems, thus the services they provide do not intentionally access the health, growth, and restoration resources of the ventral vagal system. The American Heart Association's annual 2015 report identified that in 2010, 33 million people worldwide suffered a first or recurrent stroke, a medical emergency that has an impact on the autonomic nervous system both in immediate and long-term outcome. This chapter looks at medical systems and patient and caregiver responses to stroke and stroke recovery through a polyvagal perspective.

I TEACH TRAUMA theory and practice to social work students, to newly credentialed clinicians just beginning to explore work with trauma, and to seasoned clinicians wanting to broaden their skills. My focus for the past several years has been to bring Polyvagal Theory into clinical practice. I have spent countless hours researching and creating workshops. I am intimately acquainted with Polyvagal Theory and with my own autonomic nervous system. And yet my husband's stroke and ongoing poststroke recovery brought theory up close and personal in startling ways. The necessity of unrelenting contact with medical systems that are not polyvagal-informed was, and continues to be, remarkably difficult. This chapter walks a line between personal and academic as I use my own pain to find ways to inform medical systems and my husband's recovery. In the writing of this chapter, as in the living of this experience, I move between trauma specialist and caregiver. This experience has changed my work with clients and has decidedly changed the ways I walk through the world.

Both the giving and receiving of caregiving or love has
the capacity to protect, heal, and restore.
—Stephen Porges (2011, p. 295)

On March 25, 2015, my husband, Bob, became one of the approximately 600,000 people in the United States who suffer a first-time stroke (Demaerschalk, Hwang, & Leung, 2010). It was on that day, in that moment, that we began our walk on a polyvagal path through stroke recovery. My tendency is to push myself, my vagal brake releasing to give me maximum energy without metabolic activation, but I am noticing that I am too often introducing a bigger neural challenge for Bob than he is ready for. His neuroception of safety has narrowed since his stroke. This may be natural, but I, as his wife and now suddenly transformed into a caregiver, have to regulate my energy output so I don't overwhelm him. He now experiences more cues of danger and fewer cues of safety, and I struggle to accept that change. Looking ahead is either joy filled or fear filled depending on where on the autonomic hierarchy we find ourselves. As Bob and I move through this time of brain reorganization, I've taken the responsibility to bring the benefits of ventral vagal energy to our daily living experiences as often and long and deeply as possible. Many times a challenge, this is the "medication" that will quiet his biological defense systems and support health, growth, and restoration.

Confusion and Clarity

March 25, 2015, at 3:15 in the morning—the "before and after" moment for Bob and me, although the line of demarcation has been laid down at a time unknown earlier in the night.

Something wakes me, the usual sense of safety I feel in my home with Bob replaced by a neuroception of danger. Bob is in the kitchen. The left and right sides of his face are not in synchrony. He stumbles in his walk across the kitchen. He is clumsy in his attempts to hold his phone. As I look at him, the afferent pathways of my autonomic nervous system are quick to send messages of fear. My conscious awareness takes longer to catch up as my brain pulls together the disparate images of face and feet and fingers and comes up with the word *stroke*. Although I don't yet know it, we have embarked on a journey that will stretch our neural resources. Experiences will frequently overwhelm the capacity of our vagal braking systems. We will be pulled to the extremes of autonomic response, sometimes lost in the storm of sympathetic overwhelm and other times crushed under the numbing weight of dorsal vagal collapse.

Stroke in Progress

In this moment of unfolding trauma, I look for connection. My autonomic nervous system seeks co-regulation. Relationships offer the opportunity for reciprocal interactions that regulate our physiology and moments of connection that bring a sense of safety (Porges, 2012, 2017). I reach out to Steve (Porges), and his response offers me reassurance. "Providing signals of safety, your support and reciprocity, and the sense of control that you feel will signal to Bob's 'neuroception' that his nervous system can now manage the important task of rehabilitation" (personal communication, 2015). This is the beginning of a polyvagal road map for recovery.

Bob is suffering what is called a "wake-up stroke." The time of onset is unclear and tissue plasminogen activator (tPA) treatment is not advised. His CT scan shows a large area of his anterior temporal lobe is irreversibly damaged, and a mechanical thrombectomy (stent retrieval procedure) is also deemed not an option. Bob's stroke is actually still in progress, and I learn that he is referred to as "stroking." Although this may be a commonly used descriptor in the medical world, for Bob and me even the sound of that word is distressing. Prosody, the music of language, influences our autonomic state, and the harsh consonants of *stroking* have no ventral vagal resonance for us.

As a therapist, an important clinical skill is the intentional choice of relational words and the use of phrasing and prosody to invite my client's autonomic nervous system into an experience of co-regulation. The language of medicine comes with hard edges. The communication tempo is quick. There is not a conversational pattern of give-and-take that evokes reciprocity. Cognitively, this makes sense. Autonomically, this is frightening.

Bob has moved inward. Through a polyvagal lens, it is as if he is the ancient tortoise of dorsal vagal response pulling in his head and conserving energy while the stroke eats up cortical real estate. My autonomic response is one of sympathetic nervous system mobilization. I sense danger and an intense need to find a way to stop the death march Bob's neurons are engaged in. From his dorsal vagal hideaway, Bob is unaware of the path of destruction the stroke is leaving in its wake. He and I are out of attunement, our nervous systems diverging in their individual adaptive survival responses. As the stroke continues to progress, Bob loses function on his left side. The doctors watch for brain swelling, which would bring the need for a craniectomy, and my sympathetic nervous system responds. While Bob is safely distanced from awareness by the protection of a dorsal vagal state, my body floods with a need to take charge, to will Bob's brain not to expand beyond the safety of his skull. I can feel the futility of this, but my activated sympathetic nervous system brings adrenaline and cortisol that are translated into a story of danger.

The emergency department personnel are calm, reassuring. This is not an uncommon event for them. As a designated primary stroke center, they are familiar with cerebrovascular accidents, but for Bob and me, this is foreign territory. Bob is moving away from me. I am trying to hold on to him. We are frightened and in a frightening environment. There are few cues of safety. The passive pathways of neuroception are at work monitoring the environment and finding overwhelming cues of danger. The space is unfamiliar, noisy, filled with alarms, people moving quickly, a merry-go-round of faces, a language we don't speak. Bob's autonomic nervous system is protecting him with an adaptive survival response of dorsal vagal conservation. His eyes are closed. His system is titrating the overwhelming stimuli that are a part of this confusing environment.

"In an effort to make hospitals more psychologically safe . . . a hospital concierge would enable your body to work with the treatment—to become a collaborator in the process of healing as opposed to being frightened" (Porges, 2012). I am now Bob's concierge, and although I am a therapist, a trauma specialist, I feel unprepared for this role. Mobilization of my sympathetic nervous system will not serve Bob, and the intensity of that response will exhaust me. Equally unhelpful will be collapse from a dorsal vagal activation that disconnects me from Bob and his medical team. To successfully navigate requires a flexible response system. I need to depend on my vagal brake to release, giving me access to increased energy, and to reengage keeping my social engagement system active and online.

In the human nervous system specific features of person-to-person interactions are innate triggers of adaptive biobehavioral systems, which in turn can support health and healing.
—Stephen Porges (2011, p. 287)

Fifteen hours after the first awareness of the stroke, Bob moves to Special Care Unit 3—the neurological intensive care unit. His ability to engage with others is measured in micromoments as his brain and body systems continue to conserve energy in this beginning reorganization process. His eyes are closed. His voice is flat. His face is immobilized on one side. His social engagement system, involving cranial nerves V, VII, IX, X, and XI, is now compromised. The medical staff assures me this is common in early poststroke recovery. Knowing that doesn't stop my autonomic nervous system from its predictable search for cues of connection and safety and feeling instead the distance, disconnection, and a neuroception of danger.

Months into recovery, Bob's face and voice will retain some of these features. His voice will not fully recover tone, inflection, and strength, creating an involuntary barrier to attunement, as this lack of prosody sends signals of disinterest and detachment (Porges, 2011). His face will regain movement, but the left side of his mouth will remain less active than his right, leaving him with not quite a full smile, an asymmetric smile that has a feeling of a false smile (Jaffe, 2010). His orbicularis oculi, the muscles around his eyes, won't return to their prestroke mobility and, although his intent is a genuine smile (Duchenne smile), in the absence of involvement of these muscles that wrinkle into crow's feet, his smile does not convey his emotions. Instead, these unwanted, unintentional, and seemingly unchangeable characteristics send cues of danger.

It feels as if his face–heart connection, the human autonomic gift that is a result of the intertwining of five cranial nerves, is broken. The important relational ingredient of reciprocity is missing. I learn to bring perception to neuroception, bring conscious awareness to my automatic, autonomic response, and create a habit of actively reminding my nervous system that it is not a measure of psychological disconnection; it is simply a physical relic of the stroke.

Other people who interact with Bob experience an autonomic response to the lack of safety cues and, following the nonconscious cues of neuroception, often slightly increase their physical and emotional distance, creating a subtle disconnection. The recovery process highlights the "biological rudeness" (Porges in Eichhorn, 2012, p. 53) that happens when the flow of conversation is interrupted, when the back-and-forth of talking, the move between internal and external states, is not smooth. The cues of safety that one autonomic nervous system sends and another autonomic nervous system seeks are missing. Without interruption of the passive pathways of neuroception, without use of the active pathways of intervention, the experience is one of ongoing autonomic misattunement.

I find the hospital environment with its proliferation of medical technology distressing. "The chrome, monitors, beeps, and alarms turn a modern intensive care unit into the antithesis of the 'healing environment.' . . . All the life cues to the real world are sacrificed to the needs of sterility and function" (Schulman, 2016, p. 253). Unlike me, Bob tells me he feels safe here in the special care unit, surrounded by machines and wires and noises. His autonomic nervous system takes these in as sounds of safety. The team of skilled health care professionals caring for Bob offer more cues of safety through their words and touch. The special care unit is a protective cocoon communicating to Bob's nervous system that he is safe and can rest. Without knowing Polyvagal Theory, the medical team generates for Bob the state of ventral vagal regulation that is necessary for health, growth, and restoration. This is in contrast to my experience. No one offers a friendly touch. The words spoken to me are strange. This is not a place that generates a state of safety for me. My autonomic nervous system is on guard.

Bob is paralyzed on his left side, unable to move independently. He is moved around the room with the Hoyer Lift. He describes the pleasure he gets from "flying." The sling of the lift holds him and sends signals of safety to his nervous system. As the Hoyer Lift is moved along its tracks, he feels the relief of being released from immobilization. He moves up the autonomic hierarchy through sympathetic mobilization into ventral vagal experience. When he recovers enough to begin to move on his own, he misses his "flight time."

The hospital signals a commitment to family–patient connection in the special care unit in multiple ways. Families can call anytime, day or night, and talk to their family member's nurse. Hearing a calm, familiar voice encourages ventral vagal regulation. Such is the gift of prosody and predictability to the autonomic nervous system. Families are urged to connect whenever they need. The availability of this resource supports the ability to sustain ventral vagal regulation, and the story that accompanies that autonomic state is one of hope. Another way the hospital invites connection is through the morning "rounding" of patients. This is a teaching hospital, and Bob's doctor believes that having family members join the medical discussion is a valuable learning experience for everyone. As a clinician with an understanding of neuroscience, I am fascinated by the CT scans and discussion of deficits and recovery potential. As a loving partner to the person whose brain is being discussed, I am terrified by the dark areas in the pictures and the ongoing unfolding of impact. I find myself moving along a neuroceptive continuum from curiosity and hope (ventral vagal engagement) to fear of the facts (sympathetic activation) and then into despair (dorsal vagal shutdown). I will come to know this continuum well over the next months and have some control over my placement on it. As a caregiver, maintaining my own ventral vagal state is a necessary ingredient in Bob's poststroke recovery.

Since the autonomic nervous system is a relational system, incidents of resonance and misattunement are experienced as individual nervous systems connect or collide. During the many days with Bob in a variety of hospital settings, I witness interactions between families and staff that run the spectrum of soothing to traumatizing. Staff make judgments about families, labeling them easy or difficult. Through a polyvagal perspective, the difficult families are more accurately labeled dysregulated. Neuroception surrounding the unfolding trauma is activating adaptive survival responses—responses that have been toned through repeated life experiences. Families need to be met and held in ventral vagal safety. The more regulated families often receive that ventral vagal welcome. The families under dorsal vagal influence may be seen as quiet and cooperative and thus met with the kindness of ventral vagal energy, or they may be seen as disinterested, mistakenly judged as not caring enough, and left in isolation. Sympathetically dysregulated families are sometimes met with understanding—"This must be so distressing for you, and I hope we will have some answers for you soon"—and other times receive a curt response in return—"There is nothing I can tell you right now." One response soothes while the other can trigger an increasingly dysregulated response.

The autonomic nervous system does not exist in isolation. It is a relational system and enters into a back-and-forth communication, a feedback loop, with another nervous system. This means the autonomic state of each individual hospital staff person is an important factor in determining the outcome of interactions with families. The signals conveyed, the cues of safety or danger sent from one nervous system to another, serve to either co-regulate or increase reactivity. Without one nervous system bringing ventral vagal energy to the interaction, there is an inevitable progression that will move back along the autonomic hierarchy in coherence with each person's habitual response patterns. It is the responsibility of the medical professional to bring a regulated nervous system, to emit cues of safety and enlist the family members' social engagement systems. Beyond an assumption of medical expertise, there is an expectation that medical professionals, who carry with them their own autonomic patterns of protection, will be able to maintain the autonomic regulation necessary to offer safety and welcome to families who are experiencing trauma.

What are the conditions for the possibility of an autonomically regulated staff? a) Create the necessary support for professionals to maintain ventral vagal regulation. This includes skills for in-the-moment resourcing and opportunities for long-term reshaping of autonomic profiles. b) Teach skills for active use of ventral vagal energy in distressed interactions with patients and families.

On my daily walk from the parking garage to Bob's room, my autonomic nervous system looks for cues of safety. However, this walk is not one that feels friendly. No one shares a smile or a moment of face-to-face connection. I pass people who I assume are family members lost in their own autonomic dysregulation and staff who I imagine are using moments of quiet disconnection to regulate before they return to the demands of their work. As I travel the halls of the hospital, I find a photo of my great-great-grandfather, Charles Oliver Hunt, the first superintendent of the hospital (1874–1903). I acknowledge the generational connection and experience a surprising ventral vagal response as I stand in front of his image and look into his eyes. Charles Oliver Hunt and I never actually shared a moment of reciprocity, but this imagined reciprocity brings me into a state of autonomic regulation.

Reciprocity is a key feature of Polyvagal Theory. It is an important regulator of the nervous system. In clinical work, reciprocity is a co-regulating skill that can interrupt habitual autonomic response patterns and bring disconfirming experiences to our clients. Clinical work can also utilize remembered reciprocity, a skill in which clients are supported in calling on a memory of a time of autonomic attunement with another person to activate present-moment ventral vagal regulation. With the image of an ancestor I never met, I am using "imagined" reciprocity, with the same powerful effect. I make sure my daily path to find Bob includes a stop by my great-great-grandfather's photograph.

In three days, Bob is transferred out of the special care unit—an indication of his increased medical stability. His autonomic nervous system moves toward engagement as his curiosity about recovery begins to come alive. On March 31, six days after his stroke, Bob takes an ambulance ride into the new world of rehab.

The autonomic nervous system is always listening. (Neural Surveillance)
How do we learn to listen and use the information for wellbeing? (Neural Navigation)
How do we create the right degree of neural challenge to tone the system? (Neural Exercise)
—Deb Dana (2018)

Rehab: The Year Ahead

The rehab hospital's tagline is "Hope is Here," and in the next three weeks Bob begins to strengthen his fragile connection to ventral vagal regulation. It is here that his brain and body systems are challenged to reorganize. He has moments of reciprocity with his medical team that come from shared ventral vagal states and moments of messiness that come from the mismatch of states. He is sometimes challenged with just the right degree of neural exercise to support rehabilitation, and at other times is pushed beyond his limits into the adaptive protection of dorsal vagal conservation that effectively shuts down any hope of return to well-being. The staff at the rehab hospital work hard to create an environment conducive to rehabilitation, but they don't have the benefit of knowing the science of autonomic response to bring to their interactions. With a foundation of Polyvagal Theory, cues of safety, co-regulation, activation of the social engagement system, and the importance of maintaining a ventral vagal state would be understood and intentionally utilized. Without this theory, it is a hit-or-miss proposition dependent on each staff person's particular training, the staff's ability and willingness to meet Bob's moment-to-moment autonomic needs for safety, and their own moment-to-moment movement along the autonomic hierarchy.

Over the next three weeks, Bob learns to navigate the rehabilitation hospital environment. He learns to walk again, to "look left," working with the left-side inattention that will be an ongoing challenge, and to move through the world with one functioning arm. Bob's first room seems to be in constant motion. His bed is by the door on a busy section of the floor. He is highly sensitive to environmental stimulation, his nervous system sending signals of "too much."

The Goldilocks effect, or Goldilocks principle, is a term adapted from the classic fairy tale in which Goldilocks experiments to find the "just right" porridge, chair, and bed. The Goldilocks principle states that something must fall within certain margins, as opposed to reaching extremes (Sumner, 2016). From a polyvagal perspective, the "just right" is the ventral vagal state regulated by an active, flexible vagal brake. Bob is outside the range of "just right," and the stroke has compromised his autonomic regulatory capacity.

Before the stroke, Bob's neural profile was one of successfully navigating the state shifts from ventral vagal to sympathetic back to ventral vagal that the human autonomic nervous system regularly moves through. The release of adrenaline from the sympathetic adrenal medullary response that is common in daily experience was easily regulated, and a full sympathetic hypothalamic-pituitary-adrenal (HPA) axis activation was unusual. He rarely traveled to the dorsal vagal roots of the autonomic hierarchy. His was a resilient autonomic system, flexible in meeting daily challenges with ventral vagal capacity. He was effective in addressing his environment and regulating into safety and social engagement.

In this early poststroke period, his response patterns are altered. His nervous system is sensitive, bringing him only micromoments of ventral vagal experience before moving quickly through sympathetic distress into dorsal vagal collapse. Medical professionals track his physical condition and respond with interventions. I track his autonomic state and respond with cues of safety. The dorsal vagal rescue will become a familiar pattern. For months he will continue to be pulled into this protective response when the world is too stimulating, when the expectations are too high, and the neural challenge is too great. It will be an ongoing process to discern the difference between depression and his nervous system taking a dorsal vagal time-out.

In the early days of recovery, I learn to actively challenge the dorsal vagal influence that has been my own habitual response to traumatic challenge. I can't afford to be overwhelmed and immobilized. My familiar patterns of disconnection and immobilization will not serve Bob's recovery. Although my nervous system pulls me toward the safety of submission, of not making waves, I move into a state of mobilization that is unfamiliar to me. Being quiet, not asking for more than is offered, is no longer adaptive. Bob needs me to advocate for him. His autonomic nervous system is sending clear messages and, even as my autonomic nervous system sends out the dorsal vagal call to disconnect, I learn to regulate, listen to his autonomic need, and take action to bring his system back into the ventral vagal promise of safety. This is the responsibility of a "concierge," of a caregiver.

Through a polyvagal perspective, we understand that the way systems define safety and risk is often incongruent with how our nervous system reacts. This is evident in the medical setting. The level of activity in the room is not lost on one of the nurses, who senses Bob's need for quiet. She would describe it as an experience of too much commotion that affects Bob's ability to rest. In polyvagal terms, I would describe it as an ongoing neuroception of danger that keeps him vigilant and unable to move into a state of ventral vagal ease.

Hospitals are engaged in a discussion of the benefits of private and shared rooms. From an autonomic perspective, there is no single right answer for patients nor, perhaps, a single right answer across the duration of patient stay. Since the autonomic nervous system is toned by early and repeated experience, patients have differing needs along a continuum of connection to solitude. Where along that individual continuum is the place that supports a particular patient's ventral vagal state? Does that placement change as a patient moves along in the rehab process, and how can we track the shifts and respond with the resource that fits the autonomic need?

No matter the description, both the nurse and I know Bob will not get better in this environment. When a patient is discharged next door, she moves Bob to the new room. Bob begins to breathe more deeply in this less stimulating environment. The possibility for more ventral vagal capacity brings the prospect of health, growth, and restoration. This will change in a few days, as a roommate moves in, but the environment of this room will continue to bring more of a neuroception of safety because there are autonomic cues of safety in this space. The bed is by the window, which lets in light. Light is known to positively affect psychological and physiological well-being, and we can hypothesize the involvement of ventral vagal regulation (Timmerman, Uhrenfeldt, & Birkelund, 2015). The bed is away from the door and the busyness of the hallway, with a curtain dividing the room for a bit of privacy. Here, proximity to others, another way the autonomic nervous system measures safety, is in the "just right" range for Bob. The room is located farther away from the alarms and intercoms at the nurses' station and the auditory assault that these sounds bring to the nervous system.

The Vagal Brake

For Bob, the rehab hospital experience is often a mystery. Unfamiliar, low-frequency sounds activate a sympathetic state as his auditory system is prompted to listen for the presence of predators. His physical capacities do not match his autonomic need for mobilization. He is trapped, and without the opportunity for co-regulation, his neuroception moves from danger to life-threat and a corresponding move down the autonomic hierarchy to dorsal vagal disconnection. Where a more resourced person might interrupt this autonomic reaction and use active pathways to maintain ventral vagal oversight, stroke has disrupted Bob's autonomic response system. He is sensitive to overloads. His vagal brake is less able to release and reengage.

The ability of the vagal brake to respond to challenge can be seen as a measure of resilience. How often do the neural challenges exceed the braking capacity? How long and how intense is the experience of dysregulation? How does the person engage with resources to bring a return to regulation? The following vignette is a common example of an incident in the hospital setting in which a patient's capacity for regulation is stressed.

One evening as Bob and I are enjoying the end of the day together; there is activity on the other side of the curtain, and we realize that the roommate we have grown accustomed to is moving out, and a new roommate will be moving in. We hear conversations about the change and try to piece together what is happening. It is clear that more information is needed to move from confusion to clarity, but in the world of patient privacy regulations, and with a treatment team that is unaware of the impact change can have on a compromised nervous system, how do we get that information? Bob's already taxed system finds this too much to take in. He can't respond and recover on his own. When viewed through a polyvagal lens, we recognize that illness affects the function of the vagal brake; that without a fully functioning vagal brake, transitions can move the nervous system into the extremes of mobilization or shutdown; that a face-to-face answer to the "What's happening?" question can bring safety to the system quickly. Even though this is a highly trained and compassionate medical staff, there is no acknowledgment that Bob might be experiencing fear.

Without a structure to understand normal autonomic adaptive survival responses, to consider movement along the autonomic hierarchy, there is no recognition of a patient's need. The elements of autonomic attunement, a simple face-to-face connection, a few prosodic words of reassurance, a quick experience of co-regulation that could bring a return of ventral vagal regulation are missing—not from a lack of caring, but from an absence of understanding the power of the social engagement system to signal safety. A staff fluent in the language of autonomic response could send simple messages of safety, and the patient might avoid the autonomic movement into survival response that interrupts the rehabilitation process. While this is one example, the patient's neuroception of danger and moments of autonomic misattunement are frequent within the hospital day.

In the end, we get information by experiencing the change as it happens. I wait with Bob until he feels settled enough to be on his own and I regain enough of my own regulation to feel safe in leaving him. This is one of many nights when I walk out of the rehab hospital and take a deep breath, letting it out slowly, fully feeling the power of heart rate variability in that resourcing exhale. This is followed by the painful recognition that Bob is trapped, that he can't do what his nervous system needs. He can't mobilize, walk out into the night air, and breathe deeply, as I can.

> *In the context of caregiving, the quality of the person-to-person interactions between a caregiver and those being cared for is critical for survival.*
> —Stephen Porges (2011, p. 295)

Autonomic Ruptures

The autonomic nervous system tests safety first through psychological distance and then through the more risky physical proximity (Porges & Dykema 2006). Talk before touch can reassure the nervous system. When medical staff simply appear and begin their work without first making contact through voice and eye gaze, there is often an autonomic startle. The step of offering the patient's autonomic nervous system cues of safety has been missed. Bob regularly experiences this out-of-order sequence. When the attempted psychological connection is the rote question, "name and date of birth," asked in a monotone voice without eye contact, the opportunity for staff and patient to engage in reciprocity is lost. The power of the social engagement system to connect and calm is unavailable. Bob frequently feels this absence. It leaves him on edge, his adaptive protective responses ready to activate.

The fit between patient and provider begins with autonomic attunement. Illness affects the patient's vagal brake, leaving a less flexible response system that is sensitive to neurological insult. These autonomic ruptures result in predictable moves backward along the autonomic hierarchy. It is incumbent on the medical team to first connect with the patient from a regulated, ventral vagal state and then find the degree of neural challenge that will push recovery forward and not trigger an autonomic move into protection. Bob experiences both fit and misfit with his team of medical providers. There are providers who "do for" him sometimes from a place of good intentions or feeling sorry for him, and sometimes due to a wish to get the job done quickly and efficiently. From a Goldilocks perspective, these are "not enough" experiences that don't engage his brain and body systems. When Bob isn't challenged to be an active participant in his rehabilitation, he remains shut down, without energy to fuel his recovery. Other providers work from a manualized protocol. For these providers, Bob's prestroke history is irrelevant, and he is seen instead through the lens of poststroke deficits. When this happens, reciprocity is missing, an autonomic mismatch results, and therapy stalls.

A notable misattunement with one therapist highlights the negative impact of an autonomic mismatch. This therapist activates a neuroception of danger for Bob through a nonprosodic voice, a tone that is deep and rough; with facial expression, a face that is often neutral and which when received by a person not in a ventral vagal state is perceived as dangerous; and with biological rudeness, looking away from Bob as they work, talking about Bob and not to him. These features trigger a sympathetically activated nervous system each time Bob is on his way to his rehab appointment, and a dorsal vagal collapse during the appointment, both of which negatively affect his ability for functional recovery. Although the inpatient section of the rehab hospital has a process for patients to address these types of incongruity, the "rules of rehab" in the outpatient section do not. We try unsuccessfully to manage the ongoing mismatch and autonomic ruptures. Bob suffers. I ache for Bob. And we finally terminate services with this provider.

Neuroception Observed

A striking, observable manifestation of neuroception occurs as Bob learns to stand again. This ability is not so much dependent on his physical capacities as on his autonomic nervous system's sensing of the capacities of the person assisting. At first we think success is due to muscle strength or weakness. As we explore the "stand–can't stand" phenomenon, Bob brings perception to this subcortical neuroceptive response and identifies it as a sense of trust in the ability of the other person to support his weight and catch him if he falls. This is independent of size and level of fitness. This is not a cognitive evaluation. This decision is made by his autonomic nervous system. When there is a neuroception of safety, he stands with growing ease and surety. When his neuroception brings unease and lack of trust, his legs don't support him and he doesn't rise from his bed. It is stunning to see the embodied changes when neuroception takes him away from safety. How amazing are the protective abilities of his functioning nervous system! And yet, how to convey this autonomic information to a staff that does not share the information and language of Polyvagal Theory—a staff that makes judgments based on a cognitive decision-making process, even in a medical system where the body should reign supreme. Ability is often measured by a patient's effort, and judgments are made about their level of desire or commitment to recovery. What is missing from the assessment is an understanding of the underlying autonomic state and the ways each state either supports or creates barriers to physical function. The staff formulates a story that is missing the important ingredient of the autonomic response hierarchy, and this story often follows the patient throughout his hospital stay.

Bob's physical therapist is a perfect match for him and engenders a tangible neuroception of safety. Bob feels safe with her, and she brings the right amount of challenge to move him forward and not overwhelm his system. Their sessions are not only physical exercises but also neural exercises. When Bob first stands and walks in the hallway, he is discussing vectors and the physics of this movement with his physical therapist, his left hemisphere engaged in the practicalities of walking. I watch, feeling an experience of awe, a ventral vagal response that fills my chest with a warm flow. The path to independent walking will take weeks, will include stumbles and falls, and will not always bring this ventral vagal flood. But this moment remains an embodied memory that my autonomic nervous system returns to over and over. It is a reminder of what is possible.

Bob correctly senses that he is being evaluated in his interactions with staff. This is part of the requirements of a rehab hospital—evaluating and tracking patient progress. His nervous system is on alert. If this state of alert is mitigated by an active vagal brake, Bob will be held within the edges of safety, and his ventral vagal system will support growth. Without the influence of the vagal brake, his sympathetic nervous system will take over, and recovery will be impaired. Before the stroke, Bob's work required him to coordinate complex systems. In this poststroke experience, rather than moving with his old confidence from a flexible vagal braking system, he is watchful from an active neuroception of danger. He is in an ongoing trauma, and his autonomic nervous system is looking out for him. When I ask him what feels dangerous, he tells me he feels he is at the mercy of other people's decisions, that someone is telling him what to do, when to do it, how to do it every moment of every day, and if he doesn't comply he will not be released from the rehab hospital. He feels trapped, and his nervous system is responding to these cues of danger. During the course of his rehab treatment, we never quite figure out how to effectively downregulate this protective response.

As Bob's brain tries to find new routes to transmit information, there is less resilience. In fact, great amounts of energy are going into the search for ways to rewire, and his capacity for physical and social engagement is limited. Frequently, the neural challenge is too great, and his autonomic response is a move into dorsal vagal conservation. I often feel a corresponding shift into mobilization, with a need to counter the messages his body is sending. When I do this from a release of the vagal brake that brings me into a higher level of engagement and a connecting conversation, Bob's nervous system responds with a beginning return to regulation. When I do this from a sympathetically driven state and a need to convince Bob that his experience is not accurate, his autonomic protective response is one of further dysregulation and a deeper dorsal vagal withdrawal.

The Heart Knows

With six days until planned discharge, Bob displays heart symptoms and is transported from the rehab hospital back to the medical center. He spends the day in the emergency department hooked up to wires and machines. The beeping machines and moving lines on the screen comfort him, and he seems to be in a state of ventral vagal regulation, while I'm moved into a neuroception of danger. In diverging states of autonomic activation, I am feeling the intensity of my sympathetic response, while Bob's vagal brake appears to be doing its job. The decision is made to admit him to the cardiac floor. Bob settles into his room, the familiarity of the beds and menus and systems giving him a sense of relaxation. It's as if he is having a necessary vacation from rehab. I can see the importance of this for him. It is visible in the way his body moves and the words he speaks.

Bob needs a nuclear stress test and will stay here until that has happened. He savors this time where his environment is quiet, where his brain is not being evaluated, where he feels met where he is and not asked to do more. We discover it is common for inpatient rehabilitation patients to have a day or two of withdrawal and to come out of that with increased skills. There is a need for an autonomic time-out. It seems that a mini vacation from the constant physiological and psychological challenges would be an appropriate experience to build into the rehab process.

This autonomically necessary day of rest has great benefit to the overall rehab process. Bob savors his two days of time away from rehab, passes his stress test, and returns to the rehab hospital to finish his last week. His wise body, his subcortical systems, found a way to get the break he needed. Bob's return to rehab brings a concomitant return to a vigilant, sympathetically driven state. He is scheduled for discharge at the end of the week. Although neither of us know what life outside the hospital will be like, we are counting on the environment of the home we have created together to activate our vagal pathways and bring calm to our stressed nervous systems.

Dysphagia

Dysphagia (difficulty swallowing due to impact to the muscles and nerves in the throat and esophagus) is a common concern following a stroke (Shaker & Geenen, 2011). This was one of the many facts we learned in the first hours of recovery after Bob's stroke. "Are you having any trouble swallowing?" was the commonly asked question and probably where the seed of anxiety was planted. This might be where his autonomic nervous system began experiencing the first cues of danger around eating and drinking. Bob was lucky in that his swallowing ability was left untouched, but in this new world he had been plunged into, the questioning, swallow testing, thick liquid, thin liquid, observed eating, and "red spoon" dining that is part of the poststroke protocol began to bring the possibility of swallowing problems to life.

A roommate in rehab, who did in fact have swallowing trouble, was hooked up to machines that emitted a constant humming noise in the background along with the periodic sounding of alarms. Bob, who couldn't get out of bed by himself, would call for the nurse when the alarms sounded in the night and no one responded, worried his roommate on the other side of the curtain was choking. Living in the general rehab environment in which dysphagia is common (65% of poststroke patients, as cited by the AHA), combined with the specific circumstances of his roommate, Bob's autonomic nervous system moved into a state of watchfulness. Autonomic state becomes psychological story, and for the entirety of his time in rehab, Bob teetered between the ventral vagal experience of alert and a story of capability, and the sympathetic experience of anxious with its story of vigilance.

Bob completed inpatient rehab and came home to continue his recovery on an outpatient basis. The dose of statin he was prescribed to prevent future problems had the unfortunate side effect of persistent nausea. Then, in the "when it rains it pours" way of things, we ventured out for a special event with disastrous consequences. This being Maine, the menu was lobster, and Bob had an adverse reaction to the richness of the melted butter. His pharyngeal reflex (gag reflex), there to protect us from substances our brain experiences as harmful, was triggered. He suffered that night, through the next day, and was left with a memory of that experience that persisted. The cues of safety receded, and the cues of danger overwhelmed his autonomic nervous system. He found no relief in the anxiety that his mobilized sympathetic system brought, and dropped into the conservation state of dorsal vagal shutdown.

The neuroception of life-threat continued, and the dorsal vagal state became the story that swallowing is dangerous. The result was an adaptive survival response of eating no more than absolutely necessary. Several weeks later and with Bob many pounds lighter, Bob's doctor discontinued the statin and ordered a barium swallow test. His now-habitual dorsal vagal response had left him with barely enough energy to run his basic systems. The dorsal vagal response was biologically protective, adaptive, and also stopped any possibility of restoration or growth. Rehab had come to a standstill.

Bob's stroke was a right middle cerebral artery stroke, which meant his ability to use contextual cues for meaning and decision making was impaired. Bob had a need for undeniable, concrete proof that swallowing was safe before he might begin to relax and eat and drink normally again. He needed to "see to believe." Bob went for his barium swallow test and watched on the screen as his pharynx and esophagus performed perfectly. His autonomic nervous system absorbed the information and returned him to a neuroception of safety around swallowing. As he watched the fluoroscopy, he saw that swallowing was not life-threatening. A half-hour procedure brought disconfirming information in the way Bob needed.

In a striking example of the process of neuroception to perception to story, Bob's autonomic state moved from dorsal vagal conservation to ventral vagal regulation and began to recreate a story of safety around eating. We shared this experience with the medical director of the rehab hospital where Bob was doing his outpatient rehab. Thankfully, this was not where Bob went for his swallow test, because their procedure is not to have patients watch the test but simply to report the results. If he hadn't seen the test on the screen in real time, I don't believe the outcome for Bob would have been the same. His neuroception would have continued to be one of concern, and that state would have kept the story of danger alive. The medical director was interested in Bob's experience and thought he would experiment with having patients watch their tests to see how that might affect the results.

The Path Ahead

We are wired to connect. Our autonomic nervous systems are on a quest to be in attuned communication with each other. In the new normal of poststroke living, the autonomic intimacy Bob and I enjoyed is infrequent. The experience now is more often one of autonomic misattunement. When autonomic rhythms are out of sync in our important relationships, the result is often a feeling of loneliness. The research on loneliness tells the story of impact to thoughts, feelings, behaviors, biology, and physical health (Cacioppo & Cacioppo, 2014; Hawkley & Cacioppo, 2010). Links have been made to loneliness and a sense of not feeling safe (Cacioppo & Patrick, 2008) which through a polyvagal perspective would highlight the absence of ventral vagal regulation. Research on eudaemonia illustrates protective factors in regulating loneliness. (Ryff, 2014) Eudaemonic well-being includes positive connections to others, personal growth, and purpose in life (Ryff, Singer, & Love, 2004). These experiences, considered in conjunction with the definition of eudaemonia, which includes words such as *safety, security,* and *welfare,* again bring the influence of the ventral vagal system to mind. In the landscape of poststroke recovery, loneliness and a lack of eudaemonic well-being create a significant autonomic challenge.

There isn't a scale that accurately predicts the scope of stroke recovery (Brewer, Horgan, Hickey, & Williams, 2013), nor is there consensus on a timeline for recovery. The path of recovery is an unpredictable one, and autonomically, unpredictability often triggers a neuroception of danger. In this case, however, unpredictability means that there is not an already defined end point, that all outcomes are possible. To successfully navigate stroke recovery, embracing unpredictability is necessary. In the beginning, Bob and I choose to believe the commonly reported timeline that 95% of recovery will be present at the end of the first year. There is a ventral vagal state of calm that accompanies thinking about the spaciousness of a year. The pressure of quick recovery that triggers the sympathetic nervous system or the despair of unending, undefined time that generates a dorsal vagal response are absent. As the months pass and we get closer to March, we revise our timeline, believing more is possible.

Now, many months later, well beyond the one-year mark, it is the active, ongoing, intentional use of ventral vagal energy, what Stephen Porges calls benevolence, that keeps hope for continued recovery alive and also allows us to gently make the slow turn toward compensation for deficits the stroke has left behind.

References

Brewer, L., Horgan, F., Hickey, A., & Williams, D. (2013). Stroke rehabilitation: Recent advances and future therapies. *Quarterly Journal of Medicine, 106*, 11–25.

Cacioppo, J., & Cacioppo, S. (2014). Social relationships and health: The toxic effects of perceived isolation. *Social and Personality Psychology Compass, 8*(2), 58–72.

Cacioppo, J. B., & Patrick, B. (2008). *Loneliness: Human nature and the need for social connection.* New York, NY: Norton.

Dana, D. (2018). *The polyvagal theory in therapy: Engaging the rhythm of regulation.* New York, NY: Norton.

Demaerschalk, B., Hwang, H., & Leung, G. (2010). US cost burden of ischemic stroke: A systematic literature review. *American Journal of Managed Care, 16*(7), 525–533.

Eichhorn, N. (2012, Spring). Safety: The preamble for attachment, An interview with Stephen Porges. *Somatic Psychotherapy Today*, p. 52.

Hawkley, L., & Cacioppo, J. (2010). Loneliness matters: A theoretical and empirical review of consequences and mechanisms. *Annals of Behavioral Medicine, 40*(2).

Jaffe, E. (2010). The psychological study of smiling. *Observer, 23*(10).

Porges, S. W. (2011). *The Polyvagal Theory: Neurophysiological foundations of emotions, attachment, communication, and self-regulation.* New York, NY: Norton.

Porges, S. W. (2012). Polyvagal Theory: Why this changes everything [Webinar]. In NICABM Trauma Therapy Series. Retrieved from http://files.nicabm.com/Trauma2012/Porges/NICABM-Porges-2012.pdf

Porges, S. W. (2013). Beyond the brain: How the vagal system holds the secret to treating trauma [Webinar]. Retrieved from http://stephenporges.com/images/nicabm2.pdf

Porges, S. W. (2015). *Social connectedness as a biological imperative: Understanding trauma through the lens of the Polyvagal Theory* [Lecture slides]. Retrieved from https://www.attach.org/wp-content/uploads/2015/09/Attach-Porges-handout.pdf

Porges, S.W. (2017). The pocket guide to polyvagal theory: The transformative power of feeling safe. NY: Norton.

Porges, S. W., & Dykema, R. (2006). How your nervous system sabotages your ability to relate. Retrieved from http://www.naturalworldhealing.com/images/polyvagal_interview_porges.pdf

Ryff, C.D. (2014). Psychological well-being revisited: Advances in the science and practice of eudaimonia. *Psychotherapy and Psychosomatics*, 2014;83:10–28 doi:10.1159/000353263

Ryff, C., Singer, B., & Love, G. (2004). Positive health: Connecting well-being with biology. *Philosophical Transactions of the Royal Society of London. Series B, 359*, 1383–1394.

Schulman, A. (2016). *Waking the spirit: A musician's journey healing body, mind, and soul.* New York, NY: Picador.

Shaker, R., & Geenen, J.E. (2011). Management of dysphagia in stroke patients. *Gastroenterology & Hepatology*, 7(5), 308-332.

Sumner, T. (2016, April 30). Thinking outside the Goldilocks zone. *Science News*, pp. 36–38.

Timmerman, C., Uhrenfeldt, L., & Birkelund, R. (2015). Room for caring: Patient's experiences of well-being, relief and hope during serious illness. *Scandinavian Journal of Caring Sciences, 29*, 426–434.

22

Born With a Heart Condition: The Clinical Implications of Polyvagal Theory

Liza Morton

Abstract: Being born with a heart condition presents increased vulnerability to a number of psychosocial difficulties including anxiety, depression, developmental delay, and infant feeding and oral motor problems, which have previously been accounted for by secondary factors. Here, I propose that the Polyvagal Theory offers a more holistic account. Since the heart is central to our nervous system, congenital cardiac anomalies may compromise neuroception, which could account for some of these psychosocial difficulties. This has implications across the lifespan, providing strategies to optimize normal development of social and defensive behaviors and to inform therapeutic interventions, explored here drawing on psychological theories and personal experience.

WE LOVE FROM the bottom of our hearts; our feelings are heartfelt; and when love is lost, we are heartbroken. Our hearts are linked to our feelings in our collective conscious, and this has been so since antiquity. Galen, the Greek medic and philosopher, considered the human heart the soul and seat of emotion. Yet since the 17th century, when the English physician William Harvey proposed that the heart circulates blood around the body, this organ has been relegated to a simple, functional pump: a school of thought confounded by the emergence of a Cartesian understanding of the "mind–body" problem. Still, the link between our heart and our feelings remains in everyday discourse, and recent scientific investigations are forcing us to reconsider the complex role of the heart in human emotion.

My interest in the human heart is more than academic. I was born with a heart condition, and making sense of my embodied experience has been a lifelong challenge. I have complete congenital heart block, caused by anti-Ro antibodies associated with maternal lupus in utero. Although the sinus node and right atrium of my heart respond in a normal, physiologically responsive way, this electrical signal is blocked prior to reaching the ventricle. Consequently, my heart holds an intrinsic rate (escape rhythm) of 40 beats per minute. For me, this is not life-sustaining, and by the time I was a few days old, I was in heart failure. In a world first, I was fitted with a cardiac pacemaker by thoracotomy at 11 days old (documented in Dasmahapatra, Jamieson, Brewster, Doig, & Pollock, 1986; Reid et al., 1982). Now I am 38 years old, and my survival has been a medical experiment, with limited guidance about the ways my life would be affected.

Heartfelt: The Human Heart

Modern medicine has established the human heart as a muscle that pumps blood around the body. The heart beats to the rhythm of an electrical impulse established in the sinoatrial node, known as *sinus rhythm*. Basically, the heart's function is to deliver oxygen and essential nutrients to the body, and to assist with the removal of metabolic waste. In a healthy body, it beats at a constantly changing rhythm responding to the internal and external environment (the chronotropic response). As a central part of the autonomic nervous system, it responds to sympathetic (fight-or-flight system) and parasympathetic (rest-and-digest system) nerves. However, Polyvagal Theory suggests that the role of the heart in human experience is more complex and subtle than this traditional dual-antagonistic model suggests (Porges, 1998, 2001, 2007, 2011).

Within this framework, one of the main functions of the autonomic nervous system is to assess and respond appropriately to risk, with the goal of establishing safety with others, termed *neuroception*. Polyvagal Theory proposed three hierarchical, phylogenetic levels of risk response, each managed by different branches of the autonomic nervous system. To successfully adapt to the changing environment, we need to be able to transition between these states to respond appropriately both when we feel safe (facilitating play, social interaction, and sexual intimacy) as well as unsafe (enabling defensive mechanisms such as mobilization during fight-or-flight and immobilization during extreme danger). There is an obligatory psychological experience for each of these physiological states. When we feel safe, we also feel connected and socially engaged via activation of the ventral vagal pathway. When our defenses are activated, we feel anxious and an urge to act via activation of the sympathetic nervous system. If we think our life is threatened, we may feel frozen with fear, withdrawn, and dissociate via activation of the dorsal vagal pathway. Transitioning efficiently between these states requires the ability to respond and recover, which depends on an efficient autonomic nervous system. This homeostatic variability is normally shaped during our early years. An efficient nervous system functions with rhythmic physiological variability, and the larger this variability, within normal parameters, the healthier the individuals are and the better able they are to respond to extrinsic and intrinsic stress. By controlling the vagal brake, the parasympathetic nervous system modulates stress vulnerability. Respiratory sinus arrhythmia (RSA) is a noninvasive measure of this parasympathetic tone that has been related to emotional regulatory capacity. The amplitude of RSA is used as an index of parasympathetic nervous system activity via the cardiac vagus. As such, RSA is a measurable, noninvasive way to monitor how the vagus modulates heart rate activity in response to stress, and it can be used to measure stress reactivity, providing a marker for neuroception, emotional regulation, and general well-being (Porges, 2011).

If we are to reconsider the human heart as fundamental to our emotional well-being, it becomes apparent that there may be significant implications for those born with a heart condition. If homeostatic variability in heart rate is an adaptive quality in a healthy body, what happens when a congenital defect means the heart beats irregularly, too fast or slow or is unable to respond adaptively to the body's demands? We might expect that any such disruption of the autonomic nervous system could compromise neuroception and self-regulation which, in turn, could profoundly affect psychosocial development.

Heart-Broken: "Blue Babies"

Until I was 12 years old, I depended on epicardial pacing systems, which override any physiological information, compelling my heart to beat at a fixed rate regardless of what I was doing. I vomited on exertion or with strong emotion, and my lips and fingers turned blue in the cold. I was constantly tired, always anticipating the next opportunity to sit down or, better still, take a nap. These pacemakers were bulky and unreliable, with fragile leads, which commonly displaced. Often my heart rate slowed, prompting an emergency trip to hospital to have my pacemaker interrogated or replaced. By the age of 7 I'd been fitted with five pacemakers, each by thoracotomy involving pioneering surgeries and interventions (Morton, 2015). I remember watching other children—at the gym, at sports day, in the playground, or on the street in active play, full of vitality and energy—not with envy but with sheer admiration. I could not comprehend how they battled the constant fatigue, aching joints, and breathlessness to be so active. At age 12, I was fitted with my first "as physiologically responsive as possible" variable-rate pacemaker, and I required open-heart surgery to close an atrial septal defect (a hole between the chambers in the heart). A variable-rate pacing system, designed to mimic the heart's natural electrical system, relays information from the right atrium to the pacemaker and back to the right ventricle. However, the pacing lead doesn't stimulate the heart's natural electrical conduction system, so this ventricular contraction is not physiologically normal. Modern pacemakers are still limited by malfunction (most commonly of the leads) and battery life. To date, I have been fitted with 10 cardiac pacemakers, and I face complex pacing problems resulting from the number of systems and leads that remain in situ, which limit space and present risk of infection.

Congenital heart disease (CHD) is the most common birth defect, with an incidence of approximately 8 in every 1,000 live births. Treatment of CHD is a success story of modern medicine. Advancements in medicine, surgery, and anesthesia mean that 90% of babies born with this condition now survive into adulthood, compared with just 20% in the 1940s (Warnes et al., 2001). As such, there is a growing population of adult survivors, and for the first time, there are now more adults than children living with CHD. The complexity of the defect varies widely, and many simple lesions do not require intervention. However, currently there is no cure for complex CHD; treatment is palliative; lifelong monitoring is indicated, with an increased mortality and morbidity burden (Greutmann et al, 2015). Symptoms may include arrhythmias, episodes of tachycardia (unusually fast heart rate) or bradycardia (unusually slow heart rate) or anatomically abnormal structural problems, which means that blood flow is compromised (in conditions such as transposition of the great arteries, tetralogy of Fallot, Eisenmenger syndrome or, more commonly, a hole between the heart chambers, known as an atrial or ventricular septal defect).

James and Jenny's compelling stories demonstrate the diversity of congenital cardiac conditions and highlight how living with a serious heart condition from birth can have wide-ranging implications for psychosocial development and experience. For many of today's adult survivors, their treatment has been experimental and outcomes uncertain, while care provision has not evolved in time to meet their needs, and many patients are lost to follow-up (Wray, Friglola, & Bull, 2012). Knowledge about the broader impact of living with this condition is limited, and historically broader organizations, such as schools and family doctors, have a poor understanding about how best to meet their individual needs.

James

James was born in 1980 with highly complex cyanotic congenital heart disease. Diagnosed with transposition of great arteries, straddling and overriding tricuspid valve, multiple holes, and several other defects, his condition could not be anatomically corrected. In 1987, he was one the first 20 patients to undergo the total cavopulmonary connection, providing definitive palliation but not a cure. Effectively, his right heart has been bypassed, with all blood flowing directly to his lungs.

> My heart condition and I have lived a path of uncertainty, challenge, and self-discovery. Growing up, I knew that I had a heart condition, but it was only later that I started to really want to understand it. When people asked me as an adult about my heart and I didn't really have a clear explanation for them, I realized I really ought to know more.
>
> Looking back, it is clear that I was always pretty aware of it—my sense of self is intrinsically linked to my heart. It is not like a cancer, where you may feel invaded; it is a part of me, my personality, my being.
>
> When I was born, I was very breathless and lethargic and extremely blue, and despite very early intervention to aid survival at 1 day and 2 years old, by the time I was 6 it was clear something definitive would have to be done or I would not survive. I remember living in a bit of a haze and would fall asleep easily, forget things from the exertion of walking across a room. Diagnosis was not definitive, and when I went to the operating room in 1987, the surgeon had three plans, opting for the "experimental" total cavopulmonary connection.
>
> Due to formative experience and despite wonderful parents (and consultant), I always became upset around hospitals, as well as during blood tests, which took ages due to poor circulation. The postoperative period was hard, due partly to chest drains, which I made my daily attempt to remove. When they were removed, it was too early, causing near respi-

ratory arrest. I was part of the learning curve; even the surgeons and consultants didn't know exactly what to expect.

I went on to a very slow, but steady recovery, and though left with a cardiac shunt, which means that I desaturate on exertion, I was much better and stopped forgetting things so easily. In 1996, I had an epicardial pacemaker fitted (after an unsuccessful attempt in 1992), which unfortunately interrupted my A levels (final high school exams).

It took me another 5–10 years to gain the confidence to go with my optimized circulation and electrophysiology. I was not going to be improved medically and, after a time, I began to exercise, take part in tennis, cycling, and strength training, which has proven physically and emotionally very positive.

It is very hard, as very few people understand what I have been through, how I feel in certain situations, the anxiety of pushing ahead and coping by myself. The physical burden is something I have managed to improve, which helps emotionally, but the emotional struggle is still there.

On reflection, I feel that my emotional well-being is partly linked to my heart. It makes sense that, in a challenging situation, I find it difficult simply due to feeling unwell, since the natural response to these situations does not work in harmony with my heart, and I feel shaky due to a poor a hemodynamic response. I think that understanding of the interplay between my heart and emotional well-being allows me now to adapt by giving myself time to settle. This level of understanding would certainly have helped growing up: I feel I would have been able to cope with experiences far more positively.

Recently admitted for a pacemaker change, I was confronted with a general nurse telling me to get on a bed to be wheeled to the operating room; my reaction was one of anger, fear, and I felt instantly unwell. Internally, I wanted to leave, but the inner strength I have gained through understanding myself, accepting my unique responses, held me in good stead. I expressed my feelings, refused, and walked to the operating room. After spending a childhood in the hospital without control, I was in control.

I have attended lectures on congenital heart disease to present from the patient perspective and have been upset listening to how life-limiting my condition probably is. Knowing the facts doesn't make it easier.

I have spent years researching and understanding my condition—as an engineer and student of cardiac physiology, it's been a fascinating journey. I have developed a fondness for my CHD. Without it, would I be me? I think not.

Jenny

Jenny Kumar, age 37, lives in Glasgow with her husband and runs her own communications consultancy. She has Eisenmenger syndrome, a rare, progressive heart condition that developed from a ventricular septal defect, present from birth but not diagnosed until adulthood. Eisenmenger's specifically refers to the combination of pulmonary hypertension and right-to-left shunting of the blood within the heart.

> My life completely changed when I was diagnosed in 2007, aged 28. At that point, I was frequently ill, breathless on walking, and diligently avoided hills and stairs. Diagnosis gave me an answer. There was an anatomical reason for my physical limitations which, looking back, explained a lot of my experiences.
>
> My mum tells me that as a baby, although I fed well, I cried more than my older sister as an infant. I was also very sweaty, now known as a symptom of the condition. From being a toddler, my lips went blue when I was cold, especially while swimming, and I remember being a sickly child, always catching the circulating bugs. They hit me hard, and I took longer to recover. My earliest memories are having persistent earache and sore throat with regular visits to the general practitioner for more "banana medicine" (liquid amoxicillin), which I enjoyed the taste of, along with the attention of both parents. I improved after a tonsillectomy at the age of 6 but still had numerous coughs and colds, which invariably developed into chest infections.
>
> At 9 I was diagnosed with migraines and asthma soon after, trying many different types of inhaler to control my breathing. Raynaud's disease followed with my white-cold, numb fingers, and the first mention of my fingers and toes displaying "clubbing." My shortness of breath didn't stop me being sporty early in secondary school. I was on the netball, hockey, and tennis teams, but cross-country running was impossible. Outside school, I started ballet, modern dancing, and tap dancing aged 11, which got tougher as I got older. I stopped at 16 to focus on exams, a convenient excuse, since my breathing problems were getting out of control. I thought I was unfit, not managing my asthma well, and avoided exercise thereafter.
>
> I have always been a happy, sociable person with a hatred of the cold and the rain because it affected my breathing. I refused to use my inhaler so as not to appear "weak" in front of friends. I was still unwell a lot of the time, but managed somehow and never missed school for long

because I enjoyed it. At university I struggled with the Glasgow hills and the weather and continued to be ill, but never fell behind academically. My then boyfriend, now husband, remembers how shocked he was at my continuous poor health.

So, when I was diagnosed, I felt vindicated. I'd always known something was not right. After the initial ventricular septal defect diagnosis, I spent 2 weeks in bed with flu symptoms. With hindsight, it was obviously shock. I took most of the 8-week wait to see a consultant cardiologist off work to get my head around what was happening, and a lot of experiences started to make sense. Later I would also understand the science behind why my legs died when I was gasping for breath and why I had palpitations after a night of heavy drinking and dancing in my teens and early 20s.

After diagnosis, I started making decisions that have enabled me to take charge of my life and manage my condition. In 2008, I started my own business. The freedom it gives me to plan my time to make best use of my energy—and build in recovery time to warm up after being out in the cold or rain, or to rest after a busy time with work—has been life changing.

I've learned to schedule my work and life incredibly carefully to stay healthy and conserve energy. I've found it helps to think like an athlete, focusing on marginal gains: getting enough sleep, eating healthily, staying hydrated, and exercising. Consequently, I'm the fittest and healthiest I've ever been. Most of the time I manage my condition well and sometimes forget about it completely. I love my work and thrive on being busy. I don't look like I have a heart and lung condition until I come down with a cold or bug and I'm forced to stop, rest, and let my body fully recover.

I started taking 125 mg of bosentan twice daily immediately after diagnosis, which is still working well. Monitoring the therapy involves blood tests four times a week to check full blood count levels and liver function as well as walk tests twice yearly at checkups. I enjoy competing with myself and am able to walk like a "normal" person: 600 m in 6 minutes, despite my sats (oxygen saturation level) dropping to 50%.

The toughest aspect was making the decision not to have children because of the risk it posed to my health and the child's. We ruled out surrogacy and talked long and hard about adopting but eventually, sadly, we faced the facts. I would be a good mother, but I don't want to be a sick mum. And I'm not prepared to put the burden on my husband of being both a father to a child and a caretaker for his wife. Counseling, which I've organized myself, has helped me explore my feelings about my condition and the impact it will continue to have. I'm naturally a positive person, but since diagnosis I have dark days and feel down, usually from frustration with my body's limitations. It's tiring monitoring your tiredness. I do feel different now that I've been diagnosed—alone sometimes and concerned for what the future holds. I have a good relationship with my cardiac team but wish they would focus on the holistic experience of disease, rather than just the medical aspect. However, I've learned that energy is precious and not to be wasted, especially on things we can't control. Somehow you find the reserves of strength to carry on, because, no matter what, life is for living—on your own terms.

Whole Heart: Polyvagal Vulnerabilities in CHD

Throughout my childhood, I presented to my cardiology team with "medically unexplained symptoms." Browsing my medical notes, it is hard to miss the repeated documentation of poor general health, fatigue, dizziness, headaches, nausea, stomach migraines, persistent cough, dehydration, and joint pain. I didn't walk until I was 30 months old, and I was a poor eater, finding extremes of temperature, bright lights, and noises difficult to tolerate. Although I was generally contented and always had friends, medical and school reports note that I was quiet, at times withdrawn, and a stoic child who didn't show much emotion. These symptoms left my dedicated cardiology team perplexed. They had no explanation, expecting me to be able to function normally as long as my pacemaker was enabling my heart to pump blood around my body. This left me confused; I felt frustrated with myself for not feeling as "normal" as I was told I should. I wondered if keeping up with daily life felt as much of a battle for everyone else, but I tried nonetheless, learning to ignore what my body was telling me and to push myself.

Given the high incidence of comorbid medical problems and the complex medical and surgical interventions survivors have often endured, the interplay between CHD and the tasks of the polyvagal circuit is complex. However, one poorly recognized difficulty may be compromised self-regulation and neuroception, resulting directly from cardiac dysfunction. In turn, this may have a negative impact on the tasks of the social engagement system and their development, including mastication, feeding, vocalizing, breathing, head tilt and turn, gaze, facial expression, voice perception, and listening with profound implications for psychosocial development.

We know that a large proportion of infants with CHD experience feeding difficulties, malnutrition, and a failure to thrive (St. Pierre et al., 2010; Kohr et al., 2003; Einarson & Arthur, 2003). Congenital heart disease is also associated with increased energy expenditure, poorly developed oral motor skills, uncoordinated swallowing, high respiratory rate, fatigue, and reflux (Arvedson & Brodsky, 2002; Sundseth Ross & Browne, 2002; Wolf & Glass, 1992) and a higher prevalence of low-level developmental delay including cognitive, attention, executive functioning difficulties, and problems with motor and language skills (Wilson, Smith-Parrish, Marino, & Kovacs, 2015; Mussatto et al., 2015; Karsdorp, Everaerd, Kindt, & Mulder, 2007; Dittrich et al., 2003; Mahle et al., 2002; Wernovsky et al., 2000).

Psychosocial problems have also been reported for this population. In a meta-analysis, Karsdorp et al. (2007 found that older children and adolescents with CHD had an increased risk of anxiety, depression, and social withdrawal. Czosek et al. (2012) found that living with an implantable cardiac device had a negative impact on quality of life for pediatric patients. Studies also demonstrate an increased risk for clinically significant anxiety, depression, and post-traumatic stress disorder (PTSD) in the adult CHD population, with loneliness and fear of negative evaluation as significant predictors of depression (Kovacs & Utens, 2015; Deng et al., 2015; Kovacs et al., 2009). A follow-up study, over 20–33 years, on psychosocial functioning found that the proportion of adult survivors with a history of special education was higher, and these individuals showed lower educational and occupational levels (van Rijen et al., 2002).

To date, these negative psychosocial outcomes have been accounted for by a host of secondary factors (such as feeling different, navigating a hidden disability, impaired peer relationships, parental overprotection, school absences, physical limitations, attachment problems; e.g., Verstappen, Pearson, & Kovacs, 2006; Kovacs, 2001) and, of course, such adversity likely increases vulnerability to psychosocial difficulties. However, it seems imperative to consider the direct impact of compromised physiology on self-regulation and neuroception and how, in turn, this influences the tasks of the social engagement system and psychosocial development, because this has important clinical implications, across the lifespan, for individuals born with a heart condition.

More generally, previous autonomic nervous system explanations of mood problems have drawn on classic dual-antagonistic stress models (Klonoff & Landrine, 1997). However, recent evidence is consistent with a polyvagal account; for example, Sack, Hopper, & Lamprecht (2004) found that participants with PTSD exhibited decreased RSA in response to a traumatic cue and an association between low-baseline RSA and sustained conditional arousal in PTSD, suggesting that low vagal tone may account for deficient arousal and emotional regulation associated with PTSD.

Tender Heart: Clinical Implications for the Attachment Bond

I spent the first 6 weeks of my life in an incubator, enduring cardiac catheterization, external pacing, two thoracotomies, an embolic stroke, and countless other invasive medical procedures (from infancy, the cardiac child must find a way to tolerate a range of medical interventions for survival, such as ECGs, ECHOs, stethoscopes, x-rays, venograms, stitches, chest drains, cannulas, injections, oxygen masks, and heart monitors). When I was finally home, I was underweight, fed poorly, and slept often. My mum tells me that she "loved me better" by holding me almost constantly. A clingy infant, I barely left her side until I started school. Some of my most traumatic childhood memories are of being wheeled away from her to the operating room and wakening postoperatively to her absence. Thankfully, she was present to support my mountainous recovery, from cardiac surgeries, back on the ward. Only by rubbing her thumb back and forth across my temple whilst softly singing could she get me to sleep (Morton, 2015).

It is well established that the attachment between the baby and the primary caregiver is vital for healthy psychological development (Bowlby, 1977; Harlow, 1958; Spitz, 1945). The need to be loved and cared for is an integral part of human nature especially in times of poor health. Normally, baby and primary caregiver (usually mother) engage in a biologically choreographed dance, and when this relationship is predictable, attuned, and safe, a secure attachment to each other is enabled. Such early, repeated interactions tone the infant's autonomic nervous system, creating its profile and providing the template on which future relationships are built. In this way, over time, the infant develops the capacity to self-regulate and navigate their social world. Neurodevelopmental studies demonstrate that children with a secure attachment to their primary caregiver are more resilient to traumatic life events (Rothschild, 2000).

Yet as a result of their heart condition and in the name of treatment, babies born with a heart condition face significant challenges to fulfilling their need for biologically driven connectedness with their attachment figures (Porges, 2014). Perhaps most obvious are the physical barriers; the infant may be incubated, in intensive care, and attached to medical equipment such as drips, heart monitors, feeding tubes, tracheostomy, and ventilation. Less apparent are the neuroception barriers. Co-regulation with the primary caregiver requires activation of the social engagement system for both baby and caregiver, since this autonomic attunement is achieved through eye gaze, vocalizations, feeding, head tilt and turn, facial expressions, and voice perception (Porges, 2011). To operate within this mode, baby and caregiver must feel safe to enable ventral vagal activation, yet such infants may be less likely to experience a neuroception of safety as a direct result of cardiac dysregulation, further heightened by enduring traumatic medical experiences.

The infant's physical development and recovery also depends on operating within the ventral vagal mode. This social engagement system is our most evolved and healthy way of being; it allows our bodies to develop and function uninterrupted by enabling us to feel safe and calm, and we need to be in this mode to reduce metabolic demand to grow, develop, learn, recover, and heal (Porges, 2011).

Therefore, a focus on establishing feelings of safety and stabilization is vital to ensure optimal development for the baby navigating the unique challenge of being born with a heart condition. Various strategies could be employed, such as educating parents that it may take more effort to engage and feed their baby, to better prepare them to meet the baby's needs. Validating their experience if their baby seems unresponsive, has poor eye contact, or has difficulty feeding could mean that, rather than feeling rejected by their baby, caregivers may feel better supported to provide the care necessary for healthy physiological and psychological development.

Promoting the importance of the caregiver's presence, touch, and soothing voice may promote the baby's health by resourcing the vagal brake. Touch expresses compassion and provides feelings of reward, reciprocity, and safety, building trust and connectedness. Compassionate encounters are linked to a decelerated heart rate, suggesting influence of the ventral vagus (Hertenstein, Keltner, App, Bulleit, & Jaskolka, 2006), and studies indicate that touch facilitates the tasks of the vagus nerve, such as feeding (Field et al., 1986). Compassion is also expressed through vocalization (Simon-Thomas, Keltner, Sauter, Sinicropi-Yao, & Abramson, 2009), so it is essential that the baby can hear the caregiver's soothing voice. It seems imperative that we do all we can to ensure that the baby knows love before pain and to allow caregivers to soothingly attend to their unwell child to enable autonomic attunement, healing, and development.

For some children, additional intervention may be indicated, including touch, play, and music therapies (Porges, 2011). However, while studies suggest that touch is calming, this is not necessarily the case if it is associated with previous trauma, pain, invasion of body boundaries, or a lack of control, and any such intervention needs to be individualized (Wilhelm, Kochar, Roth, & Gross, 2001; Rothschild, 2000).

To facilitate a successful caregiver–baby dyad, the caregivers also need to operate within their social engagement system. Yet dealing with the unique needs of a baby born with a serious heart condition is stressful for the entire family. Supporting the psychological health of caregivers will enable them to better navigate this sometimes overwhelming journey to be present for their child. Research suggests supportive input does improve outcomes for infants with CHD and their mothers (McKusker et al., 2009).

Together, these recent studies build on Robertson's (1958/1970) classic observations about the importance of the caregiver's soothing presence at the baby's (and child's) side, never more so than when they are doing poorly. An understanding that calls for a paradigm shift in medical care where stressors and disruptions of connectedness are proactively minimized. However, many of today's adult CHD survivors grew up during a time when cardiac interventions were experimental and it was common practice to be separated from their caregiver during hospital stays (Robertson, 1958/1970). Psychological and emotional support was limited, with nursing staff trained to focus on physical health. Emotional distress was often ignored and parental visits discouraged, lest they "unsettle" the child, even following James Robertson's (1958/1970) demonstration that such children have emotionally shut down rather than "settled," in his harrowing film *A Two-Year-Old Goes to Hospital*. Over the last 50 years, psychosocial issues have been introduced to training programs for medical professionals, with parents increasingly being allowed to stay with their child in hospital (European Association for Children in Hospital, 1988). However, it has been suggested that institutionalized defenses have contributed to a resistance to such developments. It is important to bear this historical context in mind when considering the lived experience of today's adult survivors. It is likely that, during childhood, such individuals have faced significant medical adversity, without the protective presence of their primary caregiver.

"You Must Be Used to This": Clinical Implications for Care Provision and Beyond

I was fortunate that my cardiac team was consistent throughout my childhood. I had a close bond with my pediatric cardiologist, who warmed his stethoscope before using it, spoke to me gently, and never left us in doubt that he genuinely cared. Yet there are all too many difficult experiences that I carry still, such as the endless anxious hours spent in hospital waiting areas for consultations, investigations, and interventions; lying still, a guinea pig as a team of men in white coats interrogated and explored the workings of my pacemaker, my heart rate under their control; an anesthetist telling me angrily to "stop being a baby" as I cried (for the first and last time) on yet another trip to the operating room; the doctors who have questioned their trainees about my scars, condition, and prognosis without my consent, in the third person; waking "prematurely" in intensive care unable to breathe, still attached to a ventilator; lying in a cold, sterile operating room, awake yet frozen with fear, as medics struggled to fit a catheter tube; and the regular comment, "You must be used to this" during routine investigations. Equally, I will not forget those who looked at me kindly, offered reassurance and took their time to gently treat me when I felt desperately unwell, in pain, and vulnerable, and I needed above all else to be understood.

During development, vagal tone is shaped by repeated social interactions to create the autonomic profile predicting whether we find connection with others safe or frightening (Hertenstein et al., 2006). For children spending time under the care of medical staff, this has wide-reaching implications for the importance of receiving care from a consistent team whose members are responsive to their individual needs, demonstrate good communication skills and compassion, minimize exposure to stressful experiences and disruptions of connectedness, and who can appropriately contain difficult emotions (Field, Diego, & Hernandez-Reif, 2010, Gerretsen & Meyers, 2010; Robertson, 1958/1970). Historically this has not been the case, and all too often, events that would be considered traumatic for a child, in any other walk of life, are assumed benign when they occur within a medical setting in the name of saving a life (Morton, 2011).

A polyvagal perspective calls for a paradigm shift toward humanized medical care where strategies to this end are embedded within the system—for example, minimizing stressful experiences (such as time spent in waiting rooms for difficult consultations or interventions); promoting the presence of caregivers (e.g., when going to the operating room or for new moms); allowing home comforts in the hospital; training all medical staff in providing compassionate, person-centered care and managing emotional distress; explicitly preparing patients for potentially traumatic events, including surgical interventions and surgery, with the aim of helping them form helpful beliefs and developing their internal resources (such as a sense of control over some aspects of what is happening to them); facilitating a successful fight-or-flight response, perhaps through imagery (Morton, 2011).

Further, difficulties in neuroception and self-regulation, resulting from cardiac irregularity and compounded by medical trauma, may contribute to survivors presenting as withdrawn, since immobilization (activation of the dorsal vagal pathway) may be more easily triggered by this uniquely challenging set of circumstances. As such, an alternative means to measure physiological arousal, such as RSA, may be indicated for pain management for infants who otherwise show no sign of distress.

Scarred FOR Life: Raising social awareness & promoting social connection.

Scarred FOR Life is a photography exhibition created by Jenny Kumar, Caroline Wilson, and me, on behalf of The Somerville Foundation (The UK's leading support organization for adults born with a heart condition). Kirsty Anderson captured portraits of eight adult CHD survivors to help change the perception that scars should be hidden away. The portrait exhibition aims to empower patients and raise awareness of the unique needs of adults with CHD. The story of each model's journey navigating the complexity of living with this condition, in their own words, was written on the reverse of their eight-foot high photo banners to give voice to this often hidden population. The exhibition was launched at Glasgow's prestigious Kelvingrove art gallery and museum in February 2015 and has since toured several venues including The Scottish Parliament. It has been well received by the public gaining national media attention and due to its success the project has now been replicated across the UK.

Psychoeducation about the unique challenges for healthy social, emotional, and physical development should be extended to other professionals and systems involved in the child's (and adult's) care, including schools, so they are better resourced to meet the child's needs and facilitate inclusion (for example, in gym lessons) and normal development. National campaigns and advocacy (such as Scarred FOR Life) could promote understanding and compassion within wider society to enable social inclusion (for example, facilitating employment) and feelings of connectedness and psychosocial safety.

"But You Look Normal": Clinical Implications for Development of the Self

During my mid-teens, my "unexplained medical symptoms" worsened. I felt disabled by chronic fatigue. My cardiac team could not find an explanation, referring me to neurology, psychiatry, and rheumatology, and a range of diagnoses followed, including myalgic encephalopathy, chronic fatigue syndrome, post-traumatic stress disorder, pacemaker syndrome, and physical exhaustion. I missed almost a full year of schooling. Eventually, I was prescribed a low dose of antidepressant medication (selective serotonin reuptake inhibitor—

SSRI) which, with pacing myself, seemed to help enough to enable a return to school. I experienced a similar episode during my mid-20s, following a period of stress, this time I was diagnosed with nonspecific connective tissue disorder. I guess some of these diagnoses may fit well enough, although none seemed to fully account for my symptomatology, which always seemed more of a way of being than an illness. Looking back, it makes sense to me that my autonomic nervous system is labile, as a result of my cardiac problems, leaving my body slightly out of step in responding to the world and vulnerable to other health difficulties. In all areas of my life, socially, in my education and career, and to have and raise a family (medical complications and poor care provision mean here too I was limited to one, treasured child), I have had to create opportunities to do things my way. Thankfully, with a little creativity, this has been possible, although it has not always been easy, and at times it has been isolating.

Polyvagal Theory offers a theoretical framework about the wider impact of living with a heart condition from birth. This understanding is empowering, because it can help such individuals make sense of their embodied experience, inform them about adapting their lives to accommodate their unique needs, and provide a language to communicate their experience to others. Rather than pathologizing their lived experience, it accounts for any symptoms in terms of reduced homeostatic adaptation, embedding them within their environment. This reinforces the fact that, despite being born with a heart condition, such individuals are normal and not, as they may have grown up hearing, "special," "different," a "lost cause," or a "miracle baby" (Verstappen et al., 2006). As such, this holistic account offers self-acceptance, enabling individuals to accept their hearts and all that they feel.

Empowering individuals born with a heart condition is important because several factors may contribute to them feeling oppressed. Parental overprotection has been associated with poorer psychosocial health for members of this population (Verstappen et al., 2006; Kovacs, 2001). While this is understandable, it is essential for the children's developing sense of self that they are supported to develop their autonomy. Wider prevailing attitudes about illness may also be disempowering for members of this population, since people with physical health problems are often reduced to their impairment—for example, "the girl with the heart condition" (Lago & Smith, 2008), as may an imbalance of power between doctors and patients (Verstappen et al., 2006). A polyvagal perspective has the potential to empower CHD survivors by helping individuals make sense of their embodied experience and encouraging self-management by teaching strategies to facilitate neuroception of safety and self-regulation.

Studies indicate increased vulnerability to psychosocial problems for this population (Kovacs et al., 2009; Karsdorp et al., 2007 Deng et al., 2015), although such difficulties are underdiagnosed (Bromberg, Beasley, D'Angelo, Landzberg, & DeMaso, 2003; Kiecolt-Glaser, Page, Marucha, MacCallum, & Glaser, 1998). Though a range of psychological therapies have been employed with this population, any psychological difficulties have been treated as secondary, indirect outcomes with little attention being given to the impact of compromised physiology on neuroception of safety. As a result, psychological treatment is based on the social engagement system (e.g., cognitive strategies and talking therapies) or the sympathetic nervous system (e.g., relaxation and behavioral therapies). Yet, developing strategies to promote a neuroception of safety may be more beneficial for this population (e.g., body psychotherapy and emotional regulation), and a range of psychological therapies could benefit from more thorough integration of a polyvagal perspective (Dana, 2015a, 2015b).

I was a quiet child, and I was often told how brave and courageous I was. However, I was never sure if this was an observation, expectation, or demand. Often I didn't feel very brave. I just developed a fine ability to keep very still and quiet (Morton, 2015). I remember feeling frozen with fear and floating out of my body to a safer place in my mind. As an adult, I attended personal therapy for several years, and I was able to make sense of my experiences, find my voice, and learn to listen to my body. I stopped pushing myself to function as well as everyone else and accepted that my body had its own rhythm that I needed to listen to if I wanted to feel as well as I could.

Any such polyvagal-informed psychotherapy could integrate relevant factors from existing therapeutic practice. Nonspecific factors, such as empathic listening and a focus on building a safe therapeutic alliance, may resource the vagal brake and facilitate autonomic attunement with others to help repair the attachment bond, empower patients, and improve interpersonal functioning (Rogers, 1961). Some specific therapeutic orientations may be of particular relevance. Compassion-focused therapy, which is grounded in cognitive-behavioral therapy, focuses on compassionate mind training to help people develop feelings of safeness and soothing (Gilbert, 2009). Body psychotherapy, a method of therapy that works explicitly with bodily sensations, thoughts, feelings, and emotions, aims to manage anxieties, establish feelings of safety, and process traumatic experiences (Rothschild, 2000). Emotional-focused therapy aims to improve emotional awareness and regulation within the context of an empathetically attuned relationship (Greenberg, 2011). Other strategies that could help to promote feelings of safety and stabilization include breathing and relaxation exercises, forms of therapeutic massage (Porges, 2011), and contemporary forms of meditation (loving kindness meditation and compassion meditation) and mindfulness (Hoffman et al., 2011; Grossman et al., 2010; Kabat-Zinn, 1990). Inclusion of a psychologist as an integral part of the cardiac team would better ensure holistic care that considers the emotional and psychological needs of this population.

Post-traumatic growth studies suggest that many people also report positive personal change following adversity, including increased resilience, a more positive perspective, a deeper appreciation of life, closer relationships, increased empathy, and personal strength (Hefferon, Grealy, & Mutrie, 2009; Staub & Vollhardt, 2008; Sheikh, 2004). It is interesting to consider how this fits within a Polyvagal Theory framework, and further work is required to explore this. When working therapeutically with this population, these resilience factors can be developed to facilitate healing and empowerment.

A Heart That Seeks Understanding

Polyvagal Theory offers a more holistic account of living with a heart condition from birth than has been available to date. It is attractive because it embeds individuals within their environment and, rather than pathologizing their lived experience, it accounts for many symptoms in terms of reduced homeostatic adaptation, providing the basis for compensatory strategies. These strategies could optimize the normal development of social and defensive behaviors to enable members of this population to feel as safe as possible and to better cope with any adversity they may face as a result of their condition. This understanding can enhance early attachment to the main caregivers, shape service provision for a population that will depend on medical intervention from cradle to grave, inform wider organizations that are involved in healthy development, and provide survivors with a framework to better understand their lived experience. The courage (from *cor*, Latin for "heart," literally meaning "to follow your heart") to live well with a lifelong heart condition comes easier with such understanding.

Acknowledgment: Thank you to Dr. Thomas Bacon, clinical psychologist, for his invaluable help in writing this article, and Jenny and James for their input and for sharing their stories.

References

Arvedson, J. C., & Brodsky, L. (2002). *Pediatric swallowing and feeding: Assessment and Management* (2nd ed.). Albany, NY: Singular.

Bowlby, J. (1977). The making and breaking of affectional bonds, II: Some principles of psychotherapy. *British Journal of Psychiatry, 130*, 421–431.

Bromberg, J. J., Beasley, P. J., D'Angelo, E. J., Landzberg, M., & DeMaso, D. R. (2003).

Depression and anxiety in adults with congenital heart disease: A pilot study. *Heart & Lung, 32*, 105–110.

Czosek, R. J., Bonney, W. J., Cassedy, A., Mah, D. Y., Tanel, R. E., Imundo, J. R., . . . Marino, B. S. (2012). Impact of cardiac devices on the quality of life in paediatric patients. *Circulation: Arrhythmia and Electrophysiology, 5*(6), 1064–1072.

Dana, D. (2015a). A beginner's guide to Polyvagal Theory. Retrieved from debdanalcsw.com

Dana, D. (2015b, November). The rhythm of regulation: Building safety from a polyvagal perspective [Workshop], Saco, ME.

Dasmahapatra, H. K., Jamieson, M. P., Brewster, G. M., Doig, B., & Pollock, J. C. (1986). Permanent cardiac pacemaker in infants and children. *Thoracic and Cardiovascular Surgeon, 34*, 230–235.

Deng, L. X., Khan, A. M., Drajpuch. D, Fuller, S., Ludmir, J., Mascio, C. E., . . . Kim, Y. Y. (2016). Prevalence and correlates of post-traumatic stress disorder in adults with congenital heart disease. *American Journal of Cardiology, 117*(5), 853–857.

Dittrich, H., Buhrer, C., Grimmer, I., Dittrich, S., Abdul-Khaliq, H., & Lange, P. E. (2013). Neurodevelopment at 1 year of age in infants with congenital heart disease. *Heart, 98*, 436–441.

Einarson, K. D., & Arthur, H. M. (2003). Predictors of oral feeding difficulty, in cardiac surgical infants. *Pediatric Nursing, 29*, 315–319.

European Association for Children in Hospital. (1988). *The EACH Charter.*

Field, T., Diego, M., & Hernandez-Reif, M. (2010). Preterm infant massage therapy research: A review. *Infant Behavioral Development, 33*(2), 115–124.

Field, T. M., Schanberg, S. M., Scafidi, F., Bauer, C., Vega-Lahr, N., Garcia, R., Nysfrom, J., & Kuhn, C. (1986). Tactile/kinesthetic stimulation effects on preterm neonates. *Pediatrics*, 77(5), 654–658.

Gerretsen, P., & Myers, J. (2008). The physician: A secure base. *Journal of Clinical Oncology, 26*(32), 5294–5296.

Gilbert, P. (2009). Introducing compassion-focused therapy, *BJPsych Advances in Psychiatric Treatment, 15*, 199–208.

Greenberg, L. S. (2011). *Theories of psychotherapy series. Emotion-focused therapy.* Washington, DC: American Psychological Association.

Greutmann, M., Tobler, D., Kovacs, A. H, Greutmann-Yantiri, M., Haile, S. H., Held, L., . . . Colman, J. M. (2015). Increasing mortality burden among adults with complex congenital heart disease. *Congenital Heart Disease, 10*, 117–127.

Grossman, P., Kappos, L., Mohr, D. C., Gensicke, H., D'Souza, M., Penner, I. K., & Steiner, C. (2010). MS quality of life, depression and fatigue improve after mindfulness training: A randomized trial. *Neurology, 75*, 1141–1149.

Harlow, H. F. (1958). The nature of love. *American Psychologist, 104*(1), 224–231.

Hefferon, K., Grealy, M., & Mutrie, N. (2009). Post-traumatic growth and life-threatening physical illness: A systematic review of the qualitative literature. *British Journal of Health Psychology, 14*, 343–378.

Hertenstein, M. J., Keltner, D., App, B., Bulleit, B. A., & Jaskolka, A. R. (2006). Touch communicates distinct emotions. *Emotion, 6*, 528–533.

Hoffman, S. G., Grossman, P., & Hinton, D. E. (2011). Loving-kindness and compassion meditation: Potential for psychological interventions. *Clinical Psychology Review, 31*(7), 1126–1132.

Kabat-Zinn, J. (1990). *Full catastrophe living: Using the wisdom of your body and mind to face stress, pain, and illness.* New York, NY: Delta.

Karsdorp, P. A., Everaerd, W., Kindt, M., & Mulder, B. J. (2007). Psychological and Cognitive Functioning in Children and Adolescents with Congenital Heart Disease: A Meta Analysis. *Journal of Pediatric Psychology, 32*, 527–541.

Kiecolt-Glaser, J. K., Page, G. G., Marucha, P. T., MacCallum, R. C, & Glaser, R. (1998). Psychological influences on surgical recovery. Perspectives from psychoneuroimmunology. *American Psychologist, 53*, 1209–1218.

Klonoff, E. A., & Landrine, H. (1997). *Preventing misdiagnosis of women. A guide to physical disorders that have psychiatric symptoms*. Thousand Oaks, CA: Sage.

Kohr, L. M., Dargan, M., Hague, A., Nelson, S. P., Duffy, E., Backer, C. L., & Mavroudis, C. (2003). The incidence of dysphagia in pediatric patients after open heart procedures with transoesophageal echocardiography. *Annals of Thoracic Surgery, 76*, 1450–1456.

Kovacs, A. H., & Utens, E. M. (2015). More than just the heart transition and psychosocial issues in adult congenital heart disease. *Cardiology Clinics, 33*, 625–634.

Kovacs, A. H., Saidi, A. S., Kuhl, E. A., Sears, S. F., Silversides, C., Harrison, J. L., . . . Nolan, R. P. (2009). Depression and anxiety in adult congenital heart disease: Predictors and prevalence. *International Journal of Cardiology, 137*, 158–164.

Lago, C., & Smith, B. (2008). Ethical and best practice. In C. Lago & B. Smith (Eds.), *Anti discriminatory counselling practice*. London, England: Sage.

Mahle, W. T., Tavani, F., Zimmerman, R. A., Nicolson, S. C., Galli, K. K., Gaynor, J. W., . . . Kurth, C. D. (2002). An MRI Study of neurological injury before and after congenital heart surgery [Supplemental material]. *Circulation, 106*(12), I109–I115.

Morton, L. (2011). Can interpersonal psychotherapy meet the psychological cost of life gifted by medical intervention? *Counselling Psychology Review, 26*(3), 75–86.

Morton, L. (2012). Healing hearts and minds. *The Psychologist, 26*(9), 694.

Morton, L. (2014). Addressing the psychological impact of living with a heart condition from birth. *Cardiology News, 17*(4), 6–12.

Morton, L. (2015). What your patient is thinking: The heart of medicine: Growing up with pioneering treatment. *British Medical Journal, 351*, h3881.

Mussatto, K. A., Hoffman, R. G., Tweddell, J. S., Bear, L., Cao, Y., & Brosig, C. (2014). Risk and prevalence of developmental delay in young children with congenital heart disease, *Pediatrics, 133*, e570.

Porges, S. W. (1998). Love: An emergent property of the mammalian autonomic nervous system. *Psychoneuroendocrinology, 23*(8), 837–861.

Porges, S. W. (2001). The Polyvagal Theory: Phylogenetic substrates of a social nervous system. *International Journal of Psychophysiology, 42*, 123–146.

Porges, S. W. (2007). The polyvagal perspective. *Biological Psychology*, 116–143.

Porges, S. W. (2011). *The Polyvagal Theory: Neurophysiological foundations of emotions, attachment, communication, self-regulation*. New York, NY: Norton.

Porges, S. W. (2014, December 6). *Connectedness as a biological imperative: Understanding trauma through the lens of the Polyvagal Theory*. Presented at the New England Society for Trauma and Dissociation.

Reid, J. M., Coleman, E. N., & Doig, W. (1982). Complete congenital heart block. Report of 35 cases. *British Heart Journal, 48*, 236–239.

Robertson, J. (1970). *Young children in hospital* (2nd ed.). London, England: Tavistock. (Original work published 1958)

Rogers, C. (1961). *On becoming a person: A therapist's view of psychotherapy*. London, England: Constable.

Rothschild, B. (2000). *The body remembers: The psychophysiology of trauma and trauma treatment*. New York, NY: Norton.

Sack, M., Hopper, J. W., & Lamprecht, F. (2004). Low respiratory sinus arrhythmia and prolonged psychophysiological arousal in post-traumatic stress disorder: Heart rate dynamics in arousal regulation. *Biological Psychiatry, 55*, 284–290.

Sheikh, A. (2004). Posttraumatic growth in the context of heart disease. *Journal of Clinical Psychology in Medical Settings, 11*(4), 265–273.

Simon-Thomas, E. R., Keltner, D. J., Sauter, D., Sinicropi-Yao, L., & Abramson, A. (2009). The voice conveys specific emotions: Evidence from vocal burst displays. *Emotion, 9*, 838–846.

Spitz, R. A. (1945). Hospitalism: An inquiry into the genesis of psychiatric conditions in early childhood. *Psychoanalytical Study of the Child, 1*, 53–74.

St. Pierre, A., Khattra, P., Johnson, M., Cender, L., Manzano, S., & Holsti, L. (2010). Content validation of the infant malnutrition and feeding checklist for congenital heart disease. *Journal of Pediatric Nursing, 25*, 367–374.

Staub, E., & Vollhardt, J. (2008). Altruism born of suffering: The roots of caring and helping after victimization and other trauma. *American Journal of Orthopsychiatry, 78*, 267–280.

Sundseth Ross, E., & Browne, J. V. (2002). Developmental profession of feeding skills: An approach to supporting feeding in preterm infants. *Seminars in Neonatology, 7*, 469–475.

Van Rijen, E. H., Utens, E. M., Roos-Hesselink, J. W., Meijboom, F. J., van Domburg, R. T., Roelandt, J. R., Bogers, A. J., & Verhulst, F. C. (2003). Psychosocial functioning of the adult with congenital heart disease: A 20-33 years follow-up. *European Heart Journal, 24*, 673–683.

Verstappen, A., Pearson, D., & Kovacs, A. H. (2006). Adult congenital heart disease: The patient's perspective. *Cardiology Clinics, 24*, 515–529.

Warnes, C. A., Liberthson, R., Danielson, G. K., Dore, A., Harris, L., Hoffman, J. I., Somerville, J., . . . Webb, G. D. (2001). Task Force 1: The changing profile of congenital heart disease in adult life. *Journal of the American College of Cardiology, 37*, 1170–1175.

Wernovsky, G., Stiles, K. M., Gauvreau, K., Gentles, T. L., du Plessis, A. J., Bellinger, D. C., Walsh, A., Burnett, J., . . . Newburger, J. (2000). Cognitive development after the Fontan operation. *Circulation, 102*, 883–889.

Wilhelm, F. H., Kochar, A. S., Roth, W. T., & Gross, J. (2001). Social anxiety and response to touch: Incongruence between self-evaluation and physiological reactions. *Biological Psychology, 58*, 181–202.

Wilson, W. M., Smith-Parrish, M., Marino, B. S., & Kovacs, A. H. (2015). Neurodevelopmental and psychosocial outcomes across the congenital heart disease lifespan. *Progress in Paediatric Cardiology, 39*, 113–118.

Wolf, L. S., & Glass, R. P. (1992). *Feeding and swallowing disorders in infancy: Assessment and management*. San Antonio, TX: Therapy Skill Builders.

Wray, J., Friglola, A., & Bull, C. (2012). Loss to specialist follow-up in congenital heart disease; out of sight, out of mind. *Heart, 99*(7), 485–490.

Index

In this index, *f* indicates figure, *n* indicates note, and *t* indicates table.

Also available from
THE NORTON SERIES ON INTERPERSONAL NEUROBIOLOGY

The Birth of Intersubjectivity: Psychodynamics, Neurobiology, and the Self
Massimo Ammaniti, Vittorio Gallese

Neurobiology for Clinical Social Work: Theory and Practice
Jeffrey S. Applegate, Janet R. Shapiro

The Heart of Trauma: Healing the Embodied Brain in the Context of Relationships
Bonnie Badenoch

Being a Brain-Wise Therapist: A Practical Guide to Interpersonal Neurobiology
Bonnie Badenoch

The Brain-Savvy Therapist's Workbook
Bonnie Badenoch

The Neurobiology of Attachment-Focused Therapy
Jonathan Baylin, Daniel A. Hughes

Coping with Trauma-Related Dissociation: Skills Training for Patients and Therapists
Suzette Boon, Kathy Steele, and Onno van der Hart

Neurobiologically Informed Trauma Therapy with Children and Adolescents: Understanding Mechanisms of Change
Linda Chapman

Intensive Psychotherapy for Persistent Dissociative Processes: The Fear of Feeling Real
Richard A. Chefetz

The Healthy Aging Brain: Sustaining Attachment, Attaining Wisdom
Louis Cozolino

The Neuroscience of Human Relationships: Attachment and the Developing Social Brain (Second Edition)
Louis Cozolino

The Neuroscience of Psychotherapy: Healing the Social Brain (Second Edition)
Louis Cozolino

Why Therapy Works: Using Our Minds to Change Our Brains
Louis Cozolino

From Axons to Identity: Neurological Explorations of the Nature of the Self
Todd E. Feinberg

Loving with the Brain in Mind: Neurobiology and Couple Therapy
Mona DeKoven Fishbane

Body Sense: The Science and Practice of Embodied Self-Awareness
Alan Fogel

The Healing Power of Emotion: Affective Neuroscience, Development & Clinical Practice
Diana Fosha, Daniel J. Siegel, Marion Solomon

Healing the Traumatized Self: Consciousness, Neuroscience, Treatment
Paul Frewen, Ruth Lanius

The Neuropsychology of the Unconscious:
Integrating Brain and Mind in Psychotherapy
Efrat Ginot

10 Principles for Doing Effective Couples Therapy
Julie Schwartz Gottman and John M. Gottman

The Impact of Attachment
Susan Hart

Art Therapy and the Neuroscience of Relationships, Creativity, and Resiliency:
Skills and Practices
Noah Hass-Cohen and Joanna Clyde Findlay

Affect Regulation Theory: A Clinical Model
Daniel Hill

Brain-Based Parenting: The Neuroscience of Caregiving for Healthy Attachment
Daniel A. Hughes, Jonathan Baylin

Sex Addiction as Affect Dysregulation: A Neurobiologically Informed Holistic Treatment
Alexandra Katehakis

The Interpersonal Neurobiology of Play: Brain-Building Interventions for Emotional Well-Being
Theresa A. Kestly

Self-Agency in Psychotherapy: Attachment, Autonomy, and Intimacy
Jean Knox

Infant/Child Mental Health, Early Intervention, and Relationship-Based Therapies: A Neurorelational Framework for Interdisciplinary Practice
Connie Lillas, Janiece Turnbull

Play and Creativity in Psychotherapy
Terry Marks-Tarlow, Marion Solomon, Daniel J. Siegel

Clinical Intuition in Psychotherapy: The Neurobiology of Embodied Response
Terry Marks-Tarlow

Awakening Clinical Intuition: An Experiential Workbook for Psychotherapists
Terry Marks-Tarlow

A Dissociation Model of Borderline Personality Disorder
Russell Meares

Borderline Personality Disorder and the Conversational Model: A Clinician's Manual
Russell Meares

Neurobiology Essentials for Clinicians: What Every Therapist Needs to Know
Arlene Montgomery

Neurobiology and the Development of Human Morality: Evolution, Culture, and Wisdom
Darcia Narvaez

Brain Model & Puzzle: Anatomy & Functional Areas of the Brain
Norton Professional Books

Sensorimotor Psychotherapy: Interventions for Trauma and Attachment
Pat Ogden, Janina Fisher

Trauma and the Body: A Sensorimotor Approach to Psychotherapy
Pat Ogden, Kekuni Minton, Clare Pain

The Archaeology of Mind: Neuroevolutionary Origins of Human Emotions
Jaak Panksepp, Lucy Biven

The Polyvagal Theory: Neurophysiological Foundations of Emotions, Attachment, Communication, and Self-regulation
Stephen W. Porges

The Pocket Guide to Polyvagal Theory: The Transformative Power of Feeling Safe
Stephen W. Porges

Foundational Concepts in Neuroscience: A Brain-Mind Odyssey
David E. Presti

Affect Dysregulation and Disorders of the Self
Allan N. Schore

Affect Regulation and the Repair of the Self
Allan N. Schore

The Science of the Art of Psychotherapy
Allan N. Schore

Mind: A Journey to the Heart of Being Human
Daniel J. Siegel

The Mindful Brain: Reflection and Attunement in the Cultivation of Well-Being
Daniel J. Siegel

The Mindful Therapist: A Clinician's Guide to Mindsight and Neural Integration
Daniel J. Siegel

Pocket Guide to Interpersonal Neurobiology: An Integrative Handbook of the Mind
Daniel J. Siegel

Healing Moments in Psychotherapy
Daniel J. Siegel, Marion Solomon

Healing Trauma: Attachment, Mind, Body and Brain
Daniel J. Siegel, Marion Solomon

Love and War in Intimate Relationships: Connection, Disconnection, and Mutual Regulation in Couple Therapy
Marion Solomon, Stan Tatkin

How People Change: Relationships and Neuroplasticity in Psychotherapy
Marion Solomon and Daniel J. Siegel

The Present Moment in Psychotherapy and Everyday Life
Daniel N. Stern

The Neurobehavioral and Social-Emotional Development of Infants and Children
Ed Tronick

The Haunted Self: Structural Dissociation and the Treatment of Chronic Traumatization
Onno Van Der Hart, Ellert R. S. Nijenhuis, Kathy Steele

Prenatal Development and Parents' Lived Experiences: How Early Events Shape Our Psychophysiology and Relationships
Ann Diamond Weinstein

Changing Minds in Therapy: Emotion, Attachment, Trauma, and Neurobiology
Margaret Wilkinson

For all the latest books in the series, book details (including sample chapters), and to order online, please visit the Series webpage at wwnorton.com/Psych/IPNB Series